PLATO'S UTOPIA RECAST

Plato's Utopia Recast

HIS LATER ETHICS AND POLITICS

Christopher Bobonich

CLARENDON PRESS · OXFORD

OXFORD
UNIVERSITY PRESS

Great Clarendon Street, Oxford OX2 6DP

Oxford University Press is a department of the University of Oxford.
It furthers the University's objective of excellence in research, scholarship,
and education by publishing worldwide in

Oxford New York

Auckland Bangkok Buenos Aires Cape Town Chennai
Dar es Salaam Delhi Hong Kong Istanbul Karachi Kolkata
Kuala Lumpur Madrid Melbourne Mexico City Mumbai Nairobi
São Paulo Shanghai Singapore Taipei Tokyo Toronto

with an associated company in Berlin

Oxford is a registered trade mark of Oxford University Press
in the UK and in certain other countries

Published in the United States
by Oxford University Press Inc., New York

British Library Cataloguing in Publication Data
Data available

Library of Congress Cataloging in Publication Data
Bobonich, Christopher.
Plato's utopia recast: his later ethics and politics / Christopher Bobonich.
p. cm.
Includes bibliographical references and index.
1. Plato—Ethics. 2. Plato—Contributions in political science. 3. Plato. Phaedo
4. Plato. Republic. 5. Plato. Laws. I. Title.
B398.E8 B63 2002   184—dc21   2002019754
ISBN 0–19–925143–6

1 3 5 7 9 10 8 6 4 2

Typeset by Hope Services (Abingdon) Ltd.
Printed in Great Britain
on acid-free paper by
T. J. International Ltd,
Padstow, Cornwall

To my parents, my wife, Karen,
and our two canine children,
Plato and Sappho

Acknowledgments

My work on this book has been generously supported by various institutions. I would like to thank the Princeton University Center for Human Values for a fellowship in 1994–5 and the Center for Hellenic Studies for a Junior Fellowship in 1995–6. Stanford University and its Philosophy department have been extremely supportive and I am grateful for a John Philip Coghlan Faculty Fellowship in 1997–9, a Stanford Humanities Center Fellowship in 1999–2000, and an Alden H. and Winifred Brown Faculty Fellowship, 2000–1.

I have learned much from discussions of the ideas in this book with many more people than I can remember and properly acknowledge. But the following have read all or parts of this manuscript or related papers and offered very valuable comments and advice: Julia Annas, Liz Asmis, Rachel Barney, Eric Brown, Alan Code, John Cooper, Stephen Darwall, Gail Fine, Jyl Gentzler, Christopher Gill, Eric Hutton, Terry Irwin, P. J. Ivanhoe, David Johnson, Charles Kahn, Rachana Kamtekar, Richard Kraut, André Laks, Tony Long, Susan Sauvé Meyer, Julius Moravcsik, Don Morrison, Martha Nussbaum, Reviel Netz, Andrea Nightingale, Josh Ober, Tony Price, Peter Railton, Christopher Rowe, the late Trevor Saunders, Jennifer Whiting, Christian Wildberg, Bernard Williams, and Chris Young. Erich Gruen kindly helped me understand the publication process. I have also benefited from the opportunity to present parts of this work to audiences at Brown University, Cornell University, the First International Congress on Ancient Thought at Salamanca, the Greater Philadelphia Philosophy Consortium, Johns Hopkins University, Rice University, Temple University, the University of Arizona, the University of Bristol at the Third International Symposium Platonicum, the University of Michigan, and the University of Texas at Austin. The last draft of the manuscript was much improved by the skilled editing of Laura Maguire.

I would like to thank Ann Wald and, later, Ian Malcolm whose enthusiasm for this project was deeply encouraging to a first-time author. Peter Momtchiloff and Charlotte Jenkins have been a delight to work with and have been extraordinarily patient with an author who has missed deadlines. I would like to thank Nigel Hope who did a meticulous and superb job of editing my manuscript.

Some pages of previously published articles reappear in this book. More frequently, they serve as sketches for views elaborated more fully here or provide supplementary detail. I would like to thank the following for permission to reprint published material: Oxford University Press for excerpts from Bobonich (1991) in section 2.3, excerpts from Bobonich (1996) by permission of Oxford University Press in section 2.3, excerpts from Pangle (1980) © 1980 Basic Books, Inc., reprinted by permission of Basic Books, a member of Perseus Books, L.L.C., excerpts in section 3.4 from my review of Terence Irwin, *Plato's Ethics*, *The Philosophical Review* 105 (1996), 235–240, © 1996 Cornell University, reprinted by permission of the publisher, excerpts from Bobonich (1995b) in section 5.4 and (2001) in section 5.4 by kind permission of Academia Verlag, excerpts from Bobonich (1994) in section 3.3 by kind permission of Walther de Gruyter GmbH & Co, and excerpts from Bobonich (1995a) in section 2.11 by kind permission of University Press of America, Inc.

Finally, I would like to thank John Eden, Heather Kirkorowicz, Laura Maguire, Isodora Stojanovic, and Audrey Yap for their invaluable help in checking the galley proofs of this book and in compiling the index.

Contents

1 Philosophers and Non-Philosophers in the *Phaedo* and the *Republic*

1.1 Introduction

Xenocrates [says] about true philosophers, that they alone do voluntarily what the rest of mankind do involuntarily under the compulsion of law, like dogs under the lash.

(Plutarch, *On Moral Virtue*)

Just as a man is not a good builder if he does not use the ruler or any other such instrument but takes his measures from other buildings, so presumably if a man either lays down laws for cities or performs actions by looking at and imitating other human actions or constitutions, whether of Sparta or Crete or of any other state, he is not a good or serious lawgiver. For imitation of what is not good cannot be good, nor can an imitation of what is not divine or stable in its nature be immortal and stable. But it is clear that to the philosopher alone among craftsmen belong laws that are stable and actions that are right and fine.

(Aristotle, *Protrepticus*)

Our concern, though, is not to avoid wrongdoing, but to be god . . . [The philosopher] will altogether separate himself, as far as possible, from his lower nature and will not live the life of the good man that civic virtue requires. He will leave that behind, and choose another, the life of the gods: for it is to them, not to good men, that we are to be made like.

(Plotinus, *On the Virtues*)

In these lines we find a strand of Greek ethical and political reflection that is disturbing and profoundly alien to us and yet critical for understanding Plato.[1] On this view, only a philosopher can genuinely live well and only a philosopher can lead a truly happy and flourishing life. All other human beings, no matter what else is true of them, go badly astray in their lives and actions; their lives inevitably fail to be happy and are incomplete or warped. For Xenocrates and the *Protrepticus*, ethical virtue itself is restricted to philosophers. Only the philosopher, Xenocrates assures us, voluntarily acts virtuously or finely; everyone else acts as virtue requires only under the compulsion of the law, like dogs under the whip. For the *Protrepticus*, the philosopher, in addition to being the unique craftsman of a good political constitution, is the only person whose actions are right and fine, that is, virtuous. In Plotinus, we find a radicalization of these tendencies. Our true goal or true good is to become divine, that is, to lead the contemplative life of the gods. Only the philosopher can live such a life and this requires transcending or leaving behind civic or ethical virtue.

To see how alien these views are to us, consider the following characterization of modern moral philosophy offered by one of its most distinguished historians.

The new outlook that emerged by the end of the eighteenth century centered on the belief that all normal individuals are equally able to live together in a morality of self-governance. All of us, on this view, have an equal ability to see for ourselves what morality calls for and are in principle equally able to move ourselves to act accordingly, regardless of threats or rewards from others. These two points have come to be widely accepted—so widely that most moral philosophy now starts by assuming them. In daily life they give us the working assumption that the people we live with are capable of understanding and acknowledging in practice the reasons for the moral constraints we all mutually expect ourselves and others to respect. We assume, in short, that people are equally competent as moral agents unless shown to be otherwise. There are many substantive points on which modern moral views differ from what was widely accepted at the beginning of the seventeenth century, but our assumption of prima facie equal moral competence is the deepest and most pervasive difference.[2]

In the above passage, Schneewind contrasts the 'new outlook' that emerged at the end of the eighteenth century with the medieval moral and theological conception and its successors. The medieval view, unlike the new outlook, does not accept that normal adults are prima facie equally morally competent, but rather holds that most people must remain dependent on instruction 'about what is morally required in particular cases'.³ But even the medieval Christian consensus is far closer to the modern outlook than it is to the strand of ancient thought we are considering.

The medieval consensus holds that the primary and basic principles of morality are equally well known to all men. Some are better than others at seeing what the principles require in particular cases, but the virtue that enables them to do so—prudence—does not require speculative wisdom and can be had even by the 'simple'. Although virtue is possible for human beings even in a state of nature, more is required for salvation. After the Incarnation, all humans must accept the Christian creed. The revealed truths of the creed cannot be known by unaided human reason, so even philosophers must seek instruction from authority. But revelation is designed to be accessible to all. Though some have a fuller and more explicit grasp of the implications of revealed truth than others, this knowledge does not specially equip them to lead better lives. Simple people need not have fully explicit theological beliefs and need not be concerned with the subtleties of the faith; they can rely on Scriptures tailored to their needs, on the infused virtues of baptism, and on the authority of the Church. The faith needed for salvation does not require speculative or philosophical sophistication. Both the wise and the simple can have it: all humans share a basic theological competence in that all are capable, with grace, of doing what is necessary for salvation or ultimate happiness.⁴

In sharp contrast to both the medieval and modern views, the strand of ancient thought we are considering denies the equal ethical or moral competence of people as well as their equal ability to lead happy lives. For Xenocrates, non-philosophers cannot understand what virtue really is or involves, but can only grasp what their laws or customs command. And their sole motivation for complying with these rules is that they fear the sanctions of disobedience as dogs fear the whip. But dogs have no claim to exercise the sort of excellence or virtue open to human beings. And if non-philosophers fail to attain human excellence, we cannot expect them to lead truly happy or flourishing lives.

The *Protrepticus* agrees that only the philosopher acts virtuously. It does not, however, claim that others cannot be brought to act appropriately except by the threat of sanctions. But whatever motivations and reasons for action non-philosophers may have, they are not enough to make them truly virtuous. The *Protrepticus* is also more explicit about what it is that non-philosophers lack: since they do not have exact knowledge, neither the actions they perform nor the constitutions they establish can be good. Real virtue thus seems to require the sort of theoretical knowledge uniquely available to philosophers. And because of the intimate link between virtue and happiness, neither can non-philosophers lead happy lives. Although Plotinus may hold that the civic or ethical virtues are products of the contemplative ascent of the philosopher, such virtue remains present in the philosopher only as an unactivated potentiality. Genuine happiness requires that the sage transcend these virtues by assimilating himself to the contemplative life of the gods and this is a project that is possible for the philosopher alone.[5]

Plotinus holds that the wise person will transcend political concerns, but the claims of Xenocrates and of the *Protrepticus* also have crucial implications for political philosophy. If no one but the philosopher can appreciate what is truly valuable or worthwhile, we should expect that only political communities that are founded by philosophers can be good. Presumably the continuing supervision and ordering of such communities must also be carried out by philosophers, or at least they would have to make the political and social decisions that called for more than a mechanical application of existing rules. Political authority must thus be lodged with philosophers.

But these views have deeper implications for political community and for the very nature and possibility of a good human community. The view that genuine virtue is peculiar to philosophers is not simply a threat to the claim of ordinary people to participate in political rule and decision-making. It is a fundamental challenge to what a good political community can be. If, for example, Xenocrates is right, then the best that philosophers can achieve—even given autocratic power—is to ensure that non-philosophers comply with the rules that they establish. Philosophers could, at most, establish laws and ensure compliance with them by effective compulsion; but even perfect compelled compliance is not enough to make such citizens virtuous. A good political community thus simply cannot aim at making non-philosophic citizens good or bringing it about that they lead happy lives (as opposed to the less than fully human life of exemplary coerced obedience). The *Protrepticus* is less restrictive in the motivations it allows to non-philosophers, but it is nonetheless committed to the same pessimistic conclusion that even a good constitution cannot succeed in making non-philosophers virtuous. Indeed, a human community large enough to exist as a city cannot aim at sharing a good life with all its members. On this view, a theory of a good human community will have to be a theory about an association of philosophers. If relatively few are intellectually capable of such contemplation (or if few people will find such a life attractive enough to pursue), then such a community will not be able to reproduce itself through ordinary family mechanisms. Even philosophers' children will often lack the ability or interest to sustain it. A good human association will thus almost inevitably have to be a small group existing within a larger society from which it must attract new recruits.

On both the medieval and modern outlooks, ethics is a study of the obligations or the virtues open to all normal adults. (Consensus on this point cuts across the differences among, e.g., eudaimonistic, utilitarian, and deontological theories.) The strand of ancient thought we are considering does not share this conception of what ethical philosophy is. These authors do not begin from what is for us (as well as the medievals) the starting point of ethical and moral reflection: the idea that we are seeking principles of action and living that can be shared by all normal human adults. Nor can they think of political philosophy as the search for the principles and proper arrangement of a self-sufficient community that aims at enabling all or most of its members to lead good human lives.

Although these ancient authors differ significantly among themselves, we might think that their similarity is not especially surprising: all share a common link with Plato. Xenocrates was the third head of Plato's Academy and the last to know him personally, the *Protrepticus* is widely thought to be one of Aristotle's earliest writings and to have been composed while he was still a member of Plato's Academy, and Plotinus, the last great philosopher of antiquity, is the traditional founder of Neoplatonism. Both Xenocrates and Plotinus, in different ways, saw themselves as followers of Plato and it is not unreasonable to see the author of the *Protrepticus*, whether or not it was Aristotle, as also heavily influenced by Plato. It would, however, be a mistake to see this strand of ancient thought as confined to philosophers of a broadly

Platonist perspective. We find closely related ideas in other systems of ancient thought, such as that of the Stoics.

But the problems and issues we have seen concerning the relation between the pursuit of philosophy and possessing virtue and attaining happiness and the implications of this relation for political philosophy are central to understanding Plato's ethics and politics. Although we must not infer that Plato's position is basically the same as those we have seen, the alien and disturbing nature of the views held by those so heavily influenced by Plato should prepare us to look for what is alien and disturbing in Plato himself. These issues form, I think, the essential set of ethical and political problems that occupied Plato from the great middle-period dialogues, such as the *Phaedo* and the *Republic*, to his last dialogues, including the *Laws*. In this book, I argue that Plato's resolution of these problems undergoes a fundamental change from his middle-period dialogues, such as the *Phaedo* and the *Republic*, to his late dialogues, such as the *Statesman* and the *Laws*. In the *Laws* we find a new vision of the relation between philosophy and virtue and thus a new vision of ethics and of the good political community.

In the rest of this introduction, I offer a brief sketch of the argument. The distinction between philosophers and non-philosophers is at the center of Plato's ethics in the *Phaedo* and the *Republic*. In the *Phaedo*, Plato sharply distinguishes the genuine virtue that philosophers have from the best sort of character state that non-philosophers can possess. Non-philosophers inevitably go astray or make a 'wrong exchange' in their valuing and pursuit of virtue and other goods such as pleasure and honor. The best character state that is open to them is merely 'a kind of façade' of virtue and 'is in reality, slavish and has nothing healthy or true about it'. Since Plato thinks that there is a very close connection between being virtuous and having a happy or flourishing life, non-philosophers' lack of virtue has starkly negative implications for their happiness. According to an early passage in the *Phaedo*, the uniform post-mortem fate of non-philosophers is to go to the underworld uninitiated and unpurified and, once there, to 'wallow in the mud' (*Phd.* 69B7–D3).[6] This pessimistic verdict is confirmed by a second passage in which Plato considers the possibility that human souls undergo reincarnation. In this case, the very best of non-philosophers, i.e. those who have achieved the best character open to one who is not a philosopher, remain impure because they have not been purified by learning and thus cannot enter the company of the gods. The appropriate reward for them is reincarnation into a non-human life, e.g. into the cooperative and tame races of bees or ants (*Phd.* 82A11–82C1).

As we shall see in more detail later in this chapter, although the *Republic*'s view of non-philosophers is more nuanced than the *Phaedo*'s, it is still quite pessimistic. According to the *Republic*'s official characterization of virtue in Book 4, since non-philosophers fail to possess wisdom, they fail to possess genuine virtue. Nor does their education enable them to appreciate genuine value. In Book 7 of the *Republic*, Plato considers whether the musical education received by the auxiliaries—the non-philosophical soldier class— tends to the good of leading the soul out of the Cave and into the light, that is, toward genuine reality. It does not, since this musical education does not provide knowledge, but only inculcates appropriate habits which do not in themselves furnish an appreciation of genuine reality (*Rep.* 522A4–B1). In the *Republic*, too, non-philosophers' cognitive defects and lack of genuine virtue have negative implications for their happiness. All the citizens of the *Republic*'s just city, except those who have been philosophically educated, remain in the Cave and this is a pitiable condition for a human being.

When he [one who has left the Cave] reminds himself of his first dwelling place and what passed for wisdom there, and of his fellow prisoners, do you not think that he would count himself happy because of the change and pity the others? . . . Would he not feel with Homer that he would greatly prefer to 'work the earth as a serf to another, one without possessions' and go through any sufferings, rather than share their beliefs and live their life? (*Rep.* 516C4–D7)

In sum, I shall argue that in the *Phaedo* and the *Republic*, Plato denies the following four claims.

(1) At least some non-philosophers are capable of being genuinely virtuous.

(2) At least some non-philosophers are capable of valuing virtue for its own sake, that is, are capable of believing that virtue is good for its own sake and of desiring virtue for its own sake.

(3) At least some non-philosophers are capable of valuing for its own sake the genuine well-being or happiness of others; in particular,

they are capable of valuing for its own sake in other people the most important constituent of happiness, that is, virtue.

(4) At least some non-philosophers are capable of living happy lives.

As we shall see, these ethical defects of non-philosophers originate in a fundamental cognitive defect: they are unable to appreciate and value what is genuinely valuable.

But when we turn to the *Laws*, one of Plato's late dialogues, we find signs that something quite new is going on. Near the end of the fourth book of the *Laws*, the Athenian, Plato's spokesman in the *Laws*, asks whether the legislator for their new city of Magnesia should, in making laws, 'explain straight away what must and must not be done, add the threat of a penalty, and turn to another law, without adding a single bit of encouragement or persuasion to his legislative edicts' (*Laws* 720A1–2). Plato goes on to condemn such a procedure as 'the worse and more savage alternative' (*Laws* 720E4). The better method is for the legislator to try to persuade the citizens to act in the manner that the laws require. The Athenian explains what he has in mind by means of a comparison between legislators and doctors.

[S]ick people in the cities, slaves and free, are treated differently. The slaves are for the most part treated by slaves . . . None of these doctors gives or receives any account of each malady afflicting each domestic slave. Instead, he gives him orders on the basis of the beliefs he has derived from experience. Claiming to know with precision, he gives his commands stubbornly, just like a tyrant, and hurries off to some other sick domestic slave . . . The free doctor mostly cares for and examines the maladies of free men. He investigates these from their beginning and according to nature, communing with the patient himself and his friends, and he both learns something himself from the invalids and, as much as he can, teaches the one who is sick. (*Laws* 720B8–D6)

The Athenian recommends that in founding Magnesia he and his fellow legislators follow the free doctor's method. He thus proposes attaching 'preludes' to individual laws, and to the law code as a whole that give an account of the reasons that justify the law's commands. These preludes explain the ethical basis of the law and, more generally, provide the citizens with an account of how they should live (*Laws* 858C–859B).

In the ninth book, the Athenian returns to this point and criticizes all previous legislators and legislation.

Athenian: [W]hat pertains to the laying down of laws has never been worked out correctly in any way . . . We did not make a bad image, when we compared all those living under legislation that now exists to slaves being doctored by slaves. For one must understand this well: if one of those doctors who practices medicine on the basis of experience without the aid of theory should ever encounter a free doctor conversing with a free man who was sick—using arguments that come close to phil-osophizing, grasping the disease from its source, and going back up to the whole nature of bodies—he would swiftly burst out laughing and say nothing other than what is always said about such things by most of the so-called doctors. For he would declare, 'Idiot! You are not doctoring the sick man, you are practically edu-cating him, as if what he needed were to become a doctor, rather than healthy!' Kleinias: Would he not be speaking correctly when he said such things? Ath.: Maybe—if at any rate, he thought besides that whoever goes through the laws in the way we are doing now, is educating the citizens, but not legislating. (*Laws* 857C2–E5)

In these passages, Plato requires that a good city aim at imparting to all its citizens—and not only the philosophers among them—some reasoned grasp of basic ethical truths. This requirement goes well beyond what Plato required or thought possible in middle-period dialogues such as the *Phaedo* and the *Republic*. This difference, I shall argue, is a sign of new and signifi-cant developments in the *Laws*. In particular, the *Laws* endorses the four claims whose denial is central to Plato's conception of non-philosophers in the middle period. Plato in the *Laws* accepts the following claims.

(1) At least some non-philosophers are capable of being genuinely vir-tuous.

(2) At least some non-philosophers are capable of valuing virtue for its own sake, that is, are capable of believing that virtue is good for its own sake and of desiring virtue for its own sake.

(3) At least some non-philosophers are capable of valuing for its own sake the genuine well-being or happiness of others; in particular, they are capable of valuing for its own sake in other people the most important constituent of happiness, that is, virtue.

(4) At least some non-philosophers are capable of living happy lives.

In the middle period, Plato holds that the fundamental failure of non-philosophers is their inability to recognize and appreciate what is of genuine value. It is this failure that by itself excludes them from leading virtuous and happy lives. In the *Laws*, and some of the other late dialogues, Plato comes to think that at least some non-philosophers can—albeit partially and imperfectly—come to appreciate and respond to genuine value. They can be appropriately oriented to things of real value and thus are capable of living virtuous and happy lives.

In the rest of this book, I shall argue for this new reading of the *Laws*. But let me note immediately one consideration that has convinced some that the *Laws* represents no significant change from the *Republic*, but is, rather, a scheme for implementing the *Republic*'s theories in the actual world. In Book 5, in what is nowadays perhaps the most famous passage in the *Laws*, the Athenian announces that they are to engage in the construction of a 'second-best' city. Given the importance of the passage, it is worth quoting in full.

Anyone who uses reason and experience will recognize that a second-best city [δευτέρως . . . πρὸς τὸ βέλτιστον] is to be constructed . . . But the most correct procedure is to state what the best constitution is, and the second and the third, and after stating this to give the choice among them to whoever is to be in charge of the founding . . . let us state what constitution is first as regards virtue, what is second, and what is third . . .

That city and that constitution are first, and the laws are best, where the old proverb holds as much as possible throughout the whole city [κατὰ πᾶσαν τὴν πόλιν]: it is said that the things of friends really are in common. If this situation exists somewhere now, or if it should ever exist some day—if women are common, and children are common, and every sort of property is common; if every device has been employed to exclude all of what is called the 'private' from all aspects of life; if, insofar as possible, a way has been devised to make common somehow the things that are by nature private, such as the eyes and the ears and the hands, so that they seem to see and hear and act in common; if, again, everyone praises and blames in unison, as much as possible delighting in the same things and feeling pain at the same things, if with all their might they delight in laws that aim at making the city come as close as possible to unity—then no one will ever set down a more correct or better definition than this of what constitutes the extreme as regards virtue. Such a city is inhabited, presumably, by gods or children of gods (more than one), and they dwell in gladness, leading such a life. Therefore one should not look elsewhere for the model of a constitution, but should hold on to this and seek with all one's might the constitution that comes as close as possible to this. If the constitution we have been dealing with now came into being, it would be, in a way, the nearest to immortality and second in point of unity . . .

Now then what do we say this constitution is and how do we say it comes to be such? First, let them divide up the land and the households, and not farm in common, since such a thing would be too demanding for the birth, nurture, and education that we have now specified.   (*Laws* 739A3–740A2)

It is sometimes thought that this passage settles the question of the relation between the theory of the *Republic* and that of the *Laws*. The assumption is that Plato here endorses the city sketched in the *Republic* as the best possible city, but now thinks that the demands it places on its inhabitants are too high: the city in the *Laws* is the second-best, but is the best that is likely to be compatible with human nature. It is also sometimes thought to follow from this that Plato still means to endorse the basic elements of the *Republic*'s political and ethical theory.

But such an interpretation misreads the passage. Even if Plato were to endorse the political arrangements of the *Republic* as the best possible ones, it would not follow that he also endorses all the claims concerning political theory made in the *Republic*, much less that he endorses all of the *Republic*'s claims in ethics, psychology, and epistemology. The political arrangements of the *Republic* are entailed by, and are consistent with, many different sets of premises, some of which are mutually inconsistent. Nor does the present passage endorse all of the political structures of the *Republic*, rather it endorses the community of property, women and children, and the goal of making the city as unified as possible. But what is most important is that this passage does not in fact endorse the *Republic*'s method for making the city one by introducing a certain kind of community of property and families. In the *Republic*, these institutions are restricted to the first two classes, but are rejected for the third class, the producers. The *Laws* passage presents as the 'first-best' city, not that of the *Republic*, but one in which there is, throughout the entire city, a community of property and of women and children. So the claim that the city sketched in the *Laws* is second-best does not suggest that the *Republic* still represents Plato's ideal political arrangement.[7] What the *Laws* represents as the ideal—that is to be approximated as closely as possible—is a city in which all citizens are subject to the same extremely high ethical demands.

In this book, I trace and explore the backward and forward connections to Plato's new estimate of the ethical capacities of non-philosophers. On the backward side, these changes rest on significant developments in Plato's psychology and epistemology. In particular, in the late period as a whole, we see a tendency toward a more unified view of the soul's capacities and a richer understanding of how reason structures and influences the rest of the soul's capacities. Plato's increased optimism about the ability of non-philosophers to appreciate genuine value springs from a more complex account of how our psychic capacities interact and of how non-sensible items are accessible to thought. On the forward side, these differences in the ethical capacities of non-philosophers have significant implications for Plato's political philosophy. Since non-philosophers are capable of more, the political and social institutions appropriate for them must also be different. Plato's political philosophy, for the first time, takes as its proper task the elaboration of a theory of the city or state as an association of those who share a genuine common end, in particular, the common end of leading virtuous lives. On the basis of this understanding, Plato proceeds to restrict citizenship to those capable of participating in such a common life and to rethink the appropriate relations between the citizens and the law and, more generally, the nature of a good political community.

It is, I think, only by reading the *Laws* in the context provided by Plato's other post-*Republic* dialogues—especially the *Phaedrus*, the *Philebus*, the *Statesman*, the *Theaetetus*, and the *Timaeus*—that we can see its true place in Plato's philosophy. The *Republic* is the crowning work of Plato's middle period because it provides within itself an account articulated in some detail not only of Plato's ethics and politics, but also of the psychology, epistemology, and metaphysics on which they rest. Because the *Laws* is comparatively lacking in extended argumentation on these basic philosophical issues, it is often dismissed as of little theoretical interest. But Plato is not trying in the *Laws* to provide a comprehensive philosophical statement of the sort found in the *Republic*. Questions of psychology, epistemology, ethics, and metaphysics (including the metaphysics of value) are explored in great detail and with extraordinary sophistication in the other later dialogues. Indeed, I think, they are treated in much more detail and with greater philosophical power than in the middle period. And it is these later dialogues that provide the indispensable background for understanding the *Laws*. In the *Laws*, Plato draws novel ethical and political conclusions that depend on the philosophical work done in the later dialogues, especially on developments in Plato's views of the nature and structure of the human soul. By examining Plato's philosophical positions in the other later dialogues, we can work out the deeper justification for Plato's new vision of political and ethical community in the *Laws*. And by articulating this vision, we gain greater understanding of the other later dialogues on which it rests.

We can best understand the developments in Plato's later period by examining them against the background of his previous positions and we can best appreciate the strengths of his later accounts by examining how they respond to and solve some of the problems generated by Plato's middle-period views. I cannot trace here the entire history of Plato's ethical theory or the full course of his development from the middle period on. But in the rest of this chapter, I shall explore Plato's two most important earlier discussions of non-philosophers: that in the *Phaedo* where Plato for the first time takes as a central theme the differences between philosophers and non-philosophers and that of the *Republic* which is the most extended and the philosophically richest account of non-philosophers in the middle period.[8]

1.2 *The* Phaedo*: Introduction*

More prominently and insistently than any previous dialogue, the *Phaedo* distinguishes philosophers from all non-philosophers and asserts Socrates' status as a philosopher. The dialogue that depicts Socrates' death opens by sharply contrasting philosophers' and non-philosophers' attitudes toward death. In its opening section, Plato argues that this difference in their attitudes flows from a more basic difference: philosophers and non-philosophers pursue radically different ultimate ends. Because of their radically different ultimate ends, philosophers and non-philosophers cannot have the same kind of virtue. Plato distinguishes between the kinds of virtue that each has—non-philosophers can have only a façade of genuine virtue—and shows what implications such virtue has for their possibility of happiness. Roughly midway through the dialogue, Plato returns to the subject of how the virtue of philosophers and that of non-philosophers differ and to their correspondingly divergent post-mortem fates. Finally, in the dialogue's great closing cosmological and theological myth, Plato returns for the last time to the very different post-mortem careers of their souls.

The contrast between philosophers and non-philosophers is thus a recurring and structuring theme of the dialogue. But along with this, the *Phaedo* clearly and emphatically advances strong and controversial metaphysical, epistemological and psychological claims that go beyond what is found, at least explicitly, in dialogues that are reasonably thought to be chronologically close, such as the *Meno* and the *Symposium*. The *Phaedo* offers an argument to distinguish Forms from sensibles, asserts that the objects of Recollection are Forms and holds that Forms are apprehended only by a non-sensory faculty of the soul, thought (*dianoia*) or reasoning (*logismos*).[9] As we shall see in this section, these two themes of the *Phaedo* are not independent of each other. The differences between philosophers and non-philosophers crucially depend on this newly articulated psychology, epistemology, and metaphysics.

1.3 *The* Phaedo: *Virtues and Ultimate Ends*

The *Phaedo* holds that all non-philosophers are radically ethically defective. But what is the nature of this defect and why are they subject to it? Plato begins by contrasting philosophers' and non-philosophers' attitudes toward death. The philosopher disdains the body and its pleasures and seeks to separate his soul from his body and his bodily senses so that he can better attain the truth about the Forms (*Phd.* 64C10–68B6).[10] In life, the philosopher tries to keep his soul separate from his body and he hopes that in death, when his soul is released from his body and exists apart from it, he will attain the knowledge that he seeks (*Phd.* 65E7–68B6). For this reason, the philosopher is not vexed at dying and he is not afraid of death (*Phd.* 67D12–E1, 68B5–6). All non-philosophers, on the other hand, are afraid of dying, because each is a 'lover of the body'.

Then you have sufficient indication that anyone whom you see resenting death was not a philosopher [φιλόσοφος] after all, but a lover of the body [φιλοσώματος] and also a lover of wealth or a lover of honor [φιλοχρήματος καὶ φιλότιμος], either one of these or both. (*Phd.* 68B8–C3)

The differences between philosophers' and non-philosophers' attitudes toward death are thus explained by more basic differences in their goals or ultimate ends. All non-philosophers are afraid of death because the goods that they value are conditions of the body or at least require embodiment. Plato does not make fully explicit what the goal of 'lovers of wealth' is. Some people falling into this category might value the attainment of wealth for its own sake, while others might value wealth only instrumentally insofar as it enables them to satisfy their desires for food, sex, and drink or to gain the pleasures involved in such satisfactions. (I shall call all such things 'the goods of wealth'.) Plato's lack of precision suggests that settling these questions is not necessary for his argument: whichever of these options is correct, lovers of wealth still have the same grave ethical defect. (Indeed, as I shall argue below, Plato might allow that some lovers of wealth value these conditions in others.) I shall return below to the initially surprising claim that lovers of honor are 'lovers of the body'. So we may construe the claim that all non-philosophers are 'lovers of wealth and honor or both' in the following way.

Every non-philosopher has as his ultimate end either honor or the goods of wealth or some combination of the two, that is, every non-philosopher thinks that his happiness consists solely in the goods of wealth or in honor or in some combination of the two. (I shall call all the goods sought by lovers of the body 'bodily goods'.)

This claim about non-philosophers' conceptions of the good is central to Plato's account of them in the *Phaedo*. To begin, it is their conceptions of the good that disqualify non-philosophers even from courage and moderation as understood by ordinary people. The only characteristic non-philosophers can have that resembles courage in some way is the disposition to risk death when they believe that doing so is the best available way of securing bodily goods and the only characteristic they can have that resembles moderation is the disposition to reject certain bodily desires in order to better secure other bodily goods (*Phd.* 68C5–69A4). But such 'moderation' is not sufficient to satisfy even the ordinary conception of moderation, and philosophers better satisfy the ordinary conception of courage than non-philosophers do.[11] In each case, these defects of non-philosophers stem from their ultimate ends.

What is more important for Plato is that because of their conception of the good, all non-philosophers lack genuine virtue. Because they take bodily goods as their ultimate end, their actions are guided by their fears about and desires for bodily goods even when they act as a virtuous person would. Such an aim disqualifies them from any genuine virtue.

[T]his may not be the right exchange with a view to virtue, the exchanging of pleasures for pleasures, pains for pains, and fear for fear, greater for lesser ones, like coins; it may be rather, that this alone is the right coin, for which one should exchange all these things—wisdom [φρόνησις]; and everything being bought and sold for this, or rather in the company of this, really is, perhaps, courage, moderation, justice, and, in short, true virtue namely in the company with wisdom, whether pleasures and fears and everything like that are added or subtracted; whereas their being parted from wisdom and exchanged for each other, this kind of virtue is, perhaps, a kind of façade [σκιαγραφία] and in reality it is slavish and has nothing healthy or true about it [τῷ ὄντι ἀνδραποδώδης τε καὶ οὐδὲν ὑγιὲς οὐδ' ἀληθὲς ἔχῃ]; whereas, to tell the truth, moderation, justice, and courage may in fact be a kind of purification of all such things, and wisdom itself a kind of purifying rite.   (*Phd.* 69A5–C2)[12]

Difficulties surround some of this passage's details, but Plato's main claims are clear enough. True virtue requires that

(i)   a person aim at wisdom for its own sake, and
(ii) wisdom govern all the person's exchanges involving other things, that is, that the person choose and act on the basis of wisdom.

All non-philosophers lack genuine virtue because they fail both conditions. They do not aim at wisdom for its own sake, and their choices are not governed by wisdom.[13]

All that non-philosophers can have is 'slavish virtue' and this has 'nothing healthy or true about it'. It is tempting for us to understand this defect of non-philosophers in terms of what we would count as serious ethical failures. We might think that Plato's complaint is that non-philosophers have the vice of treating virtue as instrumentally good or that they all have selfish ends and disregard the interests of others. If this were their state, we would find it reasonable to deny that they possess ethical virtue. But this also seems to us to be a wildly implausible view of ordinary people. It seems to be clear, for example, that some people who are not philosophers act honestly not out of the belief that 'honesty is the best policy', but rather out of a commitment to honesty. Similarly, it seems clear that it is not necessary to be a philosopher to avoid the vice of total selfishness. So we may think that Plato here is simply blinded to obvious facts about human beings, perhaps by his elitist and aristocratic prejudices or perhaps by a desire for a simple reductive account of human motivations. At any rate, nothing philosophically interesting hangs on this eccentricity of Plato. It is—like Aristotle's views about women or the status of non-Greeks as natural slaves—a blind spot in a great philosopher.

But such a dismissal is too fast and we should be wary of assuming that Plato shares our typology of ethical failure, but applies it eccentrically. So let us return to the issue of what the failure of non-philosophers is. According to *Phaedo* 69A5–C2, non-philosophers exchange pleasures for pleasures, pains for pains, and fears for fears: that is, they pursue as their ultimate ends the most favorable balance of bodily goods (*Phd.* 68D8–9, cf. 68E2–7, and 69A8–9 may suggest that they pursue simple maximization). They may, for example, decline a drink now in order to avoid the pain of a hangover or to be able to indulge zestfully tomorrow. Actions that are virtuous on either the ordinary conception or Plato's own conception of virtue, such as resisting certain pleasures or fears, seem to be valued by non-philosophers only insofar as they conduce to attaining their own ultimate ends which are entirely distinct from such virtues, i.e. some favorable balance of bodily goods. Similarly, if we classify the disposition to choose and act so as to attain the most favorable balance of bodily goods in the long run as a kind of virtue, e.g. 'slavish virtue', non-philosophers will, at most, see such virtue as instrumentally valuable insofar as it leads to the distinct end of bodily goods. And even what they falsely think of as their knowledge of what is good would only be of instrumental value for them. As we shall soon see, however, there are passages in the *Phaedo* that suggest a slightly different account of non-philosophers' motivations.

But such an account does not entail that non-philosophers see genuine virtue itself as instrumentally valuable. First, since neither the actions nor the dispositions just described are sufficient for genuine virtue, it does not follow that non-philosophers see genuine virtue as even instrumentally valuable. It is clear, in fact, that they do not do so. Non-philosophers do not recognize the existence of Forms and they see philosophers' pursuit of wisdom as simply a failure to appreciate what is really good: given philosophers' goals, they are as good as dead and their lives are not worth living (*Phaedo* 64A10–C2, 65A4–7). Second, even if non-philosophers could attribute non-instrumental value to actions such as helping others and keeping promises and the disposition to perform these actions, this would not be sufficient to possess genuine virtue, since genuine virtue requires aiming at and being guided by wisdom. This point is quite important, since we might otherwise think that all that excludes non-philosophers from genuine virtue in the *Phaedo* is that they non-instrumentally value only their own possession of bodily goods and take virtue or the well-being of others into account only instrumentally. But *Phaedo* 69A–C shows that Plato's requirements are stronger: genuine virtue requires both being guided by wisdom and taking wisdom as an ultimate end. The pursuit and possession of wisdom is not a higher good that may or may not be possessed by virtuous people, rather it is essential to being a genuinely virtuous person.

I shall return to the role of wisdom in virtue below, but let us turn to the issue of selfishness and the interests of others. Plato's characterization of non-philosophers so far may suggest that the ultimate ends of non-philosophers are entirely self-confined, that is, that each non-philosopher is an ethical solipsist.

A person is an ethical solipsist if and only if she values as constituents of her ultimate end (i.e. of her happiness) only states of herself and she values these states independently of any relation they have to the benefit or harm of others.[14]

A conception of happiness, for example, as the most favorable balance of one's own bodily pleasures over pains would be a form of ethical solipsism.

Being honored is a state of a person, but it is a relational state, that is, the state's definition makes essential reference to other people (in this case, to their attitudes). An ultimate end consisting in honor will count as a form of ethical solipsism as long as what the person cares about is others' attitudes toward herself and not others' benefit or harm. The characterization of non-philosophers as lovers of body, that is, of wealth and honor, may lead one to think that all that each individual cares about is her own wealth or honor. So may several other early passages in the *Phaedo* (e.g. *Phd.* 66c6–D1, but cf. 68A3–B2). Plato's description of the transmigration of souls near the middle of the dialogue suggests, however, that this may not be the case for all non-philosophers. After death, the soul of a non-philosopher will be re-embodied, since it is weighed down by the body. The bodies and sorts of lives they will re-enter correspond to the way that they lived in their former life.

Those who have cultivated gluttony, for example, and violence and drunkenness, and have taken no pains to avoid them, are likely to enter into the forms of donkeys and animals of that sort . . . and those who have preferred injustice, tyranny, and robbery will enter into the forms of wolves and hawks and kites.

. . .

And is not the direction taken by the others as well obvious in each case, according to the affinities of their training?

Quite obvious, of course.

Are not the happiest [εὐδαιμονέστατοι] even of these [i.e. non-philosophers], and the ones going to the best place, those who have practiced popular and political virtue [τὴν δημοτικὴν καὶ πολιτικὴν ἀρετὴν], which they call 'moderation' and 'justice', and which was developed by habit [ἐξ ἔθους] and training, without philosophy or reason? . . . [They are the happiest] because it is likely that they will go back into a political and tame race [πολιτικὸν καὶ ἥμερον γένος], either, I imagine, that of bees or wasps or ants, or back again into the very same one, the human race, and that respectable men are born from them . . .[15] But no one may rightly join the company of the gods who has not practiced philosophy and is not completely pure when he departs from life, no one but the lover of learning [φιλομαθεῖ]. (*Phd.* 82A11–82C1)[16]

All non-philosophers share the same basic fate in the afterlife: they are re-embodied. The only way to avoid re-embodiment and join the gods' company is to practice philosophy. The 'happiest' and the best behaved of non-philosophers, however, go back again into the bodies of 'tame and political creatures'—ants, wasps, and bees. The precise significance of this animal imagery is not obvious, but it is plausible that ants and bees are an appropriate destination for the best of non-philosophers precisely because bees and ants are not ethical solipsists. Both readily cooperate with others and are willing to make sacrifices for the community (see Cicero *De Finibus* 3.62–3). (In the *Symposium*, Plato holds that animals in general are willing to sacrifice their lives in defense of their young (*Symp.* 207A5–C1).)

In the so-called 'Socratic' dialogues, Plato held that each person's ultimate end was that person's own greatest apparent happiness and there is no reason to think that he abandons this view in the *Phaedo*.[17] So if some non-philosophers are not ethical solipsists, they will still act in order to advance, as far as possible, their own happiness.[18] The *Phaedo* does not provide an analysis of how one can both be a non-solipsist and take as one's ultimate end one's own greatest happiness, but it does not exclude the possibility for either philosophers or non-philosophers. As many scholars have plausibly argued, we may reconcile the two by allowing that people can consider the happiness of others as a part or constituent of their own happiness.[19] They can thus have a non-instrumental concern for the happiness of others while still taking their own greatest happiness as their ultimate end. So we can allow that the 'happiest' of non-philosophers might have such a non-instrumental concern for the happiness of others. Indeed, we might well expect that this is the case, since in the *Symposium* many non-philosophers have a non-instrumental concern for their children. Nevertheless, even if the possessors of popular and political virtue aim to benefit others because they consider others' happiness to be part of their own happiness, they will not possess genuine virtue. Genuine virtue, as we have seen, requires both aiming at and possessing wisdom. Non-instrumental concern for others is not sufficient.

Similarly, the above passage may suggest that it is wrong to think all non-philosophers see the sort of virtue and virtuous activity open to them as only instrumentally valuable in the production of bodily goods. The popular and political virtue displayed by the best of non-philosophers arises from 'habit and training'. Although this is not explicitly inconsistent with the calculating instrumentalist picture, it more naturally suggests that, at any rate, the best of non-philosophers perform the virtuous action as the unreflective outcome of their early ethical training and without an ulterior motive. But this, too, is not sufficient for genuine virtue. In sum, we have seen that Plato's criticism of non-philosophers in the *Phaedo* does not commit him to the idea that they are all calculating instrumentalists or that they all disregard the interests of others. Thus we cannot dismiss his position as resting on rather implausible claims about the psychology and motivations of ordinary people. This may, however, simply make Plato's pessimism more puzzling. If non-philosophers need not be instrumentalists or solipsists—defects that we would find intuitively acceptable grounds for denying them a share in virtue—why, then, does Plato see them as not merely failing to obtain certain intellectual or contemplative goods, but as actually failing to be genuinely virtuous? I shall return to this question after considering Plato's views about the happiness of non-philosophers.

1.4 The Phaedo: The Happiness of Non-Philosophers

It is a fundamental principle of Plato's ethics that genuine virtue is of the greatest benefit to its possessor. To what extent and in what ways does the virtue of non-philosophers benefit them? Plato does not explicitly address this question, but he makes his view clear. Consider again his description of slavish virtue. This sort of virtue contains 'nothing healthy or true' (*Phd.* 69B7–8).

And so those who established the rites for us really do seem not to be inferior people, but have long been saying in their riddling fashion that whoever arrives in the underworld unadmitted to the rites and uninitiated, will wallow in the mud [ἐν βορβόρῳ], while he who arrives there purified and initiated will dwell with the gods. For there really are, as those concerned with rites say, 'many who carry the thyrsus, but the initiates are few'. These latter, in my view, are none other than those who have practiced philosophy in the right way.[20] (*Phd.* 69C3–D3)

Since slavish virtue is a mere 'façade' of virtue, these implications for its possessor's happiness should not be surprising. Because non-philosophers are not guided by and do not aim at wisdom, they remain uninitiated and are destined for the mud.

The *Phaedo*'s later account (*Phd.* 82A11–82C1) which we have just seen of the transmigration of non-philosophers' souls offers no less bleak a picture. Here again, joining the company of the gods requires having wisdom as an ultimate end. Non-philosophers will either lie in the mud in Hades or will be reincarnated as a non-human animal (in the best case, as an ant or a bee). Three points are worth particular attention. First, in both pictures of the afterlife all non-philosophers are cut off from contact with the gods. Lying in the mud or reincarnation as an animal leaves them far removed from the divine. Only philosophers actualize the capacities of the human soul that are themselves divine and that bring their possessors into a divine state. Second, there is no possibility of significant improvement for non-philosophers in the afterlife. On the earlier picture, lying in the mud seems to be a permanent condition. But the later picture that allows reincarnation is no more optimistic. The best of non-philosophers pass from respectable people into various animal reincarnations and back again, but while some reincarnations are worse than others, none is a worthwhile life for a human being. Although individual souls that lead a non-philosophic life can, on the later picture, make significant progress, this would require that in one of their future reincarnations they pursue philosophy. Insofar as they do not, they cannot make significant advances in virtue or happiness. Third, even if we do not take literally the details of the post-mortem fate of the non-philosophically virtuous, Plato presents their lot as what their lives and the condition of their souls entitle them to. Since the happiness of one's life depends primarily on the condition of one's soul, the post-mortem fate of non-philosophers should not be seen as marking a genuine and radical *change* in their happiness. Cashing out the eschatological imagery, Plato is claiming that non-philosophic virtue here and now is not sufficient to provide its possessor with a human life worth living. This is a remarkable conclusion and one that deserves emphasis. Plato is denying not merely that non-philosophers can have happy lives, but that even the best of non-philosophers can have lives that are worth living.[21] We might dismiss these claims as mere aberrations that result from the *Phaedo*'s exaggerated asceticism. But as we shall see, Plato has strong motivations for these claims. In order to understand why Plato comes to such pessimistic conclusions, let us return to his psychology.

1.5 The Phaedo: The Psychology of Non-Philosophers

As we have seen, it is the ultimate ends of non-philosophers that render them unable to possess genuine virtue or happiness. What we now need to understand more fully is why non-philosophers have these defective ultimate ends and why such ends disqualify them from genuine virtue and happiness. Let us start by considering in more detail the choices and actions of non-philosophers. The non-philosophically 'virtuous' will make many of the same choices and perform many of the same actions as philosophers who possess genuine virtue. For example, on certain occasions, both courageous philosophers and 'courageous' non-philosophers will choose to go to battle and stand their ground rather than run away. Similarly, both moderate philosophers and 'moderate' non-philosophers will choose to pass up an evening symposium and will act accordingly, if this would interfere with the next day's activities. Underlying this similarity in choice and action is a certain similarity in their practical deliberation. Both virtuous non-philosophers and virtuous philosophers seem capable of

(i)   forming a conception of their overall, long-run good;
(ii) engaging in means–end reasoning and evaluating their options in light of their overall, long-run conception of the good; and
(iii) acting in accordance with their conception of the good.

But as we have seen, philosophers and non-philosophers have very different conceptions of the good, and the differences in the ends they pursue and in how they arrive at these ends are essential to Plato's understanding of their virtue and happiness. On some modern conceptions of virtue, two individuals might both possess the same virtue while differing radically in their conceptions of the good. (This is especially true for modern virtue theories that reject the doctrine of the unity of the virtues.) But on Plato's understanding of virtue, what is essential to virtue is the virtuous person's relation to the good. In the early or Socratic dialogues, Plato characterizes virtue as knowledge of the good and he thinks that all human beings always act in accordance with what they know or believe to be best. In the Republic, Plato recognizes the possibility of acting contrary to one's belief about, and perhaps one's knowledge of, what is best, but he characterizes complete virtue as knowledge of what is good along with the dispositions that allow one to act on this knowledge. In both cases, being virtuous consists in knowing and pursuing what is best, that is, the right ultimate ends. Thus the most important similarities between philosophers' virtue and non-philosophers' virtue will depend on the similarity between the content of the ends each pursues as good.

Nevertheless, one might think that even if there are significant differences between the ends virtuous philosophers and the non-philosophically virtuous pursue, the fact that both evaluate their options in light of their overall, long-run conception of the good constitutes an important formal similarity between them. But the difference in their ultimate ends reflects a significant difference in practical deliberation. Once non-philosophers' conceptions of the good have been fixed, they are capable of calculating efficient means to ends, weighing long-run costs against short-run benefits, and weighing a number of different considerations to reach an overall judgment about what is to be done. They may well be able to reach an all-things-considered or overall judgment of what is best, in the sense that they can take into account all considerations that they recognize as relevant. But this does not guarantee that their conception of the good itself has been rationally chosen. And Plato, in several passages, denies this.

If it [the soul] is separated from the body when it has been polluted and made impure, because it was constantly with the body, and paying court to this and in love with it, and been so bewitched by it, by its desires and pleasures, that it thinks nothing real except what is corporeal [τὸ σωματοειδές]—what can be touched and seen, drunk and eaten, or used for sex—yet it has been accustomed to hate and tremble before what is obscure to the eyes and invisible, but intelligible and grasped by philosophy; do you think that a soul in this condition will depart pure, and alone by itself? (*Phd.* 81B1–C2)

Lovers of learning recognize that when philosophy takes their soul in hand, it has been absolutely bound and glued to the body, and is forced to view the things that are as if through a prison, rather than alone by itself; and that it is wallowing in utter ignorance [ἀμαθίᾳ]. Now philosophy discerns the cunning of the prison, sees how it is effected through desire . . . As I say, then, lovers of learning recognize that their soul is in that state when philosophy takes it in hand . . . and tries to release it, by showing that inquiry through the eyes is full of deceit, as is that inquiry through the ears and other senses; and by persuading it to withdraw from these so far as it need not use them, and by urging it to gather itself together, and to trust none other but itself, whenever, alone by itself, it thinks of any of the things that are, alone by themselves; and not to regard as real what it investigates by other means, in other things, it [i.e. the object of investigation] being other. That kind of thing is sensible and seen, whereas the object of its own vision is intelligible and invisible. It is, then, just because it believes it should not oppose this release that the soul of the true philosopher abstains from pleasures and desires and pains, so far as it can, reckoning that when one feels intense pleasure or fear, pain or desire, one incurs harm from them not merely to the extent that might be supposed—by being ill, for example . . . but one incurs the greatest and most extreme of evils, and does not take it into account. [That] is that the soul of every man, when intensely pleased or pained at something, is forced at the same time to suppose that whatever affects it in this way is most clear and most true, when it is not so; and these things are especially visible things, are they not?

Well, is it not in this experience that soul is most thoroughly bound fast by body? Because each pleasure and pain fastens it to the body as if with a nail, pins it there, and makes it corporeal, so that it takes for real whatever the body declares to be so. Since by sharing beliefs and pleasures with the body, it is, I believe, forced to become of like character and nurture to it, and to be incapable of entering Hades in purity; but it must always exit contaminated by the body, and so quickly fall back into another body, and as if it were a seed, grow in it, and so have no part in communion with the divine and pure and uniform.   (*Phd.* 82D9–83E3)[22]

Drawing on these passages, we can first fill out our account of the motivations of non-philosophers and then turn to their psychological and epistemological basis. In these passages, and in the *Phaedo* as a whole, Plato tells us more about the defects of non-philosophers' motivations than he does about philosophers' motivations and what makes them right or good. His basic complaint is quite general and allows for considerable complexity in non-philosophers' motivations, although Plato is more interested in the root cause of their defectiveness than in the varieties of possible malfunction. Plato distinguishes the pleasures, desires, and emotions of the body from the proper activity of the soul, which is concerned with what is intelligible and non-sensible. He holds that bodily emotions and desires can, without any cooperation from the soul's proper activity, move the person to act. Nevertheless, the proper activity of the soul need not be motivationally inert: the soul can, for example, oppose bodily desires and emotions and set the person's ends.[23] In non-philosophers, the soul, and in particular the aspect or element of the soul that involves reason, fails to do its proper job: it does not shape the person's ends on the basis of its own resources, but rather, in one way or another, either fails to evaluate or endorses the desires and emotions that originate independently of reason. The person's ultimate ends are thus formed by—and the person acts on—the pleasures and desires of the body, rather than the motivations of reason. (As a first rough characterization, I shall call those motivations issuing from the proper activity of the soul 'rational motivations'; other motivations for action—in the *Phaedo* these are the pleasures, desires, and emotions of the body—I shall call 'non-rational motivations'.)

This basic picture can be filled out in many different ways. At its crudest, the sort of motivation that Plato attributes to non-philosophers could consist in the animal-like immediate pursuit of whatever bodily emotion or desire is occurrent or is strongest without any sort of intervention by the soul. But there are many ways, including some much more sophisticated ones, for the soul to go wrong. Plato need not deny that the soul endorses the non-rational desires as, in some way, appropriate. Despite some language suggesting that the body 'compels' the soul to adopt its ends, Plato need not think that non-philosophers usually experience a conflict between reason and non-rational desires in which the latter win out. And when there is a conflict, it need not be the case that non-rational desires influence the soul only through their causal force. The problem with non-philosophers is that their souls do not engage in their own proper activity in the first place, and, as a result, they may simply endorse the non-rational motivations as worth pursuing.

The soul might, for example, endorse as a general principle that it is best to act to satisfy its strongest desires. Even such a weak principle of evaluation may allow a person—unlike, perhaps, non-human animals—to have a conception of its long-run, all-things-considered good. Or perhaps especially intense non-rational desires could focus the person's attention on themselves so that the soul endorses their satisfaction as a proper ultimate end and acts to restrain other non-rational desires in light of this ultimate end.[24] But even the defective selection of some non-rational desires to form the person's ultimate end need not only be a matter of their psychological intensity. Rather than responding to the intensity of non-rational desires, the soul might subject its non-rational motivations to certain sorts of critical scrutiny. It might, for example, try to maximize the satisfaction of non-rational desires and evaluate them in light of considerations of consistency and efficiency. Or, even if not all non-rational desires are for pleasure and the avoidance of pain, the soul might try to satisfy them because the satisfaction of desire brings pleasure and its frustration brings pain. Finally, the soul might simply take over, unreflectively, the principle of selection embodied in the advice or the models provided by other people.

Although many of these defective character types might be ethical solipsists, it is important to see that nothing in Plato's basic complaint requires this. We might have non-rational desires for the well-being of some others, e.g. our offspring, or the soul might take over unreflectively non-solipsistic aims inculcated by outside training and habituation. What is essential to every form of defect, however, is that whatever critical scrutiny the soul engages in, it does so without drawing upon its own proper resources of reason. This sort of account of non-philosophers' motivations is consistent with a wide variety of psychological, epistemological, and metaphysical positions. But in the *Phaedo*, Plato goes further in sketching the psychology and epistemology that underlies his claims; he provides more detail about the genesis and content of non-philosophers' motivations and why being governed by such motivations is so serious an ethical failing.

Plato describes the soul's acceptance or endorsement of these non-rational motivations as a kind of 'pollution' or corruption of the soul by the body. This takes place, according to the *Phaedo*, in a quite straightforward way: the problem is that the soul is 'bewitched' by the desires and pleasures of the body itself (*Phd.* 81B1–C2). And Plato is emphatic in ascribing the non-rational motivations to the body.

Does [the soul] comply with bodily feelings [τοῖς κατὰ τὸ σῶμα πάθεσιν] or does it oppose them? I mean, for example, when heat and thirst are in a body, by pulling the opposite way, away from drinking . . . and surely in countless other ways we see the soul opposing bodily feelings, do we not? Well now, do we not find [the soul] dominating all those alleged sources of its existence, and opposing them in almost everything throughout all of life, mastering them in all kinds of ways, sometimes disciplining more harshly and painfully with gymnastics and medicine, sometimes more mildly, now threatening and now admonishing, conversing with our appetites and passions and fears, as if with a separate thing? That, surely, is the sort of thing Homer has represented in the *Odyssey*, where he says that Odysseus:

> Striking his breast, reproved his heart with words:
> 'Endure, my heart; even worse you did once endure.'[25]   (*Phd.* 94B7–D1)

Plato thus, at least explicitly, accepts (1).

(1) The body is itself the proper subject of certain desires and passions (*epithumiai* and *erōtes*).[26]

If the body is the proper subject and origin of these desires and passions, it must have the cognitive resources necessary to form them. The following two claims are essential to understanding the origin and status of the body's non-rational desires.

(2) The body has resources for forming beliefs and desires and these resources include sense-perception.

(3) The body's resources do not include any state or capacity that involves a grasp of non-sensible items, especially the Forms.[27]

It is these claims that provide the deeper theoretical basis for Plato's strongly pessimistic view of non-philosophers. In non-philosophers, the soul sets the person's ends by drawing on the desires already formed by the body.[28] But given its resources, the body can have access only to sensible things and properties; it cannot have access to the Forms. In each non-philosopher, the soul takes over as its end the body's desires that take as their objects sensible items. This is why non-philosophers are 'lovers of the body'.

Non-philosophers do not engage in the sort of thinking and reasoning which alone can apprehend the Forms.[29] Because of this, their goals have a twofold defect. First, non-philosophers fail to take as ends goals that involve non-sensible items. But non-philosophers do not merely fail to attain the truth, they are subject to serious error. Non-philosophers think nothing is real except what is corporeal (*Phd.* 83C5–9). In particular, they think that what makes things fine or good is the possession of various sensible properties.[30] What makes something fine is, for example, its bright color or shape (*Phd.* 100C–D); what makes something good, for example, is its being a bodily pleasure. But according to Plato's metaphysics in the *Phaedo*, it is one and the same thing that makes whatever is fine fine or makes whatever is good good. Since any sensible property will fail to account for some cases of goodness or fineness—e.g. no sensible property can account for the fineness of a geometrical circle—no sensible property ever makes anything at all good or fine. What makes any good or fine thing good or fine is, instead, some non-sensible feature of it.[31]

Since non-philosophers form their conception of the good and the fine through sensation and value as fine and good only sensible properties, they never are aware of nor desire what really makes things good or fine.[32] Plato does not present them as grasping that there are non-sensible properties, but rejecting them as candidates for what makes things good or fine. They simply do not accept the existence of such properties. Whatever non-philosophers value, including their own actions, conditions of themselves, or the apparent well-being of others, they will value it for some reason other than that it is genuinely valuable, that is, they will value it for having some feature that never makes anything at all good or fine. This explains Plato's claim that the 'greatest and most extreme of evils' comes about when satisfying bodily desires and feeling pleasures and pains: this evil is that the soul 'takes for real whatever the body declares to be so', i.e. it takes as good and fine bodily or sensible properties. This is a double misfortune:

(i) The person fails to be aware of and to value the genuine non-sensible properties of goodness and the fine.

(ii) The person values as fine and good features of things that are not genuinely valuable.

We can now see more clearly why Plato denies genuine virtue to non-philosophers and is so pessimistic about the happiness of their lives. If we accept that non-philosophers are cut off from an appreciation of genuine value, it is not unreasonable to deny them genuine virtue. If we accept the objectivity of such value properties and see it as an essential function of human reason to grasp them, it is not unreasonable to deny that non-philosophers can have good or happy lives.

Let me note a few final points. First, despite the fact that Plato explicitly attributes desires and beliefs to the body, one might argue that this language should not be pressed and that these desires really belong to the soul. If this is right, Plato would be recognizing a kind of complexity within the soul and a possibility for conflict that he did not recognize in the Socratic dialogues. The conflict noted at *Phd.* 94B7–D1 between, for example, thirst and a desire or judgment springing from reasoning is used in *Republic* Book 4 to argue for a partitioning of the soul that assigns thirst to one part of the soul and assigns the desire coming from reason to another, distinct part of the soul. I do not think that there is sufficient evidence in the *Phaedo* to suggest that Plato's language is merely metaphorical and it is natural to see the *Phaedo* as a transition point between the Socratic dialogues which have no room for such conflicting desires and the *Republic*'s partitioning of the soul itself into different subjects of belief and desire. Nevertheless, the essential aspects of my analysis of the defects of non-philosophers would not be affected, if Plato implicitly held in the *Phaedo* the *Republic*'s theory of a partitioned soul.

Second, Plato does not provide much detail about how the desires and appetites of the body are formed and exactly what resources are deployed in their formation and in their endorsement by the soul. (Whatever capacities are involved in such formation and endorsement do not require a grasp of Forms. But Plato does not, for example, tell us why souls in which reason fails to do its proper job suffer this failure. Perhaps in some souls their reason is inherently too weak to do what it should, in others their lack of proper habituation and education explains their weakness.) For his purposes, what is important is the contrast between the sort of reasoning and thought that involves grasping the Forms and that which does not. It is enough for his present purposes that non-philosophers never, when forming and pursuing their ultimate ends, draw upon reasoning that involves grasping Forms. We can thus see why Plato is not especially concerned here with whether non-philosophers act from an ulterior motive or whether they merely fail to have the right motive for acting virtuously. What is of basic importance is that non-philosophers do not appreciate the genuine standards of goodness and fineness and that they fail to appreciate what it is that makes anything good or fine.

Finally, although Plato reserves most of his criticism here for money-loving non-philosophers, he does not draw any significant ethical distinction between honor-lovers and money-lovers. Both possess the same sort of virtue, i.e. slavish or political virtue, and since this virtue contains nothing healthy or true, both seem to fail equally to be benefited by their possession of such virtue. Both are 'lovers of the body', as contrasted with philosophers who value genuine non-sensible value properties. Honor-lovers, we might think, fit awkwardly into the category of lovers of the body, since honor is not obviously a sensible property. But the essential contrast Plato is drawing is between non-sensible value properties that things have in virtue of participating in the appropriate Forms and everything else.[33] The problem with honor-lovers is that their conception of the good and the fine is not formed by thinking and reasoning about Forms and does not include a grasp of what really makes things good and fine. This parity of the two sorts of lovers of the body is not inconsistent with the idea that some non-philosophers are worse off than others. (And Plato clearly thinks that non-philosophers are worse off if they lack slavish or political virtue than if they have it.) But there is no suggestion in the *Phaedo* that a love of honor in itself involves a love of the genuinely valuable features of things.

1.6 The Phaedo: The Dependency Thesis

Although we can now better see their basis in Plato's psychology and epistemology, the claims that no non-philosopher thinks that virtue is good for its own sake, and that none has a life worth living, are still in sharp conflict with our ordinary understanding of human beings. Plato in the *Phaedo*, however, may not have been troubled by such a conflict with ordinary common sense, since one of the dialogue's central themes is that, because of their reliance on the senses rather than reason, non-philosophers' beliefs are shot through with confusion and error. Philosophy brings with it a radical transformation in our views of what is valuable.

Nevertheless, there are some continuities with Plato's earlier views. Plato in the Socratic dialogues holds that genuine virtue is necessary for happiness.

If we add to this the *Phaedo*'s claim that non-philosophers do not possess genuine virtue, it follows that they cannot be happy. This does not, however, by itself entail that they cannot have lives that are worth living, since non-philosophers might fail to be happy, yet still have lives that are well worth living. But given his views about the goals of non-philosophers in the *Phaedo*, Plato may be committed to the stronger claim by his theory of the Dependency of Goods in the *Euthydemus* and the *Meno*. I discuss a later version of this theory further in Chapter 2, but let me briefly note its relevance to the *Phaedo*.

In the *Euthydemus* and the *Meno*, Plato divides goods into Dependent and Independent Goods.[34]

Dependent Good: *x* is a Dependent Good if and only if *x* is good for a person who possesses wisdom (*phronēsis*) or knowledge of the good and *x* is bad or at least not good for a person who lacks wisdom or knowledge of the good.

Independent Good: *x* is an Independent Good if and only if *x* is good for a person regardless of what else she possesses.

Plato holds that goods such as wealth, health, honor, political office, and various other bodily and psychic qualities are Dependent Goods, that is, they are only good for a person who possesses wisdom or knowledge of the good. Wisdom itself is an Independent Good. For those who lack wisdom or knowledge of the good, Dependent Goods are either not good or bad. Since non-philosophers clearly do lack wisdom or knowledge of the good they could not be benefited by any of the goods that they possess (and may be harmed by them). Even if non-philosophers are merely not benefited by the Dependent Goods they possess, a life with no goods does not seem to be worth living. In the *Meno*, Plato on some interpretations allows that true belief is capable of rendering Dependent Goods good for their possessor.[35] But it does not seem that this weakening of the requirement for benefit will help non-philosophers in the *Phaedo*, since they do not merely lack knowledge of the good while having true beliefs about it; rather, they have false beliefs about the good. All non-philosophers suffer the 'greatest and most extreme of evils', which is that the soul 'takes for real whatever the body declares to be so' (*Phd.* 83c1–2, d6–7). Given the falsity of their beliefs about the good, it seems that they will not be benefited by any of their possessions.

The Dependency Thesis also helps us to see the place of other-regarding concern in Plato's ethics. One reason that we might have had for thinking that non-philosophers were ethical solipsists was that if we allow them a substantial degree of other-regarding concern, it might seem implausibly harsh to claim that they possessed only a façade of virtue that is of no significant benefit to them. Is it not more reasonable to see such people as possessing a reduced, but still genuine, form of virtue that is still valuable? The Dependency Thesis shows why Plato might reasonably reject this line of thought. In the *Meno*, Plato classifies courage, moderation, justice, and all other psychic qualities insofar as they do not include knowledge of the good as Dependent Goods (*Meno* 88A–B). It thus seems plausible that concern for others, like these other psychic qualities that do not include knowledge of the good, is a Dependent Good and, as such, does not benefit its possessor without knowledge.

This evaluation of other-regarding concern is a consequence of the Dependency Thesis, but Plato has further grounds for thinking that this consequence is reasonable. In the *Rhetoric*, Aristotle claims that friendship or loving involves wishing for the other person what we regard as good (1380^{b}36–7, cf. 1381^{a}7–10). This is a view that Plato shares in the *Symposium* and *Phaedrus*. (For further discussion of these dialogues, see Section 1.16.) Thus in seeking to advance the good of friends or loved ones, non-philosophers, like philosophers, will seek to give to them what they themselves find of genuine value. But the sort of goods that non-philosophers would seek to provide to one another are, by themselves, not good for their possessors at all (and may, in fact, be bad). And if what they give to others includes educating them to their own conception of the good (or sustaining them in their shared conception of the good), such an education or habituation, as long as it is retained, will make it impossible for its recipients to benefit from any of their other possessions. In sum, even non-philosophers who act so as to benefit others for their own sake will aim at providing others with things that are, in fact, not good for them and will foster and sustain in them views about the good which make it impossible for them to be virtuous or to benefit from anything. It is not clearly unreasonable for Plato to hold that such other-regarding concern makes no significant improvement in one's own virtue or happiness. Consider, for example, the case of the politician in the *Gorgias* who, like a pastry chef satisfying children's desires for sweets while ignoring their health, satisfies the citizens' desires for pleasure without really benefiting them.[36] Or consider a person who acts to bring as many other people as possible into the pleasant dream-like state of a drugged haze. I think that even if we were to discover that the politician or the drug provider were aiming at the well-being of others for their own sake, we would still not see them as being genuinely virtuous or as themselves significantly benefited by such other-regarding concern. If we find Plato's view alien, one important reason for this may be that we reject his understanding of what is genuinely beneficial, rather than that we differ with him over the value of other-regarding concern as such.[37]

1.7 The Phaedo: Wisdom

We are now in a better position to see why wisdom plays a double role in genuine virtue. It is, according to the right-exchange passage at *Phaedo* 69A–D, both an ultimate end and the basis on which choices are to be made: it is what other things should be exchanged for and it is the standard on the basis of which other things should be exchanged. This wisdom has previously been described as the object of the philosophers' pursuit; this is what they desire and love. Wisdom involves grasping, by reasoning and thought, the things that are, and this includes what justice, the fine, and the good are. As Plato goes on to make clear, wisdom takes as its objects, e.g., the just itself, the fine itself, and the good itself, that is, the Forms.[38]

Roslyn Weiss, for example, rejects this interpretation on the grounds that the *Phaedo* assumes that 'one does not attain [wisdom] *phronēsis* until death'.[39] On her view, wisdom is only an object of aspiration; it is not something that the philosopher actually possesses. But the *Phaedo*'s denial of the possibility of having wisdom while embodied is usually qualified: before death, we never 'adequately' or 'purely' attain wisdom. And later in the dialogue Plato allows that at least some people know what the equal itself is.[40] Such a qualification, however, still allows for a sharp distinction between philosophers and non-philosophers. The *Phaedo* does not give a full account of what it is to know a Form, but drawing on the case of the Equal, it seems to involve at least the following. A person who knows the Form of F:

(1) recognizes that the Form of F is not identical with sensible things or properties, and
(2) is able to give an account of the Form of F.

Although he does not explicitly claim that knowing the following principle is a necessary condition of knowing a Form, Plato thinks that it is a very basic fact about Forms that sensible things are dependent on them.

(3) All sensible Fs are F in virtue of participating in the Form of F.

Since non-philosophers do not recognize Forms in addition to sensible things and properties, they fail all three criteria. Their conception of the fine and the good will be restricted to sensible properties. And since even in the case of sensible things, these properties are not what makes them fine or good, they will not pursue things for the features that make them genuinely valuable. Plato can, on the other hand, allow that philosophers, even while embodied, satisfy enough of these criteria or come close enough to satisfying them to have a genuine sort of wisdom, although this wisdom is not fully adequate or pure. They will have recognized the non-identity of Forms with sensibles, accepted the priority of non-sensible Forms with regard to understanding and explanation, and will have made some progress toward grasping an account of what they are.[41]

The shortcomings of non-philosophers also show why wisdom should function—as the purification passage itself requires—not just as an object of aspiration for philosophers, but as a standard of value. First, genuine philosophers pursue wisdom as a very great good, but this is not merely an especially strong desire that they happen to find themselves possessing. Rather it proceeds from wisdom, that is, from a grasp of what makes wisdom valuable and thus worth desiring. Second, if wisdom were solely an object of pursuit and not a standard of value, it would not seem to give the philosopher any grounds for pursuing anything other than contemplation. In the *Phaedo*, Plato stresses that philosophers avoid ordinary unjust actions because their goals do not lead them to pursue the objects that prompt such actions, e.g. violent pleasures. But the *Phaedo* does not exclude philosophers from pursuing things other than contemplation, and the requirement that genuinely virtuous people act on the basis of wisdom shows how philosophers can have a positive motivation for performing virtuous actions. They will be able to respond, in an appropriate way, to whatever is good or fine in virtue of their grasp, albeit imperfect, of what they really are.[42]

1.8 The Phaedo: Political Implications

The *Phaedo* does not explicitly discuss political theory, but the dialogue offers a view of non-philosophers and we should consider its implications for what Plato's political theory could be. Its conception of the nature of non-philosophers commits Plato to a radically pessimistic understanding of the possibilities of political association. 'Popular and political' virtue might be inculcated in citizens by actual states that are comparatively well-governed. But, as we have seen, this sort of virtue is not sufficient to make the citizens' lives worth living. Such a problem, however, does not arise only for existing polities; in fact, no possible reorganization of the political and social structure of the city seems capable of solving it. Given Plato's account of their ethical psychology, non-philosophers must pursue goods which are not capable of making their lives worth living and the *Phaedo* does not make room for any sort of education for non-philosophers that could make their lives worth living without making them into philosophers. On this view, there is no way to encourage individuals to be genuinely virtuous, except by encouraging them to lead philosophical lives.

So what can a city and its laws do for non-philosophers? Let us assume that the goal of a city's laws should be to foster the virtue and happiness of its citizens.[43] Even if the lives of non-philosophers cannot be made worth living, this does not entail that all non-philosophers' lives are unimprovably bad: some possible lives which are not worth living may be less bad than others and Plato seems to think that having no virtue at all is even worse than having only slavish virtue. If the laws aim at both increasing the happiness of those who really are capable of virtue and happiness, and decreasing the misery of those who are not, then they should try to make all non-philosophic citizens into reliably non-philosophically virtuous people. There are two main ways to do this. First, an extensive and effective system of sanctions and penalties could affect people's calculations concerning pleasure, pain, and fear so as to give them greater reason to act in accordance with non-philosophical virtue. But such a system of sanctions would be costly and individuals' adherence to the standards of non-philosophical virtue would be contingent upon their calculation of the gain of the violation and the likelihood of avoiding the penalty. Other sorts of education and habituation are possible, however, for non-philosophers. Such training would seek to foster in them the belief that, at least in most cases, long-run calculations concerning bodily goods support acting in accordance with non-philosophical virtue, or, perhaps more effectively, the sort of habitual attachment to non-philosophical virtue attributed to the 'happiest' of the non-philosophers along with whatever forms of non-instrumental concern for others they can have. But none of this removes their false beliefs about the nature of the good. Thus it remains the case that the lives of non-philosophers are not worth living and there is nothing which suggests that any sort of education or training which does not make its recipient into a philosopher can provide him with a life worth living.

Concerns remain, however, about the sort of political arrangements that are actually possible. To begin, the radically different ultimate ends of philosophers and non-philosophers make it difficult for them to reach a stable agreement on the political and legal structure of the city. Both philosophers and non-philosophers will favor arrangements which best allow them to realize their own ultimate ends. And since bodily goods are especially subject to competition, agreement would seem to be very difficult to achieve. (They are, Plato stresses, the source of wars and faction, *Phd.* 66C6–D1.) It is possible that bargaining might produce an agreement which was acceptable to all, and that each person would realize that no agreement more favorable to him could be agreed upon, but those whose ultimate ends are bodily goods would be prone to engage in free-riding and defections from the agreed-upon scheme when they believed that they could do so without suffering sanctions.

These questions point to the more general issue of the relations among the individual goods of the members of a city composed of both philosophers and non-philosophers. (Problems about these relations cannot be reduced to the problem of what sort of agreements are possible, since, for example, even if a certain agreement maximally advanced the real interests of each person, some people might not be able to realize this.) The *Phaedo* does not tell us all we need to know in order to settle the issue, since we need to know more about the proper relation between the individual's happiness and the happiness of others. We shall return to this issue in our discussion of the *Republic*, but we can now note some of the challenges Plato will have to face there.

Problems of conflict among individuals' goods would tend to be lessened if individuals considered the happiness of others to be a part of their own good. As we have seen, Plato's position in the *Phaedo* on whether non-philosophers are capable of such other-regarding concern and, if they are, how far it can extend is not entirely clear. Yet even if they are capable of such other-regarding concern, difficulties persist. Since other non-philosophers do not have lives that are worth living, an individual non-philosopher would seem to have little or nothing to gain by considering their happiness as part of his own. The individual non-philosopher, on the other hand, would be benefited by considering the good of philosophers as part of his own good. But since he does not recognize what it is that makes philosophers' lives good and in fact rejects their ends as valueless, he would not be motivated to consider their good to be part of his own. Yet even if he were so motivated, he does not seem entitled to benefit in this way from their happiness. This would be too easy a way to avoid the requirements of the Dependency Thesis and of the 'right exchange' passage (*Phd.* 69A5–C2), which requires that one's choices and actions aim at and be guided by wisdom. Both demand a re-orientation of one's life based on one's own wisdom.

There are also problems in the case of philosophers. The *Phaedo* does not explicitly address the question of how far the philosopher is interested in the welfare of others. Given his conception of the good, he will avoid obvious harm to others, but it is not clear what motive he has to act to benefit them or to consider their good as part of his own good. But as we have seen, nothing in the *Phaedo* excludes the possibility that the philosopher is motivated to bring about good states of soul not only in himself, but also to attempt to do this in others. (Although it is not a theoretical claim, see *Phd.* 115B5–C1.) If this is right, it may well give the philosopher reason to foster genuine virtue in other potential philosophers, but it does not seem to provide him with a clear motive to act on behalf of non-philosophers, since he cannot foster genuinely good states in them. If, for example, the philosopher's other-regarding concern for non-philosophers takes the form of including their happiness within his own, this would seem simply to diminish his own happiness. And even if the philosopher could be motivated to improve non-philosophers' lives without making their happiness a part of his own, the fact that he could not produce genuinely valuable states seems to suggest that such activity may have a relatively low priority for him.

Nevertheless, even if the *Phaedo*'s account allows that individuals' well-being need not come into conflict (no one must be made worse off to make someone else better off) and that all individuals can recognize this, its view of non-philosophers has profound implications for Plato's understanding of political association. Any political association will inevitably be divided into two quite different groups: philosophers, who are capable of genuine virtue and happiness, and non-philosophers, who are not. Even if there were a complete coincidence between the interests of philosophers and non-philosophers, their agreement could only be an agreement on what best coinstantiates radically different ends. Both Plato and other Greek political thinkers hold that there should be a consensus or concord (*homonoia*) among the citizens of a good city, but the *Phaedo*'s account of non-philosophers' motives rules out the possibility of a substantive consensus, that is, a consensus on the nature of the ultimate ends that the laws and social institutions should aim at. No matter how stable the consensus is, it will not be one in which all the citizens 'wish for what is just and advantageous, and these are the objects of their common endeavor as well' (*Nicomachean Ethics* 1167^{b}8–9). For this reason, it will not be possible for philosophers and non-philosophers to form a city that is, as Aristotle, for example, thinks a good city must be, a common association aiming at the goal of living the good life (*Politics* 1252^{b}30, 1280^{a}31–2). Non-philosophers could not participate in such a goal. A city which was a *common* association for living virtuously and happily could only be formed by excluding all non-philosophers from citizenship.

1.9 The Phaedo: Conclusion

Let us take stock. We have seen that the *Phaedo* denies (1)–(4).

(1) At least some non-philosophers are capable of being genuinely virtuous.

(2) At least some non-philosophers are capable of valuing virtue for its own sake, that is, are capable of believing that virtue is good for its own sake and of desiring virtue for its own sake.

(3) At least some non-philosophers are capable of valuing for its own sake the genuine well-being or happiness of others; in particular, they are capable of valuing for its own sake in other people the most important constituent of happiness, that is, virtue.

(4) At least some non-philosophers are capable of living happy lives.

Since non-philosophers neither possess nor aim at wisdom, (1) is false. Although non-philosophers need not be solipsists, their ultimate ends do not include pursuing wisdom or genuine virtue or fostering them in others, so (2) and (3) are false. And given the tight connection that Plato thinks holds between virtue and happiness, (4) is false.

We have also seen that Plato's denial of these four claims rests on his psychology and epistemology. The fundamental failure of non-philosophers is epistemic: they do not grasp what is genuinely fine or good and do not appreciate the genuine good-making and fine-making features of people, actions, and things. Thus their ultimate ends are formed independently of such appreciation. In particular, the body, entirely apart from any operation of reason, has its own desires for certain sorts of objects. In individual non-philosophers, the soul or the reasoning element or aspect of the soul takes over these desires as ultimate ends and does not engage in the activity proper to it of pursuing wisdom and forming its ultimate ends in light of this. It is only by grasping non-sensible value properties that a person's soul develops what is divine within it and undergoes the radical transformation necessary for genuine virtue and happiness. Without undergoing this transformation, the soul is cut off from any appreciation of genuine value. And the only way that Plato recognizes of effecting such a transformation and bringing the soul into good condition is by bringing it to grasp Forms.

[W]henever [the soul] studies alone by itself, it departs yonder toward that which is pure and always is and immortal and unvarying, and in virtue of its kinship with it, enters always into its company, whenever it has come to be alone by itself, and whenever it may do so; then it has ceased from its wandering and, in relation to those things, it stays identically in the same state, because it lays hold of things of a similar kind; and this condition is called 'wisdom' [φρόνησις], is it not?   (*Phd.* 79D1–7)

[T]he soul of a philosophic man . . . would not think that philosophy should release it, but while philosophy is releasing it, it should of its own accord surrender itself to pleasures and pains, to bind it back in again to the body, and should perform an unending task of a Penelope working at some web of hers in a reverse fashion. Rather, securing rest from these feelings, by following reasoning and always being occupied in this, and by beholding what is true and divine and not the object of belief [τὸ ἀληθὲς καὶ τὸ θεῖον καὶ τὸ ἀδόξαστον], and being nurtured by it, it believes that it must live thus for as long as it lives, and that when it has died, it will enter that which is akin and of like nature to itself, and be rid of human ills. (*Phd.* 84A2–B3)

Other-regarding concern is not enough to bring about such a transformation, and even if a non-philosopher were to pursue a just distribution of bodily goods for all the citizens, he would still be trapped by his false conception of the good. In sum, the *Phaedo* presents a starkly pessimistic view of non-philosophers. But might Plato think that the environment provided by an ideal political and social arrangement could allow non-philosophers to attain a truly valuable sort of virtue and happiness without engaging in philosophy? To see whether this is the case, we must turn to the *Republic*.

1.10 The Republic: *Introduction*

We saw that in the *Phaedo* Plato holds that all non-philosophers are radically ethically defective. All non-philosophers lack genuine virtue and they lack genuine virtue because they have the wrong ultimate ends. They are oriented towards sensible objects and not towards genuine non-sensible value properties. As a result, their lives fail to be happy and, in fact, do not seem to be worth living. The fundamental problem was not that all non-philosophers violated ordinary standards of just behavior, pursued solipsistic ends, or simply that their views about the good and the fine were unreflective and not as fully grounded as philosophers'. Rather theirs was the deeper failure to appreciate what really is of genuine value. Thus if Plato's view of non-philosophers is substantially more optimistic in the *Republic*, this will require deep changes in other aspects of his views. It cannot simply be the case that non-philosophers in ordinary Greek society have only solipsistic ends and that the education in the just city of the *Republic* expands their sympathies. What we would need to show is that Plato's psychology and epistemology have changed so as to allow them to appreciate what is of genuine value without receiving a philosophic education or that Plato no longer thinks that such appreciation is necessary for living a good life.

The *Republic* attempts to provide an account of what justice is and to show that justice is good by itself for its possessor and that a just person is always better off than an unjust person, no matter how other goods and evils are distributed between them. Since Plato proceeds to develop an account of the virtues of individuals by first giving an account of the virtues of a city, the *Republic* sketches a picture of a just city. But an adequate sketch of a city requires a characterization of the vast majority of its inhabitants, that is, non-philosophers, and in the *Republic*, Plato explicitly and in some detail examines their nature and capacities and works out the political implications of his views of non-philosophers. He gives an account of how they are to be educated, of the ethical character they can attain, and of what role they are to play in the city.

1.11 The Republic: The Virtues of Non-Philosophers

The just city of the *Republic* is divided into three classes of citizens: the philosopher rulers or complete guardians, the auxiliaries, and the producers.

The auxiliaries form the military class, the producers engage in various kinds of craft production and farming as well as trading, shopkeeping, and so on, and all non-philosophers fall into one of these two lower classes.[44] Does Plato allow that they can possess the virtues? To begin, none of the members of the two lower classes satisfies the *Republic*'s official and explicit characterization in Book 4 of any of the four virtues of an individual: courage (*andreia*), moderation (*sōphrosunē*), justice (*dikaiosunē*), and wisdom (*sophia*). In Book 4, Plato divides the soul into three parts—the Reasoning part (*to logistikon*), the Spirited part (*to thumoeides*), and the Appetitive part (*to epithumētikon*)—and defines the virtues in terms of the parts of the soul. (I discuss the *Republic*'s partitioning of the soul and later developments in Plato's psychological theory in more detail in Chapters 3 and 4.) The virtue of wisdom requires the possession of knowledge (*epistēmē*). A person is 'wise [σοφὸν] by that small part [of the soul] that ruled in him and handed down these commands, by its possession in turn within it of the knowledge [ἐπιστήμην] of what is beneficial for each and for the whole, the community composed of the three [parts of the soul]' (*Rep.* 442C5–8). Courage consists in the Spirited part's preservation in the face of pleasures and pains of the commands of the wise Reasoning part about what is to be feared (*Rep.* 442B11–C3). Moderation consists in the agreement of all three parts that the wise Reasoning part should rule (*Rep.* 442C10–D1). In the case of both courage and moderation, the Reasoning part of the soul must be wise. Justice requires that each part of the soul do its own job with regard to ruling and being ruled and this requires the possession of the other three virtues, including wisdom (*Rep.* 443C4–444A6).[45] Thus each virtue requires the possession of wisdom and this, in turn, requires the possession of knowledge. Although it is not yet apparent to Socrates' interlocutors by the end of Book 4, this characterization excludes all non-philosophers from virtue since, as Books 5–7 proceed to make clear, the auxiliaries and the producers lack knowledge.[46]

Thus the *Republic*, like the *Phaedo*, rejects the claims of non-philosophers to possess any genuine virtue. One might object, however, that from the fact that non-philosophers fail to satisfy Book 4's accounts of the virtues, it does not follow that they are as badly off as non-philosophers in the *Phaedo*. Although they fail to have the 'highest grade' of virtue or 'perfect' virtue, that is, 'philosophical' virtue, non-philosophers might still have a lower grade or imperfect form of virtue. But Plato never character-izes the virtues defined in Book 4 in any of these qualified ways. The Book 4 characterization is not merely an account of one species of genuine virtue that is restricted to philosophers, while other species of genuine virtue are had by non-philosophers. The Book 4 characterization is, rather, Plato's account in the *Republic* of what genuine virtue is. The *Republic* does, how-ever, sometimes apply to non-philosophers virtue terms that are verbally qualified in some way. They might, for example, possess 'political courage' or 'moderation for the masses'. But in the *Phaedo*, too, Plato was willing to attribute to non-philosophers verbally qualified forms of virtue such as 'popular', 'political', and 'slavish' virtue. To see how closely such psycho-logical states approximate genuine virtue and how far they benefit their pos-sessors, we must turn to the relevant passages.

In Book 4, Plato gives an account of 'political courage'.

Socrates: Courage [τὴν ἀνδρείαν] is a certain kind of preserving ... The preserv-ing of the belief [τῆς δόξης] produced by law through education about what—and what sort of thing—is terrible. And by preserving through everything, I mean preserving that belief and not casting it out in pains and pleasures and desires and fears ... This kind of capacity and this kind of preservation, through everything, of the right and lawful belief about what is terrible and what is not, I call courage; and so I set it down, unless you disagree.
Glaucon: But I do not disagree. For, I think that you regard the right belief [τὴν ὀρθὴν δόξαν] about these same things that comes to be without education—that found in beasts and slaves—as not at all lawful and call it something other than courage.[47]
. . .
Soc. : Yes, do accept it, but as political courage [πολιτικήν γε] ... (*Rep.* 429C5–430C3)

This passage comes in the course of a discussion of what makes the city cour-ageous, not during Plato's account of the virtues of individuals. It is thus unclear whether it attributes a qualified sort of courage to the auxiliaries (i.e. 'political courage') or whether it merely claims that the preservation by the auxiliaries of the opinion handed down by the philosopher rulers makes the city courageous without taking a position on what this condition in the

auxiliaries is to be called.[48] But in either case, the passage identifies a characteristic of the auxiliaries that resembles a genuine virtue. Genuine courage
consists in the preservation by the Spirited part of the soul of the commands
that the Reasoning part hands down on the basis of its own wisdom; political
courage consists in the auxiliaries' preservation of the commands handed
down by the philosopher rulers. Plato also explicitly gives an account of non-
philosophic moderation: 'For the masses, are these not the main points of
moderation: to be obedient to their rulers and themselves to be rulers over the
pleasures of drink, sex, and food?' (*Rep.* 389D9–E2).[49]

We should not yet, however, accept that there is a significant and substantive resemblance between the virtues of philosophers and those of
non-philosophers or that the virtues of the latter are sufficient to provide
them with a good life. In neither of the above cases of courage and
moderation is the sort of qualified virtue attributed to non-philosophers
described in a manner analogous to genuine virtue, that is, in terms of the
condition of the parts of the soul. In particular, in neither case do we
receive an account of the Reasoning part of those with non-philosophic
virtue or of their ultimate ends. Auxiliaries may preserve the rulers' commands and both of the lower classes may control their desires for food,
drink, and sex, but why do they do so? With respect to courage and moderation, the sort of virtue attributed to non-philosophers is described only
as a disposition to engage in certain sorts of behavior. Neither in the case
of political courage nor in the corresponding sort of moderation does
Plato characterize the ultimate ends of its possessor. We cannot infer from
the claim that those with political courage have 'right belief' that they
share, without knowledge, the philosophers' ends: although he does not
think it is enough for 'political courage', Plato accepts that animals and
slaves can have right belief about what is to be dreaded (*Rep.* 430B–C). But
an account of non-philosophers' motivations and ends is necessary for
evaluating their condition, since having the wrong ultimate ends was the
problem with non-philosophers in the *Phaedo*.

1.12 The Republic: The Ultimate Ends of Non-Philosophers

What is the *Republic*'s position on the ends pursued by non-philosophers? The most important passage occurs in Book 9 where Plato correlates the different parts of the soul with different objects of pursuit and claims that the ultimate end of an individual is determined by the part of the soul that rules in him.[50]

Since the soul of each individual is divided into three parts, in just the way that a city is, it [the claim that the most just person is the happiest] will, I think, admit of another proof. The three parts [of the soul] have also, it appears to me, three kinds of pleasure, one peculiar to each, and similarly three desires and ruling principles [ἀρχαί].

One part, we say, is that with which a man learns, one is that with which he feels anger. But the third part, owing to its manifold forms, we could not easily designate by any one distinctive name, but we give it the name of its chief and strongest element; for we called it the appetitive part because of the intensity of its appetites concerned with food and drink and sex and their accompaniments, and likewise the money-loving part, because money is the chief instrument for the gratification of such desires. And if we should also say that its pleasure and love were for gain or profit, should we not thus bring it together under one head in our discourse so as to understand each other when we speak of this part of the soul, and justify our calling it the money-loving and gain-loving part [φιλοχρήματον καὶ φιλοκερδές]?

And, again, of the spirited element, do we not say that it is wholly set on control and victory and good repute [πρὸς τὸ κρατεῖν . . . καὶ νικᾶν καὶ εὐδοκιμεῖν]? And might we not rightly call it the victory-loving and honor-loving part [φιλόνικον . . . καὶ φιλότιμον]?

But surely it is obvious to everyone that the part by which we learn is always wholly straining to know where the truth lies, and that it least of the three is concerned for wealth and reputation. Lover of learning and philosopher [φιλομαθὲς δὴ καὶ φιλόσοφον] would be suitable designations for that.

Is it not also true that the ruling principle of people's souls is in some cases this part and in others one of the other two, as it may happen? And that is why we say that the three primary classes [τὰ πρῶτα τριττὰ γένη] of people are also three, the philosopher, the lover of victory and the lover of gain [φιλόσοφον, φιλόνικον, φιλοκερδές].[51]   (*Rep.* 580D3–581C4)

This passage states general psychological principles that apply to people both inside and outside the just city.[52] Plato here returns to the three parts of the individual soul for whose existence he argued in Book 4: the Reasoning part, the Spirited part, and the Appetitive part. He adds to the account given in Book 4 and here attributes to each part of the soul certain distinctive pleasures, desires, and ruling principles. He claims people's ultimate ends and their objects of pursuit should be explained in terms of the parts of the soul. In each person, one part of the soul rules and establishes its own ends for the whole person.[53] Thus the philosopher rulers of the first class along with the non-philosophic members of the second class, the auxiliaries, and the members of the third class, the producers, will each be ruled by one of the three parts of their souls. The identity of the part of the soul that rules in the individual determines to which of the 'three primary classes' of human beings—the philosopher, the lover of victory, and the lover of gain—the person belongs. The members of the just city's first class, the complete guardians or the philosopher kings, are clearly ruled by the Reasoning part of the soul and belong to the first of the three primary categories, i.e. 'philosopher'.

Since these are general psychological principles, the members of the second and third classes should also fall within these three categories. Given their education, political and social roles, and Plato's description of their interests, the second and third classes cannot fall into the category 'philosopher' and thus must fall into one of the other two. In those ruled by the Reasoning part, the Reasoning part seeks knowledge of the truth and this, as we have seen in Books 5–7, requires knowing (or at least seeking knowledge of) the Forms. But the education of the two lower classes does nothing to lead them toward knowledge of the truth or toward a desire for such knowledge. In Book 7, Plato considers whether the musical education the auxiliaries receive (which is the most advanced education that they get) tends to the good of leading the soul out of the Cave and toward the 'intelligible' or 'knowable region'. The answer is that it does not, since musical education 'educated the guardians through habits. Its harmonies gave them a certain harmoniousness, not knowledge; its rhythms gave them a certain rhythmical quality; and its stories, whether fictional or nearer the truth, cultivated other habits akin to these. But there was nothing in it that aimed at any such subject as you are now seeking'[54] (*Rep.* 522A4–B1). Since the Reasoning part of the auxiliaries does not value or pursue such learning, the auxiliaries cannot be ruled by the Reasoning part. In Book 5, Plato sketches the extraordinarily limited place of bodily satisfactions in their lives: e.g. they have little or no private property, they are not allowed to possess money or private homes, they have few chances to engage in sex, and receive only limited and plain food and drink. If the auxiliaries were ruled by the Appetitive part of the soul, they would be very frustrated, but Plato thinks that they will be highly satisfied with the rule of philosophers. Since honor is the primary good that their training establishes for them, we should see the auxiliaries as being ruled by the honor-loving part.[55]

The producers certainly receive no more education than the auxiliaries and probably do not even receive a musical education.[56] Since Plato thinks that they, too, will be highly satisfied with their lives despite their lack of opportunities for gaining honor, we should see them as ruled by the money-loving part. (All that is essential to my argument, however, is that they are not ruled by their own Reasoning parts.)[57] There are several subtypes within those ruled by the third part, but the producers in the just city seem to pursue, in an orderly way, the satisfaction of the necessary bodily appetites. (Necessary appetites are those that are unavoidable or whose satisfaction is beneficial, *Rep.* 558D–559C.) In sum, both the auxiliaries and the producers will be ruled by one of the two lower parts of the soul: the auxiliaries by the Spirited part and the producers by the Appetitive part. Thus the ultimate ends of the auxiliaries and the producers are set by one of the lower parts of the soul without any distinctive contribution by the Reasoning part. The objects of these lower parts are fixed in kind: even in the virtuous person, the Spirited part pursues honor and the Appetitive part pursues the satisfaction of bodily desires or their attendant pleasures.[58] (In the virtuous person, the Spirited part will pursue as honorable what the Reasoning part, on its own grounds, identifies as good.)

One might object that Plato only says that he has described the 'three primary classes' of people; he does not say that everyone falls into one or another of these classes. Indeed, perhaps none of the citizens in the just city falls into the three psychological classes Plato has just marked out. We should not, however, accept this objection. To begin, Plato in the *Republic* recognizes only three parts of the soul: the Reasoning part, the Spirited part, and the Appetitive part. There are no further parts that might have some other distinct ultimate end. Nor is there some further entity over and above the three parts of the soul. So any account of the ultimate ends of individuals will have to be given in terms of these three parts.[59] We also have further direct textual evidence for these identifications of the auxiliaries and the producers.

1.   The long passage above from Book 9 (*Rep.* 580D3–581C4) opens with the claim that the soul and the city are divided into three classes in the same way (*Rep.* 580D3–4). This picks up a passage from Book 4 in which Plato provides accounts of the virtues of the city and of the individual and says that he uses the former to arrive at the latter.[60] In doing so, he makes the following two claims.

(A) There are three classes in the city and the city is virtuous on account of the affections of these three classes. (*Rep.* 435B4–7)

(B) The individual has the same classes in his soul and is virtuous on account of the same affections of these classes. (*Rep.* 435B9–C2)

It is not yet clear what makes a class in the city the same as a class in the soul. For example, the second class in each might be the same on account of the fact that each is, e.g., naturally suited to supporting the ruling class; if so, nothing substantive follows about the ultimate aim of the second class in the city or the soul. But Plato goes further.

[W]e surely must agree that each of us has within himself the same classes and characters that are in the city? They could not get there from anywhere else. It would be absurd to suppose that the spirited part [τὸ θυμοειδὲς] in cities was not derived from private citizens who are held to have this quality, as do the Thracians and the Scythians . . . or the quality of love of learning [τὸ φιλομαθές], which would chiefly be attributed to the region where we dwell, or the love of money [τὸ φιλοχρήματον], which we might say is not least likely to be found in Phoenicians and Egyptians.   (*Rep.* 435E1–436A3)

Thus the thumotic part or class of the city is due to the presence of people of a thumotic character, the money-loving class to those of a similar character. (Note that *Rep.* 435E1–436A3 applies both to the just city as well as to various unjust cities.) This passage does two crucial things. First, it identifies the three classes in the city as the spirited, the learning-loving, and the money-loving. Second, it claims that each class owes its identity to the presence in it of people with the corresponding character. For example, the spirited class is due to the presence of spirited people, the learning-loving class to those who love learning, and the money-loving class to those who love money. Plato does not offer here a further analysis of what makes people spirited, lovers of learning, and so on. He proceeds, rather, to the difficult question of whether the individual has three distinct parts in his soul, since this is what he needs to establish in order to define the virtues of persons. But Plato does return to this question in Book 9 (cf. *Rep.* 544D–E) and there offers an analysis of what it is, e.g., to be a learning-loving person: it is to have the learning-loving part of one's soul rule. Members of the second class will thus be ruled by the Spirited part of the soul, members of the third class by the Appetitive part.

2. Those ruled by the Reasoning part of the soul in Book 9 are philosophers and lovers of learning. These clearly are the people who comprise the class of the philosopher rulers in the just city. We thus should expect the second and third classes of the city to be discussed. On the basis of this classification of types of people, Plato goes on to rank the different character types with regard to the pleasantness of their lives and sees this as relevant to judging their happiness (*Rep.* 580C–588A). It would leave an odd gap in our understanding of the happiness of the city not to discuss the second and third classes at all.

3. Plato also clearly subsumes the auxiliaries under the timocratic classification. In his discussion of the timocrat, Plato takes as interchangeable the contrast between 'the honor-lover' (ὁ φιλότιμος) and 'the philosopher' (ὁ φιλόσοφος) and that between 'the courageous man' (ὁ ἀνδρεῖος) and 'the philosopher' (ὁ φιλόσοφος) or wise man (cf. *Rep.* 582B8–C1 and 582C6–9), and he attributes 'courage' to the honor-lover (*Rep.* ἀνδρεία, 582E4). While the musically educated auxiliaries do not possess courage as defined in Book 4, Plato does sometimes refer to them as 'courageous' (e.g. *Rep.* 416D8–E1) and there is no one else, besides the philosopher, whom we could expect Plato at this point in the *Republic* to classify as 'courageous'.[61]

In sum, we have good reason to hold that Plato's division of the city into three classes is based on his tripartite psychology. Each of the three parts of the soul has its own characteristic object and in each individual one of the parts' ends constitutes the ultimate end of the whole person. There are thus three basic classes of people who have different ultimate ends. In the members of the two lower classes, the Reasoning part does not do its own proper job of establishing the ultimate end of the individual by drawing on its own resources. The Reasoning part in the auxiliaries and producers endorses or goes along with the goal established by the Spirited part or the Appetitive part. Thus the auxiliaries and producers take, respectively, as their ultimate ends, the characteristic objects of the Spirited part or the Appetitive part.

1.13 The Republic: The Happiness of Non-Philosophers

Let us now consider the possibility of happiness for non-philosophers. While it might be the case that non-philosophers are as happy as they can be in the just city (that is, they are better off, or less badly off, in the just city than outside it), this is only a comparative judgment and does not tell us whether they in fact are happy, how happy they are, and what it is that gives them the kind or degree of happiness that they have.[62] We might find it obvious that citizens of any of the city's three classes can have happy lives and so think that Plato would as well, but we have already seen enough evidence to make us wary of relying on our modern intuitions as a guide to Plato's views. And Aristotle, for example, finds it entirely obvious that the members of the third class could not have happy lives: 'But if the guardians are not happy, what other class is? For clearly the artisans and the mass of laborers are not' (Politics 1264^{b}22–4).[63]

One of the strongest reasons for thinking that Plato denies that non-philosophers can have happy lives is that we have good grounds for pessimism, even if we do not explicitly rely on the claims that they fail to possess genuine virtue or that they are either honor-lovers or money-lovers or that they are ruled by one of the lower parts of the soul. Since all non-philosophers, even in the just city, are in the Cave, Plato could only hold that the auxiliaries or producers could be happy if he held that some in the Cave are leading the good life or at least lives that are good or choiceworthy for human beings. First, Plato says that he introduces the metaphor of the Cave to illustrate 'the effect of education and the lack of it on our nature' (*Rep.* 514A1–2). He then proceeds to consider the nature of life in the Cave from the point of view of the released and escaped philosopher.

If he reminds himself of his first dwelling place and what passed for wisdom [σοφίας] there, and his fellow prisoners, do you not think that he would count himself happy because of the change and pity them [αὐτὸν μὲν εὐδαιμονίζειν τῆς μεταβολῆς, τοὺς δὲ ἐλεεῖν]?

And if there had been honors, praises or prizes among them for the one who is sharpest at identifying the shadows as they pass and best able to remember which usually came earlier, which later, and which simultaneously, and who could thus best divine what was to come, do you think that he would desire these rewards, or envy those among the prisoners who were honored and held power? Instead, would he not feel with Homer that he would greatly prefer to 'work the earth as a serf to another, one without possessions', and go through any sufferings, rather than share their beliefs and live their life? (*Rep.* 516C4–D7)

Like non-philosophers in the *Phaedo*, the Cave dwellers are cut off from the surface of the true earth. And just like non-philosophers in the *Phaedo*, the state of the Cave dwellers is deeply undesirable: their lives, and not merely their cognitive condition, are objects of pity. The philosopher, that is, the person who sees things as they really are, would prefer to go through any sufferings rather than live their life. In the *Republic*, all non-philosophers are in the Cave and thus a pessimistic conclusion about their happiness is warranted.

While it is true that non-philosophers' lives and not just their cognitive condition are pitied, their lives are pitied because of their cognitive condition. The Cave metaphor makes it clear that no change that leaves them within the Cave can succeed in making their lives truly desirable. We would not stop pitying them, even if we were assured that they helped each other in spotting shadows or devoted time and energy to helping their children learn how to spot shadows. The fundamental problem lies in the failure of their education to make a sufficient improvement in their cognitive condition.

When the eye of the soul is really buried in a sort of barbaric mud [βορβόρῳ βαρβαρικῷ τινι], dialectic gently pulls it out and leads it upwards, using the arts we described to help it and cooperate with it in turning the soul around.   (*Rep.* 533C7–D4)

These arts are the mathematical disciplines that, unlike the auxiliaries' musical education, lead the person outside of the Cave. Plato's phrasing here echoes his description of the fate of non-philosophers in the *Phaedo*. There the souls of non-philosophers, on arriving in Hades, will 'lie in the mud'; in this passage from the *Republic*, their souls (or the best part of their souls) now really are buried in the mud.[64] A page later, Plato goes on to describe explicitly their fate in the afterlife. The non-philosopher is 'dreaming and asleep throughout his present life, and, before he wakes up here, he will arrive in Hades and go to sleep forever' (*Rep.* 534C3–D1). A life of eternal sleep should again seem deeply undesirable to us: it is one in which the best capacities of human beings are not exercised at all.[65]

There are further grounds for a pessimistic view. First, as we have seen, non-philosophers fail to satisfy Book 4's definitions of the virtues because they fail to possess knowledge. At the end of Book 4, Plato describes the failure to possess justice as a vice (*kakia*).

Come here then, so that you can see how many kinds of badness or vice [κακία] there are, I mean those that it is worth examining. From the vantage point we have reached in our argument, it seems to me that there is one form of virtue [ἓν ... εἶδος τῆς ἀρετῆς], and an unlimited number of forms of badness, four of which are worth noting.   (*Rep.* 445C1–7)

Plato goes on to claim that there are as many kinds of constitution as there are kinds of soul. The one right form of constitution is monarchy or aristocracy (depending on the number of rulers), but in either case philosophers rule. Correspondingly, the one virtuous form of soul is the one that satisfies the Book 4 definition and is ruled by knowledge. In Book 8, after the long discussion in Books 5–7 of epistemology and metaphysics which makes it clear that non-philosophers lack knowledge, Plato reaffirms that all the character types, except the one satisfying the Book 4 account, are kinds of badness or vice.[66]

Second, the Dependency Thesis again seems to rule out a positive evaluation of the lives of the non-philosophic lower classes. Both the auxiliaries and the producers fail to possess knowledge and if they are ruled by one of the lower parts of the soul, they have false beliefs about the good. Thus if Plato continues to hold the Dependency Thesis, they will fail to be benefited by whatever Dependent Goods (e.g. health and wealth) they have. We might try to avoid this conclusion by weakening the Dependency Thesis. The simplest solution would be to allow a Dependent Good to benefit its possessors as long as they had a true belief *that* the Dependent Good was good, regardless of why they believed it good. But this is too weak, since it would allow the slavish virtue of the *Phaedo* to benefit its possessor. A second possibility is to allow the belief that honor or the satisfaction of necessary desires is the good to play the role which is played by genuine knowledge of the good in the Dependency Thesis. I shall discuss Plato's Dependency Thesis in more detail in the next chapter, but the prospects for a Dependency Thesis weakened in this way are not promising. This suggestion would at least require an account of how the belief that honor or the satisfaction of necessary desires are good in themselves for their possessor could be a necessary condition of the Dependent Goods being beneficial. But the idea that lies behind the Dependency Thesis, I shall argue, is that a necessary condition of Dependent Goods being good for their possessors is that they have some appreciation of why they really are worth desiring, that is, some appreciation of their value. Neither the belief that honor or predominance is good in itself, nor the belief that the satisfaction of bodily desires is good in itself (or, more generally, that desire satisfaction is good in itself) offers an adequate explanation of why these things are good. An adequate explanation will require some grasp of how these things instantiate or are related to genuine value properties and that, as we shall see when we turn next to the *Republic*'s epistemology, is something that the auxiliaries' and the producers' education does not provide.[67]

But as we shall also see in the next chapter, Plato does not unequivocally assert or deny the Dependency Thesis in the *Republic*. This omission is surprising, since the Dependency Thesis would provide strong support for the *Republic*'s claim that just people are always better off than unjust people. From this thesis it would follow, for example, that unjust people's false beliefs about the good render whatever other goods they possess either unbeneficial or actually harmful.[68]

The Dependency Thesis makes benefiting from one's Dependent Goods a discontinuous matter: they simply fail to benefit someone who does not possess knowledge of the good (or the appropriate sort of true belief, if this is possible). In the later books of the *Republic*, Plato may suggest a more scalar conception of benefit. In Book 9, Plato ordinally ranks the five character types—kingly, timocratic, oligarchic, democratic, and tyrannic—in that order with respect to virtue and happiness (*Rep.* 580B6–7). But we cannot infer from this that all the types are virtuous and happy to some extent: the tyrant, for example, is most unjust and most miserable (*Rep.* 580C2). It is not possible, I think, to read off from this ranking exactly how happy non-philosophical types of lives can be. Nevertheless, the classification of everything below the kingly life as a kind of badness suggests that neither the timocrat nor the oligarch will have a significantly good life.

Plato proceeds in Book 9 to offer a further demonstration of the superiority of the just person's life and this is an argument to show that he has the truest pleasures and thus the most pleasant life (*Rep.* 583B–588A). Once again, the timocrat has the next most pleasant life followed by the money-lover (*Rep.* 583A). As the argument progresses, however, Plato at times seems to suggest that only the philosopher has true pleasures at all.[69] But even if some true pleasures are allowed to non-philosophers, they do not seem to be significant. Plato here understands pleasure as a sort of replenishment and correlates the truth of the pleasure with the nature of the replenishment. Specifically, Plato contrasts, in the case of bodily pleasures, the body being filled with food and drink with the soul being filled with knowledge of the Forms. The body and its fillings *are* much less than the soul and its fillings, so the pleasures or replenishments connected with the body are much less true pleasures than those connected with the soul (*Rep.* 585B–E). These claims about pleasure present difficulties of interpretation, but what is important for us is the very low ranking assigned to bodily pleasures. As Gosling and Taylor put it, '[T]he thought seems to be that a firm lasting container filled with firm lasting contents can truly be said to be filled, whereas when one has a non-stable container and volatile contents it is only in a dubious sense to be called a filling at all: can one fill a hair-sieve with liquid?'[70] If bodily pleasures are replenishments at all they are such low-grade replenishments that they are properly described as 'façades' and 'images' of true pleasures and as 'bastard' pleasures (*Rep.* 586B7–C5 and 587B14–C1). Thus even if the pleasures of non-philosophers count as real pleasures, they are barely such. If this scalar theory of pleasures is transferred to the case of the good, it would suggest that the goods of non-philosophers, although truly good for them, are such low-grade goods that they are only barely good at all.

Finally, let us consider the myth of Er, the myth of the afterlife and reincarnation that closes the *Republic.* According to this myth, some non-philosophers are admitted to heaven. So we might think that some non-philosophers are capable of or deserve some form of genuine happiness. But we have reason to be skeptical of this conclusion. After death, there is a judgment and souls then either travel an upward path through the heavens or a downward path under the earth for 1,000 years. This judgment, however, is not a final judgment. After their 1,000-year journey, all souls, except those of the incurably bad, choose another life.

[T]he one who came up first chose the greatest tyranny. In his folly and greed [ἀφροσύνης τε καὶ λαιμαργίας] he chose it without adequate examination and did not notice that, among other evils, he was fated to eat his own children as part of it. When he examined at leisure the life he had chosen, however, he . . . bemoaned his choice. And, ignoring the warning of the Speaker, he blamed chance, daimons, or guardian spirits, and everything else for these evils but himself. He was one of those who came down from heaven, having lived his previous life under an orderly constitution, where he had participated in virtue through habit and without philosophy [ἔθει ἄνευ φιλοσοφίας ἀρετῆς]. Indeed, so to speak, most of those who were caught out in this way were souls who had come down from heaven and were untrained in suffering as a result . . . If, however, someone pursues philosophy in a sound manner when he comes to live here on earth and if the lottery does not make him one of the last to choose, then . . . it looks as though not only will he be happy here, but his journey from here to there and back again will not be along the rough underground path, but along the smooth heavenly one.[71] (*Rep.* 619B7–E5)

We might take this myth to suggest that at least some non-philosophers, when living in a good city, pursue virtue and the good because they are living in a constrained environment under supervision. Once released from such constraint, they will go wrong. But while under supervision, they can be virtuous and have good lives. We should, however, reject this interpretation.[72]

The myth assumes that there are just two ways of participating in virtue: through habit or by philosophy. Habitual virtue, which includes that possessed by the auxiliaries in the just city, is not, even on the above interpretation, of long-run benefit. But even more pessimistic conclusions about habitual virtue are warranted. Souls make their choices of new lives on the basis of their conception of the good and choose in accordance with the habits and character of their previous life. So the non-philosopher's choice is a reflection of his judgment of what is good. This is not undermined by the fact that he denies responsibility for his choice and that he made his choice without sufficient examination (*Rep.* 619B9–C6). We are told that he is wrong to deny responsibility and that he, in fact, chose it out of 'folly and greed' (*Rep.* 617E4–5, 619B8–9). In particular, he goes wrong because of his false judgments about what is genuinely valuable; that is why, for example, he is attracted by the specious benefits of the tyrant's life (e.g. its honors and bodily pleasures). Although he immediately regrets his choice, he never says or hints that he was mistaken in what he did value about it; he only regrets that it has unnoticed consequences. And although the habitually virtuous non-philosopher laments that the tyrant's life involves eating his own children, he does not regret that such a life will tend to make his soul worse. (Nor does he suggest that he chose such a life because he mistakenly thought it conduced to virtue.)

Even if his false judgment of the good causes the habitually virtuous non-philosopher to go wrong in his choice, we might think that the delights of heaven have corrupted his judgment of the good. But the nature of their journey through heaven is the outcome of a just judgment by god and Plato does not think that just judgments harm people. No just judgment would put them in circumstances that would reliably corrupt them. If non-philosophers had started off with an attachment to genuine virtue, they would be better off undergoing the physical punishments described for those passing underground as long as that would allow them to retain a just character. The myth thus suggests that the non-philosopher has had false judgments about the good all along. Non-philosophers choose in accordance with their previous character and have only themselves to blame. What they value thus remains the same; the opportunity to choose another life merely reveals what they valued all along. The non-philosophically virtuous do not appreciate what is genuinely valuable and their orderly lives do not entitle them to any progress in their next life. Their existence is simply a depressingly endless cycle of interchanged paths.[73]

In the case of both the *Phaedo* and the *Republic*, it would be wrong to think that the only problem with non-philosophical lives is that they have bad post-mortem consequences. In both dialogues, the post-mortem fate of non-philosophers vividly expresses what it is like simply to lead such a life: that kind of life is what it is precisely because it is cut off from the most important good, that is, an apprehension of genuine reality and value. Wallowing in the mud or leading a tyrant's life is not a sharp change in the real quality of their lives, but rather is an indication—in the terms they can understand—of what their lives really are like. In the *Republic*, as in the *Phaedo*, it is philosophy alone that gives one a genuine appreciation of the fine and the good and thus gives one a good life now and hereafter. In the myth of Er, it is only the philosopher who will in successive choices pick the sort of life that leads to his returning to heaven. It is also worth stressing that there is nothing in non-philosophical virtue that leads to progress in the afterlife. (Note that this is true whether or not one thinks that non-philosophers are corrupted by their sojourn in heaven.) Non-philosophical virtue does not bring with it, nor does it merit, any closer approach to genuine virtue in the next life. As we shall see, in some of the dialogues following the *Republic*, especially the *Phaedrus* and the *Laws*, we find important changes in Plato's eschatology with respect to non-philosophers and their chances of ethical and cognitive progress in the next life.

1.14 The Republic: *Epistemology*

We have seen so far that the fundamental problem for non-philosophers stems from their cognitive condition: this explains both their failure to possess virtue and their failure to have good lives. In particular, I have argued that what they fail to do in both the *Phaedo* and the *Republic* is to recognize the genuine non-sensible value properties of things. So we must now turn explicitly to the epistemology and metaphysics of the *Republic*.

These topics have generated, and continue to generate, an enormous literature and many sharp controversies. I do not intend to offer here a full interpretation of the *Republic*'s epistemology and metaphysics or to take a position on each point of controversy. But what I shall try to show in this section is that my claims about non-philosophers are compatible with a very wide spectrum of reasonable interpretations of the *Republic*'s epistemology and metaphysics. I shall concentrate on the topics most relevant to the issues at hand.

On what we may call the 'traditional' interpretation of the *Republic*'s epistemology, Plato distinguishes belief or opinion (*doxa*) and knowledge or understanding (*epistēmē*) in terms of their different objects. Opinion can only be of sensibles (sensible properties and particulars), and not of Forms; knowledge can only be of Forms, and not of sensibles.[74] The traditional interpretation draws on two sorts of evidence from the *Republic*: (i) the argument in *Republic* 5, which distinguishes the philosopher from the non-philosophic lover of sights and sounds, and proceeds by distinguishing knowledge from opinion, and (ii) the further elaboration of Plato's epistemology and metaphysics in Books 6 and 7.

Let us begin with the argument in Book 5. This argument distinguishes knowledge from opinion in the following way.

(1) Knowledge is of (or is set over) what is.
(2) Opinion is of (or is set over) what is and is not.

Claims (1) and (2) can be understood in different ways and recent scholarship has clearly marked out the main options. To begin, 'is' (*einai*) can be used in several ways: (i) existentially, (ii) predicatively, (iii) veridically, and (iv) in an overdetermined or fused way.[75] Depending on which use of 'is' is in play, (1) (and (2)) will be construed differently. On the existential reading, (1) asserts 'Knowledge is of what exists'. On the predicative reading, (1) asserts 'Knowledge is of what is F' (where F is specified by the context or left unspecified). On the veridical reading, (1) asserts 'Knowledge is of what is true'. The overdetermined use is more complex, since a single occurrence of 'is' may display more than one of the three other uses. These options allow us to draw a further distinction. On reading (iii), it is natural to see (1) as correlating knowledge with the contents of a cognitive condition, that is, with certain propositions. On the other readings, it is natural to construe Plato as correlating knowledge instead with certain objects, that is, with certain features of the world (e.g. sensible or non-sensible properties and particulars).

On perhaps the most plausible version of the traditional interpretation, the Book 5 argument claims that knowledge is of what is (really or completely or unqualifiedly) F. Plato's point is that knowledge is restricted to objects that are F and not not-F, that is, knowledge is of objects that do not suffer the 'compresence of opposites'. This restricts knowledge to Forms, since on this interpretation only the Form of F is F and not not-F; all sensible Fs are both F and not-F. For example, the Form of Justice is just and not not-just, but the act of returning what is owed is sometimes just and sometimes not just. The Form of Beauty (or the Fine) is beautiful and not not-beautiful, but a beautiful woman is beautiful compared with other women, not-beautiful compared with the gods; the Form of Equal is equal and not not-equal, but equal sticks and stones are equal in some ways, but not-equal in others.[76] So on this interpretation, we should understand (1) and (2) as:

(1a)   Knowledge is of Forms.
(2a)   Opinion is of sensibles.

Accepting (1a) and (2a), it should be uncontroversial that non-philosophers do not grasp or appreciate—they have no knowledge of or opinion about—genuine value properties. It is clear that non-philosophers do not have knowledge as the Book 5 argument understands knowledge. All that they can have is opinion, but opinion is only of sensibles and genuine value properties are not sensible.[77]

Proponents of the traditional interpretation can also point to other passages from Books 6 and 7 to provide independent evidence that Plato endorses (1a) and (2a) in the *Republic*.

Let us agree that philosophical natures always love the sort of learning that makes clear to them that being that always is and does not wander around between coming to be and passing away.   (*Rep.* 485A10–B3).

When [the soul] focuses on something illuminated by truth and what is, it understands, knows, and seems to possess understanding; but when it focuses on what is mixed with obscurity, on what comes to be and passes away, it believes and is dimmed, changes its beliefs this way and that, and seems bereft of understanding. (*Rep.* 508D4–9)[78]

Some commentators, most notably Gail Fine, reject this traditional account of Plato's epistemology in the *Republic*. Fine argues that the Book 5 argument is not committed to either (1a) or (2a) and that later passages, such as those above, that may seem to assert (1a) and (2a) can be brought into line with the correct interpretation of Book 5. Fine endorses a veridical understanding of 'is' in the Book 5 passage. On this view, (1) and (2) should be understood as follows.

(1b)   Knowledge is of what is true.

(2b)   Opinion is of what is true and not-true.

More precisely, knowledge is of the members of the set of true propositions, that is, the set of propositions that can be known includes only true propositions; the set of propositions that can be believed includes both true and false propositions. So on this reading, knowledge and belief have different contents, that is, they range over partially overlapping, but different sets. But this does not entail that the objects that the propositions in each set are about are entirely distinct; a true proposition from the set of true propositions, a true proposition from the set containing true and false propositions, and a false proposition from the same set could all be about or concern the same object.

A traditional account of Plato's epistemology is, as we have seen, sufficient for the claim that non-philosophers do not recognize the genuine non-sensible value properties of things. It is not, however, necessary. Indeed, for my purposes, I do not need to decide whether we should accept the traditional account of the *Republic*'s epistemology, Fine's account, or some other option. To begin, the traditional account accepts (2a) and thus rejects knowledge of sensibles, while Fine accepts this possibility. Agreeing with Fine that knowledge of sensibles is possible does not entail that non-philosophers can have knowledge of or opinion about genuine value properties. Indeed, on Fine's view, non-philosophers cannot have knowledge of any sort, since they do not satisfy Plato's conditions for knowledge of Forms and she holds that all knowledge requires knowledge of Forms. Although knowledge of sensibles is possible, it will be restricted to philosophers, since they are the only knowers of Forms.[79] (The denial of a grasp of genuine value properties to non-philosophers does not require even this much and is consistent with the claim that knowledge of sensibles is possible even without knowledge of Forms.)

This illustrates an important point. Fine holds that (1b) and (2b) are the proper interpretation of (1) and (2). (1b) and (2b) are, by themselves, consistent with the claims that (A) one can have knowledge of sensibles without knowing anything else and that (B) one can, regardless of the rest of one's cognitive condition, have opinions about Forms. But one could hold that a full interpretation of the *Republic*'s epistemology must supplement (1b) and (2b) and that such a supplement, while leaving (1b) and (2b) intact, nevertheless excludes (A) and (B). And, as we have seen, Fine herself rejects (A).

What, then, is my analysis of the ethical defects of non-philosophers committed to? It is, I think, uncontroversial that non-philosophers have no knowledge of Forms, so the important question concerns the possibility of non-philosophers having beliefs about Forms.[80] So consider

(i)   Non-philosophers have no opinions about Forms.

Although this is sufficient for my claim, it is not necessary. The problem with non-philosophers on my account is that their valuing of things and actions is not based on a grasp of genuine value properties. Whether they can have true beliefs about, e.g., the Form of Bed or of Finger (if there are such Forms) seems to be independent of this claim.

What, then, of (ii)?

(ii)   Non-philosophers have no opinions about value Forms.

Nor is (ii) necessary for my claim, since even if non-philosophers had opinions about value Forms, they might simply have false beliefs about them which would result in their systematically misvaluing things. What, then, of (iii)?

(iii) Non-philosophers have no true opinions about value Forms.

This, too, is not necessary, since some non-philosophers might have various sorts of true opinions about value Forms, but still be subject to the ethical

defect I suggest. They might, for example, think that the Form of the Fine
has no temporal or spatial location, but have no opinion about whether the
Form of the Fine is what makes fine things fine. Or perhaps they only
endorse claims of the sort 'The Form of the Fine is either fine or not fine'.
Such true opinions do not enter into their valuing of things. So let us consider

(iv) Non-philosophers' valuing of things and actions is not based on
their opinions about value Forms.

This is clearly not necessary for my position, since non-philosophers'
valuing of things and actions might be based on their false opinions
about value Forms. So consider, as a first approximation:

(v) Non-philosophers' valuing of things and actions is not based on
their true opinions about value Forms.[81]

Let us begin by considering some textual evidence. In Book 5 of the
Republic, Plato faces up to the task of showing that if cities are going to be
happy they must be ruled by philosophers. To do this, he needs to show
what a philosopher is.

And once that is clear, we should be able to defend ourselves by showing that the
people we mean are fitted by nature both to lay hold of philosophy [ἅπτεσθαί τε
φιλοσοφίας] and to rule in the city, while the rest are naturally fitted to leave
philosophy alone and follow their leader [τοῖς δ' ἄλλοις μήτε ἅπτεσθαι
ἀκολουθεῖν τε τῷ ἡγουμένῳ]. (*Rep.* 474B7–C3)

Thus only the first class in the just city will lay hold or engage in philosophy.
Plato proceeds to distinguish between philosophers who 'love the sight of
truth' [τοὺς τῆς ἀληθείας ... φιλοθεάμονας, *Rep.* 475E4] and the 'lovers of
sights, lovers of craft and practical people' [φιλοθεάμονάς τε καὶ φιλοτέχνους
καὶ πρακτικούς, *Rep.* 476A10].

The lovers of sights and sounds see and embrace fine [καλὰς] sounds, colors, and
shapes, and everything fashioned out of them, but their thought is unable to see
and embrace the nature of the fine itself ... there are very few people who would
be able to reach the fine itself and see it by itself ... What about someone who recognizes fine things, but does not recognize the fine itself and is not able to follow
anyone who could lead him to knowledge of it? Do you not think he is living in a
dream rather than a wakened state? Is not dreaming this: whether asleep or awake,

to think that a likeness is not a likeness but rather the thing itself that it is like? (*Rep.* 476B4–C7)

The lover of fine sights is one who 'thinks there is no fine itself and no one character of the fine itself that remains always the same in all respects but who does believe in the many fines—the lover of sights . . . would not allow anyone to say that the fine itself is one or that the just is one or any of the rest' (*Rep.* 479A1–5). Only the philosopher 'thinks there is some fine itself, and is able both to see it and the things that participate in it and does not think that the things that participate in it are it nor that it itself is the things that participate in it' (*Rep.* 476C9–D3).

The lover of fine sights and sounds believes that there are many properties, and not just one, that make things fine and thinks that these are sensible properties, e.g. colors and shapes.[82] It is crucial to see that such a condition is not restricted to the early stages of human development or to those who are, by normal human standards, stupid or unsophisticated. Such a condition is not confined to children or to those who lack a conventionally good education. The lovers of sights and sounds, after all, 'take pleasure in learning things' (*Rep.* 475D2–3) and are enthusiastic connoisseurs of the products of high culture. They enjoy and appreciate painting, sculpture, and especially music and poetry. They do not, however, accept the existence of non-sensible Forms, but instead hold that the beauty or fineness of beautiful or fine actions and things can be accounted for without reference to Forms and in terms of sensible properties. They satisfy (v), since their valuing of things and actions is not based on their true opinions about value Forms.

We have good reason to think that no non-philosopher in the *Republic* advances beyond this level. First, as we have seen, musical education—which is the most advanced education that non-philosophers receive—does not lead its recipients toward being. In Book 7, after having established earlier that philosophers must rule in the just city, Plato asks what sort of education can produce philosophers. This study is a 'turning of the soul from a day that is a kind of night to the true day—the ascent to what is, which we say is true philosophy'; it is a study that 'draws the soul from the realm of becoming to the realm of what is' (*Rep.* 521C6–8, 521D3–4). Plato proceeds to inquire whether any sort of education they have discussed can accomplish this. Music, poetry, physical training, and all the other arts fail to accomplish this (*Rep.* 521D13–522B5). The only study that can do this is mathematics when undertaken in the proper way, but no one uses it correctly, that is, in such a way as 'to draw one toward being' (*Rep.* 523A2–3). Thus the education of all people in the just city, except that of philosophers, simply does not turn them toward genuine non-sensible value properties and this claim is neutral on whether we can, as a result of an appropriate education, have opinions about these properties or can have only knowledge.[83] Second, the members of the lower two classes, even in the just city, remain in the Cave and while in the Cave they recognize nothing beyond participants.[84]

What about Recollection? If the objects of Recollection are non-sensibles and non-philosophers recollect, then they might at least have some sort of grasp of some non-sensibles. (Note that this is perfectly consistent with (v).) The *Republic* makes no explicit reference to Recollection.[85] Nevertheless, even if Recollection has a place in the *Republic's* epistemology, it does not seem to play a role in non-philosophers' beliefs about the fine and the good. First, consider, for example, Fine's account of the *Republic's* epistemology. On Fine's view, the transition from the lowest level of the Divided Line, imagination, to the next higher level, opinion, is accomplished via the elenchus and the elenchus involves Recollection. We can accept this while still maintaining (v), since we can also agree with Fine that most citizens do not make such a transition about ethics and thus do not recollect.[86]

Second, as we shall see in more detail in Chapter 4, Recollection is not invoked by Plato in the middle period to explain the ordinary acquisition of concepts or basic language competency, but only to explain some more sophisticated cognitive achievement. In the *Phaedo*, the dialogue whose account of Recollection is most relevant to the *Republic*, Recollection requires an explicit recognition of non-sensibles. In recollecting the Form of the Equal, one recognizes its non-identity with sensible equals.[87] We have seen no reason to think that the education of non-philosophers in the *Republic* gives them a belief in the existence of Forms and their non-identity with sensibles. (Allowing that mathematicians accept the existence of non-sensible properties or particulars, whether or not this involves explicit acceptance of Forms, would not help non-philosophers, since their musical education does not include these sorts of mathematical studies.)

Third, if there is Recollection in the *Republic*, it is plausible to associate it with the 'turning around' of the soul that is accomplished only by the sort of mathematical training that goes beyond musical education. Here, again, Recollection will be associated with the first recognition of non-sensible properties and principles of order. The final reason for denying that Recollection is involved in non-philosophers' ethical views is that, as we have seen, their conceptions of the good are those of the two lower parts of the soul. The Reasoning part of the soul takes over these conceptions of the good, but does not effect essential changes in them. But like the body in the *Phaedo*, the lower parts do not have access to the Forms. (As we shall see in Chapter 4, this is a claim that Plato unequivocally endorses in the *Phaedrus*.)

In sum, the fundamental problem of non-philosophers is that they do not accept the existence of non-sensible value properties and do not base their valuing, in an appropriate way, on such properties.[88] So whether or not we accept a traditional interpretation of the *Republic*'s epistemology, we should still accept that the fundamental failure of non-philosophers is this epistemic defect. We thus see that there is a gradual unfolding of Plato's views about non-philosophers in the *Republic*. Books 2 and 3 give an account of what seems to be the only education that the citizens of the just city are to receive and an education that thus seems to be sufficient for virtue. The construction of the just city is finished in Book 4 and this allows Plato to give a definition of the virtues. This is a definition that non-philosophers will not satisfy, although their failure to do so is not yet clear to Socrates' interlocutors. The reasons why they fail cannot be clear until the long discussions of epistemology and metaphysics in Books 5–7. Once this account has been given, Plato returns to his account of the tripartite soul. We receive a classification of different kinds of people and then, in Book 9, an explicit characterization of the goals of people based on an account of the goals of the parts of the soul.

1.15 The Republic: Non-Philosophers—Solipsism and Instrumentality?

Once again, we must be careful not to overstate Plato's pessimism about non-philosophers and not to misidentify its source. As in the *Phaedo*, Plato in the *Republic* need not hold that all non-philosophers are ethical solipsists or that they value all forms of virtue only instrumentally. We can see that at least some non-philosophers seem to be capable of forms of other-regarding concern by turning to a dialogue chronologically close to the *Republic*, the *Symposium*.[89] In the *Symposium*, Plato holds that each person desires to have the good always and understands this as a desire to possess the good and be immortal (*Symp.* 206A, 207A). This desire, however, can take different expressions.

In the case of each of us, old parts of our bodies are lost, but generate new ones and old opinions, desires, habits, and so on are lost, but also generate new ones. We can also generate in other ways; we can engage in physical generation and leave behind children, or in a higher and better kind of generation and leave behind the sort of offspring that Homer and Hesiod did (*Symp.* 207D–209D). Everything naturally 'values its own offspring' and seeks to preserve them (*Symp.* 208B4–5). Our desire for our own eternal possession of the good can thus be expressed in different kinds of generation and it is this desire that grounds the fact that everything naturally values its own offspring. Although it is not clear exactly what the relation is between our desire for immortality and our concern for our own offspring, Plato seems to be claiming that our desire for our own immortal possession of the good gives us a non-instrumental concern for what we generate, that is, our own offspring.[90] Such non-instrumental concern, however, is hardly sufficient for genuine virtue. A concern for one's own offspring is, after all, common to all mortal creatures. In each case, this concern is conditioned by the person's own conception of the good and the fine. 'Those pregnant in body' seek physical generation, that is, having children (*Symp.* 208E1–5). The second group of lovers mentioned in the *Symposium*, who also do not progress to the 'Greater Mysteries' which involve philosophic contemplation, seek 'deathless glory forever' and encourage their beloved to similar pursuits

(*Symp.* 208C5–6).[91] For both of these groups of lovers, other-regarding concern is manifested by trying to make sure that the other attains what you yourself regard as good and fine.

The *Republic* does not explicitly invoke the *Symposium*'s theory of love and my account of non-philosophers does not require it to be present in the *Republic*. Nevertheless, what the *Symposium*'s theory licenses is also, roughly, what the social scheme of the *Republic* suggests. We should expect to find that many producers love their children and seek to obtain for them the bodily goods that they themselves value. Similarly, the auxiliaries will encourage all the children of their own class to seek and attain honor.[92] Many non-philosophers, it thus seems, will not be ethical solipsists. But supplementing the *Republic* in this way does not fundamentally alter our picture of non-philosophers. Such love does not affect the primary determinant of their condition: it does not give them any more accurate insight into what is really valuable (cf. *Symp.* 211D2 and 216A1–2).

We can now turn to non-philosophers' attitudes toward virtue. To begin, what is their attitude toward genuine virtue? Genuine virtue involves knowledge of the good and one of the most important genuine goods is contemplation. But, as we have seen, in non-philosophers the Reasoning part of the soul simply endorses or takes over the goals of one of the two lower parts of the soul. Thus non-philosophers do not value contemplation. And since they would think that genuine virtue is not directed to the good, they will not value it for its own sake. Given their ends, neither will they think that engaging in such contemplation is even instrumentally valuable for themselves.

Nor does Plato explicitly claim that non-philosophers value for its own sake the sort of virtue open to them. Political courage and the 'main points' of moderation both fail to make any reference to the agent's good, but in order to explain why agents should be interested in controlling their appetites or obeying their rulers we need to see why doing so is, from their own point of view, best for them (*Rep.* 389D–E, 429C–430C). If these are the virtues of non-philosophers and non-philosophers really do value them for their own sake, they would have to find controlling their appetites and obeying their rulers good for their own sake. We might, however, think that the typology of character states in Book 9 of the *Republic* (at 580D ff., discussed above) suggests a straightforwardly instrumentalist account of the value that non-philosophers accord to the sort of virtue open to them and to the sorts of virtuous actions that they can perform. On such an account, they will value their own virtue only insofar as it conduces to their own naturally preferred ends of honor or the satisfaction of the necessary appetites. Ordinary manifestations of the virtues—avoiding harm, giving help, and the dispositions to perform such actions—would also be valued by non-philosophers only insofar as they conduce to their own preferred goods.[93]

Such a reading is not without some support. Plato, in the later dialogues, explicitly expresses a very bleak view of the ethical capacities of the sort of people who would occupy the *Republic's* producer class. As we shall see in Chapter 5, those who would occupy the class of producers are excluded from the city of the *Laws* on the grounds that they cannot share in virtue. Such functions are assigned to slaves and resident aliens, since the badness of their ethical condition—unlike that of citizens—is not a direct concern of the city's laws. The more challenging case is provided by the auxiliaries. We might think that a character motivated by honor rather than virtue is a rather rare kind of ethical pathology.[94] But this is not a view that Plato shares. In the *Symposium*, Diotima makes the following defense of her claim that all people desire immortality.

Look, if you will, at how human beings seek honor. You would be amazed at their irrationality . . . if you had not pondered the awful state of love they are in, wanting to become famous and 'to lay up glory immortal forever', and how they are ready to brave any danger for the sake of this, much more than they are for their children; and they are prepared to spend money, suffer through all sorts of ordeals, and even die for the sake of glory. Do you really think that Alcestis would have died for Admetus or that Achilles would have died after Patroclus, or that your Codrus would have died to preserve the throne for his sons, if they had not expected the memory of their virtue—which we still hold in honor—to be immortal? Far from it. (*Symp.* 208C2–D7)

Diotima finds it entirely obvious that these great heroes would not have acted virtuously unless they thought that they would be remembered for doing so and that they were more inclined to run risks in order to gain fame for themselves than to save their own children. The cost of acting virtuously for these extraordinary heroes is death, but it is worth noting that Diotima finds it obvious that the thought that they would be doing what is honorable (although not actually honored) would not be sufficient motivation.

So exactly how pessimistic is the *Republic*? Does Plato think that all that the auxiliaries value for its own sake is honor insofar as it consists in being honored?[95] Such a claim would have one very unpalatable consequence. The auxiliaries would then be, *ceteris paribus*, indifferent between acting honorably and merely seeming to act honorably as long as they received the same honor in each case. (We should note an important clarification. The above formulation might suggest that the auxiliaries are ethical solipsists, but as we have already seen, this need not be the case. They will, it seems, have non-instrumental interests in furthering what they take to be the actual well-being of others and thus in doing, rather than seeming to do, what is required for this.) But leaving aside those sorts of cases in which the well-being of others is relevant, are the auxiliaries indifferent between being honored for actually acting according to the standards the philosophers set for them and being honored for merely seeming to act according to them? This is a question that within the context of the *Republic*'s just city may not have great practical importance. The auxiliaries' education is designed to insure that they do not have to face such questions. They will habitually conform to the city's standards of honor and will be educated to believe that the gods' judgments are inescapable. Insofar as their education is effective, they will not feel tempted to try to seem honorable without acting honorably.

Nevertheless, one might feel that this still underestimates the auxiliaries' character. And it is crucial to see that Plato is not committed to such a view. Plato in the *Republic* is not committed—and my interpretation does not require that he be committed—to thinking that the auxiliaries inevitably take as their ultimate end the goal of being honored and consider everything else as instrumental to this. The fundamental problem for non-philosophers is not that they must consider only instrumentally good the happiness of others or what they themselves think of as virtue. Rather their fundamental problem is that they fail to appreciate what is genuinely good and fine. They thus fail to grasp what genuine virtue is and fail to value for the right reasons the sort of virtue that they can have as well as everything else. Plato can allow that the auxiliaries hold that striving for honor is good in itself or even that they consider good in itself being honored for actually living up to the standards that apply to them in the just city.[96] Indeed, Plato could, compatibly with his pessimistic evaluation of their ethical character, allow that the auxiliaries come to value as good in themselves the actions and dispositions for which they are honored. They might think that actually acting in this way is good in itself and see this end as something having a certain authority, that is, as deserving to override the other motivations they may have. None of these options requires that non-philosophers appreciate the genuine goodness of virtue or of the other things that might be the appropriate ground of honor.

To see why, consider an example. Suppose that the auxiliaries in fact value virtuous actions only insofar as they are instrumental to the entirely distinct end of being honored. Suppose also that there is a psychological mechanism which results in the gradual transference of valuation from the original end to the instrument so that as a matter of psychological fact auxiliaries will come to value virtuous action non-instrumentally. Plato should not think that this sort of transition makes an essential ethical difference. It might make an essential difference if the notion of being good in itself were exhausted by the role of being an ultimate terminus for choice and desire. But this is not the only role played by the good for Plato: the good is constituted by those features which make a thing rationally worthy of being an ultimate end. So merely treating something as an ultimate end is not sufficient for appreciating it as deserving such a response. Plato thus could allow the auxiliaries to consider as good in themselves their dispositions to conform to the just city's standards of what is honorable and virtuous without thinking that this puts them in a good ethical state. And this might not be the result of such a psychological mechanism, but because they take over, unreflectively, their society's standards.

The central and persisting defect in the auxiliaries' motivations is that they do not stem from reason's seeking out and finding what is really good. The spirited motivations, even when taken over by the Reasoning parts of the auxiliaries, are not in themselves ways of grasping the truth about value.[97] To put the point in terms of the psychology of the *Republic*, the Spirited part of the soul is not capable of grasping the good-making features of things. This is not to deny that coming to have honor-based motivations is a crucial and perhaps indispensable stage in the virtuous person's ethical development.

Such motivations will focus the people's desires on actions and objects they may later find better reasons to pursue and such motivations, even after the acquisition of the right reasons, can be a powerful additional support for right action. Indeed, insofar as the motivation of honor might develop so as to lead people to hold that certain ends deserve to override their other motivations, it will be an important preparation for genuine virtue.[98]

We should thus reject a commonly held account of the difference between genuine virtue and the virtues of non-philosophers in the *Republic*. It is, for example, often claimed that the ethically significant difference between the genuine virtue that philosophers have and the sort of virtue that non-philosophers can have is simply that between knowledge and true belief.[99] But this is at best a misleading way of characterizing the difference between philosophers and non-philosophers, since it suggests that they agree on the content of the good and differ only in their epistemic states: what philosophers know is good, non-philosophers truly believe is good. But if the above interpretation is correct, the difference between philosophers and non-philosophers is much deeper than this, since it concerns the very content of the good itself. Non-philosophers will have false beliefs (or at least lack true beliefs) about the most important issue in ethics, that is, what makes things good or fine, and will thus fail to recognize, among other things, why virtue is good and fine.

1.16 The *Republic: Political Philosophy*

Given this understanding of non-philosophers, what follows for Plato's political theory? I cannot discuss here the entire political theory of the *Republic*, but I shall focus on two related issues. First, as we saw in our discussion of the *Phaedo*, there are worries about the possibility and stability of a political association comprised of philosophers and non-philosophers. The just city of the *Republic* requires extensive, highly structured, and complex forms of social interaction and cooperation among all the citizens. Given Plato's understanding of the nature of non-philosophers, can they be reliably motivated to engage in the sorts of cooperation required by the just city?

Although this is a very important question for Plato's political philosophy, it is not the most important question. Perhaps the most fundamental part of Plato's political philosophy is its conception of what a just city is and of the relations that should bind the citizens to each other and to the political and social structure itself. What is the nature of the political association whose overwhelming majority is comprised by non-philosophers as Plato describes them in the *Republic*? What goals can such an association have? What is the ethical value of the ties that bind the citizens together and of their activities in support of the political association? We shall find that in order to underpin the sort of cooperation he expects, Plato must appeal to several factors which allow non-philosophers to approximate the actions of a genuinely virtuous person without actually being genuinely virtuous. But this is only an approximation of what genuine virtue requires and this fact has deep implications. First, it is not clear that the factors that Plato appeals to are sufficient to sustain the extensive sort of cooperative activity he requires from non-philosophers. But more significantly, even if such cooperation can be sustained without attributing to non-philosophers the capacity to be genuinely virtuous or to value genuine virtue for its own sake, Plato must adopt a very restricted conception of some of the most basic aspects of political association, for example, citizenship, concord, and friendship.

Cooperation   The demands on the citizens in the *Republic* are high. The legal system aims at making the city as happy as possible, that is, at maximizing the overall happiness of the citizens.[100] Thus the laws will require all citizens to perform the special job assigned to members of their social class (guardians will rule, auxiliaries will defend the city, and producers will engage in appropriately regulated productive activity) and do whatever else is necessary to maximize overall happiness. What explains their willingness to do so? Even if genuine virtue requires such a concern for overall happiness, this does not show that non-philosophers have such a concern, since they are not genuinely virtuous.

Let us start by considering a view that makes the most minimal demand on non-philosophers' concern for others. On this account, the happiness of each person is entirely self-confined, that is, roughly, it consists solely in states of herself and these states are valued independently of any relation they have to the benefit or harm of others.[101] Nevertheless, all citizens recognize that they are members of a mutually beneficial cooperative enterprise and this is sufficient to sustain all the forms of cooperation that Plato requires.[102] One might worry that if the happiness of each citizen is entirely self-confined, the range of cooperation would be significantly restricted by the possibility of conflict among individuals' goods and that there would be frequent conflict between the goods of individual citizens. But this account holds that each person is maximally happy in the just city and that no person can maximize his happiness only in such a way that another person ends up with less than the maximal happiness open to him. Conflict will occur if people neglect their long-run happiness or form false conceptions of the sort of honor or bodily satisfactions that contribute to their long-run pleasure or happiness. But in the just city, people will be educated to true beliefs on these points.

It is difficult, however, to accept these claims. Even if members of both classes will be satisfied with relatively modest amounts of their natural goods, it seems that conflicts among individuals' goods remain possible. Given a relative scarcity of goods, there will be circumstances in which some individuals are not maximizing happiness. They will thus be motivated to seek these goods and since people are entirely self-interested on this interpretation, considerations of others' welfare will not in themselves give these individuals a reason to restrain their pursuit of these goods. Even if the cooperative scheme is mutually beneficial, free riding is an ever present possibility. We can appeal to the possibility of sanctions, the long-run undermining effects of defections, and perhaps the long-run effects of defections on one's own character, but it seems highly implausible that these would always be sufficient to rule out the possibility of gaining at the expense of others.[103]

We do seem, however, to have textual evidence that Plato intends to build other-regarding concern directly into all citizens' motivations. For example, in Book 5, Plato holds that the 'greatest good' at which legislators should aim in designing the city is that the whole city be one rather than many (*Rep.* 462A2–7). Specifically, legislators should aim at creating a community of pleasure and pain (*Rep.* 462D8–E2). We can see this as the requirement that all citizens count the happiness of their fellow citizens as part of their own happiness. If all of the citizens were to do this, conflict among the happiness of individual citizens would tend to be reduced (although not necessarily entirely eliminated). Nevertheless, there are serious worries about the possibility of this arrangement.

First, the community of pleasure and pain is supposed to exist among all the citizens, not just the philosophers and the auxiliaries. But this community of pleasure and pain is especially fostered by the community of women, children, and property and is undermined by their absence; and these institutions are limited to the first two classes.[104] (We might, of course, also share Aristotle's skepticism about whether such a wide extension of family sentiments is in fact possible.) For the producers, it seems that their goals and ends make it impossible for them to share in the institutions which foster unity and that, in turn, the institutions they live under only increase their reluctance to count the happiness of their fellow citizens as part of their own. The more heavily the happiness of others counts in the producers' own happiness, the greater will be the difficulty of showing that they will accept such a conception of their own happiness.

Second, there is a more general worry about the demand that citizens include the happiness of others within their own. If this strategy is to explain how cooperation within the just city is possible, Plato needs to show not only that citizens will be happier by including the happiness of others within their own happiness, but also that citizens will, in general, recognize this. But there are significant difficulties on both points. Given their conceptions of the good, the members of a higher class will consider the lives of members of a lower class deeply unsatisfactory. (The Dependency Thesis, for example, would suggest that the philosopher would consider no one else's life worth living; honor-lovers, it seems, would consider money-lovers' lives not worth living (*Rep.* 581D).) Further, producers will not find the philosophers' or the auxiliaries' lives good given the meagerness of their satisfaction of the appetitive desires; the auxiliaries, however, may find philosopher rulers' lives good because, e.g., they are honored. So except in the case of auxiliaries with regard to philosophers, it is not clear that members of one class would think that they would increase their happiness by including within it the happiness of members of other classes. Moreover, philosophers would be right in denying that the lives of the lower classes are good (and the auxiliaries would seem to be right in thinking that the lives of the producers are significantly worse than their own). And, as we noted in connection with the *Phaedo*, even if the producers and the auxiliaries could be brought to consider the happiness of philosophers as part of their own, it is not clear that they are entitled to benefit in this way from their happiness, since they do not recognize what makes philosophers' lives good and in fact reject their ends as lacking in value.

As a response to the motivational worry, we might try to appeal to benefits. The *Republic*'s just city provides benefits to members of all three classes and Plato at times seems to suggest that those who recognize that they have been benefited will tend to benefit their fellow citizens in return (cf. *Rep.* 412D, 463A–E, and 590D–E). It is the recognition that they are benefited by their fellow citizens that is supposed to be one of the main grounds of the friendship (*philia*) which citizens are expected to have for their fellows. It is intuitively plausible that, at least in many cases, it is just for the recipient of benefits to provide benefits in return. To determine whether such a principle could ground the range of cooperation that Plato expects from citizens of the lower two classes, we would have to consider more carefully the many factors relevant to the obligation, e.g., the actual and the just relation between benefits received and benefits returned, the effect of the attitude of the giver and the recipient on the obligation incurred, and so on.[105] Nevertheless, we should grant that both auxiliaries and producers are, in general, better off within the just city than outside it.

So will the auxiliaries and the producers be motivated to benefit their fellow citizens? The clearest instance in the *Republic* of the appeal to benefits as a motivational factor presents the requirement to repay benefit as a requirement of virtue and Plato expects philosophers to respond to this appeal because they are just (*Rep.* 519E–520E). Since the auxiliaries and the producers are not genuinely virtuous, the appeal to benefits does not show that they have a non-instrumental motivation to return benefits.[106] So we might pursue a two-track strategy. For philosophers, the appeal to benefits functions as an appeal to their sense of justice. (For a full justification, we would need a further account of what makes such a response just and of why acting justly in this way benefits philosophers.) For non-philosophers, the appeal to benefits is an appeal to a psychological principle: to the extent that people realize that they are benefited by others, they have a tendency to desire to return benefits for its own sake. But even if Plato accepts such a psychological principle, it is not clear what the relation is between such a tendency and the auxiliaries' and the producers' conceptions of their own good. Even if such a principle describes an innate human tendency, to the extent that it interferes with their achieving their own conception of the good, non-philosophers would be motivated to try to rid themselves of the tendency or at least to limit its expression. What Plato would need to show is that such a tendency to return benefits for its own sake is part of the auxiliaries' and the producers' happiness and would be accepted as such by them. Building such a tendency into non-philosophers' conceptions of the good without some such account threatens to be an *ad hoc* attempt to rely on an appeal to a natural tendency to do the work that cannot be done by their attachment to virtue. (It is possible, of course, to find some plausible motivations for, e.g., the auxiliaries and producers to act in accordance with such a principle: the philosopher rulers might honor such a tendency and its expression and try to habituate the auxiliaries to accept such a norm without doing their own calculations of good and bad. But in this case, the appeal to benefits does not do independent work.)

Perhaps the most interesting and sophisticated attempt to show how other-regarding concern can be a part of a person's own happiness is made by Terence Irwin. Irwin proposes that we supplement the *Republic*'s account of philosophers' motives with the theory of love developed in the *Symposium* and *Phaedrus*; although he does not suggest applying this strategy to non-philosophers, it seems reasonable to consider this possibility.[107] Restricting ourselves to the case of a philosopher, Irwin claims that when he comes to understand that contemplation of the Forms is the greatest good for him, 'he will also have reason to value other activities expressing his view of the best activities for his whole life'.[108] Irwin characterizes this 'expressive' desire, in part, as follows: '[W]hatever someone comes to value in the ascent he will also want to propagate . . . the just man values for itself his own p-justice [i.e. psychic justice, that is, the genuine virtue of justice as defined in the *Republic* Book 4], and so he will want to produce p-justice in other people's lives too.'[109] So the philosopher will seek to embody in his beloved the qualities he finds most valuable. In the *Phaedrus*, for example, philosophers are followers of Zeus, but various non-philosophers are followers of other gods in accordance with what they value. Philosophers will seek to make appropriate others into followers of Zeus; it is not suggested that this gives a philosopher a motive to make appropriate others into good exemplars of their corresponding god (*Phdr.* 252C–253C).

But what about non-philosophers? If they are capable of a similar expressivist motivation, they will also desire to replicate in others what they find valuable. Honor-loving auxiliaries will thus desire to make their loved ones into good honor-lovers; money-loving producers will desire to make their loved ones into good money-lovers. But it is not clear that such an account will justify the full range of cooperation required for the just city. First, this expressivist motivation gives non-philosophers no motive for acting with regard to members of other classes. Second, honor-loving auxiliaries and money-loving producers may find it difficult to extend this concern even to all those who share a similar conception of the good, since as this concern becomes more widespread, there will be a greater threat of conflict (a) between their realizing their own self-regarding good and others realizing theirs, and (b) among the self-regarding goods of those others in whom they are trying to replicate what they find admirable or fine.

Finally, even if we could find an argument showing that there is in fact such a coincidence of interests among the members of the three classes, the lower classes may fail to realize this. Their members may often have to forego certain benefits because philosophers realize that they would have bad effects (either on the characters of the individuals involved or on the political system itself). But the producers and auxiliaries are unlikely to grasp or accept the philosopher-rulers' reasoning in all cases: why, for example, should we expect them to accept the results of Plato's theory of the degeneration of the soul?

The nature of a city Whether the sort of cooperation that Plato envisages can be stably maintained is not the most important question for Plato's political philosophy.[110] Plato's understanding of non-philosophers brings with it an understanding of what a good city can be and of what it can offer to its citizens. I shall explore the issues surrounding this point more fully in

Chapter 5, but let us now briefly note three significant implications of the *Republic*'s view. First, concord (*homonoia*) is a fundamental notion in the political theory of the *Republic*, since Plato identifies the virtue of moderation, both in cities and individuals, as a kind of concord: 'this concord, this agreement between the naturally worse and the naturally better as to which of the two is to rule both in the city and in each individual, is rightly called moderation' (*Rep.* 432A6–9). This agreement between the naturally worse and the naturally better in the citizen body is an agreement on the same rulers and the same political and social arrangements (e.g. *Rep.* 431C9–432A9). But since citizens have different goals, the reasons for their endorsement will differ. The *Republic*'s account of non-philosophers' motives rules out the possibility of a substantive consensus, that is, a consensus on the nature of the ultimate ends at which the laws and social institutions should aim. No matter how stable the consensus is, it will not be one in which all the citizens 'wish for what is just and advantageous, and these are the objects of their common endeavor as well' (*Nicomachean Ethics* 1167^{b}8–9).[111] Even if a stable consensus is possible, it is ethically significant that it is not sustained by a cooperative effort to foster virtue among all those who are cooperating. Such cooperation lacks an important kind of ethical value because it is not aimed at producing genuine virtue.

Second, we have seen that Plato in the *Republic* stresses the importance of binding the citizens together by the ties of friendship. This friendship is based on the recognition that one is engaged in a mutually beneficial relationship with one's fellow citizens and, in the case of the guardians and auxiliaries, on an extension of family sentiments owing to the community of women and children. But only within the philosopher class will friendship be based on genuine virtue and aim to foster such virtue. The friendship that binds together citizens as such does not require seeing one's fellow citizens as participating in the common pursuit of virtue and does not aim at fostering virtue in all of them.

Finally, what does this conception of a just city and its citizens suggest about the place and value of political activity? Although his language is somewhat dated, Aristotle's great nineteenth-century commentator, W. L. Newman, captures well part of the contrast between Aristotle's ideal city and that of the *Republic*.

Aristotle's dream is of a State, not composed of protectors and protected . . . but of *spoudaioi* [excellent]—men of many-sided excellence, intensifying by their mutual relations as parts of a society each other's virtue . . . His ideal State is . . . one composed of fully-developed men, rejoicing in each other's manhood . . . The best State is that which is all gold, not that which is tipped with gold . . . The secret of a State's excellence lies in the fact of its consisting of a large body of excellent citizens organized aright.[112]

In the *Republic*, political activity seems to be restricted to the philosopher rulers.[113] The political activities of the rulers will be based on their knowledge of the Forms and will derive the primary part of their value from being an expression of the philosophers' knowledge. The members of the lower two classes are excluded from the defining activities of genuine citizens in that they do not have a share in the city's deliberative or judicial functions. The activities they can engage in to support and protect the state will rather be faithful obedience to the laws and commands of the philosophers, and prompt and efficient performance of their assigned social functions. Their exclusion from the city's deliberative and judicial functions, and thus from a role in helping to guide and shape their own and the community's future, is an indication of how far they fall short of the citizens of Aristotle's ideal city. But this is not the fundamental point. (A significant degree of exclusion from such functions might be warranted even if they were capable of handling them well as long as there were others who could do it much better.) Once again, what is of the greatest importance is the motivation for, and the value of, the activity they do engage in. The activities of the citizens in Aristotle's city aim at fostering virtue in all the citizens, and the political activity of the citizens is itself an especially fine expression of virtue and is a major component of their genuine happiness. Whatever activities the *Republic's* lower two classes engage in to support the city, they will not be motivated by genuine virtue and these activities will not proceed from and express an appreciation of the genuine value at stake. Thus they will lack a basic ethical value.

1.17 The Republic: Conclusion

Although in the *Republic* Plato's evaluation of non-philosophers is not as unrelievedly negative as it was in the *Phaedo*, Plato still rejects (1)–(4). (It is clearer, for example, that not all non-philosophers are solipsists in the *Republic*.)

(1) At least some non-philosophers are capable of being genuinely virtuous.

(2) At least some non-philosophers are capable of valuing virtue for its own sake, that is, are capable of believing that virtue is good for its own sake and of desiring virtue for its own sake.

(3) At least some non-philosophers are capable of valuing for its own sake the genuine well-being or happiness of others; in particular, they are capable of valuing for its own sake in other people the most important constituent of happiness, that is, virtue.

(4) At least some non-philosophers are capable of living happy lives.

As in the *Phaedo*, the fundamental problem for non-philosophers is their failure to appreciate genuine value. Thus their fundamental defect is epistemic. Non-philosophers' ethical education does not develop reason's capacity to grasp genuine value. Also, as in the *Phaedo*, this epistemological claim is bound up with Plato's psychology. The epistemic defect of non-philosophers is part of the more general problem that the ends of non-philosophers are set inappropriately. In the *Phaedo*, they are set by the body which is too epistemically limited to grasp genuine value properties. In the *Republic*, in non-philosophers the Reasoning part takes over the goals of the lower parts without engaging in the task of determining, through its own resources, what is truly good.

The *Republic*, nevertheless, provides a brilliant attempt to solve a problem that may have seemed irresolvable in the *Phaedo*: how can philosophers and non-philosophers be united into a just political community? We have seen so far some of the costs of the *Republic*'s solution and in the coming chapters we shall consider some of the respects in which the *Republic*'s solution comes undone. In the *Laws*, we shall find a new account of the ethical capacities of non-philosophers that rests on significant developments in Plato's epistemology and psychology and which, in turn, gives rise to a new vision of the just political community.

But before turning to the first signs of significant developments in the *Laws*, let us pause to consider some of the essential aspects of the *Phaedo–Republic* position. On this view, genuine virtue requires that the person engage in a very special sort of reasoning. Unreflective action that is in accordance with what justice requires, or even such action motivated by a sympathetic desire to help others, is not sufficient for genuinely virtuous action; and it, along with the dispositions that give rise to such action, lacks significant ethical value.

The idea that only philosophers can be virtuous and thus that only they can act virtuously is, as we have noted, quite alien to modern moral thought. But the claims that genuine moral motivation is a very special kind of motivation (which may be very rare) and that it requires the person to engage in a very special kind of reasoning are not alien to modern moral thought. Both are found in Kant. Consider, for example, the following passage from Kant's *Groundwork of the Metaphysics of Morals*.

To be beneficent where one can is a duty, and besides there are many souls so sympathetically attuned that, without any other motive of vanity or self-interest, they find an inner satisfaction in spreading joy around them and can take delight in the satisfaction of others so far as it is their own work. But I assert that in such a case an action of this kind, however it may conform with duty and however amiable it may be, has nevertheless no true moral worth. Rather it is on the same footing with other inclinations, for example, the inclination to honor, which, if it fortunately lights upon what is in fact in the common interest and in conformity with duty and hence honorable, deserves praise and encouragement, but not esteem; for the maxim lacks moral content, namely, that of doing such actions, not from inclination, but *from duty*... [I]f nature had put little sympathy in the heart of this or that man ... would he not still find within himself a source from which to give himself a far higher worth than what a mere good-natured temperament might have? By all means! It is just then that the worth of character comes out, which is moral and incomparably the highest, namely, that he is beneficent, not from inclination, but from duty.[114]

Let us pursue this comparison a little further and begin with Kant's psychology.[115] Kant holds that desires do not directly cause actions in rational beings. Instead, desires produce actions only by being incorporated into a maxim, that is, a practical principle. A desire presents an incentive for the agent or the agent's will. Such an incentive has a complex structure and presents both an action to be performed and the end to be realized by that action. Its typical structure is thus 'I will perform action A to achieve purpose P'. The incentive, however, by itself is not sufficient to bring about the action and the agent must decide whether or not to act on it. She regards these incentives as possible grounds for her choice. To decide to act upon an incentive, the person needs a reason to do so, thus she will need a reason for adopting the purpose of the action. The principle that she acts upon, that is, her reason for adopting *this* action for *this* purpose, is her maxim.

This account of the structure of action allows us to make clearer what Kant thinks gives moral value to action. What determines whether the action has moral value is its maxim, *not* its purpose. In the famous example from the *Groundwork* above, both the sympathetic person and the one who acts from duty have the very same purpose, that is, to help someone. The sympathetic person need not have any conscious or unconscious selfish motive. He may perform the helping action 'for its own sake', that is, because he finds it immediately desirable. Yet even if he does not have such an ulterior selfish motive, the action lacks moral value. Only the action that is performed from duty has moral value, that is, the only action having moral value is one whose maxim or principle of volition has the appropriate relation to the thought of the agent's duty. The dutiful person may share the sympathetic person's purpose of helping another, but the crucial difference between them lies in the dutiful person's maxim, that is, the practical principle on which he acts. In choosing to help, the dutiful person's purpose is not to do his duty, but what gives his action moral value is that he adopts for the right reason the purpose of helping, that is, he adopts it on the principle of morality. His maxim expresses the thought that he chooses the purpose of helping because it is required. In particular, on Kant's view, the dutiful person's principle of volition is to act on a maxim having the form of a law. We do not need to go into the details of what this involves, but, roughly, it requires the person to consider whether he can will the universalsation of his proposed maxim. To adopt as a principle of volition acting only on maxims having the form of a law is to act only on maxims you could will everyone to follow. For Kant, acting on the basis of duty in this sense, or having a good will, is the only source of moral value.

I shall return shortly to some of the important differences between Kant and Plato. But some of the similarities are worth stressing. In order for an action to have any moral value at all for Kant, it must proceed from a very special kind of reasoning. Although philosophical sophistication is not needed to engage in this sort of reasoning, unreflective performance of an action out of habit, or merely out of the belief—unbacked by further reasoning—that it is good or morally required or desirable for its own sake is not sufficient for it to have moral value. Nor is sympathetic motivation— such as finding helping others immediately desirable—sufficient. What is required is 'an intelligent view of *why* the action is required'.[116] Specifically, what is required is thinking about whether the proposed action and purpose have the right kind of universalizability. Genuine moral reasoning and choice that has moral value requires a very special form of reflection upon and appreciation of the grounds of your action.

For Plato, as for Kant, virtuous action requires a very special sort of reasoning. (I leave aside here complications about cases of sudden action.) Genuinely virtuous action must proceed from the correct direction of the Reasoning part. Even if the desires and emotions of the two lower parts of the soul prompt the person to perform the same sort of action that the virtuous person would perform, this is not sufficient for the action to be virtuous. Nor is it sufficient that the action not be based on an ulterior selfish motive; it might aim at benefiting others for their own sakes, it might be seen as something that simply is required, and it can even be endorsed under this description by the Reasoning part. Nevertheless, such an action fails to be virtuous unless it is based on the right direction of the Reasoning part and, in particular, on the Reasoning part's appreciation of why the action is fine or good.

We can thus see what is wrong with one common account of the difference between the philosopher and others for Plato. On this view, the difference is that the non-philosopher has 'the correct opinion as to what ought to be done but will not be able to give an account or justify his opinion' while the philosopher is able to justify his opinion as to what 'ought to be done'.[117] The problem with this account is that it suggests a mistaken understanding of the nature of virtuous reasoning and choice for Plato. It makes it seem as if the essence of ethical reasoning is to determine which actions have the property that they 'ought to be done'. The philosopher and the non-philosopher share this same ethical belief and the difference is that only the former can go on to give a theoretical justification of the belief that they share. On such a picture, it seems arbitrary to deny that the non-philosopher's action is (basically) virtuous or that it possesses a significant degree of ethical value. The action is responsive to the fundamental ethical value that is at stake here, it is chosen because the action is seen to be one that 'ought to be done'.

Such an action would, however, lack moral value for Kant precisely because it is not responsive to the fundamental ethical value at stake. The agent does not engage in the right sort of moral reasoning and thus the action is not chosen on the basis of duty or with a good will. For Plato, the essential task of ethical reasoning is to form and act upon an appreciation of the features that make justice and everything else that is choice-worthy genuinely fine or good and thus genuinely deserving of choice. The ethical value of an action requires the right sort of direction by the Reasoning part because the ethical value of the action is (at least partially) constituted by the fact that it expresses an appropriate response to, that is, an appreciation of, genuine value.

Both Kant and Plato require the agent to engage in a special form of reasoning in order for her actions to have moral or ethical value. They differ, however, over what the form of the reasoning should be and how it is related to value. For Kant, it is the good will itself, that is, willing according to duty, that confers value on what is chosen.

[J]ust as to explain a thing fully we would have to find its unconditioned first cause, so to *justify* a thing fully (where justify is 'to show that it is objectively good') we would have to show that all the conditions of its goodness were met, regressing on the conditions until we came to what is unconditioned. Since the good will is the only unconditionally good thing, this means that it must be the source and condition of all the goodness in the world; goodness, as it were, flows into the world from the good will, and there would be none without it . . . Value in this case does not travel from an end to a means but from a fully rational choice to its object. Value is, as I have put it, 'conferred' by choice . . . the Kantian approach frees us from assessing the rationality of a choice by means of the apparently ontological task of assessing the thing chosen: we do not need to identify especially rational ends. Instead, it is the reasoning that goes into the choice itself—the procedures of full justification—that determines the rationality of the choice and so certifies the goodness of the object. Thus the goodness of rationally chosen ends is a matter of the demands of practical reason rather than a matter of ontology.[118]

For Plato, the good will or the reasoning underlying ethical choice and action is not value-conferring in this way; fineness and goodness are, rather, a matter of ontology. Fineness and goodness are objectively real properties and actions and objects are fine or good in virtue of their participation in the corresponding Forms. Kant made willing on the basis of an intelligent appreciation of one's duty essential to the moral value of one's action. Plato's picture of the virtuous agent in the *Republic* makes his intelligent appreciation of the objective properties of fineness and goodness essential to virtuous action. The virtuous and rational agent, for Plato, is one who is properly responsive to the real value of actions and things. Without a grasp of these true value properties, the person must fail to be appropriately responsive to genuine value. So part of Plato's pessimism in the *Republic* about the virtue of non-philosophers rests on his understanding of a virtuous agent as one who is responsive to genuine value.

The other part rests on his conception of the psychological and epistemological capacities of non-philosophers. Genuine value properties are non-sensible and a proper conception of them cannot be derived from the contents of perception.[119] Such a proper conception requires that the Reasoning part of the soul does its own proper work and comes to an explicit appreciation or conception of these non-sensible properties. In non-philosophers, the Reasoning part of the soul does not do its proper work. Non-philosophers do not recollect value Forms according to the *Phaedo*'s criteria for Recollection nor do they undergo the sort of education that the *Republic* requires in order to grasp non-sensible value properties. Their ultimate ends are thus not formed by the proper appreciation of genuine value, but rather are set by the lower parts of the soul. As we have seen, Plato may hold that when the Reasoning part of the soul in the auxiliaries takes over the goals of the Spirited part, it does not aim merely at being honored, but instead endorses certain ways of acting as having to be done or as ultimate ends. But in the auxiliaries, the Reasoning part fails to go on to achieve a proper appreciation of the non-sensible value properties that constitute the ethical value at stake in the action.

What of non-philosophers' happiness? With this picture of the virtuous agent in place, we can better appreciate Plato's pessimism. Plato's conception of happiness is based on an understanding of what people are most fundamentally and people are, most fundamentally, their Reasoning parts.[120] This is not to suggest that Plato must adopt a purely contemplative view of happiness, since the natural purpose of the Reasoning part is both to know the truth and to rule the soul. What is essential to the good functioning of the Reasoning part and thus to happiness is an appropriate response to value and this may include both knowing it and ordering things in accordance with it. So the failure of non-philosophers is not simply their failure to grasp value, but also their failure to express it appropriately in action. The full extent of this failure can best be seen in light of Plato's teleology. Consider the senses themselves. They exist for a purpose and that purpose is to lead the person to a grasp of non-sensible properties of order.

We must next speak of that supremely beneficial function for which the god gave them [the eyes] to us. As my account has it, our sight has indeed proved to be a source of supreme benefit to us, in that none of our present statements about the universe could ever have been made if we had never seen any stars, sun, or heaven. As it is, however, our ability to see the periods of day and night, of months and of years, of equinoxes and solstices, has led to the invention of number, and has given us the idea of time and opened the path to inquiry into the nature of the universe. These pursuits have given us philosophy, a gift of the gods to the mortal race whose value neither has been nor ever will be surpassed. I am quite prepared to declare this to be the supreme good our eyesight offers us. Why then should we exalt all the lesser good things, which a non-philosopher struck blind would 'lament and bewail'? (*Tim.* 46E7–47B5, cf. 47C ff.)

To the extent that non-philosophers' appreciation of the sensible world does not lead them to such principles, their senses do not merely put them in touch with a lesser good than they could attain, rather their provision fails to attain its purpose and the senses themselves are wasted and in vain. Similarly, the lower parts of the soul in the *Republic*, insofar as they are not simply the unfortunate byproduct of embodiment, serve a purpose: they exist to enable the proper functioning of the Reasoning part. To the extent that they serve only their own purposes, they, too, are in vain. In light of this conception of the ultimate end of human beings as knowing and expressing the truth about basic value principles which are themselves the first principles of order, Plato's conception of a virtuous agent in the *Republic* is not merely an intellectualist eccentricity.

2 Virtue, Goods, and Happiness in the *Laws*

2.1 *Overview*

The following chapters explore in detail Plato's later psychology and ethical and political philosophy, but let me begin by sketching in broad outline some of the central differences from the *Phaedo* and the *Republic*. In the opening books of the *Laws*, Plato insists that correct legislation must be founded on a true view of the goal to be attained, and criticizes Crete and Sparta for their mistaken understanding of the goal of legislation. As interpreted by his Cretan and Spartan interlocutors, the goal of their laws is victory in war (*Laws* 625D–626B). But the true goal of all correct legislation is the whole of virtue: the laws of a just city must aim at inculcating all the virtues in the entire citizen body and this is the goal of the laws in their new city of Magnesia. This understanding of the goal of law rests on the claims that Plato goes on to make about the goodness of virtue and the relation between its goodness and the goodness of other things.

[T]he good man, since he is moderate and just, is happy and blessed whether he is great and strong or small and weak, whether he is rich or not . . . For the things said to be good by the many are not correctly so described . . . To speak plainly, I say that the things said to be bad are good for unjust men and bad for just men, while the good things are really good for good men, but bad for bad men. (*Laws* 660E2–661D3)

Plato here endorses a Dependency Thesis about goods. Every good, other than virtue, is only good for its possessor on the condition that its possessor is virtuous. Virtue, in contrast, is good for its possessors no matter what else they have or lack, and thus virtue is good by itself. Since virtue is not only a great good in itself, but being virtuous is a necessary condition of benefiting from any other good, the law code aims at fostering virtue in all the citizens. Moreover, Plato's statement of the Dependency Thesis is directed not just at a philosophical elite, but to all the citizens. Thus non-philosophers as well as philosophers are expected to come to believe the Dependency Thesis and to order their lives accordingly. So in the *Laws*, unlike the *Phaedo* and *Republic*, Plato accepts

> (1) At least some non-philosophers are capable of valuing virtue for its own sake, that is, are capable of believing that virtue is good for its own sake and of desiring virtue for its own sake.

Although the laws and the city's system of education will surely fail in some cases, Plato does not think that the laws' goal of fostering virtue throughout the body of non-philosophical citizens is unattainable, and thus he accepts

> (2) At least some non-philosophers are capable of being genuinely virtuous.

Accordingly, Plato does not assign honor as the best motivation open to non-philosophers and we find in the general prelude to the law code—which is emphatically addressed to all the citizens—the claim that everyone must pay the appropriate honor to virtue.

Of all the things that belong to one, the most divine—after the gods—is the soul, the thing that is most one's own. It is the case with everybody that all one's possessions fall into two classes. The superior and better sort are masterful, while the inferior and worse are slavish. Hence one's masterful possessions should always be honored above one's slavish possessions. So I speak correctly when I urge that one honor one's soul second after the gods. . . . There is no one among us, so to speak, who assigns honor correctly, though we are of the opinion that we do. For honor is presumably a divine good, and cannot be bestowed through what is bad: he who thinks that he is making his soul greater with words or gifts or certain indulgences, yet fails to change its condition from worse to better, seems to honor it, but in fact is not doing so at all. (*Laws* 726A6–C1)

To speak generally, 'honor' means for us following the better things and, in the case of the worse things that allow for improvement, bringing them as close as possible to the same end. And hence no human possession is more naturally well-suited than the soul for fleeing the bad or for tracking down and capturing what is best of all, and, after capturing it, dwelling in common with it for the rest of one's life. That is why it was assigned the second rank of honor. (*Laws* 728C6–D3, cf. 707D1–6)

Honor here is not the passive condition of being the object of others' attitudes; it is, rather, the activity of honoring one's own soul, which consists in efforts to bring it into a good, that is, a virtuous, condition. Although non-philosophers, unlike philosophers, do not possess knowledge, Plato now thinks that they are capable of appreciating the goodness of virtue and thus are capable of instantiating the genuine value of virtue and so of being genuinely benefited by the goods they possess. Thus Plato also accepts that

(3) At least some non-philosophers are capable of living happy lives.

As we saw in our discussion of the *Phaedo* and *Republic*, it was not entirely clear how far non-philosophers could aim at the good of others for their own sake. But, more important, even if they were capable of this, they were not capable of valuing for its own sake in other people the most important constituent of happiness, i.e. genuine virtue. But in the *Laws*, this is expected of the citizens generally: '[T]he man who is to attain the title "Great" must love neither himself nor his own belongings, but things just, whether they happen to be actions of his own or rather those of another man' (*Laws* 732A2–4). This is part of the general prelude to the laws and is addressed to all the citizens. Virtue is presented as having a worth or goodness of its own that gives everyone, including non-philosophers, reason to promote it both in themselves and in others. The *Laws* thus accepts

(4) At least some non-philosophers are capable of valuing for its own sake the genuine well-being or happiness of others; in particular, they are capable of valuing for its own sake in other people the most important constituent of happiness, that is, virtue.

These developments in Plato's views of the ethical capacities of non-philosophers have both a backward and a forward connection. The backward connection is to Plato's epistemology and psychology, which must have changed so as to allow these developments. Plato has come to think that non-philosophers can have at least a partial and imperfect grasp of genuine value. This requires that non-philosophers' goals are no longer set by entities which cannot grasp genuine value properties, such as the body in the *Phaedo* or the lower parts of the soul in the *Republic*. In Chapter 3, I argue that the *Laws* abandons the *Republic*'s theory of parts of the soul. The abandonment of the theory of the parts of the soul allows non-philosophers to appreciate genuine value properties, but it does not, by itself, entail that it is possible nor does it explain how it is possible. In Chapter 4, I argue that in the later period Plato develops a new understanding of how the soul's rational faculties structure and influence the rest of the soul's capacities. This account both provides a deep ground for Plato's more unified conception of the soul and allows him to explain how more ordinary forms of belief and cognition can involve an appreciation of genuine value.

The forward connection is to Plato's political theory which I discuss further in Chapter 5. Since non-philosophers are capable of genuine virtue, new conceptions of what a good city is and of what a good citizen is are both possible and required. Plato in the later period—tentatively in the *Statesman* and then decisively in the *Laws*—moves to an understanding of the good city as an association aiming at the common goal of living happy and thus virtuous lives. This goal is common to all the members of a just city, that is, its citizens, in a strong sense: it is a goal that each citizen is supposed to have and the content of the goal is that each person live happily and virtuously. The concord that sustains the pursuit of such a common goal will be more than an agreement—motivated by different basic concerns—on who should rule; it will rather be a shared agreement on what ends should be pursued. The common goal of the laws, as we shall also see, establishes a criterion of membership in the good city. Citizenship is restricted to those capable of sharing in the end of the city's laws and thus of living a virtuous and happy life. Those who perform the tasks assigned to the producer class in the *Republic* are excluded from citizenship and their tasks are given either to aliens or to slaves for the simple reason that their corruption does not directly harm the city.

I go on to examine the implications that this new conception of a city and its citizens has for basic aspects of Plato's political philosophy. I shall consider its implications for Plato's views about the appropriate relations between the citizens and the laws, the nature of political rule, and the value of political activity. We shall also see that Plato's new conception allows the good political association to have a deep theological and ethical significance that it previously lacked.

I begin in the next section by examining some of Plato's programmatic remarks in the *Laws* about the nature and the role of law. By seeing what law can and should be in a just city, we can learn something about the nature and capacities of those it is designed to govern, that is, the citizens.

2.2 *Reason and Law*

The *Laws* begins with the following exchange.

Athenian: Is it a god or a man, visitors, who is responsible for the arrangement of your laws?
Kleinias: A god, visitor, a god, to say the most just thing. We Cretans call Zeus our lawgiver; while among the Spartans, where this man [Megillus] is from, I think they claim Apollo as theirs.   (*Laws* 624A1–5)

The Athenian then asks about the semi-divine legislator of the Cretans, Minos, and the end of the laws that he established. Kleinias readily answers that all the Cretan laws were established for the sake of victory in war (*Laws* 625C–626B).

As we shall see, one of Plato's most fundamental—and his most frequently reiterated—political principles in the *Laws* rejects this as a normative claim. Despite their reputation for excellence, Crete and Sparta are radically mistaken in their conception of the ultimate end of law: the correct end for the entire legal code is not victory in war or the inculcation of any one virtue, but rather the inculcation of the whole of virtue. Similarly, insofar as the Cretan and the Spartan interlocutors claim a divine foundation for their law codes, they are radically mistaken.[1] Plato does accept, however, that in a good or just city, god, in a way, rules. Here, as elsewhere in the *Laws*, we see that unreflective common sense often hits upon the truth, but only a small part of the truth. The best existing cities recognize the formal aspect of the truth that god rules in a just city, but do not grasp what the content of such rule is.

[T]here can be no rest from evils and toils for those cities in which some mortal rules rather than a god. Our argument indicates that we should imitate by every device the way of life that is said to have existed under Kronos; in our public life and private life—in the arrangement of our households and our cities—we should obey whatever within us partakes of immortality, giving the name 'law' to the distribution ordained by reason [τὴν τοῦ νοῦ διανομὴν ἐπονομάζοντας νόμον]. (*Laws* 713E4–714A2)

For of all branches of learning, those that have the most sovereign influence in making the learner become better are the ones that pertain to the laws—if, that is, they should be correctly set up; and they would be, or else our divine and marvelous law [νόμος] would in vain possess a name akin to reason [νῷ]. (*Laws* 957C4–7)

The word for 'reason' is '*nous*' and that for 'law' is '*nomos*', so Plato claims the support of etymology for the link he asserts between reason and law.[2] Since reason is itself divine, god rules insofar as reason rules and reason can rule, if it finds expression in correct or just law. Reason 'strives to become law' (*Laws* 835E5) and Plato describes law as a 'calculation' or 'reasoning' (λογισμός) about good and bad that has become 'the common judgment of the city [δόγμα πόλεως κοινὸν νόμος]' (*Laws* 644D1–3).[3]

   The claim that law can be a good expression of reason in its highest form, that is, god's reason, should be surprising. God's reason fulfills perfectly the inherent task of reason to know the truth and thus it is a state of perfectly clear, accurate, and synoptic knowledge of the first principles of value and order and of the truths that flow from these principles. Law can be a good expression of reason, however, since reason is not exclusively directed to knowing the truth. In Book 10 of the *Laws*, Plato offers a refutation of certain atheists. These atheists hold that everything that comes into being does so either by nature, by chance, or by art. The 'greatest and finest' things come into being by nature and chance, while only lesser things are produced by art. They hold that the elements and their qualities exist by nature and chance and that it is by nature and chance that the entire kosmos comes to be. The political and legislative arts as well as justice and the gods (that is, human stories and conventions about non-existent gods) do not exist by nature, but are later products of art (*Laws* 888E–890A). Plato argues against these views that soul and the things 'akin' to it are what set bodies in motion and continue to order them (*Laws* 891E–899B).[4]

Belief, then, and supervision, reason [νοῦς], art, and law [νόμος] would be prior to hard things, soft things, heavy things, and light things. And, indeed, the great and first deeds and actions would be those of art, since they are among the first things, while the things that are by nature, and nature, which they incorrectly name in this way, would be later and would have as their ruling causes art and reason [νοῦ]. (*Laws* 892B3–8)

God's reason is responsible for the ordering of the world for the best. Reason 'governs' or 'rules' the world (*Phil.* 28D5–E6, *Stsmn.* 272E3–4, 273C2–3); reason orders and arranges the heavens and the entire kosmos (*Laws* 966E2–4, 967B5–6; *Phil.* 28D5–E6, 30C2–7; *Stsmn.* 273D4–5; *Tim.* 30A2–6, 37D5–7, 53A5–B4, 69B2–C3). This emphasis on divine reason as the cause of order in the world is a theme that runs throughout the late dialogues, including the *Laws*, the *Philebus*, the *Statesman*, and the *Timaeus*.[5] Reason has an inherent tendency both to grasp what is best and to order things so as to bring them into the best condition. Reason in the individual soul grasps what is best for the individual and directs the person in the pursuit of it (e.g. *Laws* 644C–645C). Reason, as embodied in law, also pursues this ordering goal at the level of the city as a whole. Reason determines that the proper ultimate end or *telos* for the city's laws and political and social institutions is the best condition of the city itself, that is, its greatest happiness. At the level of the kosmos, god perfectly instantiates reason and orders both bodies and souls so that, as far as possible, their best condition is attained (*Laws* 903B–905D, 967B). In each of these cases, reason, insofar as it aims at what is best, aims at fostering virtue (*Laws* 906A2–B3).

Good or just law can be an especially fine expression of reason. Reason as expressed in ordinary craft production can impose good order on inanimate materials and then employ the worked up materials as a tool to order something further. Architects, for example, can construct a straight-line that they then use in building a house. Although the straight-line possesses or instantiates a kind of good order, it does not possess reason and is not itself the origin of the ordering of the other materials. Reason as expressed in law, however, can bring order to creatures that can themselves possess reason and creatures possessing reason are the finest products of reason. This is why, for example, the Demiurge endows the universe itself with a soul.

It was not permitted (nor is it now) that one who is supremely good should do anything but what is best. Accordingly, the god reasoned and concluded that in the realm of things naturally visible no unreasoning thing could as a whole be finer than anything that does possess reason as a whole, and he further concluded that it is impossible for anything to possess reason apart from soul. Guided by this reasoning, he put reason in soul, and soul in body, and so he constructed the universe. (*Tim.* 30A6–B5)[6]

And part of the explanation of why creatures possessing reason are the finest products of reason is that they can themselves be originating principles of order.

Now all of the above [the four elements] are among the auxiliary causes employed in the service of the god as he does his utmost to bring to completion the character of what is best. But because they make things cold or hot . . . and produce all sorts of similar effects, most people regard them not as auxiliary causes, but as the actual causes of all things. Things like these, however, are totally incapable of possessing any understanding or reason about anything. We must pronounce the soul to be the only thing there is that properly possesses reason . . . So anyone who is a lover of reason and knowledge must of necessity pursue as primary causes those belonging to intelligent nature, and as secondary all those belonging to things that are moved by others and that set still others in motion by necessity . . . we must describe both types of causes, distinguishing those that possess reason and thus fashion what is fine and good, from those which, when deserted by wisdom, produce only haphazard and disorderly effects every time. (*Tim.* 46C7–E6)

Reason can move itself and in virtue of moving itself can move and order other things. It does not simply transmit orderly motion that is imposed by some external necessity.[7] We shall return to some of the metaphysical issues surrounding the idea that reason or souls possessing reason are self-movers in Chapter 4. But it is important to see that the connection between reason and the active origination of order is embedded in Plato's ethics and politics. Law can be an especially good expression of reason insofar as it helps bring to order human beings who come to possess reason within themselves and are not always subject to external direction.

Even good law, nevertheless, falls short of being a complete expression of reason on two related grounds. In each case, the problem concerns the relation between the law and the action performed in accordance with the law.

First, law is relatively fixed and cast in general terms, so that it will fail in some cases and circumstances to recommend what is best (*Laws* 875C3–D5, cf. *Stsmn.* 294A–296A). This failure of law stems from the fact that its directives cannot be as fine-grained or flexible as those issuing from living reason. But there is also a more fundamental concern stemming from the nature of law as an order. Near the end of the fourth book of the *Laws*, the Athenian asks whether the lawgiver for the new city of Magnesia should in making laws 'explain straight away what must and must not be done, add the threat of a penalty, and turn to another law, without adding a single bit of encouragement or persuasion to his legislative edicts' (*Laws* 720A1–2). A few lines later, the Athenian himself condemns such a procedure as 'the worse and more savage alternative' (*Laws* 720E4). The better method is for the lawgiver to try to persuade (*peithein*) the citizens to act in the manner that the laws prescribe. As André Laks has rightly noted, law here is seen as violent not only insofar as it threatens a penalty, but also simply in virtue of issuing a command with no explanation.[8] As a response to this problem, Plato proposes attaching preludes (*prooimia*) to particular laws and to the legal code as a whole. Such preludes are an essential supplement to the bare commands of the law in Magnesia. So I shall now turn to a consideration of the preludes in the *Laws*.

2.3 Preludes to the Law

In Plato's own view, one of the most important innovations in the political theory of the *Laws* is the requirement that good lawgivers try to persuade the citizens and not simply issue commands to them by means of laws. '[N]one of the lawgivers has ever reflected on the fact that it is possible to use two means of giving laws, persuasion and force [βία] . . . They have used only the latter; failing to mix compulsion with persuasion in their lawgiving, they have employed unmitigated force alone' (*Laws* 722B5–C2).[9]

In a series of passages from Books 4, 9, and 10, Plato introduces the notion of a prelude and offers a theory of why they are needed and of what roles they are to perform. Let us consider these passages in order.

Is [the one in charge of our laws] just going to declare straight away what must and must not be done, add the threat of a penalty, and turn to another law, without adding a single encouragement or bit of persuasion to his legislative edicts? There is one sort of doctor who used to proceed in this way, and another sort who used to proceed in another way each time he took care of us. (*Laws* 719E8–720A3)

The analogy between lawgivers and doctors is one that Plato has appealed to in previous dialogues. But there Plato's point was that since the doctor, unlike the patient, knows what is best for the patient in the long run, he is justified in imposing on the patient, even by force, painful courses of treatment that the patient would reject. Here Plato uses the old analogy for quite different purposes and proceeds to work out a new analogy between lawgivers and these two kinds of doctors.

We assert that there are certain persons who are doctors; and then, that there are in addition doctors' servants, whom we also call 'doctors' . . . Whether they are free men or slaves, they acquire the art by following their masters' command, by observing, and by experience, but not by following nature, as the free doctors do, who have themselves learned in this way and who teach their disciples in this way. (*Laws* 720A6–B5)

These two kinds of doctors also differ in the sort of patients they treat and the manner of their treatment.

[S]ick people in the cities, slaves and free, are treated differently. The slaves are for the most part treated by slaves . . . None of these doctors gives or receives any account [οὔτε τινὰ λόγον . . . δίδωσιν οὐδ᾽ ἀποδέχεται] of each malady afflicting each domestic slave. Instead, he gives him orders on the basis of the opinions he has derived from experience. Claiming to know with precision, he gives his commands stubbornly, just like a tyrant, and hurries off to some other sick domestic slave . . . The free doctor mostly cares for and examines the maladies of free men. He investigates these from their beginning and according to nature, communing with the patient himself and his friends, and he both learns something himself from the invalids and, as much as he can, teaches [διδάσκει] the one who is sick. He does not give orders until he has in some way persuaded; once he has on each occasion made the sick person gentle by means of persuasion, he attempts to lead him back to health. (*Laws* 720B8–E2)

Plato unequivocally condemns the method of the slave doctor as 'the worse and more savage of the two' (*Laws* 720E5). The lawgiver in

Magnesia must instead follow the model of a free doctor treating free people.

What was called a tyrannical command, and likened to the image of the commands of the doctors we said were unfree, seemed to be unmixed law; what was spoken of before this, and said to be persuasive on behalf of this, really did seem to be persuasion, but seemed to have the power that a prelude has in speeches. For it has become clear to me that this whole speech, which the speaker gives in order to persuade, is delivered with just this end in view: so that he who receives the law uttered by the legislator might receive the command—that is, the law—in a frame of mind more favorably disposed and therefore more apt to learn something [ἵνα γὰρ εὐμενῶς, καὶ διὰ τὴν εὐμένειαν εὐμαθέστερον].   (*Laws* 722E7–723A6)

As a means of engaging in the right sort of persuasion—although it is not the only means to be employed in Magnesia—the lawgiver must attach preludes to the laws and the Athenian distinguishes two kinds of prelude. First, he claims that the preceding books of the *Laws* constitute a general prelude to the legal code of Magnesia and he later requires that the entire *Laws* be read by all the citizens. Second, especially important individual laws will receive their own preludes: in addition to the body of the law which specifies the offense and the attendant penalties, citizens will receive an account of why they should act as the law prescribes.

In Books 9 and 10, the Athenian expands on this account of what the preludes are supposed to achieve. But before turning to these passages, it is important to note that the explanation we have just received of why persuasion and thus preludes are necessary is not merely a claim about what would be desirable in some ideal circumstances that will not obtain in Magnesia. Rather they are intended to justify and regulate the actual use of preludes in Magnesia.

In Book 9, in the course of setting out the provisions of a law concerning theft, the Athenian explicitly refers back to the Book 4 passages we have just considered.

Athenian: [W]hat pertains to the laying down of laws has never been worked out correctly in any way . . . We did not make a bad image, when we compared all those living under legislation that now exists to slaves being doctored by slaves. For one must understand this well: if one of those doctors who practices medicine on the basis of experience without the aid of theory [ἄνευ λόγου] should ever encounter a free doctor conversing with a free man who was sick—using arguments that come close to philosophizing [τοῦ φιλοσοφεῖν ἐγγὺς χρώμενον μὲν τοῖς λόγοις], grasping the disease from its source, and going back up to the whole nature of bodies—he would swiftly burst out laughing and would say nothing other than what is always said about such things by most of the so-called doctors. For he would declare, 'Idiot! You are not doctoring the sick man, you are practically educating [σχεδὸν παιδεύεις] him, as if what he needed were to become a doctor, rather than healthy!'

Kleinias: Would he not be speaking correctly when he said such things?

Ath.: Maybe—if at any rate, he thought besides that this man who goes through the laws in the way we are doing now, is educating [παιδεύει] the citizens, but not legislating.   (*Laws* 857C2–E5)

Such education is, however, an essential task of the good lawgiver precisely in his role as lawgiver.

But is the lawgiver alone, among writers, not supposed to give advice about the fine, good, and just things, teaching what sort of things they are and how they must be practiced by those who are going to become happy? . . . Or is it not correct that of all writings in the cities, the things written about the laws appear, when opened up, by far the finest and the best, and that the writings of the others either follow those or, if they speak in dissonance, be laughed at? . . . should the writings [about the laws] appear in the shapes of a father and mother, caring dearly and possessing reason [νοῦν], or, like a tyrant and despot, should they command and threaten, post writings on the walls, and go away?   (*Laws* 858D6–859A6)

The difficulty that prompted this interruption in the statement of the proposed statute in Book 9 concerns the theory of punishment. The general issue is how to match appropriately the particulars of the offence with the attendant penalty. Should, for example, larger thefts have greater penalties? But the Athenian quickly moves to what is one of the central and most pressing issues for Plato's entire theory of punishment. Both law and common sense give great weight to the distinction between voluntary and involuntary wrongdoing. Voluntariness is often an essential factor in determining whether an offense has, in fact, been committed and in fixing the appropriate punishment or other treatment of the offender. (The voluntariness of the action also, of course, affects our attitude toward the offender, even apart from the question of legal sanctions.) This distinction, however, must seem highly problematic to Plato, since he accepts the

'Socratic paradox' that no one does wrong voluntarily (*hekōn*). If no one does wrong voluntarily, must we give up our ordinary common sense and legal distinction? If so, can it be replaced with a different distinction that better captures what the old distinction inadequately marked?

The Athenian explicitly draws our attention to this conflict and considers whether they should simply proceed to legislate in accordance with the view that all wrongdoing is involuntary.

Well, we have not found our way clear of the difficulty in these matters, nor defined what the difference is between these things, which, in all the cities by all legislators who have ever existed, have been held to be two forms of injustices, voluntary and involuntary, and have been so legislated. Is this argument now being uttered by us going to say only this much and depart, as if it were being spoken by a god, giving no argument as to why it has spoken correctly, and just legislating in defiance of the difficulty in some way? That is impossible. Before legislating, it is necessary to make clear somehow that these things are two, but that the distinction between them is a different one, so that whenever someone imposes the judicial penalty on either of them, everyone may follow the things that are being said and may be able to judge . . . what is fittingly laid down and what is not.   (*Laws* 861B1–c6)

What follows is a detailed and philosophically sophisticated discussion of how to resolve the conflict, consistently with the rest of Plato's ethics and psychology. And this discussion itself serves as a prelude to the laws concerning theft which it interrupted (*Laws* 861c–864c). The purpose of this discussion, as the passage just quoted shows, is to make clear to the Magnesians the deeper basis underlying the laws' treatment of offenders. Such an explanation must be provided in order to help the citizens to fulfill better their function as judges who will impose penalties—all citizens have a share in the exercise of judicial functions in Magnesia—and to judge whether the system of justice is being correctly carried out (cf. *Laws* 957c–958a).

The last set of Plato's programmatic remarks about the nature and the role of preludes occurs in Book 10. Here the Athenian is led to reflect on the purposes of the preludes just prior to proposing Magnesia's law against impiety. Here the Athenian imagines a dialogue between the interlocutors in the *Laws* and a young atheist. The young atheist demands just as you demanded in regard to the laws, that before you direct harsh threats at us, you try to persuade and teach us [διδάσκειν] that there are gods, adducing adequate evidence [τεκμήρια λέγοντες ἱκανά] . . . From lawgivers who are claiming to be not savage but gentle, we demand that persuasion be used on us first. And perhaps we would be persuaded by you, even if you did not speak more eloquently about the existence of the gods than others, as long as you spoke better as regards the truth.   (*Laws* 885C8–E5)

The Athenian accepts the challenge and in the rest of Book 10 proceeds to give several elaborate and philosophically sophisticated arguments for the fundamental theses of Magnesia's theology. These include, for example, a version of the cosmological argument that tries to establish that we must account for motion in the world by means of a psychic first cause of motion and order. In considering the need for preludes, the Athenian holds that (i) those acting, or tempted to act, contrary to the laws have no good reason to act in this way (they are either akratic or hold false beliefs), and (ii) the good lawgiver should try to teach the citizens—not only about the gods, but also about what is fine and what is just—so that they do more than simply conform their actions or beliefs to what the law requires. (As we shall see below, it is also the task of the good lawgiver to bring it about that the citizens' emotions and desires do not subvert reason either by prompting them to akrasia or by deforming their reasoning processes, although the preludes are not themselves the primary way of doing this.)

As he begins his argument, the Athenian comments that the young atheists do not have a rational basis for their beliefs. They hold their view

without a single adequate argument [οὐδὲ ἐξ ἑνὸς ἱκανοῦ λόγου]—as anyone having even a small amount of reason would admit. How could someone use gentle arguments to admonish, and at the same time to teach [διδάσκειν], these people about the gods, and first that they exist? Yet it must be dared. For it should not be the case that both of us are maddened at the same time—some of us by gluttony for pleasure, and others by spirited anger at such men. Let some such preliminary speech as the following proceed, without spiritedness, for those who are corrupted in their thinking [τὴν διάνοιαν διεφθαρμένοις], and let us speak gently, quenching our spirited anger.   (*Laws* 887E8–888A6)

The Athenian proceeds to urge the young atheist to consider what he is about to say carefully and to investigate it well.

If you should be persuaded by me, you will wait until you have a view about these matters that has become as clear as it can be, and meanwhile you will investigate [ἀνασκοπῶν] whether things are thus or are otherwise, and will inquire from others, and especially the lawgiver. During this time, you would not dare to do anything impious concerning the gods. The one who establishes the laws for you should try, now and in the future, to teach [διδάσκειν] how these very things are. (*Laws* 888C7–D5)

The Athenian then states the following terms to the young atheist: 'either to teach [διδάσκειν] us that we are not speaking correctly ... or, if he is not able to speak better than we, to be persuaded by us and live believing in the gods' (*Laws* 899C6–D1). What the disbeliever needs, the Athenian claims, is an 'argument', and he appeals to his reason: 'if you should still be in need of some argument [λόγου τινὸς], hearken to us as we speak ... if you are at all reasonable [εἰ νοῦν καὶ ὁπωσοῦν ἔχεις]' (*Laws* 905C7–D1, 891B7–D4). At the conclusion of his arguments for the first two of the three basic claims of Magnesia's theology, the Athenian pronounces himself satisfied with the proofs given: 'That there are gods and that they exercise supervision over human beings, I would say has been demonstrated [ἀποδεδεῖχθαι] by us in no mean fashion' (*Laws* 905D1–3, cf. 899D1–2).

Once again, Plato here emphasizes the need for the lawgiver to persuade with respect to all facets of his legislation and for the citizen to do more than blindly accept the theological and ethical beliefs recommended by the laws.

Athenian: Is the lawgiver merely to stand up in the city and threaten all the people, that if they do not affirm that the gods exist and do not think and believe that they are such as the law affirms—and about what is fine and what is just and all the greatest matters [περὶ καλῶν καὶ δικαίων καὶ περὶ ἁπάντων τῶν μεγίστων], the same speech, and about whatever tends to virtue and vice, that it is necessary to act in these respects while thinking in the way the lawgiver has instructed in writing—is he to say that whoever does not show himself obedient to the laws must in one case die, and in another case be punished with blows and prison, and in another case with dishonors, or in other cases, with poverty and exile? Is he to present no persuasion for human beings, mixed in with his speeches as he gives them laws, so as to make them as gentle as he can?
Kleinias: Not at all! If there happens to be even some small bit of persuasion as regards such matters, the lawgiver of even slight merit should in no way grow faint

. . . if [such arguments] are difficult to listen to at the beginning, there is no need to fear, so long as the slow learner can go and examine them often. Even if they are lengthy, if the arguments are beneficial, it does not seem to me to be at all reasonable or pious for any man to fail, on this account, to help these arguments as best he can.   (*Laws* 890B5–891A7)[10]

These programmatic remarks in Books 4, 9, and 10 about the preludes, which we have now examined, possess the following main features.

(1)   What the person who is to be persuaded is asking for is to be 'taught', that is, to be given good epistemic reasons for thinking that the principles lying behind the legislation are true (*Laws* 885D–E).

(2)   What the lawgiver and the preludes actually do is characterized as 'teaching', that is, giving reasons to the citizens and bringing it about that they 'learn' (*Laws* 718C–D, 720D, 723A, 857D–E, and 888A).

(3)   The preludes are thus designed to be instances of rational persuasion, that is, attempts to influence the citizens' beliefs through appealing to rational considerations. They are not intended to inculcate false but useful beliefs or to effect persuasion through non-rational means. The citizens are expected *to do* something rather than have something *done to them*. A certain kind of activity is required of them: they are to learn (*Laws* 722E–723B, 807C–D, 858D, and 890B–891A). (Here the contrast between activity and passivity is at the level of common sense, but as we shall see in Chapter 4, activity comes to have a deeper significance in Plato's theory of the operation of reason and the nature of the soul.) As we saw in the case of the question of whether wrongdoing can be voluntary, such learning will be essential to carrying out their political responsibilities.

(4)   The preludes are meant to provide quite general ethical instruction. The lawgiver is to be a primary source of instruction about what is fine, just, and good. Thus the citizens will learn why the laws are fine and just and should also learn why following the laws and, more generally, acting virtuously is good for them. They are to receive a true and reasoned account of what is good for human beings. The preludes advocate that the citizens adopt a certain way of evaluating their actions, choices, and lives: they provide an account of what goods are to be pursued, why they are to be pursued, and of the relations among these goods.

(5) These passages also give a first answer to the question of why such instruction, rather than simple commands or non-rational persuasion, is appropriate for the citizens. The Athenian introduces the preludes as the analogue in the case of a city's laws and its citizens to the sort of treatment given by a free doctor to a free patient. As Plato presents the analogy, it is the fact that both are free that determines what is appropriate in their relationship. In the case of two free persons, even when the first possesses knowledge of what is good for the second that the second lacks, it is ethically appropriate that the one try as far as possible to persuade the other rationally; because of the patient's status as a free person, he deserves to be rationally persuaded.

But we can still ask for a further justification of why treatment as a free person benefits the citizen. Stepping back, what we have found in the case of the preludes is an instance of a recurring pattern in the *Laws*. The Athenian begins by deferring to tradition and by accepting a divine foundation, and correspondingly high status, for the laws of Crete and Sparta. What gradually emerges is that legislation can have a divine origin only insofar as it expresses reason, and this necessity of expressing reason leads to a radical criticism of all previous legislation on two related grounds. First, all existing constitutions fail to recognize the true value of virtue and thus fail to establish the proper goal for the laws. Second, all existing constitutions and legislators treat their citizens as slaves, not as free people, insofar as the citizens do not receive an account of the reasons justifying the laws. We should expect from what we have seen so far that these criticisms have a common basis: it is because citizens must be educated so as to be virtuous that this new way of treating them is required (*Laws* 718B–C). The aim of the laws in Magnesia is to make all the citizens virtuous and the preludes along with the rest of the citizens' education express Plato's continued commitment to the idea that rational understanding is necessary for genuine virtue. The lawgiver should aim to give the citizens the sort of grasp of the fine and the good that is analogous to the grasp of health that a free doctor should give to a free person. Such a doctor should use arguments that 'come close to philosophizing' and go back, in his explanation, to 'the whole nature of bodies' (*Laws* 857D2–4).

The contrast with the *Republic* is both sharp and significant. The *Republic*, too, connected freedom to rational understanding and slavery to a condition of following orders without understanding. This is why Plato describes members of the lower two classes as slaves of the rulers: 'Therefore, to insure that someone like that [one whose reason is not strong enough to rule himself] is ruled by something similar to what rules the best person, we say that he ought to be the slave [δοῦλον] of that best person who has a divine ruler within himself' (*Rep.* 590C8–D1). In the *Laws*, however, the crucial distinction between the free and the unfree is not, as it is in the *Republic*, that between philosophers and non-philosophers. It is, rather, between those who have been brought up and successfully educated under the Magnesian system of laws and those educated under any other sort of constitution.

We have so far examined Plato's programmatic account of the preludes. But some scholars have suggested that we must take a far more bleak view of them. As I shall argue in the next section, these worries can be met. But Plato's programmatic account does raise other serious and deep philosophical issues and in the next section I shall also try to make clear what they are.

2.4 *The Place of the Preludes*

Preludes and Education in Magnesia   Before turning to worries that some have raised about the preludes, let us put them in their larger context within Magnesia. As the Athenian notes in Book 8, the preludes are a means of 'educating' the citizens (*Laws* 857D6–E5). Given this function, the preludes are continuous with the rest of the citizens' education. Even within the text of the *Laws*, Plato does not, and need not, draw a sharp line between stretches of text that are explicitly designated 'preludes' and those parts of the text that also explain the purpose of the laws, but are not officially designated as 'preludes'. Passages explaining the law or encouraging people to obey it are often found in connection with proposed statutes and are only sometimes termed 'preludes'. We are told that the legislator will make available to the citizens his writings on topics related to the laws, that is, on the fine, justice, virtue, and happiness, and the Athenian expects that the study of these writings will help to make the citizens more virtuous. Further, the entire text of the *Laws* itself will be read by all the citizens and such study of the lawgiver's writings—both in the preludes and in the text of the *Laws* as a whole—is a central aspect of the citizens' political life.

The preludes are, however, only part of the citizens' education. This education begins with gymnastics and music. The citizens' musical education includes reading and writing, the study of the lyre, and the study of appropriate literature: appropriate literature is especially the text of the *Laws* and then whatever other prose and poetry accords with the ethical principles of the *Laws*.[11] The auxiliaries' education in the *Republic* was an education in music and gymnastics; the first part of the citizens' education in Magnesia will be similar in that it, too, is an education in music and gymnastics. The content of the musical education will be significantly different, however, in that it will include the principles and arguments enunciated in the text of the *Laws* itself.

But this is not the only difference. For all free citizens, there are three further branches of study (*mathēmata*): calculation and arithmetic (*logismos, ta peri arithmous*), measurement (*metrētikē*) of lengths, surfaces, and solids, and astronomy (*Laws* 817E5–818A1). This program begins with simple problems in numbering and calculation. It progresses to the measurement of lines, surfaces, volumes, sounds, and motions. Such measurement is not, however, purely an empirical matter and it includes the study of plane and solid geometry, acoustics, and kinetics. The study that the Athenian places special emphasis on is that of incommensurable magnitudes. In recommending the study of incommensurable magnitudes for the whole city, the Athenian says that when he recently learned of them and thus of the ignorance he previously shared with the rest of the Greeks, 'it seemed to me to be the condition not of human beings, but of pigs, and I was ashamed, not only for myself, but for all the Greeks' (*Laws* 819D7–E1).

The purpose of these mathematical studies is not merely their usefulness for the practical affairs of household management, civic administration, and warfare.[12] The study of numbers is of the greatest importance because it 'awakens him who is by nature sleepy and unlearned, making him better at learning [$\epsilon\dot{v}\mu a\theta\hat{\eta}$], memory, and sharpness, and thus making him surpass his nature by a divine art [$\theta\epsilon\acute{\iota}a$ $\tau\acute{\epsilon}\chi\nu\eta$]' (*Laws* 747B3–6).[13] These studies will acquaint all the citizens with 'divine necessities' ($\dot{a}\nu\acute{a}\gamma\kappa a\iota$ $\theta\epsilon\hat{\iota}a\iota$,

Laws 818B3–8) and they will do so in at least two ways. First, such preparatory mathematical studies are essential to enable the citizens to carry out the astronomical studies that are an essential part of ordinary Magnesian theological instruction. All Greeks now commit the 'absolutely intolerable' error of speaking falsehoods and thus 'blaspheming' against the heavenly gods (*Laws* 820EII–821D4).[14] This blasphemy consists in claiming that the sun, the moon, and the stars follow many irregular paths. The truth is, rather, that each of them always moves in a circular path and that the apparently slowest moving of them is, in fact, the fastest (*Laws* 821B–822C). The ordinary Greek belief is a blasphemy because it fails to perceive the real divine order of the heavens (*Laws* 817E–822C). Ordinary Greek theological beliefs are thus radically in error and it is a central task of Magnesia's educational program to give the citizens sufficient mathematical and astronomical training to enable them to revise their beliefs intelligently in accordance with the truth. This recognition of the order of the stars plays an essential role in the arguments in Book 10 that the universe is ordered by intelligent gods who exercise supervision over it and over human affairs. The exact nature of the astronomical theory that Plato has in mind here is not entirely clear, but whatever he has in mind will be a mathematical theory of considerable complexity and sophistication.[15]

The second and related point concerns Plato's emphasis on incommensurability as an essential topic of knowledge for all the citizens. (As we saw above, insofar as people lack precisely this knowledge, they fall short of their own rational nature as human beings.) As Ian Mueller elegantly notes, one of the most striking features of the existence of incommensurables is its 'incompatibility with empirical facts': the assertion of the incommensurability of the side and the diagonal of the square 'is always disconfirmed by careful measurement'.[16] The recognition of incommensurability is thus in itself a recognition of a non-sensible property. It is, as we have seen, part of the metaphysical theology that is a fundamental part of the studies of all Magnesians. All citizens will learn that

(i)   the stars are moved by souls, and
(ii)   the real motion of the stars is circular and invariant, not wandering and irregular.

But the circularity of the stars' motion is not simply a neutral fact that has no normative implications. The inherent connection between circular motion and intelligence, which Plato frequently asserts in the later dialogues, is an explicit part of the theology taught in Book 10's impiety prelude.[17]

> [T]he [motion] that moves always in one place must necessarily move around some center . . . and it must in every way have the greatest possible kinship and resemblance to the revolution of reason [νοῦ] . . . [M]oving according to what is the same, in the same way, in the same place, around the same things, toward the same things, and according to one proportion and order characterizes both reason and the motion that moves in one place. (*Laws* 898A3–B2)

So the citizens' mathematical education is essential for them to grasp the following basic theological truth.

(iii) The circular motion of the stars is an expression of the rationality of the divine souls moving the stars.

The education of all Magnesians is designed to bring it about that they recognize non-sensible properties and that they grasp the role of such non-sensible properties as principles of good order. This mathematical education thus does what the musical education of the auxiliaries in the *Republic* could not do. So our examination of the rest of the citizens' education supports the Athenian's own account of the preludes' purpose.

Nevertheless, some scholars have suggested that we should take a far more pessimistic view of the preludes.[18] Although Plato's programmatic discussions of the preludes do suggest that he is recommending rational persuasion, the reality, they think, is far more depressing. The actual preludes in the *Laws*' text, it is claimed, fall dismayingly short of rational persuasion. How then are we to explain this gap? The most moderate and perhaps best worked-out attempt to do so is made by André Laks. Laks holds that Plato's programmatic remarks in Book 9 about the preludes are best understood as part of the 'legislative utopia' sketched in the *Laws*.[19] They are deliberately hyperbolic and present an idealized picture of the activity of the lawgiver. This idealized picture proposes to do away entirely with the violent aspect of law and replace it with fully rational argumentation. But Plato throughout the *Laws* is sensitive to the inevitable gap between what is best in theory and what is practically attainable. According to Laks, the actual preludes that are attached to proposed statutes work not through rational argumentation, but rather by means of a rhetoric of praise and blame. And this is the sort of prelude that we should expect to find in any city, even a just city, that is compatible with human nature.

There are, I think, four main reasons to reject this interpretation. First, it is both true and important that Plato in the *Laws* is highly sensitive to the fact that human nature sets limits on the attainment of what would be ideally best. Indeed, the recognition of this fact plays a central role in the *Laws'* political theory and in the construction of Magnesia. Consider the two most important examples. Although a community of property and women would be the best political arrangement, such a city would have to be inhabited by 'gods or the children of gods' (*Laws* 739D6).[20] Because the Athenian recognizes that such a system would be 'too demanding for the birth, nature, and education' of the actual citizens (*Laws* 740A1–2), he goes on to provide explicitly a quite different and incompatible economic system for Magnesia. Similarly, the best political arrangement would be to have an autocratic ruler who possessed full knowledge of what is best for the whole city and was always willing to act on this knowledge. But among humans, such a character can be found 'nowhere or in any way, except to a small extent' (*Laws* 875D2–3). Accordingly, the Athenian explicitly rejects autocratic rule in Magnesia and proposes a quite different sort of constitution.[21] Plato never makes similar remarks about the possibility of educating the citizens through preludes that engage in rational persuasion. He never says that he thinks that this, like a community of property or autocratic rule, is not possible given what human nature actually is. Indeed, the Athenian (and his interlocutors) repeatedly stress that this is the model that the Magnesian lawgiver should follow (*Laws* 722A–723B, 723C–D, 858E–859B, 890E–891A, cf. 811C–E). Nor does Plato in these passages suggest that providing such preludes frees us from the necessity of attaching penalties to these laws. We thus have good reason to think that Plato believes that such persuasion is possible, at least in moderately favorable (but empirically possible) circumstances. The Athenian notes that the legislator will have some range of preludes from which to choose (*Laws* 723A–D). It is, in fact, reasonable to expect that the tendency over time in Magnesia will be toward greater rational argumentation in the persuasion and education of the citizens, rather than less. The first population for whom the preludes are crafted is chosen from prospective colonists drawn from all of Greece. Although there is an examination of the prospective citizens as part of their selection procedure, their education will be radically inferior to that received by the future citizens of Magnesia.[22]

Second, Laks' interpretation does not make good sense of Plato's extremely emphatic claim that such preludes are an entirely novel innovation: no previous lawgiver has ever noticed the possibility of employing the sort of persuasion that a free doctor uses in his treatment of a free person. Plato is unlikely to have thought that no previous lawgiver ever noticed the possibility of employing rhetorical and other non-rational means of persuasion to bring about greater compliance with the laws.[23] Third, such an interpretation of the preludes' purpose cannot account for instances of sophisticated rational argumentation that we do find in some of the preludes. The prelude to the impiety law includes a version of the cosmological argument providing an account of the origin of motion and a sophisticated classification of kinds of motion. The prelude to the law on theft, as we saw, attempts to reconcile a basic and quite revisionary principle of Plato's psychology with common sense and universal legal practice. Nor can such an interpretation account for the sort of mathematical education provided to all citizens. Why insist on the study of incommensurable magnitudes for those who will otherwise receive only a simple rhetoric of praise and blame? The final reason for rejecting this interpretation is that we do not need to adopt it in order to account for the variety of preludes—some more sophisticated, some less—that we do find in the *Laws*. Such variety can be explained consistently with the interpretation I have already offered. This claim, of course, requires an argument and I shall offer one after considering some further worries.[24]

Less moderate critical interpretations, unlike that of Laks, do not hold that Plato acknowledges the fact that his programmatic remarks only present an unattainable ideal. R. F. Stalley, for example, suggests that 'The discrepancy between what the Athenian actually does and what he says he is doing could result either from deliberate deceitfulness or from a waning of Plato's own rational powers.'[25] Having to choose between attributing to

Plato such deception or a grave loss of mental acuity is not an attractive dilemma and I think that we can make better philosophical sense of what is going on. But before turning to this, let us consider some further grounds that commentators have suggested for rejecting the claim that Plato intends to appeal to, and to develop, the citizens' powers of reasoning.

This second set of worries centers on the political and social conditions that provide the context for education and persuasion in Magnesia. Some have thought that Magnesia's environment is so restrictive that the citizens cannot really develop rationally grounded beliefs. The arts are subject to extensive and restrictive censorship and even children's games are highly regulated and are to undergo little change. Contact with the outside world, and ideas coming from it, is carefully circumscribed for almost all citizens. There are criminal sanctions for certain kinds of false religious belief and there is extensive legal regulation of many aspects of the citizens' private lives. On a wide range of topics, the lawgiver sets out recommendations that, although lacking the force of law, are backed up by substantial social pressure (e.g. *Laws* 762C, 880A, 914A, 917C, and 936B). Does Plato's endorsement of these practices show that he is not, despite the passages we have considered, genuinely committed to the goal of developing in most citizens rational grounding for the beliefs that they are to hold? Interpretations such as Stalley's and similar ones that appeal to the second set of worries are open to some of the same objections brought against Laks' view. What we need to provide is an interpretation that makes sense of all that we do find in the *Laws*. We should try to find an interpretation that explains the full range of preludes and allows us to see Plato's programmatic remarks as sincere.

Let us begin by considering one of the critics' favorite examples of a prelude, that to the law on hunting.

Friends, may you never be seized by a desire or lust for hunting on the sea, for angling, or in general for hunting of animals that dwell in water, or for those basket-traps that perform the toil of a lazy hunt, whether the hunters are awake or asleep. (*Laws* 823D7–E2)

The passage continues in the same vein. Strictly speaking, this is not designated as a prelude, but we cannot avoid the worry that easily: as I have argued, we should not draw a sharp distinction between passages explicitly designated as preludes and the rest of the text. The prelude to the hunting law illustrates one important facet of the lawgiver's communication with the citizens. Plato repeatedly stresses that the above prelude is addressed to the 'young'; although it will be read by all, it is especially intended for the young (*Laws* 823C5–6, D5). The more general point is that the lawgiver's task is to address all the citizens and thus he will have to speak with a great variety of people at different stages of ethical development and different levels of ethical attainment. As we shall see in more detail in Chapter 5, Plato explicitly restricts Magnesia's political community to the virtuous (or those with the potential for virtue). Nevertheless, although capital punishment or the deprivation of citizen rights are penalties for a very wide range of offenses, there is no systematic institutional attempt, apart from the penal law, to locate and reform, or exclude from the political community, everyone falling short of virtue. The Athenian stresses that the very fact that the laws have penalties attached to them is shameful, but even in Magnesia law has to deal with citizens of varying degrees of imperfection.[26] We should expect that the same is true of the lawgiver's teaching and instruction and we do, in fact, find a wide range of preludes.

There are the rationally sophisticated discussions in the prelude justifying Magnesia's theology and in the prelude to the law on theft. In other preludes, the reasons lying behind a law or practice are stated with relatively little argument and sometimes with rhetorical elaboration. And there are some instances in which the legislator appeals to religious myths that Plato is unlikely to endorse literally. A favorite example of many of those who are pessimistic about the preludes is found in connection with the laws concerning murders springing from the desire for pleasure or from envy. Here the Athenian recommends repeating the stories told by those involved in the mystery rites to the effect that such wrongdoers will suffer the appropriate crime-specific penalty in a future reincarnation: parricides will be killed by their sons and so on. And the Athenian hopes that such stories will serve to prevent murders by inducing fear (*Laws* 870E4–5). But as Trevor Saunders perceptively notes, these stories follow a long and discursive preamble that appeals to the value of virtue as opposed to external goods (*Laws* 870A–D). Such stories are designed for those who have failed to benefit from the education given to all and are the next resort when persuasion and education have failed. They are followed by the last resort, which is the statement of the penalty attached to violation of the law (*Laws* 871A–C).[27]

The presence of preludes of all three types does not undermine the significant differences between the *Laws* and the *Republic*. This diversity cannot justify reading away the examples of more sophisticated preludes and holding that Plato's real intent is to provide only preludes of the second and third type. Plato did not expect that each and every citizen in Magnesia would attend carefully to the more sophisticated preludes. And he certainly expected that some would obey the law only out of fear of legal or divine punishment and that others would not be dissuaded even by fear of punishment. The education of the Magnesians is, however, designed to give them all the ability to follow the more sophisticated preludes and such preludes are addressed to the whole citizen body and are not restricted to an elite class.[28]

Finally, we should not be surprised to find that the prelude to the impiety law is exceptional in its detail and we cannot infer from this that Plato thought it would be desirable for there to be only one prelude of this sort in Magnesia. The *Laws'* text is already extremely long and shows various signs of incompleteness. The impiety prelude by itself occupies almost all of Book 10. It would have been an unmanageable task to provide similar preludes on all the central issues in ethics. To see what such preludes might look like, we can turn to the better worked-out example in Book 10 and to Plato's programmatic remarks. (Book 10 also introduces material that is partially new. Offering simplified versions of topics already treated must have seemed a less interesting and pressing task to Plato, especially near the end of his life.) This is fully compatible with the idea that there will be other preludes that are intended for citizens at a lower level of ethical development.

Since I have discussed the issues arising from Magnesia's restrictive social environment in detail elsewhere, I shall be relatively brief here.[29] Plato forbids the citizens access to certain sorts of information (e.g. some sorts of poetry are banned, as are works advocating atheist conclusions) and strongly encourages the citizens, in part by social sanctions including customs of approval, to adopt certain other beliefs. Further, some of the processes by which citizens come to be favorably disposed to approved ethical beliefs do not appeal to reason in a strong sense. For example, the right sorts of games and dances are supposed to give rise in children to a tendency to take pleasure in appropriate activities and stably taking pleasure in them disposes the children to approve of and value such activities.

But none of this requires Plato to reject the goal of fostering rational beliefs. First, the items that are banned do not merely contain false claims; they also tend to distort people's reasoning capacities. Inappropriate poetry, for example, corrupts people's capacities to arrive at and maintain true beliefs. Such poetry fosters desires and emotions that tend to bring it about that we acquire false beliefs and lose true ones by non-rational processes (and it also tends to make such processes more pervasive and deeply rooted). Second, social encouragement and various kinds of habituation can lead citizens to adopt true beliefs by processes other than rational argumentation. This, however, need not be inimical to fostering rational reflection in those citizens capable of it. Even if citizens do not adopt some of their ethical beliefs through rational argument, Plato also provides for explanations of the reasons behind the law to be available and to be studied. The preludes and the lawgiver's other writings serve as a lifelong encouragement and opportunity for the citizens to come to appreciate the rational basis of the beliefs they may have adopted on other grounds.

Further, such habituation will proceed in large part through fostering certain emotions, such as shame, and appealing to certain sorts of pleasure. But such appeals to emotions and to pleasure need not undermine people's capacity to have a reasoned appreciation of their ethical beliefs. Cultivation of the right emotions and pleasures can both help prepare for the development of a reasoned appreciation of the good and help sustain it once it is in place. Such emotions and pleasures can (i) help block the formation of bad desires and emotions which would tend to corrupt people's rational capacities, and (ii) attach people to objects and courses of action for which they can come to develop a reasoned appreciation. And even in people who possess a reasoned appreciation of what is good and fine, such pleasures and emotions can serve as a separate and additional sort of motivation for acting rightly.

These are ways in which the cultivation of the right emotions and pleasures can still be indirectly rational. But they might also contribute to a person's rationality in a stronger sense by developing, at least at a fairly basic level, some of the very capacities that are involved in higher exercises of reason. This is the most ambitious defense of Plato's practice in Magnesia in that it aims to show that the restrictive measures in fact directly further the goal of bringing citizens to have rational grounds for their beliefs. Such a strategy may also help to account for the remarkable emphasis that Plato gives to developing in the citizens a highly determinate pattern of pleasures and emotions. It does so, however, via commitments to strong claims in Plato's psychology and epistemology. Seeing whether this account can be made good will thus have to await our longer discussions of non-rational motivations in Chapter 4.

There are, of course, also less ambitious ways of justifying the restrictions we find, without holding that Plato is not genuinely committed to encouraging rationally grounded beliefs among the citizens. This goal, for example, may compete with others such as maintaining the long-run stability of the city and Plato might think that although restrictive measures may curtail some rational inquiry, the long-run results justify doing so. He may also both overestimate the fragility of true beliefs and underestimate the negative consequences of such restrictions. But none of this suggests that Plato is deceptive in his characterization of the intent of the preludes and of the citizens' education or that he thinks that rational persuasion is an unattainable ideal.[30]

Let us close this section by considering two broader issues. First, since Laks, for example, holds that the argumentative preludes are confined almost entirely to the 'legislative utopia' (he would also have to hold that this is true of other aspects of the citizens' education that aim at developing rationally grounded beliefs), he is left with the task of explaining how persuasion is supposed to work in Magnesia. Laks suggests that the primary means of persuasion is by appeal to praise and blame, pleasure and 'the opinions and attitudes normally shared by most people'.[31] But it is difficult to see how these resources alone could produce the sort of city Plato intends Magnesia to be. Plato's proposal of an entirely new model for legislation is part of a radical criticism of all previous constitutions: this includes those of Crete and Sparta, which both did an especially good job of appealing to praise and blame and commonly shared beliefs.[32] But allied with Plato's criticism of the manner of legislation in Crete and Sparta there is, as we shall see in Section 2.5, a radical criticism of the results that such constitutions achieve. The citizens brought up under both constitutions have very grave ethical failings. Although they are steadfast in war, they do not know what to do with peace or leisure. A sign of this is that their own citizens think that both constitutions are designed only to cultivate the virtue of courage. These flaws ultimately rest on the failure of the constitutions to foster an appreciation of the nature and value of virtue. Genuine courage, for example, cannot exist apart from the other virtues, especially a correct conception of the ultimate end, and even the best citizens of these constitutions value pleasure and honor more than virtue. It is not incoherent to suppose that an ethical education whose primary appeals were to shame, honor, and pleasure might develop a character that valued virtue for its own sake. But even if pleasure and honor were to fix people exceptionlessly on the right actions, such an education gives them neither a grasp of what virtue is nor any reason to pursue virtue for its own sake. Even if some psychological mechanism were to bring such people to value acting in approved ways for no further end, this would not give them a rational appreciation of what is good about such action. To see whether Plato thinks that ordinary citizens in Magnesia are capable of this, we shall have to examine, in Section 2.5, the *Laws'* understanding of the goodness of virtue.

We can see Plato facing a related problem in the *Statesman* and resolving it in a way that supports the idea that rational persuasion is required. In the *Statesman*, Plato holds that among the citizens there are two types of character that are potentially good: the courageous character and the moderate character. The courageous tend toward vigorous lives and are prone to act aggressively, especially when facing opposition. The moderate seek quiet lives, mind their own business, and tend to be cautious and conservative. These differences in action and character type are ultimately founded on disagreements about what is good and fine (*Stsmn.* 307A–308A and 311A).[33] These sorts of courage and moderation, however, fall well short of genuine virtue and one clear sign of this is that, unlike genuine virtues, they are not such that one can have one of them only if one has the other. In fact, such tendencies to courage and moderation are incompatible and those who have them are hostile to and in conflict with each other. The only way of establishing harmony in the city sketched in the *Statesman* is by imparting to citizens 'the divine bond' of 'really true and firmly settled true opinion' about the fine, the just, and the good (*Stsmn.* 309C1–8). Such a bond is divine because it is akin to what is immortal in the soul, that is, reason (*Stsmn.* 309C).[34] It is only because they possess such a bond that citizens having either one of these natural tendencies can come to have a character that is genuinely fine and, in particular, can come to possess all the virtues, including genuine courage, moderation, and wisdom (*Stsmn.* 309A8–B7, 309E5–7). The initial discrepancy between these basic character types cannot be resolved by appealing to common pleasures or to a shared sense of shame or a desire for honor. It is only by giving citizens the same true ethical opinions about the fine, the just, and the good—and excluding those not capable of sharing in them—that genuine concord (*homonoia*) and friendship (*philia*) can be achieved in the city. Although Plato is not fully explicit about this, such opinions seem to consist in grasping—albeit in a way that amounts to less than knowledge—the reasons behind the law, that is, grasping why they are fine, just, and good.[35]

There is a second set of concerns that raise important philosophical questions that will occupy us in the next section and in Chapters 3 and 4. I have argued so far that the lawgiver's persuasion of the citizens helps solve the two problems that we noted at the beginning of this chapter for the claim that law could be an expression of reason. Insofar as the law itself is supplemented with an explanation of the reasons behind it, the citizens receive more than a bare command and violent compulsion. Second, although law itself is too general to address adequately all the varied circumstances of life, if it succeeds in giving citizens an intelligent appreciation of the basis of the law and the whole legal system, it will help equip them to deal with novel situations.[36]

We have, however, so far concentrated on what education in Magnesia might provide for the citizens, but have not considered its limitations. The condition of the vast majority of the citizens falls short of genuine knowledge: they do not have a synoptic grasp of any body of knowledge, they are not capable of articulating and defending against all challenges an account of the basic ethical notions, and they do not seem to have extensive training in the use of the elenchus. Nevertheless, the *Laws* leads us to believe that the citizens can grasp, at least to a significant extent, what virtue is and can value virtue for its own sake. This leaves us with several important issues. First, if Plato's educational project is to succeed, it requires us to show that there can be a realm of ethical reflection that, although falling short of philosophical knowledge, involves a recognition of and response to genuine value. But is such reflection sufficient to bring it about that non-philosophers can possess the virtue of wisdom (*phronēsis*)? Can ordinary citizens have such a virtue without genuine knowledge and without possessing knowledge of the Forms? Second, it was precisely their inability to attain a recognition of and appropriate response to genuine value that constituted the fundamental defect of non-philosophers in the middle period. This was the reason for Plato's bleak assessment of their ethical capacities and lives. How, then, has Plato's psychology and epistemology changed so as to allow for such recognition without philosophical knowledge?

This second question sets the agenda for Chapters 3 and 4. In the next section, I shall focus on the first question. I shall begin by showing why this question is especially pressing in the *Laws*. The Dependency Thesis, as we saw in Chapter 1, seemed to exclude non-philosophers from happiness because it required a person to possess knowledge in order to benefit from any other good. As we shall see in the next section, the *Laws* places the Dependency Thesis at the very center of its ethical theory. So I shall now turn to consider why the Dependency Thesis has such a central place in the *Laws* and whether the non-philosophical citizens of Magnesia can satisfy its demands.

2.5 The Goal of the Laws

In the *Republic*, Plato holds that the goal of the laws is to bring about the greatest possible happiness in the city (e.g. *Rep.* 419A–421C). As we have seen, however, the *Republic* does not aim at bringing it about that all of the citizens are genuinely virtuous. The crucial difficulty is that knowledge is necessary for the virtue of wisdom and wisdom is necessary for the other virtues. Since non-philosophers lack knowledge, they lack genuine virtue. The laws thus aim at doing the best for non-philosophers that can be done without making them genuinely virtuous or happy.

In the *Laws*, Plato still holds that the ultimate end of the legal system is to bring about the greatest possible happiness in the city.[37] But this is not the claim that Plato gives the greatest emphasis. In all his legislation, the lawgiver must aim at a single goal and that is virtue. In particular, the lawgiver must aim at fostering all the virtues—courage, justice, moderation, and wisdom—in the citizens as a whole.[38] Plato announces this claim with a fanfare at the beginning of the *Laws*, returns to it at its end, and repeatedly stresses it throughout the text.

[A]ny lawgiver worth much of anything will never set down laws with a view to anything but the greatest virtue. And this is . . . that quality which someone would call complete justice. (*Laws* 1. 630C3–6)

Keep in view what was said at the beginning, about how the Cretan laws looked to one goal. You two said this was what pertains to war. I then interrupted, saying that it was fine that such legal institutions looked somehow to virtue, but that I could not at all go along with them when they looked only to a part and not almost to the whole. Now you two in your turn, as you follow the present legislation, must guard against my legislating something that does not aim at virtue, or that aims at a part of virtue. For I assert that the only law correctly laid down is this: one which, just like an archer, aims each time at what alone is constantly accompanied by something fine, one which leaves all the rest aside, even if there is a chance of producing some wealth and other such things by ignoring the things just mentioned. (*Laws* 4. 705D3–706A4)[39]

In our consideration of the nature of the land and the order of the laws, we are looking now to the virtue of the constitution. We do not hold, as the many do, that preservation and mere existence are what is most honorable for human beings; what is most honorable for them is to become as good as possible and to remain so for as long a time as they may exist. (*Laws* 4. 707D1–5)[40]

In brief, this was the substance of the agreement: in whatever way a member of the community, whether his nature be male or female, young or old, might ever become a good man, possessing the virtue of soul that befits a human being—whether this be as a result of some practice, or some habituation, or some possession, or desire, or belief, or certain things learned at some time—toward this . . . every serious effort will be made throughout the whole of life; no one of any sort is to be seen giving precedence in honor to any of the other things that are impediments, not even, finally, to the city. (*Laws* 6. 770C7–E1, cf. 807C1–D5)

[I]f our founding of the country is to have an end, there must be something in it that knows, in the first place, this goal we are speaking of (whatever our political goal may be), and then in what way it ought to attain this . . . But if some city is devoid of such a thing, it will not be surprising if, lacking reason and senses, it acts haphazardly each time in each of its actions . . . [T]here is nothing surprising in the fact that the legal customs of the cities wander, since different parts of the legislated codes in each city look to different aims. And in most cases there is nothing surprising in the fact, that, for some, the definition of justice is what allows some to rule in the city, whether they happen to be better or worse, while for others it is what allows them to become wealthy, whether they are slaves of certain people or not, and that others are set into motion by the spirited zeal for the free way of life. Others, again, have a twofold legislation that looks to both—that they may be free and may also be despots over other cities; then the wisest, as they suppose, look to these and all such aims, but not to any one, being unable to give an account of anything that is honored preeminently and toward which their other affairs should look. So then would not our principle have been set down in the correct way a long while ago? For we declared that everything pertaining to our laws ought always to be looking to one thing, and this, we presumably agreed, was very correctly said to be virtue.   (*Laws* 12. 962B4–963A4)[41]

This requirement that the laws aim at inculcating all the virtues in the citizens gains special significance from the contrast between what Plato proposes for Magnesia and the practice of all other constitutions. Early in Book 1 in reply to a question from the Athenian, Kleinias explains the goal of Cretan legislation.

[O]ur Cretan lawgiver ordained all our legal usages, both public and private, with an eye to war, and he therefore charged us with the task of guarding our laws safely, in the conviction that, without victory in war, nothing else, whether possession or practice, is of any value [τῶν ἄλλων οὐδενὸς οὐδὲν ὄφελος], but all the goods of the vanquished fall into the hands of the victors.   (*Laws* 626A5–B4)

Although the *Laws* is not one of Plato's more elaborate literary productions, it still is constructed with some subtlety. Kleinias' statement does not make determinate the relations among victory in war, the goods the victors obtain, and the aims of the legislator. The Athenian chooses to construe this remark as the claim that the Cretan laws aim at what helps to bring about victory, that is, at courage. Cretan laws thus aim at 'part' of virtue, although not at the whole of virtue. Even understood this way, this fact shows that the

Cretan constitution is radically defective because it does not aim at all the virtues. This defect is reflected in the character of the citizens brought up under it. There is no reason to think that Kleinias and Megillus represent corrupted citizens of Crete and Sparta: rather we can take the Athenian at his word that they are its best products. The very fact that Kleinias does not hold that the constitution aims at virtue as a whole shows that it has failed in its proper task, since no virtuous person could see such a state of affairs as satisfactory.

But Kleinias has even more grave ethical shortcomings. His view that victory in war is the proper aim of the laws springs from his more fundamental view that just as each city should be organized so as to be victorious in war over all other cities, this is the right attitude for a village to adopt towards another village, for a household to adopt towards another household, and for every person to adopt towards everyone else: 'All people are publicly and privately the enemy of all' (*Laws* 626D7–9). As Kleinias spells out his view, we see that he

(i) rejects the claim that the value of other goods depends on their possessor being virtuous, and

(ii) even allows that a person who possesses all goods other than virtue and 'has within himself only injustice and insolence' lives basely, but also holds that he lives happily, pleasantly and profitably to himself (*Laws* 661E2–662A8).

Kleinias and Megillus are often portrayed as ethically impeccable, although slow-witted, interlocutors. But it is important to see that this is mistaken. The best products of Crete and Sparta think that goods other than virtue are much more important than virtue itself and may well think that virtue is worthwhile only insofar as it produces these goods. It is reasonable to connect this failure with the other great failure of Cretan and Spartan laws that we have already seen, that is, their failure to treat the citizens as free people. Without some further account of the point of virtuous practices, Plato suggests that we will tend to see them as aimed at goods other than virtue. The injunctions of the Cretan and the Spartan law codes to act bravely must be brought under some conception of the good, and ordinary ethical education is not enough for their citizens to get it right.

The *Laws'* claim that the constitution ought to aim at fostering all the virtues in the citizens as a whole sets two issues for us. First, what is the relation between making the citizens as happy as possible and fostering all the virtues in the citizens? We would expect that fostering the virtues plays a central role in making them happy, but we need a more specific account of the relation between virtue and happiness in the *Laws*. Is virtue the only good, that is, does happiness consist solely of virtue? Or if there are other goods besides virtue, what is the relation between virtue and these goods? Second, can the lawgivers in Magnesia really aim at inculcating all the virtues in the citizens? Can they foster the virtue of wisdom in any but the small elite who possessed it in the *Republic*? The *Statesman* suggested that 'firmly settled true opinion' about the fine, the just, and the good could help produce a kind of wisdom and we must see how the *Laws* develops this idea. From what we have seen, we do not have to worry that the lawgiver only tries to encourage in citizens the tendency to do what the virtuous person would while not aiming at virtue for its own sake, but rather at pleasure or honor. But we may have further concerns. If we no longer require knowledge for the possession of the virtue of wisdom, can we still retain what is distinctively valuable about wisdom? If what is valuable for the possessors of wisdom is, at least in large part, theoretical understanding, how can a lesser state still benefit them? Might it do so, for example, by being purely practical as opposed to theoretical? We can turn to these issues, however, only after first taking up the relation between virtue and other goods.

2.6 *Dependent Goods in the* Laws

In two passages early in the *Laws*, Plato announces a radical thesis about how the value of other goods depends on the possession of virtue.

Passage A
It is not without reason that the laws of Crete are held in especially high esteem by all the Greeks. The reason is that they are correct laws—and they are correct because they make those who use them happy. For they provide all the goods. Now goods are twofold, some human, some divine. The former depend [ἤρτηται] on

the divine goods, and if a city accepts the greater, it will also acquire the lesser.[42] If not, it is bereft of both. The lesser goods are those of which health is the leader; in second place is beauty; in third place is strength, in running and in all other bodily movements, and in fourth place is wealth—not blind, but sharp-sighted, insofar as it follows wisdom. Wisdom, in turn, is first and leader [ἡγεμονοῦν] among the divine goods; second, after wisdom, is a moderate disposition of soul; from these two mixed with courage comes justice in third place; and fourth is courage. All of these goods are by nature placed prior in rank [ἔμπροσθεν τέτακται φύσει] to the former goods, and the lawgiver must rank them in this way.   (*Laws* 631B3–D2)

Passage B

You compel the poets to say that the good man, since he is moderate and just, is happy and blessed, whether he is great and strong or small and weak, whether he is rich or not. Even if someone were richer than Cinyras or Midas, if he is unjust, then he is miserable [ἄθλιός] and lives wretchedly [ἀνιαρῶς] . . . For the things said to be good [τὰ . . . λεγόμεν' ἀγαθὰ] by the many are not correctly so described. It is said that the best thing is health, and second is beauty, and third is wealth—and then there are said to be innumerable other goods: sharp sight and hearing, and good perception of all the objects of the senses; and further, being a tyrant and doing whatever one desires; and the perfection of all happiness is to possess all these goods and then to become immortal, as quickly as possible. But you and I say this: that all these things, beginning with health, are extremely good [ἄριστα] for just and pious men, but all are extremely bad [κάκιστα] for unjust men. To see, to hear, to perceive, and, in general, to live as an immortal for the whole of time, while possessing all the things said to be good except for justice and the whole of virtue, is the greatest of bads [μέγιστον . . . κακὸν]. The bad is less when such a man lives a very brief time . . . I say plainly that the things said to be bad are good for unjust men and bad for just men [τὰ μὲν κακὰ λεγόμενα ἀγαθὰ τοῖς ἀδίκοις εἶναι, τοῖς δὲ δικαίοις κακά], while the [things said to be] good really are good [ὄντως ἀγαθά] for good men, but bad for bad men . . . Given a man who possesses in a lasting way health, wealth, and tyrannical power—and for you, I add exceptional strength and courage along with immortality and that he has nothing else of the things said to be bad—but given that he has within himself only injustice and insolence; perhaps I do not persuade you that a man living in this way is unhappy and is manifestly miserable [ἄθλιον]?   (*Laws* 660E2–661E4)

(I prefer the awkward 'bad' to 'evil', since 'evil' may suggest purely moral badness and we should not build this assumption into our translation.) In

Passage A, Plato distinguishes 'divine' or 'greater' goods from 'human' or 'lesser' goods and claims that the latter 'depend on' the former. In Passage B, he calls the human goods 'things said to be good', which suggests that the difference between the two kinds of goods is more fundamental than, for example, a difference of quantity. In the rest of Passage B, Plato elucidates the nature of this dependency.

Let us begin by considering the classifications that Plato makes and then turn to his account of dependency.

(1) The human goods comprise a rather varied group. Elsewhere in the *Laws*, Plato distinguishes among goods of the soul, goods of the body, and goods external to the soul and body (e.g. 697B–C). Human goods are drawn from all three categories. They include external goods, such as wealth; bodily goods such as health, beauty, and strength; as well as goods that are partly bodily and partly psychic such as keen perceptual capacities. But they also include some purely psychic goods. In Passage B, Plato allows that an unjust person can possess 'courage' (*andreia*, *Laws* 661E1, cf. 696D4–6), although such courage, like the human goods, does not benefit its possessor if he is unjust. This sort of courage seems simply to be an ability to resist fear in the service of whatever ends the person has and since its value, like that of the human goods, depends on its possessor being virtuous, it should count as a human good. There are indefinitely many other human goods, including immortality and the ability to do whatever one desires. In sum, human goods seem to include all the things that common sense classifies as good, insofar as they are entirely distinct from the divine good of virtue. Pleasure is not mentioned in Passages A and B, but at the beginning of Book 5, Plato distinguishes divine from non-divine possessions and classifies pleasure among the human possessions (*Laws* 726A2–3 and 732D8–E7). It seems reasonable to take this as entailing the claim that pleasure is one of the human goods and thus is a Dependent Good.

(2) The divine goods consist of the four virtues: courage, justice, moderation, and wisdom. Within this group, wisdom has a special place as the 'leader' of the other virtues. The possession of all of the four virtues is what makes someone a 'good' or 'just' person (*Laws* 660D2–3).

(3) In Passage B, the Athenian refers to 'the things said to be bad'. Although he does not give examples, the natural contrast with 'the things

said to be good' shows that these include sickness, ugliness, and so on. As in the case of the human goods, the positive or negative value of these 'bads' depends on whether their possessor is virtuous. Finally, corresponding to the divine good of possessing all the virtues is the bad of vice or injustice. Having this bad is, as we have seen, compatible with possessing the sort of courage or moderation that is a human good.

The value of the human goods or the things said to be good is, in some way, dependent on the divine good of complete virtue: 'the things said to be bad are good for unjust men and bad for just men, while the [things said to be] good really are good for good men, but bad for bad men' (*Laws* 661D1–4). Thus we may call these items, 'Dependent Goods' and 'Dependent Bads'.

G is a Dependent Good if and only if G is good for a just or good person and G is bad for an unjust or bad person.

B is a Dependent Bad if and only if B is bad for a just or good person and B is not bad for an unjust or bad person.[43]

So the value of Dependent Goods is dependent on their possessor having wisdom, courage, and moderation, and thus justice. I shall call the claim that all goods that are entirely distinct from virtue are Dependent Goods, the 'Dependency Thesis'.

Corresponding to this account of Dependent Goods and Bads, we can give an account of Independent Goods and Bads.

G is an Independent Good if and only if G is good for a person regardless of what else she possesses.

B is an Independent Bad if and only if B is bad for a person regardless of what else she possesses.

Justice is an Independent Good and vice an Independent Bad.

Let me immediately note one refinement. The above definitions of Dependent Goods and Dependent Bads are based quite closely on Plato's phrasing in Passage B. As I shall argue below, they must be complicated slightly to capture Plato's intentions. Plato need not (and I think does not) hold that every Dependent Good is bad for an unjust person; what he should hold is that no Dependent Good benefits a person apart from virtue. This is true if either the Dependent Good is bad for unjust people or if it is simply not good for them. Nor should Plato hold that a Dependent Bad is actually good for an unjust person; *nothing* is good for an unjust person. What Plato intends is that, for example, unjust people are worse off if they are wealthy than if they are poor. But even the small amount of money that they have (their 'poverty') is not actually good for them. So what Plato should (and I think does) hold is that for an unjust person having a Dependent Bad is not good, although it is less bad than not having that Dependent Bad or than having the corresponding Dependent Good. This more precise formulation allows us to say that nothing is good for people unless they are just or virtuous. I discuss this, and some connected complications, further in Section 2.8.

2.7 *Preliminary Clarifications*

Goods can be distinguished in many different ways and to understand Plato's claims, it is essential to get clear about the nature of the dependency he is asserting. Let us begin by noting that in Passages A and B, Plato is classifying different sorts of things as good *for* (or bad *for*) individual persons; he is concerned with what contributes to a person's well-being or happiness or is a benefit for him. The notion of goodness that Plato is exploring here is essentially relational and, moreover, is relative to particular individuals. We can make this idea clearer by comparison with some modern theories of value. Thomas Nagel distinguishes two sorts of reasons for action: agent-relative reasons and agent-neutral reasons. An agent-relative reason for performing action A is a reason only for a particular person to perform A; an agent-neutral reason is a reason for anyone to perform A. Let us assume a direct correspondence between reasons for action and goodness.[44]

In Passages A and B, Plato is not concerned to establish what has agent-neutral goodness, that is, what things or states of affairs are good for all agents from an impartial point of view, or more precisely, from a point of view that is neutral with respect to the identities of individual agents.[45] For example, Plato's claim here that health is good for a virtuous person entails that if I am virtuous, my possession of health is good for me and that if you are virtuous, your possession of health is good for you. Plato does not go on to assert that my virtuous possession of health is good for both of us or for people generally.

Although some philosophers use 'intrinsic value' to capture the idea of agent-neutral value, there is a stronger notion of intrinsic value that is also relevant. On this stronger notion, intrinsic goodness is the objective, non-relational property of goodness that is independent of all persons. This is, for example, the conception of goodness that G. E. Moore explored in *Principia Ethica*. This is again not Plato's concern in Passages A and B: he is not, for example, claiming that the world is a better place because of my being virtuous or my virtuous possession of health.[46] I am not claiming that the notions of agent-neutral goodness or intrinsic goodness (or something like them) play no role in Plato's ethics or that they have no connection to the distinction drawn in Passages A and B. Indeed, I shall argue that they have intimate connections to what is good for a particular person. Nevertheless, in these passages, the only sort of goodness that Plato explicitly considers is being good for a particular agent.

But even within the category of what is good for particular agents, Plato in his corpus draws several different distinctions. First, as we have noted, he employs a trichotomy of goods: goods of the soul, goods of the body, and goods external to both. Such a classification is especially natural within the category of things good for particular agents, since it specifies, so to speak, the location of the good with respect to the agent herself. From the perspective of a person acting to acquire or enjoy goods for herself, their location with respect to herself is a fundamental fact. But this distinction is obviously not identical to that between Independent and Dependent Goods nor is it extensionally equivalent, even if we group together both kinds of non-psychic goods, since as we have seen, Dependent Goods include psychic goods.

We must also keep the Independent/Dependent Good distinction apart from another distinction that Plato draws among things good for a particular agent. Plato recognizes the more familiar distinction between final goods and instrumental goods, that is, the distinction between things good as ends and things good as means. And he sometimes, for example at the beginning of Book 2 of the *Republic*, uses the means–end distinction as a way of classifying things that are good for particular agents.

Glaucon: Tell me, is there a kind of good that we would choose to have not because we are aiming at what comes from it [οὐ τῶν ἀποβαινόντων], but because we welcome it for its own sake [αὐτὸ αὑτοῦ ἕνεκα]—such as enjoyment and such pleasures as are harmless and nothing results from them afterwards save to have the enjoyment?
Socrates: In my opinion, there is a good of this kind.
Gl.: . . . Is there a kind we love both for its own sake and for what comes from it [τῶν ἀπ᾽ αὐτοῦ γιγνομένων], such as thinking and seeing and being healthy? Surely we welcome such things for both reasons.
Soc.: Yes.
Gl.: And do you see a third form of good, which includes exercise, medical treatment when sick, as well as the practice of medicine, and the rest of moneymaking? For we would say that they are laborious but beneficial to us; and we would not choose to have them for their own sake, but for the sake of the wages and whatever else comes from them.   (*Rep.* 357B4–D2)

An instrumental good, such as undergoing surgery, insofar as it is an instrumental good, is valued only for the sake of some distinct effects it brings about, e.g., the state of being healthy. To call something instrumentally good is not to claim that it possesses goodness, but rather to state a fact about its causal powers: it can be used to bring about some distinct effect that does possess goodness.[47] Thus if I could obtain the end without using the means then, *ceteris paribus*, I would have no reason at all to adopt the means. A final good, in contrast, *qua* final good, is good apart from anything that it may bring about, that is, it is good apart from its causal effects. Even if it were causally inert, I would, *ceteris paribus*, have reason to choose it. This does not, however, entail that, so to speak, it carries its goodness within it. It does not entail that it is good apart from everything else. In particular, it may be good only when it occurs in conjunction with another good (that is not a causal consequence of the final good). All that finality in itself entails is non-instrumentality; it does not, by itself, entail independence.

A Dependent Good, on the other hand, is something such that a necessary (and sufficient) condition of its being good is the presence of something other than the Dependent Good. (In the case of the *Laws*, the dependency is on virtue; there could be formally similar relations in which some goods were dependent for their goodness on the presence of something else besides virtue).[48] Thus, if we assume (what I shall shortly question) that all instrumental goods require wisdom to be beneficial and are not good in its absence, all instrumental goods are Dependent Goods, but even so, not all Dependent Goods need be instrumental goods. In Passages A and B, Plato is careful not to claim that the Dependent Goods are instrumental goods and he does not characterize the difference between divine and human goods in terms of the distinction between the value of a thing apart from its consequences and the value of its consequences. The relevant distinction is, rather, that between a thing being good for its possessor without the presence of anything else, and its being good for its possessor only in the presence of some distinct thing. We do not yet know why Dependent Goods require the presence of virtue to be good for their possessor, but it need not be the case that Dependent Goods are valuable solely for their causal effects. The notion of a Dependent Good, as we have seen it in Passages A and B, allows for the possibility that, in the presence of virtue, a Dependent Good is good for its possessor independently of any effects it brings about. Understanding how this could be so is a task I shall take up, but to illustrate the idea, consider a non-Platonic example. If I am colorblind, seeing a Rothko painting is of no value to me, but it is of value to me in conjunction with the ability to see colors. Seeing a Rothko is a kind of dependent good: its goodness is dependent on an ability to perceive (or perhaps the actual perception of) colors. But seeing a Rothko in color need not be instrumental to anything else; it may be of value to me independently of any effects it brings about. And it is certainly not a *means* to the thing on which its goodness depends, that is, in this case, the ability to see colors.

Finally, it is important to keep in mind that this is a distinction between *goods* and not a distinction between things that are real goods and those that merely seem to be goods. Dependent Goods 'really are good' for good people, while Dependent Bads are bad for them. If virtue were the only genuine good, this would seem to undermine the claim that the goodness for people of their possession of other things *depends* on their possession of virtue.

2.8 The Difficulties of Dependency

In the following sections, I shall consider how Plato can ground the Dependency Thesis, but we should begin by recognizing the difficulty of justifying this claim. Plato himself in the first two books of the *Laws* draws our attention to some of these difficulties. We find there a pair of claims that formally resemble the Dependency Thesis, but differ from it in important ways; seeing their limitations will allow us better to appreciate the Dependency Thesis's demands.

Let us return to Kleinias' claims about the goal of Cretan legislation (*Laws* 626A5–B4, quoted above). Kleinias' language closely echoes some of Plato's statements of the Dependency Thesis, but Kleinias' claim is that all other goods depend on victory in war: without victory in war, no other good is of any benefit to its possessor. This is a very simple form of dependence: the other goods are dependent on victory because without it the practices of the citizens will be disrupted and their possessions taken away. Victory in war, as Kleinias presents it, is a necessary condition of the actual existence of these goods, or, more precisely, of their existence as the possessions of the citizens: without victory in war, the goods of the losers will become the goods of the winners. A similar point is made in the *Menexenus'* funeral oration: wealth is not desirable for a coward, since he is simply 'rich for another, rather than for himself' (*Mx.* 246E2–4).

This dependency claim, however, cannot survive much reflection. First, victory in war is not a genuinely necessary condition of the citizens' possessing or benefiting from all other goods, since at least some of the citizens of a losing city can retain some goods and thus, on Kleinias' view, will be benefited by them. This objection is quite simple, but it points to some deeper features of the notion of dependency. On Kleinias' view, the goods gained or preserved by victory carry their goodness, so to speak, with themselves: all that is required on the side of the agent to benefit from them is to possess them and victory is only a mechanism for assuring possession. The goodness of the good things preserved by war is independent of such victory and all that victory affects is the identity of the people who have them. A person need not do anything special or have any distinctive characteristics in order to gain the benefit. Benefiting is, on this view, passively receiving good things and the person is like a container that can be occupied by different bundles of goods. Benefiting people is thus only a matter of assigning to them certain goods. Since all that is required to benefit is to have the goods, no particular mechanism of acquisition is essential and so victory (or courage) must fail to be a necessary condition. Kleinias' proposal thus has two shortcomings: (i) it does not isolate a genuinely necessary condition of other goods being good for people, and (ii) it ignores the features of people that may affect whether they benefit from the goods they possess. We should wonder whether these two shortcomings are related: one way of finding a genuinely necessary condition of benefit would be to find some distinctive characteristic such that people had to have it in order to make the goodness of the Dependent Good available to themselves.

There is a second difficulty for Kleinias. In the above quotation from *Laws* 626A5–B4, he moves directly from the claim that nothing is good without victory in war to the claim that such victory is the appropriate ultimate end of the laws. The Athenian, however, objects.

The best good, however, is neither war nor civil strife—the necessity for these things is regrettable—but rather peace and goodwill towards one another. Moreover, it is likely that even that victory of a city over itself is not one of the best things, but one of those that are necessary. To think otherwise is as if someone held that a sick body, after it had received a medical purgation, were in the best active condition, and never turned his mind to a body that had no need of such remedies at all. Similarly, with regard to the happiness of a city or an individual, anyone who thought this way would never become a correct statesman, if he looked primarily and solely to external wars, and would never become a lawgiver in the strict sense, if he did not legislate the things of war for the sake of peace, rather than the things of peace for the sake of what pertains to war. (*Laws* 628C9–E1)[49]

The way in which the other goods depend on victory in war does not entitle victory to play the role of an ultimate end of the laws. The goal of legislation is the best or highest good and even if victory were necessary for attaining the highest good, it is only a precondition. In the case of sick people, medical treatment only puts them in a position to act and use the goods they have; in the case of a city, victory allows it to pursue ends other than self-preservation. Kleinias ignores this distinction, since he thinks that once victory has secured goods for the citizens, benefiting from them is easy. But even if Kleinias were to hold that these goods automatically benefit when possessed, he should recognize the need to choose among them and use them efficiently. Such a concession, however, would only require Kleinias to give instrumental value to the knowledge required to organize and order these goods. By making virtue an ultimate end of the laws, Plato gives virtue a double role: it is both the most important non-instrumental good all by itself and it is responsible for other goods being beneficial. The challenge Plato faces is to show how virtue plays both these roles.

We find a second sort of dependency claim in the *Laws*' first two books. The Athenian puts forward Tyrtaeus, the Spartan war poet, as offering a dependency thesis. Tyrtaeus, on the Athenian's interpretation, claims that if a man does not possess justice he deserves no praise even if he possesses all the other things said to be good or fine (*Laws* 629A4–B4, 629D7–E7, 660D11–661A4). Wealth or boldness in fighting, for example, is only praiseworthy if the person possessing it is virtuous. The praiseworthiness of anything is thus entirely dependent on virtue: no possession of a person is praiseworthy unless the person is virtuous.[50] Kleinias agrees with Tyrtaeus that nothing is praiseworthy unless its possessor is virtuous (*Laws* 661E6–662A4). But Kleinias also accepts what Plato's Dependency Thesis rejects, which is that unjust people, although not praiseworthy in any respect, can be benefited by the things they possess and can live happily (*Laws* 661E–662A). Kleinias' divided reaction raises two issues. First, we again see what Kleinias thinks about the nature of the goodness possessed by the things that Plato classifies as Dependent Goods. For Kleinias, goods such as health and life possess at least some of their goodness in a non-dependent way. By their very nature, they benefit human beings regardless of their ethical character. Although virtue may be a necessary condition of praiseworthiness, benefit works differently. On this point, Kleinias' position is surely in far better accord with ordinary intuitions, both Greek and modern. Even if virtue is an Independent Good and always adds to the goodness of other things, the goodness of the Dependent Goods is, it seems, at least to some extent, independent of virtue. Why, after all, is health not beneficial to unvirtuous people? It does, for example, allow them better to attain whatever ends they have and may be sought even apart from such usefulness. Healthy people avoid the pains of sickness and the frustration of desires that sickness often brings, and health itself seems to have its own pleasures. So it seems reasonable to think that if people can be benefited by something other than virtue, then this benefit should not always depend on whether they are virtuous. If there are goods other than virtue, then why do at least some of them not benefit both the virtuous and the unvirtuous alike?

A second issue concerns the grounding of the dependency claim attributed to Tyrtaeus. This claim seems intuitively easier for Kleinias, and us, to accept, but why does this claim seem more plausible? Perhaps the line of thought underlying the intuition is this: without virtue, one's possessions are not praiseworthy at all or fine in any respect because virtue is the only proper object of praise and thus *constitutes* what is fine or noble about the possession of Dependent Goods. Plato's Dependency Thesis, however, also involves a more complex notion of dependency. Plato, it seems, both wants to make the goodness of Dependent Goods depend entirely on virtue (i.e. the agent who lacks virtue does not benefit at all from them) and to sustain this claim without holding that virtue is the only thing that benefits the agent. But is Plato committed to the view that the goodness of Dependent Goods is entirely dependent on virtue? The claim that the Dependent Goods are bad (or not good) for their possessors unless they are virtuous is open to stronger and weaker interpretations. On less stringent interpretations of the Dependency Thesis, Plato is only claiming that, although at least some Dependent Goods benefit their possessors in some respects or in the short run, even if they are not virtuous, this benefit is outweighed so that these Dependent Goods are, all things considered, bad for them. Which of the following claims does Plato hold?

(1) No Dependent Good is good for unjust people in any respect, for any length of time.

(2) Some Dependent Goods are good for unjust people in some respects or for some length of time, but none is good for them all things considered.

(3) Some Dependent Goods are good for unjust people, all things considered, but most are not good for them, all things considered.[51]

Plato's earlier statements of the Dependency Thesis in the *Euthydemus* and the *Meno*, as well as Passages A and B in the *Laws*, suggest the strongest interpretation, (1). The *Euthydemus*, for example, concludes that the other goods, when separated from virtue, are 'by themselves of no value' (αὐτὰ δὲ καθ᾽ αὑτὰ … οὐδενὸς ἄξια, *Euthyd.* 281D8–EI, cf. 292B1–CI, 280B7–281AI, 288E2–289B4). In the *Laws*, Plato claims that for a person lacking virtue, the Dependent Goods are 'the worst things' (*Laws* 661B6–8, cf. 710A2) and that such a person is simply 'bereft' of the Dependent Goods insofar as they are goods (*Laws* 631CI). There is no suggestion that this claim admits of exceptions in certain cases or that this is an overall judgment that the bad factors outweigh the good. Further, (1) should be welcome to Plato, since it allows him to give a satisfying explanation of why virtue is necessary for happiness and at least greatly facilitates justifying the claim that the just person is always better off than the unjust.

On the other hand, weaker claims about the Dependent Goods, although they may be initially more plausible, present difficulties for Plato. For example, a weaker and thus more plausible claim, such as (3), may threaten Plato's claim that an unjust person who possesses all the Dependent Goods is 'miserable' (*Laws* 661E4, cf. 661CI–2) and might also call into question the claim that the just person is always better off than the unjust.[52] Neither thesis is inconsistent with (3), since (a) most Dependent Goods will still be bad for the unjust person and we might hold that (b) the disvalue of injustice by itself vastly outweighs the benefit of the Dependent Goods he possesses. But we shall then need a principled explanation of why (a) and (b) are true in order to show that they are not simply *ad hoc* stipulations. (2) may seem to avoid the difficulties of both (1) and (3), but it also threatens to collapse into (3). Once again, if we allow an unjust person to benefit from a Dependent Good in some respects or for some length of time, it may be difficult to give a principled reason for holding that, for the unjust person, the possession of no Dependent Good is ever good (or is always bad) all things considered. (If someone is benefited even for a short period of time, then one who dies at the end of that interval might be benefited all things considered.) We can make progress on these issues only by considering why Plato accepts the Dependency Thesis.

The two dependency claims we have considered suggest the challenges that a satisfactory interpretation of the Dependency Thesis must meet.

(A) It must show that virtue is a genuinely necessary condition of bene-fiting from Dependent Goods (and is not just usually required). To do this, it must show why virtue is necessary for benefiting from Dependent Goods or is a condition of their being valuable for their possessor.

(B) It must show not only that virtue is the condition of Dependent Goods being valuable for their possessor, but that virtue itself is good and is an Independent Good.

(C) To show that the goodness of Dependent Goods for their possessor is genuinely dependent on virtue, an interpretation should show that these other things when conjoined with virtue are really good for their possessor and that their value is not simply reducible to the value of virtue.[53]

2.9 Previous Attempts to Ground the Dependency Thesis

The Laws' Dependency Thesis has not attracted much philosophical atten-tion. But scholars have discussed a dependency claim found in the Euthydemus and the Meno.[54] There Plato holds that knowledge of good and bad is necessary and sufficient for an agent to benefit from any Dependent Good. Since in the pre-Republic dialogues, Plato identifies virtue with knowledge of good and bad, he holds in the Euthydemus and the Meno that virtue is necessary and sufficient for an agent to benefit from any Dependent Good. (It makes no difference for these purposes whether each virtue is identical with some distinct part of the knowledge of good and bad or is identical with the whole of knowledge of good and bad.) Despite the appar-ent resemblance between this claim and that in the Laws, we should not assume that Plato holds exactly the same theory in all three dialogues. If we think that Plato does not have a fully determinate ethical theory in the early period, we might look to the late dialogues for clarification, deepening, and, perhaps, revision of some of his earlier central claims. We would expect Plato to take up unresolved issues here and, in particular, to work out or rework the underpinnings of some of his earlier claims; and in the process of doing so, these claims may be given more determinate content as well as a firmer grounding. We shall find, for example, important connections between the later version of the Dependency Thesis and the value theory of the *Philebus*, and the epistemology and psychology of the *Theaetetus* and the *Timaeus*. Nevertheless, I shall begin by considering in this section two attempts that have been made to ground the *Euthydemus–Meno* version of the Dependency Thesis. Examining these attempts will help us to see at least part of what Plato needs in the *Laws*. Neither account can justify the claim that virtue is a genuinely necessary condition of benefit and neither explains how virtue can be both a condition of value for other goods and itself an Independent Good.

Moral Knowledge Account   In his seminal work on Plato's theory of goods, Gregory Vlastos offers an account of the *Euthydemus–Meno* Dependency Thesis. We must begin with Vlastos' account of the relation between virtue and happiness. Vlastos distinguishes sharply between 'moral virtue' and 'moral value' on the one hand, and 'non-moral value' on the other. He holds that there are components of happiness other than virtue and argues for this claim as follows. As a eudaimonist, Plato holds that 'the attainment of [the agent's own] happiness [is] the final reason for [his] every rational choice.'[55] If virtue were the only component of happiness, it would follow that there is 'no rational ground for preference between states of affairs differentiated only by their non-moral values'.[56] Thus I would have sufficient grounds for choice when faced with the options of, e.g., stealing Philoctetes' bow or refraining from theft. But I would have no reason for choosing one option rather than another when faced with a myriad of everyday decisions about when to have my hair cut, what wine to drink with dinner, or, in a memorable example of Vlastos', whether to spend the night in a vomit-covered bed or a fresh one. Here, no moral value is at stake: the differences between the states of affairs are 'non-moral: hedonic, economic, hygienic, aesthetic, sentimental or whatever'.[57] Thus if the thesis that virtue is the sole component of happiness were true it would bankrupt the power of eudaemonism to give a rational explanation of all our deliberate actions by citing happiness as our final reason for them. On that theory, if happiness were identical with virtue, our final reason for choosing anything at all would have to be only concern for our virtue; so the multitude of choices that have nothing to do with that concern would be left unexplained.[58]

According to Vlastos, the Dependency Thesis is the claim that it is 'moral virtue', i.e. 'precisely what we understand by moral virtue', which 'makes all other things good'.[59]

Although I agree that Plato recognizes components of happiness other than virtue, Vlastos' way of distinguishing virtue from the other components of happiness undermines his own account of the *Euthydemus–Meno* Dependency Thesis. Vlastos claims that it is 'moral virtue' that makes all other goods valuable. What Vlastos seems to mean by 'moral virtue' is 'moral knowledge,' i.e. knowledge of the moral values at stake in the circumstances of choice (for example, knowing that stealing Philoctetes' bow or harming another is morally bad).[60] Given this identification of moral virtue with moral knowledge, the claim that moral virtue is what makes all other goods good for their possessor is equivalent to the claim that moral knowledge is what makes all the Dependent Goods valuable. But this account has two problems. First, in the *Euthydemus* and the *Meno*, Plato claims that Dependent Goods are dependent on people's knowledge of the good, i.e., on their knowledge of what is good or bad for themselves all things considered, and Plato simply does not draw any distinction between moral goodness and other kinds of goodness or restrict knowledge of good and bad to knowledge of the morally good and bad.[61] Second, Plato does not merely fail to draw this distinction explicitly. Rather, such a distinction would be unwelcome to him because it would undermine the claim that the value of all Dependent Goods is dependent on the person's knowledge of the good. In cases in which making moral use of Dependent Goods is good for the person, moral knowledge *might* be a plausible source of value. We would still need, however, an explanation of exactly *why* this is so, that is, of how moral knowledge makes the moral use of Dependent Goods good for a person.

But what of cases in which the Dependent Good is not being put to moral use and moral value is not at stake? Consider one of Vlastos' own examples. Vlastos asks us to imagine a person faced with the choice of spending the night in one of two beds: one covered with vomit from its previous drunken occupant or a clean, fresh bed. Vlastos uses this case to show that happiness has components other than virtue: he argues that since the two choices do not differ with respect to virtue, but the person who chose the clean bed would be happier, virtue is not the sole component of happiness. But this example also undermines Vlastos' account of dependency. Vlastos claims that the person's 'virtue would be unimpaired if, clenching [his] teeth and holding [his] nose, [he] were to crawl in between those filthy sheets for a bad night's sleep'.[62] But, on Vlastos' understanding of virtue, not only is it the case that the person's virtue is unimpaired if he is virtuous, but also that the condition of his soul, whether virtuous or unvirtuous, is simply unaffected by the choice. Neither would the unvirtuous person's moral condition be *improved* by crawling between the same filthy sheets or impaired by getting into the clean bed. The choice involves only 'non-moral value' and we have not been given any reason to think this non-moral value cannot be had by a person lacking moral knowledge. Specifically, the person's moral knowledge cannot be what makes this non-moral good good for him: knowing that choosing either bed is morally permissible does not make the choice of the clean bed better from the point of view of non-moral value. If one got into the clean bed without at least implicitly believing that this was permissible, this might be a moral flaw that results in a loss of moral value. But that does not show that benefiting from the non-moral value at stake requires moral knowledge. (We could avoid this problem by claiming Plato is an ethical egoist, i.e. holds that each person is morally obligated to do what is all things considered best for herself, but this would give moral value to states of affairs that Vlastos says are non-moral.) The problem is more general than it seems, since the moral knowledge explanation fails to account for benefit not only in cases in which the choice concerns wholly 'non-moral' value, but even in cases in which moral value is also at stake. Moral knowledge might include the knowledge that non-moral value is always outweighed by moral value, but this does not explain why or how non-moral value itself depends on knowledge of moral value.

So we are left with several worries. First, this account does not show that virtue is a necessary condition of benefiting from all Dependent Goods

because it does not show why moral knowledge would be necessary to benefit from non-moral value. People lacking virtue or wisdom may do or be
willing to do bad things in order to gain some Dependent Goods such as
health, they may use their health unvirtuously, or their possession of it
might cause them to go wrong in some further way, but considered just by
itself, apart from the cost of obtaining it and the consequences of its possession, why is health not good for them? The moral knowledge account does
not provide a satisfactory answer. Second, even if we accept that moral
knowledge is a necessary condition of benefiting from moral goods, why is
this so? The moral knowledge account does not yet provide an explanation
of the relation between moral knowledge and moral value that justifies the
dependency of Dependent Goods. Finally, this account does not explain
why virtue is an Independent Good.

The Productive Account There is a second explanation of the
Euthydemus–Meno Dependency Thesis to consider. Given Plato's claim
that wisdom is the 'leader' both of the other virtues and the Dependent
Goods (*Euthd.* 281B1 and *Meno* 88A3; cf. *Laws* 631C6, 631D5–6), we may suppose that Dependent Goods are dependent on wisdom because wisdom is
necessary and sufficient for their proper use. On this account, the relevant
wisdom is the knowledge of good or correct use, that is, it consists in the
knowledge of how to use Dependent Goods in order to produce a good for
their possessor. (Let us call this the 'productive account'.) Although this
interpretation goes naturally with the idea that knowledge is only an instrumental good, it does not require it; it leaves open the possibility that knowledge is a non-instrumental good and an Independent Good. Further, this
interpretation leaves it open how the correct use of Dependent Goods
benefits their possessor: the correct use can be a means to some further
goods or can itself be non-instrumentally good for the agent. But if the productive account holds that correct use of Dependent Goods is valuable solely as a means to some further good, it will ultimately have to be filled out by
specifying the goods to which the correct use of Dependent Goods is an
instrument and showing that wisdom is a genuinely necessary condition of
their production. Given Plato's views from at least the *Republic* on, the most
promising version of the productive account for the *Laws* will treat both

wisdom and at least some instances of the correct use of the Dependent Goods as non-instrumental goods.

The productive account has some intuitive plausibility and it is superior to the moral knowledge account in that it attempts to explain the dependency of 'non-moral' goods on virtue. 'Non-moral' goods, like any other goods, must be used correctly in order to benefit the agent and this requires wisdom, i.e. knowledge of correct use. Nevertheless, the productive account cannot explain the Dependency Thesis. We can best see its strengths and limitations by turning to the *Euthydemus*. The productive account is suggested, for instance, by some of the examples that Plato uses there: carpenters are not benefited by possessing tools and raw materials unless they know how to use them and carpentry provides knowledge of how to use means to bring about beneficial ends (e.g., *Euthd.* 280C4–E2).[63] More generally, the productive account seems to fit well with the overall line of argument in the *Euthydemus*.

(1) Right use of a Dependent Good is a necessary (and sufficient) condition of its possessor benefiting from the possession of a Dependent Good.

(2) Wisdom is a necessary (and sufficient) condition of the right use of a Dependent Good.

Therefore,

(3) Wisdom is a necessary (and sufficient) condition of its possessor benefiting from the possession of a Dependent Good.[64]

The goodness of the Dependent Goods for their possessor is thus dependent on knowledge of the good because such knowledge is necessary and sufficient for using the Dependent Goods correctly. If you do not know how to use the resources available to you, you will not be able to use them rightly and if you do not use your resources rightly, they will not benefit you. If, on the other hand, you do know how to use your resources, you will use them rightly and they will benefit you.

Bad luck provides well-known difficulties for the claim that wisdom is sufficient for benefiting from a Dependent Good. Although Plato holds that the wise person will have no need of luck (*Euthd.* 279D6 and 280A6–B3), it is hard to justify this claim on the productive account. It seems that even wise people may have so few resources that they can derive no benefit from their use and that any amount of wisdom, short of omniscience, will be subject to accidental misuse. Further, even omniscience, much less anything else, will be subject to outside intervention in the productive process. (Omniscience might only guarantee that you will know that you will be interfered with.) Wisdom, even if it is sufficient for making the best possible use of the Dependent Goods in one's possession, does not seem to be sufficient for benefit.

But there is also a little-noticed problem about good luck. Why cannot people lacking knowledge sometimes be lucky and benefit from their accidentally correct use of Dependent Goods? Although knowledge of correct use is more reliable in producing benefit, it is not necessary. Even if such cases of good luck are rare, they still are counterexamples to the claim that knowledge is a necessary condition of benefit. One might dismiss such counterexamples as trivial exceptions to the Dependency Thesis because they are empirically unlikely. And even in these cases, one could hold that knowledge is better, even apart from its results, than the state of mind of the agent who accidentally gets things right and thus hold that, although both the lucky and the knowledgeable agent benefit from their correct use of Dependent Goods, the knowledgeable agent is still better off.[65]

But cases in which a person uses a Dependent Good correctly, i.e. in the way that a wise person would, while lacking knowledge or even true belief about the good, need not be rare and if we allow that the Dependent Goods benefit an agent in such cases, the Dependency Thesis is gravely undermined. Such cases need not be rare, since wrong motivations, such as thinking the good consists in honor or in the satisfaction of necessary appetites, can lead the agent, at least in many cases, to perform the same actions that virtuous people would perform because of their true understanding of the good. If all that Plato intends is to require this sort of correct use in order to benefit from Dependent Goods, the Dependency Thesis would be a clumsy way of attaining his end. If this interpretation were right, then the Athenian's emphatic and severe rejection of the Cretan and the Spartan law codes in favor of the Magnesian law code which is based on the Dependency Thesis would be misplaced, since the sort of behavior the

Cretan and the Spartan law codes require overlaps to a significant degree with that required by Magnesia's (*Laws* 625C–628E and 629B–632E). And in the case of the virtue of moderation, Plato in the *Laws* rejects the possibility of benefit in such cases. People who possess moderation, construed as a natural self-restraint with regard to pleasures, but lack the other virtues and thus lack knowledge of the good, will still act, on many occasions, as a virtuous person would in rejecting certain pleasures. Nevertheless, Plato holds that this sort of moderation is of no benefit to the agent and will not make the Dependent Goods good for their possessor (*Laws* 696A–E and 709E–710B).

Moreover, the idea that the knowledgeable agent is better off than one who acts correctly on the basis of, e.g., a lucky guess because knowledge is a good 'over and above' correct action is simply another way of losing the very notion of *dependency*. On this account, the value of other goods is not dependent on the possession of wisdom; rather, wisdom is a reliable guide to correct use and a good in addition to correct use. The knowledge of the good found in the *Protagoras'* 'art of measurement' might illustrate such a productive role. Without such an art, one may often go wrong in choosing and combining pleasures. But the role of wisdom is simply to guide one's use of things so as to produce the greatest balance of pleasure over pain in the long run. Wisdom is a reliable guide to getting and keeping what is good, but pleasure carries its own goodness with it and all that one has to do in order to benefit is possess the pleasure. Further, on the productive account it is difficult to see why such knowledge should be more than instrumentally good. The productive account is not inconsistent with attributing non-instrumental value to such knowledge, but it does not give us reason to think that what is independently good about such knowledge is its capacity to produce some distinct good for the agent.

The productive account is thus too weak to justify the Dependency Thesis. But if we are to appreciate the strength of the Dependency Thesis, we must not conflate the present objection with a related idea. It is standard Platonic doctrine that genuine virtuous action requires the proper motivation: merely doing what the virtuous person would do is not sufficient for genuinely virtuous action, if one acts on the wrong reason. Agents' motivations are (partially) constitutive of the virtuousness of their action. This is an idea we find intuitively plausible, if we think of morally virtuous action. Agents who refrain from theft solely out of fear of punishment or benefit orphans solely out of a desire to have a good reputation for justice do not act in a morally virtuous way, that is, they deserve no moral credit for their actions. But the Dependency Thesis demands much more: it holds that the use or possession of a Dependent Good does not benefit agents unless they possess knowledge of the good. This does not clearly accord with our intuitions which have a tendency to a kind of dualism. We tend to think that there are two very different kinds of value, one of which is such that it must be appreciated, at least to some degree, in order to be realized (e.g. aesthetic and moral value) and one of which does not require such appreciation (e.g. that involved in having pleasure, being healthy, or having one's desires satisfied). We need to see what justification Plato can provide for a claim which may seem so implausible to us.

A second concern for the productive account is its restriction of the things which can be good for agents. Specifically, if Dependent Goods are valuable for the agent apart from their use, the productive interpretation cannot account for this value. Although Plato insists on the distinction between having and using a Dependent Good in the *Euthydemus*, he does not there give the distinction a hard edge.[66] In the *Laws* passages, Plato does not invoke this distinction and does not claim there that no Dependent Good is of any benefit unless it is used. And it does, in fact, seem that certain Dependent Goods have at least some value apart from their use. For some goods, we can, with difficulty, give sense to the idea of using them: e.g. we might think of using certain pleasures as means to recover our energies for further virtuous activity. But the *Philebus*, by including some pleasures as constituents of the good life (62E–64A, 66C), makes it clear that some pleasures are non-instrumentally good.

For other goods, there seems to be no plausible way to give sense to the notion of using them. For example, if, as is often thought, Plato's account of justice and other-regarding concern involves the idea that the good of others can count as part of my own good, there seems to be no sense in which I must 'use' the happiness of others for it to count as part of my good. (This is not to require that using *x* always results in some product separate from *x*; e.g. I use my body in dancing, but dancing is not a separate product.) And even in the case of Dependent Goods for which we can give sense to the idea of using them—e.g. harmless pleasure and awareness of beauty, both of which can be used in virtuous activity—at least some of them seem to have a value beyond their use. It seems reasonable to prefer having harmless pleasure and awareness of beauty even apart from the opportunities they provide for increased virtuous activity. More generally, virtuous actions aim at achieving some end independent of themselves, and achievement of these ends seems to have value apart from the activity of trying to attain them. For example, virtuous action may aim at harmless pleasure or at benefiting others and it is reasonable to think that agents are better off (apart from an increase in their opportunities for further virtuous activity) if they succeed than if they fail; that is, it seems that actually obtaining the end is of benefit to the agent over and above the activity aimed at bringing it about and the further activity it enables. If this is right, then at least some Dependent Goods have some value for their possessor apart from their use. If not all the value of a Dependent Good comes from or is constituted by its use, the productive account cannot explain why knowledge is necessary for this benefit.[67]

In sum, the productive account fails to show why knowledge of the good is a necessary condition of benefiting from Dependent Goods. Nor does it show why such knowledge is an Independent Good and, in fact, seems to fit best with an instrumentalist view of the value of knowledge.

2.10 Grounding Dependency

Let us take stock and consider what conditions a good explanation of the Dependency Thesis must meet.

(1) Virtue must be necessary for benefiting from any Dependent Good, not only those Dependent Goods that are instances of 'moral value'.

As we saw, the moral knowledge account did not meet this condition.

(2) Virtue must be genuinely necessary for benefiting from any Dependent Good and a good explanation must make clear why it is necessary.

What we need is an account of the Dependency relation that isolates a feature of the knowledge required that makes it a genuinely necessary condition of benefiting from other things. In trying to find this, we are following the strategy of locating some distinctive feature of the person herself that is required for her to benefit from anything. Neither of the two accounts we have considered meets condition (2). A crucial shortcoming of the productive account was that it made knowledge valuable simply in virtue of its role in producing (and perhaps coordinating) various goods. But once the goods were produced, knowledge had no further role. The person needed to be active in using and producing goods, but after their production, was once again left passive: nothing special on the side of the agent was required to enjoy the benefit. On the productive account, even if knowledge were an Independent Good and had some value apart from its role in production, the value of the knowledge was simply added on to the benefit coming from the use of the goods. This leaves the person's knowledge extrinsic to the actual benefit enjoyed.

(3) Virtue must be an Independent Good.

The moral knowledge condition, although consistent with this claim, did not provide an explanation of it. Although the productive account is also consistent with it, as we saw, it does not isolate a feature of the knowledge required that would make it an Independent Good. In cases in which you obtain goods without using your knowledge, the knowledge seems to be of no benefit.

A further condition is not explicitly stated by Plato, but is nevertheless quite plausible. The goodness of virtue should not be accidentally related to its role as a source of value for the Dependent Goods. It is because virtue is itself good that it makes other things good. This suggests the following fourth condition.

(4) The feature of virtue that makes it an Independent Good is essential to explaining why virtue is a source of value for the Dependent Goods.

Let us begin by focusing on requirement (2). We can make knowledge a genuinely necessary condition of benefit by making the agents' knowledge itself partially constitutive of their benefiting. To see how this might work, consider an important suggestion made by Richard Kraut about the notion of happiness. Kraut has argued that both we and Aristotle share the idea that an important aspect of happiness is the fulfillment of certain 'subjective' conditions, such as being satisfied or being content. Happiness requires that a person have

certain attitudes towards his life: he is very glad to be alive; he judges that on balance his deepest desires are being satisfied and that the circumstances of his life are turning out well. . . a major human good is the second-order good which consists in the perception that our major first-order desires are satisfied.[68]

This is, I think, an intuitively attractive suggestion. Kraut isolates two conditions that are relevant to happiness: (i) an awareness that one's major desires are being satisfied, and (ii) a positive attitude toward the satisfaction of these desires; one is 'glad' that they are being satisfied. Applying this to the case of Dependent Goods, we would require (i) an awareness that one has (and in appropriate cases is using) the Dependent Good, and (ii) a positive attitude toward this, for example, a belief that one is benefited by the Dependent Good.

The idea that such an awareness of a Dependent Good and a belief about its goodness are partially constitutive of benefiting from the Dependent Good is very plausible. How could a Dependent Good benefit me, if I am unaware that I have it or I perceive it as a great evil? Such a proposal seems to succeed in solving the requirement of necessity that previous accounts failed to do. Nevertheless, this is still too weak for Plato's purposes. To see why, consider some examples. First, it is reasonable to hold that I can be benefited by an appropriate awareness of fine or beautiful objects. Let us grant that I have the appropriate productive knowledge. I know how to produce fine objects and how to use them: I know how to produce fine paintings and know that they should be placed at a proper viewing height, adequately separated from other adjacent paintings and looked at frequently. I am also aware that I have such a painting and that I am looking at it and I believe that viewing this painting is a great good. Nevertheless, it seems that I shall not be benefited by the painting or such experiences of it, if what I find good about such things is, for example, the intense sexual excitement I derive from looking at the picture or the excitement I get from seeing it as a depiction of myself as an omnipotent tyrant. Similarly, suppose that a person possesses superb argumentative skills. She reasons quickly and cogently and is especially good at producing conclusive counterexamples to complicated positions. She is aware of this ability and considers it a great good. But suppose that what she finds good about it is her ability to humiliate others and impress bystanders. Once again, it seems reasonable to deny that she is benefited by her argumentative skills.

The problem in both cases is that there is not an appropriate relation between the person's beliefs and the goodness of the Dependent Good. What is potentially beneficial about fine objects is that they allow me to have an awareness of real beauty and this requires that I appreciate the features of the object that make it genuinely good or fine. Similarly, what is potentially valuable about fine reasoning abilities is that they allow for (or, when exercised, constitute) a grasp of the truth. What the person needs in both cases is an appreciation of the genuinely valuable features of the Dependent Good.

Let us apply this idea to the Dependency Thesis. The knowledge in question here is wisdom (*phronēsis*), that is, knowledge of the good. An adequate explanation of why this is required for benefit should appeal to what is essential to such knowledge. Although such knowledge may allow its possessor to produce good things and use them correctly or well, this is merely a consequence of the essential nature of such knowledge. What *is* part of the essence or nature of such knowledge, however, is that it is knowledge of what goodness is, or of what makes something good.[69] Holding that knowledge of the goodmaking features of a Dependent Good is partially constitutive of the beneficial use or beneficial possession of a Dependent Good resolves the problem of necessity that the other accounts failed to handle. The Dependency Thesis can now be seen to be exactly what Plato needs and not too strong a claim as it was on the productive account. Even if correct use is possible without knowledge, the Dependency Thesis still holds, because an appreciation of the good is partially constitutive of benefit. We at last have an account that makes knowledge of the good a genuinely necessary condition of benefit.

Since knowledge of the good is not limited to knowledge of what is morally good, condition (1) is satisfied. Condition (3) is satisfied, since knowledge of the good is an Independent Good for Plato. Finally, on this account, it is precisely the feature of wisdom which makes it such an important Independent Good that allows it to play the role of the condition or source of value for the Dependent Goods. Knowledge of the good is itself a great good because it is knowledge of what goodness is, and this is the feature of such knowledge on which the goodness for the agent of other goods depends. The agents' knowledge of the good is what puts them, so to speak, in contact with the goodness inherent in things. The appreciation of the goodness of a thing forms a bridge between the objective goodness of a thing that is independent of my desires and beliefs and my benefiting from it.[70]

The present interpretation of the Dependency Thesis also guarantees, at least for practical purposes, that certain subjective conditions are fulfilled when virtuous people benefit from a Dependent Good: they will recognize that they possess the Dependent Good and appreciate that such possession is good for themselves. The Dependency Thesis thus guarantees the fulfillment of the sort of subjective conditions that Kraut suggests, and it is reasonable to think that the person is benefited by this. Indeed, as we shall see in our discussion of the *Philebus* in the next section, Plato does require the satisfaction of similar 'subjective' conditions in the good life. Nevertheless, this does not exhaust the idea behind the Dependency Thesis. The Dependency Thesis requires not merely the awareness *that* one's desires are satisfied, but also an appreciation of the fact that the objects of one's desires are good. The fundamental difference is between the awareness or belief that one's desires have been met (which is all that is necessary for being satisfied or content) and an appreciation of the features of the objects of one's desires which make them really worth desiring. (And insofar as our rational desires are for what is really good, it is the fact that certain objects of our desires possess genuine goodmaking features that explains why we rationally desire them.) More is required for such correct appreciation than the awareness of the satisfaction of a higher-order desire that one's first-order desires are satisfied, or a higher-order endorsement of one's first-order evaluations.

We shall need to see in greater detail why Plato thinks that more is required. I have so far simply appealed to our intuitions to support this interpretation of the Dependency Thesis. I shall turn in the next section to show how this explanation of the Dependency Thesis is supported by Plato's views in the later dialogues, especially by the *Philebus'* claim that wisdom is the cause of the good life.

But let us begin by considering some basic issues that this interpretation immediately raises. First, we might be concerned that we are attributing to Plato a far too subjective account of the good. Specifically, this interpretation makes the benefit people receive, that is, what is good for them, depend on their attitudes or beliefs. Thus on one prominent contemporary account of what is objectively good for a person, Plato is not an objectivist about the goodness of Dependent Goods. On an 'Objective List' conception of well-being, things are good or bad for people, independently of their attitude toward them.[71] But we cannot avoid denying that Plato is an objectivist in this sense. Simply by making the goodness of Dependent Goods depend on the agent's virtue, Plato makes their goodness depend on the agent's beliefs about and desires for the good. The Dependency Thesis is just inconsistent with making the benefit of Dependent Goods independent of the agent's attitude toward them. Plato is not, however, committed to stronger and more controversial forms of subjectivism. The Dependency Thesis does not entail that a Dependent Good is good for people, if they believe that it is. Indeed, since it makes knowledge (which is truth-entailing) a necessary condition of benefit, it is inconsistent with such a claim. Nor is it Plato's view that the agent's desire or belief constitutes the value in the Dependent Goods; rather his idea is that the agents' appreciation or recognition of the genuine goodmaking features of Dependent Goods is a necessary condition of their benefiting from them. Objects, activities, and states of soul possess these goodmaking features independently of our beliefs about them or desires for them, but the possession and use of these Dependent Goods only benefit a person when these goodmaking features are recognized as such. The appreciation or recognition of the thing's value does not confer value or goodness on the thing in question: that is determined by whether the thing possesses objective goodmaking features. But our appreciation of these features helps to determine that it benefits us.

We should not, however, understand the sort of appreciation required in too passive a way. In order to benefit, we must not only appreciate the value of the Dependent Good (and its possession and use), but this awareness must actually structure and govern our engagement with the Dependent Good. Mere appreciation of the value of a Dependent Good, if it is causally idle and not the focus of one's engagement with the Dependent Good, will not suffice for benefit.[72]

Our first worry was that the Dependency Thesis was too lax, but our next concern is that it is too stringent. Does it, for example, give an implausibly stringent account of instrumental goods or of the benefits in ethical character that a person can enjoy without becoming wise? Suppose, for example, that taking a certain drug allows me to continue living a virtuous life. Taking this drug, it seems, benefits me even if I have no beliefs (or have false beliefs) about its goodness or even if I am unaware that I am taking it. But Plato should not want to deny that the drug is instrumentally good and need not do so. The requirement for appreciation should be restricted to non-instrumental goods and non-instrumental goodmaking properties. This is not an unprincipled restriction, since the value of instrumental goods is entirely derivative from their causal consequences (what really possesses the good are the causal consequences) and the Dependency Thesis will apply, e.g., to both the possession and use of health.

We might also be concerned about cases in which the agent undergoes what intuitively seems to be an improvement in ethical character without acquiring wisdom. Consider the ethical education of children. Until this education is at least well-advanced, children may lack the knowledge necessary for recognizing the goodmaking features of things. Nevertheless, although the children might not think that they are benefited by their ethical education, we think that they are and this is what justifies our action in providing for such education. But Plato can, consistently with the Dependency Thesis, justify such educational practices. Even if children are not really benefited until they acquire a virtuous appreciation of the goodmaking features of things, even the early stages of education are in children's interests, since they bring the children closer to the stage at which they will actually be benefited. Further, since some mistakes about the good are worse than others, even early education can move children from worse states to states that are less bad.

But even if we accept the idea that appreciation of value is essential to certain kinds of benefit (e.g. in cases of aesthetic or ethical value), is it plausible to hold that appreciation is required for all kinds of benefit? The example above concerning a beautiful painting involved a case of what we would think of as aesthetic value and there it seemed not unreasonable to think that appreciation was required for benefit. Similarly, it is plausible to think that benefit from ethical action requires appreciation of the value at stake. But what of cases not clearly falling in either of these groups? For example, is it really the case that benefiting from harmless pleasures or from health requires some appreciation of their goodmaking features? If so, what is such appreciation like? We shall have to return to this issue after our discussion of the *Philebus*. But even now, we might start from cases that seem plausible and hope to extend the account. The example concerning the ability to reason well may also give us some encouragement. The person's desire to humiliate others is an ethical failure, but we may be inclined to judge not merely that she acts wrongly, but that she herself fails to benefit from her abilities because she does not recognize the value of knowing the truth. A further reason for hope is provided by the fact that Plato does not think ethical and aesthetic value are fundamentally different from each other or from other sorts of value: it is one and the same goodmaking property that makes all good things good. If the notion of being benefited has a common content in all cases, then it would be puzzling if it were instantiated by two radically different ways of standing in the right relation to the fundamental goodmaking property.

A final but important concern is that of how much knowledge the Dependency Thesis requires, and whether it requires knowledge in the strict sense (*epistēmē*). If knowledge of the Form of the Good or of the highly abstract account hinted at in the *Philebus* were necessary, then few people in Magnesia would be benefited. As we saw in Chapter 1, Plato's pessimistic view of non-philosophers in the *Phaedo* and the *Republic* rested on his view that they failed to appreciate the genuine value of things. If he is to avoid this result in the *Laws*, Plato needs to develop an account of the virtue of wisdom that allows for an appreciation of the good that falls short of full-blown philosophical knowledge. As we shall see below, one important route of access to such appreciation is through Magnesia's theology. But most citizens of Magnesia will be neither philosophers nor theologians. What Plato needs to explain is the value of the active ethical and political life that the citizens actually live.

So it will not be an easy task to show how the Dependency Thesis can play a role in justifying the citizens' actual lives. But we have good reason to look for such an account. The Dependency Thesis itself plays a fundamental role in the ethical and political theory of the *Laws*. It explains why the proper ultimate end of the laws is to foster virtue in as many citizens as possible, and it also explains Plato's insistence that the citizens receive a true ethical account of the basis of the laws that govern them and his low estimation of legal systems which do not provide such accounts. What we need to see is exactly how the requirements of the Dependency Thesis might be met by Magnesia's citizens.

2.11 *The* Philebus

The *Philebus* is a wide-ranging dialogue. Its topics include the place of knowledge and pleasure in the good life, philosophical methodology, and basic issues in metaphysics. But one theme that unites the dialogue is its concern with goodness or value: Plato not only discusses the role of knowledge and pleasure in the happy human life, but also sketches a metaphysical analysis of goodness. We may thus hope to find here some further account of the relation between what is good for me and what possesses the non-relational property of goodness itself. And as part of its examination of goodness, the *Philebus* provides a subtle exploration of different ways in which the goodness of a thing, including states of soul, depends on the cognitive condition of its possessor.

Mollusks and the Dependency of Pleasure   In the *Philebus*, Plato argues that the good life for human beings is a mixed life composed of both pleasure and knowledge. He begins his argument for this claim by showing us the unsatisfactoriness of any life composed solely of either pleasure or knowledge. Early in the dialogue, Socrates asks his hedonist interlocutor, Protarchus, whether he would find choiceworthy (αἱρετός) a life of the 'greatest pleasures' which has no wisdom in it (*Phil.* 21B3–4).

If you did not possess reason [νοῦν] or memory [μνήμην] or knowledge [ἐπιστήμην] or true opinion [δόξαν . . . ἀληθῆ], in the first place, is it not necessary that you be ignorant about this very thing, that is, whether you were enjoying yourself or not, given that you were empty of all wisdom [φρονήσεως]? . . . And likewise, if you had no memory, you could not remember that you ever did enjoy yourself and no recollection at all of pleasure encountered at one moment could remain. If you had no true opinion, you could not judge that you were enjoying yourself when you were and if you were deprived of the power of calculation you would not be able to calculate that you would enjoy it in the future. Your life would not be that of a man, but that of some mollusk or one of those sea creatures whose bodies are encased in shells.[73]   (*Phil.* 21B6–c8)

All that Socrates does in this passage is appeal to Protarchus' immediate and untutored intuitions (*Phil.* 21A4). Plato does not try here to show that this conclusion follows from a deeper philosophical theory. Nor should we assume that Protarchus' conception of knowledge or of why it is valuable is adequate. This opening counterexample calls Protarchus' simple-minded hedonism into question, but it is only a starting point for the hard philosophical work done in the rest of the dialogue.

Although this counterexample justifies only a much weaker conclusion than that Plato comes to at the end of the dialogue on the basis of some strong philosophical claims, it has more content than is usually thought. It is sometimes suggested that what this thought experiment shows is the importance of memory and practical reason in anything that can count as a distinctively human life. But this still leaves unclear what it is about memory and practical reasoning that makes them valuable and how it is that they add value to one's life. And as we shall see, Plato goes out of his way to suggest that Protarchus fails to appreciate what sort of cognitive attainments are distinctive of a human life and what role they should play within it. To begin, what the counterexample shows is that a life of pleasure without the presence of something else is not desirable; the greatest pleasures are only worthy of choice on the condition that the person possesses something else. The desirability or goodness of pleasure is thus *dependent* on something else, in particular, on some other state of the person. Let us now fill in the details.

First, since the failure of the two lives of unmixed pleasure and unmixed knowledge prepares the conclusion that the mixed life is the good life, all that Plato needs to establish is the weak claim that neither unmixed life is the good life according to the strong conditions specified at *Philebus* 20C8–21A3. Two of these three conditions require the good life to be 'complete' (τέλεον) and 'sufficient' (ἱκανόν) and Plato understands these to require that the good life is unimprovably good.[74] Thus the failure to satisfy these conditions is consistent with the rejected lives being very good, yet allowing of some improvement. But it seems clear that we should have a far more negative view than this of the unmixed life of pleasure. Socrates' characterization of this life as that of a mollusk and Protarchus' reaction that such a life would not be 'sufficient or choiceworthy for any human being or animal' (*Phil.* 22B1–2) suggest that such a life is not worth living for a human being and that its pleasures would be of little or no benefit to us.[75] It seems fair to conclude that for Protarchus, most, if not all, of the value of pleasure depends on the person possessing the sort of knowledge lacking in the counterexample.

So exactly what sort of lack of knowledge causes the unmixed life of pleasure to be undesirable? Plato mentions three forms of knowledge here:

(a) knowing that you are presently having pleasure;
(b) remembering that you had pleasure in the past;
(c) calculating that you will enjoy pleasure in the future.

(a) is the primary case of missing knowledge, while (b) and (c) apply (a) to the past and the future.[76] All three are very simple forms of knowledge or reason: (a), for example, seems only to involve basic self-awareness along with the ability to grasp that what one has is 'pleasure'. But they still have more content than is usually thought.

Consider, first, how the life of unmixed pleasure will seem to Protarchus (and the counterexample is supposed to appeal to his judgment). Protarchus takes over Philebus' claim that pleasure is the good: 'good' and 'pleasant' are two names for the same thing, that is, for the same 'nature'.[77] Thus, from Protarchus' point of view, this is a life in which, because he has the 'greatest pleasures', he has the 'greatest goods'. Nevertheless, he is not aware that he has them. This identity between pleasure and the good is central to the correct understanding of the counterexample's force. It is the fact that he would be unaware of having *the good* and not merely the fact that he would be unaware of having pleasures, that should account for the life's undesirability. If Protarchus held that pleasures are indifferent or bad, he would have no reason to find his lack of awareness of them undesirable. This change in the counterexample asks us to imagine him rejecting hedonism and then considering the imagined life. But, similarly, if he retained his hedonism, but imagined a life in which he had the greatest pleasures and was aware of them as pleasures, but within that life held that pleasure was bad or indifferent, it seems that he should also find such a life deeply undesirable.

This thought experiment's place in the text also directly supports the idea that the unmixed life's undesirability is a result of the person's lack of awareness of his possession of the good. It immediately follows Plato's statement of the third and 'most necessary' of the three conditions on the good life (*Phil.* 20D7). '[E]verything capable of knowing hunts for it, and desires to take hold of it and possess it, caring nothing for anything else [τῶν ἄλλων οὐδὲν φροντίζει] unless its accomplishment involves some good' (*Phil.* 20D8–10).[78] Thus a human living a mollusk's life would not be aware that his ultimate desires for the good were being satisfied to any extent. By itself, this seems to make such a life deeply undesirable. One might object that the third condition is not relevant, since within the unmixed life, the person would neither register the apparent absence of goods nor retain the desire for the good that the third condition attributes to people. But while the unmixed life of pleasure seems to have these cognitive limitations, this does not count against the suggestion that the undesirability of such a life is a result of a lack of awareness not merely of pleasure, but also of the good. A person living such a life would equally fail to register the apparent absence of pleasure and to be aware of deep, unsatisfied desires for pleasure. In either case, if the counterexample is to work, Socrates and Protarchus will have to accept that the proper standpoint for evaluating such a life is not from within that life, but rather that provided by the correct standpoint. And since Protarchus accepts the third condition (*Phil.* 20D11), it is reasonable for it to enter into his judgment of proposed lives.

On this understanding of the counterexample, pleasure should only be a special case of a more general thesis that it is undesirable to possess a good without being aware that what one has is good. Such a generalization is suggested by the third condition itself. The good, whatever it may be, is the ultimate end of our desires and thus it seems that any life in which we were completely unaware of whatever good we possessed would be deeply undesirable.[79] This is not to hold that the only thing that is bad about our failure to be aware of possessing the good is the experienced frustration of desires. If that were so, then we should not be so quick to accept the undesirability of the mollusk's life: it lacks such desires for the good (or at the very least is unaware of them) and suffers no frustration. Indeed, if the frustration of our desire for the good were the only thing bad about such lack of awareness, the mollusk's case might lead us to think that we should try to rid ourselves of such desires for the good. Part of what our intuitive response may suggest upon reflection is that having such desires is an essential aspect of having a good human life. Seeing why this is so will have to wait, however, until much later in the dialogue.

A final point to note about the counterexample is that there is a striking gap between the language that Plato uses in discussing the thought experiment and the lessons that Protarchus draws from it. What Plato takes the case to show is the need for knowledge (*epistēmē*), reason (*nous*), and wisdom (*phronēsis*) in the good life. But the sort of awareness that Protarchus finds crucial falls well short of anything that Plato would count as genuine instances of these. A sign of this disparity is that Plato stresses that the sort of life he is describing is simply not a 'human life' (*Phil.* 21C6–8), thus suggesting that the sort of wisdom we are seeking is something distinctively human. But Protarchus began with the claim that the good is the same for all animals (*Phil.* 11B4–6, C5–8) and the counterexample does not convince him that the good must involve anything distinctively human: the life described is not choiceworthy for 'any human being or animal' (*Phil.* 22B1–2).[80] The sort of awareness of pleasure or the good that is missing there should be found, Protarchus thinks, in any good human or animal life.

What role, then, does the counterexample suggest for knowledge in the good life? First, concentrating on one's present experience, the only sort of knowledge the counterexample justifies is the simple awareness that what one has is good. What it justifies is thus something like the subjective conditions on happiness discussed above. For Protarchus, this is the self-awareness involved in being aware of oneself as having pleasure and the capacity to recognize this as the good. It is not clear exactly what mental resources are necessary for doing this, but it is plausible to think that what Protarchus has in mind is, roughly, the ability to treat pleasure as the ultimate end of action. To treat something as the good is to treat it as satisfying the three conditions stated at *Phil.* 20C8–D10. The good is always desired and is the ultimate criterion guiding our choices and actions.[81] Treating something as the good in the thin sense of the counterexample need involve nothing more than giving it (or recognizing that it has) this role in our thought and action. Since our thoughts and actions are temporally extended, this will involve memory, calculation, and thus some ability to discriminate the good from other things and reidentify it over time. But it need not involve considering whether pleasure is entitled to play this role or grasping the features that make it worthy of being an ultimate end. The awareness that Protarchus demands requires more than the passivity of a mollusk, but it still involves only a low-grade form of activity. The person need only be aware of his own states, find himself drawn to pleasant states, and be capable of some simple kinds of reflection. In doing so, he will satisfy the subjective conditions on happiness: he will perceive that his ultimate desires are being satisfied (and expect future satisfaction of them).

Nor does the counterexample justify a strong role for practical reason in the form of rationally weighing different courses of action and making a choice on the basis of good reasoning. Expecting to get the recognition of the value of such a conception of practical reason out of the counterexample is unfair to Protarchus' original position. A hedonist need not concede so much and we can find a weaker and more acceptable interpretation of the reference to 'the power of calculation' at *Phil.* 21C5–6. If you value pleasure as your ultimate end, it also seems reasonable to value remembering your past pleasures and anticipating your future pleasures. Lovers of wine and Don Juans value not only their present experiences, but also dwell lovingly on the past and keenly anticipate the future. They value such memories and anticipations because they value wine or sex, not because they value the exercise of practical reason. Such anticipation need not involve a rich conception of weighing different options and choosing among them, but only projecting into the future more instances of the present valued experience.

The counterexample thus gives only minimal content to the sort of knowledge required. It also establishes only weak claims about the value of such knowledge. All that hedonists need do is attribute value to their knowledge of pleasure; they need not, and will not, attribute value to any other kind of knowledge or true belief.[82] Thus the hedonist has been given no reason for valuing knowledge or true belief as such, that is, for the characteristics which make them knowledge or true belief. The counterexample does not establish that knowledge or true belief as such have any value. So despite Protarchus' reaction, the hedonist should not yet be especially worried. Nothing we have so far seen suggests that it is the goodness of knowledge or true belief that contributes to the goodness of the good life.

Nevertheless, Plato's position so far bears a formal similarity to the Dependency Thesis, which is sufficiently significant to make it unlikely that it is unintentional. Plato does not, for example, criticize hedonism by raising the standard objection (which he himself has previously made) that there are bad pleasures or that we all do, in fact, recognize goods other than pleasure. His point simply is that pleasure is a kind of dependent good, i.e. it is only good for its possessors if they possess something else. Even on the weakest reading of the counterexample, pleasure's goodness is dependent on a kind of knowledge, that is, the knowledge that one is having pleasure. On a stronger reading, the resemblance is closer: the value of one's possessions depends on one's knowledge that they are good. But on either reading, there are important differences from the Dependency Thesis. On a weak reading, all that is required is awareness of pleasure as pleasure, not as something good. I have argued, however, that awareness of pleasure as a good is also needed and, once we accept this, Plato's third condition on the good life suggests that we extend the requirement to other goods, if we reject hedonism. Plato, however, has not yet justified these steps, nor has he given us reason to require genuine knowledge or any appreciation of why a thing is good. But seeing Plato's criticisms as involving some version of dependency prepares us for a deeper account of the sort of dependency involved in the good life. Such an account will require a more adequate understanding of the knowledge required for leading a good life. Plato will eventually argue that the sort of reason required is related to divine reason and is intimately related to the virtue of wisdom, genuine knowledge, and art.

The Metaphysics of the Mixed Life   Plato proceeds in the rest of the *Philebus* to offer a richer account of the place of knowledge in the good life. This involves both a general metaphysical account of what makes anything good, that is, an account of non-relational goodness (and not just an account of what is good for human beings), as well as a fuller description of the sorts of knowledge that are ingredients in the good life. Plato characterizes different forms of knowledge in terms of truth (ἀλήθεια) and purity (τὸ καθαρόν) and includes all these forms of knowledge in the good life (*Phil.* 55C–59E and 61E–62D).

But knowledge has another role besides that of an ingredient. As we have seen, Protarchus' intuitions require the good life to be a mixture of pleasure and knowledge. But the rest of the *Philebus* shows that this conclusion has a deeper metaphysical basis. Plato begins by sketching a division of 'everything that really exists now in the universe' into four ultimate kinds (*Phil.* 23C4). These are:

(1)   the indeterminates (*apeira*),
(2)   the determinants (*peras echonta, perata*),
(3)   mixtures (*summeikta*) arising from the combination of a determinant with an indeterminate, and
(4)   the causes (*aitiai, aitia*) of these mixtures.

On the theory that Plato develops, all good things are mixtures in that they are mixtures of the indeterminate (*apeiron*) and the determinant (*peras*).[83] Plato's examples of the indeterminate include things such as the hotter and colder, drier and wetter, faster and slower, greater and smaller, and higher and lower. These are things whose nature takes on 'the more and the less', that is, these are things that lack a definite quantity or measure (*Phil.* 24A6–D7). The determinants are numerical ratios or proportions, such as double or equal, that do not admit of the more and less and that impose order on the indeterminates and make them measured and harmonious (*Phil.* 25A6–B3, D11–E2). 'So the mixture of the indeterminate and the determinant is responsible for good climate and generally for everything we have that is fine [καλά] . . . There are countless other things which I pass over: the fineness [κάλλος] and strength of health, and many other very fine things in souls' (*Phil.* 26B1–B7). Since the goodness of a thing consists in its being an appropriate combination of a determinant and an indeterminate, all good things are essentially mixtures. And what makes a thing good is its being the mixture of the indeterminate and the determinant that it is. This provides a general theory of what makes anything good that will be refined later in the *Philebus*.

But in addition to the determinant and the indeterminate and the resulting mixture, Plato posits a fourth kind of entity, the cause (ἡ αἰτία, τὸ αἴτιον) of the mixture (*Phil.* 23D7–8). Plato seems, however, to give two characterizations—which are not obviously equivalent—of the cause of the mixture that is the good life. First, he claims that reason (*nous*) is the cause and second, that the three properties of fineness (τὸ κάλλος), proportion (ἡ συμμετρία), and truth (ἡ ἀλήθεια) are the cause. To understand these claims and their relation to each other, we need to start with Plato's first account of the cause of the good life.

I will not now champion reason for the prize against the combined life, but we must look and see what to do about second prize. It may be that each of us will claim his own candidate as the cause [αἰτιώμεθ᾽] of this combined life—one of us, that reason is the cause [αἴτιον]; the other, that pleasure is—so that while neither is the good, one might claim that one of them is the cause [αἴτιόν] of it. On this point I should be even readier to contest Philebus. I should hold that in this mixed life, whatever it is the possession of which [ὃ λαβὼν] makes the life at once both choiceworthy and good, it is reason that is more akin to it and more nearly resembles it [συγγενέστερον καὶ ὁμοιότερόν]. According to this account, it would never be truly claimed that pleasure had a share in either first or second prize. If my reason is at all to be trusted at the moment, it will not even get third prize. (*Phil.* 22C7–E3)

Plato here distinguishes (a) reason (*nous*) which he explicitly characterizes as the cause of the mixed or good life, that is, the cause of its goodness, and (b) that whose possession by a life makes that life good. The latter is the property or properties in virtue of which a life is good. (I shall call these the 'goodmaking' properties or the 'goodmakers'.) Later on, Plato explicitly calls these goodmakers the 'cause' of the good life.

But it is certainly not difficult in the case of every mixture to see the cause on account of which it is either of the highest value or of none at all [δι᾽ ἣν ἢ παντὸς ἀξία γίγνεται ἡτισοῦν ἢ τὸ παράπαν οὐδενός] . . . any mixture whatever that fails of measure [μέτρου] or the nature of proportion [συμμέτρου] necessarily destroys its ingredients and, most of all, itself.[84] For it is no mixture, but truly an unmixed jumble, and always is really a disaster for what it afflicts . . . So now the power of the good has fled and taken refuge in the nature of the fine [τὴν τοῦ καλοῦ φύσιν]. For measure [μετριότης] and proportion [συμμετρία] everywhere turn out to be fineness [κάλλος] and virtue [ἀρετὴ] . . . And we said that truth [ἀλήθειάν] was mixed with them in the mixture . . . Then if we cannot capture the good by means of one idea [μιᾷ . . . ἰδέᾳ], let us take hold of it with three: fineness, proportion, and truth. Let us say, treating them as one, that this is the element in the mixture that we should most correctly regard as the cause [ὀρθότατ' ἂν αἰτιασαίμεθ'], and that it is on account of this as being good that the mixture itself has become good . . . So now anyone could judge adequately between pleasure and wisdom and decide which is more akin to the highest good and is of greater honor among men and gods.   (*Phil.* 64D3–65B2)

These three goodmakers—fineness, proportion, and truth—are the cause of the good life in that they are the properties that constitute what it is for a thing to be good, that is, they constitute the goodness of any mixture. As such, they are necessary and sufficient conditions of the goodness of any mixture and, in particular, are both the necessary (*Phil.* 64A, 64D3–E3) and sufficient conditions (*Phil.* 22D6–7, 64D3–65A5, 65A1–5) of the goodness of the good life.[85] Indeed, they are necessary conditions of the mixture having any value at all: whatever fails to have them is not a genuine mixture and lacks all value (*Phil.* 64D3–E3). Since they account for the goodness of all mixtures and not just the goodness of the good life, they must be non-sensible and non-psychic properties.

Now that we have seen how the goodmakers are the cause of the goodness of the good life, we need an explanation of how reason is the cause of the good life. Any satisfactory interpretation must do justice to Plato's claim (*Phil.* 22C7–D4) that being the cause of the good life is sufficient to entitle reason to second place after the mixed life itself and this at least requires that reason in its role as cause is non-instrumentally good. Let us first consider the suggestion that reason is the cause of the goodness of the mixed life because it is the best ingredient in the mixed life. On this line, we could argue that since the value of reason is much greater than the value of pleasure, reason will be responsible for the goodness of the mixed life by being responsible for most of its value. But this is not an adequate explanation.

The three goodmakers are the cause of the good life because they constitute the determinant which is imposed on all the ingredients of the good life. If reason is to be a cause of the mixed life in a similar way, it must in some way be involved in the imposition of order on the mixed life as a whole, that is, it must be responsible for the mixed life being the mixture that it is. If reason were the cause of the goodness of the good life only insofar as it is the best ingredient in it, reason would have no role to play in explaining the goodness of the other ingredients of the good life; in particular, it would have no role to play in explaining the goodness of pleasure.

The requirement that reason account for the goodness of the ordered whole that is the good life is supported by Plato's application of his fourfold classification to pleasure and reason (*Phil.* 23B–31A), which immediately follows the initial claim at *Phil.* 22C7–D4 that reason is the cause of the good life. Here Plato characterizes the cause of the mixture as what produces the mixture or brings it into being (*Phil.* 26E2–27C2). This suggests that reason is the cause of the mixed life insofar as practical intelligence acts to produce the proper order within one's life, that is, insofar as it is an efficient cause of the mixture or, more precisely, the efficient cause of the mixture's instantiation of the goodmakers.[86] But the fact that reason is the efficient cause of the mixed life is not, as such, sufficient to explain why reason, in virtue of being the cause of the mixture, is non-instrumentally good, since an efficient cause, *qua* efficient cause, is only instrumentally good. Nor does this interpretation give any significant point to Plato's use of divine creative activity as his illustration of reason as a cause. If Plato's only point were that reason can exercise efficient causality, then appealing to the productive crafts would be simpler and less controversial. Indeed, if the point only concerned efficient causality, there would be no reason to appeal either to god's creative activity or to craft production. Any run-of-the-mill instance of deciding to do something and then acting to bring about a result would serve just as well as an illustration. Plato, rather, seems to be suggesting that there is a deeper resemblance between the way that god's reason is the cause of the orderly whole of the world and the way in which individual reason is the cause of the orderly whole that is the good life.

In order to see how the practical aspect of reason has more than instrumental value, Terence Irwin suggests returning to Socrates' opening counterexample against the life of unmixed pleasure. On Irwin's account, the kind of knowledge involved here is the sort of rational consciousness 'involved in being aware of myself over time; memory, self-consciousness and rational calculation'.[87] To show that reason is the cause of the mixed life, Irwin suggests that

Plato might reasonably appeal to his argument against the unmixed life of pleasure. [He] argues against Protarchus that such a life lacks the essential element of rational consciousness and planning that connects the different episodes of pleasure into a life for a rational agent. If they are unconnected, the different pleasures are still goods, and they are the raw material for a good life; but they do not constitute parts of a good life until they are connected and arranged by the right sort of rational consciousness.[88]

On Irwin's interpretation, the sort of reason that is the cause of the good life is the sort of knowledge missing in the mollusk-like life of the counterexample.

This is, however, too weak an account of how reason is the cause of the good life. First, on this interpretation, the notion of reason as the cause of the good life undergoes no development from the beginning to the end of the dialogue. But our understanding of reason has grown much deeper and we have seen that the sorts of knowledge for which the counterexample shows a need are not genuine instances of reason or knowledge. We should thus seek a stronger interpretation of how reason functions as a cause of the good life. Second, immediately following the initial claim that reason is the cause of the goodness of the mixed life (*Phil.* 22C7–D4), Plato explains how reason is the cause of mixtures by discussing how god's reason is the cause of the mixture that is the world. In the same section, he also draws a more intimate connection between the microcosm and the macrocosm.

Socrates: Each element in us is small and insignificant, and is in no way pure at all or endowed with the power that is worthy of its nature . . . There is something called fire that belongs to us, and then again there is fire in the universe . . . And is not the fire that belongs to us small, weak, and insignificant, while the fire in the universe overwhelms us by its size, fineness, and every power that belongs to fire . . . is the fire in the universe nourished, generated, and ruled by the fire that belongs to us, or, on the contrary, does my fire, and yours, and that of all living beings, owe all this to the universal fire?

Protarchus: That question does not even deserve an answer.

. . .

Soc.: Realize that the same holds in the case of what we call the cosmos. It would be a body in the same way, since it is composed of the same elements . . . Does the body of the universe as a whole provide for the sustenance of what is body in our sphere, or is it the reverse, and the universe possesses and derives all the goods enumerated from ours?

Prot.: That, Socrates, is another question not worth asking.

. . .

Soc.: But where does [our soul] come from, Protarchus, unless the body of the universe were ensouled, since that body has the same elements as ours, although finer in every way?

Prot.: Clearly from nowhere else.

Soc.: We surely cannot believe, Protarchus, that those four kinds (the determinant, the indeterminate, their mixture, and their cause—which is present in everything)—we cannot believe that this last item, the cause, while it is recognized as all wisdom of every kind, since among us, it gives souls to our bodies and provides training for the body and medicine for its ailments and in other cases order and restitution, but has nevertheless failed in the case of the elements of the whole universe (although they are the same elements that pervade the whole heaven on a great scale and are fine and pure) to contrive what is finest and most honorable . . . [W]e had better pursue the alternative account and affirm, as we have often said, that there is in the universe a plentiful indeterminate and a sufficient determinant, and that there is, above them, a by no means insignificant cause that orders and arranges the years, seasons, and months, and may justly be called wisdom and reason. (*Phil.* 29B6–30C7)

Plato does not spell out the relation that holds between the universe's body and our bodies and between the reason that rules the universe and our reason, but he clearly intends something more than the assertion of causal dependence. At least part of what he is asserting is that the orderliness of the world provides a paradigm for us in ordering our own lives and that, in particular, the activity of divine reason as the cause of good order in the world provides a paradigm for individual reason in its role as the cause of order in the good life. What appears to ground the idea that divine reason is a paradigm for our reason is sameness in composition. Although the fire in us is weak and insignificant it is the same sort of stuff as that which is in the universe; similarly, both our bodies and the body of the universe are ensouled.

We are invited to see our reason as the same sort of thing as divine reason and thus as having similar capacities.

God is certainly aware of himself as a rational agent over time and possesses memory, self-consciousness, and is aware of planning for the future (or at least he has some non-temporal analogues), but these are not the most significant features of god's creative activity. What is, rather, most significant about this activity is its orientation toward the good. In the first characterization in the passage above of the cause in the universe we learn that it orders and arranges years and seasons and Plato concludes that his account 'confirms the utterances of those who declared of old that reason always rules the universe' (*Phil.* 30D7–8). This is a reference to Anaxagoras and should remind us of the *Phaedo*'s claim that reason orders all things for the best. This claim is also very prominent in the *Timaeus* and the theology of Book 10 of the *Laws*. Divine reason possesses perfect knowledge of the good and the goodmakers and because it is itself good, it orders the universe so that it instantiates the good as far as possible (e.g. *Laws* 903B ff. and *Tim.* 29E ff.). Thus reason insofar as it is in its best state both knows the good and seeks to instantiate it. (Plato stresses that the pattern used by god is apprehensible by *logos* and *phronēsis, Tim.* 29A6–7.) If, as the parallel suggests, we should seek a common feature between the way that divine reason and our reason are the cause of mixtures, what we should expect is that individual reason's awareness of the good and intention to impose good order on the individual's life is the feature of individual reason that entitles it to be the cause of the goodness of the mixed life.

We can begin our search for a stronger interpretation than Irwin's by returning to a passage quoted above, *Philebus* 22C7–E3. In this passage, Plato claims that reason is akin to the goodmakers and that reason is the cause of the good life, but what is the relation between these two claims? This is an important point, since Plato here appears to make two different suggestions.

(1) Reason deserves second place, after the mixed life, in virtue of being the cause of the good life.

(2) Reason deserves second place, after the mixed life, in virtue of being more akin to, and more like, the goodmakers than pleasure is.

Some scholars hold that (2) simply replaces (1) as Plato's 'real' view: Hackforth, for example, holds that here 'Socrates corrects or modifies his first suggestion, that reason, rather than pleasure is the cause of the goodness of the Mixed Life.'[89] But such an interpretation is unattractive. First, Plato reiterates (1) later in the dialogue.[90] Second, jettisoning (1) renders pointless Plato's long discussion of how reason acts as the cause of mixtures (*Phil.* 28D–31A). Third, rejecting (1) results in an undesirably restricted understanding of the goodness of knowledge, since it seems to commit us to the view that knowledge is good only insofar as it is one of the ingredients of the good life and has a high value as an ingredient. On the other hand, Plato stresses (2) at the end of the dialogue (*Phil.* 61A4–5, 65A7 ff., and 67A10–12) and mere efficient causality is not enough to warrant giving reason second place.

But we do not have to give up either (1) or (2). Plato can and should hold that reason deserves second place in virtue of being a cause, but in virtue of being a special sort of cause. What Plato needs to hold is

(3)   Reason deserves second place because it is the cause of the good life in virtue of the properties which render reason akin to the good-makers.

Understanding (3) will lead us into some of the more difficult aspects of Plato's later metaphysics and epistemology, so let me briefly sketch what we shall find. The notion of reason being akin to the goodmakers is complex.

1.   Reason is akin to the goodmakers in the straightforward sense that reason instantiates the goodmakers. Reason is not simply some mental capacity or other, but is the best condition of the soul. Indeed, the claim that reason is the best condition of the soul is true in two ways. First, the psychic state that is best for people, that is, most benefits them, is one in which they have attained or exercise reason. But, second, the possession of the goodmakers is what makes a thing non-relationally good. A soul possessing the goodmakers is, so to speak, the best thing that a soul can be.

Since reason is the best condition of the soul, it is more than merely the capacity to reason correctly. As Plato understands it here, reason is a state of the soul that instantiates knowledge. And it is the instantiation of knowledge that makes reason good. So we can refine (3). Reason is the cause of the good life insofar as it instantiates knowledge. Thus (3) is the claim that knowledge is the cause of the good life because of the features that make it the knowledge that it is. And since it is the instantiation of knowledge that makes reason good, reason is the cause of the good life insofar as reason is itself good. We can thus give sense to the idea that reason by its own goodness makes the good life good.

2.   But there is another strand of Plato's argument. In virtue of what sort of knowledge is reason the cause of the good life? The knowledge in question will be knowledge of what makes the ingredients of the good life worthy of rational choice and of how these ingredients are to be ordered and mixed. This will be an appreciation of the goodness of the ingredients and of their proper mixture. Thus reason will stand in a double relation to the goodmakers: it will know them and in virtue of knowing them it will instantiate them.

Let us turn to the details. Plato describes reason as 'more akin and more similar' and 'more attached and fitted to' and 'more naturally related' to the goodmakers than pleasure is.[91] There are two lines of argument leading to this conclusion. The first begins from Plato's analysis of different kinds of knowledge at the end of the *Philebus*. The most important distinctions Plato draws (*Phil.* 55C–59B) are with respect to accuracy (*akribeia*), clarity (*saphēneia*), purity (*katharotēs*), and truth (*alētheia*). As we shall see, the degree to which different kinds of knowledge possess these features is relevant to the question of why knowledge and reason are akin to the goodmakers. In particular, the more fully knowledge is accurate, clear, pure, and true, the more akin it is to the goodmakers. And it is more akin to the goodmakers because it knows them and instantiates them.

Purity has a central role among these distinctions and we can begin to see what Plato means by the purity of knowledge by considering other items he classifies as pure.

How can there be purity in the case of whiteness, and what sort of thing is it? Is it the greatest quantity or amount, or is it rather the complete lack of any admixture, that is, where there is not the slightest part of any other color? . . . this is the truest and the finest of all instances of white, rather than what is greatest in quantity or amount . . . a small portion of pure white is to be regarded as whiter than a larger quantity of an impure whiteness, and at the same time, finer and truer. (*Phil.* 53A5–B6)[92]

Insofar as the white is purer, it is also finer and truer.[93] Plato immediately applies this understanding of purity to the case of pleasure. '[T]his example suffices to prove that in the case of pleasure, too, every small and insignificant pleasure that is pure from pain [καθαρὰ λύπης] will turn out to be pleasanter, truer, and finer than a greater quantity of the impure kind' (*Phil.* 53B8–C2). A pleasure is pure to the extent that it is unmixed with pain. And insofar as a pleasure is purer, it is also finer and truer.

Knowledge will thus be impure insofar as it is mixed with error or ignorance and will be pure insofar as it is unmixed with error or ignorance.[94] This understanding of the purity of knowledge allows us to see two important connections that purity has. First, the accuracy, clarity, and truth of knowledge go along with its purity. Second, purity goes along with determinacy and impurity with indeterminacy. The sort of mixture that makes either knowledge or pleasure impure also makes the resulting mixed state indeterminate.[95]

Knowledge is accurate, clear, and true insofar as it grasps the nature and structure of the objects with which it deals. What Plato emphasizes toward the end of the *Philebus* is that knowledge is clearer, more accurate, and truer insofar as it more precisely grasps the nature of its object in mathematical terms or in the way that mathematics grasps the nature of its objects. Subject matters differ in the extent to which such clarity and accuracy is possible. Plato, for example, contrasts music and shipbuilding.

But let us first find out whether within the manual arts there is one side more closely related to knowledge itself, and the other less closely; second, whether we should treat the one as purest, the other as less pure . . . If someone were to take away arithmetic and the sciences of measurement and weighing from all arts, the rest might be said to be worthless . . . All that would be left for us would be to conjecture and train our senses through practice and experience. We would have to rely on our ability to make guesses that many people call art, once it has acquired some proficiency through practice and labor . . . This is clear, to start with, in the case of music. The harmonies are found not by measurement, but by guesswork based on practice, and flute music throughout tries to find the measure of each note as it is produced by guess. So the amount of unclarity mixed up in it is great, and the amount of security small ... But the art of building, I believe, employs the greatest number of measures and instruments which give it great accuracy and make it more scientific than most arts.   (*Phil.* 55D5–56B6)

Music suffers a relatively great degree of unclarity not because it cannot produce harmonies, but because in its productive efforts it can only discriminate more or less accurately the underlying structure of musical order.

But there is a greater difference between arts such as building and the 'most accurate' arts of arithmetic and especially, dialectic (*Phil.* 56E, 57D, 59B–C). This difference in their accuracy depends on their subject matter. Arithmetic is divided into two kinds: that of arithmeticians and that of the arithmetically naive.

The difference is not a small one, Protarchus. For some arithmeticians calculate with unequal units, for instance two armies and two oxen and two very small or incomparably large units. But the others refuse to agree with them, unless it is declared that none of the countless units differs in the least from any of the others. (*Phil.* 56D9–E3)[96]

The units of the naive, unlike those of genuine arithmeticians, suffer compresence with regard to their numerical properties. Dialectic, on the other hand, deals with 'being, the real and what is always the same' (*Phil.* 58A2–3). Although Plato does not explicitly call these items Forms here, it is reasonable to hold that this is what he has in mind and, in any case, they share with Forms the feature of being purely and determinately F.[97]

The purest and most accurate sort of knowledge thus grasps objects that are themselves pure and determinate. Nor is this link accidental: it is the fact that such objects are themselves pure and determinate that allows the knowledge that grasps them to be pure and determinate. The features that make such objects pure and determinate are those that make them knowable.[98] Knowledge itself is purest and most determinate when it grasps principles of order and structure, that is, when it grasps what makes its objects determinate.

The different kinds of knowledge differ not only with respect to accuracy, clarity, purity, and truth. The arts of measurement are the 'ruling' or 'leading' parts of the productive arts and what is left after they have been removed is 'worthless' (*Phil.* 55D10–11, 55E1–3). Indeed, those arts employing measurement more accurately are 'more fully arts' than the others (*Phil.* 56B4–6). These different kinds of knowledge can also be ranked along a dimension of value that is not their value to us.

> Secure and pure and true and what we may call unalloyed have to do with the things that are forever in the same state, without anything mixed in, or with that which is most akin to them. Everything else ought to be regarded as secondary and later . . . And of the names applied to such matters, would it not be just to give the finest names to the finest things? . . . Are not reason, then, and wisdom the names that we should honor most? . . . Then these names are applied most accurately and correctly to cases of thinking about true being . . . And these are the very names that I brought forward at the beginning for our verdict.   (*Phil.* 59C2–D8)[99]

Pure and true knowledge is the sort of knowledge that has the highest non-relational value. This should not be surprising, since the second important connection that purity has is with determinacy. Just as impure pleasure is indeterminate insofar as it is impure, impure knowledge is indeterminate insofar as it is impure.[100] And as we have already seen, determinacy is a value property: what makes anything good is that it consists in the appropriate combination of a determinant and the indeterminate.[101] So what makes knowledge non-relationally good is that it grasps the order and structure of its objects, that is, the features making the objects determinate and thus good.

This is not, however, unrelated to the question of what is best for us. There are two immediate indications of such a connection. First, as Plato notes at the end of the above quotation, his candidate for the sort of knowledge that makes a life happy was that which has just been ranked as finest. Second, shortly before this when Plato considered what knowledge is clearest, most accurate, and truest, he said that he was putting to one side the question of which kind of knowledge most benefited us (*Phil.* 58B9–C2). But he did note in passing that there is a faculty of our souls that 'loves the truth and does everything for its sake' (*Phil.* 58D4–5).[102]

At the end of the *Philebus*, Plato returns to the question of what is best for us and draws together the themes of the preceding discussion. This is the second line of argument leading to the conclusion that reason is more akin to the goodmakers. He first gives an explicit account of what makes 'any mixture whatsoever either of the highest value or of none at all' (*Phil.* 64D3–5). This is an account of what makes any mixture good or valuable; it is not simply an account of what makes the mixed life or other things that we can have good for us. It is thus a characterization of what makes things non-relationally good.[103] What makes anything non-relationally good is its possession of the three goodmaking properties: fineness (κάλλος), proportion (συμμετρία), and truth (ἀλήθεια, *Phil.* 65A2). This is a way of specifying the idea that it is the imposition of the appropriate determinant on the indeterminate that makes anything good and thus it gives us a second line of argument.

Plato then undertakes to compare wisdom and pleasure directly to the three goodmakers (*Phil.* 65B5–7). On the basis of the fact that knowledge is much more akin to the goodmakers than is pleasure, knowledge is judged to be a better thing for us. Thus Plato moves from the claim that something is non-relationally good to the claim that it is good for us. For now, it is enough to note that he does this, later we shall have to consider what justifies such a move.

So what, then, settles the question of whether wisdom or pleasure is more akin to the three goodmakers? With regard to each of the three goodmakers—truth, proportion, and fineness—reason is judged to be more akin to the goodmaker in virtue of instantiating it or instantiating it more fully (*Phil.* 65B10–66A3). Let us start with truth.

Socrates: Take truth [ἀληθείας] first, Protarchus. Take it, and after looking at all three, reason, truth, and pleasure, take plenty of time, and answer whether you think pleasure or reason is more akin [συγγενέστερον] to truth.
Protarchus: What need is there to take one's time? For the difference, I think, is great. For pleasure is the greatest of impostors. And the story goes that in the pleasures concerning sex, which seem to be the greatest pleasures, even perjury is pardoned by the gods, as if pleasures, like children, did not have the smallest share of reason. But reason is either the same thing [ταὐτὸν] as truth or, of all things, the most like it and the truest [πάντων ὁμοιότατόν τε καὶ ἀληθέστατον]. (*Phil.* 65B10–D3)

Truth, as a goodmaking property, is non-cognitive and non-propositional: a true F is an F that displays all the features found in the definition of F and does not display any of the features that are the opposite of F. As we have seen, the truest instance of white is the 'most unmixed, in which there is no trace of another color' (*Phil.* 53A6–B2), true pleasures are those unmixed with any pain, and the truest forms of knowledge are those that provide a full and accurate representation of their object, unmixed with ignorance or error.

How, then, is reason akin to truth as a goodmaking property? Reason can possess truth in a straightforwardly propositional way, that is, it is an instance of knowledge. It is 'akin to' and 'like' non-propositional truth in several related ways.

(1) A true F is an especially valuable cognitive item: since it instantiates F without defect or admixture of the opposite of F, it provides a good basis on which individual reason can form a clear and accurate understanding of F.[104]

(2) When reason expresses knowledge about what is F, what it grasps are the definitional features that make it the case that the F is F.

We must also remember that these principles of order and determinacy are goodmaking properties, that is, value properties. When reason fully possesses the truth about its subject matter, it is in its best state, that is, it instantiates the goodmaking properties.[105] But for reason fully to possess the truth about its subject matter is for it to grasp fully and completely the nature of its subject, that is, its order and structure. This is to grasp what makes it determinate, that is, to grasp its goodmaking features. So reason instantiates the goodmakers by knowing them. Similar remarks should apply to the other two goodmakers.[106]

We thus have an account of what makes reason akin to the goodmakers and thus of the grounds that Plato gives for its being good for us. But we still face an important concern. Accepting the link between what is non-relationally good and what is good for us, what the above argument seems to show is that theoretical wisdom or reason, that is, knowledge of the goodmaking properties, is the best good for human beings. This would entitle it to a prominent place in the good life as a main ingredient. But showing that reason is the most valuable ingredient of the good life does not yet show that reason is the cause of the good life. And this is what we need to show. This brings us back to the issue that Irwin rightly noted (although I argued that we should not accept his solution).

The cause of the good life, as we have seen, should play a role in bringing it into being. One might think that this would exclude theoretical intelligence from being the cause of the good life, because theoretical intelligence in itself is causally idle. This is a worry of which Socrates shows himself to be aware. When he considers what sort of knowledge must be present in the mixed life, he reminds Protarchus that they distinguished two kinds of knowledge: 'one kind deals with a subject matter that comes to be and perishes, the other is concerned with what neither comes to be nor perishes, but is always unchangingly the same' (*Phil.* 61D10–E3). The latter is the truest kind of knowledge, but Socrates asks whether this is enough for a human being.

Suppose, then, there is a person who possesses wisdom [φρονῶν] about what justice itself is, and can give an account in accordance with his knowledge [τῷ νοεῖν], and has the same kind of comprehension about all the rest of what there is . . . Will this person have sufficient knowledge, if he has an account of the divine circle and sphere themselves, but is ignorant of the human sphere and these, our circles, using even in housebuilding those other yardsticks and those circles? (*Phil.* 62A2–B2)

Strikingly, this is the first and only time that the *Philebus* states that justice is an object of the highest sort of knowledge. Immediately after Socrates claims that justice is an object of the best sort of knowledge, he reminds us of the need for human beings to act. His point cannot only be that human life will require the practice of certain sorts of arts, such as housebuilding. The lesson that we should draw is, rather, that the best sort of knowledge of justice must be appropriately related to action. (There is, as it stands, an odd gap in the argument of the *Philebus*. This passage might be thought to suggest that although the best life includes the highest sort of knowledge, the next best life is composed rather of the knowledge of housebuilding and similar arts without an explicit place for virtue. We can fill this gap by recognizing the need for the knowledge necessary for selecting the ingredients of the good life. Such selection should proceed in accordance with the ranking that Plato does give of the goodness of various kinds of knowledge.) Nor is the need to act simply an unfortunate aspect of our limited human condition that we would be better off without. As we have already seen, the love of truth need not be purely theoretical but can also be a desire to order. Plato has stressed that god's reason orders the world and this indicates what the best sort of reason will do by its own nature.

Reason thus has a place as a productive cause. When reason acts as a productive cause that includes the recognition of value, then it acts in virtue of what it is essential and it acts in its best state. Moreover, since its appreciation of goodness and order is what makes it good, its own goodness is productive of the goodness of the mixed life. But this is not yet enough to settle our original concern. What of the other constituents in the mixed life, that is, the various forms of knowledge and pleasure that are admitted? Do they have some value for the person, even if they are not selected by reason in its best condition or in something approximating its best condition? If they do, we might worry that we have not shown that their value to the person is dependent on reason.

That their value is dependent on reason in this way is what we should expect, if reason at the end of the dialogue plays as important a role in the good life as it did in the opening counterexample. There we saw that no other pleasure or possession was of benefit to a human being without reason. Specifically, no other pleasure or possession benefited a person unless he was aware of its goodness. But as we saw, the sort of awareness of goodness required by the counterexample was of a very weak sort. In the end, after Plato's conception of reason has been enriched by showing its relation to objectively goodmaking properties, is reason still of such central importance? Is it a condition of benefit?

The *Philebus* does not provide a full explanation of its answer to this question, but it points to the most important part of what is missing. Any account of what is good *for* a creature must be grounded in an account of that creature's essential nature. Our attention was drawn to this fact by the opening counterexample itself. Protarchus rejected the original unmixed life lacking reason because it would not be 'sufficient or choiceworthy for any human being or animal' (*Phil.* 22B1–2). But at that point in the dialogue, that is as far as he is willing to go. He concedes a place only for the sort of reason that is needed for something more than the life of a mollusk. He shows no sign of recognizing that reason might have very different roles to play in the lives of humans and of non-human animals that are nevertheless higher than mollusks. (Nor is he especially motivated to do so, given the version of hedonism he endorses.) As we have seen, the *Philebus* stresses that there is an intimate kinship between our reason and god's reason (although the difference between our reason and god's gives pleasure a place in our lives that it does not have in his). To see what grounds Plato's answer, we shall have to turn to his account of what human beings are and this will come in Chapter 4 when we consider the psychology of the *Timaeus*.

Nevertheless, the *Philebus* points to an answer to our question. Let us first consider some textual evidence.

(1) Protarchus is willing to admit the other kinds of knowledge into the mixed life only on the condition that the person has the 'first' or highest kind (*Phil.* 62D1–3). This first kind of knowledge includes knowledge of the good, and the other kinds of knowledge will not do harm, and will be beneficial, only if the person has such knowledge.

(2) With regard to the admission of pleasures, Socrates says on their behalf: 'It is neither possible nor beneficial for any kind to remain alone, in isolation and in its pure form. Of all kinds, comparing them with one another, we think the best to live with is the one that brought knowledge of everything else, but especially as perfect knowledge as possible of each of us' (*Phil.* 63B7–C3).

The text provides some difficulties here, but pleasures are admitted only on the condition that the person has knowledge of them. Specifically, the knowledge required is the best kind of knowledge which knows these pleasures and all other things. This knowledge is thus more than simple self-awareness and, if it is the best sort of knowledge, it will know the pleasures as they really are. The admitted pleasures are 'akin' to reason and are thus determinate. The knowledge will be the knowledge of what makes them the determinate things they are and thus knowledge of what makes them good. These are the pleasures that personified reason itself claims as desirable in light of its goal 'to discover in this mixture [the mixed life] what is good in man and in the universe and to get some vision of the nature of the good itself' (*Phil.* 64A1–3).

(3) Insofar as reason is causally productive of the mixed life, it orders its ingredients and imposes measure on them. Whatever lacks such

measure is a pseudo-mixture that lacks any value (*Phil.* 64D3–E3). If reason is the cause of the goodness of the good life, it should be a necessary condition of its goodness.[107]

Making an appreciation of goodness a necessary condition of the other sorts of knowledge benefiting us also helps to explain why the other kinds of knowledge should count as constituents of the good life at all. Although human beings may need shelter from the weather in order to lead a good life, this hardly shows that knowledge of housebuilding is a necessary component of the good life or is good except for its products. But Plato ranks such arts in respect of non-relational goodness in terms of the extent to which they employ measurement. This ranking is in terms of the extent to which they grasp the determinate features of mixtures, that is, the features that make the mixtures good. Plato, as we have seen, accepts an inference from the fact that something is non-relationally best to the claim that it is best for us. Thus if such kinds of knowledge are to be non-instrumentally good for us, their benefit to us should consist in the fact that they constitute a grasp of order (albeit not the truest or purest sort of grasp). If they are to be non-instrumentally good for human beings, it will not be because of the needs of the human body for shelter. It will rather be because they constitute one of the ways that human beings can, given their cognitive limitations, grasp the good. Similarly, pure pleasures will constitute a kind of grasp of the orderly features of their objects and even sensory pleasures, insofar as they are valuable, will be an appreciation, in a sensory mode, of order.

Reason thus has a twofold role in the good life. First, it is a constituent of every ingredient and insofar as it is a constituent it is there because it grasps the order and determinate nature of things and thus is a grasp of objective goodness. Music, for example, insofar as it is included, is the art (and exercise) of musical theory that grasps the proportions and ratios that regulate pitches, tones, and lengths and imposes a determinate structure upon an indeterminate sound. It is, by its very nature, an appreciation of goodness: musical theory does not simply catalog various possible combinations of determinants and the indeterminate, but picks out the ones that are fine and good by their nature (*Phil.* 26B1, 7). A person able to catalog, even in a mathematically precise way, various sounds, but who does not recognize the appropriate harmonies as fine and good, fails to possess the musical art as Plato understands it. Similarly, a person who produces a harmony by accident, perhaps by dropping a lyre with a lucky bounce, does not possess the musical art and is not benefited by such production.

A fuller account of how reason can enter into pleasures must await the psychology of Chapter 4, but even now we can see that the pleasures that Plato allows as good are, or intimately involve, a perception of order. True pleasures, which Plato counts as good, include, for example, pleasures of sight, and these are pleasures taken in things that are fine by themselves by their very nature and not things that are merely fine relative to something else (*Phil.* 51B–C). These things include sensible objects possessing the appropriate geometrical shapes, and such pleasures are an appreciation of good and fine order in a sensory mode. Plato may also allow certain impure but necessary pleasures to count as good and as constituents of the good life.[108] These, perhaps, include even pleasures associated with eating and drinking. But the value of these pleasures also depends on their being a perception of fine order. Insofar as what one enjoys in satisfying one's appetites is the intense release from prior tension, such pleasures are indeterminate and are not good or are bad for the person. So even the pleasures of health, when enjoyed in this way, do not benefit their possessor. The sort of pleasure taken in health that could count as good for the person would require not valuing the intensity of the release from tension, but enjoying and valuing the activity of maintaining one's physical constitution and the good order of the body. This is also, albeit in a less elevated form, a perception in a sensory mode of something as determinate and thus is a perception, in a sensory mode, of good order.[109]

But in addition to reason's role as an ingredient in kinds of knowledge and pleasure, it has a role in selecting and ordering the constituents. This includes a grasp of why they are worthy of choice and of how they are to be ordered so as to form a life that is itself determinate and well-ordered and is thus both non-relationally good and good for the person who lives it. It is both by grasping order insofar as it functions as a constituent of the ingredients of the good life, as well as by grasping the determinate order of the life as a whole, that reason brings itself into an orderly and good state (cf. *Tim.* 42E–44C and 89E–90D).

This theory of the *Philebus* thus does not rest simply on our intuitions, but is rather part of a complex account involving strong metaphysical claims, especially claims about the nature of the objective goodmaking properties of things, and about how reason is akin to or similar to these goodmakers. As we have noted, the *Philebus* does not answer all our questions. First, we have seen that reason bringing itself into a good state by grasping order is a constituent of every good for a human being. But if humans consist both of reason and some distinct faculties or capacities, why should this be true? To answer this question, the *Philebus'* account must be supplemented by an account of what human beings are. Second, we need some further explanation of how ethical activity involves the grasping of good order. Finally, we have not said how pure, clear, accurate, and true one's grasp of goodness must be in order for a person to benefit. Insofar as the *Philebus* counts as constituents of the good life things other than the highest exercise of reason, however, it shows that such a grasp can be less than complete. In Chapter 4, I say more about the first of these issues and in the next section, I discuss the last two. But the value theory that we have explored in the *Philebus* does, I think, show that Plato holds that a grasp of objective goodness is a necessary condition of benefiting from things and shows at least part of the justification for this claim.

2.12 *The Dependency Thesis*

My main concern in this section will be to consider how the Dependency Thesis is embodied in the ethical life of Magnesia. Doing so will raise questions about Plato's psychology and epistemology and in Chapters 3 and 4, I take up these issues. Let us begin by drawing together the strands of our discussion in order to give a fuller account of the Dependency Thesis.

Benefits and Harms   I have argued that knowledge of the good is a genuinely necessary condition of agents benefiting from the Dependent Goods they possess and use. This knowledge is required in order to appreciate the goodmaking features of the Dependent Goods and of their use and to appreciate how the various Dependent Goods fit together into a good life. Thus Dependent Goods can be good for the just agent in several ways. First, a Dependent Good can be used in virtuous action and such actions can be non-instrumentally good for the virtuous agent. For such use to be beneficial, the agent has to recognize the goodmaking features of the action and value them for their own sake. Some other Dependent Goods, such as certain pleasures (e.g. those associated with the perception of fine objects) or forms of knowledge, or the welfare of others benefit the agent apart from use of them. But once again, to benefit from these Dependent Goods, the agent has to value them for their genuine goodmaking features. For example, the pleasure associated with the awareness of fine objects should be valued because it is pleasure taken in genuinely fine objects. Further, some of the agent's virtuous actions, in addition to being non-instrumentally good insofar as they are virtuous actions, will be of benefit by improving or maintaining the agent's ethical character or producing Dependent Goods that can be used in further virtuous actions or that benefit the agent apart from their use.

We can also now give an account of the disvalue of the Dependent Bads. For the just person, Dependent Bads can be bad for more than one reason. First, the possession of Dependent Bads, such as sickness and poverty, may reduce the agent's opportunities to act virtuously. Serious ill health may also interfere with the agent's ethical character: e.g. chronic pain can disrupt one's thoughts and the unhealthy, Plato thinks, have more difficulty resisting bad sexual desires. But certain Dependent Bads, such as pain, can be bad for the just person even apart from the effects they have in diminishing virtuous activity. Given a choice between two virtuous lives that are equal in all other respects, a rational person has reason to avoid the one containing significant pain. (Pain is or involves the perception of a disordered and unmeasured state and is regarded as bad by the virtuous person for that reason.)

What we now need is an explanation of Plato's claim that Dependent Goods are bad for unjust people and that Dependent Bads are good or, rather, less bad for them than the corresponding Dependent Good would be. Dependent Goods can be bad for unjust people in several ways. There are two straightforward ways in which Dependent Goods can be bad for unjust people, both of which focus on the ways in which unjust people use their Dependent Goods. (It is important to see that another straight-forward account does not work. Unjust people's use of Dependent Goods will tend to be defective. They will, for example, use their wealth to pursue intense pleasures and such a course of behavior will tend to undermine their chances of gaining and keeping other Dependent Goods. Their pursuit of intense bodily pleasures will, for example, tend to undermine their health. But they are better off, or, more precisely, less badly off without Dependent Goods.)

(1)   Unjust people's use of Dependent Goods will tend to have bad effects on their ethical character. Since not all unjust states of character are equally bad, there is room for ethical degeneration even among the unjust. This ethical degeneration will usually be hastened by the possession of more Dependent Goods. The satisfaction of some akratic desires by an autocrat speedily leads to complete injustice and the immoderate satisfaction of desires for food, sex, and drink tends to encourage the growth of bad desires and thus to make the person even more unjust.

(2)   Injustice is sufficient for misery and thus the lives of unjust people are not worth living. So any Dependent Good that prolongs their lives, e.g. health, will only prolong their misery and so make them worse off overall.

Although these are important reasons why Dependent Goods are bad for unjust people, they do not provide a full explanation. For example, Plato asks us to consider a person who permanently possesses all goods except jus-tice and claims that even for such a person, all his Dependent Goods are 'the worst things' for him (*Laws* 661B6–7). Nothing suggests or requires that this unjust person's character continually grows worse. Moreover, it is implausible that each Dependent Good that the unjust person has extends his life. But even if it did, this does not entail that no Dependent Good benefits him for some length of time or in some respect.

We can begin by noting that, to a first approximation, Plato holds that any action springing from an unjust character is an unjust action (cf. *Laws* 862A7–B4). In particular, even when an unjust person does what a just per-son would do in the same circumstances, his action is still unjust. Since all unjust actions are non-instrumentally bad, any use of a Dependent Good by an unjust person is bad for him. This argument is a useful beginning, since it gives us reason to hold that any use of a Dependent Good by an unjust person is bad for him. But we need to go further to say why this is the case. Such an explanation will help explain why Dependent Goods do not benefit, even if use of them is not required, and why they do not benefit even partially or temporarily.

Plato should appeal to the special role of wisdom in explaining this harm or lack of benefit. Unjust people suffer serious harm in their dealings with Dependent Goods because they have the wrong attitude toward genuine value. They will both fail to appreciate (and may disvalue) what is good about the Dependent Good and what they value about it is something bad or at least not good. For example, a fine painting will be valued for the sexual pleasure it gives rise to, and the pleasures of health will be valued as the intense release of the tensions of deprivation.[110] They will fail to appreciate or find tedious the abstract symmetry of the fine object (and will thus find unappealing some of the best instances of fine objects, the crafted geometrical shapes of the *Philebus* that are non-relatively fine or the intelligent, orderly motions of the heavens) or the healthful activity of self-maintenance. Unjust people will value their argumentative skills, if they possess some, because, for example, these skills allow them to bend others to their own will or because they allow them to humiliate others in debate. They will not value them because they provide insight into the fine, orderly structure of knowable objects (nor will they see these skills themselves as instances of such order).[111] Their lack of wisdom thus cuts them off from the genuine value inherent in things and leaves them with the double misfortune of disvaluing the good and valuing the bad or the worthless.[112] Such valuing will have two aspects: judging good and desiring or loving. Plato can reasonably hold that unjust people suffer something bad both with respect to what they judge good and what they love.[113]

Filling out this story completely would require a full examination of the various Dependent Goods and the varieties of psychopathology found among the unjust. We might wonder, for example, whether Plato holds that an unjust person always fails to appreciate the goodmaking features of every Dependent Good. Plato does think that judgments of goodness—whether correct or incorrect—tend to hang together more tightly than most contemporary philosophers would think they do. Since Plato thinks that there is a single goodmaking property, recognizing value is recognizing the same property in its different instantiations. Getting it right in some cases will tend to increase one's chances of getting it right in others to a much greater extent than it would on more pluralistic theories of goodness. Nevertheless, the same property is not equally evident in all cases and one cannot mechanically apply the account of goodness to different kinds of things. (Even in relatively nearby cases, such as fine or good shapes and sounds, recognizing the goodmaking features in one case still leaves a great deal of work to be done in the other.[114]) Thus anything less than perfect knowledge will fail to get some cases right. Further, one can approximate more closely or more distantly the correct account in any particular kind of case. Even the account of the good that Plato offers in the *Philebus* is not fully adequate and requires much further specification. With regard to incorrect views about goodness, Plato tends to think that there is a fairly limited range of unjust characters and that within each type, the person's ultimate ends are fairly uniform, e.g. maximizing honor or satisfying intense pleasures. So each type of unjust character will tend to make the same sort of mistake in all cases. And even if we were to hold that an unjust person could adequately recognize the goodmaking features of a Dependent Good in some particular case, this would be consistent with the account of the Dependency Thesis we have developed. If there is benefit in this case, what explains this benefit is an appreciation of the good.

Finally, we may turn to the effect of Dependent Bads on the unjust. At *Laws* 661D1, Plato claims that Dependent Bads are actually 'good' for unjust people. But it seems clear that we should not take this assertion literally. What Plato means is that for an unjust person having a Dependent Bad is less bad than not having that Dependent Bad (and, in particular, is less bad than having the corresponding Dependent Good: e.g. for an unjust person health is worse than sickness). Nevertheless, having a Dependent Bad is not genuinely good for anyone, even for an unjust person. To see why this is so, consider the ways in which it is 'preferable' (a description neutral between 'less bad' and 'good') for an unjust person to have the Dependent Bads. First, since an unjust person's life is not worth living, a Dependent Bad that kills him shortens a life of negative value. A fatal disease that kills him in five days reduces the total amount of misery in his life, but it does nothing more than that. This does not constitute a positive benefit for the agent, but only the avoidance of further harm. It does not make any segment of an unjust person's life (or any aspect of his life) better than or equal to non-existence.[115] Second, Dependent Bads can forestall ethical degeneration. Consider two character states both of which are bad, but one of which is worse than the other: for example, that of a tyrannical man who is not an actual tyrant and the state of soul he would be in if he were an actual tyrant. The power and wealth of a tyrant would allow him to indulge his bad desires, which will then grow and make his character even worse. Lack of power and poverty forestall this, but if he deals with them unjustly, they simply help constitute a way of life that is not worth living. Third, the Dependent Bads hinder people from performing unjust actions (which are non-instrumentally bad for them). Nevertheless, since these Dependent Bads only help minimize the number of unjust actions and prevent the further deterioration of an already unjust character, they do not constitute a positive benefit, but only prevent further harm.[116] Finally, there are cases in which a Dependent Bad leads to ethical reform, especially those in which it serves as an effective punishment. Although these do not seem to be the main cases that Plato has in mind in the *Laws'* passages, they are possible. But even when the punishments succeed, if the person moves from one more unjust state to another unjust state that is less unjust, the improved portion of the person's life still is not worth living. If the move is from injustice to justice, then we could say that the Dependent Bad is instrumentally good for the person and being just is non-instrumentally good for him. The pain, though, considered in itself, seems to have no positive value for the person.[117]

Although the *Laws* gives wisdom a special place as the leader of the other goods, it makes the value of the Dependent Goods depend on the agent's possession of the whole of virtue which includes, but is not limited to, knowledge of the good. In what way, then, are the Dependent Goods dependent on the other non-wisdom virtues, in particular, on courage and moderation?

Courage and moderation (which I discuss in more detail in Chapter 3) are the two virtues that prevent akratic action and conflict. They play two roles in doing so. First, they have a direct role in preventing the agent from acting akratically: roughly, courage is a disposition that allows a person to resist desires and emotions that prompt to akratic action and moderation is a harmony between one's desires and emotions and one's knowledge of the good. Second, they also have an indirect role, since Plato thinks that desires and emotions can, not only lead people to act against their overall judgments of what is best, but also can bring it about that agents irrationally form an overall best judgment or irrationally change a true overall judgment they already possess. Thus the value of Dependent Goods depends on courage and moderation in at least three ways. These virtues enable agents to use Dependent Goods in virtuous action, by (1) enabling them to form and retain rational overall judgments, and (2) to act on their rational overall judgments once formed. And (3), by enabling the agent to form and retain rational judgments about the good, these virtues enable the agent to benefit from Dependent Goods apart from their use.

Finally, we may wonder whether wisdom itself is an Independent Good or whether it requires courage and moderation in order to have value. Some passages, for example, might seem to suggest that wisdom itself does not benefit a person without moderation (e.g. *Laws* 709E7–710A2). Without courage and moderation, (a) wisdom will sometimes not find expression in action, and (b) may itself be undermined. But we might still see this as a case of wisdom retaining (at least part of) its value, while the person loses other goods. Plato, however, may not have been especially concerned to insist that wisdom retains at least some of its value even in these cases, since in the absence of courage and moderation, wisdom itself is quickly undermined.

Dependency in the Republic   Before considering in more detail how the Dependency Thesis is embodied in Magnesia's ethical life, we can gain a valuable contrasting perspective by looking back at the *Republic*. It is surprisingly difficult to determine the *Republic*'s position on the Dependency Thesis. As a first sign of this difficulty, consider the *Republic*'s first and best-known classification of goods. As we saw in Section 2.7, the famous classification of goods at the beginning of Book 2 that sets the terms for Plato's task in the rest of the *Republic* is the distinction between things good as ends and things good as means. As we also saw, this is a different distinction than that between Dependent and Independent Goods. But further, it is tempting to see the *Republic* 2 passage as giving a verdict about certain goods that is incompatible with the Dependency Thesis. There Plato counts sight, health, hearing, and harmless pleasures as things that are good for their own sake or good as ends (*Rep.* 357B–C, 367D1). Since there is no hint of any qualification to the claim that these are good for their own sake, we might understand this as asserting that although sight and health may have bad consequences for some people (i.e. those lacking virtue), they are, at least to some extent, good for anyone who possesses them.[118] But according to the *Laws*, sight, health, and hearing are Dependent Goods and thus only good for virtuous people (*Laws* 661B–C).

But perhaps we need see no conflict here. The *Republic* passage comes early in the text and the specific examples may not matter much: perhaps all that Plato is trying to do here is to make the means/end distinction clear with the help of a few intuitively plausible examples and is not concerned with the ultimate analysis of particular cases. Moreover, Plato does not explicitly say that hearing and so on benefit people regardless of their character, and adopting the means/end distinction does not exclude also holding the Dependency Thesis. Plato can go on to claim that keen hearing is a non-instrumental Dependent Good for virtuous people and that it is neither instrumentally nor non-instrumentally good for the unvirtuous. Indeed, asserting the Dependency Thesis at this point in the *Republic* would either be question-begging or a case of laying down a promissory note that could only be redeemed much later.

Nevertheless, there are obstacles to such a compatibilist interpretation. First, on this line, we might expect Plato at some point in the *Republic* to state the Dependency Thesis explicitly. We should especially expect this, since the Dependency Thesis would be an enormous help in proving the *Republic*'s central ethical claim, that is, that a just person is always better off than an unjust person, no matter how other goods are distributed between them. The Dependency Thesis would allow Plato to show that no Dependent Good is of any benefit to an unjust person. But, as we shall see shortly, there is no unequivocal textual evidence in the *Republic* for the Dependency Thesis. Second, the Dependency Thesis sits uneasily with the rest of the *Republic* and Plato at least flirts with a different sort of theory.

Let us first consider some of the textual evidence. I shall consider three passages that might be thought to assert the Dependency Thesis. The first is Plato's description in Book 4 of the just person.

One who is just does not allow any part of himself to do the work of another part or allow the various classes within him to meddle with each other . . . he harmonizes the three parts of himself like three limiting notes in a musical scale—high, low, and middle. He binds together those parts and any others there may be in between, and from having been many things he becomes entirely one, moderate and harmonious. Only then does he act.   (*Rep.* 443D1–E2)

The most that this passage claims is that before pursuing anything the *Laws* would count as a Dependent Good, one should establish a just condition of soul and then give priority to maintaining this condition of soul over the attainment of any Dependent Good. Since the just person is right to do this, we may conclude that the course of action that establishes and maintains one's own justice is always better for the person than any other course of action, no matter how other goods are distributed among the available courses of action. But this only requires that the good of justice should always outweigh the benefit of any amount of other goods; it does not require that other goods are only good for the just person.

The second passage comes from Plato's first statement, at the end of Book 4, of the answer to the question of whether justice is more profitable than injustice. This passage goes on to claim that the just person is always better off to give priority to a just condition of soul.

This inquiry looks ridiculous to me now that justice and injustice have been shown to be as we described. Even if one has every kind of food and drink, lots of money, and every sort of power to rule, life is thought to be not worth living when the body's nature is ruined. So even if someone can do whatever he wishes, except what will free him from vice and injustice and make him acquire justice and virtue, how can his life be worth living when his soul—the very thing by which he lives—is ruined and in turmoil?   (*Rep.* 445A5–B3)

In this passage, Plato goes further and claims that an unjust condition of soul is sufficient to make one's life miserable, no matter what other goods one has. But Plato does not claim that no other good can be of any benefit to the unjust person. In the terms of the metaphor of bodily health, Plato claims that a person with a ruined physical constitution is miserable, no matter what kind of food and drink he has. He does not claim that a person with a ruined constitution is not better off if he has some food and drink. (He might, so to speak, be better off dead, but while living with his disease, it may be better for him to have food and drink than to suffer hunger and thirst.) Perhaps Plato means to suggest the stronger point that if one's health is totally ruined, then no external good is of any benefit at all. If I am unable to move and wracked with great pain, perhaps no external good would be of any use to me. Is Plato claiming that injustice is the psychic equivalent of such a complete physical collapse? He does not say this and he does not think that every form of injustice involves a complete collapse of one's ability to set and fulfill goals. If we accept the intuitive appeal of the idea that justice is a form of psychic health, we shall expect that injustice will tend to interfere seriously with the proper use of one's other goods, but this is a much weaker claim than the Dependency Thesis.

The first two passages refrain from asserting the Dependency Thesis, but the third suggests that Plato is not willing to rely on it. In Book 2, Socrates claims that justice is both good for its own sake and for its consequences. But his interlocutors demand that Socrates leave entirely aside any appeal to the good consequences of justice; he is to show that the life of the just person is always better than that of the unjust without taking into consideration the 'rewards and reputation' that come from justice. Plato accepts the challenge and is satisfied that he has met it by the close of the dialogue (*Rep.* 612B). But near the very end of the *Republic*, Plato lets the 'rewards and reputation' coming from justice, back into consideration. He makes two points. First, the gods have arranged things so that the bad things the just person suffers turn out to be better for him in the long run.

[E]verything that comes to someone who is loved by the gods, insofar as it comes from the gods themselves, is the best possible, unless it is the inevitable punishment for some mistake he made in a former life . . . the same is true of a just person who falls into poverty or disease or some other apparent evil, namely, that this will end well for him, either during his lifetime or after he has died, for the gods never neglect anyone who eagerly wishes to become just . . . and must we not suppose that the opposite is true of an unjust person?　(*Rep.* 612E8–613B4)

Plato's point is not that poverty or disease is not in any way bad for the just person, but that the present harm is outweighed by future benefits.[119] The 'opposite' that we would expect to happen to unjust people is that the present gains they make in goods such as health are outweighed by future harms. The idea that goods such as health are of short-run benefit to the unjust but are outweighed by future evils, is strongly suggested by Plato's second point here. This is that, even leaving the gods aside and looking only at consequences coming from human beings, just people 'for the most part' by the end of their lives have a favorable balance of good consequences and the unjust an unfavorable balance. Just people usually have a good reputation, rule if they wish, and marry and give children in marriage to whom they wish (*Rep.* 613D). Clever but unjust people are like 'runners who run well for the first part of the course, but not for the second. They leap away sharply at first, but they become ridiculous by the end and go off uncrowned with their ears drooping on their shoulders' (*Rep.* 613B10–C2).

> As for the unjust people, the majority of them, even if they escape detection when they are young, are caught by the end of the race and are ridiculed. And by the time they get old, they have become wretched, for they are insulted by foreigners and citizens, beaten with whips, and made to suffer . . . punishments, such as racking and burning . . .   (*Rep.* 613D5–E2)

These empirical generalizations about unjust people are dubious, but they would be entirely inept if Plato held the Dependency Thesis. If the benefit of the sorts of goods that unjust people could acquire were dependent on their possessor being virtuous, there would be no need for the hazardous claim that unjust people usually lose these goods and acquire evils when they get older. If Plato held the Dependency Thesis what he should do when he reintroduces external goods is point out that their benefit is dependent on their possessor being virtuous. (Moreover, the Dependent Bads that the unjust are usually supposed to suffer when older would, in fact, be better or less bad for them than the Dependent Goods they had when younger.) Plato does not do this and simply pursues a line of argument that is only needed if he is no longer willing to rely on the Dependency Thesis and which rests on what he himself must have thought was at least a highly controversial premiss.

Although these passages are not decisive, we can also see why Plato might be uncomfortable with the Dependency Thesis in the *Republic* and discern the inchoate outlines of an alternative approach.[120] I have argued in Chapter 1 that if virtue is required in order to benefit from the possession of Dependent Goods, then neither auxiliaries nor producers can benefit from their possession of Dependent Goods in the *Republic*. This is not simply because they lack the sort of knowledge required for virtue in *Republic* Book 4. As we saw, both classes have false beliefs about the good and the goodness of virtue that would disqualify them from benefiting, even if all that were required to benefit from Dependent Goods were true beliefs about what justice is and what sort of good it is. Although, as we saw in Chapter 1, Plato is quite pessimistic about non-philosophers in the *Republic*, there are some signs that he may have allowed them to benefit from the possession of some Dependent Goods. Instead of explicitly making virtue a necessary condition of benefit, Plato ordinally ranks with regard to virtue and happiness the different kinds of lives he distinguishes, by reference to which part of the soul rules in the person—the philosophic or just life, the timocratic, the oligarchic, the democratic, and the tyrannical lives. This ordinal ranking is not in itself inconsistent with the sharp cut-off postulated by the Dependency Thesis, since an ordinal ranking does not commit Plato to the claim that each class of person is happy to some degree: the tyrant, for example, is clearly miserable. Plato might think that since all classes other than philosophers lack virtue, they all fail to benefit from their Dependent Goods, although the timocrats are the least badly off.

But there are further reasons that suggest a modification of the Dependency Thesis beyond the mere fact that Plato supplies an ordinal ranking of kinds of lives. The ordinal ranking comes during Plato's discussion of the different kinds of lives led by people who are ruled by different parts of the soul. This division of the soul may give Plato reason to recognize exceptions to the Dependency Thesis. The next chapter discusses the *Republic*'s psychological theory in greater detail, but as we have already seen in Chapter 1, the *Republic* divides the soul into three parts—the Reasoning part, the Spirited part, and the Appetitive part. Each of the three parts seems to have its own good and the person's good seems to be the common good formed by the composite of the goods of the three parts. Plato does not provide much detail about the exact nature of the good of each of these parts or about how they combine to form the good of the whole soul (the composite is not necessarily a simple aggregate).[121] Nevertheless, we can see how an alternative theory to the Dependency Thesis could be developed on this basis. Presumably the good of the Spirited part consists, roughly, in the long-run satisfaction of its desires for honor and predominance, and the good of the Appetitive part consists in the long run satisfaction of its desires for bodily goods. Plato need not think that it is *pro tanto* beneficial, e.g., to the Appetitive part to satisfy each of its desires; perhaps there are certain insatiable, bestial, or unnecessary desires whose satisfaction is in no way good for the Appetitive part. But it seems plausible that the good of the Appetitive part consists in the long-run satisfaction of at least some subset of bodily appetites. On the basis of this account, Plato can explain in the *Republic* how things other than the welfare of the Reasoning part affect the person's happiness. In addition to achieving what the Reasoning part thinks of as good for itself, the person can attain the goods of the lower parts of the soul and thus be benefited by goods other than virtue and knowledge, such as honor and the satisfaction of certain bodily appetites.

If we take seriously the idea that each part of the soul has its own good consisting in the satisfaction of its own characteristic desires and that the good of the person is a composite of these, then there may be reason to allow that some goods can be attained for the lower parts of the soul (and thus for the person), even if the person lacks virtue. We thus have reason to recognize exceptions to the Dependency Thesis and such exceptions could occur in more than one sort of case. Consider, for example, a case in which the overall good of the soul requires some significant sacrifice of bodily goods. Here the bodily goods sacrificed are the objects of exactly the sort of moderate and wholesome appetites whose satisfaction the Reasoning part would endorse, if they did not in this case conflict with the more important goods of the other parts of the soul. But the Appetitive part cannot take into account the welfare of the other parts of the soul. From its point of view, it is simply missing out on the sorts of items that it values. It thus seems plausible to hold that, at least in some cases, the Appetitive part of the soul would be better off if the person pursued the bodily goods and did not act in accordance with a true judgment of what is best overall. Even if the person would be better off rejecting the bodily goods in order to gain honor or some good of the Reasoning part, why would the Appetitive part never be better off if its desires had been satisfied? (Even if the Appetitive part is not on the whole better off, there may be a conflict with the Dependency Thesis if it benefits to some extent or in some degree.) Exceptions to the Dependency Thesis seem even more likely where there is no conflict between the goods of the different parts, but the person pursues, e.g., moderate bodily pleasures, while lacking virtue. Even if people lack a genuine appreciation of what is good and are unaware of what benefits the soul as a whole, it seems possible for them to identify and pursue, with some degree of adequacy, long-run healthful bodily satisfactions. In a virtuous person, the Reasoning part will endorse (some) of these satisfactions as benefiting the Appetitive part and the whole person. But why should the same satisfaction not benefit the Appetitive part and the whole person, if the Reasoning part fails to have a proper conception of the end and endorses the Appetitive part's desires without reflection?[122] In sum, once Plato allows that the parts of the soul have the characteristic desires that they do, it seems that the most he can plausibly hope for is that, in the long run, the goods of each part tend to coincide. There seems to be no clear rationale for ruling out the possibility that the lower parts can benefit from Dependent Goods, even in a person who lacks virtue.

The possibility of benefiting from Dependent Goods without virtue also seems to be accepted by Plato in his two arguments in Book 9 about the pleasantness of the just life. Although Plato argues that the philosopher has by far the most pleasant life, he allows that both timocrats and oligarchs, although they lack virtue, have some pleasures: the timocrat enjoys the pleasures of the Spirited part and the oligarch enjoys those of the Appetitive part. Since Plato presents considerations about pleasure as part of his answer to the question about the happiness of different kinds of lives, it seems reasonable to hold that such pleasures benefit those who have them, even if they are not virtuous.

This alternative theory fits well with the passages in the *Republic* that seem only to claim that the badness of unjust action outweighs any possible benefit. Plato can hold that the good of justice always outweighs any good of the lower parts without holding that the goods of the lower parts benefit the lower parts (and thus the person) only when the whole soul is just. Although the Reasoning part may usually be much better than the lower parts of the soul even at determining what is in the long-run interest of the lower parts themselves, it is hard to see why attaining something good for the lower parts of the soul requires that the Reasoning part possess the sort of knowledge of the good needed for virtue.

I have argued that the *Republic* does not explicitly endorse the Dependency Thesis and that some of Plato's remarks show how an alternative theory may be developed. The *Republic* at times also seems to suggest that the satisfaction of the lower parts of the soul is relatively trivial.[123] But we must distinguish two different ways in which their satisfaction may seem trivial. First, it may be the case that the Reasoning part never finds much good in the sorts of things that the lower parts go for: the lower parts characteristically have (nearly) worthless objects. Although Plato does not think that honor and the satisfaction of the bodily appetites are the most important things in life, he need not deny that some of these are genuine goods and that reason can endorse their pursuit as genuinely worthwhile. The more troubling point about the satisfaction of the lower parts concerns the limitations of their point of view. The Spirited part pursues its objects because it desires honor or predominance, not because these honors are genuinely good or fine. Similarly, the Appetitive part pursues its own satisfactions for its own reasons. For the Spirited part, for example, to achieve its own good is for it to satisfy the moderated desires it has for honor. In achieving its own good, however, it does not come to adopt the outlook of the Reasoning part. But the importance to the Reasoning part of the Spirited part's being satisfied is not clear. The Reasoning part might think it is good to pursue certain honors because such honors are good (they are a deserved response to real merit), but this is not the same as finding it good that the Spirited part of the soul is satisfied. (Similarly, certain bodily or sensory pleasures may have something fine about them, but the Appetitive part is not sensitive to the fineness of its replenishments.) The Spirited part is satisfied, not because it shares the Reasoning part's view about why such honors are worth pursuing, but because its own partial, and thus faulty, conception of what is worthwhile has been achieved. If the Spirited part is unsatisfied, it may interfere with the other parts and the Reasoning part may have reason to avoid the frustration of the lower two parts. But this does not make it reasonable for the Reasoning part to attribute much intrinsic importance to the satisfaction of the lower parts. Seeing to their satisfaction will be important primarily in order to prevent disruption of the soul's harmony. Attaining certain honors or certain bodily or sensory pleasures may be good from the Reasoning part's view and by its own standards, but this requires more than that the desires of lower parts are satisfied or that they enjoy their characteristic pleasures.

We have thus seen one way to avoid the Dependency Thesis in the *Republic* which requires taking seriously the idea that the parts of the soul have their own evaluative outlook and their own good. If Plato does not, in fact, hold the Dependency Thesis in the *Republic*, he may have a somewhat less pessimistic, although still low, evaluation of the lives of non-philosophers than he did in the *Phaedo*. But this view requires a troubling lack of integration between the Reasoning part's standards of valuation and the person's own spirited and appetitive desires. In Chapter 3, we shall see that Plato has a more unified conception of the soul in the *Laws*.

The Wisdom of Non-Philosophers   We can set our following discussion of whether non-philosophers can possess the virtue of wisdom in a broader context by considering an alternative to the account I have developed. As we have seen, the central problem for non-philosophers in the *Republic* is that their ends are set by the lower parts of the soul and the lower parts of the soul fail to grasp the features that make things genuinely valuable. So one way in which the ethical standing of non-philosophers might be improved is if Plato revised upward the capacities of the lower parts of the soul. On such an account, even if the education of non-philosophers does not give them a rational appreciation of the good, more sophisticated desires and emotions of the lower parts might allow for a significant improvement in their ethical character. I shall argue in Chapter 3 that the *Laws* gives up the *Republic's* partitioning of the soul. But even now, it is clear that Plato in the later period is not sympathetic to the view that a good ethical character can be constituted simply by improving the emotions and desires that the *Republic* associates with the lower parts of the soul. We can see this by turning to the *Statesman* and the *Timaeus*.

In the *Statesman*, as we have seen, Plato holds that there are two broad classes of people: the courageous and the moderate. Although it is a mistake to read the *Republic*'s theory of parts of the soul into the *Statesman*, the character of each class of people is formed, more or less, around a natural tendency to pursue ends that the *Republic* would associate with the lower parts of the soul. The courageous are self-assertive and pursue predominance and honor; the moderate pursue a comfortable and peaceful life. Should we infer that Plato now thinks that these natural tendencies, although not the highest or best form of virtue, are sufficient for a significant sort of excellence of character? Despite the fact that Plato calls these natural tendencies 'virtues', it is clear that the answer to this question is 'No'. These character states are not near misses at genuine virtue, but are serious defects. People who have only these natural tendencies without further education are excluded from citizenship in a good city ruled by the science of statesmanship because they fail to achieve genuine virtue. The persistence of these two natural conditions, without further education, results in the destruction of cities (*Stsmn.* 307D). What these people require is an education that imparts to them 'genuinely true and firmly settled opinion about what is fine, just, and good' (*Stsmn.* 309C5–7). These true opinions are a 'divine bond' that is akin to the 'immortal part' of the soul and this bond binds or works upon the rational part alone and not upon the mortal part. Thus these true opinions should be supported by reasons and not just trained emotions and desires. The *Statesman* is insistent that the sort of virtue necessary for citizenship in a good city requires an education that inculcates a rational grasp of what is fine. It is essential that the citizens be brought to see and accept good reasons for their views about the actions and character states that they recognize as fine, just, and good. Reliance on anything less is a sufficient ground for exclusion from citizenship in a good city.

Toward the end of the *Timaeus*, Plato again considers the role of reason, as opposed to the emotions and desires associated with the lower parts of the soul, in leading a good life.

Let these remarks suffice, then, on the subject of . . . how a man should both lead and be led by himself in order to have the best prospects for leading a rational life [κατὰ λόγον]. Indeed, we must give an even higher priority to doing our utmost to make sure that the part that is to do the leading is fitted for that task in the finest and best possible way . . . There are . . . three distinct types of soul that reside within us, each with its own motions . . . We ought to think of the most sovereign part of our soul as god's gift to us, given to be our guiding spirit. This, of course, is the type of soul that . . . resides in the top part of our bodies. It raises us up away from the earth and toward what is akin to us in heaven . . . For it is from heaven, the place from which our souls were originally born, that the divine part suspends our head . . . So if a man has become absorbed in his appetites [ἐπιθυμίας] or his ambitions [φιλονικίας] and takes great pains to further them, all his thoughts are bound to become merely mortal . . . But if a man has seriously devoted himself to the love of learning and to true wisdom [τὰς ἀληθεῖς φρονήσεις], if he has exercised these aspects of himself above all, then there is absolutely no way that his thoughts can fail to be immortal and divine, should truth come within his grasp . . . [C]onstantly caring for his divine part as he does, keeping well-ordered the guiding spirit that lives within him, he must indeed be supremely happy. Now there is but one way to care for anything, and that is to provide for it the nourishment and the motions that are proper to it. And the motions that have an affinity to the divine part within us are the thoughts and revolutions of the universe. These, surely, are the ones which each of us should follow. We should redirect the revolutions in our heads that were thrown off course at our birth, by coming to learn the harmonies and revolutions of the universe, and so bring into conformity with its objects our faculty of understanding [τῷ κατανοουμένῳ τὸ κατανοοῦν], as it was in its original condition. And when this conformity is complete, we shall have achieved our goal: the best life offered to humankind by the gods, both now and for evermore. (*Tim.* 89D2–90D7)

Plato goes on to describe the different sorts of reincarnation that the different kinds of soul undergo.

Land animals in the wild, moreover, came from men who had no tincture of philosophy and who made no study of the universe whatsoever, because they no longer made use of the revolutions in their heads but followed instead the lead of the parts of the soul that reside in the chest [i.e. *thumos*]. (*Tim.* 91E2–6)

We do not need to decide whether to take such talk of reincarnation literally. But in the *Timaeus* as well, Plato insists that a decent human life requires an advanced form of rational education and that genuine excellence in character cannot be achieved simply through the training of spirited emotions and appetitive desires. Specifically, it is by studying orderly objects by means of mathematics that our thoughts become orderly and in the condition requisite for leading a good life. The *Timaeus* attributes special prominence to the study of astronomy in attaining our own proper condition. And, as we have seen, all the citizens of Magnesia are expected to develop a fairly sophisticated, mathematically based grasp of the movements of the stars.

The late dialogues thus seem to agree that the training of spirited emotions and appetitive desires is not enough to produce a good state of character and a good life. Given the sort of creatures that we are, the perfection of our non-rational faculties by themselves is not sufficient for a good life. This is precisely what we should expect on the basis of the Dependency Thesis and the two passages at *Laws* 631B–D and 660E–661E that make the possession of wisdom a necessary condition of benefiting from one's Dependent Goods.

Let us now turn to the question of how far reason will be developed in non-philosophers in Magnesia. The minimal formal requirement in Plato's statement of the Dependency Thesis is that non-philosophers possess the virtue of wisdom (*phronēsis* or *nous*) which is the leader of the other virtues and of the Dependent Goods (*Laws* 631C6, D5, 660E3). In Book 3, which follows the two earlier statements of the Dependency Thesis, Plato returns to the importance of wisdom. '[O]ne should not pray or be eager to have everything follow one's own wish, but rather to have one's wish follow one's wisdom [φρονήσει]. This is what a city and each one of us should pray and strive for—to possess reason [νοῦν]' (*Laws* 687E5–9). So having wisdom or reason is a goal that is to be pursued by 'each one of us', that is, by all the citizens. Nevertheless, we might worry that Plato in the *Laws* sometimes distinguishes wisdom from true opinion and suggests that only those who have gone through very advanced studies will have wisdom. '[T]he one who frames the laws will set up guards—some grounded in wisdom [φρονήσεως], some in true opinion [ἀληθοῦς δόξης]—so that reason [ὁ νοῦς] will knit together all these things and may declare that they follow moderation and justice rather than wealth or love of honor [φιλοτιμίᾳ]' (*Laws* 632C4–D1). But even here, Plato emphasizes that the laws are to aim at inculcating justice in the citizens and has just said that justice includes wisdom (*Laws* 631C7–8).

A second passage helps to resolve the apparent inconsistency. In Book 3, the Athenian reminds his interlocutors of their opening discussion about the proper goal of the laws.

[Y]ou two maintained that the good lawgiver should lay down all his enactments for the sake of war; I, on the other hand, maintained that this would constitute an exhortation to set up laws for only one virtue out of four, whereas what should be done was to look to the whole of virtue, and especially at the first part, the leader of all virtue, which would be wisdom, and intelligence and belief [φρόνησις δ᾽ εἴη τοῦτο καὶ νοῦς καὶ δόξα], with *eros* and desire following upon these.   (*Laws* 688A4–B4)

What this passage suggests is that the cognitive condition that is to play the role of the leader of the other virtues and that is a condition of the Dependent Goods being valuable for their possessor includes both some kinds of true opinion, as well as more epistemically advanced states.[124] Nevertheless, insofar as 'wisdom' is the name of a virtue, it is partly honorific and applies in a strict sense only to the highest sort of cognition.[125] But since some sorts of true opinion are sufficient to make the Dependent Goods valuable for their possessor, Plato is quite willing to call such a state 'wisdom' and to hold that the goal of Magnesia's laws is to bring about at least such a state in all the citizens.[126]

Directly after the passage quoted above (*Laws* 687E5–9), in which Plato claims that wisdom is the goal for all citizens, he goes on to elaborate what he has in mind by means of a contrast with the vice of ignorance (ἀμαθία) or foolishness (ἄνοια): '[D]issonance between pleasure and pain and the belief that is according to reason [τὴν κατὰ λόγον δόξαν] I assert to be the ultimate and greatest ignorance [ἀμαθίαν]' (*Laws* 689A7–9). This belief 'according to reason' is the person's belief about what is fine or good (*Laws* 689A5–6).

[N]othing that pertains to ruling is to be given to citizens who are ignorant in the above respects; and they are to be blamed for their ignorance, even if they are shrewd at calculating . . . It is just the opposite sort who are to be proclaimed wise [σοφούς]—even if, as in the proverb, they 'know neither how to read or swim'— and the ruling offices are to be handed over to them on the ground that they are the wise ones [ἔμφροσιν]. For without consonance, my friends, how can wisdom [φρονήσεως]—even in its smallest form—come about? It is not possible. But the finest and greatest of consonances would most justly be called the greatest wisdom [σοφία], and whoever partakes of this evidently lives according to reason [κατὰ λόγον]. (*Laws* 689C7–D8, cf. 696C–D and 710A–B)

If all that Plato requires for wisdom is consonance between one's judgments of what is overall fine and good and one's desires, then he seems to count as wisdom cases in which these judgments are entirely unreflective and do not involve any appreciation of their rational basis.[127]

But as we have seen, we have good reason not to attribute such a view to Plato. Most citizens will not undergo the advanced studies received by members of the Nocturnal Council and they will not possess the sort of knowledge or understanding (*epistēmē*) that Plato contrasts with true belief. Thus they will not, for example, be able to give the sort of account of how virtue is both 'many' and 'one' that is expected of the members of the Nocturnal Council, nor does Plato say that they will have explicit beliefs about Forms as such. Magnesia will not be a city composed solely of philosophers, and most citizens will always lack the synoptic grasp of a field and the ability to respond to all sorts of challenges that Plato associates with genuine knowledge (*epistēmē*). Thus they could, unlike genuine knowers, be persuaded to adopt false beliefs—and this is why censorship is required (cf. *Tim.* 51E). What we would like to show, however, is that non-philosophical citizens can still grasp and appreciate the basic non-sensible properties of goodness and fineness although they do not possess understanding (*epistēmē*) in a strict sense. Seeing how this is possible will require the examination of Plato's psychology and epistemology I undertake in Chapters 3 and 4. In the rest of this chapter, I consider what sort of education the citizens do get and the role of such wisdom in their ethical life.

All citizens are to learn that virtue is non-instrumentally good, that it is an Independent Good, and that it is a condition of value for all other goods. Unlike the producers and auxiliaries of the *Republic*, the non-philosophers of the *Laws* will be educated to value reason for its own sake. In the *Laws*, the 'golden cord' of reason is found within each individual and non-philosophers are capable of cooperating with reason because they recognize its value. The Athenian's justification for providing preludes to the laws also makes it clear that simply following reasonable commands, without grasping for oneself the reasons underlying them, is the condition of a slave. Thus the citizens' education will employ arguments that 'come close to philosophizing' in order to provide them with a rational grasp of the principles underlying the lawgiver's account of the good life. Although they are to accept the guidance and superior knowledge of some, they should recognize that reason is the most valuable aspect of each human being and that thus they cannot simply accept the laws' guidance about the good life without themselves trying to grasp why what the law commands is good.

Non-philosophical citizens will, it seems, even be educated to have some true beliefs about the value of more strictly contemplative goods. And, as we also saw, they receive a sophisticated education in mathematics and in astronomy, which for Plato is a branch of theology. In both mathematics and astronomy they become aware of non-sensible principles of order. Indeed, the fundamental principle of Plato's theology in Book 10 is that the fineness and good order of the universe is explained by an intelligent, non-material cause. The stars are animated by gods and thus insofar as the motions of the stars are studied, citizens take as actual objects of study and contemplation the movements of the gods. The goodness of the heavens is connected to its order and this order is explained in non-material and non-sensible terms: that is, by reason acting for the best in mathematically determinate ways. And as we saw in the *Timaeus*, such contemplation is one central way of bringing order to the reason inside each of us. The *Philebus* provided a further account of how this is so. The study of mathematics and of mathematical astronomy involves grasping principles of order and determinacy and such principles are themselves value properties. By grasping them, reason brings itself into a state that is both non-relationally good and good for its possessor.

A comparison with Kant may provide further illumination of Plato's views. Plato is a metaphysical or substantive realist about value. He holds that the value of things and actions is a non-relational property that they have independently of our attitudes. As Kant rejects realism as a solution to the traditional problems of metaphysics, so he rejects metaphysical or substantive realism about value. For Kant, the good will or the power of purely rational choice is 'the source and condition of all the value in the world; goodness, as it were, flows into the world from the good will, and there would be none without it.'[128] The only thing that has unconditional value is the power of purely rational choice and thus what makes any thing or action good is that it is the object of rational choice. It is rational choice that confers upon anything its value.

For Plato, the direction of explanation runs in the opposite direction. It is the possession of the non-relational goodmaking properties that makes whatever is good good and thus it is these properties that confer goodness on reason itself. Practical rationality, for Plato, must be characterized in terms of objective value. Reason itself is made good by the fact that it constitutes a grasp of non-relational goodmaking properties. To be practically rational is to recognize the value inherent in things and to respond appropriately to it. Such appropriate recognition and response to objective value has both cognitive and desiderative aspects: it involves grasping the good and loving the good. This is not to say that any sort of practical pursuit of one's own good, even if it is correct and successful, is a seeking after what is objectively valuable. There might be creatures—e.g. various non-human sorts of animals—that could seek out what is good for them, although what is good for them is not something possessing objective value. This sort of practical inquiry, even if complex, would not be an activity of reason for Plato. Yet even in non-human animals, we should, at least in general, expect a significant coincidence between what is good for a creature and the possession of objective value. But this is not because the notion of what is good for a creature gives content to the notion of what is objectively good, but rather, because the world is providentially ordered.

This understanding of practical rationality may allow us to make progress with three important remaining issues. First, as we saw, Plato justifies explaining the basis of the law to the citizens by an appeal to freedom. In virtue of being free, people are owed an explanation of the principles governing their conduct. Nevertheless, one of the most disturbing features of Magnesia's political and social structure is its tight restrictions on the lives of citizens and on the information available to them. If Magnesia's social structure violates people's autonomy, can Plato's appeal to freedom really be sincere?

Second, in both the *Phaedo* and the *Republic*, the contemplative ideal was a prominent component of the good life. Especially in the later dialogues, we find Plato relying on the idea that the goal of human life is an assimilation to god (*homoiōsis theōi*), e.g. in the digression in the *Theaetetus* (171D–177C), the Book 10 theology of the *Laws*, and in the *Timaeus* passage we have just examined. This claim may suggest an ideal that similarly calls into question the value of action. David Sedley provides a fascinating account of how this tension was reflected in later Platonists.[129] Focussing on the *Timaeus*, we can ask what the result will be of assimilating our reason to the patterns provided by the World Soul. For Xenocrates and the Middle Platonists, this ideal was essentially what we would describe as moral. The patterns of the World Soul produce the cycles of the seasons and thus sustain the good order of the entire universe. Assimilation to it is the source of benevolence and other-regarding concern. In particular, against the Stoics who saw justice growing out of our natural affinity to other human beings, these Platonists saw justice deriving not from human nature, but from our assimilation to the benevolence of the World Soul.

But as Sedley points out, there is another tendency in Platonism. Plotinus, for example, sees assimilation to god as a purely intellectual assimilation to a higher being. The moral virtue of justice as psychic harmony described in *Republic* 4 is simply a quasi-virtue produced by habituation that must be transcended in the effort to reach pure intelligibles. Sedley suggests that Plotinus' interpretation, although extreme, may well be right and Sedley refers to a passage from *Republic* 7 that dismisses courage and moderation as 'so-called virtues of the soul [that] are akin' to the virtues of the body (*Rep.* 518D9–10) and to the *Timaeus* passage quoted above (*Tim.* 89D2–90D7) that locates human happiness in the godlike state of the rational soul, not in the harmony of all three parts. If this is right, it suggests a bifurcation: intellectual activity for the philosopher and a very different kind of practical virtue for others.

A third set of concerns is provided by Plato's particular conception of value properties. We may feel that a considerable range of value is missing. Mathematics and mathematical astronomy might be a salutary propaedeutic to abstract ethical reasoning, but what will ethical reasoning itself look like? And how is it related to the breathtakingly abstract notion of value sketched in the *Philebus*?

Finally, let me note a related set of issues that I shall postpone to Chapter 4. It is a standard objection against realism about the good that it creates a motivational mystery. If the good is specifiable independently of our contingent motivation and of our capacities of rational choice, what guarantees that it is motivating *for us*? If the good is specified independently of actual human motivation, might it not be the case that human beings simply are indifferent to it? This problem faces Plato in an especially acute form. On the account developed, Plato accepts a very tight connection between objective value and what is good for people. First, there is something approaching direct proportionality between the objective goodness of things and actions and their goodness for people. Second, an awareness of objective, non-relational value is a necessary condition of benefit *for the person*. These are much stronger claims than simply holding that it is good for a person to value the objectively valuable. What grounding can Plato give them? I shall take this issue up in Chapter 4, since Plato's answer to the question of why a grasp of objective goodness and fineness is good *for us* depends on his account of the sort of creatures that we are.

In the dialogues we are considering, Plato does not raise these questions explicitly in these forms. What his answer would be is, I think, clearest in the case of freedom and autonomy. On the other issues, Plato may not have a fully worked-out view and this may be reflected in controversies among later Platonists. Indeed, further reflection on the relevant issues sometimes raises problems that are more adequately articulated only later in the Greek tradition. Nevertheless, the problems are sufficiently important to warrant inquiry.

Autonomy There are aspects of Plato's thought that suggest a striking concern for freedom and autonomy. As we have seen, the appeal to the idea that Magnesia's citizens deserve to be treated as free people and benefit from such treatment is at the heart of Plato's justification of preludes in the *Laws*. But even in the *Republic* there are passages that seem to attribute value to autonomy. Consider, for example, the notorious passage from Book 9 quoted above (*Rep.* 590C–D) in which Plato advocates that members of the lower classes be 'slaves' to the philosopher rulers so that all citizens are, in one way or another, ruled by reason. What draws our attention in this passage is the suggestion—which we inevitably find shocking—that in a just city almost all citizens will occupy the position of 'slaves', at least insofar as their lives are directed by others. But we should also notice that in this passage Plato takes it as obvious that it is better for a person to be ruled by an inner principle than by something external: 'it is better for everyone to be ruled by divine reason, preferably within himself and his own' (*Rep.* 590D3–5). It would not be wrong to be reminded of certain modern theorists.

I wish my life and decisions to depend on myself, not on external forces of whatever kind. I wish to be the instrument of my own, not other men's, acts of will. I wish to be a subject, not an object; to be moved by reasons, by conscious purposes, which are my own, not by causes which affect me, as it were, from outside. I wish to be somebody, not nobody; a doer—deciding, not being decided for, self-directed and not acted upon by external nature or other men as if I were a thing, or animal, or a slave incapable of playing a human role, that is, of conceiving goals and policies of my own and realizing them.[130]

Insofar as we find the ideal of autonomy as self-direction attractive, we will tend to see Plato's use of the language of freedom in the *Laws* as disingenuous or as applying to only a few people or to ideal circumstances. But we can better understand what is going on in terms of Plato's theory of value.

For Plato, what is essential to rationality and to the possibility of benefit is that one actually grasps and responds to genuine value. The value of ethical reflection itself is constituted by the value of the psychic states and activities it involves and issues in: ethical reflection is good for the person to the extent that it replaces false beliefs or ignorance with true beliefs, develops rational support for true beliefs, and eventually attains knowledge. If one thought, as for example Kant did, that the goodness of any end depends on its being the object of free, rational choice, then paternalistic attempts to restrict and guide inquiry will be deeply problematic. Indeed, insofar as paternalistic means render the choice less than fully rational, they rob such choice of any value. Using paternalistic means that infringe upon the rationality of the person's choice in order to make it more likely that the person chooses well is simply an impossible strategy.[131]

Plato's evaluation of such cases must be more nuanced. Many things that would be rejected by a Kantian would also be seen as problematic by Plato. Getting people to do the right thing out of unreflective habit or because they are deceived about the reasons for doing it, would fail to bring them into the right relation to values and would thus not benefit them. (Although Plato might think that even this is less bad for such people than allowing their bad desires to have free expression.) Nevertheless, if one could be brought to grasp and love genuine value by a route that did not fully respect the person's autonomy, Plato would not have the grounds for objection that Kant would. Moreover, the case for paternalistic restrictions may be stronger if one is trying to develop something less than full-blown knowledge (*epistēmē*).[132]

Why, then, for Plato is it better for rational direction to come from inside rather than outside? It is not because self-determination is valuable in itself or is a condition of value.[133] The claim that it is better for rational direction to come from inside is simply an affirmation of the ultimate end as knowing the truth and ordering things in accordance with it. Unless rational direction comes from within, the person's reason is not grasping values in the best way. Only when directing reason is within oneself is one's own Reasoning part doing what it is intended to do, that is, bringing itself into good order by appreciation of genuine value and ordering other things accordingly. It is better to have something akin to such rule imposed on one from outside than to have no kind of order in one's life, but this is a *lower* sort of value, the realization of which frustrates the higher capacities of the soul. Reason is an inherent orderer and thus it fails to realize its own nature insofar as it serves as passive material to be ordered from without.

Assimilation to god and the virtues   Sedley rightly calls attention to a little-noticed passage from the *Republic*, that is, Plato's claim that courage and moderation are 'so-called' virtues that are, unlike wisdom, 'akin' to the virtues of the body (*Rep.* 518D9–10).[134] This passage presents an issue of central importance to Plato's ethics that has not received much attention, although I do not think it is the issue to which Sedley himself points. The *Republic* passage suggests, Sedley holds, an 'unfavourable contrast of moral with intellectual virtue'.[135] But what the passage draws is, rather, an unfavorable contrast between the good condition of the lower parts of the soul and the good condition of the Reasoning part. This is not to draw an unfavorable contrast between moral and intellectual virtue or between strictly contemplative goals and other-regarding goals, since nothing rules out the possibility that we might have *rational* motivations for moral virtue or other-regarding concern. If so, Plato's relative dismissiveness of the good condition of the lower two parts would not call such concern into question.

There are two lessons to draw from this passage. First, the *Republic* passage does raise doubts about the value of the good condition of the lower parts of the soul and in so doing raises doubts about the value of the virtues of courage and moderation insofar as they consist in such conditions.[136] The fundamental reason for Plato's relatively low estimation of these conditions is that even at their best the lower parts cannot grasp the truth about value and appropriately respond to it. This is an important point, since modern virtue theory often sees as one of its advantages the fact that it gives a central place to feelings and emotions in its understanding of a good human character. Insofar as Plato sees such emotions and desires as associated with the lower parts of the soul, he cannot give them such primacy.

The second point is that in order to see other-regarding concern as having a higher value we need to see it as not cut off from the values grasped in contemplation. On some interpretations of Aristotle, for example, there is such a split between contemplative activity at its best and fine practical activity. On such an interpretation, philosophy and other forms of contemplative activity might recognize, among other things, the value inherent in fine ethical activity. Nevertheless, this sort of contemplation does not, even in part, constitute the value of ethical practice; the value of good ethical practice is complete before contemplation enters the picture. The understanding of the Dependency Thesis that I have advanced points to a way of bringing contemplative activity and fine practical activity more closely together. What the Dependency Thesis requires is that good ethical practice, including that displaying a concern for others, should proceed from a grasp of the value of such activity. In its most perfect form, practice will proceed from the sort of knowledge of the good and the fine that the philosopher seeks in contemplation.[137] But as I shall argue in Chapter 4, good ethical activity of the sort open to non-philosophers still proceeds from a less clear and accurate grasp of the very same properties. And in Chapter 5, I argue that Plato grounds the other-regarding concern involved in good ethical activity in a response to objective value.

Value Properties   Finally, we must take up the question of the content of value properties for Plato and, in particular, of how far they are mathematical. This is an unusually contentious and often obscure issue. Rather than argue for a particular interpretation, I shall try to show that the account developed so far is consistent with a wide variety of reasonable interpretations. The strongest interpretation would be that all value properties *are* mathematical properties. This is, perhaps, suggested by Myles Burnyeat.

No-one would feel the force of the answer [to the question 'What is the Good?'] 'Good is One' let alone believe it unless they had previously come to feel the force of the idea that goodness resides in abstract mathematical harmony and proportion . . . and that these are the bonds of unity . . . It is still harder to believe that the goodness which resides in mathematical relationships is one and the same as the goodness that one needs to govern oneself and others . . . Speusippus, like Aristotle, had every reason for resisting Plato's proposal for mathematizing ethics and moralizing mathematics. But the very fact of resistance shows us what Plato's proposal was.[138]

Does this mean that ethical properties such as good, fine, justice, and virtue are identical with various mathematical properties?[139] Even if Plato holds such a view, it is neither one that he works out in detail in the dialogues nor one that we find (nor would he expect us to find, prior to the appropriate mathematical studies) intuitively plausible.

Nevertheless, whatever the proper account of the nature of value properties is, it is important to show that non-philosophers' thought about values can be continuous with philosophers' knowledge of the same values. We see two tendencies in the *Laws*. First, Magnesia is committed to the central importance of political and social structures designed to encourage ethical and political discussion. We have seen the emphasis placed on the ethical education of citizens and, in Chapter 5, we shall see that the political arrangements of the city require citizens to devote a considerable amount of their time to political and ethical conversation as part of carrying out their civic duties. The citizens are expected to find such political activity not a burdensome necessity, but a valued part of their lives. This discussion will not make explicit reference to Forms. There will, however, be discussion about what justice or courage requires. Other advanced topics that are less directly practical will receive something like metaphorical treatment. As we have seen, for example, the idea that free citizens deserve a certain sort of treatment is a publicly available regulative principle in Magnesia. But underlying it is a complicated story about the objectivity of value and, ultimately, a psychological and epistemological theory about how Forms enter into everyday thought.

The theology advanced in Book 10 is based on what Plato takes to be true claims about divinity. Moreover, Magnesia's theology gives Plato a way to articulate a standard of objectivity that does not require full metaphysical detail. The main targets of Plato's attack on atheism are those who deny the objectivity of value. And in an implicit rejection of Protagorean relativism, Magnesians are taught that god, not man, is the measure of all things (*Laws* 716c). This is not, however, to make Euthyphro's mistake, since although the Athenian does not go into details, he makes it clear that ethical standards are not dependent on god. God is seen as bringing the world into its best condition and doing so because he is responding to the goodness of this order. As such, he provides a paradigm for the citizens' own actions and also allows them a way of understanding that certain Dependent Goods are objectively good. They, for example, will not be able to choose health on the basis of a Timaean account of the good order that health instantiates. But they will choose health because it allows them to engage in virtuous activity and because it instantiates what they can recognize, at a very general level, as the proper kind of providentially designed natural order.

The second tendency is more explicitly mathematical. The citizens of Magnesia will be educated from youth onwards to understand goodness as constituted by the order imposed on what is disorderly. In the simple forms of harmony in song, and rhythm in dance, goodness is constituted by the order (*taxis*) imposed on the naturally disorderly movements of voice and body. But the citizens are also educated to grasp more sophisticated forms of order. Their study of incommensurable magnitudes is valuable because such truths are worth knowing apart from their application and the mental acuity they develop (*Laws* 817E ff.). But such studies also allow the citizens to realize for themselves that the motions of the heavens are not, as is usually thought, disorderly, but rather display the divine order of circular motion which is akin to the movement of reason itself. The instantiation of this order in the stars and planets allows Plato to infer that the intelligence which is the cause of this order must be 'good with every virtue' (*Laws* 899B6). The teaching in the prelude to the theological law goes further and claims that it is fundamentally the same form of order that constitutes virtue in souls as well as in bodies and in the world at large (*Laws* 906C2–6).

We may see a related development in the *Statesman*. In the *Philebus*, Plato suggests that virtue can be understood as a mixture of the unlimited and a determinant (*Phil.* 26B5–C2). The *Statesman* seems to try to work this idea out. Plato flirts with the claim that virtuous actions and states of soul can be understood as mean states in a sense that is at least quasi-mathematical. The particular version of this view sketched in the *Statesman* is not worked out in much detail and does not seem especially promising.[140] Nevertheless, perhaps more important than the details of the proposal is that it suggests a quasi-mathematical account of the ethical value of particular actions and character states.

We shall be able to spell out more precisely the continuity between non-philosophers' thought about value and philosophers' knowledge of value only after considering Plato's psychology and epistemology in Chapters 3 and 4. In Chapter 4, I shall argue that non-philosophers can have access in their ethical thinking to the very same non-sensible value properties that philosophers know.

2.13 Virtue and Happiness

We began this chapter by looking at some of Plato's claims in the early books of the *Laws* about the goodness of virtue and the relation between its goodness and the goodness of other things. Let us end the chapter by examining the *Laws*' position on the relation between virtue and happiness. Plato, throughout his career including the *Laws*, held the principle of rational eudaimonism.[141]

The principle of rational eudaimonism: For each individual, the ultimate end of all her rational actions is her own (greatest) happiness.

Insofar as she is rational, each person pursues her own greatest happiness for its own sake, not for the sake of anything else and she pursues everything else for the sake of her own greatest happiness. Thus if rational agents are to be virtuous and act virtuously, virtue must contribute optimally to their own happiness. The relation between virtue and happiness was a central concern of Plato's ethics at all stages and much scholarly attention has been devoted to analyzing the positions of various dialogues. So we can begin by focusing on some of the claims that were prominent in previous dialogues. I use 'virtue' here to mean 'complete virtue', that is, the state consisting in the possession of courage, justice, moderation, and wisdom.

Most straightforwardly, Plato in the *Laws*, like all other ancient ethical theorists, holds that being virtuous is necessary for being happy. The necessity of virtue for happiness follows easily from the Dependency Thesis and Plato explicitly draws our attention to this fact (e.g. *Laws* 660E5–661E4).[142] Since nothing benefits or is good for a person who lacks virtue, and happiness requires having at least some goods, an unvirtuous person can never be happy. The Dependency Thesis is not, however, required for holding that virtue is necessary for happiness, since it might be the case that virtue is so great a good that a person cannot be happy without it.[143] But if we were to allow that things such as health and pleasure have value and benefit people apart from virtue, we would need to show why virtue is of so much greater value. The Dependency Thesis allows us to avoid such calculations of weight.

A greater challenge is provided by the question of whether virtue is sufficient for happiness. But before turning to the relevant texts, there are two important preliminary issues. First, does Plato in the *Laws* think that happiness is a maximally or unimprovably good state or does happiness come in degrees such that A can be happier than B, although both A and B are happy?[144] Second, does Plato think that happiness consists solely in virtue or does he allow that there are other components of happiness besides virtue?[145] An awareness of these possibilities will allow us to avoid some fruitless disputes. If, for example, one scholar cites evidence that Plato thinks that virtue is sufficient for happiness, another might argue that those passages should not be taken literally since we have other compelling evidence that Plato recognizes components of happiness besides virtue. If the first scholar assumes that Plato holds a scalar conception of happiness while the second assumes that he holds a maximalist conception, then the real grounds of their disagreement may remain obscure and we might dismiss the *Laws*' position as simply muddled.

Let us begin with the second question, since if happiness consists solely in virtue, then answering the question of whether virtue is sufficient for happiness is considerably easier.[146] The view that Plato holds that happiness is identical to virtue has not attracted much support in modern scholarship, but it has recently been skillfully defended by Julia Annas.[147] She argues that Plato held such a view throughout his career and that, in particular, he holds it in the *Laws*. She interprets the *Laws'* distinction between divine and human goods along the lines of the Stoic distinction between the genuine good of virtue and preferred indifferents. Plato, Annas holds, thinks that only virtue is good and only vice is bad. Human goods motivate us to pursue them and human bads motivate us to avoid them, but actually obtaining them does not affect our happiness at all.

Concentrating on the *Laws*, we find that some of Plato's claims are, as they stand, inconsistent with the Stoic view that only virtue is good. For example, Plato claims that things such as health and good perceptual capacities are 'very good' (ἄριστα, *Laws* 661B6) for just people and, indeed, 'really are good' for them (ὄντως ἀγαθά, 661D2–3). Similarly, ill health and other such things are 'bad' for just people (κακά, *Laws* 661D2). This is a clearer commitment to the goodness or badness of these things when possessed by virtuous people than Plato makes in the *Euthydemus*.[148] But Annas holds that despite Plato's actual use of 'good' and 'bad' here, we should interpret him as claiming that Dependent Goods and Dependent Bads are, respectively, good or bad for a person only insofar as they 'encourage' or 'retard' virtue. She gives two reasons for this. First, in the same passage, Plato asserts that virtue all by itself is sufficient for happiness. Since I do not think it is clear that the passage says this and even if it does, it would not entail that virtue is the only good if Plato holds a scalar conception of happiness, I shall leave this aside for the moment.

Annas' second reason is that taking these claims literally produces an odd asymmetry in Plato's views. She argues that we face an awkward asymmetry if we allow any conventional goods (e.g. health) to contribute to a person's happiness in any other way than by encouraging virtue. Conventional evils or bads (e.g. sickness) when possessed by an unjust person are not bad in the way that we conventionally think that they are bad. Indeed, they are good insofar as they make the unjust person more capable of becoming virtuous. If we allow conventional goods to be good for virtuous people in any other way than by contributing to their virtue, we would allow that conventional goods benefit in a conventional way (the way that most people think they do), while conventional bads do not harm in a conventional way.[149]

Such an asymmetry does not produce an incoherence in Plato's position and we might accept it. But there is not, in fact, the sort of asymmetry that Annas describes, since Plato does not hold that Dependent Goods benefit the virtuous person in the way that most people think. As we saw in the case of our interlocutors, most people think that virtue is *for the sake of* the Dependent Goods. Or at least they think that Dependent Goods benefit people whether or not they are virtuous. On the interpretation of the Dependency Thesis I have argued for, Dependent Goods must be appreciated in order to benefit their possessor. Keen sight, for example, is good for a just person because it allows for the perception of fine objects that are appreciated for the features that actually make them fine, and not because it allows for the better appreciation of sexually stimulating scenes. The benefit of Dependent Goods for the virtuous person requires a correct appreciation of value and is thus apparent only from the perspective of the virtuous person. So we can accept that Plato's actual usage fairly reflects his position while avoiding the asymmetry.

There are, in addition, considerable costs to Annas' interpretation. First, in the *Philebus* some pleasures are a necessary part of a life that is completely happy. Similarly, in the *Laws* Plato holds that the most just life will be the happiest only if it is also pleasant. In neither case is it plausible to think that Plato is confusing pleasure being part of the good life with its being an indifferent.[150] Moreover, attributing the Stoics' position to Plato would leave very awkward gaps in his theory. It is a notorious problem for the Stoics whether they can explain the rationality of the just person's pursuit of preferred indifferents (and rejection of dispreferred indifferents) since they hold that getting these things is not good (and that getting the dispreferred indifferents is not bad) for the person. The Stoics develop an elaborate theory to meet the challenge. Whether or not we think they are successful, they acutely feel the gap in their position without such a theory and this issue was an obvious and frequent source of criticism. Plato shows no signs of recognizing such a gap nor does he ever hint at anything like the Stoic solution. Further, Annas' interpretation seems to require not only that we attribute to Plato a Stoic theory of the good and of indifferents, but also a

Stoic theory of action as an entirely inner process.[151] In sum, we have good reason to hold that Plato does allow that happiness has components other than virtue and that Dependent Goods can benefit people in ways other than encouraging or increasing their virtue.

So are there passages that claim that virtue is sufficient for happiness? The most promising passage occurs in Book 2, in which the Athenian iron-ically compliments his interlocutors:[152] 'You compel your poets to say that the good man, since he is moderate and just, is happy and blessed, whether he is great and strong or small and weak, whether he is rich or not' (*Laws* 660E2–5).[153] This passage and others in the *Laws* fall short of claiming that a person can be happy without any Dependent Goods, although it does suggest that the virtuous person does not need many goods in order to be happy. This passage's significance, however, depends on our first question, which is whether Plato in the *Laws* has a maximal or scalar conception of happiness. There are passages in the *Laws* that suggest, although they do not conclusively establish, that Plato holds a scalar conception of happiness such that A can be happier than B, although both A and B are happy (*Laws* 662D–663A, 662E, 734C–E, 742E–743E). And even if Plato held an official definition of happiness as an unimprovably good state, we can see why he might choose to employ scalar language. If happiness is a maximally good state including virtue and the possession of some other goods, then it seems reasonable to hold that some of these other goods might be subtracted from such a life while still leaving the person a life well worth living, although not one that attains happiness. There should be many such virtuous lives that are filled with goods, although they are not maximally good and for most practical purposes our concern will be with picking out lives that are well worth living. Calling such lives 'happy' as long as they are sufficiently high up among lives that are well worth living would not be unreasonable and is not such an abstruse and sophisticated move that it could only occur as the culmination of a long dialectical debate.[154]

The more pressing issue is how badly off a virtuous person can be, while still remaining virtuous. Is virtue by itself, no matter how few Dependent Goods one has and how many Dependent Bads, always sufficient to give a person a life well worth living or even a life worth living at all? Some schol-ars have argued that Plato in some dialogues usually classified as early or middle held that a life might be virtuous, but still not worth living.[155] The *Laws* does not explicitly address this question, although *Laws* 660E2–5 suggests that virtue is sufficient for lives that are well worth living, even if they include few Dependent Goods and many Dependent Bads.[156] Plato does not, however, explicitly say that the virtuous person always has a life worth living no matter what and Plato may have thought that, from the point of view of practice, it was not necessary to address this question. First, the practical question that agents face is what course of action is best for themselves in the long run, overall. Plato thinks that a person is always better off pursuing virtue. So even if virtue can be subject to great misfortunes, this does not affect the question of whether people should pursue virtue. Second, the misfortunes of the virtuous are not permanent, since in the long run god apportions happiness to justice. We do not need to invoke this theological claim to show that the virtuous person is always better off than the unvirtuous one (if we did, we could not meet the challenge of the *Republic*), but it does give virtuous people added reason to be content with their lives.

What it is important for Plato to show, given his eudaimonism and his categorical demand that each person pursue justice, is that people are always better off being just no matter what misfortune they may suffer and no matter what goods an unjust course of action may bring.[157] Given the Dependency Thesis, it will be the case that nothing benefits unjust people. But this is not sufficient to settle the comparative question, if we allow that enough misfortunes can make the just person's life not worth living. (If such misfortunes could at most render life of no value, then the just person would always be better off.) What Plato needs to show is that both the goodness of virtue and the badness of vice have a special prominence. Here again an appeal to the sort of argument we shall consider in Chapter 4 may help. The basic idea of this argument is that each of us is identified in some especially intimate way with our rational capacities and that these rational capacities, in turn, have the function of standing in the appropriate relation to objective value. Standing in the right relation to objective value thus helps constitute what it is for the individual to benefit. The metaphor that Plato uses several times in the *Laws* to describe the condition of the unjust is one of darkness: the unjust are caught in a fog or create a darkness within themselves (e.g. *Laws* 663B, 875C). Their central problem is that they fail to appreciate (where appreciation involves both a cognitive grasp as well as love) what is really good and instead value what is bad or lacking in value. If what is most essential to human beings is that they are by nature formed to seek and act upon the truth, this is the greatest of misfortunes. No matter how badly impaired virtuous people's appreciation of value may be and no matter how poor their surroundings, it is not unreasonable to think that they will be better off than the unjust. If we consider, for example, what is good for the eyes as eyes, it is reasonable to think that seeing eyes, even if their vision is impaired and they have an impoverished visual environment, are better off than eyes that are blind. Indeed, this metaphor puts the case for justice too weakly. The objects of thought are more reliably available to a person than the objects of vision. Even more important, unjust people, insofar as they have a false conception of the good (and Plato thinks that this is the typical outcome of akrasia), are not merely failing to grasp the good, but are attributing value to what lacks it and loving what is not deserving of love. This would be more like having eyes that loved their own blindness and darkness itself.

Just people can have Dependent Bads and these are genuinely bad for them. There is thus an important asymmetry between goods and bads: while virtue is a necessary condition of gaining any benefit, vice is not a necessary condition of suffering some bad. Sickness can cut short their lives and pain can disrupt, without destroying, the good order of their soul.[158] Moreover, if acting on and expressing their appreciation of what is good benefits people, the failure of their efforts may be bad for them. Nevertheless, by being virtuous they will have realized, at least partially, the most essential aspect of their identity: they will have some appreciation of what is objectively good. Plato's value theory, along with his understanding of what human beings are, may thus be capable of sustaining the importance that he attributes to virtue.[159]

3   Parts of the Soul and the Psychology of Virtue

3.1 Introduction

In Chapter 1, we saw that Plato's middle-period view of the capacities of non-philosophers to acquire genuine virtue and thus to lead happy lives was deeply pessimistic. In the previous chapter, I argued that there is a substantial shift in Plato's views by the time of the *Laws*. As we saw, Plato thinks that good or correct law is an expression of reason (*nous*), that is, an expression of the excellent condition of our capacity to reason. In Magnesia, there will be an intimate relation between reason as expressed in good law and the reason of the individual citizen. The education of Magnesia's citizens provides them with rational grounds for accepting their political and legal system as well as for their basic ethical and theological beliefs. The citizens are to believe that virtue is good for its own sake and to desire it as such and the education of all the citizens is intended to bring it about that they possess genuine virtues.

As we also saw in the last chapter, that citizens must acquire genuine virtue in order to benefit from whatever other goods they possess. This benefit requires that they display an excellence of reason. Specifically, as part of their acquiring genuine virtue, they will develop an ability to recognize and appreciate, in an imperfect but nevertheless significant way, the goodmaking features of things.

In the next two chapters, I shall examine the ways in which these shifts in Plato's position depend on developments in his psychology and epistemology. The specific changes we have just noted in Plato's views of the ethical capacities of non-philosophers must rest on corresponding changes at a more fundamental level. If non-philosophers are now capable of forming and possessing beliefs and desires that suffice for genuine virtue, Plato's psychology and epistemology must have changed so as to make this possible. We must show how non-philosophers are capable of attaining the excellence of reason involved in recognizing the goodmaking features of things.

In this chapter I focus on the following set of issues. A fundamental aspect of Plato's psychology in the *Phaedo* and the *Republic* is its commitment to a partitioning thesis. On this account, individual human beings consist of distinct agent-like parts. This partitioning is sometimes thought to be nothing more than Plato's response to one problem, that is, the issue of akrasia. In the early dialogues, Plato denies the possibility of akrasia; in the *Republic*, he accepts its possibility and the *Republic's* partitioning of the soul is intended to explain how akrasia is possible. But the *Phaedo* suggests that Plato's commitment to partitioning is not motivated exclusively by accepting the possibility of akrasia, since although the *Phaedo* does not clearly recognize akrasia, in that dialogue Plato partitions the person into the distinct agent-like parts of the soul and the body.

The fundamental claims constituting the partitioning strategy are that (1) the person is a compound of distinct agent-like parts that are themselves the proper or ultimate subjects of beliefs, desires, and other psychological states and activities, and (2) these parts have different characteristic beliefs, desires, goals, and abilities. These basic ideas are elaborated in different ways in the *Phaedo* and the *Republic*: in the *Phaedo*, the body is treated as the subject of certain psychological states; in the *Republic*, the soul itself has distinct parts that are the subjects of different psychological states.

This partitioning of the soul does much important work for Plato in the middle period. It provides Plato with a theory of non-rational motivations, that is, a theory of the desires, emotions, and beliefs that come into being and persist, although they do not spring from and are not maintained by reason.

(1) Partitioning enters Plato's thought in the *Phaedo* along with a radical distinction between philosophers and non-philosophers in terms of their goals and their ethical and epistemic capacities. These developments are not coincidental and partitioning is intended to provide the explanatory

basis for this distinction. The different capacities and characteristics of philosophers and non-philosophers are ultimately to be explained by the different capacities and characteristics of the parts of the person and by facts about which part dominates or rules within the individual.

(2) Since the partitioning theory grounds Plato's account of the basic ethical and cognitive distinctions among people, it is essential to the *Republic*'s political theory, which assigns, on the basis of such distinctions, fundamentally different sorts of education, duties, and social roles to each class within the city.

(3) The four virtues recognized in the *Republic* are characterized wholly in terms of the parts of the soul and their features. The nature of the virtues can only be fully understood in terms of the relevant features of the parts of the soul. Thus we can only understand the goodness of the individual virtues by understanding the goodness of the conditions of the parts of the soul that constitute these virtues.

(4) All people have all three of the parts of the soul. Even in the virtuous, the lower parts retain some of their characteristic functions. Thus the partitioning theory provides Plato with a general account of the origin and persistence of different sorts of beliefs and desires in all people. In particular, Plato's account of the Spirited and Appetitive parts of the soul provides the basis for a theory of non-rational motivation in both the virtuous and unvirtuous.

(5) Although the partitioning theory is not exclusively a theory of akratic conflict and action, one of its great philosophical accomplishments is to provide Plato with a theoretical framework that allows him to recognize the possibility of akratic conflict and to attempt to explain its origins and resolution.

In this chapter, I argue that the *Laws* rejects the sort of partitioning theory found in the *Republic* and moves decisively beyond any form of partitioning that involves agent-like parts of the soul. As the middle-period form of partitioning does much work for Plato and has several distinct lines of motivation, so its rejection has more than one basis. I begin by arguing in Section 3.2 that the *Republic* is, in fact, committed to the partitioning strategy. In Section 3.3, I examine the most impressive achievement of middle-period partitioning, that is, the *Republic*'s theory of akrasia, and try to show that although the *Republic*'s theory is powerful and subtle, it faces severe problems. In the second half of this chapter, I argue that the *Laws*' theory provides a superior account of akrasia that avoids these problems and I consider some more general issues concerning the *Laws*' new more unitary understanding of the nature of the soul.

The argument in the second half of the chapter, if successful, shows that Plato can offer a better theory of akrasia without the parts of the soul. But we can also develop a deeper account of why Plato abandons partitioning. Drawing on the *Phaedrus*, the *Theaetetus*, and the *Timaeus*, I argue that we see a significant shift in Plato's epistemology. First, the lower parts of the soul lose their autonomy as the sources of concepts and beliefs that are independent of the Forms. All belief and conceptualized desire involves some grasp of non-sensible properties and this fact exerts pressure for recognizing only a single subject of all belief and desire. Second, no longer is there a sharp discontinuity between the ethical cognitive resources of philosophers and non-philosophers, with the former alone having access to non-sensible properties, while the latter are limited exclusively to sensible properties. Although the difference in degree may still be great, the difference in their cognitive states, at least in some cases, is that between the clearer and dimmer grasp of the same thing, not that between states focused on different kinds of things.

3.2 *Parts of the Soul and Akrasia in the* Republic

Parts of the Soul   The *Republic* divides the soul into three parts: the Reasoning part, the Spirited part, and the Appetitive part (*to logistikon, to thumoeides,* and *to epithumētikon*). (*Faute de mieux,* I use the standard translations, although they may be misleading: for example, all three parts, not merely the Appetitive part, have desires.) Plato characterizes each of these three parts in agent-like terms: each is treated as the ultimate subject of psychological affections, activities, and capacities that are normally attributed to the person as a whole.[1] In particular, each part

(1) has its own desires (ἐπιθυμίαι), and can wish and want (βούλεσθαι and ἐθέλειν),

(2) has conceptual and cognitive capacities:
   (i) each has beliefs,
   (ii) each has practical goals,
   (iii) each can engage in some forms of reasoning, including reasoning about what to do, and
   (iv) each can communicate with the others: one part can persuade another and they can all agree.[2]

(3) has its own pleasures.

In Section 3.3, I consider in more detail the distinctive features of the parts of the soul, but we can now see the broad outlines of Plato's theory. Each part has the basic capacities needed to be a source of action. Each has a grasp of a practical goal, desiderative impulses toward it and the capacity to engage in at least simple sorts of practical thought. Each has its own pleasures which involve characteristic ways of experiencing the world that are automatically bound up with desire and pursuit. As we shall also see, items within one part fit together with each other in ways that they do not with items in other parts. Finally, each can, without the cooperation of the others, move the agent to act.

To illustrate Plato's treatment of the parts of the soul in the *Republic*, consider his characterization of the virtues in Book 4.

Courageous, too, then, I take it, we call each individual because of this part, when, namely, his spirited part preserves in the midst of pains and pleasures the rule handed down by reason . . . But wise by that small part that ruled in him and handed down these commands, by its possession in turn within it of the knowledge of what is beneficial for each and for the whole, the community composed of the three . . . And again, was he not moderate by reason of the friendship and concord of these same parts, when namely, the ruling principle and its two subjects are at one in the belief that the reasoning part ought to rule [ὁμοδοξῶσι δεῖν ἄρχειν], and do not raise faction against it? (*Rep.* 442B11–D1)

All three parts here have beliefs, engage in communication, and the Spirited part and the Appetitive part are capable of agreeing that the Reasoning part ought to rule.

Yet should we take literally these attributions of psychological affections and activities to the parts of the soul? Before turning to Plato's argument in Book 4 to partition the soul, let us consider a preliminary worry. We might think that Plato is unreflectively, and without serious theoretical commitment, engaging in the common personification of psychic (or quasi-psychic) entities. When Hippolytus claims that his tongue swore, but his heart remained unsworn, we need not attribute to him the view that his tongue literally has beliefs.[3] But we cannot simply read away Plato's language in this way, since he treats the parts of the soul as agent-like not only when he is defining the virtues, but throughout the *Republic* and, in particular, in Book 4, when he tries to get clear about the real nature and capacities of the soul (*Rep.* 435B–440C). One might then argue that Plato's language, although reflective, does not represent an ultimate theoretical commitment. Perhaps Plato thought that agent-like parts of the soul had some explanatory value, even if the ultimate correct account of the soul would not attribute, e.g., beliefs and desires to the parts of the soul.

But we also have general reasons for doubting this subtler claim. First, Plato's commitment to agent-like parts of the soul pervades the *Republic* and he never suggests that such talk is intended as a metaphor or as a convenient way of speaking and not as a literal truth claim.[4] Thus we would be left to our own devices in cashing out Plato's claims and would risk reading into Plato, as the obvious meaning lying behind his metaphor, whatever assumptions about mind and action seem plausible to us. Second, we would need to see what Plato could have thought the explanatory benefit was of postulating agent-like parts even if he did not take them literally. Some contemporary philosophers of mind, such as Daniel Dennett, have argued that homunculi can be of significant explanatory value in psychological theory, especially in cognitive psychology. But Dennett's hope is to find progressively simpler homunculi which can be reduced ultimately to a non-intentional level.

One starts in AI [artificial intelligence] with a specification of a whole person or cognitive organism—what I call, more neutrally, an intentional system . . . and then breaks that largest intentional system into an organization of subsystems, each of which could itself be viewed as an intentional system (with its own specialized beliefs and desires) and hence formally as a homunculus. In fact, homunculus talk is ubiquitous in AI, and is almost always illuminating. AI homunculi talk to each other, wrest control from each other, volunteer, sub-contract, supervise and even kill . . . Homunculi are *bogeymen* only if they duplicate *entire* the talents they are rung in to explain . . . If one can get a team or committee of *relatively* ignorant, narrow-minded, blind homunculi to produce the intelligent behavior of the whole, this is progress . . . If we then look closer at the individual boxes we see that the function of each is accomplished by subdividing it via another flow chart into still smaller, more stupid homunculi. Eventually this nesting of boxes lands you with homunculi so stupid (all they have to do is remember whether to say yes or no when asked) that they can be, as one says, 'replaced by a machine.' One *discharges* fancy homunculi from one's scheme by organizing armies of idiots to do the work.[5]

These intentionally characterized homunculi are not in themselves ultimately explanatory and we attain a scientifically acceptable explanation only when we reach a level at which no intentionally characterized homunculi remain. For Dennett, the intentional characterization of homunculi, persons, or any intentional system is simply a strategy for predicting the entity's observable behavior or identifying global patterns in its dispositions to peripheral behavior.[6] But these are not Plato's ambitions: he is not attempting to go below the intentional level and he is trying to do more than predict or find patterns in behavior. For Plato, any explanatory gain would have to be a gain in identifying and describing the real nature and operations of soul and it is not clear how postulating agent-like parts would do this, if they do not actually exist. Even if non-existent agent-like parts could, in certain circumstances, have some explanatory value (as, for example, an idealized model), Plato, as we shall see, introduces them precisely in order to answer the question of whether the soul has the same sort of complexity as the city and a satisfactory answer to this can only be had by establishing whether conflicting desires should be assigned to different subjects.

Finally, some of the reluctance to take seriously Plato's attribution of psychological states to the parts of the soul may be because of the idea that such parts are necessarily unexplanatory, since they reintroduce at the level of the part what we were trying to explain at the level of the whole. But as Dennett notes, such a move is obviously unexplanatory only if the parts 'duplicate *entire* the talents they are rung in to explain'. But it is not obviously incoherent to think that the real nature of the soul is such that it is composed of intentionally characterized parts that are all necessary to explain the psychology of a single human person. To see whether intentionally characterized parts are, at least potentially, explanatory, we have to turn to the details of Plato's view.

The Book 4 Argument We can better see what Plato is committed to by examining his careful and elaborate argument in Book 4 for partitioning the soul. The fundamental principle used in this argument is a claim we may call the 'Principle of Contraries'. 'The same thing cannot do or undergo contraries with respect to the same thing and in relation to the same thing at the same time [ταὐτὸν τἀναντία ποιεῖν ἢ πάσχειν κατὰ ταὐτόν γε καὶ πρὸς ταὐτὸν οὐκ ἐθελήσει ἅμα]' (*Rep.* 436B8–9).[7] Thus there are two ways of reconciling with the Principle of Contraries cases in which what seems to be one and the same thing, e.g. a person, does or suffers contraries. First, it may be that the contraries are not, in fact, with respect to the same thing and in relation to the same thing at the same time. In such a case, the Principle does not exclude the possibility that one and the same thing can possess both contraries. (I shall call contraries that are with respect to the same thing and in relation to the same thing at the same time 'complete contraries' and contraries that fail to be either with respect to the same thing or in relation to the same thing or at the same time 'incomplete contraries'. The Principle holds that the same thing cannot coinstantiate complete contraries.) Option #1 dissolves the apparent exceptions by qualifying the contraries, that is, by showing that they are incomplete, and thus allowing their coinstantiation.

The second option for avoiding conflict with the Principle is that what seems to be one thing is not, in fact, a single thing, but is composite, that is, there are two distinct subjects, each of which is qualified by, or is the proper subject of, one of the complete contraries. Option #2 thus resolves apparent exceptions by distinguishing two different subjects for complete contraries that are non-coinstantiable. In the case of the soul and the conflict of desires he considers, Plato adopts the second alternative. Specifically, Plato argues for the separation of the Reasoning part of the soul from the Appetitive part by claiming that a person can, at the same time, both desire to drink and reject drinking and thereby does or undergoes contraries with respect to the same thing and in relation to the same thing at the same time. This option of attributing different contraries to different parts of the soul makes the parts distinct subjects which have the relevant complete contraries, that is, each part has one of the conflicting desires. If we are to block this conclusion, we need to show that the apparent contraries can be handled by the Option #1 strategy.

Two recent interpreters of this passage, A. W. Price and Michael Woods, argue that we do have good reason to resist this line of interpretation. They hold that Plato's solution to the conflict of desires is not to distinguish different subjects, but rather to distinguish different ways in which the same subject is qualified. They hold that Plato thinks that, in the case of drink, the same thing is undergoing contraries with respect to different things at the same time.[8] To settle this question, we must examine the details of Plato's argument.

The argument for the partitioning of the soul occurs in the course of Plato's attempt in Book 4 to give an account of the virtue of justice in individuals. Plato has previously established that the four virtues of the city consist in the appropriate condition of the classes in the city (*Rep.* 428A–434C): e.g., the city is just because each of the classes—the guardians, the auxiliaries, and the producers—performs its own job. Appealing to the general principle that the same name applies to different things (e.g. a city and a person) in the same way,[9] Plato infers that 'we shall thus expect that the individual also has these same forms [εἴδη] in his soul, and that on account of the same affections [πάθη] of these [forms] with those [forms in the city] he rightly receives the same names as the city' (*Rep.* 435B9–C2).[10] Note that even at this introduction of the notion of forms of the soul, Plato treats them as having affections, that is, as subjects.

Nevertheless, Plato admits that it is not clear whether we should endorse the above inference: determining whether the individual really has these forms in his soul is difficult (*Rep.* 435C4–D7, 436A8–9, 436B2–3). The first step, however, in settling the matter is not difficult.[11]

[W]e surely must agree that each of us has within himself the same classes and characters [εἴδη τε καὶ ἤθη] that are in the city? They could not get there from anywhere else. It would be absurd to suppose that the spirited part in cities was not derived from private citizens who are held to have this quality, as do the

Thracians and the Scythians . . . or the quality of love of learning, which would chiefly be attributed to the region where we dwell, or the love of money which we might say is not least likely to be found in Phoenicians and Egyptians.   (*Rep.* 435E1–436A3)

It is important to be clear about what Plato thinks he has shown here. The forms or classes and characteristics found in a city are due to the presence in it of people who have the same characteristics: e.g. the cities of Thrace and Scythia and the auxiliary class of the just city are spirited because the people in them are spirited. This does not yet show that the souls of people are divided into forms or parts which are the subject of different desires. In the examples that Plato chooses, cities possess the characteristics they do because of the presence in them of entities that are the more basic subjects of these characteristics.[12] Thracian cities are spirited because Thracian citizens, the basic entities composing the cities, are spirited. If the parallel holds true in turn for persons themselves, then people will possess these characteristics in virtue of the fact that their souls are composed of parts that are the more basic subjects of these characteristics. It is determining whether *this* is the case that is the more difficult question which has not yet been satisfactorily answered and this is the task that Plato takes up next. (I have added reference marks in the following passage.)

Passage A
(I)   But this is hard. Do we do each of these things with the same thing [τῷ αὐτῷ] or are there three things and we do one thing with one and one with another [ἄλλο ἄλλῳ]? Do we learn with one part [ἑτέρῳ] of ourselves, feel anger with another [ἄλλῳ], and with yet a third [τρίτῳ] desire the pleasures of nutrition and generation and their kind, or is it with the entire soul [ὅλῃ τῇ ψυχῇ] that we act in each case once we begin? That is what is really hard to determine [διορίσασθαι] properly.

I think so too.

(II)   Let us then attempt to determine in this way [ὁρίζεσθαι] whether they are the same as one another or different [εἴτε τὰ αὐτὰ ἀλλήλοις εἴτε ἕτερά ἐστι].[13]

How?

(III)   It is clear that the same thing cannot do or undergo contraries with respect to the same thing and in relation to the same thing at the same time. So that if we ever find these contraries in them we shall know that it was not the same thing but a plurality [οὐ ταὐτὸν ἦν ἀλλὰ πλείω].   (*Rep.* 436A8–C1)

This passage sets the basic question to be answered in the rest of the argument—in order to account for the variety of human desires and characters, should we posit a plurality or a single thing? Connecting this passage with the issue which set off this whole inquiry—whether there are *eidē* in the soul as in the city—our question takes the following form.

(Q) Does an individual learn with one *eidos* of the soul, feel anger with another *eidos* of the soul, and desire bodily pleasures with a third *eidos* of the soul or does he do each of these with the entire soul?

What is not yet clear is the exact sense we are to give here to the notion of doing something 'with' something.[14] If, for example, we hold that we do not learn with the whole soul, but learn with X, does this imply that X is the ultimate subject of learning, that is, that it is the thing which actually does the learning and acquires wisdom? If so, then this option would commit Plato to *eidē* which have beliefs, desires, and so on and thus to agent-like parts.

Socrates' next sentence (II) helps answer this question. Although it is hard to 'determine' (*Rep.* 436B2) the answer to (Q), Socrates here proposes a strategy for 'determining' (*Rep.* 436B5) the answer: 'Let us then attempt to determine in this way whether they are the same as one another or different.' (*Rep.* 436B5–6). The next sentence is the first statement of the Principle of Contraries and thus it becomes clear that the way to determine whether an individual performs different psychic activities with different *eidē* of his soul is by applying the Principle: 'It is clear that the same thing cannot do or undergo contraries with respect to the same thing and in relation to the same thing at the same time. So that if we ever find these contraries in them we shall know that it was not the same thing but a plurality' (*Rep.* 436B8–C1). Once again, we face a choice between a single thing and a plurality and Plato suggests that the task of the following argument is precisely to settle the question of whether a conflict of desires can be resolved by attributing them to one thing or to a plurality.[15] But it is now clearer exactly what this choice involves. If the contraries are not complete, we can attribute them to 'the same thing'. But if the contraries are complete, then we cannot attribute them to the same thing. We must attribute these contraries to a plurality of subjects: one thing does or undergoes one of the complete contraries, while the other thing does or undergoes the other of the complete contraries. The Principle thus presents us with an explicit choice between two ways of resolving a conflict of desires: one that attributes the conflicting desires to different subjects and one that does not.

Since applying the Principle is the way that Plato proposes for answering (Q), we can now give a more precise sense to (Q). To hold that we learn, grow angry, and desire the pleasures of nutrition and generation with 'the same thing' (*Rep.* 436A8), that is, with 'the whole soul' (*Rep.* 436B1), is to hold that the contraries involved in the conflict of desires that Plato goes on to consider are not complete contraries and can be attributed to the same subject, i.e. the whole soul. On the other hand, to hold that these are done not 'with the same thing', but with three is to hold that the relevant contraries are complete and must be assigned to different subjects. Thus we should here construe the claim that a person 'does F with X' as the claim that 'X is the proper subject of F'. To hold that both the case in which we act with 'the whole soul' and the case in which we act with three different things are cases in which, according to the Principle of Contraries, it is really 'the same thing' acting is to ignore the link that Plato explicitly forges between (Q) and the task he sets in his statement of the Principle of Contraries (*Rep.* 436B8–C1)—that is, the task of determining whether the facts about conflict allow us to hold that 'the same thing acts' or whether we must acknowledge a 'plurality'.

The argument has not yet established that the different parts of the soul are the subjects of the conflicting desires. If they are, then when the contraries are attributed to the parts, they will characterize the parts in the same way that they would characterize the soul if they were attributed to the soul. But if Plato is to reject the different subjects option, then we should expect him to show that the conflicting desires are not complete contraries and that it is the whole soul that acts in these three ways.

Plato proceeds to illustrate the Principle by showing how it can avoid two prima-facie counterexamples. Price and Woods rely on these examples to show that Plato's real intent is not to distinguish different subjects of conflicting desires, but rather to show that apparent contraries can both be attributed to the same subject, since they are with respect to different things. Let us consider Plato's two examples.

If anyone should say of a man standing still but moving his hands and head that the same man [ὁ αὐτὸς] is at the same time at rest and in motion we should not, I take it, regard that as the right way of expressing it, but rather that a part of him is at rest and a part in motion [τὸ μέν τι αὐτοῦ ἔστηκε, τὸ δὲ κινεῖται] ... Then if our interlocutor should carry the jest still further with the subtlety that tops at any rate stand still as a whole [οἵ γε στρόβιλοι ὅλοι ἑστᾶσί] at the same time that they are in motion when, with the peg fixed in one point, they revolve and that the same is true of any other case of something moving around in a circle in the same place— we should reject the statement because such parts in respect of which [κατὰ ταὐτὰ] they both stand still and move on such occasions are different parts of them. We would say that there was a straight line and a circumference in them and that in respect of the straight line [κατὰ μὲν τὸ εὐθὺ ἑστάναι] they are standing still since they do not incline to either side, but in respect of the circumference [κατὰ δὲ τὸ περιφερὲς] they move in a circle; but that when they revolve they incline the upright to the right or the left or forward or backward, then they are in no way at rest.[16]   (*Rep.* 436C9–E6)

These alleged counterexamples illustrate the two ways of resolving apparent violations of the Principle: in the first (head and hands/the body), the contraries are complete and thus must be assigned to different subjects; in the second (the spinning top), the contraries are incomplete because they are not 'with respect to the same' and thus can be coinstantiated by one and the same subject. Price accepts this characterization of the options, but claims that these two options are not exclusive and that in the apparent counterexamples 'Clearly Plato could have reversed the redescriptions, qualifying predicate instead of subject, and subject instead of predicate: the man moves in respect of his head and hands, but not of his legs and torso; it is not the axis, but the circumference of the top that moves.'[17]

But, to begin, the two descriptions cannot always be equivalent. Consider a case in which the same thing has complete contraries except that they are not at the same time. Here one description allows for the identity of a thing over time; the closest redescription would attribute the contraries to different temporal stages. But these are two different options. Nor is it plausible to think that Plato held that there is no truth of these matters independent of description. Plato shows no sign of thinking that the sort of reversal that Price endorses is possible and repeatedly affirms that there is one correct description of the alleged counterexamples (*Rep.* 436C9–D1,

436E1–2, 439B8–10). Plato rarely stresses terminological exactitude, but when he does so repeatedly, we should take the distinction seriously. Upon examination, we can see that in each of the two cases in the above quotation a reversal of the sort that Price recommends would be a mistake.

Let us first consider the more complicated case of a top. Price holds that it is equally satisfactory to say that the axis is standing still while the circumference moves. But this is not equally satisfactory.

(1) Plato describes the top case as one in which the same thing has incomplete contraries.

(2) The two-subjects analysis of the top case that Price gives does not capture all that Plato wants to say about the top.

(3) Price's two-subjects analysis does not remove the contradiction.

As we have seen, the Principle of Contraries will allow us to resolve apparent counterexamples either by showing that the contraries are not complete or that they are complete but belong to two different things. In the case of the man, Plato does not use the *kata* locution and finds two different subjects for motion and rest: hands and head/the rest of the body. This is to resolve the apparent counterexample by means of the latter strategy, that is, Option #2. Plato immediately proceeds to consider the second, more sophisticated counterexample of a spinning top. The qualification at *Rep.* 436D5 that it is 'as a whole' that a rotating top fixed on a point both moves and is at rest is significant. Plato has just disposed of the man counterexample by showing that different parts of the same thing are the proper subjects of the contraries. What a good counterexample should next try to find is a case that cannot be resolved in the same way. And this is, in fact, what we find; the counterexample claims that the *whole* top both remains at rest and moves. Here Plato does not use 'the one part'/'the other part' vocabulary he used above to resolve the conflict, rather he claims the top is at rest 'in respect of the straight line' and moves 'in respect of the circumference'.[18] This seems to be a straightforward instance of showing that the contraries are not in fact complete because they fail to be in respect of the same thing.[19] Because motion and rest are not 'in respect of' the same thing, the contraries are not complete and thus are coinstantiable. But Price holds that Plato here could reverse the description, that is, the conflict could be resolved by claiming that one part of the top moves while another part stands still, i.e. the circumference of the top moves while the axis stays at rest. This is the claim that is crucial to Price's and Woods' strategy of avoiding two different subjects for the contraries.

But Plato does not say this and there is good reason to reject this claim.

(1)   This interpretation does not say all that Plato wants to say. It is not true that the circumference of the top alone moves in a circle. All the concentric circles of the disk or sphere (or all the coaxial points in the sphere) are moving in a circle. This description is, however, still ambiguous. More precisely, all the coaxial points are moving in a circle around the axis. They are not revolving, that is, they are not moving in a circle around some fixed point off the sphere's axis.

(2) Nor is it true that only the axis is standing still. As long as the top does not incline with respect to its original axis (*Rep.* 436E3), either forward or backward or to the right or left (*Rep.* 436E4–6), the whole top is standing still: it continues to occupy the same space. The same is true of the concentric spheres or disks within the original sphere. If we choose to consider individual points within the sphere, every point remains in the original plane it lies in perpendicular to the axis. When the top inclines forwards or backwards or to the right or left, all such points will then move with respect to the original axis. Note that this is precisely the sort of motion that Plato emphasizes the top as a whole lacks. The top as a whole is no longer at rest in any way when the top inclines forwards/backwards or right/left.[20]

(3)   But Price's redescription strategy of analyzing spherical rotation in terms of some parts that are simply moving while others are simply at rest not only fails to say all that Plato wants to say. What is more important is that it fails to remove the attribution of motion and rest to the same thing and thus would be an unsatisfactory response to this more sophisticated counterexample. Consider, for example, a torus in a rotating sphere. The torus is both moving and at rest: it rotates around the axis of this sphere but does not move right/left, or forwards/backwards (or up/down) with respect to the axis. But since a torus does not contain an axis (Plato here considers physical objects as well as geometrical objects), we cannot say that its axis remains at rest. Similarly, for any point not on the axis, it is true that in the

case described it is both moving and at rest. It is moving around the top's axis while remaining in its original plane perpendicular to the axis. We cannot resolve this case by distinguishing further parts within the point some of which are moving while others are at rest. Only by recognizing different kinds of motion can we resolve the problem.

In the *Timaeus*, we see an elaboration of this basic idea (34A1–7, 40A2–B8, 43A6–B5). There Plato distinguishes six motions in addition to rotation. These are: movement forwards and backwards, to the right and left, upwards and downwards (*Tim.* 43B2–5). At 40A ff. Plato describes the motion of the fixed stars.

He [the Demiurge] bestowed two movements upon each of them [the fixed stars]. The first was rotation, an unvarying movement in the same place, by which the god would always think the same thoughts about the same things. The other was revolution, a forward motion under the dominance of the circular carrying movement of the Same and uniform. The gods are devoid of motion and stand still in respect of any of the other five motions [τὰς δὲ πέντε κινήσεις ἀκίνητον καὶ ἑστός], in order that each of them may come as close as possible to attaining perfection. (*Tim.* 40A7–B4)

Plato here explicitly describes the fixed stars as both moving and not in motion because they are rotating and not, e.g., moving up/down or right/left.

Nor in the case of the man is it, as Price suggests, equally satisfactory to say that he is moving 'in respect of' his head and hands. Just like the top, this is a case of spatial motion (*Rep.* 436C5–6). As we saw in the case of the top, the 'in respect of' qualification specifies the direction of motion, but this produces a straightforward falsehood here. It is not the case that the man, as a whole, is moving in the direction of his head and hands, while remaining still in the direction of his body. All that we have is a simple case in which the head and hands possess the property of moving, while the remainder of his body has the property of being at rest.

Woods' unease at Plato's description of the man case may, however, have another source. This may be the intuition that the head and hands are the wrong subjects of motion because there is a single subject, i.e. the man who is moving his hands and keeping the remainder of his body at rest. But this is to misconstrue the example. Nothing suggests that Plato is here concerned with the complex question of the causal origins of bodily movements (and episodes of causing to stay still). This would require some account of how the soul brings about motion or rest in the body and thus would focus on movement in a transitive sense and on the soul as the subject of action. But what Plato needs is a simple and obvious example to illustrate the Principle and he focuses on rest and intransitive motion in the body.[21] And if we consider spatial rest and motion, it is true that there are different subjects having the properties of rest and motion; denying this just gets wrong the facts about physical bodies and physical motion. Hands and heads are not, of course, the ultimate subjects of motion, since they, in turn, could be at rest and in motion at the same time. If there are any physical units for Plato, they lie far below the macroscopic level. But this complication is not relevant to Plato's purpose of giving a clear example to illustrate the strategy of removing the contradiction by finding different subjects of motion and of rest.

Having shown that there are these distinct two ways to avoid counter-examples to the Principle of Contraries, Plato restates the Principle (*Rep.* 436E8–437A2) and says that they will assume it without further argument (*Rep.* 437A3–10). He then offers an elaborate argument (*Rep.* 437B1–439B1) to show that thirst and the rejection of drink are contraries (*Rep.* 437B3–6, 437C8–10, cf. 439B5–6).

The crucial step of the argument occurs at *Rep.* 439A9 ff.

Passage B
The soul of one who is thirsty then, insofar as it thirsts, wishes nothing else than to drink, and yearns for this and its impulse is for this ... Then if anything draws it back when thirsty it must be something different [ἕτερον ἄν τι ἐν αὐτῇ] in it from that which thirsts and drives it like a beast to drink. For it cannot be, we say, that the same thing, at any rate, with the same part of itself at the same time acts in contrary ways about the same thing [οὐ γὰρ δή, φαμέν, τό γε αὐτὸ τῷ αὐτῷ ἑαυτοῦ περὶ τὸ αὐτὸ ἅμ' ἂν τἀναντία πράττοι]. (*Rep.* 439A9–B6)

Plato's language here picks up on his earlier contrasts in this section between a single subject and a plurality of subjects (*Rep.* 436A8–B6 and 436B8–C1). I have argued above that Plato links together the option of finding different forms in the soul and the option of finding plural subjects for complete contraries in the Principle of Contraries. The claim that what draws back from drinking must be 'something different' from that which desires to drink echoes the language of the head and hands/rest of body case and attributes the thirst to one subject and the rejection to another. (Note that this phrase echoes the resolution in the head/hands case; cf. *Rep.* 439B3–4 with 436D1.) One might suggest that Plato leaves us some more room than this, since the closing sentence in the above quotation does not express the 'in respect of' qualification. Perhaps Plato here suggests that in the case of thirst and its rejection, the same thing is not acting 'with the same part of itself' and by this means that the contrary activities are not 'in respect of' the same thing so that, after all, one and the same thing can thirst or desire drink and reject it. There are several reasons to reject such a suggestion.

(1) We have seen that Plato in this passage construes doing F with X as a case in which X is the ultimate subject of F.[22] So to hold that the soul thirsts with the Appetitive part is to hold that the Appetitive part is the proper subject of the thirst.

(2) In this passage, Plato never uses the 'in respect of' qualification to describe the case of thirst and its rejection: he never says that the soul thirsts 'in respect of' the Appetitive part, but rejects the drink 'in respect of' the Reasoning part. What he does do in Passage B and the passages that follow is distinguish different subjects for the contrary desires.

(3) But even if we were to think that Plato would accept that the soul thirsts 'in respect of' the Appetitive part and rejects 'in respect of' the Reasoning part, this would not affect the question of what the ultimate subject of the desires is. As long as the claim that the soul F's 'in respect of' one part of the soul is intended to attribute one of the contraries to that part, it is still the case that the parts are the ultimate subjects of the contraries.

Plato proceeds to try to make his meaning clearer with an example. 'Just as, I suppose, it is not well said of the archer that his hands at the same time push away the bow and draw it near, but we should say that there is one hand [ἄλλη μὲν] that pushes it away and another [ἑτέρα δὲ] that draws it to' (*Rep.* 439D8–11).[23] This case is supposed to be 'just like' (ὥσπερ γε, *Rep.* 439B8) that of thirst and is clearly intended to remind us of the earlier example of the man whose head and hands are moving, while the rest of his body stays still

(*Rep.* 436C9–D3). There as well as here, Plato stresses that there is a right thing to say about such cases and that it is that there are two subjects for the contraries. Here, too, Plato is seeking a simple case in which the right answer is obvious and he goes back to cases of physical bodies and spatial motion. The apparent conflict is that one and the same thing—'the hands' (*Rep.* 439B9)—are at the same time pushing away and drawing towards. The resolution is to treat these as complete contraries and apportion each to its own proper subject.[24] The fact that there is a single causal origin, i.e. the soul, for each of the motions does not undermine the fact that we must posit different subjects for the opposed spatial motions.[25] Nor should we be bothered by the fact that the archer's hands are not ultimate subjects, since they could be decomposed by similar examples. It is enough for Plato's purposes that further analysis would take the same strategy of finding distinct subjects for (potentially) opposed motions.[26]

If we instead try to resolve the contradiction by seeing the archer as the ultimate subject of the properties of pushing one part of himself outward and drawing in another part, an unattractive picture of agency results. The parallel in the case of the soul would be that an ultimate subject over and above the parts of the soul sets one part in motion toward and another in motion away from the same object. The soul as the ultimate subject thus brings it about that one part desires drink while another part rejects it. But it is at best very difficult to give sense to the idea that there is a further ultimate subject above and beyond all three parts.[27] Nor is it clear that the two contraries 'bringing it about that the Appetitive part desires drink' and 'bringing it about that the Reasoning part rejects drink' are really coinstantiable by a single subject.

At *Rep.* 439B3–5 in Passage B, Plato asserted the conditional that if we find both thirst and a drawing back from thirst in the soul, then that which draws back must be something different from that which thirsts. He proceeds to establish that there is something that opposes thirst in the specified way.

> Would we assert that sometimes there are thirsty people who do not wish to drink?
> Certainly, it happens often to many different people.
> What, then, should one say about them? Is it not that there is a something in the

soul that bids them drink and a something that forbids, a different something [ἄλλο ὄν] that masters that which bids?

I think so.

Does not that which forbids in such cases come into play—if it comes into play at all—as a result of calculation, while what draws and drags them to drink is a result of affections and diseases?

Apparently.

Hence it is not unreasonable for us to claim that they are two, and different from one another [αὐτὰ διττά τε καὶ ἕτερα ἀλλήλων]. We shall name that in the soul with which it calculates [τὸ μὲν ᾧ λογίζεται] the reasoning [part] and that with which it loves [τὸ δὲ ᾧ ἐρᾷ], hungers, thirsts, and gets excited by other desires, the irrational and appetitive [part] . . .[28]   (*Rep.* 439C2–D8)

Here Plato claims that there are such cases and applies the archer paradigm.[29] (All that Plato needs to show is that such cases are *possible*, but showing their actual existence is the most convincing way to establish their possibility.) The contraries are conceived of as conflicting imperatives each of which is attributed to a different subject. This allows him at last to answer the original question posed in Passage A: the different psychic activities of learning and bodily desires are done with different *eidē* of the soul and the different *eidē* are the ultimate subjects of their respective activities.[30] Plato then proceeds to give a less elaborate argument for the separation of the Spirited part of the soul from both the Appetitive and Reasoning parts (*Rep.* 439E3–441C7).

3.3 *Akrasia in the* Republic

In this section, I shall fill out the *Republic*'s theory of akrasia and show how it can be defended against one important attempt to show that it falls prey to a straightforward confusion. Better appreciating the strengths of this theory will let us see more clearly its genuine weaknesses, which I turn to in the next section. Plato's argument in Book 4 that establishes the existence of the three parts of the soul is not enough to provide a full characterization of them. But one important further claim that he makes in Book 4 is that the Reasoning part is the part that makes judgments about what is good for the whole soul (*Rep.* 442C7–8). Thus it is the Reasoning part that has an overall judgment about what is best for the whole soul as well as a corresponding desire for what is best. On the *Republic's* account, in every case of akratic conflict, whether or not it issues in akratic action, an essential part of what is going on in the person is a conflict between the desire of the Reasoning part for what is overall best and a desire of at least one of the other two parts of the soul. As the example of a thirsty man in Book 4 shows, Plato intends these desires to be the sort of contraries that fall under the Principle of Contraries and he offers at least two ways of describing desiring, wanting, and wishing so as to make their inclusion plausible. (I shall simply speak of desiring from here on.[31])

Would you not set down all such things as contraries to one another: assent to dissent, striving to take something to rejecting it, drawing something in to thrusting it away, whether they are actions or affections? That will not make any difference . . . What about being thirsty and hungry and generally the desires [τὰς ἐπιθυμίας], and further, wishing and wanting [τὸ ἐθέλειν καὶ τὸ βούλεσθαι]? Would you not set all these somewhere in the classes just mentioned? For example, will you not say that the soul of a man who desires either strives for what it desires or draws toward itself that which it wants to become its own; or again, that, insofar as the soul wishes that something be supplied to it, it nods assent to itself as if answering a question and reaches out toward its attainment?

I shall.

What of not-wanting, and not-wishing, and not-desiring [τὸ ἀβουλεῖν καὶ μὴ ἐθέλειν μηδ’ ἐπιθυμεῖν], shall we not class these with the soul's thrusting away from itself and driving away from itself and generally with all the contraries of the former?

Of course.   (*Rep.* 437B1–D1)

Plato here distinguishes assent/dissent and drawing in/pushing away as two distinct pairs of opposites. This first characterization of desiring as a form of interior assent allows Plato to redescribe the opposition between desiring and not-desiring in terms of the logical and psychological opposition between assent and dissent.[32] The second description characterizes conflicting desires as forces acting in opposite directions. The possible object of desire is conceived of as either being drawn in or pushed away. A second passage, quoted above, fills out these descriptions. In the case of thirsty people who do not wish to drink 'there is a something in the soul that bids them drink [τὸ κελεῦον] and a something that forbids [τὸ κωλῦον], a different something that masters [κρατοῦν] that which bids' (*Rep.* 439c5–7). Here the description in terms of opposed forces is given a more precise form. No longer is the object of desire the recipient of the force applied; rather the soul, or more accurately, one part of the soul, is seen as moving toward the object, while the other part drags the soul back.

These two different ways of describing desires suggest two aspects of all desires and these, in turn, suggest two ways in which akratic conflict can be resolved. To begin with, assent and command are both linguistic notions. Plato presents desires not as blind forces that lack any sort of representation of their object, but rather as involving some linguistic and non-pictorial representation of their objects. And even in its most primitive manifestation, a desire involves some conceptualization of its object. Since desires have conceptual or propositional content they can enter into interactions with other psychic items in virtue of their own content. (We can think of this as a type of rational interaction. As an illustration, compare the way in which, in normal cases, the desire to drink a Coke and the belief that the Coke machine I am standing in front of charges $1 produce a desire to put $1 in the machine and the way in which Ella Fitzgerald's singing 'I get a kick out of you' interacts with a glass to produce a shattering of the glass.)

Since *all* desires are forms of assent or command, such a command is not essentially the outcome of practical reasoning (or even of a default process that takes desires as input). The notion of a command does not pick out an intention or a decision as opposed to an ordinary desire; the command is essential to any desire as such, since it expresses the idea that the desire prompts to action. (Plato treats desires—perhaps in conjunction with the appropriate beliefs—as capable, at least on some occasions, of initiating action without the generation of another psychic item and without belonging to or being endorsed by the Reasoning part.) Similarly, we should not attribute very sophisticated content to the assent as such: at a minimum, it might involve only something of the form 'Do X!' or 'Take X!', rather than, e.g., 'Do X because it is good or best!' (*Rep.* 437c4–6, cf. 439c5–6, suggests something imperatival.) But there are desires with richer content and the fact that desires have content leaves open the possibility that they can change in the light of new information and that the desires of one part could change in response to communication with another part.

Plato's conception of desire also involves the idea that a desire has a certain force or strength. The strength of a desire is distinct from the desire's content and is a non-representational property. A desire pulls the agent to act in virtue of its strength and thus, as a first approximation, we can think of the strength of a desire as its capacity to bring about action.[33] Indeed as the example of thirst suggests, Plato seems to think that a desire can bring action about without necessarily involving deliberation, reflective endorsement, decision, or choice.

A final important point to note is that since the strength of a desire or its causal power to bring about action is distinct from the content of that desire, the strength of a desire is a non-rational determinant of what the person does. When a person acts on a desire what seems to bring about the action is the strength of the desire, not her belief as the belief with the content it has or her desire as a desire for a particular sort of object. Intuitively, this seems to be a different sort of explanation than we normally give in cases of action issuing from practical deliberation. There we might say that Mary considers her options, reflects on their merits, decides to do A, and then tries to bring A about. Plato does not, however, try here to work out a full metaphysics of agency. To do so, we would, for example, need to consider the metaphysical commitments of our ordinary explanatory practices: do they, for instance, commit us to some form of agent-causation and is such a commitment desirable or even coherent?[34] Moreover, we can find a broader sense in which causation by the strength of a desire can be, at least indirectly, a form of rational causation, that is, a form of causation in which the content of the desire has a causal role. Compare the case of desire and action to the following case. Ella Fitzgerald's singing a phrase of a song may shatter a glass, but the meaning of the words she sings are simply irrelevant to this effect. The effect of her utterance on the glass would be the same even if the sounds produced meant something else or nothing at all.[35] Here something with content (the sung phrase) can be causally efficacious without its possessing that content or without its meaning being at all relevant to its causal powers. The causal effect of the sound co-occurs with a sound having a certain meaning, but the causal effects are not in any way dependent on the sound's having the meaning it does. The relation between a desire's strength and its content may, however, be tighter than this. Its strength may be, at least in part, dependent on its particular content. But as we shall shortly see, the possibility of mis-alignment between a desire's content and its strength is crucial to Plato's explanation of the possibility of akrasia.

The representation of a desire as a command registers both that desire's link to action and its having a content. Desires, by their very nature, press for fulfillment or satisfaction. Less figuratively, the notion of a command involves the idea of an intimate link to action at least to the extent that having the desire that p by itself, *ceteris paribus*, disposes its possessor to try to bring about p. This is why the desire that p, unlike belief that p, can persist in the face of realization that not-p. (This is a fact about the relation between a desire and the subject of this desire: the mere recognition that one part has a desire does not automatically dispose the other parts to try to bring it about.) Commands, also by their very nature, are part of a process of communication and invite examination of their grounds.[36]

These two aspects of desires, the linguistic and the causal, suggest two fac-tors that are relevant to what happens and thus are relevant to the resolution of akratic conflict: the content of the desire and the force of the desire.

Thirsty Man Many philosophers have thought that the motivational strength of a desire plays an important role in the explanation of akrasia. Let us compare Plato's account of akratic action to the following non-Platonic account. A person is confronted with two courses of action, X and Y. She believes that action X is her best option overall and, in particular, that it is better overall than action Y and believes that she can do either X or Y, but not both. Nevertheless, the person's desire to do Y is stronger than her desire to do X. Thus if the person acts, she will do (or try to do) Y. And the sim-plest way to reach the conclusion that the person will try to do Y is to accept the general claim that if a person tries to do anything at a given time, she will try to do whatever she most strongly desires to do.[37] How close is this account to the one that Plato offers?

We can distinguish in Plato's account of the thirsty man, on the one hand, the overall judgment that it is best not to drink and the corresponding desire not to drink, and, on the other hand, the desire to drink. Since what forbids comes to be from calculation and calculation is concerned with what is better and worse for the whole soul (*Rep.* 439C9–D1, 442C5–8), we may take this as a judgment of what is overall best for the whole soul. Plato does not explicitly say that a desire for what the agent believes to be overall best is also at work here, but it is reasonable to infer that it is, since Plato holds that all people do desire what they believe to be overall best for themselves (*Rep.* 413A4–5, 505D5–E8). The two desires are tugs or pulls on the agent which can be stronger or weaker; thus Plato accepts the idea that desires can vary in strength.[38] Plato does not systematically investigate the notion of the strength of a desire here, but it is introduced as a kind of pulling and pushing, that is, as an instance of the sort of forces that are found in physical objects. What psychic pulling and pushing share with physical pulling and pushing is something like efficient causality.[39] Desires pull their possessors towards certain actions (e.g. *Rep.* 439B3–5); less metaphorically, the strength of a desire is its capacity to bring it about that the agent acts in a particular way (or is, perhaps, what grounds such a capacity).

Plato's example also encourages us to think that what the person does is determined by the strength of the opposing pulls: the person will act on whatever desire pulls most strongly.[40] His description suggests that as long as a desire for drink persists, the only way that the person can reject the drink is if the strength of his desire not to drink is greater (*Rep.* 439A9–B5). And as the example of the thirsty man shows, the strength of a desire can come apart from the person's judgment of the goodness of the desire's object. Even if rejecting the drink is thought to be better than drinking, it seems that the attempt to pull back from drinking is not always successful (as the desire for what is overall best is defeated in the case of Leontius, *Rep.* 439E–440A).

But there is an important difference between these accounts. The non-Platonic explanation just sketched invokes the idea of the strength of a desire, but it is a crucial part of its explanation of akratic action that the same subject can both believe that X is better overall than Y, but still desire more strongly to do Y. The causal power of a desire and the agent's ranking of the goodness of the desire's object are distinct features of a desire and they can, in some cases, come apart. The Platonic account, on the other hand, explains akratic action by positing that one agent-like part believes that X is better overall than Y and thus desires to do X while a different agent-like part desires to do Y, along with the fact that the desire for Y is stronger than the desire for X. Akratic action is possible because of the fact that the strength of the Appetitive part's desire is distinct from, and is not always directly proportional to, the Reasoning part's judgment of the goodness of the desire's object.

This difference between the non-Platonic account and the *Republic*'s account suggests one straightforward but quite powerful objection to Plato's strategy. Does the partitioning of the soul have genuine explanatory value on Plato's account? We might think that the following argument shows that it does not. The first step in explaining the possibility of akratic action is to distinguish between the strength of a desire (its power to bring about an action) and the judgment of the object of that desire in terms of overall goodness. This distinction is not yet sufficient to show that akratic action is possible, since, for example, it might be the case that one's desire for the object judged overall best is always stronger than any other desire. The second crucial step is to show that these two properties can come apart so that one's strongest desire can be for something other than what one judges best.[41] But this is all that we need to explain akratic action. The misalignment between strength and evaluation is why akratic action occurs: it is because the causally stronger desire can have as its object something not ranked best overall that akratic action can occur. The placement of the akratic desire and the desire for what is overall best in different parts is explanatorily idle, since there is no further work left for it to do.

If successful, this would be an extremely damaging criticism, since partitioning, as we shall see in more detail in Section 3.4, has high costs. If partitioning is not needed to explain the occurrence of akratic action, then its costs are not counterbalanced by any benefits. Yet since we have seen that the explanation of akratic action is not the only purpose of partitioning, this is not a decisive objection. Even if Plato is wrong to think that partitioning is necessary to explain akratic action, he may have other good reasons to adopt it. But Plato has a stronger reply and can, in fact, defend the explanatory value of *Republic*-style partitioning. Once we allow that there are two desires with misaligned force and evaluation, then we need nothing further to explain how such desires can issue in akratic action.[42] Their location is not a further fact needed to explain how the misalignment issues in akratic action. But this does not show that partitioning is explanatorily idle. The above objection rests on the assumption that such misalignment is possible. But Plato might think that such misalignment between strength and evaluation may only be possible if these two desires are in different parts. In particular, the partitioning may explain the origin or the persistence of the akratic desire itself or of the fact that it is stronger than the desire for what is overall best. We can only see whether the partitioning is explanatorily relevant by finding out more about the nature of the parts and of the relations among them.

Communication and Persuasion   Competition between desires in terms of strength is not the only way in which akratic conflicts can be resolved. As we have seen, the desires of each part of the soul have linguistic content and each part also has beliefs. The parts can communicate and such communication can affect the parts' desires. We find several examples of such communication in the *Republic*. As we saw above, it is built into Plato's account of courage and moderation (*Rep.* 442B11–D1). Second, in Book 8, Socrates criticizes the oligarchic man, in comparison with the philosopher, for failing to attain 'the true virtue of a soul that is of one mind [ὁμονοητικῆς] and harmonious' (*Rep.* 554E4–5). In the oligarchic man's public dealings 'where he enjoys the reputation of being just, his better part keeps down his other evil desires by force [βίᾳ]—not persuading them that it is not better [ὅτι οὐκ ἄμεινον] [sc. that they be satisfied], nor making them gentle by reasoning [λόγῳ] with them—but by compulsion and fear [ἀνάγκη καὶ φόβῳ]' (*Rep.* 554C11–D3).[43] In the case of the virtuous person, that is, the philosopher, Plato is more concerned with the long-term education or training by the Reasoning part of the lower parts of the soul than with its attempt to avoid a particular instance of akrasia by altering, by means of persuasion, the akratic desires (or the strength of these desires) of the lower parts. But nothing rules out such interventions and Plato accepts that they occur (e.g. *Rep.* 441B–C). Nor does the possibility of such persuasion threaten the idea that the person always acts on his strongest desire. Even if, prior to persuasion, the Appetitive part's desire to drink is stronger than the Reasoning part's desire to refrain, we might hold that the persuasion of the

Appetitive part by the Reasoning part affects the strength of the former's desires so that after persuasion, the Appetitive part's strongest desire is not to drink. (Although if the Appetitive part retains its desire to drink, there may be a problem about the further division of this part.)

But when the Reasoning part persuades the Appetitive part, exactly what happens? Consider the case of the oligarchic man. For this criticism to have a point, Plato must think that the philosopher can persuade his Appetitive part by communication, by means of *logoi*, that it is better for it to go along with reason. The Reasoning part does not merely suppress the worse desires or somehow block them from bringing about an action; the effect of the Reasoning part's communication on the Appetitive part is not simply causal. This persuasion is a form of rational interaction: the Reasoning part's communications interact with the Appetitive part's desires because of the content that the communications and desires have. We have already seen that the desires of each part are conceptualized and propositional; they are not, for example, non-representational Humean desires. So if the Reasoning part's communications are to interact rationally with the desires of the lower two parts, this requires, as a first approximation, that these communications must have at least some conceptual overlap with the concepts in which the lower parts' judgments are framed. The lower parts must be able to recognize the terms in which they are addressed. (This is only a first approximation, since successful communication may require only a weak sort of 'recognition' that falls short of conceptual overlap.)[44]

In the case of the oligarchic man, the Appetitive part initially wants to satisfy certain desires, but is persuaded by the Reasoning part that, in light of other considerations, e.g., the long-run consequences of drinking, it is better not to do so. Thus the sort of judgment that the Appetitive part ends up making here is a comparative judgment of goodness. The Appetitive part seems capable of judging of what is best for itself, taking more than one consideration into account, even if it cannot judge of what is overall best for the whole soul (*Rep.* 442C5–8).[45] The idea that both of the lower parts are capable of making judgments about their own good explains why the lower parts are friends to the Reasoning part and why they agree that it should rule (*Rep.* 589A6–B6, 590C8–D6, 612B2–4). The lower parts believe the Reasoning part ought to rule because they realize that the Reasoning part's rule is in their long-run best interest and their friendship with the Reasoning part requires the belief that the Reasoning part seeks their good. The lower parts may not be able to take all relevant considerations into account and will not be as good as the Reasoning part at calculating long-run consequences, but they are capable of weighing costs and benefits. And there are other passages in the *Republic* that also suggest that the lower parts are capable of making judgments about their long-run good.[46]

Despite this evidence, we might still worry whether the lower parts have the conceptual resources necessary for doing this. As we have seen, Plato attributes some beliefs to them, so the objection should not be that they cannot form beliefs at all. Even the Appetitive part is capable, according to Plato, of means–end reasoning.

[W]e called it the Appetitive part because of the intensity of its appetites concerned with food and drink and sex and their accompaniments, and likewise the money-loving part, because money is the chief instrument for the gratification of such desires . . . And if we should also say that its pleasure and love is of gain . . . [would we not be right] in calling it the money-loving and the gain-loving part? (*Rep.* 580E2–581A7)[47]

It is because it calculates that money is an effective means to satisfying its desires that the Appetitive part desires money. But can the lower parts form beliefs about their overall good? Plato does indicate that the lower parts have certain cognitive limitations: they cannot come to know and contemplate the Forms and they do not care about the good of the soul as a whole.[48] But neither of these two limitations suggests that the lower parts cannot form beliefs about their own good. The most important passage occurs in Book 9 (*Rep.* 580D–581C, quoted above) where Plato correlates the different parts of the soul with different objects of pursuit and claims that the ultimate end of an individual is determined by the part of the soul that rules in him.[49]

According to this passage, each part of the soul takes a particular object as its end. In light of this end, each part develops subsidiary ends: the Appetitive part desires money as a means to the satisfaction of its desires and it desires more rather than less money. The Appetitive part's desires are divided into 'necessary' and 'unnecessary' desires and at least many of its necessary desires are aimed at its long-run benefit.[50] The Spirited part can delay the satisfaction of its desires and accept short-run evils for the sake of its long-run interest. Given their ability to form long-run conceptions of their interests, take various considerations into account, and engage in means–end reasoning, the lower parts have the notion of an ultimate end of action. Their other desires are (more or less) regulated by their conception of their ultimate end. Such regulation is possible even if the lower parts do not form a conception of the good of the whole soul; they may fail to be consistently impartial with respect to time and will, at least sometimes, fail to take into account all the considerations they themselves think relevant.[51] But this cluster of abilities makes it reasonable for Plato to describe them as he does: they have some conception of their overall good insofar as they can form a conception of some ultimate end, take various considerations into account, and regulate, at least to some extent, their other desires in light of such an end.

There is one other important feature of the Book 9 passage. There are at least two ways in which one might characterize mental partitions. One way we can describe as functional. Here different partitions are defined by the failure of mental items to interact in rational ways. The belief that drinking is not best and the desire not to drink do not interact in a rational way with the desire to drink, since this latter desire does not cease to prompt to action. Given this failure, we assign these items to two different parts. Since the parts are defined in terms of a failure of rational interaction, their different location cannot *explain* their failure to interact rationally. A second way of characterizing mental partitions offers an independent criterion of identity for the parts and thus can allow the placement of different items in different parts to explain their failure to interact appropriately. The Book 9 account is of the latter sort. Each part has a nature that accounts for the content of its desires; the location within a part explains why the items interact (more or less) appropriately with each other, but not across parts.[52]

Explanatory Value of Partitioning   We can now return to our earlier concern about the explanatory value of the *Republic*'s partitioning. We considered the objection that the possibility of a misalignment between the force or strength of a desire and the evaluative ranking of the object of that desire was sufficient to explain akratic action. The objection holds that since the possibility of misalignment is sufficient, the placement of the conflicting desires in different parts of the soul does no explanatory work. We can now see how Plato can respond to this objection by arguing that it misconstrues the explanandum of the partitioning theory. In the case of thirst, once the Appetitive part's desire to drink is stronger than the Reasoning part's desire to do what is best overall, i.e. not drink, then the fact that the Appetitive part's desire to drink is stronger does suffice to explain why the person acts akratically. But this is not all that requires explanation. Although the strength of the thirst explains the agent's action, we can still ask for an explanation of the origin of this desire and for an explanation of why it persists and prompts to action even in light of the judgment that it is better not to drink. Plato can reasonably hold that both of these facts are to be explained by the nature of the part that desires drink and by facts about how this part interacts with other parts.

Consider the point about persistence first. The Reasoning part's desire not to drink because it is not best overall to do so, does not by itself destroy or reduce the strength of the Appetitive part's desire to drink. Only because of some further persuasion of the Appetitive part does such a change come about. (Or perhaps by the Reasoning part acting directly to suppress the Appetitive part's desire, if this is possible.) On the other hand, beliefs and desires within any one part, e.g., the Appetitive part, do tend to interact in more or less rational ways. Once the Appetitive part, for example, realizes that money is instrumental to the satisfaction of its long-run goals, it forms a desire for money. And at least in the oligarchic person, the awareness that drinking will interfere with the long-run satisfaction of bodily desires leads to the loss (or diminishment of the strength) of the desire for drink. The location of beliefs and desires helps explain the sorts of interactions they can enter into. In particular, their attribution to different subjects or to the same subject explains their interactions.[53]

The location of these beliefs and desires in different parts of the soul can only explain their failure to interact rationally if there is an independent criterion for the identity of the parts. But Plato has the resources to offer such an account and partitioning helps to explain the characteristic origins of human desires. It is a prominent fact of our psychological life, Plato has come to think by the time of the *Republic*, that we find ourselves with desires for bodily satisfactions and self-assertion that do not stem from the operations of reason. We can explain why this is the case by seeing these desires as originating in subjects that have characteristic goals, including beliefs about the good or about ultimate ends. Particular desires for these things are explained by the overall goals of the lower parts. We may also be able to provide a further account about how some more basic features of the parts explain their characteristic ends. Plato does not try to work out such an explanation fully in the *Republic*. But we can see one central way in which the features of the parts shape their ends.[54] The epistemic limitations of the lower parts crucially limit the nature of their ultimate ends. Neither of the lower parts can be aware of Forms, so they do not value their contemplation and they cannot desire anything the conception of which requires some grasp of a Form.[55]

Once Plato attributes such ends to the parts of the soul the Principle of Contraries will apply so that we need to postulate two distinct subjects as the havers of the potentially incompatible beliefs. To show that the person is a compound all that Plato needs to show is that it is possible that there is such conflict and it is possible that the Reasoning part will disagree with the Spirited part over whether certain pleasures are good for the Spirited part and with the Appetitive part over whether the satisfaction of certain bodily pleasures is good for it. (The incompatible beliefs need not include the term 'good'. A similar problem arises if they hold incompatible beliefs about what is pleasant or simply about what is to be pursued.) Once we allow that incompatible beliefs are involved, the case for partitioning is stronger, since it does seem impossible that a single subject should consciously believe an explicit contradiction. The *Republic's* partitioning theory is not the only way to explain akratic action or conflicting desires and in the second half of this chapter I shall argue that the *Laws'* theory is superior. Nevertheless, the *Republic's* theory does have explanatory value and is not so easily refuted.

3.4 *Problems with the* Republic's *Account of Akrasia*

The *Republic's* theory is subtle and powerful and can avoid an important line of objection. It is, however, subject to great difficulties.

The Regress Problem   As we have seen, it is sometimes thought that all psychological theories positing homunculi are subject to regress objections. But as we also saw, this is a mistake and at least some theories can accept homunculi without such problems. Nevertheless, the *Republic's* partitioning theory is vulnerable to a specific form of the regress objection. Full examination of this criticism will be somewhat complicated, so let us begin with a quick sketch of the objection's reasoning. If conflict of desires is sufficient for partitioning the soul, why can there not be a conflict of desires within one part that forces us to subdivide that part? The *Republic's* theory allows the lower parts to have beliefs about and desires for their own ultimate ends. Why might it not be the case that sometimes one part has a desire for one course of action that best realizes its ultimate end and a persisting desire for something else? If this is possible, we shall have something like akrasia occurring within one of the parts and the Principle of Contraries will license further subdivision. To determine whether such a case is possible, we must consider more carefully what sorts of conflict license the application of the Principle of Contraries. This is made more difficult by the fact that it is not clear exactly what sorts of conflict fall under the Principle. There is an extensive literature on this issue, but I shall consider here one of the most recent and perhaps the most philosophically sophisticated and ingenious attempt to show that the Principle of Contraries can be interpreted so as to block such objections.

In *Plato's Ethics*, Terence Irwin considers this sort of regress objection brought against the Spirited part of the soul. Irwin agrees that Plato's attribution of beliefs and desires to the parts of the soul is not merely metaphorical. Since the parts of the soul can have beliefs and desires, we must consider whether we can find within them the sorts of conflicts that license the application of the Principle of Contraries. To do this, we need a more determinate account of how the Principle applies to the conflict of desires than we find in Plato's text. Intuitively, what is required is that one opposing desire oppose acting on the other opposed desire 'as such'. This, Irwin rightly thinks, requires more than that (i) the two desires are contingently non-co-satisfiable, or (ii) the one desire is an aversion to the object of the other desire, or (iii) the one desire is an aversion to the second desire itself. What is required is that the opposing desire employ, in the right way, the notion of the good. Irwin holds that the following are the three sorts of contrariety that license the application of the Principle of Contraries.

#1. Desire for what is best overall for the agent vs. desire which does not aim at any form of the good.

#2. Desire for what is best overall for the agent vs. desire for what is good for the agent.

#3. Desire for what is good for the agent vs. desire which does not aim at any form of the good.

This account is intended to establish the distinctions among the three parts that Plato finds and to rule out the possibility of conflict *within* any of these parts. #1 establishes the distinction between the Reasoning part and the Appetitive part, #2 between the Reasoning part and the Spirited part, and #3 between the Spirited part and the Appetitive part. Let us consider, in the case of the Spirited part, whether this account avoids the regress noted above.

According to Irwin, the Spirited part's desires rest 'on some belief about the goodness or badness of its object, apart from the fact that it is simply an object of desire'; the Spirited part values objects 'in the belief that [they have] some further property that deserves to be valued'.[56] The 'spirited part *conceives of its objects* as good for the agent without conceiving of them as best, all things considered, for the agent'.[57] This restriction is crucial to Irwin's argument. If the Spirited part had desires for what is best overall for the agent and not just desires for what is good for the agent, then there could be conflict within the Spirited part licensing the Principle of Contraries if the Spirited part also had persisting, incompatible desires for what is good for the agent (that is, there could be a type-#2 conflict). Does Irwin give us sufficient reason to think that the Spirited part cannot make judgments of what is overall best?

Since Irwin grants to the Spirited part the concept of 'good for the agent', the objection must concern the notion of being 'best overall for the agent'. But we should allow that the Spirited part can distinguish its short-run from its long-run good and prefer the latter as such (Irwin agrees that the more primitive Appetitive part can prefer, as such, its long-run to its short-run satisfaction).[58] Nor, I think, would Irwin deny that the Spirited part can take more than one consideration into account or make various comparative judgments of goodness (e.g., *ceteris paribus*, doing two equally honorable things is better than doing one). Irwin's point is, rather, that the Spirited part does not form a judgment about what is best for the whole agent composed of the three parts of the soul.[59]

But while it is true that the Spirited part does not form such a judgment, this fact does not undermine its claim to judge of what is best overall *for itself*, that is, to form a judgement of what is best for itself taking into account all things it can consider or thinks it relevant to consider. Indeed, Irwin's claim that the Spirited part desires (i) what is good for *the agent*, but not (ii) what is best overall for *the agent* seems to involve an equivocation. If 'agent' in (i) and (ii) denotes the whole soul, then it is just false that the Spirited part desires even what is good for the agent. On Irwin's account, the Spirited part has 'no conception of itself as a part of a whole'.[60] Thus it will not desire things on behalf of the larger whole. But this does not undermine the Spirited part's claim to conceive of *itself* as a temporally extended entity and to desire the good on its own behalf, make comparative judgments, and so on. But if the Spirited part can judge of what is best overall for itself, if it does not do so explicitly in terms of the strength of its desires and it has desires which are not automatically responsive to its overall judgments, then it seems liable to one of the sorts of contrariety which licenses the Principle of Contraries. And it is one of the most characteristic features of the Spirited part that it is subject to desires and emotions which are good-dependent, but are not fully responsive to rational judgments. Since Irwin allows the Spirited part to have an interest in virtue and honor, as well as angry impulses, there are many opportunities for such conflict. The Spirited part may find it more honorable not to act on an angry impulse (e.g. it is more honorable to ignore small slights from inferiors), but why must its angry impulse always be perfectly responsive to this judgment? Irwin's account does not provide sufficient reason to think that such conflicts are impossible within the Spirited part and thus to think that it is immune from conflict which breaks it down further.[61]

A similar argument can be given for the possibility of conflict within the Appetitive part. As we have seen, the Appetitive part has a conception of its ultimate end, that is, of its long-run satisfaction. But it also has many particular desires for, e.g., food, sex, and drink. So if the Appetitive part has a desire for what is overall best for itself, it seems that this desire can come into conflict with its other desires in several ways. Plato's description in Book 4 (*Rep.* 437D2–439B1) of at least some of the desires of the Appetitive part, e.g., those for food and drink, may suggest that these desires are not directed at the good of the whole individual, nor at the good of the Appetitive part, nor are they derived from such desires.[62] If so, what guarantees that such desires will not come into conflict with the Appetitive part's desire for its overall best? While this account of the desires for food and drink does not by itself rule out the possibility that these desires disappear or diminish in strength once an appropriate judgment is made by the Appetitive part, it does make it difficult to see why this should happen. Such conflict also seems possible if we allow some of the desires of the Appetitive part to aim at pleasure or at something conceived of as good rather than overall best. But even if we think that the Appetitive part does not have desires for what is overall best but does have desires for what is good for itself, these seem able to come into the appropriate sort of conflict with either desires for the pleasant or with those simply for food and drink.

Even if this shows that Irwin's account does not prevent the subdivision of the lower parts, it does not, of course, show that it is impossible to avoid such subdivision. We might, for example, try to avoid the possibility of akratic conflict within the lower parts by excluding them from having one or the other type of conflicting desires. First, we could hold that each of the lower parts can avoid akratic conflict within itself by preventing the formation of desires that prompt to akratic action. But this leaves it quite puzzling how the lower parts manage such prevention given the nature of the contrary desires, and Plato's description of the persuasion of the Appetitive part shows that this persuasion goes on while the Appetitive part still has akratic desires. We might, instead, hold that each of the lower parts is such that (1) its desire for what is overall best for itself is always its strongest desire, or (2) it can act in accordance with its own desire for what is overall best for itself even if this is not its strongest desire. But both of these seem to be *ad hoc* expedients. (1) seems hard to reconcile with Plato's emphasis on the unruliness of the lower parts. (2) requires an exception to the rule that the strongest desire always wins, and if we allow that the lower parts are capable of overriding their strongest desire, why cannot the Reasoning part always override stronger desires in the other parts?

But even if we were to accept (1) or (2), this is not sufficient to prevent the subdivision of the lower parts. (1) or (2) might guarantee that in each part the desire for what is best for it always wins out, but this does not show that akratic conflict within the parts is not possible. After all, in the case of thirst that establishes the division of the soul, all that Plato requires is persistent opposition between the desire for the best and some other desire. The desires are assigned to different parts even if the appetitive desire to drink never actually wins out. And Plato's description of the lower parts does not suggest that each lower part is by nature perfectly continent, i.e. such that once a desire for what is best overall is formed, all other desires cease to prompt to action.[63]

The above strategies attempt to avoid akratic conflict by guaranteeing that within each part nothing opposes in an inappropriate way that part's desire for its own ultimate end or long-run satisfaction. We might try the alternative strategy of removing from the lower parts the other potentially conflicting item, that is, the desire for and belief about its ultimate end. We have seen that the *Republic* does attribute such capacities to the parts of the soul. But even if Plato makes such a claim, we might think that it is an inessential aspect of the partitioning theory and that we could save the basic structure of his view by dropping this claim. But Plato has good reason for not making this move. First, suppose that we allow the lower parts only to have desires that are like thirst as it is presented in Book 4. On this view, none of the desires in the lower parts would be for objects conceived of as good. As thirst is just a desire for drink, not for good or pleasant drink, so all the desires of the lower parts would be for particular objects that are not characterized as good or pleasant. Thus the lower parts will lack the desires for long-run satisfaction or overall good that are essential to akratic conflict. But such a view avoids possible subdivision at too high a cost.[64] It cannot account for some of the desires and judgments that Plato wants to count as non-rational motivations and thus attribute to the lower parts. At least some of the desires of the Spirited part, such as some cases of anger, involve a conception of the good. Further, some appetitive desires seem to involve a conception of a long-run end: e.g. the appetitive desires of the oligarch include some that are for the long-run satisfaction of bodily appetites. Moreover, without this sort of conceptual overlap, it is quite difficult to make sense of the Reasoning part's persuasion of the lower parts. So such a view would require drastic revision of the *Republic*'s understanding of non-rational motivations.

But even apart from these concerns, there is another reason that such a modification of the *Republic*'s theory is unattractive. Once we make the non-rational motivations so primitive, it is no longer clear that we need to house them in a separate agent-like part. We do not seem to need to assign these desires to different agent-like parts in order to explain the possibility of an agent (1) having these desires simultaneously, or (2) acting akratically. The presence of such opposed desires does not seem to be the sort of failure of rationality that requires us to attribute them to different subjects. For example, one might think that consciously believing an explicit contradiction is so irrational that we must assign the different beliefs to different subjects. But this does not seem to be the case with the different kinds of desires the modified view posits. Even if we consider the beliefs that correspond to the desire in each part, there is no contradiction or apparent unacceptable irrationality in believing that not A-ing is best for me overall and A-ing is something I desire. Nor is partitioning needed to explain why the person acts on the desire opposed by the Reasoning part. Here the explanatory work is done by the idea that the strength of desires can be out of proportion to the ranking of the objects of desires and that agents act on their strongest desires. There seems to be no need to invoke agent-like parts, rather than different classes of desires or distinct capacities for different kinds of desires. *Republic*-style partitioning is a strategy that carries high costs. Since the costs of partitioning are so high, we should show that we are driven to it by conflicts that simply cannot be accommodated within a single agent except at the cost of unintelligible or nearly unintelligible irrationality. We need, for instance, to see the parts as the subjects of incompatible beliefs or of inconsistent intentions or as operating on each other in ways that a single agent cannot operate on herself.[65] And one important way of doing this is by seeing them as offering *competing* claims about the good and the best.

Finally, it is by seeing the parts in this way that they are able to play another of partitioning's basic roles. In both the *Phaedo* and the *Republic*, the agent-like parts that Plato recognizes are crucial to explaining why different people pursue the goals that they do. The parts are rival claimants to the Reasoning part in setting the person's ultimate ends. To the extent that we see the parts as genuine end-setters, they become liable to conflict, thereby licensing further subdivision.

Unity of the Self The *Republic*'s partitioning theory commits Plato to denying the unity of the person. Specifically, it commits him to denying that there is a single ultimate subject of all of a person's psychic states and activities. What seems to be a single psychic entity is in fact a composite of three distinct and durable subjects. These subjects have their own points of view: they are concept-possessing, subjects of beliefs, desires, and so on. They are centers of agency, since the beliefs and desires they possess are capable of producing action.[66] We should not underestimate the conflict between such a theory and our ordinary intuitions. One important sign of this is the near impossibility of imagining what it would be like to be such a compound. It seems that one ends up either imagining possessing all the psychological states simultaneously (thus losing the idea that they belong to different subjects) or one imagines being each of the parts of the soul (thus losing the idea that they form a single person).[67] Although troubling, this is not fatal to Plato's view, since he might reject the idea that introspective imagination is a reliable guide to psychic reality.

But there are other costs to such a partitioning. Trying to work out in detail how the parts interact leads to puzzles. First, all the parts seem to share some information, for example, they are aware of the person's environment. But how are we to explain this? It seems hard to see how the same token belief could be shared by the different parts, but postulating three token beliefs with the same content (one for each part) seems uneconomical. Second, exactly how does communication between the parts happen? It is especially difficult to see how the parts can register the fact that they are communicating. When the Reasoning part rehearses the bad long-run bodily consequences of taking a fifth glass of whiskey, the person does not seem aware of this as an act of communication. On the other hand, how is the Appetitive part to conceive of the Reasoning part's communications? The problems are especially acute if we think that the lower parts are not aware that they are parts of a whole.[68] But even if we do attribute such awareness to them, what is it like to receive such communications? Does the Reasoning part directly produce a change in the beliefs of the Appetitive part or is the Appetitive part actually aware of some sudden external communication? Finally, on this account akratic conflict and action should be fairly common. Although we can describe mechanisms that tend to produce agreement, it is difficult to see why harmony should be attained as often as it is.

Another set of concerns is brought out by several passages in Books 9 and 10. Consider the following passage from Book 9 in which Plato presents 'an image of the soul in words' (*Rep.* 588B10).

[F]ashion a single kind of multicolored beast with a ring of many heads that it can grow and change at will—some from gentle, some from savage animals . . . Then fashion one other kind, that of a lion, and another of a human being. But make the first much the largest and the other second to it in size . . . Now join the three of them into one, so that they somehow grow together naturally . . . Then, fashion around them the image of one, of the human being so that anyone who sees only the outer covering and not what is inside will think it is a single creature, a human being. (*Rep.* 588C7–E1)

This image identifying the Reasoning part with a human being and the two lower parts with animals is a vivid and memorable metaphor. It invites us to identify with the human being and to see the animals as alien to us. In Book 10 in the course of an argument for the immortality of the soul, Plato goes on to give an account of the origin of psychic complexity. The two lower parts are 'added onto' the Reasoning part when the soul is embodied (*Rep.* 611D4, 612A2, cf. 611B5–7).[69] This passage in Book 10 appears to extend the idea of the Book 9 metaphor that the lower parts are alien to the person and at least broaches the possibility of a significant revision in the Book 4 account of the soul. On the Book 4 account, the soul or person is identical with a compound of the three parts. In Book 10, Plato seems to suggest that once the soul is no longer embodied, the Reasoning part loses the other two parts. Since I persist after my death, I am then identical with the Reasoning part. But Plato may be suggesting that even before death, I am identical with my Reasoning part; the lower two parts are not really parts of me.[70] If so, this would be quite a radical revision in several basic aspects of our self-understanding. First, it seems to undermine the idea that the person is responsible for actions resulting from the lower parts winning out. The problem is not just that the strength of the lower parts' desires might be so great that the person could not do otherwise, but the more basic worry that the akratic desires and emotions are not really *his* desires and emotions. All that it seems the person is responsible for is how he responds to these alien forces, not for having them. Second, if I really am identical with the Reasoning part and not with the composite, why should I attach more than instrumental value to the well-being of the lower parts? Any non-instrumental concern would seem to be a peculiar form of altruism rather than self-interest. Finally, this view would have the unattractive result that the unity of the self is not required for (nor even usually goes together with) co-consciousness.

But if we retain the claim that I am identical with the composite of the three parts of the soul, the *Republic*'s view also has unattractive results. First, it produces a strikingly disunified picture of motivation. Since the lower parts do not have access to concepts drawn from an awareness of the Forms, the concepts that structure these emotions and desires cannot include genuine value concepts. This will be especially awkward for spirited motivations. Anger and the other spirited motivations will never respond to justice or fineness as such, but will at most coincide in the outcome that the Reasoning part prefers on distinct grounds.[71] The person is not even partially united by the integration of reason.

Further, this fact about the epistemic limitations of the lower parts calls into serious question the worth of their good condition and thus of all the virtues except wisdom. Since even in their best state the lower parts cannot be responsive to genuine value, how much non-instrumental value does their good condition have? They may be soothed and kept satisfied so that they do not interfere with the operations of reason and provide a motivational boost to rational desires, but do they have any more important place in the life of a virtuous person? If not, their good condition seems to be important only in the way that the good condition of the body is.

A final concern about the *Republic*'s explanation of akrasia is that it leaves the person troublingly passive. (This is logically independent of the partitioning hypothesis, since we could see activity even in parts of the soul. But it is a feature of the *Republic*'s account.) Nothing in the passages we have seen in Book 4 suggests that people can control the strength of their desires (except perhaps indirectly) and the only causally relevant antecedent to action seems to be a competition among the person's desires with regard to strength. A person's judgments about what it is best to do overall is distinct from the motivational strength of her desires. In the best case, a person's judgment about what is best is aligned with her strongest desire, but this is not something that she herself can determine. She seems to be left as a passive spectator of the competition of her own desires, and thus of her own actions. I shall return to this issue about passivity at greater length in the second half of this chapter.

Before turning to the *Laws*, a closing point about the partitioning strategy is worth emphasizing. We have seen so far some of the motivations for partitioning as well as some of the problems to which it gives rise. But there is an additional reason for partitioning that connects up with issues I shall discuss at greater length in Chapter 4. As we have seen, the desires, emotions and beliefs that Plato associates with the body in the *Phaedo* and with the lower parts of the soul in the *Republic* do not draw upon a grasp of the Forms and cannot engage in reasoning based upon such a grasp. (I shall speak hereafter simply of the lower parts of the soul, but the claims will apply, with appropriate modification, to the body in the *Phaedo*.) The content of these motivations is not even partially framed in terms of concepts drawn from the Forms and they do not rationally interact with beliefs and desires that draw upon such concepts. Their cognitive resources derive from perception and whatever simple reasoning can go on without a grasp of Forms, e.g. means–end reasoning.[72] The lower parts are, to borrow some contemporary terminology, relatively 'informationally encapsulated'.[73] Moreover, this condition is permanent: no amount of training can bring it about that the lower parts have access to the Forms. This permanent lack of integration along with the fact that the lower parts' beliefs, desires, and emotions do interact with a fair degree of minimal rationality makes it not unreasonable to think of the lower parts as subjects of psychic states and activities.[74] As we shall see in Chapter 4, the fundamental motivation for the rejection of a partitioning theory is Plato's rejection of such a sharp and permanent cognitive division between reason and the non-rational motivations.

3.5 Plato's Later Views: Introduction

Controversy already surrounds Plato's later psychology. According to some scholars, Plato moves from a tripartite theory of the soul at the time of the *Republic* to accept, in some of the later dialogues, a bipartitioning of the soul into rational and irrational elements. One, for example, holds that '[c]oncerning the *Laws* there is little need to argue that Plato works primarily with an implicit or unformulated bipartite psychology. This is almost a commonplace among scholars today.' In opposition, another scholar has argued that '[t]he bipartite analysis can never *exclude* the tripartite. Tripartition always presupposes bipartition and bipartition is always capable of expansion into tripartition.'[75] I shall argue, however, that we should reject both of these options.

Let us begin with the claim that bipartitioning can always be expanded into a tripartition. According to the *Republic*, it is the application of the Principle of Contraries that establishes the division of the soul into parts. If it has been shown that the possibility of psychic conflict requires a division of the soul into two parts, it is still a further substantive question whether there are other conflicts that require a further division of the soul. Bipartition is not always capable of expansion into tripartition and this is why in *Republic* 4 Plato offers an argument for recognizing the Spirited part of the soul as a separate part that crucially depends on the existence of certain kinds of psychic conflict. Using the *Republic*'s criteria for dividing the soul, a bipartition of the soul into two distinct and non-overlapping parts *A* and *B* is consistent with tripartition if and only if:

(a) there can be conflict within one and only one part of the soul, say, *A*, which licenses the application of the Principle of Contraries, and
(b) neither of the parts resulting from the subdivision of *A* is subject to the sort of conflict that would license further application of the Principle of Contraries.

But although bipartitioning and tripartitioning are distinct and incompatible options, they share a common and controversial claim: both hold that the soul is a composite of at least two parts which are themselves the proper subjects of psychological states and activities.

I shall argue that the *Laws* rejects this claim and does not partition the soul into agent-like parts: on its view, the soul is neither bipartite nor tripartite, but unitary. The soul is the single subject of all psychological states and activities. Since explaining the possibility of akrasia was one of the central goals of the *Republic's* theory, I shall first turn in Section 3.6 to examine the *Laws'* account of akrasia. I argue that the *Laws'* theory recognizes and explains akratic conflict and action and successful resistance to akratic conflict, while not partitioning the soul, and that it thus avoids the problems that faced the *Republic's* account. Although I think that the abandonment of partitioning in the *Laws* and some other late dialogues is clear, Plato has not worked out all the details of his psychology and the new account raises many more interesting issues than it resolves. In Section 3.7, I take up some of the issues stemming from the *Laws'* theory of akrasia. Plato's late psychology is concerned, however, with issues beyond akrasia. The *Laws* still recognizes complexity within the soul and a division between rational and non-rational aspects. In Section 3.8, I consider the nature of this division and some of its broader implications for Plato's ethics.

This still leaves several important tasks. One might think that this account of the *Laws'* psychology is implausible because Plato clearly recognizes agent-like parts in other dialogues between the *Republic* and the *Laws*, especially the *Phaedrus* and the *Timaeus*. In Chapter 4, I argue that, on the contrary, we see in the *Phaedrus*, the *Theaetetus*, and the *Timaeus* the development of Plato's rationale for the abandonment of the *Republic's* psychological theory. Picking up the thread of the argument from Chapter 3, I argue that Plato comes to deny to the lower parts of the soul the sort of epistemic independence that they had in the *Republic*. In particular, the perceptual resources they drew upon in the *Republic* are no longer sufficient to allow them to be goal-setting agents or the possessors of beliefs and desires. Finally, in Chapter 4, I examine the implications of the late psychology's more subtle view of how the soul's rational faculties structure and influence the rest of the soul's capacities for Plato's understanding of the place of the emotions and pleasure in the virtuous life.

3.6 Akrasia and the Divine Puppets of the Laws

Divine Puppets   In the *Republic*, it was akratic conflict that brought to light the soul's division.[76] In this section, I shall argue that the *Laws* explains akrasia without relying upon the division of the soul and examine how it does so. In the first few pages of the *Laws*, Plato focuses our attention on the old problem of psychological complexity and conflict within the individual. In order to justify the Cretan practice of designing their laws to assure victory at war, Kleinias claims that what is called 'peace' is an illusion and that every city is always at war with every other city (*Laws* 626A2–5). At the Athenian's prompting, Kleinias extends the point: the same relation holds between each village and every other one and even between each person and every other person (*Laws* 626C6–12). The Athenian then invites Kleinias to carry his reasoning one further, unexpected step: is there such a conflict within each individual? Kleinias accepts the invitation and asserts that there is a basic, ongoing conflict within each of us: 'Here, visitor, is the first and best of victories, the victory of oneself over oneself; and being defeated by oneself is the most shameful and at the same time the worst of all defeats. These things indicate that there is a war going on in us, ourselves against ourselves' (*Laws* 626E2–5).

Thus the existence of motivational conflict becomes a central issue at the very beginning of the *Laws*. The Athenian acknowledges that there is something puzzling about the idea that the worse element in a person could ever be stronger than the better and he returns to this issue later in Book 1 when he attempts to explain the puzzle by means of the most striking metaphor in the *Laws*: the great puppet image that portrays each human soul as a kind of divine puppet. (The mention of 'opposed' affections (*pathē*) lifts the description out of pure metaphor.) I shall begin by looking carefully at this image to see what it tells us about the nature of psychic complexity and conflict in the individual.

Let us suppose that each of us living beings is an ingenious puppet of the gods— whether contrived as a plaything of theirs or for some serious purpose, we do not know. But this we do know, that these affections in us [ταῦτα τὰ πάθη ἐν ἡμῖν], like sinews or cords, draw us along [σπῶσίν τε ἡμᾶς], and being contrary to each other, pull one against the other [ἀνθέλκουσιν] to contrary actions; and herein lies the dividing line between virtue and vice. For, as our argument declares, there is one of the pulling forces [μιᾷ ... τῶν ἕλξεων] which each person ought always to follow [συνεπόμενον] and in no way abandon, thereby pulling against the other sinews: this is the golden and sacred pull of calculation [τὴν τοῦ λογισμοῦ ἀγωγὴν], called the common law of the city. The other cords are hard and iron and have every sort of shape, while this one is soft since it is of gold. With that finest pull of the law we should always cooperate; for since calculation is fine, but gentle rather than forceful, its pull needs helpers to assure that the golden kind within us may always vanquish the other kinds.[77]   (*Laws* 644D7–645B1)

Let us now fill out the details of this account. To begin, there are only two basic kinds of element in the story the Athenian tells: a person's affections (πάθη) and the person himself (*Laws* 644C4–7, E1, E6). (We do not need to hold that this exhausts the contents of soul: there might also be, e.g., durable states or *hexeis*. But the metaphor suggests that this is all that is needed to explain akrasia.) Although these affections may oppose each other, there is only a single subject of the opposed affections and that is the person. There are no nested puppets within the puppet itself that are the possessors of some of the affections. Although the puppet image is only a metaphor, this detail is significant. Plato's other great images of a partitioned soul—that in Book 9 of the *Republic* portraying the soul as a composite of a human being, a lion and a hydra-headed beast, the *Phaedrus'* charioteer and two horses, and the *Theaetetus'* wooden horse with people inside—make it clear that the parts are the sorts of things that can be subjects of psychic states. In the *Laws'* image, all of the affections attributed to the person seem to be occurrent psychic states of some sort: they are occurrent beliefs, desires, or emotions. None is described as a part or as agent-like and no affection is the sort of thing that could *have* beliefs or desires.[78] In this passage, spirit (θυμός) is listed right along with various occurrent psychic states, e.g., pleasure and pain: there is no suggestion that spirit is agent-like. In sum, we find here desires (including those characteristic of the lowest part of the soul in the *Republic*), but not the Appetitive part; we find spirited emotions, but not the Spirited part.

One might suggest that although the metaphor has no place for the parts of the soul, Plato may simply have overlooked this or chosen a bad image.

Perhaps we should place no weight on the image's details, since Plato's only point is the simple one that people do act akratically and he does not intend to provide any further account of akrasia. But such a dismissive attitude to this metaphor is unwarranted. Just before he introduces the puppet metaphor, Plato reminds us that he is returning to the earlier puzzle in Book I about motivational conflict: 'Long ago we agreed that those who are able to rule themselves [ἄρχειν αὐτῶν] are good, and those who cannot are bad ... Let us consider again in a clearer way what we mean by that. Allow me to clarify it for you, if I can, by means of an image' (*Laws* 644B6–C2). Immediately after presenting the image, Plato claims that it should make 'clearer' the meaning of the phrase 'being stronger (or weaker) than oneself' (τὸ κρείττω ἑαυτοῦ καὶ ἥττω, *Laws* 645B1–3). It was designed, he adds, to clarify the nature of virtue and vice and it does so by giving a 'true account' of the impulses or pulling forces within us (τὸν μὲν λόγον ἀληθῆ ... περὶ τῶν ἕλξεων, *Laws* 645B4, 645C1). Since failing to rule oneself and being weaker than oneself are standard descriptions of akratic conflict within the soul that can issue in akratic action, we have Plato's own assurance that the puppet image is designed to make clear what goes on in a person during akratic conflict.[79] Although any metaphor inevitably possesses features that are irrelevant to its meaning, we should begin by assuming that the image's main features to which Plato draws our attention are significant and will repay some effort to work them out.

Plato's ultimate theoretical basis for rejecting the parts of the soul will not become clear until Chapter 4. There I shall argue that Plato's late epistemology leads him to this rejection. In the *Phaedrus* and the *Timaeus*, Plato emphasizes that the lower parts of the soul are incapable of any contact with the Forms at all. But in the later dialogues, Plato has come to think that such contact is required for a very wide range (perhaps all) of human cognition and so the lower parts become increasingly cognitively impoverished. By the time of the *Timaeus*, Plato holds that the lower parts are no longer capable of belief or conceptualized desires, and thus can no longer be agent-like in the way that the parts were in the *Republic*.

But even before we turn to this argument, we have good reason to take seriously the possibility that Plato no longer accepts a *Republic*-style partitioning of the soul. Such an account is strikingly absent from the places in the late dialogues where we would expect to find it. As I shall argue, it is absent from the *Laws'* account of akrasia. But also the *Sophist* distinguishes akrasia and ignorance without invoking the parts of the soul and the *Philebus'* extensive analysis of pleasure and grading of different kinds of pleasures significantly fails to follow the *Republic's* lead and does not mention the parts of the soul.[80] Moreover, the sophisticated account in *Laws* 10 of the soul as the source of motion presents the soul as the unitary subject of all its affections and there is no sign of partitioning (e.g. *Laws* 896C–D).[81] Finally, as we have seen in the first half of this chapter, it is the *Republic's* partitioning of the soul that is responsible for many of the problematic features of its account of akrasia. So even before the confirmatory argument of Chapter 4, it is worthwhile to work out how the *Laws'* account of akrasia proceeds without assuming that Plato is still committed to agent-like parts of the soul.[82]

So let us return to the details of the puppet image. Among the affections of the soul that Plato recognizes here, the fundamental distinction is that between those represented by the soft and golden cord and those represented by the hard and iron cords. Although the Athenian does not provide an exhaustive list of the soul's affections, he tells us more at other places in the *Laws*. In a passage that shortly follows, he claims that drunkenness affects the puppet by making its pleasures, pains, spirited emotions (θυμούς), and loves (ἔρωτας) more intense (*Laws* 645D6–7). On the other hand, drink will take away its perceptions, memories, beliefs, and knowledge (φρονήσεις) (*Laws* 645E1–2).[83] A later passage claims that we can be said to be weaker or stronger with regard to pleasure and spiritedness and goes on to spell out what this means: being weaker includes the 'tyranny in the soul' of spirited emotion, fear, pleasure and pain, envy and desire (*Laws* 863E6–8).[84] So we can include among the hard and iron cords the affections made more intense by drink along with those whose 'tyranny' in the soul makes one 'weaker than oneself'. We can thus be akratic with regard to a number of things, including appetitive desires and spirited emotions. The golden cord of calculation is also included among the affections and should pick out instances of reasoning. Specifically, calculation is concerned with judgments about what is good and bad for the person in the long run (*Laws* 644D1 ff.). The desire for the good associated with the judgment is a desire of reason itself rather than a desire originating independently of reason which reason then endorses.

The iron strings are independent of the golden string. Thus they do not stem from this sort of reasoning. Since they are forceful rather than gentle, it seems that their motivational strength is often quite high. Finally, their hardness as contrasted with the softness of the golden cord suggests that they are relatively resistant to outside influence. These emotions, fears, and desires persist in spite of calculation pulling in the opposed direction, whereas the golden cord is open to the influence of further reasoning.[85]

The fundamental division between reasoning and everything else is emphasized by the choice of the kinds of metals that compose the cords: Plato makes no room here for silver cords. This seems surprising in light of the *Republic*, since there the Spirited part is the natural ally of the Reasoning part (*Rep.* 440A–E). It is perhaps less surprising in the *Laws*, given the sharp distinction in kind Plato draws in his theory of Dependent Goods between the value of reason and that of everything else. As in the *Republic*, these affections produce or help to produce action by 'drawing' the agent to various actions; they thus seem to be among the causes of action. The agent who can intervene in the contest also seems to have, at least potentially, a causal role.

Finally, in several passages in the *Laws* Plato seems to accept the possibility that not only a person who has true belief about the good, but also one who has knowledge can act akratically. In Book 3, Plato characterizes akrasia as a kind of ignorance: 'So when the soul opposes knowledge, or beliefs, or reason [ἐπιστήμαις ἢ δόξαις ἢ λόγῳ]—the natural rulers—this I call "ignorance" [ἄνοιαν]' (*Laws* 689B2–4). In Book 10's theology, Plato rejects the possibility that the gods 'know [γιγνώσκοντας] what should be done, and as the most worthless human beings are said to do, they know [εἰδότες] it is better to act otherwise than the way that they are acting, but they do not do so on account of certain weaknesses in the face of pleasures or pains' (*Laws* 902A8–B2). One might worry that Plato is using 'knowledge' loosely in these passages, but in Book 9 he makes it clear that even a person who is in the cognitive state that a fully educated philosopher is in can act akratically. This possibility is important for the political theory of the *Laws*, since here Plato rejects autocratic rule because he holds that even a philosopher who rules autocratically will almost inevitably eventually become corrupted.

[T]here is no one among humans whose nature grows so as to become adequate both to know [γνῶναί] what is in the interest of humans as regards a political constitution and, knowing this, to be able and willing always to do what is best. For, in the first place, it is difficult to know that the true political art must care not for the private but the common . . . Second, even if someone should advance sufficiently in the art to know that this is the way that these things are by nature, and after this should rule the city without being audited, and as an autocrat, he would never be able to adhere to this conviction and spend his life giving priority to nourishing what is common in the city, while nourishing the private as following after the common. Mortal nature will always urge him towards getting more than his share and towards private business, irrationally [ἀλόγως] fleeing pain and pursuing pleasure, and putting both of these before what is more just and better. Creating a darkness within itself, it will completely fill both itself and the whole city with everything bad. (*Laws* 875A1–C3)

Such people are eventually filled with darkness and thus lose their knowledge and acquire false beliefs, but especially in light of the two earlier passages it is reasonable to see the process of corruption as beginning with akrasia.[86]

The Dynamics of Akrasia   We now need a more detailed analysis of the dynamics of akratic conflict and its resolution. Drawing on the puppet passage, Plato's account should run roughly as follows. One of the iron cords, say a desire, pulls a person to perform a certain action, X. This desire does not spring from any calculation about what is best overall for the person, but nevertheless it can, perhaps when joined with an appropriate belief (e.g. 'I can do X now.'), move the person to act. At the same time, the person knows or believes that action Y is better overall than any other option and that he can do either X or Y, but cannot do both X and Y. His desire to do X pulls more strongly than his calculation that Y is overall best (or the desire for Y that is associated with his calculation). Thus the person believes that Y is better overall than X, but he is more strongly motivated to do X. So in the *Laws* as well as the *Republic*, the strength of a person's desire to perform an action is distinct from his evaluation of that action. His desires can vary in strength and the strength of his desire to perform a particular action is not always directly proportional to his judgment of the object's goodness. Indeed, given his warning that the iron cords are forceful and that reason needs helpers, Plato seems to think that akratic conflict and, perhaps, even akratic action will not be very rare.

But unlike the *Republic*, the *Laws* accepts these claims while locating all the beliefs and desires involved within a single person: none is located within an agent-like part of the soul. Agent-like parts of the soul have no role in the description or analysis of akratic conflict and action. To continue the story: if nothing else happens, the person will do X or try to do X. This, if it takes place, would be an instance of 'hard akrasia'. I shall characterize as 'hard akrasia' any case in which a person believes that one course of action is best for herself overall and believes that it is open to her to perform that action, and yet, without being physically compelled, takes (or tries to take) what she believes is an incompatible and overall worse course of action.[87] I shall consider below several kinds of 'weak akrasia' in which a person's judgment of what is best for herself overall is blocked, rendered inoperative, or deformed in some other way.

Yet there is still one further factor beyond the strength of the competing desires that is relevant to the outcome. The person may follow (συνέπεσθαι) the golden cord of calculation and pull along with it against the others (*Laws* 644E5–6). This is a striking reworking of the original image. Although Plato makes no use of the idea that some external agent is pulling the strings, the puppet image initially emphasizes the passivity of the person. We are presented as being moved to act as the outcome of the cords pulling against one another. The person seems to be nothing more than the passive container of affections that pull against one another, or the passive spectator of these pulling forces. But as E. B. England perceptively remarks, with the idea that the person can pull along with the cord of reason, 'we are no longer a *spectacle: we can pull our own wires*.'[88] Less metaphorically, the person is no longer passive with respect to his affections, but can somehow intervene in their interactions. This active power or capacity of the agent frees him from having his actions determined solely by the forces of the interacting affections. What the person does is affected not just by the force of the affections, but also by the person's own intervention in the process. At least in some cases, the outcome of the interaction is not determined purely by forces that happen to attach to the conflicting desires, but is also affected by the person acting in support of reason. This does not entail that the causal role of the force of a desire is entirely superseded, since the person's intervention is characterized as a pulling along with the cord of reason and Plato may think that the resultant action is determined by which desire is strongest after the intervention. (Although, as we shall see in more detail below, the initiation of the person's intervention or pulling along with reason need not, it seems, be the outcome of the previous balance of forces.) The most direct way of understanding this would be that the person intervenes to increase the strength of his rational judgment or of the associated desire for what is overall best. This, at least in some cases, will bring it about that the person does Y. Yet we have no reason to think that this pulling along with reason will always be successful; sometimes the person's counter-pull will be insufficient and he will still do X. This would also be an instance of hard akrasia: the person performs what he concurrently realizes is not overall the best course of action available to him. The akratic desire directly defeats the person's judgment of what is overall best (or his desire associated with such a judgment).

Let us now turn to some of the issues raised by the *Laws'* new account.

3.7 Varieties of Weak Akrasia

Let us begin by considering the circumstances in which akrasia may occur. A person believes that she can do either X or Y, but cannot do both X and Y, and at the same time believes that action Y is better overall than any other option. If without any further reasoning or change of mind, she knowingly does (or tries to do) X without being physically compelled, this is a case of hard akrasia. This description, however, also suggests several ways in which the person might go wrong that, while they are not instances of hard akrasia, are intimately related to it. Although this is not an exhaustive list, three options are worth special mention.

(1) The person does not reach a judgment about what is overall best before she acts and she acts without one.

(2) The person does form the judgment that Y is overall best, but this judgment is undermined before she acts and she acts without (fully) possessing an overall best judgment.

(3) The person changes her mind about what is best overall and comes to accept that X is overall best and she acts on this judgment, but this change of belief is irrational.[89]

All three of these characterizations require more precise description in order to capture the intended phenomena and doing so is made more difficult by the fact that Plato (unlike Aristotle in *Nicomachean Ethics* 7) does not try to anatomize the deliberative process. Nevertheless, these three categories do correspond to real distinctions in Plato's discussion.

Let us begin with cases of (1). According to our description, in this sort of case the person fails to reach an overall best judgment. We have so far assumed that reaching such an overall judgment is a normal precursor of action, but we might raise questions about the psychological reality of such an assumption. Whether or not the overall judgment is the result of a full-blown deliberative process, is such a judgment normally explicitly present before action? Or is it normally present only in potential form? Although Plato's language suggests that such a judgment is normally explicitly present, we perhaps do not need to settle the issue for our present purposes.

More important are two other omissions in (1). First, (1) does not distinguish between cases in which the resulting action conflicts with what the agent would have done if she had carried out her deliberation well or with some general policy that she already has and those in which it does not.[90] It is the cases involving such a conflict that primarily concern us. Finally, we are interested only in cases in which desires and emotions in some way disrupt or deform the agent's deliberation and action. So we can put on one side cases in which the failure to form such a judgment is fully explained by, e.g., the fact that the person is habitually unreflective, or just careless on this occasion. The cases that we are concerned with are those in which the presence of desires and emotions helps to explain why the person fails to form such a judgment. So in these cases, although the person might be aware that she is acting without having deliberated, she cannot be aware that she is acting contrary to what is overall best for her. We may call these cases of 'impetuous' akrasia (cf. *Nicomachean Ethics* 1150ᵇ19–22).

Anger, in particular, is especially likely to be a cause of such impetuous akrasia. In Book 9, in the course of discussing gradations of punishment for legal offenses, the Athenian distinguishes three causes of wrongdoing (ἁμαρτήματα): spirit (*thumos*), pleasure, and ignorance (*Laws* 863B1–C2). Spirit 'is by nature quarrelsome and pugnacious, overturning many things with irrational violence . . . And pleasure, we proclaim, is not the same as spirit, but, we assert, holds absolute rule through a strength opposite to it: through persuasion and forceful trickery she does whatever her intention wishes' (*Laws* 863B3–9).⁹¹ Plato here suggests a difference in the way that anger and pleasure typically work: anger 'overturns' things, while pleasure works by 'persuasion' and 'trickery'. The claim that anger overturns many things should not, however, lead us to think that anger always brings about wrongdoing by leading the person to act contrary to an overall best judgment that he concurrently possesses. (And as we saw in the puppet passage, pleasure, too, can lead the person to act against an overall best judgment that he concurrently possesses.) Plato goes on to distinguish two kinds of wrongful killings caused by spirit or anger. In the first, the killing 'is done out of spirit by those who act on a sudden impulse, who all at once and without intending to kill beforehand destroy someone with blows or some such thing and feel regret immediately after the deed is done' (*Laws* 866D7–E3).⁹² In such cases, the person acts without prior deliberation.⁹³ Although the text is not entirely decisive, this seems to be a case in which at the time of action the person has no overall judgment about what is best. Moreover, this failure to form such a judgment is explained by the presence of the angry impulse. After acting, the person realizes that his action is contrary to his own overall judgment of what is best and thus regrets performing the action and, presumably, his failure to deliberate as well.⁹⁴

We can see cases of type (2) as displaying a deeper disruption of reason. In these cases, unlike impetuous akrasia, the person has formed an overall judgment of what is best. But in the face of certain desires or emotions, the person loses his grip on this judgment, although he does not go on to form a new overall judgment endorsing the action to which his desire or emotion prompts him. In Book 1, the Athenian considers some of the effects that drinking can have on a person.

Athenian: Does not the drinking of wine make pleasures, pains, the spirited emotions, and the erotic emotions, more intense?
Kleinias: Very much so.
Ath.: What about perceptions, memories, beliefs, and knowledge? Do they become more intense in the same way? Or do they not desert anyone who becomes thoroughly drunk?
Kl.: Yes, they entirely desert him.   (*Laws* 645D6–E4)

The person is then left with the 'disposition of soul' that he had as a young child (*Laws* 645E5–6). In this sort of case, I might lose my belief that Y is overall best. But this will also undermine my desire for Y because this desire is dependent on a belief arrived at by reasoning. At least, I will no longer desire Y *as* what is overall best. At the same time, the strength of my desire for X increases. In some cases, I might then do X without engaging in further deliberation. In the case of drunkenness, once the effects of the wine wear off, I will tend to regain my previous overall judgment. The case that Plato considers here is one in which complete drunkenness causes a complete loss of certain beliefs, but he does not exclude the possibility of intermediate cases in which the person's grasp of his belief is undermined or his awareness of it is clouded without totally losing the belief.[95] Such cases are on the borderline between hard and weak akrasia. In these cases, the person's loss of his overall judgment (and of the associated desire) helps explain why he does X.

But we also need to explain the loss of judgment itself. In the above passage, Plato suggests that drunkenness acts in two distinct ways: (a) to undermine the initial overall judgment and (b) to increase the strength of non-rational desires. He does not say that it is the increase in the strength of desires that causes the loss of belief. Elsewhere in the *Laws* he allows that intense pleasures, anger, desire (*erōs*), insolence, love of gain, and fear can by themselves bring about such changes (649D2–7). But Plato might think that there is more than one mechanism at work in these cases. Sometimes the strength or intensity of an emotion or desire might directly bring about the loss of judgment. On the other hand, in the *Timaeus*, Plato seems to suggest that the relation between the strength of the non-rational desire and the loss of judgment is not a direct causal link, but that both share a causal origin in some bodily condition.⁹⁶ But what both of these sorts of cases share is perhaps more important than their differences. In all of them, the causal relation, like the case of Ella Fitzgerald's singing breaking the glass, fails to be rational causation in the following sense: the conceptual content of the pleasure or desire does not play a causal role. It is the pleasure's or desire's strength rather than what the desire is for that explains what happens.

But here, too, there are interesting borderline cases. In the *Philebus*, Plato focuses on how pleasure can bring about a loss of opinions. When reason and intelligence are asked whether, in addition to true pleasures, they wish to live with the strongest and most intense pleasures, they reject them: 'They are a tremendous impediment to us, since they infect the souls in which they dwell with madness or even prevent our own development altogether. Furthermore, they totally destroy most of our offspring, since neglect leads to forgetfulness' (*Philebus* 63D5–E3). Such loss of knowledge is not limited to practical judgments, but should include them. In the case of the destruction of reason's offspring, Plato seems to suggest that intense pleasures focus the person's attention on themselves and thus lead at first to inattention to one's overall best judgment which may be followed by a more lasting loss of awareness of such a judgment. Here it may be the case that the person's attention is not merely caused to shift by the intensity of the pleasure independent of the content of the pleasure, but that the particular content of the pleasure helps to focus his attention. The content thus can play a role in explaining the person's attention to the pleasure, but it cannot provide a reason for the neglect of the overall judgment. This seems simply to be a causal effect.

In both cases of types (1) and (2), reason is frustrated, but the interference is, so to speak, external. Reason is prevented from beginning to operate in its normal way, or its end result in the form of an overall judgment is destroyed before it issues in action. The desire or emotion then produces action on its own without any contribution of reason or reasoned deliberation. But Plato also recognizes a more intimate interference with the operations of reason. In such cases, the akratic emotion or desire seems to work by interfering with the operations of reason itself so as to produce a distorted overall best judgment. This is an internal corruption of reason. Such cases are especially interesting, since some philosophers think that recognition of this possibility is a peculiarly modern contribution. According to them, it is the modern view that

overturned a view of reason, common since antiquity, according to which it is a completely independent force. Evidently, it is a force that is stronger in some people than in others, and, when it comes to action, it is less often frustrated in some agents than in others. But the old idea was that there was no interfering with its inner working. A good analogy would be the engine of a car, which may be more or less powerful and more or less frustrated by what happens beyond the clutch, but, if it itself malfunctions, the trouble is entirely its own.[97]

In cases of internal corruption, the fault is not entirely reason's own.

We may broaden (3) to include not only cases in which the person irrationally changes her overall judgment once it has been made (which seem to be the primary cases that Plato has in mind), but also some cases in which the initial overall judgment is irrationally formed. Plato does not distinguish these possibilities sharply and for the purposes of designing a good ethical education for the young, it may not be necessary to do so. But one or the other accounts for the 'persuasion and forceful trickery' of pleasure (*Laws* 863B8).[98] In all such cases, the person forms a mistaken judgment, but it is essential to these cases that the error is not simply an instance of intellectual incompetence (e.g. reasoning from false beliefs or making a bad inference), but is brought about by a desire or an emotion.[99] I might, for example, misread the sign saying 'Please do not feed the animals' as 'Please do feed the animals' either because I am nearsighted or because I have been hoping to give some fruit to the monkeys.

The mechanisms noted above can help to explain some such cases. If I have lost my grip on my correct overall judgment and some of its grounds either as a causal effect of a strong desire or because my attention is focused on such a desire, then I might judge that pursuing the pleasure is best overall because I no longer take all relevant considerations into account. This will especially be the case with respect to emotions and pleasures that are only circumstantially bad. We can thus understand and explain type (3) cases with the resources already available.

But such cases also point to some more general issues. We have so far explained some mistaken judgments about what is best in particular circumstances that are influenced by a non-rational emotion or desire. But this is not yet to explain how the person's judgments about what is overall best come to be systematically mistaken rather than wrong in particular cases or how a person comes to have wrong beliefs about the goodness of certain *types* of, e.g., pleasures, since the effects of the clouding desire will tend to be temporally limited. It will also be more difficult to explain how such errors happen in the case of a person who has knowledge or well-supported true beliefs about what is good. Here, too, some mistakes about circumstantially bad emotions or desires may be possible in such people even if their non-rational motivations have, in general, been well trained. But Plato thinks that this sort of process is what explains the striking and eventually complete ethical degeneration of the philosopher who rules as an autocrat.

Neither the *Republic* nor the *Phaedo* seems to recognize the possibility of such corruption of the philosopher. Indeed, their psychology would make such corruption very puzzling. The non-rational motivations associated with the body or the lower parts of the soul are so sharply and obviously distinct from the desires and judgments of reason that more than circumstantial error would require quite a radical disruption of reason. A fuller explanation of the *Laws'* position will require, it seems, that rational and non-rational motivations be brought more closely together. I shall consider how this might be so in Chapter 4, after a fuller discussion of non-rational motivation in the *Laws*.

3.8 Psychic Intervention

As we saw in Section 3.6, one important way in the *Laws* in which a person can prevent akratic action is by intervening to support his overall best judgment. In this section, I shall consider this phenomenon in more detail. Such intervention is open to stronger and weaker interpretations. These interpretations differ with regard to the ubiquity of the person's intervention and its implications for the nature of the soul. We may begin with a minimalist interpretation.

On a minimal interpretation, such intervention is a type of self-control. This is a minimal interpretation in at least two ways. First, the intervention of the person occurs only on some occasions before action, that is, those in which the person tries to overcome stronger bad desires. It is not an inevitable accompaniment of all action. There is, for example, no space for such intervention when the person lacks bad desires or they are weaker than his rational desires and there is no actual intervention when the person does not even try to intervene. Second, this interpretation makes no claims about the nature of the soul that allows such intervention. We may find that there is good reason to think that Plato goes beyond such a minimal account, but this is all that is immediately required by the puppet metaphor. Let us first consider some issues arising out of this minimal interpretation.

The above account assumes that the person's intervention is to support his rational judgments and rational desires. But is this necessary? In terms of the image, could the person ever pull along with one of the iron cords? Nothing in Plato's language suggests such a possibility. With regard to the iron cords, the person is seen only as passive, that is, as sometimes giving in to their pull (e.g. *Laws* 644E5–6). When a person gives in in this way, we do not have to say that he *chooses* not to intervene, that is, that he knowingly chooses the worse or that he endorses acting on the worse desire: he may just fail to intervene on the side of reason. Such a choice of the worse desire is possible, for example, in the theories of some medieval Christians who have a conception of the will as independent of reason and desire and capable of choosing between them (I shall call this a 'strong conception of the will').[100]

If the person either pulls along with the golden cord of reason or remains passive, he seems to have a special affinity with reason. We can begin to make this idea more determinate by holding that this pulling along requires a certain sort of reflection by the person on his desires and beliefs and that such reflection is the act of reason. Seeing this intervention as an act of reason does not require that we see it as the act of a distinct Reasoning part of the soul. We can identify it as rational, for example, in virtue of its content: it involves stepping back from one's desires and endorsing and supporting one of them because it expresses an overall conception of the good that is rationally determined. Here it is not the mere fact that this endorsement is a higher-order one that makes it rational, but the fact that it satisfies independent criteria of rationality. This does not entail that such an intervention cannot be in some way mistaken, since the person might pull along with the golden cord although it embodies a mistaken judgment while still acting on behalf of his judgment of what is overall best.

Nor does allowing such intervention obviously lead to some sort of troubling regress. We could allow, for example, that the person sometimes undertakes deliberation to decide whether or not to intervene. (If the best option is only slightly better than its competitor, we might wonder whether it is worth intervening.) This would generate a regress only if we held that some yet higher-order deliberation was always required before actual intervention and there is no need for such an assumption.[101] Nor would a regress be forced by allowing the possibility that, even after such deliberation ends with the belief that it is overall best for him to intervene, he might akratically fail even to try to intervene.

If we allow that such intervention is a coherent possibility, what psychic resources does it require? Is it compatible with a belief–desire psychology? There is more than one issue involved here and we can begin to sort them out by considering two accounts of deliberation, one in Hobbes and one in Schopenhauer, respectively.

When in the mind of man, appetites and aversions, hopes and fears, concerning one and the same thing arise alternately, and diverse good and evil consequences of the doing, or omitting the thing propounded, come successively into our thoughts, so that sometimes we have an appetite to it, sometimes an aversion from it, sometimes hope to be able to do it, sometimes despair or fear to attempt it, the whole sum of desires, aversions, hopes and fears, continued till the thing be either done or thought impossible, is that we call DELIBERATION . . . In deliberation, the last appetite or aversion, immediately adhering to the action, or to the omission thereof, is that we call the WILL, the act (not the faculty) of *willing*.

Now by means of his ability to think, a human being can represent to himself the motives whose influence he feels on his will in any order he likes, alternately and repeatedly, in order to hold them up before the will; and this is called *reflecting*. He has a capacity for deliberation and, by virtue of it, a far greater *choice* than is possible for the animal . . . [T]he capacity for deliberation . . . gives us nothing but a *conflict of motives*, one that is very often painful, over which irresolution presides, and whose scene of conflict is the whole mind and consciousness of the human being. For he allows the motives repeatedly to try their strength on his will, one against the other. His will is thus put in the same position as that of a body that is acted on by different forces in opposite directions—until at last the decidedly strongest motive drives the others from the field and determines the will. This outcome is called decision and, as the result of the struggle, appears with complete *necessity*.[102]

Intuitively, both of these conceptions of deliberation present the person as disturbingly passive. But it is important here to get clear on exactly what the problem is. One reasonable concern is that these views make no room for reflection on what is good or bad about the objects of choice. Deliberation, on this view, is simply a matter of presenting to oneself the various desires one has until one, the strongest one, drives the others from the field and brings about the action. What we want to make room for is the idea that action can depend upon the reflective control of the agent, in particular, that practical reasoning about the good can affect what the person does.

We can now ask, more precisely, whether such reflective control and guidance requires more than a belief–desire psychology. Plato does not put the question this way. This may either be because he does not come to this issue, as we do, with an assumption that a belief–desire psychology is the default account of human psychology and that any extension requires an explicit proof that the additional item is not reducible to beliefs and desires or simply because he does not develop a full account of practical deliberation. Indeed, I do not think that we can attribute to Plato a fully worked-out account. But we should consider what directions his views indicate, since it is often just assumed that Plato has a belief–desire psychology. Some Neoplatonists, for example, may go beyond this and it is worth trying to see whether their views have genuine Platonic antecedents or at least can be seen as responding to gaps or problems in Plato's own views.

To begin, a belief–desire psychology does not have to be committed to such a weak notion of deliberation. We can allow that a person can both reflect on her present beliefs and desires and engage in reasoning about what to do that goes beyond calculating how best to satisfy desires that she already has. We do not need to see our practical judgments simply as expressions of desires that we just find ourselves with. If we allow that deliberation can include reasoning about proper ends, we then have several ways of accounting for action without introducing anything more than an appropriate desire.[103] We can, it seems, allow rational deliberation to affect action without introducing anything beyond beliefs and desires.

It is, of course, still possible to be dissatisfied with this picture of deliberation and action. We might, for example, think that it still leaves the person passive: the rational desire resulting from deliberation is simply one more force competing with the force of other desires. What we need in order to capture the idea that the person is genuinely active is the notion of some further capacity to choose among all of her desires, including her rational desires. Whether or not we find this a plausible (or even coherent) picture of agency, it seems to be asking for something that Greek psychology notoriously did not recognize, that is, a strong conception of the will. But it would be a mistake to think that such a conception is the only alternative to the enriched belief–desire account of deliberation just sketched.

What the puppet passage shows, I think, is that such a dichotomy is too simple. Although Plato does not have a strong conception of the will, he may need more than what is offered by the above account of rational deliberation. Plato's worry is not that we have not made room for the capacity to choose to act against our rational desire. His worry is, rather, that in certain cases my rational desire for what I judge overall best is weaker than one of my non-rational emotions or desires. If we accept that I shall try to do whatever I am most strongly motivated to do, it then seems inevitable that I shall act on the non-rational desire or emotion. Part of what Plato tries to show by means of the puppet image is that such an outcome is not inevitable. And even if there is the proper alignment between the strength of my desires and my evaluation of their objects, this alignment is not up to me. What does the work for Plato in showing that such an outcome is not inevitable is the notion that I can intervene in the competition of desires. The question for us is exactly what is involved in such a capacity to intervene. There are at least three possibilities that are worth considering.

First, insofar as the worry is that a person's non-rational motivations might be stronger than his rational desire, a natural suggestion is that we might try to enlist on the side of reason some powerful non-rational motivations that change the balance of forces. David Sedley insightfully points out that we can see the Spirited part of the soul playing exactly this role in the *Republic*. Spirit is a natural ally of reason and can, when well trained, add its motivational force to that of our rational desires. Although spirit does not play the role of the medieval Christians' will, it can account for the person's willpower.[104] In the *Laws*, Plato no longer posits a Spirited part of the soul, but he does hold that good ethical training requires enlisting certain non-rational motivations on the side of reason. Following the puppet passage in Book 1, Plato goes on to discuss this possibility and, in particular, stresses that shame can play such a role.[105] Such a solution perhaps requires nothing more than further beliefs, desires, and emotions, but it does not seem to capture all that Plato wants. First, the puppet image presents us with a case in which the person must intervene while all the non-rational motivations are, so to speak, already on the scene. The problem is that, even taking the support of non-rational motivations into account, the balance of motivation is against reason. Second, spirited emotions might support reason in many cases, but it is implausible to think that they are always active in cases of conflicted choice. Finally, even if spirited motivations were capable of playing such a role, we may again worry that this leaves the person, insofar as she is a rational agent, too passive. Non-rational motivations might support reason, but reason gets its way only by virtue of the force of something other than reason. Reason does not directly determine what the person does.[106]

So far we have seen a place for beliefs and desires and that Plato posits a capacity for self-control. One way to develop Plato's view would be to hold that this capacity involves some further psychic item mediating between beliefs and desires and action. Self-control would be exercised via some psychological item other than raising the strength of the good desire so that raising the strength of the good desire is not a basic act. Moreover, in the sorts of cases that Plato describes it is plausible to see room for such an explanation. The person in the puppet case realizes that one of his emotions, e.g. his anger prompting him to strike back, is right now stronger than his desire not to do so based on his judgment that it is better overall to refrain. It still seems possible, however, for him to commit himself to refraining or to decide not to strike back. What this calls for is recognizing some psychic state—settling upon, deciding, committing, or intending—that is not determined by the balance of the strength of the person's motivations and, once formed, can bring about action. We can still make room for the notion of motivational strength by holding that the formation of such a state brings with it, usually or at least sometimes, a shift in the person's motivational balance. (On this account, the strength of a desire still does the work of bringing about the action when the agent goes for the right thing: pulling is not just the way that non-rational motivations work nor is it an indication that the action is compelled.) This goes beyond what Plato explicitly recognizes in the text, but it is one plausible way to explain the capacity for self-control to which he is committed. Further, insofar as decision is an expression of reason, this suggestion avoids some of the objections raised against the first proposal. Such a suggestion also points beyond cases of self-control. If decision mediates between the person's desires and beliefs and action in cases of conflict, it may have a wider role in practical deliberation. We might see deliberation, for example, as usually issuing in decision.[107]

There is a third possibility worth noting that has implications for Plato's understanding of the nature of the soul. Although we might not want to press the details of the puppet image too far, it at least suggests that the person affects the strength of his good desire or judgment directly, that is, without doing something else. Specifically, he does not form another state, a decision or intention, that has a different motivational force from the good desire. But it is important to see that even if we thought that we should not take such direct intervention literally, the above account points toward a need for something that goes beyond our current analysis. Both the idea that the agent directly intervenes and the alternative that the agent, after reflection on his beliefs and desires, forms an intention or a decision, gives some role to the agent himself. They both present the agent as active with respect to his beliefs and desires and as the initiator of the coming into being of psychic states or changes. Although we could adopt either suggestion in a form that cancels this apparent implication, throughout the later dialogues Plato appeals to the idea that the soul actively engages with some of its affections and beliefs and shows no sign of wanting to reduce this activity or agency to something else (e.g. the interactions of the affections themselves).[108] Moreover, such a view seems to fit well with some of Plato's other claims about the soul in the late dialogues.

Let me first say what this picture of agency suggests and then go on to connect it with some of Plato's later views about the soul. Such a sketch once again goes beyond anything that Plato explicitly says and I shall not try to work out the view in full detail. Nevertheless, the connections between this picture of agency and Plato's metaphysical claims about the soul are not unnatural, and some Neoplatonists, I think, explore related ideas. To begin, on this sort of view, we can distinguish between beliefs and desires on the one hand and various psychic acts on the other. Such acts may include pausing to reflect, actually engaging in reflection on one's beliefs and desires, and various other operations on one's beliefs and desires, including perhaps the formation of desires and the sorts of intervention just described.[109] In order to explain such activity, we may think that we need to recognize, as a first step, a category of psychic *acts* distinct in kind from beliefs and desires. Beliefs and desires are both affections (*pathē*) or things that we undergo. We should allow that such psychic acts, like beliefs and desires, have some content. A second step goes beyond this and recognizes a third sort of item different in kind from both beliefs and desires and acts. This is the soul, which is the source of these psychic acts. The soul is an active principle, distinct from and not entirely constituted by its beliefs, desires, and acts.[110]

It is an important principle of Plato's post-*Republic* views that the soul is a self-mover in a strong sense. Aristotle, too, holds that animate creatures are self-movers, but argues that self-movers are complex wholes. One part of these wholes is unmoved or unchanged, but is the agent of change; another, distinct, moved part undergoes the change. This analysis of self-motion is intended as a rejection of the stronger Platonic position that does not recognize such a distinction within a self-mover. Plato holds that the soul is both the source and subject of its own motion and is not moved by anything else. The soul that changes or moves is itself the source of this change.[111] This does not entail, so to speak, that every aspect of the soul is itself self-moving. We can distinguish, for example, such things as having beliefs or desires (affections or *pathē*), that is, being in a certain state which is itself not identical with a self-change from the formation of certain psychic states or operations upon them. There is a striking passage from the *Timaeus* that draws a special connection between the self-motion of the soul and certain sorts of reflection on its own affections. I shall discuss this passage in more detail in the next chapter, but it is worth looking at it in this connection.

Certainly what we are talking about now [i.e. plants] partakes of the third kind of soul, the kind that our account has situated between the midriff and the navel. This kind is totally devoid of belief and calculation and reason [ᾧ δόξης μὲν λογισμοῦ τε καὶ νοῦ μέτεστιν τὸ μηδέν], but does share in perception, pleasant and painful, together with desires. For it is always wholly passive [πάσχον γὰρ διατελεῖ πάντα]; its formation has not by nature permitted it, revolving in itself around itself, repelling motion from without, and using its own native motion, to discern and reflect on itself. Therefore, to be sure, it lives and is not other than a living thing, but it remains stationary and rooted down since it lacks self-motion [τῆς ὑφ' ἑαυτοῦ κινήσεως].[112]   (*Tim.* 77B3–C5)

Although Plato does not work out the details, what this passage suggests is that there is an intimate connection between self-motion and self-awareness, reflection and having beliefs. Simply having sensory affections is a passive state of receiving transmitted motion and to advance from it to the formation of beliefs requires higher-order reflection on these affections.[113] Such reflection is not a passive state, but rather an activity that expresses the self-motion of the soul: it is an example of unreduced agency. It is natural to extend this idea so that any higher-order reflection on lower-level states is also an activity that is an expression of self-motion. So the sort of intervention that a person is capable of according to the *Laws*' analysis of akrasia would be such a case of a psychic activity that is caused by or expresses the self-motion of the soul.

In the later dialogues, we thus see the starting points for this way of understanding reflection or self-awareness and the role of reflection in other psychic states and activities. This line of thought finds fuller and more complicated expression in the Neoplatonists. But there are two final points to notice. First, the distinction that Plato draws in the *Timaeus* passage is between the original and natural self-motion of the soul and motion that comes from outside. So insofar as acts of reflection are expressions of the original, circular motion of the soul, they will have a special affinity with reason. This is the case since, as we learn elsewhere in the *Timaeus*, circular psychic self-motion is the motion of reason. Such affinity shows that reflection and psychic intervention are not expressions of a faculty separate from reason, but are themselves activities or expressions of reason.

Second, what worries Plato about motions that come from outside is that they are non-rational in origin and distort the inherent rational activities of the soul. The resulting motion is partially caused or brought about by the non-rational force of these outer motions; it is not entirely an expression of the inherent activity of reason. Plato shows no sign, however, of being worried by the problem of determinism itself. It is not the idea that the external motion causally determines the resulting deformation of reason that Plato focuses on, it is rather that the outside motions are a disruption of the inherent activities of reason.[114] The idea that the self-motion of reason provides the metaphysical grounding for a libertarian understanding of choice and other mental activities is a later, but important development in Neoplatonism.[115]

3.9 Origins and Persistence

We have so far considered various explanations of why something other than one's desire for what is overall best can win out. But we also need to consider why there is such competition in the first place. An important task for the new account is to explain the origin and persistence of akratic emotions and desires without invoking agent-like parts of the soul. If there is just one source of deliberative agency, how can we account for the origination of non-rational desires and for their failure to interact rationally with the person's overall judgments and desires? We do not receive an explicit and full account of these issues in the late dialogues, but neither should we expect it. These issues remain difficult problems that Aristotle wrestles with and I do not think that we have a satisfactory account of them today. Nevertheless, I shall briefly indicate the directions opened up by Plato's later views.

To vindicate the possibility of hard akrasia, we need to show, to a first approximation, that

(1) desires can originate in something other than the outcome of practical deliberation, and

(2) desires prompting to akrasia can persist after a conflicting overall best judgment has been reached.

(1) is something that Plato clearly believes and it seems to us a weak requirement. That Plato believes (1) is clear from the puppet image's description of

the different kinds of cords in a person. None of the iron cords stems from the golden cord of calculation, thus these desires and emotions do not arise from reasoned deliberation about what is overall best for the person. Indeed, this shows something stronger than (1), since (1) would be satisfied even if the akratic desires arose only during practical deliberation, but were not always identical with the desire for what is overall best that deliberation issues in. Once we accept (1), we may be able to analyze many cases of apparent hard akrasia as varieties of the less problematic weak akrasia. We can in this way avoid some of the worries surrounding persistence. In cases of weak akrasia, the person does not at the time of the action act against an overall best judgment that he possesses. In impetuous akrasia, the person's overall best judgment is forestalled so that he does not reach one before he acts. In other cases, his overall best judgment is undermined before he acts so that he acts while not fully possessing such a judgment. And even in cases in which the akratic emotion or desire works by interfering with the operations of reason itself so as to produce a distorted overall best judgment, we do not have to account for the persistence of the akratic desire in the face of a conflicting overall judgment.

It is (2) that provides the greater challenge. One important worry here is that the akratic desire and the desire for what is overall best may involve conflicting judgments and in the first part of this chapter we saw that it was this possibility that provided the most plausible reason for accepting agent-like parts in the *Republic*. A first step to avoid such conflict is to see akratic desires as representing their object as something other than overall best. There is no incoherence in thinking that A is good, but B is overall best or that A is pleasant, but B is overall best. And this is a strategy that Plato pursues in the *Laws*. Specifically, Plato thinks that it is especially desires for pleasure that lead to akrasia.[116]

Nevertheless, problems lurk here. First, our beliefs about what is overall best and our desire for it are not entirely insulated from our beliefs about and desires for what is good or what is pleasant. Indeed, the *Laws* more clearly than the *Republic* allows that our judgments about what is good (or best) and fine can influence what we take pleasure in and that our overall judgments can be corrupted by our non-rational desires. Second, does Plato think that it is impossible that when rational deliberation indicates that a certain course of action is not merely not best overall, but simply not really good or not really pleasant, that non-rational desires for such a course persist? Third, our judgment of what is overall best is not merely different from the judgments embodied in non-rational motivations, but in some way is supposed to subsume them or take them into account. In deciding what to do, reason takes into account the good features that the non-rational desires respond to (whether the object of the desire is pleasant or has something else good about it). So we may find A pleasant, but realize that it is not best overall. Yet it still seems reasonable to ask why we are sometimes moved to pursue A rather than just register the fact that it is pleasant and why we are sometimes moved all the way to action. On the *Republic*'s theory, this was not at all surprising. The lower parts of the soul had, so to speak, their own points of view. They had their own characteristic ends and thus their desires continue to press for fulfillment even in the face of the judgments of the Reasoning part, unless they are persuaded that the course of action recommended by reason is the best way to pursue their own ends. Such persistence is much more puzzling once we think that there is a single source of deliberative agency. All the judgments involved in these desires and emotions are made by the same subject. So why are they not better integrated?

It is not enough to explain this persistence that one's non-rational desire and one's desire for what is overall best are distinct entities or distinct affections. Consider, for example, the parallel with belief. In the course of reasoning out what I think is true, I will take into account my initial judgments and preliminary conclusions. But once I reach a final judgment about what is true, these preliminary beliefs, if they conflict, tend to disappear.[117] Why is this not true in the case of my non-rational motivations? The following very simple story about belief may help to clarify some of the issues. Belief, let us say, is taking a certain proposition to be true. If I did not lose my earlier beliefs when I came to my conflicting judgment, I would be in the situation of, at the same time, taking the same proposition to be true and taking it to be false. And it is very hard to see how I could do this. The case of desire is quite different. There is nothing especially troubling in seeing how I could have both a pro- and a con-attitude toward the proposition 'I eat sweets now.' Although the parallel with the case of belief is not exact, what would be problematic is both intending (or trying) to eat sweets now and intending (or trying) not to eat sweets now. But no such phenomenon is necessary for akratic action. Although there is a single subject of both desires, the impulse to action is not under its direct control. Desires, in addition to having content and often being backed up by beliefs, have motivational force and this force is a non-representational feature of the desire that is independent of the judgment-making capacity.

We have seen that it is a central part of Plato's explanation of akrasia in the *Laws* that a desire has motivational force and that this force can be misaligned with the evaluation of the object of the desire. Nevertheless, we should not want to make the motivational strength of a desire too independent of its content. Akrasia is not the result of freely floating motivational force simply attaching to some desire or other. Akratic temptations both across individuals and within the lives of individuals have typical patterns. Plato, for example, stresses that the pleasures of food, sex, and drink are the main sources of hard akrasia. In these cases, a strong impulse to action is not inexplicable and although not pursuing them is sometimes overall best, even in these cases the desire is backed by a certain kind of rationality. Can we explain this without falling back into accepting agent-like parts of the soul? What it seems that we need is something less than an agent that still in some way rationalizes, to a certain extent, the akratic pursuit of the object.

We do, I think, find an intriguing suggestion in the *Philebus*. In the course of an inquiry into the nature and origin of desire, Plato gives an account of the desire of thirst. This is especially interesting, since thirst was the example used in the *Republic* to establish the partitioning of the soul. Plato here characterizes thirst as a desire for filling with drink. So it is more than the uncomfortable registering of a lack, it is already an impulse to action. Insofar as a person is thirsty, his desire is not for what he is currently experiencing, since what he is experiencing is rather an emptying. His desire is for filling.

Something in the person who is thirsty must somehow be in contact with filling . . . But it is impossible that this should be the body, for the body is what is emptied out . . . The only option we are left with is that the soul makes contact with the filling, and it clearly must do so through memory . . . This impulse, then, that leads him [the person] towards the contrary of its own state signifies that it has memory of that contrary state . . . it is this memory that directs it towards the objects of its

desires ... [τὴν ... ἐπάγουσαν ἐπὶ τὰ ἐπιθυμούμενα ... μνήμην]   (Phil.
35B6–D1)[118]

What is especially interesting about this passage is that, according to it, it is
the memory that leads towards the thing desired. The memory of fullness,
conjoined with the present awareness of emptiness, produces a directed
desire toward filling with drink. It is not suggested that this is a description
of rational deliberation producing the judgment that it is best overall to
drink, rather it is simply the description of the genesis of an ordinary desire
to drink. Such a desire is more than just the awareness of a certain kind of
current discomfort, but is a goal-directed movement towards action. If such
a psychic process need not be an instance of practical deliberation, it is
tempting to think that it need not be fully responsive to it either. The perception of emptiness goes together with the memory quasi-automatically to
produce a desire as an actual impulse toward action that displays goal-
directed rationality.

Such an account would need a great deal of further filling out, but it has
the potential to offer an explanation of why such desires can continue to
prompt to action and sometimes move the agent all the way to action even
in the face of a conflicting overall best judgment. Memory is sub-agential,
but it has a certain structure that allows it to play a role in forming goal-
directed impulses to action, that is, desires. If the process does not require
the independent concurrent action of reason, it seems that we can explain
why the desire can produce akrasia. The appeal to memories which are
embedded in perceptual and physiological processes will also help to
explain why akratic temptations take certain characteristic forms.
Moreover, if such interactions between perceptions and memories are not
always open to direct influence by rational thought and reflection, then we
may also be able to explain certain sorts of akrasia that suggest something
like the persistence of conflicting judgments or at least a tendency to make
a conflicting judgment. (Desires for such pleasure may be additionally reinforced by the tendency to rationalize the desires that one has. And it seems
possible that the rationalized desire might not employ the same conceptualization of the pleasure as is embodied in the memory.) Memories have a
certain conceptual structure. The memory invoked above seems, for exam-

ple, to use the concept of fullness. If memories are not fully open to revision by rational reflection (or at least are not always actually so revised), the concepts embedded in them might remain the same while rational reflection leads to conceptual development. For example, early on in development, the person may take as pleasant ridding himself of pain. If memories are then laid down employing this concept of pleasure and function as the memory involved in the production of thirst does, the person would tend to have desires in certain circumstances for something as pleasant because it consists in ridding himself of pain. Such desires may persist even when the person's rational reflection has enabled him to see that ridding himself of pain or the absence of pain itself is not really a pleasure at all. This line of thought goes beyond what we explicitly find in the text, but it is one reasonable way to fill out Plato's position and it uses resources that he develops in the *Philebus*.

But memory's capacity to render us susceptible to akrasia can also be used to form an important ethical safeguard. Even in Magnesia's controlled environment, citizens are subject to influences that can corrupt their ethical character. Memories laid down in childhood and youth, however, can help to fix what it is that adults find pleasant. Insofar as these memories do embody some grasp of genuinely valuable pleasures, for instance, those that embody some grasp of good order, they can serve two beneficial functions. First, they provide a persistent source of motivation: adults will tend to continue to find these old pleasures pleasant. Doing so will help make them more resistant, for example, to corrupting innovations in music. The old pleasures provide a standard by which adults can judge—even if this judgment is not fully explicit and proceeds by using an unarticulated standard of similarity—whether the new pleasures are worth pursuing. The old pleasures can thus serve to fix their judgments and experiences of pleasure upon the appropriate pleasures without argument and perhaps even in the face of spurious arguments (that they cannot answer) in favor of new pleasures. Second, as we have seen, Plato thinks that the value embodied in certain valuable pleasures is the very same value that makes things good or fine. We should thus expect adults' fixed tastes in pleasures to help protect them not only against innovation in pleasures, but also against ethical change more generally. Faulty ethical innovations, beyond those found in new poetry or music, will fail to accord with their pleasures. Here, too, entrenched memories that are not easily open to revision will help to make the citizens resistant to deceptively attractive innovations without and, perhaps even in the face of, argument.

3.10 The Virtues

In the final section of this chapter, I shall briefly consider some of the implications of Plato's psychology for his understanding of the virtues and shall focus on courage and moderation. As we have seen so far, virtue as a whole consists in knowledge of (or true belief about) what is good along with the proper orientation to the good. Although this orientation includes dispositions to make certain choices and to perform certain actions, it is not restricted to such dispositions and includes, for example, a wide variety of emotions, desires, and tendencies to take pleasure and pain in various things and activities. Nor must such states always consist in some attitude toward the good as such. What is important is that these states affect the person's capacity to know and pursue the good.

We may approach courage by considering the initial views of Kleinias that the Athenian starts from and reacts against. Kleinias holds that courage does not require the rest of the virtues either to exist or to be beneficial for its possessor and he seems to see courage as primarily directed against fear and pain.[119] Plato insists on a much broader conception of courage: it opposes, in the appropriate way, not only fear and pain, but also longing or desire and pleasure.[120] Courage is the general ability to resist all such things in the appropriate way. This account of courage immediately reflects the difference between the *Laws* and the *Republic* over the partitioning of the soul. The *Republic* defined courage as the preservation by the Spirited part of the soul of the command handed down by the Reasoning part in the face of pleasures and pains (*Rep.* 442B11–C3), but the *Laws* rejects the idea that the Spirited part can have beliefs and instead focuses on the relation between the person and his various affections.[121] Insofar as courage involves a disposition to struggle in the appropriate circumstances, it seems that a courageous person may still have fears or pleasures that conflict with his other aims or desires. Even when courage is basically properly directed by wisdom, conflicting fears or desires may still persist. Thus even when courage is properly led by wisdom, a courageous person may not be entirely free from misdirected fears and desires (or desires that have an inappropriate degree of strength), but rather is able to resist them.[122]

Kleinias' view that a person can have courage while lacking the other virtues conflicts with one of the central claims about the virtues in the early and middle dialogues, the Reciprocity of the Virtues. (Indeed, this claim is prominent in Greek ethics in general.)

Reciprocity of the Virtues: A person has a virtue if and only if the person has every virtue.[123]

In the *Laws* and elsewhere in the later dialogues, Plato sometimes uses 'courage' and 'moderation' to refer to psychic conditions that can exist in a person apart from the other virtues.[124] Courage, for example, at times seems to be the ability to resist fears, pleasures, and so on in support of one's beliefs about what is overall best, even if these beliefs are mistaken.[125] This ability to resist fears, pleasures, and so on is usually exercised by enlisting certain emotions, especially shame, on the side of one's desire for the overall best outcome. If Plato allows such cases, they will violate the Reciprocity of the Virtues.

The possibility that one might have courage or moderation, but lack wisdom is not the only challenge that the Reciprocity of the Virtues faces. One might also worry, for example, about the possibility of possessing wisdom, but lacking one of the other virtues.[126] But I shall focus here on the concern about courage and a similar one concerning moderation. Plato presents two different accounts of moderation in the *Laws* and he makes it clear that they are different. The first describes moderation as the ability to resist pleasures: it is a kind of self-restraint (*enkrateia*) with regard to pleasures (with regard to pleasure: e.g. *Laws* 673E5, 840B5–C9; perhaps with regard to fear: e.g. 648D3 with E6). As in the case of courage, direction toward what is actually best for the agent is not built into this conception of moderation and it is thus possible that such self-restraint may be exercised in the service of bad ends. Such an account of moderation, however, makes it difficult to distinguish from courage and is too weak to capture Plato's full view.[127]

In other passages, Plato identifies moderation with a kind of consonance. On this account, moderation is consonance (*sumphōnia*) between one's desires, especially one's desires for pleasure and the avoidance of pain, and one's judgments about what is overall best. A moderate state of soul is one in which the person's desires are directed toward what he believes to be overall best for himself and in which he has no desires, or only few and weak desires, for something other than what he thinks overall best.[128] This is not to say that in a moderate person all of his desires aim directly at what is overall best for himself, but only that there is a coincidence between the object of his desire for what is overall best and his other desires. He may, for example, desire certain things simply as pleasant, but he will still be moderate if the object of these desires is what he also judges overall best. But even on this conception of moderation as consonance, we might have a worry parallel to the case of courage. Why might there not still be, in a person lacking virtue, such a consonance between his overall best judgments and his desires and pleasures?

Nevertheless, we should not be too quick to assume that there is a fundamental change in Plato's position on the Reciprocity of the Virtues. To see why this is so, we must take into account Plato's claim that such 'virtues' do not benefit their possessor apart from wisdom.[129] The Reciprocity of the Virtues is endangered, however, only if what exists apart from the other virtues is itself a genuine virtue and Plato might reasonably deny that any psychic quality that does not benefit its possessor is a virtue. Does such a defense make the Reciprocity of the Virtues trivial? The worry is this. Suppose that two people differ in that one person possesses all the virtues including wisdom, but the other has false beliefs about what is overall best. If it were possible for this difference with respect to knowledge about what is best to be the only psychological difference between these two people, we might worry that denying that the one lacking wisdom possesses courage and moderation makes the Reciprocity of the Virtues uninteresting. If the intrinsic properties of the psychological state that grounded the virtuous person's courage and moderation were the same as the intrinsic properties grounding the non-virtuous person's 'courage' and 'moderation', then denying that such courage and moderation are really virtues because the relational properties of these states were different (one is guided by knowledge, the other by false belief) might seem to make the Reciprocity of the Virtues true by fiat. Plato will be able to avoid this outcome if there are intrinsic differences between these two grounding states. The most promising way of showing this will be by allowing that reason in a virtuous person shapes the non-rational motivations such that they must differ from the corresponding motivations in a non-virtuous person.[130]

Thus once again we find that Plato's more general views about psychology affect his understanding of the virtues. Insofar as Plato allows for greater overlap between reason and the non-rational motivations, his defense of the Reciprocity of the Virtues will be stronger and more interesting. For example, as I shall argue in the next chapter, Plato gives a prominent place in ethical education in Magnesia to the development of certain sensory pleasures that involve a low-level grasp of genuine value. They are, so to speak, ways of apprehending value in a sensory mode. Insofar as genuine moderation involves having such pleasures, it will differ in a significant way from the 'moderation' of the non-virtuous.

Plato's acceptance of a unified understanding of the soul offers some hope that the non-rational motivations may, insofar as they can now draw upon reason's resources, have a larger and more important place in the life of the virtuous person. If their content can, at least partially, be determined by the person's grasp of genuine value properties, the non-rational motivations might themselves embody some sort of awareness of value. As I have argued, this will make Plato's defense of the Reciprocity of the Virtues stronger and more philosophically interesting. But it would also help with the problem we noted in Chapter 2 about the value of the good condition of the lower parts of the soul and, thus, of courage and moderation. There we saw that given the content of the emotions, desires, and beliefs of the lower parts in the *Republic*, we might reasonably worry whether their good condition was of significant value or even of more than instrumental value. A more unified conception of the soul suggests a way of vindicating the value of the non-rational motivations.

Nevertheless, this increased optimism about the non-rational motivations is only part of the story about them in the later dialogues. We also find there what is, in some respects, an increasingly pessimistic picture. The *Phaedrus* seems to rule out the possibility that reason can persuade the Appetitive part of the soul and the *Timaeus* offers a strikingly impoverished conception of the Appetitive part's capacities. There is also concern about the Spirited part. *Thumos* no longer seems to have the natural function, as it did in the *Republic*, of putting into effect the commands of the Reasoning part. If reason is capable by itself of ruling the appetites, spirit understood as anger might be grouped together with the appetites and Plato in both the *Statesman* and the *Laws* is increasingly sensitive to the negative and dangerous aspects of anger. To make progress on these and related issues, we must turn to some new topics.

4 Parts of the Soul and Non-Rational Motivations

4.1 *Introduction*

Let us begin by taking stock. We have seen that in the *Republic* Plato draws a sharp distinction between philosophers and non-philosophers and holds that the latter cannot be genuinely virtuous or happy. This claim rests on Plato's psychology and epistemology and, in particular, on his partitioning of the soul. In the *Republic*, Plato partitions the soul into three parts, the Reasoning part, the Spirited part, and the Appetitive part. These parts have characteristic beliefs, desires, pleasures, ends or goals, and epistemic resources. In non-philosophers, one of the two lower parts rules and in ruling determines the content of the end for the person, but this is the proper task of the Reasoning part. Thus in non-philosophers the Reasoning part fails to do its job of determining, on the basis of its own resources, the person's end; rather, it simply takes over, unreflectively, the goals and desires of the lower parts. Since the lower parts do not—and, given their epistemic limitations, cannot—aim at genuine virtue for its own sake or at what is genuinely good in itself, non-philosophers also fail in these basic ways. Ordinary people are bound to live deeply defective lives because they are incapable of grasping the features of things that make them genuinely valuable. Further, it is this understanding of the parts of the soul that allows Plato to give an account of akrasia and of non-rational motivation in general.

In Chapter 1, I argued that these ethical defects of non-philosophers originate in their epistemic limitations. In the *Republic*, the Spirited part is the home of emotions such as anger and of the desire for honor; the Appetitive part is the home of desires for the bodily satisfactions of food, sex, and drink. I argue that Plato's view, in the *Republic*, is that we can have such emotions and desires without, either explicitly or implicitly, drawing on knowledge of Forms. We can form concepts of the objects involved, discriminate them from other kinds of objects, and engage in some forms of reasoning about them (e.g. means–end reasoning) without drawing on an awareness of Forms. In non-philosophers, the Reasoning part of the soul does not reach a higher cognitive level: in its valuing of things it, too, operates with concepts drawn from perception, not with concepts arising from an awareness of value Forms. It is only in philosophers that the Reasoning part comes to have an awareness of such Forms and thus comes to grasp the fundamental intelligible properties (and the relations among them) that must be grasped in order to understand whatever order and structure there is in the world or to understand what is genuinely good, fine, or beautiful.

If, as I have argued, Plato is more optimistic about the ethical capacities of non-philosophers in the *Laws*, then his psychology and epistemology must have changed in some important respects. I argued in Chapter 3 that Plato in the *Laws* rejects the *Republic's* tripartitioning of the soul into agent-like parts. He still holds that the soul is complex and has both rational and non-rational elements or aspects, but in the *Laws* he recognizes only a single subject of beliefs, desires, emotions, and so on. This is an essential step toward the *Laws'* more optimistic understanding of non-philosophers, since the defects of non-philosophers in the *Republic* stemmed from the fact that they were ruled by one of the lower parts of the soul.[1] It is not yet sufficient, however, for we must still establish that non-philosophers possess the resources needed for valuing virtue for its own sake and being genuinely virtuous. But it is the partitioning of the person that underlies Plato's earlier pessimism about non-philosophers.

This leaves me with three tasks in this chapter. First, I shall offer an account of Plato's post-*Republic* psychology that shows why it develops into the more unitary conception of the soul that I find in the *Laws*. This account will allow us to fit together and make sense of a number of hitherto disconnected developments in Plato's later psychology and epistemology. Second, I shall take up the implications of Plato's later views about the soul for his understanding of what sort of creatures we are and of what benefits us. Finally, I shall examine the implications of Plato's later psychology and epistemology for his understanding of the non-rational motivations, especially some aspects of his views about spirited emotions and pleasure.

4.2 The Impoverishment of the Lower Parts of the Soul

Introduction   One might find it simply quixotic to search for evidence of a more unitary conception of the soul in the late dialogues, since the *Phaedrus* and the *Timaeus* might be thought to present nearly insuperable problems for the idea that there is a change of this sort in Plato's late ethical psychology. Specifically, one might object that it is most unlikely that the *Laws* abandons the claim that the soul is composed of agent-like parts, since the *Phaedrus* and the *Timaeus*, both of which also post-date the *Republic*, unequivocally endorse the *Republic*'s partitioning of the soul. Both the *Phaedrus* and the *Timaeus* divide the soul into three parts and freely attribute beliefs and desires to these parts.

We could make several replies to this worry. If the *Phaedrus* is dated relatively close to the *Republic*, there is ample time for Plato's position to change. Even if the *Timaeus* is to be dated relatively late, for example after the *Theaetetus*, we may still hold that there is sufficient time for Plato's views to develop in the direction of the *Laws*.[2] Or we might argue that discrepancies between the *Laws* on the one hand and the *Phaedrus* and the *Timaeus* on the other can be explained not by appeal to chronology, but rather by the literary character of the latter two dialogues. Neither the account of the tripartite soul in the discourse of the *Timaeus* nor the account found in the myth of Socrates' second speech in the *Phaedrus* is intended as literally true psychological theory. Yet even if we were to accept both of these points, they would simply give us reason to read away the apparent claims of the *Phaedrus* and the *Timaeus*; they would not provide any positive reason to think that Plato's thought is developing in the direction of the *Laws*' position. Even this much, however, might leave us sympathetic to the more unitary interpretation, since, as I have argued, Plato has strong philosophical reasons to reject *Republic*-style partitioning and such partitioning is absent from several late dialogues where we would expect to find it. (I shall also argue that we find additional reason to reject partitioning in the *Theaetetus*.)

But a more direct argument is available. A closer examination of the *Phaedrus* and the *Timaeus* reveals a more interesting situation than so far suggested. What I shall argue is that we do not need to explain the *Phaedrus* and the *Timaeus* away; rather the two dialogues help to show why Plato's views evolve in the way that they do. Beginning in the *Phaedrus*, Plato starts to make some sort of awareness of the Forms a part of ordinary, i.e. non-philosophic and non-scientific, cognition. Recollection of the Forms is invoked to explain some of the judgments, including judgments about value, that non-philosophers make. The *Timaeus* and the *Theaetetus* (another post-*Republic* dialogue) go further and require that in order to make any judgment at all, the soul must draw on an awareness of non-sensible properties or Forms. (I note below some possible qualifications to these claims that do not affect the main argument.) Neither the *Timaeus* nor the *Theaetetus* requires the person to be aware of Forms, as such, in ordinary judgments, but they do hold that even the most basic judgments require the use of concepts that are drawn from an awareness of Forms, not simply from perception. Non-philosophers are thus not entirely cut off from an awareness of genuine value and the right sort of education can bring it about that they are aware of, albeit still partially, the genuinely valuable features of things and value them as such.

Embedding an awareness, even if often very imperfect, of Forms in ordinary cognition also has drastic consequences for the *Republic*'s theory of parts of the soul. In the *Phaedrus* and the *Timaeus*, Plato emphasizes that the lower parts of the soul are incapable of any contact with the Forms at all. Thus, since such contact is required for more ordinary sorts of cognition, the lower parts are increasingly cognitively impoverished. By the time of the *Timaeus*, Plato holds that the lower parts are incapable of belief or opinion (*doxa*). The consequences of this for his psychology are momentous. If the lower parts are no longer capable of belief or conceptualized emotions or desires, then they can no longer be agent-like in the way that the parts of the soul were in the *Republic*. They are no longer subjects at all, since they can no longer have conceptualized states. This is, as we shall see, a sufficient motivation for the

Laws' abandonment of agent-like parts of the soul and it brings with it the new and large project of understanding non-rational motivations as involving distorted or partial applications of reason.

So let us turn to the *Phaedrus* and the *Timaeus*. We find in both dialogues, although to a more marked extent in the *Timaeus* than the *Phaedrus*, two tendencies. First, Plato adopts in an exaggerated way the strategy of recognizing agent-like parts, that is, he attributes beliefs and desires to entities which he does not think literally have beliefs or desires or he attributes to the parts of the soul more sophisticated beliefs and desires than the rest of this theory allows. Second, Plato works out epistemological and metaphysical reasons that undermine the capacity of the parts of the soul to have beliefs and contentful emotions and desires.

Let us begin by considering some instances of exaggeration. In the *Timaeus*, for example, the penis and the womb are each ensouled living creatures (ζῷον . . . ἔμψυχον, *Tim.* 91A2–3) that have their own desires and the womb, at least, is capable of something like anger in addition to its desire for childbearing (*Tim.* 91B3–C4).[3] Similarly, consider Timaeus' description of the Spirited part of the soul.

That part of the soul, then, which partakes of courage and spirit, since it is a lover of victory, they settled nearer the head, between the midriff and the neck so that it might hearken to reason and, together with it, forcibly [βίᾳ] restrain the part consisting of desires whenever it should utterly refuse to yield willing obedience to the word of command from the citadel. And the heart, which is the junction of the veins and the fount of the blood which circulates vigorously through all the limbs, they set in the guardhouse, in order that, when the force of the spirit boils up, as soon as reason passes the word round [τοῦ λόγου παραγγείλαντος] that some unjust action is being done which affects them, either from without or even from the desires within, every sentient part of the body [πᾶν ὅσον αἰσθητικὸν ἐν τῷ σώματι] should quickly perceive through all the channels both the exhortations and the threats and in all ways obey and follow them, thus allowing their best part to be the leader of them all. (*Tim.* 70A2–C1)

The pumping of the blood throughout the body when the person, or his *thumos*, is angry at an injustice is portrayed here as passing on information to a sentient body. But neither in this case nor in that of the penis and the womb is there any temptation to take literally these attributions of beliefs or desires. The *Timaeus* is concerned with the interaction of the soul and the body and in these passages is especially concerned with the bodily effects of psychic states, but this does not give us a good reason to think that these attributions of belief are meant literally. Nor, as we shall shortly see, could we attribute the beliefs and desires of the penis and the womb to the Appetitive part itself; nor could the *thumos* pass on words of encouragement or threats to the Appetitive part. In the *Timaeus*, the Appetitive part is no more capable of belief than the penis or the womb.

In the *Phaedrus*, on the other hand, the exaggeration concerns the capacities of the parts of the soul. For example, when the Reasoning and Spirited parts reject having sex with the loved boy, the black horse (the symbol of the Appetitive part in the *Phaedrus*), 'breaks forth into angry reproaches, bitterly reviling his mate and the charioteer for their cowardice and lack of courage in deserting their post and breaking their agreement' (*Phdr.* 254C6–D1). But this either attributes to the Appetitive part a concern with courage and keeping one's agreements or something like the deceptive intent to make such claims, without itself accepting them, in order to talk the other two parts around. Either of these possibilities, however, seems implausible in light of the intellectual limitations of the Appetitive part in the *Phaedrus*. It is a horse that is 'shaggy-eared, deaf, and scarcely yielding to whip and goad together' (*Phdr.* 253E4–5); it is trained only by the use of force, not by words of command.[4] To see how the capacities of the Spirited part might also be exaggerated, we need to consider in more detail the ways in which Plato restricts both of the lower parts in the *Phaedrus* and the *Timaeus*.

Recollection in the Phaedrus *(I)*   It is a common theme of both the *Phaedrus* and the *Timaeus* that the lower two parts of the soul are epistemically highly impoverished. The *Timaeus* explicitly goes further than the *Phaedrus*, so let us begin with the *Phaedrus*. In the *Phaedrus'* myth, both human and divine souls are portrayed as tripartite and the individual soul is depicted as a charioteer driving two horses, one white and one black. The Reasoning part of the soul is the charioteer and the two horses represent the two lower parts. The myth describes how the gods' souls and disembodied human souls interact with the Forms which are located in a region 'above the heavens'. Let us first consider the account given for the gods and then that for humans.

The region above the heavens has never yet been celebrated as it deserves by any earthly poet ... What is in this place is without color and without shape and without solidity, a being that really is what it is [i.e. Platonic Forms], the subject of all true knowledge, visible only to reason [νῷ], the soul's steersman. Now a god's thought [θεοῦ διάνοια] is nourished by reason and pure knowledge, as is the thought of any soul that is concerned to receive what is appropriate to it, and so is delighted at last to be seeing what is and watching what is true, feeding on all this and made happy until the revolution brings it around in a circle to the same place. On the way around, it has a view of Justice as it is; it has a view of Moderation; it has a view of Knowledge—not the knowledge that is close to change, that becomes different as it knows the different things that we consider real down here. No, it is the knowledge of what really is what it is.   (*Phdr.* 247C3–E2)

Now that is the life of the gods. As for the other souls, one that follows a god most closely, making itself most like that god, raises the head of its charioteer up into the place outside and is carried around in the revolution with the others. Although distracted by its horses, this soul does have a view, just barely [μόγις καθορῶσα], of the things that are. Another rises at one time and falls at another, and because its horses pull it violently in different directions, it sees some things and misses others. (*Phdr.* 248A1–6)

According to the myth, human souls fall and become embodied and after death rejoin the procession. But Plato is emphatic that it is not only in one cycle of birth that the lower parts of the soul fail to see the Forms: at no point in their entire eternal span of existence do they see any of the Forms, however briefly or however indistinctly. Something in their constitution apparently renders them by nature incapable of any contact with the Forms. This is a radical and permanent difference in kind between the higher and lower parts. The inability of the lower parts to see the Forms is for Plato a central part of the myth's message, since he insistently draws our attention to it by repeating the point with variation: once for the gods, once for human beings, once non-metaphorically (the Forms are accessible only to reason (*nous*) and thought (*dianoia*)), and once metaphorically (only the charioteer's head rises to the region beyond the heavens).

The fact that in humans the lower parts of the soul never see the Forms, while the highest part sees, at least indistinctly, at least some Forms, may seem to be a tedious and philosophically uninteresting detail of the myth's machinery. But this fact is, I think, central to Plato's later psychology and ethics and it has a homelier version. Leaving aside for the moment the issue of the agent-like status of a part of the soul, we can say quite generally that each part of the soul specifies, in terms of a characteristic grouping of beliefs, desires, capacities, and (at least in some cases) emotions, one of the fundamentally distinct ways in which human beings can be motivated to act. The rational part is bound up with our capacities and desires for theoretical understanding and with the application of reason to determine what is genuinely good and to seek the agent's genuine good. But there are characteristic kinds of motivation that are not caused by our desire for theoretical understanding or our rational pursuit of the good, such as anger, the bodily appetites, and desires for bodily pleasures. If such emotions and desires do not spring from reason, it is then appropriate to ask what sort of cognitive resources are involved in the origin and persistence of such motivations and in the determination of their content. What sort of thinking and what sort of capacities enter into our non-rational motivations? Answering these questions will be essential for understanding the nature of the non-rational motivations and thus for understanding how they can interact with our rational motivations and the sort of worth our non-rational motivations can have.

On the *Phaedrus'* account, non-rational motivations cannot include as part of their content concepts drawn from an awareness of Forms. So these motivations cannot discriminate objects using such concepts and they cannot respond to objects as possessing the properties that correspond to these concepts. This in turn has implications for how they can interact with rational motivations. Consider, for example, Alcinous' account of such interaction.

And because there exists neither science nor art in any other part of the soul than the reasoning element, the virtues that relate to the appetitive part are not such as to be teachable, because they are neither arts nor sciences (for they have no proper object of study). Indeed wisdom, in its capacity as science, bestows on each of the other virtues their proper objects, even as the helmsman instructs the sailors about certain things that are not visible to them, and they obey him . . .[5]

The reasoning part gives the proper objects to the lower parts because these objects are not visible to the lower parts. But the commands of the reasoning part have to be such that the lower parts can understand them. What the lower parts can understand depends on the concepts that they have and such communications from the reasoning element do not impart to them the new concepts necessary for possessing the arts and sciences. What they receive are commands framed in terms of the concepts they can apply.

Plato's view in the *Phaedrus* is that the lower parts do not ever see the Forms, but how severe a limitation is this? If the lower parts do not ever see the Forms, they cannot recollect them and thus cannot possess the concepts derived from such recollection.[6] So in order to see how great a limitation this is, we must consider the *Phaedrus'* account of recollection. Such an inability to recollect would not impose a severe restriction if, for example, Dominic Scott were right that 'recollection starts only with the process of philosophizing.'[7] On Scott's view, non-philosophers do not even begin to recollect and although their souls do contain deeply buried knowledge of the Forms, this knowledge does not influence in any way their beliefs, desires, current epistemic abilities, or ways of seeing the world: for the non-philosopher 'the memory of the forms is playing no role in his life at all.'[8] If this were right, then the lower parts of the soul would, in virtue of failing to see the Forms, be no more cognitively limited than ordinary non-philosophers. But for the *Phaedrus*, this account of the role of the Forms is not correct.

Seeing why it is not correct will give us a better understanding of some important aspects of Plato's later ethical psychology: in particular, it will give us a better understanding of what non-philosophers can do, but the lower parts of the soul cannot. First, consider the *Phaedrus'* account of the different kinds of lives that people live. When in one of its passages through the heavens, the soul

fails to see [μὴ ἴδῃ] because it could not keep up, and by some mischance takes on a burden of forgetfulness and badness, then it is weighed down, sheds its feathers and falls to the earth. At that point, according to the law, the soul is not born into a wild animal in its first incarnation; but a soul that has seen the most [πλεῖστα ἰδοῦσαν] will be planted in the seed of a man who will become a philosopher, or a lover of beauty, or a lover of the Muses, or an erotic man. The second sort of soul will be put into someone who will be a law-abiding king, or someone fit for generalship and ruling; the third into that of a politician, or a household manager, or a businessman . . . (*Phdr.* 248c5–d7)

The list continues through another six lives (for a total of nine kinds of life): doctor or trainer, seer or expert in mystic rites, poet or imitative artist, craftsman or farmer, sophist or demagogue, and tyrant. So for this entire range of people, the different kinds of lives they lead is determined by how much of the Forms they have seen (and how distinctly) in their passage through the heavens prior to the transit in which they saw none.[9] Those below the philosophical life have seen some of the Forms and it is not the case that the knowledge is so deeply buried that it cannot influence them. The amount of Forms they have seen is supposed to *explain* the different goals they have and so it must influence their thinking. (Since there are close connections among the Forms, differences in numbers of Forms seen and in the clarity with which they are seen should ramify.) Put into the framework of the myth, the choice they make among these lives is determined, or at least constrained and influenced, by the Forms that they have seen.

The details are, admittedly, hard to spell out. Presumably we do not want to say that the difference is that, e.g., a doctor saw the Form of Health, a craftsman the Form of Bed, and so on.[10] But while trying to fill in these details is not a philosophically significant task, it is philosophically significant that it is hard to do so. What such difficulty indicates is how deeply enmeshed ordinary cognition is with the recollection of the buried awareness of Forms. Recollection is not limited to philosophers nor must it occur only as part of an elenctic inquiry, even at its earliest stages (since there is no reason to think that all engage in the elenchus). Plato also deliberately makes room for one's degree of Form-awareness to have quite widespread effects on one's mental life. The various sorts of lives differ in quite complex ways in the kinds of cognitive capacities they involve and especially in the sort of goals pursued as good. These complex differences will be explained, at least in part, by the complex differences in the buried knowledge of Forms that different people possess. The buried amount of knowledge which can be triggered by experience differs in the extent of Forms known and the clarity with which each is known.[11] Even ordinary non-philosophic and non-scientific cognition will depend on a complicated structure of (at least partially) recollected knowledge.

One might object here that Plato does not explicitly say that the soul's amount of Form-awareness determines the kind of life it enters into or is the basis on which the soul chooses its kind of life: all that he explicitly asserts is a correlation between the two.[12] It is, however, quite implausible to think that the correlation is merely accidental, and I think it is clear that *Phdr.* 248C5 ff. conversationally implies the stronger thesis. But a persistent objector might argue that although one's amount of Form-awareness and one's kind of life are not merely accidentally correlated, they have no direct relation, but are both merely outcomes of a common cause. This is not, at least in the abstract, a purely idle skeptical possibility, since one might hold that bad desires are the common cause of the amount of Form-awareness one has and of the sort of life one leads or chooses. Bad desires keep one from seeing the full range of Forms clearly while discarnate and they entirely explain one's choices in an embodied life: one's buried awareness of Forms has no causal role in the formation of one's beliefs and desires while embodied and such awareness does not account for any of their content. This still seems, however, to make the close association between Form-awareness and kind of life in *Phdr.* 248C5 ff. highly misleading. But we also have other reasons to reject this interpretation: for example, it gets wrong the order of the soul's decline at *Phdr.* 248C5–8. The soul's forgetfulness results in its growing heavier and losing its wings: in other words, its loss of knowledge results in the lower two parts growing stronger and more burdensome, not the other way around.[13] We do not need to deny that bad desires can lead to further or deeper forgetfulness, and could even grant that bad desires are partially responsible for individuals' initial forgetfulness while recognizing that individuals' degree of Form-awareness influences their actual choices.[14]

But we also have further decisive evidence that Form-awareness plays a significant role in the choices and lives of at least some non-philosophers. All 'mad' lovers are engaging in recollection, but not all mad lovers are philosophers or have started to engage in philosophizing. ('Mad' lovers are the only sort of lovers that Plato approves of in the *Phaedrus*.) The fourth kind of madness that Socrates distinguishes in his second speech characterizes a man who sees beauty on earth, recollects the 'true Beauty' (τοῦ ἀληθοῦς ἀναμιμνῃσκόμενος), and whose wings begin to grow (*Phdr.* 249D4–7, cf. 249A7–B1).[15] The man who loves the beautiful and partakes in this madness is called a lover (*Phdr.* 249E1–4). When such lovers see here

a likeness of the things up there [τι τῶν ἐκεῖ ὁμοίωμα], they are driven out of their wits and lose control of themselves, although they do not know what has happened to them because of their lack of clear perception [ἐκπλήττονται καὶ οὐκέτ' αὐτῶν γίγνονται, ὃ δ' ἔστι τὸ πάθος ἀγνοοῦσι διὰ τὸ μὴ ἱκανῶς διαισθάνεσθαι].   (*Phdr.* 250A6–B1)

Although this group is 'few', it includes more than philosophers. For an especially clear case, consider the second pair of lovers that Socrates contrasts with those who lead a life in which philosophy prevails (*Phdr.* 256A–B). The second pair lead a life that is 'coarser and without philosophy, but ruled by the love of honor [φορτικωτέρᾳ τε καὶ ἀφιλοσόφῳ, φιλοτίμῳ]' (*Phdr.* 256B7–C1). As a result, they inappropriately indulge their sexual desires.[16] Nevertheless, their wings have begun to grow (*Phdr.* 256D3–5, cf. 249A7–B1), that is, they have begun to recollect (*Phdr.* 249D4–7 and 251A1–D7, especially 251B6 and D2). But there are other non-philosophical lovers. In the progression of souls through the heavens, each follows a different god (*Phdr.* 246E4–247A7, cf. 250B5–C6). Only the followers of Zeus have a philosophic nature (*Phdr.* 250B6–8, cf. 252E1–5), but followers of all the gods have seen the Forms (*Phdr.* 250B5–C6). And some of the followers of all the gods can be mad lovers; Socrates explicitly mentions only Ares, Hera, and Apollo (*Phdr.* 252C4–253C6), but he extends the point to all the gods (*Phdr.* 252D1, 253B3). It would be pedantic to try to match up the nine kinds of lives with the twelve gods, but this shows that recollection extends well down the list of lives (including the second and sixth lives). The followers of the other gods display the standard signs of participating in a mad love: they seek to educate their beloved and appear to neglect their own interests (*Phdr.* 253A–C).

The recollection of Beauty in each case starts with seeing a likeness of the Form of Beauty (*Phdr.* 250A6, 251A1–5), but not all mad lovers see these likenesses *as* likenesses of the Form of Beauty. Nevertheless, although their response is highly partial and imperfect, they are for the first time responding to a likeness of Beauty *because* it is a likeness of the Form of Beauty, that is, they are responding to it in virtue of their (dim) recollection and thus are responding to it in ways that are (to varying degrees of approximation) appropriate. They seek, for example, to educate their beloved and to instantiate in him what they take to be good and fine characteristics. In this they differ from the non-mad lover who acts as if he did not see the Form at all (*Phdr.* 250E4–5).[17]

Seeing a likeness of the Form of Beauty will, in the mad lover, trigger the buried awareness that he has of the Form of Beauty. This link is causal: recollecting will not be noticing that one's experience is already conceptualized in accordance with one's buried knowledge, but rather consists in making the buried knowledge available. This does not (at least in non-philosophers) necessarily result in coming to believe that there is a Form of Beauty or that the Form is not identical with its sensible instances. Such awareness does not enable its possessor to answer the 'What is F?' question about beauty, nor does it guarantee that the possessor has only true beliefs about beauty and beautiful things. What it does involve is, for the first time, distinguishing beautiful objects from, say, possible objects of sexual pleasure. Doing so involves not only thoughts about beauty or the fine, but also thoughts about the good: for example, that the characteristics of the beloved have a value that makes it the case that he deserves education and, perhaps, the belief that such education benefits both the beloved and the lover. The now accessible dim recollection of the Form of Beauty will both allow a more accurate grouping of beautiful or fine objects, and be connected with other concepts that the person has, such as that of the good. (Unlike the *Phaedo*, recollected knowledge of the Form will be used in conceptualizing particulars even when this conceptualization does not involve the idea that particulars fall short of the Form.) The recollection of one Form brings with it the recollection of others. This will be genuine recollection of the Form of Beauty, since there is the right causal link between the rest of the person's thoughts and his buried knowledge of the Form and the obtaining of this causal link brings with it an appropriate change in content.

Recollection in the Phaedrus *(II)*   These facts about the details of the *Phaedrus'* myth are thus philosophically important for what they tell us about the nature of recollection more generally. Specifically, they give us good reason to reject, at least for the *Phaedrus*, one simple and tempting principle of recollection that finds support in Plato's middle-period theory.

Recollecting the Form of F involves thinking of the Form of F as such.[18]

The existence of non-philosophical lovers gives us sufficient reason to reject this principle, since, as we have seen, they are recollecting, but do not think of the Forms as such. Indeed, what Plato says is consistent with the possibility that some who are recollecting (e.g. the aphilosophic followers of Ares and Apollo) may even deny that there are things such as Forms.[19]

This principle does have, however, a good Platonic heritage. In the *Phaedo*'s account of recollection of the Form of Equal, this is exactly how recollection functions: in recollecting the Form of Equal, one necessarily recognizes its non-identity with sensible equals.[20] It is in this way that the notion that sensible equals are likenesses of the Form of Equal enters the argument: recollection from a likeness always requires that one consider whether the likeness falls short of that of which it is the likeness, that is, of the thing that is recollected (*Phaedo* 74A5–7). Whenever the perception of, say, equal sticks triggers the buried knowledge of the Form of the Equal, one considers whether the likeness, that is, the equal sticks, fall short of the Form of the Equal. Recognizing that they do fall short, the person is immediately aware of the non-identity between the Form of the Equal and sensible equals. The *Phaedo* has no room for recollection from a likeness that is not recognized *as* a likeness of a Form which is not identical with its sensible likeness. The *Republic* does not explicitly mention recollection, but the notion that sensibles are likenesses of the Form plays an epistemological role, as opposed to an ontological role, only at the third level of the Divided Line. It is here that thought sees sensibles as likenesses of the non-sensible: e.g. geometers use and talk about visible shapes, but they are not thinking about them, but rather about that of which they are a likeness (*Rep.* 510D6–7). Exactly what the objects of geometers' thoughts are is controversial, but they do recognize that they are thinking about non-sensible objects or properties and their state is described by Plato as one of knowledge. This is well beyond what many of those who have begun to recollect in the *Phaedrus* do.

Commentators sometimes complain that, although the textual evidence of the *Phaedo* clearly shows that Plato holds that recollection from a likeness always requires that one consider whether the likeness falls short of that of which it is the likeness, that is, of the thing that is recollected, such a requirement is implausible and not philosophically well motivated.[21] But such a requirement expresses a line of thought that is quite natural to theories of innate ideas. The standard challenge facing such theories is the empiricist objection that the content of allegedly innate ideas is in fact derived from the resources of sense perception. Those concepts thought to be innate, the objection runs, are instead acquired either directly from sensory experiences of objects or from the operations of quite general capacities of reason, such as comparison or abstraction, upon the concepts acquired directly from experience.[22] A theory of innate ideas must show either, in its most radical form, that no concepts can be derived from experience in these ways or, in a less radical form, that there are at least some concepts, the innate ones, that cannot be derived in these ways.

Perhaps the most straightforward way of showing that a concept is innate is to show that its content is non-sensible and cannot be, or is not, the result of some general-purpose operation upon the contents of sense-experience. (This is the most straightforward way, but even if the content were wholly sensible, it might be the case that innate resources were needed to form it.) So the sort of recognition of distinctness that the *Phaedo* claims is part of the recollection of a concept might be understood as a way of satisfying a crucial step in the innatist strategy. In the case of the recollection of the concept *equal*, the recognition of distinctness is the realization that the property corresponding to the concept of *equal* does not suffer the compresence of opposites found in sensible properties. Such a realization might play one of two roles. First, without such a recognition the person does not have even prima-facie reason to think that the concept is innate and thus not derived from sense-experience. But all that this tends to show, it seems, is that such a person would have no reason to think that this concept was innate or recollected; it would not tend to show that such a concept is not in fact innate or recollected. Plato might think, however, that we can give such recognition a more central role. He might think that such a recognition is (at least partially) constitutive of having the relevant concept.

Nor is this an entirely implausible requirement for concept possession. For example, even without an explicit account of concept possession, it seems intuitively plausible that a person lacks the concept *greater than* if she applies the concept that she does have, G, only to pairs of physical objects that are such that one is longer than the other.[23] We may find it similarly intuitively plausible that having the concept *equal* requires grasping that the concept is not definable in purely sensible terms. Such a conclusion might well follow if, for example, one held what has historically been a very common account of concept possession, that is, to have the concept F (where F is not a primitive concept) one must grasp the definition of F.[24] (But note that our intuitive judgment about the case of *greater than* does not require that we accept the strong requirement of definitional knowledge embodied in this common account.)

On this understanding, the *Phaedo* denies that non-philosophers possess the concept of *equal* and, for similar reasons, that they possess, for example, the concepts of *fine* or *just*. Is this such an implausible conclusion that we should be reluctant to ascribe it to Plato? One might have two worries. First, it is uncontroversial that non-philosophers do correctly classify many cases of just, fine, and equal things. How can we account for their capacity to make these correct discriminations without attributing to them the possession, in some form or other, of the relevant concepts? Second, if philosophers and non-philosophers do not share the same concept of, e.g., justice, then it is no longer clear, as it should be, that they are disagreeing when one asserts 'Justice is (or just things are) G' and the other asserts 'Justice is not (or just things are not) G'. Indeed, consider people who make the transition from being non-philosophers to being philosophers. On this theory, it is not the case that once they recollect Justice they come to grasp truths about something that they previously had false beliefs about. They instead come to be thinking about something altogether different. Is Plato really committed to these claims?

In this chapter, I shall argue that Plato comes to adopt a new and better theory of recollection in the *Phaedrus* and other late dialogues, so I do not want to argue that the *Phaedo*'s theory is not open to objection. But I do think that we can make some progress in showing that it is not as obviously unacceptable as the above objections suggest. Let us begin with the first worry that non-philosophers do possess discriminatory capacities that allow them to recognize and respond differentially to, e.g., fine things. This is, however, a fairly weak reason to attribute to them the possession of the concept *fine*. The mere fact that a creature can, with considerable success, discriminate many instances of F may not require that we attribute to it any concepts at all. Ticks, for example, might be quite good at distinguishing warm-blooded animals from the rest of their environment and respond differentially to them, but we might think that they have no concepts at all. Non-philosophers, of course, have many capacities that ticks lack including a wide variety of linguistic capacities, but the example shows that successful detection of things falling under *F* is not in itself an intuitively compelling reason to attribute possession of the concept *F*. If we compare non-philosophers to philosophers with respect to their uses of *F*, we find important differences.

(1) Non-philosophers lack many of the beliefs that philosophers have about the fine and fine things. (They do not, for example, believe that the fine is a single, non-sensible property and do not think that geometrical objects are especially good instances of it.)

(2) Non-philosophers do not group together fine things into one class. (They would not group together Alcibiades, Helen, and Euclid's proof that any solid angle is contained by plane angles less than four right angles (XI, 21).)

(3) Non-philosophers often lack the ability to distinguish false cases of *F*. (They will often judge inappropriate poems, songs, and paintings to be fine.)

More generally, philosophers and non-philosophers will differ significantly in what they count as falling under the concept *fine*: the latter will not include non-sensible items and there will be differences even with respect to sensible items. Further, non-philosophers will give accounts of the fine in sensible terms, philosophers in non-sensible terms.

Nevertheless, it should not be surprising that in many cases, non-philosophers and philosophers, although employing different criteria, identify the same things as *F*. There should be, for example, considerable overlap with respect to their judgments about fine or beautiful bodies. Consider, for example, one possible explanation for some of this overlap. Non-philosophers' standards for beauty will, at least quite often, be based, in some way or other, on sexual attractiveness. Sexual attractiveness, in turn, will bear some rough correspondence to outward signs of vigor and healthy functioning. Such healthy functioning of a natural organism will, in turn, ultimately be explained in terms of non-sensible properties, e.g., symmetry and order. So non-philosophers' terms may, in these restricted cases, roughly track the extension of the philosophers' concept. (Although even in the case of physical beauty, Plato stresses that non-philosophical devotees of it are led astray in their judgments by their sexual desires, e.g. *Rep.* 474D ff.) Similarly, it is reasonable to think that social rules will, in general, tend to promote, in certain basic respects, the tranquillity and material prosperity of society. They will encourage and require people to refrain from various kinds of violence and deception against their fellows. Actions that tend to contribute significantly to the community's safety and prosperity, even at considerable risk or cost to the individual, will receive especially high praise and honor as, e.g., heroically just. Philosophers will have their own reasons for endorsing many of these actions: most common forms of deception and violence will be in the service of appetitive goals that they reject and they also have positive reason to engage in some other-regarding activities. As in the case of the fine, such overlap will not be perfect: creating and maintaining the just city of the *Republic* will, for example, require forms of violence and deception that the average Athenian would reject as unjust.

Nor does the fact that some ordinary people's beliefs about, e.g., the fine are inconsistent with one another require that they are engaging in recollection. Given the somewhat haphazard way these concepts are formed—being drawn from the person's own experiences as well as often conflicting cultural influences—the fact that they are frequently inconsistent should not be surprising, especially since, as we have seen, some terms of non-philosophers will track the philosophers' concept in a range of cases.[25]

The second set of worries may be more concisely stated by availing ourselves, somewhat anachronistically, of the notions of sense and reference. If non-philosophers' concepts determine the senses (that is, the cognitive content) of their linguistic expressions and so fix the reference of their terms, we seem to get very unattractive and unintuitive results. As already noted, we seem to get puzzling cases of reference shift that might interfere with communication. But we may also have to assign surprising truth-values to many of the assertions of non-philosophers. For example, if some non-philosophers' concept of justice is 'obedience to the laws' and their concept of virtue is 'a way of behaving that is always beneficial', then it seems that the truth-value of their utterance of 'Justice is a virtue' is false.

Such results, although unintuitive, are not incoherent and this position does not obviously preclude the possibility of successful communication and inquiry.[26] Yet Plato need not be committed to them. In particular, he can allow for greater space between what speakers intend to communicate by the use of their words and what their words convey and between what they intend to talk about, pick out, or refer to, and what they, in fact, talk about. Consider, for example, one plausible interpretation of the *Cratylus'* theory of language. On this account, words such as 'justice' or 'the fine' have a descriptive content by themselves, but this descriptive content is not fixed by what the speaker has in mind.[27] Rather, the descriptive content has been fixed by the name-giving of the original name-giver who coined, e.g., 'justice'. This descriptive content picks out something and when the name is correct, it picks out the real nature of a natural kind and correctly describes it. So the descriptive content of 'justice' might still correctly describe justice and pick out its real nature, even if what is 'in the head' of the speaker is badly mistaken. So if the cognitive content of even non-philosophers' linguistic expressions corresponds to this descriptive content and the descriptive content fixes the reference of these terms, Plato can avoid the counterintuitive results that we have noted.[28]

It is worth noting, however, that if we accept this theory and also take seriously the etymologies offered in the *Cratylus*, we might come to quite pessimistic conclusions about not only what is in ordinary speakers' heads, but also about what their words convey and pick out. As Gail Fine notes, in the *Cratylus* Plato holds that most people refer to the same nature, justice, even though their beliefs about justice vary widely.[29] But the problem is that the original name-giver has done a poor job with the words concerning knowledge and value.[30] All such words tie value and knowledge very intimately to change and instability. 'Just' (*dikaion*), for example, is so called because those who think that 'the universe is in motion' hold that there is a very thin and rapid element that 'superintends and passes through' [*diaïon*] all other things' (*Crat.* 412D2–E3). In this case, 'justice' will badly fail to convey the right descriptive content and will not pick out the real nature that it should.

Since the *Phaedrus* seems to abandon the *Phaedo's* controversial requirement for recollection, it faces the challenge of showing that we need to invoke recollection at all. In the *Phaedo*, the supposedly recollected concept, the concept of equal, has non-sensible content and thus it is at least prima facie plausible that it is not derived from sense-experience. (This is not enough to show that the idea is innate, since an empiricist opponent might claim that the non-sensible content can be generated by some operation on sensory contents such as abstraction. But it may not be unreasonable to hold that the burden of showing that there is such a mechanism falls on the opponent.[31]) I have argued that in the *Phaedrus* recollection is more deeply embedded in ordinary thought and is not explicitly tied to the conscious awareness of concepts that have non-sensible content. So the challenge of showing that we need to acknowledge recollection in these cases is greater. It is no longer clear that there is an unbridgeable gap between what sensory experience provides and the concept or end state at which we arrive.

Consider, as an illustration, a case drawn from Descartes. It is the fact that we have a concept of a chiliagon, unlike the fact that we have a concept of a triangle, that gives us reason to think that some of our ideas are innate. Since there are no sensory instances of chiliagons, I could not have derived the idea from sense-experience, whereas there is no such obvious gap between my sense-experience and my concept in the case of triangle. We might not find this a compelling argument for the innateness of the concept *chiliagon*, but it illustrates the difficulty that Plato faces in the *Phaedrus*.[32] And one promising strategy in response to this is to undermine the assumption that sense-experience by itself, without the addition of innate ideas, can provide the initial content that the empiricist relies on. One way of doing this is to argue that the very sort of sense-experience and operations upon it that seem to provide the empiricist's starting point require the possession and use of concepts that cannot themselves be derived from sense-experience. This is not a strategy that we find in the *Phaedo*, nor is there an explicit suggestion of it in the *Phaedrus*. Pursuing it will require a more detailed examination of the nature of perception and its relation to thought and this points us toward the *Timaeus* and the *Theaetetus*.

Recollection and Reincarnation in the Phaedrus   There is a final passage to consider in connection with the question of how far Forms are involved in ordinary cognition in the *Phaedrus*. This famous passage occurs during

Plato's explanation of why, when souls choose their next life, any human soul can choose to pass into an animal's body and life, but the only soul that can take the reverse path is one that had once been human. Souls, after having led an embodied life, reach a place where they can again chose the sort of life they will enter into.

From there, a human soul can enter a wild animal, and a soul that was once human can move from an animal to a human being again. But a soul that never saw the truth [τὴν ἀλήθειαν] cannot take a human shape,

[Passage 1]

for a man must grasp what is said in accordance with form [kat'eidos legomenon], arising from many perceptions and being collected together into one through reasoning.

[δεῖ γὰρ ἄνθρωπον συνιέναι κατ'εἶδος λεγόμενον, ἐκ πολλῶν ἰὸν αἰσθήσεων εἰς ἓν λογισμῷ συναιρούμενον, Phdr. 249B6–C1]

And this is a recollection of those things which our soul once saw, when it was travelling with a god and, lifting its vision above the things we now call real, rose up into what is truly real instead. (Phdr. 249B3–C4)[33]

What is controversial about this passage is exactly what claim is made in Passage 1. Compare, for example, Hackforth's translation: 'seeing that a man must needs understand the language of Forms, passing from a plurality of perceptions to a unity gathered together by reasoning' (Phdr. 249B6–C1). Hackforth's 'language of Forms' for kat'eidos legomenon construes 'eidos' here as meaning, that is, having the sense of 'Platonic Form'. Thus Scott, who adopts Hackforth's translation, thinks that what the passage claims a man must do is understand or have knowledge of an account or definition of a Platonic Form. But this is unlikely to be correct.

Up to the beginning of the myth's account of the soul's passage through the heavens, eidos has always been neutral with respect to the existence of Platonic Forms: it simply means 'class' or 'kind' (e.g. of centaurs or songs) and this is what it continues to mean throughout the myth. (Idea too is similarly neutral up to and throughout the myth.[34]) But it is striking and surprising that throughout the entire myth, Plato carefully refrains from calling the residents of the region above the heavens either eidē or ideai, although they clearly are Platonic Forms. He refers to them instead by a truly remarkable number of periphrases (e.g. at Phdr. 247C6–7 and 247E3).

We thus should start by understanding *eidos* as meaning 'class' or 'kind'. After the myth, the notion of a class or kind is connected to Plato's method of collection and division and the project of finding the natural joints of things (*Phdr.* 265C ff.). We may eventually come to think that these collections and divisions must be underpinned by complex relations among Platonic Forms.[35] Indeed, the sentence immediately following Passage 1 points us in this direction, since it tells us that—in some way—our ability to grasp natural classes or kinds is grounded in recollection. Filling out this line of thought is the task of the rest of the *Phaedrus* and the thematically connected late dialogues. But given Plato's careful use of language, we cannot take the sentence to concern our *de dicto* knowledge of Platonic Forms.[36] Any temptation to read it this way should already have been removed by seeing that Plato in the immediately preceding section has stressed that some form of recollection is found in all sorts of human lives (*Phdr.* 248D–249B). We should thus prefer the traditional interpretation of this passage according to which Plato is claiming that some form of recollection is necessary for understanding language, since language reflects, however dimly or inaccurately, the division of the world into natural kinds. The *Phaedrus* does not attempt to make the commitments of this claim as precise as we would like, since as we saw in the last subsection, it does not provide an argument as to why this is the case.[37] This is enough to show, however, that some form of recollection is deeply embedded in ordinary thought and language.

The Lower Parts of the Soul in the Phaedrus   If recollection is so deeply involved in ordinary cognition, what capacities can the lower parts of the soul have? It is clear that Plato is less optimistic than he was in the *Republic*. In the *Phaedrus*, he appears to have given up the idea that the Appetitive part can be persuaded by the Reasoning part that obedience to it is in the Appetitive part's own interests. It responds not to commands or speeches (*logoi*), but only to the whip (*Phdr.* 253E4–5). At the end of its training, it cannot realize that the Reasoning part knows best, but rather, 'nearly dies of fright [φόβῳ]' of it (*Phdr.* 254E8). It is not part of the myth's purpose to give a precise account of the reasons for this limitation, but as we shall shortly see, the *Timaeus* echoes exactly this claim about the Appetitive part and attributes the defect to the Appetitive part's total incapacity to grasp speech. Such a deeply pessimistic understanding of the Appetitive part may be suggested by some of the myth's other details.[38]

Plato seems more optimistic about the Spirited part, but he also clearly thinks that it is fundamentally more similar to the Appetitive part than to the Reasoning part. And although the myth does not employ analytic terms, it makes it clear that the fundamental point of similarity between the lower parts and of dissimilarity between them and the upper part is epistemological. Neither of the lower parts can in any way draw upon resources arising from any awareness of the Forms. Since we saw in the case of the Form of Beauty that doing so is a necessary condition for beginning to be aware of and respond to beauty even in a minimally appropriate way, the lower parts will be unable to be aware of genuine virtue or what is genuinely fine (*kalon*) as such, much less value these for their own sake. Thus language which suggests that the Spirited part ever responds to justice as such is misleading.

Indeed, since the lower parts are excluded from any contact with the Forms, they would seem to be limited to whatever perception by itself can provide. If recollection is needed for having a grasp of any form or *eidos* that articulates the natural joints of things, the epistemic capacities of the lower parts will be radically restricted. But even leaving aside any controversial point of interpretation, Plato makes it entirely explicit that the lower parts are quite radically restricted. Since the lower parts of every human soul are excluded from any contact at all with the Forms, the lower parts of the soul have, in kind, the same epistemic resources as do the souls of non-human animals (*Phdr.* 249B5–6, 249E4–250A1). The metaphorical representation of the lower parts as horses thus contains a literal psychological truth. More precisely, the lower parts have the same epistemic resources as do the souls of non-human animals that have never animated a human body: many animals, if we take transmigration seriously, are animated by human souls that once saw the Forms. As we shall see in examining the *Timaeus*, it is not clear how such parts of the soul could fit in and interact with other human capacities. What is also clear is that if we have such a conception of the lower parts of the soul, any attempt to educate non-philosophers will have to be aimed at educating their rational parts: non-rational motivations alone, no matter how well trained, are incapable of constituting a virtuous *human* condition.

Yet while impoverishing the lower parts of the soul, the *Phaedrus* allows to non-philosophers (even in their earthly incarnation) access, of a sort, to the Forms themselves. This does not commit Plato to the idea that all non-philosophers value, e.g., beauty or the fine for its own sake. Not even all mad lovers do that. But it does open the possibility that some non-philosophers can come to value virtue and the fine for their own sakes. Their conception of, and responses to, fine objects are grounded in their recollection of Forms. We can now turn to the *Timaeus*.

The Timaeus   Let us begin with the following passage that describes how the divine offspring of the Demiurge settled the Appetitive part of the human soul in the body.

Passage A
The part of the soul that has appetites for food and drink and whatever else it feels a need for, given the body's nature, they settled in the area between the midriff and the boundary toward the navel . . . Here they tied this part of the soul down like a beast, a wild one, but one they could not avoid sustaining along with the others if a mortal race were ever to be. They assigned it its position there, to keep it ever feeding at its trough, living as far away as possible from the deliberative part, and creating the least possible turmoil and din, thereby leaving the supreme part to deliberate in peace concerning what is beneficial for one and all. They knew that this part of the soul would not grasp *logos* [λόγου . . . συνήσειν] and that, even if it did have some share in the perception [αἰσθήσεως] of *logoi*,[39] it would have no natural instinct to pay heed to any *logoi*, but would be bewitched for the most part both day and night by images and phantasms. Hence the god conspired with this very tendency by constructing a liver, a structure which he situated in the dwelling place of this part of the soul. He made it into something dense, smooth, bright, and sweet, though also having a bitter quality, so that the power of thoughts which proceed from reason [ἡ ἐκ τοῦ νοῦ φερομένη δύναμις], moving in the liver as in a mirror which receives impressions and provides visible images, should frighten [φοβοῖ] this part of the soul. (*Tim.* 70D8–71B5)

Passage A seems to reflect on, only to reject, a central part of the *Republic*'s account of the Appetitive part. In the *Republic*, Plato criticizes the oligarchic person because, unlike the virtuous person, he controls his Appetitive part in the wrong way. Specifically, the oligarchic person suppresses the desires of his Appetitive part 'by compulsion and fear [ἀνάγκῃ καὶ φόβῳ]' (*Rep.*

554C11–D3).[40] According to the *Republic*, virtuous people or, more precisely the Reasoning parts of virtuous people, can persuade their Appetitive parts that it is better for the Appetitive part that the Reasoning part of the soul rule and thus that the Reasoning part should rule. The *Timaeus* rejects this picture. Here the Appetitive part is not open to persuasion by the Reasoning part that appeals to the Appetitive part's capacities to have a conception of its own good and to engage in even simple forms of reasoning. The Appetitive part in the *Timaeus* lacks the capacity

(i) to form or possess a conception of its own good,
(ii) to recognize or try to act on long-run reasons, and
(iii) to engage in means–end reasoning.

The denial of (i)–(iii) to the Appetitive part leaves it, at most, the subject of immediate inclinations to objects which it does not conceptualize as good. In Passage A Plato seems to go yet further in impoverishing the Appetitive part, but let us first consider the differences from the *Republic* resulting from the denial to the Appetitive part of capacities (i)–(iii). First, the Appetitive part will not be able to recognize that the Reasoning part seeks the long-run good of the whole soul and therefore it will not 'agree that the Reasoning part should rule' (*Rep.* 442B5–D1, cf. 554E3–5). We thus lose the *Republic*'s distinction between philosophers' relation to their Appetitive part and the oligarchs'. Further, it will no longer be possible for a person to possess the virtue of moderation as the *Republic* understands it, that is, a condition in which all three parts agree as to which part should rule. At most, the Appetitive part might reliably respond to the frightening or cheering ministrations of the Reasoning part. The Appetitive part's training cannot involve bringing it about that the Appetitive part either (a) has any grasp of the good or worthwhile features of the objects of its desires, or (b) even responds appropriately to reason because it recognizes that the Reasoning part is seeking its good. In this case, it is no longer clear that the virtues of the Appetitive part are in themselves of serious importance. It becomes quite hard to see, for example, how they can be of more than instrumental value.

Second, if the Appetitive part is this limited, it does not seem capable of exercising the sort of rule over the soul that it could in the *Republic*.

Without capacities (ii) and (iii), it cannot aim at capturing the Reasoning part as it sometimes did in the *Republic*. But on this account, it does not even form a conception of the good or of an end which the Reasoning part can take over and endorse.[41]

Third, if the Appetitive part cannot engage in any means/end or long-run reasoning, then its desires cannot change in the ways that they should in the light of new information. (The Appetitive part in the *Republic* was quite capable of such reasoning; it desired money, for example, as a means to the satisfaction of its other desires.) How could an Appetitive part of the *Timaeus* sort ever move from the desire for a Coke to forming a desire to put a coin in the Coke machine? Attributing the relevant reasoning to the Reasoning part will not solve the problem of showing how such desires are acquired by the Appetitive part.[42] One could, of course, simply posit some mechanism that produces the right result without attributing to the Appetitive part a capacity to engage in the relevant sort of reasoning, e.g. some form of associationist connections. Plato shows no signs, however, of thinking that associationism could provide the right sort of solution.

But Plato seems to be making an even more radical claim than these; he is not only denying *logos* to the Appetitive part when this is understood in terms of the capacities involved in (i)–(iii). Rather the contrast is that between being able to grasp or understand speech and the capacity to respond to an image (or to pain). The only way that the 'power of reason' communicates with the Appetitive part is by creating frightening images or by contracting and compressing the parts of the liver so as to produce pains and nausea, not through any sort of words (*Tim.* 71B2–D4). Instead of (even a very simple) agent acting for a reason, that is, on beliefs and desires, we simply have a response of withdrawal to an aversive stimulus.

Indeed, it is not even certain that the images cast on the liver are representational pictures of states of affairs (as opposed, for example, to patches of gloomy colors). In any case, it seems clear that these images do not serve as representations *for* the Appetitive part. The Reasoning part may select frightful images, but what seems to do the work in bringing about an effect in the Appetitive part is the pain produced by making the liver rough and contracting it or the release from pain resulting from making it smooth again. This effect is caused by the fact that the image on the liver is painted in bile and bile contracts the liver. What the image signifies is not accessible to the Appetitive part and thus is not, as such, part of the explanation of why it does what it does.[43] Plato's ingenuity in constructing this account so that none of the representational features of the image as such (but only the non-representational property of producing contractions) affects the Appetitive part is further good evidence that he denies any capacity to the Appetitive part to grasp significance or content.

A second passage confirms this interpretation.

Passage B
[The appetitive part of the soul] is totally devoid of belief and calculation and reason, but does share in perception, pleasant and painful, together with desires. For it is always wholly passive; its formation has not by nature permitted it, revolving in itself around itself, repelling motion from without and using its own native motion, to discern and reflect on itself.[44]   (*Tim.* 77B5–C3)

This passage, which we noted in the last chapter, denies belief or opinion to the Appetitive part and this is a remarkable limitation. Plato does stress, however, the connection between perception and the Appetitive part. From this passage alone, we can see that perception in the *Timaeus* is not rich enough to provide the Appetitive part with belief or *logos*. I shall return to this issue below.

According to the *Theaetetus* and the *Sophist*, thought (*dianoia*) is silent speech (*logos*) with oneself that ends in forming a belief (*doxa*).[45] Since the Appetitive part lacks belief or *logos* altogether, it is entirely excluded from thought as Plato understands it in the late period. On this conception of the Appetitive part, its ethical training cannot involve any modification of its beliefs or the intentional content of its desires. At the most, this training could aim at reliably setting up the responses that reason approves of and such a state seems to be of little, if any, non-instrumental value.

But there are yet more drastic consequences of this limitation. An Appetitive part of this sort cannot interact with the simplest belief in appropriate ways. If, for example, I acquire the belief that the stuff in the glass is turpentine or just solid plastic, this should not lead the Appetitive part, as characterized in the above *Timaeus* passage, to lose its desire for the stuff in the glass. (Except through the deus ex machina of intervention by the Reasoning part.) But even my very basic appetitive cravings do interact in appropriate ways with my beliefs, e.g., even when desperately hungry or in need of a fix, if I learn that the bread or the heroin is locked away in the cabinet, I come to desire the key to the cabinet. If the Appetitive part lacks *logos* and is thus incapable of grasping it, these desires should belong to reason, but this simply seems to be the wrong answer. Finally, the uncombinability of the Appetitive part's states with beliefs makes it implausible to think of these affections in the Appetitive part as desires at all. One of the central roles that desires play in Greek psychology as well as in our own is to help to explain action when conjoined with the appropriate beliefs. But the non-intentional states of the Appetitive part cannot combine with beliefs in order to explain anything.[46] My believing there is a glass of water in front of me when combined with a motion in the Appetitive part (or in my liver), does not explain my reaching for the glass nor does it explain anything else.

These limitations explain why Passage A is right to deny to the Appetitive part capacities (i)–(iii). But these limitations also undermine our reasons for thinking of the Appetitive part as a genuine agent-like part of the soul at all. On the present account, the Appetitive part is simply no longer agent-like: it is not a subject of beliefs and contentful desires. Moreover, understanding the desires of the Appetitive part as non-intentional tendencies to action also undermines our original reason for partitioning the soul. Such tendencies do not seem to be contraries to judgments about what is overall best that must be assigned to different subjects. (As we saw in Chapter 3, the argument in Book 4 of the *Republic* for the partitioning of the soul depends on the idea that the contrary desires which must be assigned to different parts of the soul have content. They are seen, for example, as imperatives.) Indeed, they do not seem to be contraries of any judgments at all. Finally, without belief or concepts, all that the Appetitive part could be is a subject of unconceptualized awareness with action tendencies. But while it may be right to recognize an unconceptualized element as a feature or aspect of our mental lives, there is no need to posit a second subject for the unconceptualized element.[47] Attributing action tendencies to such a subject only leaves such tendencies inappropriately cut off from the rest of our beliefs and desires.

These limitations, however, are so far only limitations of the Appetitive part. What about the Spirited part? Timaeus, at times, sounds rather optimistic; he suggests, for example, that the Spirited part not only has some beliefs, but that it has some beliefs about justice (*Tim.* 70B3–5). Attributing to it a concern for justice as such is, however, too optimistic. In the *Republic*, the Spirited part's ultimate end was not justice; the *Phaedrus*, as we saw, seems to suggest that the Spirited part cannot respond to justice as such and Timaeus stresses here its central concern for victory and pre-dominance (*Tim.* 70A2–3). We should thus see as exaggeration any talk of the Reasoning part passing information about justice on to it. The more pessimistic interpretation seems confirmed by Timaeus' account of the ingredients of the Spirited part (it appears to be made of the same stuff as the Appetitive part, *Tim.* 69C8–D5) and by the fact that following the goals of the Spirited part leads to reincarnation as a non-human animal (*Tim.* 91E2 ff.).

None of this explicitly removes belief or *logos* from the Spirited part and we ultimately cannot answer this question about the Spirited part, I think, without an account of why the Appetitive part has the limitations it does. But the Spirited part is still a mortal part and thus shares its origins and end with the Appetitive part, not with the Reasoning part. It is created by younger gods and, like the Appetitive part and unlike the Reasoning part, it is not shown 'the nature of the universe' (*Tim.* 41E2).[48] Why, then, should the Spirited part be grouped with the Reasoning part cognitively as a sharer in belief and *logos*?

I do not want to suggest that Plato is moving toward a conception of the non-rational parts of the soul in which they both lack beliefs and the capacity to conceptualize. This would be, as we have seen in the case of the Appetitive part, a disaster for Plato's ethical psychology. (It would be an even greater disaster to try to accommodate the Spirited part's anger, self-assertion, and desire for honor in a *logos*-lacking part of the soul.) What Plato seems to be showing us is that there is something profoundly wrong with thinking of the parts of the soul as having the epistemic resources nec-essary for belief or *logos* or as being genuinely distinct subjects if they lack them. But how, then, are we to understand human appetitive desires and spirited emotions? Plato's ethical psychology requires that we see them as standing in an intimate relation to belief and *logos*, but the *Timaeus* does not clearly explain how this is possible. It is the *Theaetetus* that provides the material needed to do the work that the *Timaeus* requires. (This claim is neutral on the relative chronology of the dialogues.) But an examination of the *Timaeus* suggests the outlines of a solution.

The Resources of Perception in the Timaeus   Let us return to the *Republic*. Perception in the *Republic* has propositional content, that is, it involves perceiving that objects have certain features. Nor is perception there limited to grasping the proper sensibles, e.g., colors and sounds. It can, rather, grasp a fairly open-ended set of features, including, for example, that something is a finger.[49] Although the *Republic* does not make fully clear the relation between perception and the lower parts of the soul, the lower parts do have access to perception and the beliefs that are a part of perception, while they lack higher sorts of cognitive abilities such as thought (*dianoia*) and knowledge (*epistēmē* and *nous*).[50] It is often thought that the *Theaetetus* breaks with the *Republic* and empties perception of all propositional content.[51] (I shall return to the *Theaetetus* below.) Seeing something as F is divided into a non-conceptualized element plus a belief that, e.g., 'This is F.' If this is right, then the belief- and *logos*-lacking Appetitive part of the *Timaeus* is what would result from combining the idea that the lower parts, especially the Appetitive part, have only the resources of perception with the idea that perception has no propositional content.

And the *Timaeus* seems to suggest such a story. Here I can only pick out the details of the *Timaeus'* psychology that are most relevant to the issues at hand. We should begin by turning to Plato's description of the World Soul, since Plato provides more detail about it and claims that the rational or immortal part of the human soul has the same composition as the World Soul in a less pure form (*Tim.* 41D). The composition of the World Soul is notoriously puzzling and problematic, but it is tolerably clear that this soul includes in the mixture that composes it (parts of) the Forms of Being, Sameness, and Difference.[52] It is this composition that accounts for the World Soul's cognitive capacities. Both knowledge and true belief are found only in the soul. The soul is capable of judging of the sameness and difference of both sensibles and non-sensibles and making other sorts of judgments about them and expressing these judgments in language. What grounds this ability of the soul to make these judgments is its composition;

for example, it is able to judge of sameness and difference because it is (partially) composed of them. This applies to any judgment of the type 'x is the same as (different from) y', and not only to judgments about Forms. This inherent composition is equally necessary for judging that one sensible particular is the same as (or different from) another sensible particular. Plato here seems to assume that unless something is composed of F, it cannot grasp F or, more generally, he seems to assume a principle according to which like is known by like. I shall not try to explicate this principle further, but it does have one important implication: the soul's ability to make such judgments involving being, sameness, and difference cannot be explained in terms of concepts (e.g. of being, sameness, and difference) whose content comes solely from perception. It is only because of its non-sensible (and innate) resources that the soul can form any such judgment.

Since the immortal part of the human soul, the rational part, is composed of the same kind of ingredients as the World Soul, albeit in a less pure form, roughly the same account should hold true of it. It is only because of its non-sensible resources that the soul can form any such judgment. In addition to these facts about its composition, after the creation of the immortal part, the Demiurge 'setting each as it were in a chariot, showed them the nature of the universe [τὴν τοῦ παντὸς φύσιν]' (*Tim.* 41E1–2). Whether or not we think that the *Timaeus* hereby shows a commitment to some form of a theory of recollection, the passage must be intended to echo the *Phaedrus*' claim that only the Reasoning part of the soul sees the Forms, while the lower two parts are excluded from seeing Forms.

The construction of the immortal part of the soul and its seeing the nature of the universe have both happened before the mortal parts of the soul are on the scene. Indeed, Plato goes out of his way to emphasize their distinctness from the immortal part. The Demiurge gives to the younger gods the task of 'adding on' (*Tim.* 42E1) the mortal parts of the soul; these gods 'built [them] onto' the immortal part of the soul (*Tim.* 69C8). We are encouraged, then, to see the lower parts as quite distinct in nature and capacity from the immortal reasoning part. In the words of one leading commentator on the dialogue, 'Since [they] are not made from the same components as the rational soul, [they] do not possess the cognitive capacities that characterize the rational soul.'[53] (Plato maintains a tactful silence on their composition.) If the lower parts are not partially composed of Forms, they will be unable to judge of being, sameness, and difference, either with respect to sensibles or non-sensibles.

The lower or mortal parts of the soul are, however, associated with perception (*Tim.* 42A3–B1 and 69C6–D6).[54] Moreover, such perception seems to be unconceptualized. Timaeus claims that in addition to the tumult caused by processes such as nourishment, interactions with external bodies set our own bodies in motion.

The motions produced by all these encounters [of the immortal part of the human soul with parts of the body and with external bodies] would then be conducted through the body to the soul, and strike against it. That is no doubt why these motions as a group came afterwards to be called 'perceptions' [αἰσθήσεις] as they are still called today. (*Tim.* 43C4–7)[55]

These movements are in themselves unconceptualized and the conceptual content is provided by the rational part of the soul (*Tim.* 64B4–6).[56] So the lower parts of the soul would have unconceptualized perception as their epistemic resource, while belief and *logos* would be confined to the immortal part.[57] And it is the adding on of the lower parts of the soul that Timaeus seems to present as the explanation of irrationality in human beings.

And within the body they built another kind of soul as well, the mortal kind, which contains within itself those dreadful but necessary disturbances: pleasure, first of all, evil's most powerful lure; then pains, that make us run away from what is good; besides these, boldness also, and fear, foolish counselors both; then also spirit hard to assuage and hope easily led astray. These they fused with irrational perception [αἰσθήσει δὲ ἀλόγῳ] and all-venturing lust, and so, as was necessary, they constructed the mortal type of soul. (*Tim.* 69C7–D6)

But this is not the only story of the origin of irrationality in the *Timaeus* and it cannot be the full story. We have so far only considered Timaeus' account of the origin of knowledge and true belief, but he also provides an explanation of the origin of false beliefs involving sameness and difference. The motions involved with perception

joined with the continually flowing channel to stir and violently shake the soul's revolutions. They completely bound that of the Same by flowing against it in the opposite direction, and hindered it in its ruling and its going. And they further shook the orbit of the Different right through so that . . . they produced all manner of twistings . . . They mutilated and disfigured the circles in every possible way so that the circles barely held together and though they remained in motion, they moved irrationally [ἀλόγως] . . .[58] Whenever the revolutions of the soul encounter something outside of them characterizable as same or different, they will speak of it as 'the same as' something, or as 'different from' something else when the truth is just the opposite, so proving themselves to be false [ψευδεῖς] and lacking reason. And at such times, souls do not have any revolution that rules and guides . . . It is then that these revolutions, however much in control they seem to be, are actually under their control. All these disturbances are no doubt the reason why even today and not only at the beginning, whenever a soul is bound within a mortal body, it at first lacks reason. But as the stream that brings growth and nourishment diminishes and the soul's orbits regain their composure, resume their proper courses and establish themselves more and more with the passage of time, their revolutions are set straight, to conform to the configuration each of the circles takes in its natural course. They then correctly identify what is the same and what is different, and render intelligent the person who possesses them. And to be sure, if such a person also gets the proper nurture to supplement his education, he will turn out perfectly whole and healthy, and will have escaped the greatest of illnesses. But if he neglects this, he will limp his way through life and return to Hades uninitiated and lacking reason.[59] (*Tim.* 43c8–44c4)

This passage also gives an account of 'irrational' (*alogos*) motion, but this is quite different from the sort of irrational motion in which perception itself consists. The latter is irrational in that it is unconceptualized, but the former is irrational because it consists in an incorrect or false assertion and thus it must be conceptualized. The irrational motions of this passage are motions of the immortal or rational part of the soul; in particular, they are the distorted motions of the soul's circles composed of the Same and the Different. These false judgments thus also draw upon the soul's non-sensory resources.

But as the end of the passage shows, these distortions in the circles of the soul's rational part account not just for mistaken judgments of sameness and difference, but also account for the mistaken ethical beliefs and other ethically relevant affections that influence the person's afterlife.[60] The case seems to be parallel to that of perception. Strictly speaking, perception consists in an unconceptualized motion in the soul. Nevertheless, in human beings in the appropriate condition there is also conceptualization of the perception and this is the work of the rational part and takes place in the rational part. We should apply the same lesson to the affections that Plato attributed to the lower parts of the soul at *Tim.* 69C7–D6: e.g. pleasure and pain, boldness and fear, and anger. We can recognize that all of these have as an aspect some unconceptualized motion. (This may not be the same in all cases: for example anything desire-like has a certain motivational force that is an unconceptualized property, but this is distinct from the unconceptualized part of perception.) But as in the case of perception, the role that these items play in psychology is not exhausted by their being a unconceptualized motion. In human beings in the appropriate condition, there is also an accompanying conceptualization. (For example, fear involves the belief that something bad is in the offing, e.g., *Laches* 198B8–10, *Laws* 646E7–647A2, *Prot.* 358D5–E1.) Here, too, the conceptualization must be the work of the rational part and must belong to it. So on this account, the content of these non-rational motivations is supplied by the rational part and the belief or conceptualization belongs to the rational part. On this position, the content of non-rational motivations consists in the partial or distorted exercises of the rational part's capacity to conceptualize.

Once we accept this, it is no longer very tempting to think either that the unconceptualized motion that strictly is identified with perception is had by one subject while the conceptualization is had by another subject or to hold the corresponding story for non-rational motivations such as desire. But this is the only story that we could tell about the lower parts of the soul in the *Timaeus* if we see them as genuine subjects. The philosophical lesson that the *Timaeus* suggests is that emotions, pleasures, and desires have both a conceptualized content and a non-conceptual aspect, but these are both aspects of a state of a single subject.[61]

The Theaetetus   In the *Theaetetus*, we find three important developments that are relevant to the issues we have been discussing.[62]

I.   It radically impoverishes perception and may remove from it all propositional and conceptual content.

II. It attributes to all human beings some contact with non-sensible properties, the commons (the *koina*), and holds that contact with them is involved in forming most, if not all, judgments. This contact need not involve an explicit recognition of the commons, as such, that is, it need not involve recognizing them as non-sensible properties. (The commons include being, sameness, difference, fineness, and goodness.)

III. It holds that there is a single subject of both thought and perception.

Since these claims about the *Theaetetus* are not novel, I shall discuss each of them only briefly. First, how limited is perception on the *Theaetetus'* account? At *Theaetetus* 184B–186E, Plato argues that perception cannot be knowledge, since knowledge requires attaining truth, but perception fails to attain truth because perception cannot attain being. What is it for perception to fail to attain being? There are two main options.

(1) Perception has no propositional or conceptual content.

On this interpretation, perception fails to attain being insofar as it is unable to identify what is perceived as being F, for any F at all; that is, perception cannot make any judgments of the form 'x is F'. Perception cannot, for example, even make the judgment 'This is red'. Predicating anything at all of x requires applying to x the common of being and thus is beyond the capacity of perception.

(2) Perception includes judgment of the proper sensibles, but nothing more.

On this interpretation, perception by itself can produce judgments of the form 'x is F' when (and only when) F is restricted to the proper sensibles (color, sounds, tastes, etc.). Thus I can see that x is red without drawing on anything beyond perception, but any further judgment requires more than perception.[63]

Whichever of these interpretations we prefer, a lower part limited to perception will not be a subject that initiates choice and action. Perception cannot get to (even a very crude conception of) 'good' or 'pleasant' and cannot engage in any form of reasoning about the future or undertake any sort of comparison. A lower part limited to perception understood in this way could not possibly play the end-setting role that the lower parts did in the *Republic* and we would have to appeal to more than perception to explain why items (e.g. emotions and desires) associated with the lower parts have the content that they do. (Perhaps, at most, we might have impulses for, e.g., sweet things, unless the desire for sweet things is a desire for sweet things as pleasant.)

Second, we saw that the *Phaedrus* and the *Timaeus* attributed to non-philosophers some sort of contact with the Forms and held that this contact is necessary for forming certain judgments. (The *Phaedrus* attributes this sort of contact with Forms certainly to many and perhaps to all non-philosophers; the *Timaeus* attributes it to all humans.) Are the commons Forms? Are they recollected?[64] For our purposes, we do not need to decide these questions. What is important for our purposes is that the *Theaetetus* holds that all judgment-makers, simply in virtue of making judgments, come into contact with non-sensibles. (If you hold interpretation (2), read this as all judgment-makers beyond those restricted to judgments of proper sensibles. This includes all normal humans beyond infancy.) Such use of the commons does not require recognition of their non-sensible status or full awareness of what they are.[65] But both philosophers and non-philosophers are now drawing on the same kind of epistemic resources; they differ in their grasp of the same items.

Finally, the *Theaetetus* explicitly commits Plato to the unity of the soul. Consider Myles Burnyeat's statement of the point. The argument that being, sameness, and unity are not grasped through the senses, but through thought establishes

> that it is with one and the same part of ourselves that we do all our perceiving . . . it proves this by showing that there is something in us, the soul or mind, which can think and reason about whatever we perceive. The unity of the perceiving subject is demonstrated from the unity of the thinker who surveys and judges the proper objects of different senses, for which purpose the thinker must also be a perceiver capable of exercising and coordinating a plurality of senses . . . [this] is nothing less than the first unambiguous statement in the history of philosophy of the . . . unity of consciousness.[66]

This conclusion is, I think, basically right although there are two objections to consider. The unity of psychic subjects is not, one might argue, shown by the need for something other than the senses to judge of the application of the commons. Even granting this and the claim that the applier of commons alone can actively manipulate the senses, this still leaves room for other subjects. First, even if we think that perception has no conceptual or propositional content, we might think that the senses (or the lower parts of the soul) serve as subject(s) of unconceptualized awareness. But although such a subject is a logical possibility, it does no useful work and within a single subject, we can distinguish between her experience and her conceptualization of that experience. (It would be even less promising to think of the lower parts as subjects in virtue of possessing perceptions that are unconceptualized and do not include awareness.)

Second, a more serious worry is that we might concede the above roles for the judger of commons, but see the senses as passing on to the judger conceptualized ('Red') or propositional information ('This is red'). (Since the senses are not a promising subject of judgments, it would be tempting to see the judger of proper sensibles as the lower part(s) of the soul, but I leave this issue aside.) It does not, however, matter greatly for our understanding of the overall development of Plato's ethical psychology how we decide this issue. Even if we allow the senses or the lower parts of the soul to apply the concepts of (or make judgments about) the special sensibles, this will not give us separate subjects who make judgments of 'good' or 'pleasant'. Such subjects will not be end-setters or rich enough to force partitioning or to account for the conceptual content of our non-rational emotions and desires. To allow the lower parts to go further than this, they would have to have contact with the commons and allowing this is both extravagant in itself and flatly inconsistent with the tendency in the *Phaedrus* and the *Timaeus* to exclude the lower parts from the non-sensible. The *Theaetetus* thus at least guarantees the unity of the thinking, desiring, and emotional subject.

Let us take stock. The *Phaedrus* and the *Timaeus* cut the lower parts of the soul off from any cognitive contact with the Forms. This makes explicit what Plato is clearly committed to and assumes in the *Republic*. In the *Republic*, such a limitation on the lower parts excluded them from an awareness of genuine value properties. Nevertheless, it did allow the lower parts to have a rich variety of beliefs, since in the *Republic* Plato holds that perception is conceptual and propositional and allows the lower parts to engage in various kinds of reasoning without drawing on an awareness of the Forms. The *Phaedrus* explicitly draws attention to this exclusion of the lower parts from contact with the Forms, but Plato also finds it increasingly problematic, since Forms become more deeply embedded in ordinary cognition. In the *Phaedrus*, recollection is needed to develop at a fairly minimal level—the level separating humans from non-human animals—concepts that reflect, perhaps often dimly, the natural kinds that articulate the world 'at the joints'. These natural kinds include not only the basic kinds of physical things or the basic kinds of living organisms, but should also include the basic kinds of things relevant to ethics, including value properties. Thus even in the *Phaedrus*, which might reasonably be thought to be transitional to the later dialogues, the lower parts are cognitively quite impoverished: failing to have any awareness of the Forms leaves them with the same epistemic status as the souls of non-human animals.

As we have seen, the *Timaeus* and the *Theaetetus* go further. Both dialogues (along with other late dialogues, especially the *Sophist*) display a new interest in formal properties that apply quite generally to subjects of thought and discourse, such as being, sameness, likeness, and difference. Grasping and applying such properties will be necessary for even quite primitive kinds of thinking. Applying likeness and difference will be necessary for grouping together and discriminating any objects. Indeed, applying sameness and difference are, for Plato, intimately bound up with identifying any subject of discourse. (Plato's interest here is not so much in the structure of sensory experience itself—e.g. how it must be structured spatially and temporally for it to be an object of experience—as it is in what is required for something to be an object of thought and discussion.) Finally, applying being to a thing is necessary for identifying a subject as being anything at all, that is, it is necessary for any sort of predication. Such concepts cannot be derived from perception and perception itself in the *Timaeus* and the *Theaetetus* is non-propositional and non-conceptualized. Lower parts that are excluded from a grasp of non-sensible properties and limited to perception would be, as the *Timaeus* holds, deprived of belief and conceptualization.

These considerations concern the epistemic necessity for having some grasp of these non-sensible properties, but the *Timaeus* also suggests a metaphysical deficiency in perception. Perception is a form of passivity; insofar as the soul is moved by the body, it merely passively registers an unconceptualized motion. The *Timaeus* suggests that any sort of reflection on these affections (e.g. that involved in forming a belief or making a comparison) must involve psychic activity that Plato classifies as the self-movement of the soul. Such self-movement of the soul will involve operations of reason that draw on non-sensible resources.[67]

This examination of the dialogues between the *Republic* and the *Laws* shows why Plato ends in the *Laws*, as I have argued that he did, with a commitment to a unitary soul. In the late dialogues, Plato continues to believe that non-rational desires and emotions have content. Anger necessarily involves an awareness of injury or injustice and even primitive bodily desires conceptualize their objects as being, e.g., water or thirst-quenching or pleasant. But all such content requires the application of non-sensible properties and is the work of a single judgment-maker. The unity of the soul thus rests on the need for a single judgment-maker that must apply non-sensible properties. This allows for great variety in the sorts of judgments a unitary soul makes. Some are conscious, others may be unconscious. Some are the outcome of investigation or practical deliberation; others do not involve such investigation or deliberation (although they may, for example, involve stored memories). But the soul is no longer divided between a subject that has access to the Forms and a subject limited to sense-perception and what can be derived from it.

4.3 Non-Rational Motivations: An Overview

In the middle period, non-rational desires and emotions—for example, the spirited emotions connected with anger and the desire for honor as well as appetitive desires for bodily satisfactions or pleasures—find their home in the two lower parts of the soul. Owing to the epistemic limitations of these parts, non-rational motivations are generated without drawing in any way on contact with the Forms and are aimed at sensible objects and properties. This does not mean that the non-rational motivations always prompt the person to act contrary to reason. Spirited emotions and desires, for example, can be trained so that they tend to support the course of action that reason approves. Indeed, as we have seen, the Spirited part of the soul in the *Republic* plays a very important role in ensuring that reason's choice is put into effect. But even in cases in which there is such a coincidence, the agent will have irreducibly plural motivations. Reason, for example, may generate a desire to do *x* because *x* is the just thing to do and thus genuinely best for the agent. Spirited emotions have their own special object—predominance or honor—and may pursue *x* because doing so is honored. Nevertheless, the spirited desires are not responding to *x* because it is good or just, but because it is an object of honor.[68] Similarly, the Appetitive part of the soul is an independent source of motivation with its own special objects.

On Plato's later psychology, such a simple story is no longer possible. Non-rational motivations, as in the middle period, are conceptualized and are intimately bound up with beliefs. But perception, by itself, is no longer sufficient to provide this conceptualization and the soul is capable of such conceptualization and beliefs only by drawing on its awareness (perhaps quite dim and indistinct) of Forms. What are the implications of this for the non-rational motivations? We might expect a far more optimistic account of their place in the life of a virtuous person. Their content is now fixed, at least in part, by the person's awareness of Forms; thus they can, so to speak, be suffused with an awareness of genuine value. What had to be suppressed or eradicated in Plato's middle period can now be cultivated. Non-rational motivations can thus play a more significant role in the ethical education and development of the virtuous person. And perhaps, even in a fully virtuous person, they can play an important role in expressing the person's grasp of the good.

The account that we find in the later period is, however, more complex and far more ambivalent. First, even in the middle period, eradication is not a possible option. At least as long as a person is embodied, she is a compound of the three parts of the soul. Further, the ends of the lower two parts are fixed in basic outline. Although proper training can ensure that the Spirited part finds honor in fine objects and that the Appetitive part prefers the satisfaction of necessary bodily appetites to the satisfaction of unnecessary appetites, neither part can be brought to value these objects because they possess what reason would recognize as genuine value. The non-rational motivations must be cultivated because they cannot be eradicated, but no sort of cultivation can bring about a fundamental change in the nature of their objects. Thus they may always, even in a virtuous person, seem to reason to be, in some important way, alien to itself.

There is in the *Republic* a certain tension in the virtuous person's attitude to the lower parts. On the one hand, the virtuous person has something like a concern for the well-being of the lower parts of the soul for their own sake. The well-being of the lower parts seems to make a claim in its own right on the Reasoning part's calculation of what is best for the whole soul. The Reasoning part's virtue of wisdom consists in 'knowledge of what is beneficial for each [part of the soul] and for the whole, the community composed of all three' (*Rep.* 442C6–8). But there is also a tension in Plato's views, since the Reasoning part's judgment of what is of genuine value gives a low ranking to the objects that the Spirited and the Appetitive parts pursue.[69] Given the rather minimal value of their objects, it is difficult to see why the virtuous person's primary concern is not simply to ensure that the lower parts do not disturb the Reasoning part and that the lower parts are in such a condition that they are instrumentally useful in supporting the Reasoning part's activities. (For example, an Appetitive part in good condition will help secure the health that a virtuous person requires.) And there are passages in the *Republic* that suggest such a reading:

[T]he other [i.e. other than wisdom] so-called virtues of the soul do seem akin to those of the body. For they really are not there beforehand, but are added later by habit and practice. But the virtue of wisdom seems to belong above all to something more divine. (*Rep.* 518D9–E3)

Someone who is healthy and moderate goes to sleep only after having done the following: First, he rouses his reasoning part and feasts it on fine words and investigations; second, he neither starves nor feasts his appetitive part, so that it will slumber and not disturb his best part with either its pleasure or pain, but will leave it alone, pure and by itself, to get on with its investigations ... third, he soothes his spirited part in the same way ... And when he has quieted these two parts and quickened the third, in which reason resides, and so goes to his rest, you are aware that in such cases he is most likely to apprehend the truth.[70] (*Rep.* 571D6–572A8)

But here I shall focus on the later period's complexities. Since non-rational motivations can now draw upon reason's resources, they may have a larger place in the virtuous person's life. Certain sensory pleasures can, for example, directly embody a dim awareness of genuine value. This allows Plato, as we shall see, to offer a new and more subtle account of the role of pleasure in ethical education and training. Enjoying the proper pleasures can in itself be a way of coming to learn more about genuine value. But this is only part of the story. The non-rational motivations are now open to far more radical transformation. In the middle period, the only way for the Reasoning part to persuade the Spirited part was by appealing to considerations of what would move it, for example, honor. If there were a conflict between the two parts, the Reasoning part could enlist the Spirited part on its side only by trying to show that the course of action it proposed better satisfied the Spirited part's own desires. If non-rational motivations can respond to a wider range of considerations, they may be reworked in more fundamental ways. It may be possible for their content to take over, at least in part, reason's own outlook. The greater the extent to which such reworking of the content of non-rational motivations is possible, the closer we may come to eradicating them, at least as they are understood in the middle period. As we shall see, for example, anger in the *Laws* is subject to such a reworking that leaves it strikingly little place in the life of a virtuous person.

But the new greater closeness between reason and the non-rational motivations has implications running the other way. The more closely non-rational motivations resemble rational judgments and desires formed after rational deliberation, the more dangerous they are. It is much easier to see how—especially in conditions in which reason may in some way be impaired or cannot function in a fully adequate manner—non-rational motivations can corrupt rational beliefs and desires. Lowering the barriers between rational and non-rational motivations has serious consequences for both sides.

4.4 *Psychology and Dependency*

One important theme of our discussion will be how non-rational motivations are distinct from rational motivations and what the good condition of the non-rational motivations consists in, in Plato's later period. Let us begin by returning to an issue that arose in our consideration of Plato's theory of goods in Chapter 2. There we saw that Plato thinks that there is a very tight connection between what is non-relationally good and what is good for a person. Since what is good for a person depends on what sort of creatures human beings are, we may now, especially with the aid of the *Timaeus'* psychology, be able to make further progress on the question of why Plato thinks that such a tight connection holds. This issue is important for our investigation of the non-rational motivations, since as we saw in Chapter 1, one of the most serious threats to the Dependency Thesis arises from Plato's claims about the lower parts of the soul in the *Republic*.

So let us first return briefly to the *Republic*. In Chapters 1 and 2, I argued that the *Republic*'s partitioning theory along with its apparent commitment to the idea that each part of the soul has its own good presents a problem for the Dependency Thesis. If we take seriously the idea that each part of the soul has its own good that consists, roughly, in the satisfaction of its own characteristic desires, then it is not clear why the Dependency Thesis should hold. Consider, for example, the Appetitive part of the soul. Suppose its good consists in the appropriate satisfaction of necessary bodily appetites. In cases in which virtue requires the sacrifice of such appetites, the person is better off sacrificing them, but why think that the Appetitive part itself would be better off if they were sacrificed? And even if we were to accept (the surely dubious) claim that failing to do the virtuous thing in this case would so undermine the control of the Reasoning part that it could no longer reliably guide the Appetitive part to its own long-run good, this only shows that foregoing these bodily satisfactions would be better for the Appetitive part in the long run, overall. It does not show that satisfying them could not be good for the Appetitive part. But there are more troubling worries. Pursuit of the necessary appetites might be the usual recommendation of the Reasoning part in a virtuous person, but there is no reason to think that such pursuit of necessary bodily satisfactions could spring only from a virtuous disposition of the Reasoning part. In cases in which it does not, the non-virtuous condition of the Reasoning part might be so great a bad that the person could not be happy, but why should the satisfaction of the necessary appetites not be of *some* benefit to the Appetitive part and thus of some benefit to this person?

In the first half of this chapter, I argued that in some later dialogues Plato comes to accept a unitary soul and holds that the conceptualization and belief formation that are involved in both rational and non-rational motivations are caused by a single subject that draws on non-sensible resources. These claims by themselves do not, of course, resolve the above worries. But we can supplement them by drawing on the *Timaeus'* account of the immortal rational part of the human soul. Once again, we should begin by considering Plato's account of the World Soul. The best condition of the World Soul is one in which it possesses knowledge and understanding about non-sensibles and secure and true beliefs and convictions about sensibles (*Tim.* 37A2–C5). This state is one that the World Soul can attain since it is (partially) composed of Sameness, Difference, and Being. But this composition also grounds more than the mere possibility of the World Soul attaining such a state. Given the essential nature of the World Soul, it naturally seeks such a condition as good and such a condition is good for it.

The immortal rational part of the human soul has the same composition in a less pure form and thus the same should hold true of it, at least while it is disembodied. What effect does embodiment have? It does not result in the addition of a further subject or subjects of beliefs and concepts, such as the body in the *Phaedo* or the lower parts of the soul in the *Republic*. Thus it does not introduce a further subject that has its own specific good. What it does, rather, is produce a distortion of the circles of the rational soul themselves. Because the motions of these circles are distorted, the soul judges falsely of sameness and difference and, more generally, becomes 'lacking in reason [ἀνόητος]' (*Tim.* 44C3). If these disturbances calm down, the original revolutions of the soul reassert themselves, the circles of the soul return to their natural courses, and 'they correctly identify what is the same and what is different and they make the person who possesses them have reason' (*Tim.* 44B6–7). The rationality inherent in the natural motions of the circles of the soul, if the person is properly educated, structures and assimilates the motions impinging on the soul from external bodies and the person's own body. If successful, this process results in a return to a condition that is close to the soul's original and best state.

> And he would have no rest from these toilsome transformations until he had dragged that massive accretion of fire and water and earth and air into conformity with the revolution of the Same and similar within him, and so subdued that turbulent, irrational [ἄλογον] mass by means of *logos*. This would return him to his original and best state.[71] (*Tim*. 42C4–D2)

So in this best condition of the soul, the person should again have knowledge and understanding about non-sensibles and true beliefs about sensibles. This condition of the soul is best both non-relationally and also best for the individual soul itself. We have already seen in greater detail in our discussion of the *Philebus* why Plato thinks that the condition in which the soul possesses knowledge and true belief is non-relationally good. Both knowledge and true belief instantiate the objective goodmaking properties.

Plato does not provide an explicit argument in the *Timaeus* for the claim that such a state is also good or best for the individual soul. It is clear, however, that he is committed to it.

> [I]f a man has seriously devoted himself to the love of learning and to true wisdom, if he has exercised these aspects of himself above all, then there is absolutely no way that his thoughts can fail to be immortal and divine, should truth come within his grasp ... [C]onstantly caring for his divine part as he does, keeping well-ordered the guiding spirit that lives within him, he must indeed be supremely happy [διαφερόντως εὐδαίμονα] ... We should redirect the revolutions in our heads that were thrown off course at our birth, by coming to learn the harmonies and revolutions of the universe, and so bring into conformity with its objects our faculty of understanding, as it was in its original condition. And when this conformity is complete, we shall have achieved our goal [τέλος]: the best life offered to humankind by the gods, both now and forevermore. (*Tim*. 90B6–D7)[72]

Within the *Timaeus*, we can find a straightforwardly teleological justification for this understanding of the individual's good. The soul has been constructed so that its natural end is to stand in the appropriate relation to truth. But a literal interpretation of the *Timaeus'* account of the soul's creation is not crucial to Plato's argument. What is crucial is Plato's account of the composition of the soul: the claim that it is composed out of sameness, difference, and being specifies the soul's essential nature. This composition grounds not just the soul's ability to stand in the appropriate relation to truth; rather the soul's composition makes it the case that its essential nature is expressed by the actual tendency to seek the truth. The claim that attaining the appropriate relation to the truth is good for the agent thus can be supported by the idea that individuals' good consists in the full or perfect expression of their nature.[73]

The *Timaeus*, in fact, makes it clearer than did the close of the *Philebus* why true belief and less pure forms of knowledge are good for the individual. The World Soul does not need true belief in order to find its way to the marketplace nor does Plato suggest that true belief's only role is to conduce to knowledge and understanding. Attaining true belief is in itself a necessary part of the full exercise of the soul's essential nature. Even if it is not as great a good as higher forms of knowledge, it is a perfection of the soul's capacity to stand in the appropriate relation to truth. Thus we can see why sensory appreciation of geometrical shapes, in addition to thinking about them, is good for a person. (Moreover, such sensory appreciation is necessary for the reordering and harmonizing effects that Plato describes at *Tim.* 90B6–D7.)

We can now make some further progress on why Plato thinks that there is such a close connection between what is non-relationally good and what is good for the individual and the associated problem of motivation this raises. The essential nature of the rational part of the soul is to seek to stand in the appropriate relation to the truth. This essential nature is realized when the soul attains knowledge about non-sensibles and true beliefs about sensibles. These states of the soul are non-relationally good because they possess the objective goodmaking properties, and they are a good condition for the soul to be in because they constitute the realization of the soul's essential nature. This account of the soul's essential nature also allows Plato to respond to the common complaint against realist theories of value that they create a motivational mystery. If the good is not defined, even partially, in terms of our contingent motivations, what guarantees that it is motivating for us? Why might we not, even insofar as we are rational, be indifferent to the objective, non-relational good? Plato does not think that the notion of what is non-relationally good is given its content by facts about human nature, not even facts about the essential nature of the soul. But the essential nature of the soul is characterized as a form of rational activity that aims at standing in the appropriate relation to the truth. Since realizing its nature is constitutive of what is good for individuals, individuals insofar as they are rational cannot be indifferent to seeking to stand in the appropriate relation to truth.[74]

This line of argument does more than establish that those states of soul that are non-relationally best are also best for the individual. Supporting the Dependency Thesis requires that we give further content to what is best for the individual. Given the *Timaeus'* account of the rational part of the soul, any failure to grasp the truth is a corruption of or an imperfection in the realization of the soul's essential nature and thus bad for the soul. To put the point in the *Timaeus'* language of circles of the soul, any failure to grasp the truth is a deformation or imperfection of the circles that constitute the soul and is as such bad for it. Anything that is good for the soul is constituted at least partially by the proper movement of these circles, that is, by the realization of the soul's essential nature. So anything that is good for the soul is partially constituted by an appreciation of the truth. We can rely on the *Philebus* for a further specification of the sort of truth at stake here. The sort of truth that is grasped most clearly in the case of non-sensibles and less clearly in the case of sensibles is the truth about the order and structure of things and these are both basic explanatory properties as well as value properties. Given what the soul essentially is, an awareness of genuine value is constitutive of anything that can benefit it.

This line of defense does not answer all the questions that we may legitimately ask of Plato's position. But it does suggest how his metaphysics of value and his later psychology can support the basic principle of his late ethics, the Dependency Thesis. Here I shall concentrate on one particularly important gap in the above line of argument. We have so far spoken as if the only essential function of the soul were to have knowledge of and correct belief about the truth. But we still need to provide an account of the good condition of the soul insofar as it consists of things other than knowledge and belief; for example, desires, emotions, and pleasures. Nor will all of these count as non-rational motivations: the late dialogues agree with the middle-period dialogues, such as the *Republic*, that reason is not a purely calculative faculty and that it has its own desires. Specifying the good condition of the rational soul will thus require specifying the good condition of the rational desires. As for non-rational motivations, including some desires, emotions, and pleasures, we may adopt a strategy suggested by Plato's own treatment of the rational soul. Although possessing knowledge and understanding about non-sensibles may be the highest or best expression of the soul's essential activity of seeking to stand in the appropriate relation to truth, we have seen that it is not the only such expression. Attaining true beliefs about sensibles is an instance of the same activity. We may thus be able to extend the notion of standing in the appropriate relation to truth to these other psychic states.

Let us first consider how the argument can be extended in a way to apply to rational desires. Insofar as Plato is a rational eudaimonist, he thinks that rational desires aim, in an appropriate way, at the agent's overall good, that is, at what is overall good or best for her. Rational desires will thus aim at fully realizing the essential nature of the soul and will thus aim at those states that stand in the appropriate relation to the truth. Moreover, rational desire itself insofar as it involves taking something to be good can stand in an appropriate relation to truth. In Chapter 5, I consider in more detail the connection between rational desire and what is non-relationally good. This line of argument, however, already gives us reason to hold that the good condition of rational desires is to aim at the good.

But what of the non-rational motivations? Does the *Timaeus'* psychology provide an account of their good condition? Let us begin with spirited emotions such as anger, shame, and the emotions connected with honor. Such psychic activities and states involve a conceptualized or propositional element that draws upon the soul's non-sensible resources. So we can try to apply to them the account developed above for the soul's beliefs and rational desires. In these cases, the good condition of beliefs and desires consists in their standing in the appropriate relation to truth and the good. This suggests a relatively straightforward account of the good condition of non-rational spirited emotions. The good condition of the soul with respect to anger is to be angry at the bad and the unjust. The good condition of the soul with respect to shame is to feel shame at acting badly and basely, and so on.

Such an account, however, threatens to assimilate non-rational spirited emotions to rational beliefs and motivations. If spirited emotions and their associated desires are so responsive to the truth and the good, in what way are they still non-rational? The idea that non-rational motivations are incomplete or partial applications of the soul's reasoning capacities may provide a solution. In the *Republic*, spirited emotions in addition to their having their place within the Spirited part of the soul differed from rational motivations with respect to their object. Spirited emotions took honor as their special object as opposed to the genuine good or what is good for the whole soul. On a unitary account of the soul, forming even the desire for honor as such will involve drawing upon the soul's non-sensible resources. But we no longer need restrict the object of spirited emotions to honor. They can, however, still be distinguished from rational motivations as long as their content differs in some respects from rational motivations or if their content is not determined in the same way.[75] For example, as we saw in Chapter 3, anger is especially likely to prompt the person to impetuous akrasia. Impetuous akrasia involves being motivated to act on something less than all the relevant considerations. This suggests that we might understand anger, as a non-rational motivation, as a psychic state that is not responsive to all relevant considerations. This does not require that anger cannot be responsive to some of the very same considerations, including considerations of value, to which rational judgments and desires are responsive. On this view, anger might be responsive to injustice although it is not responsive to all the considerations that reason takes into account in the formation of a judgment about what is best overall. Anger, for example, might be differentially responsive to injustice directed against the agent herself or against those to whom she feels especially akin. Such an account of anger may provide good reason to understand it as a non-rational motivation, although it still belongs to a unitary subject that draws on non-sensible resources. (Similarly, shame might be an emotion that can move us all the way to action in response to perceived shortcomings in ourselves or in those with whom we feel a special kinship.) As we shall see in greater detail below, on this account, the dividing line between rational and non-rational motivations becomes less fixed and less sharp. Insofar as non-rational motivations, such as anger, can be more fully responsive to reason's considerations, these emotions can be more thoroughly reworked and reshaped. And if such reshaping is sufficiently radical, it may come close to a form of eradication.

Can we similarly extend this account to cover the non-rational motivations connected with pleasure? These are especially important, since the only elements that the *Philebus* counts as constituents of the happy life are kinds of knowledge and true belief, and kinds of pleasures. What we need to show is that these non-rational motivations can stand in the appropriate relation to truth and the good. One way in which we might try to fulfil this condition is by requiring that approved pleasures do not involve any false beliefs and that they take as their objects things that are, in fact, good. But here we face, in an especially acute form, the worry that this replaces pleasure and the desire for pleasure with something quite different. Even if pleasure and the non-rational motivations associated with it are structured by the application of the soul's non-sensory resources, an adequate account should preserve the following two claims: (1) desiring something as pleasant is not the same as desiring it as good, and (2) finding something pleasant is not the same as finding it good.

It would be easy to see how we might maintain both of these claims, if we held that pleasure is a particular sort of non-representational sensation or feeling like, for example, a tingle. On this view, to find something pleasant is to experience it as the right sort of feeling or sensation. This seems to be quite distinct from finding that thing good. Similarly, desiring something as pleasant is to desire it as a particular sort of sensation or feeling and this is quite distinct from desiring it as good.

But as we shall see in more detail below, Plato does not hold such a theory of pleasure and allows pleasure to have conceptual or propositional content. As we shall also see, Plato gives pleasure an important cognitive and ethical role in the *Laws*. Experiencing the right sort of pleasures is both a crucial step in ethical development, specifically, in the cognitive aspect of the development of a virtuous character and can be in itself a cognitive accomplishment. Our account of pleasure will have to show why Plato holds these views and how he can do so while maintaining the distinctness of pleasure and its associated non-rational motivations.

4.5 Spirited Emotions

In the *Republic*, the Spirited part of the soul plays an essential role in the psychology of the virtuous person. When the person receives the right upbringing, it is a natural ally of the Reasoning part and lends its own motivational force to the force of the Reasoning part's commands. In the later dialogues, Plato is considerably more ambivalent about spirited emotions (e.g. *Stsmn.* 306A–311B and *Tim.* 89D1–90B6). Let us begin by considering anger, which is for Plato one of the primary manifestations of the spirited emotions.

Every real man should be of the spirited type [θυμοειδῆ], yet also as gentle as possible. For there is no way to avoid those injustices done by others that are both dangerous and difficult, or even impossible to cure, except to fight and defend oneself victoriously, in no way easing up on punishment. This, every soul is unable to do, if it lacks a high-born spiritedness. On the other hand, in regard to the curable injustices men commit, one must first understand that no man is ever voluntarily unjust. For no one anywhere would ever voluntarily acquire any of the greatest evils . . . So the unjust man, like the man who possesses bad things, is pitiable in every way, and it is permissible to pity such a man when his illness is curable; in this case one can become gentle, by restraining one's spiritedness and not keeping up that bitter, woman's raging. But against the purely bad, perverted man who cannot be corrected [ἀκράτως καὶ ἀπαραμυθήτως], one must let one's anger have free rein.   (*Laws* 731B3–D4)[76]

Although Plato begins this passage with the claim that 'every real man should be of the spirited type', he goes on to impose a radical restriction on the place of anger in the life of the virtuous person: it is only appropriate against those who are incurable. This would involve a remarkable reordering of typical emotional responses: the just person should, for example, not be angry with someone who assaults his mother or burns down his house unless he thinks that that person is incurable.[77] What the Athenian is attempting to do (and thinks we can achieve some success in doing in virtuous people) is to make spirited emotions directly responsive to reason's outlook. The consideration that is supposed to block anger is not an appeal to the honor or status of the agent, but rather to an extremely unintuitive conclusion of reason that applies to the wrongdoer, that is, that no one does wrong voluntarily.

Anger begins in children with a primitive realization that they have suffered what they take to be a harm; it is a painful, disturbed state that involves a desire to retaliate.[78] In the course of development, the notion of harm quickly becomes associated with the idea of an affront to one's status or honor that can include harm to those with whom one has a close relation. Anger has a conceptual aspect and even in its early stages can be influenced by rational judgments: I eventually learn not to experience any anger at all at a doctor cleaning my wound; I do not grow angry, but then override it. The development that Plato envisages here in a virtuous person, however, goes considerably further.

In the course of ethical education, anger can become directly responsive to the rational judgment that all injustice is involuntary. This might happen either because (i) although anger initially takes only a limited range of considerations into account, it fades in the light of further rational considerations, or (ii) the relevant rational considerations are already taken into account in the formation of anger so that one does not experience anger to begin with. Plato, quite reasonably, does not distinguish sharply between the two. The emotion that replaces anger in most cases, pity, is also responsive to reason's judgments about curability and the worth of curing the wrongdoer. These are fairly sophisticated judgments, but this is not surprising, since anger can operate directly with a more or less adequate conception of injustice and justice. It need not be mediated by or grounded upon considerations of the agent's own status or honor, since it can draw directly on the conceptual resources of reason. As the Athenian's anger against the imaginary atheist of Book 10 shows, anger may simply take wrongdoing or injustice as its object (e.g. *Laws* 832A4–B8, 885C2–888A7).

But even in the just person, reason's control over anger will be precarious. The Athenian's own anger against the atheist is inappropriate, since he considers him curable (and thus the Athenian 'quenches' his anger, *Laws* 888A6). This precariousness springs, in part, from the fact that even when anger is appropriate for just people, getting angry is not the outcome of a process of deliberation about what it is best to do overall. In the case of incurables, for example, just people allow their anger to take its course, they do not decide or choose to become angry. Anger comes into being without overall deliberation and it can prompt the person to action without, or even against, such deliberation. An awareness of injustice, for example, brings with it a desire to put an end to the wrongdoing and to strike back against the wrongdoer. Anger's characteristic defect is that it involves a (frequently very powerful) desire and it prompts to action on this ground alone. In addition to prompting people to act before they form a rational desire and continuing to prompt to action even after such a desire has been formed, anger can deform the deliberative processes, e.g., by focusing the agent's attention on the injustice done to the exclusion of other considerations. Nevertheless, Plato thinks that anger can be informed by rational considerations to quite a significant degree. Anger can be so trained that it is not merely responsive to the occurrence of certain action types that are typically the product of psychic injustice, nor even to the actual occurrence of genuine injustice. It can become sensitive to more than one consideration, including, in particular, whether the offender's state of soul is curable.[79]

So what place is left for spirited emotions in the virtuous person? To begin, they must either embody or be responsive to more than the consideration of injustice or harm done, but also to considerations that primarily concern the well-being and reformation of the wrongdoer. And insofar as they are so reworked, they come to resemble more closely overall judgments and the desires based on such judgments. (The resemblance will be even closer if we allow that rational judgments and desires need not issue from a psychologically real process of deliberation as long as they are sensitive to the right considerations.[80]) These 'purified' emotions will thus be appropriate only in quite a restricted subset of the occasions on which anger is normally felt; they will be appropriate only when we think that the offender is incurable.[81]

But Plato's critique of anger may have even more radical consequences. On the occasions on which anger might be appropriate on Plato's criteria, is anger really a good condition of soul? Consider the passage quoted above (*Laws* 731B3–D4). Its primary justification for anger seems to be that it provides an important motivational boost in circumstances in which following reason's commands is difficult. But problems lurk here. First, this only seems to show that anger can be instrumentally useful. In dangerous circumstances, fear for a person's physical well-being might undermine his willingness to fight and resist and in such circumstances anger may play a crucial role as an additional motivational force on the side of reason's judgments. But anger here is useful because of the infirmities of rational motivation and this argument only shows its instrumental usefulness. Getting soldiers drunk before battle might have a similar effect, but this does not show that there is something good in itself about such a state.

So is there something intrinsically good about giving one's anger free rein against the incurable? If there is, it should not matter whether the circumstances are dangerous, all that should be relevant is the incurability of the wrongdoer. But if we consider the case of an imprisoned wrongdoer who is incurable, anger seems problematic: the desire to inflict harm on the wrongdoer is not one that Plato finds much room for in his penology. Plato standardly appeals instead to the idea that death is not bad for the incurably unjust, since it puts an end to an existence that is worse than nothing.[82] Nor would accepting the claim that deterrence is a legitimate justification for punishment require that the just person have a desire to harm the wrongdoer: the deprivation of wealth or freedom that might deter others is not the infliction of a harm, since wealth and freedom would not benefit the wrongdoer.

Perhaps the best we can do is to appeal to a parallel with loving the good: as it is appropriate to love the good and loving the good is a state that is good to be in, so it is appropriate to hate the bad and hating the bad is a state that is good to be in.[83] The theological claim of Book 10 that god apportions good and bad things to souls after death in accordance with their ethical character might also be thought to suggest some form of retributivist theory according to which it is good that bad people suffer something bad. It is not clear that these passages endorse retributivism or that they require that hating the bad excludes the sort of pity for the incurable that finds expression in the idea that they are better off dead. But even if we interpret them in this way, anger is still quite restricted in its scope. Indeed, since ethical progress in the afterlife seems possible according to Book 10's theology, anger may never be justifiable for human judges.

Plato's later psychology shows why anger has such a limited place in the life of the virtuous person. Because it can be informed by rational considerations, anger is appropriate, at most, with respect to incurables (and might not be justifiable for humans at all.) To the extent that spirited emotions are open to being informed by rational considerations, the development of a virtuous character will require a long and difficult process of extirpating anger from most aspects of ethical life (cf. *Sophist* 229E1–230E4). Anger finds its place in a virtuous character only insofar as it comes increasingly close to rational judgments and desires, although Plato does not seem to think that even in the virtuous such a process can be entirely successful. The features of anger that remain most distinctive of it—that it does not proceed from overall deliberation and that the desires it involves are experienced as intense and painful—are expressions of the weakness of human nature, rather than of its excellence. Anger, even when appropriate, will be of only rather marginal non-instrumental value. But consistent with the Dependency Thesis, insofar as anger can be a good condition of soul, it is such because it embodies and is responsive to true value judgments.[84]

Anger is, however, only one of the manifestations of spirited emotions and there are two others that deserve consideration, shame and those connected with honor. In the *Laws*, Plato has a more positive view of both of these motivations than he does of anger.[85] Honors are a common incentive for the citizens, and the lawgiver in Magnesia tries to inculcate in all the citizens a sense of shame and assigns to shame some of the functions that spirit had in the *Republic* of supporting reason's judgments. Plato does not attempt to do away with appeals to honor and to shame, but he attempts to re-educate and refashion the desires and emotions involved in order to attach the motivation more directly to the genuinely valuable object.[86]

The case of shame provides an especially interesting illustration of how this non-rational motivation is educated so as to undermine and transcend itself.[87] Indeed, we see an attempt to develop in a mature virtuous agent a sense of shame that directly undermines its earlier manifestations. Early in the *Laws*, the Athenian offers the following account of shame: 'we often fear opinion, when we think that we shall be considered bad if we say or do something ignoble. This is the sort of fear that we . . . call "shame"' (*aischunē*, *Laws* 646E10–647A2). The Athenian goes on to praise this sort of shame as valuable in maintaining moderation and as one of the features especially responsible for the safety of Athens at the time of the Persian Wars.[88]

In it [the Athenian constitution at the time of the Persian invasion] was a certain despotic mistress—Shame [*aidōs*]—on account of whom we were willing to live as slaves [δουλεύοντες] of the laws that then existed. In addition, the magnitude of the invading force, on land and sea, struck us with a helpless feeling of fear: this made us all even more the slaves [δουλεῦσαι] of the rulers and the laws.   (*Laws* 698B4–C2)

What is relevant to us is the way in which shame is linked to the opinions of others. Shame, as it is conceived of here, is not merely felt at others' awareness that you have violated a norm that you and they both endorse; it also involves a willingness to accept and defer to a superior's judgment of the norms. What is shameful is rejecting the control of a superior, not being in a state in which you need control.[89] The conception here is quite similar to that in Plato's justification of the philosophers' rule over the lower classes in *Republic* 9: it is 'in order that such a one may have a like government with the best man that we say he ought to be the slave [δοῦλον] of that best man who has within himself the divine governing principle' (*Rep.* 590C8–D1).[90]

But as the *Laws* progresses, its notion of what is shameful undergoes development. Here I shall pick out two examples. First, when he suggests making incommensurable magnitudes a subject of study for all the citizens, the Athenian comments on his previous ignorance: 'it seemed to me to be the condition not of human beings, but of pigs, and I was ashamed [*ēischunthēn*], not only for myself, but for all the Greeks' (*Laws* 819D7–E1). Shame here is not felt at rejecting the judgment of one's superiors, but at one's own failure to have at least a partial grasp of the rational order of the world. And insofar as people fail to have such a grasp themselves, they fall short of their own rational nature as human beings. For this reason, the Athenian requires not merely that citizens refrain from prayers which contain false assertions about the motion and speed of heavenly bodies, but also requires that the citizens learn enough astronomy to grasp demonstrations about their motion and speed and about the consistency of their real motion and speed with what we seem to observe.

Kleinias accepts the Athenian's proposal to include the study of incommensurables, but does not appreciate the reason for this. He sees such studies, rather, as entertaining amusements: 'draughts and these studies do not seem to lie so very far apart' (*Laws* 820D1–2). But if these studies are only like draughts, then a failure to engage in them might be unfortunate, since one would miss out on a source of refined enjoyment, but is not shameful. Although Kleinias is open to such studies, he understands them in such a way that his own failure to pursue them is not really shameful.

Second, as we have seen, in justifying the use of preludes to the laws Plato appeals to the contrast between slaves and free men. Here again, the citizens' shame is redirected. The Athenian, unlike Plato in the *Republic*, does not try to upgrade the condition of slavery, and slavery, even to the good lawgiver, is rejected as an appropriate model for the citizen. Slavery remains shameful and what is shameful about it is being unable to grasp the reasons for the rules governing one's own behavior. The relationship between the two parties is still unequal: the lawgiver exceeds the citizen as a doctor exceeds a patient and the lawgiver guides the citizen in acquiring an explanation. Plato complains that the need to explain the laws is something that no lawgiver has ever realized before and that must include the Athenian lawgivers who were earlier praised for developing in their citizens a sense of shame that made them slaves to the laws and to the rulers. It is precisely such a condition that is now seen as degrading and is meant to arouse the intensely negative emotional reaction that any self-respecting Greek would have at being classed as a slave. Here the shame lies in a failure to grasp the explanation oneself. This sort of shame is similar to that engendered by the elenchus: insofar as you fail to grasp the reasons for your ethical views, you fall short of being the sort of person you should be.[91] There are still important differences between the reaction of the philosopher in training to the elenchus and that of the citizens to these appeals to shame.[92] The demands of philosophic knowledge are unrestricted: the goal is a complete explanatory account and any falling short leaves the desire for truth and knowledge unsatisfied. Non-philosophers will, no doubt, be satisfied with less, but insofar as they accept these appeals they will come to have a genuine desire for a grasp, based on argument, of rational explanatory principles.

A passage at the end of the *Laws* reflects this tension between the unrestricted demands of philosophic understanding and the restricted sort of explanations that the citizens receive. During the closing discussion of the Nocturnal Council, the Athenian asks Kleinias whether its members will know that virtue is one, but be unable to give a proof of this in speech, and

Kleinias replies: 'Impossible—for this is the condition of a slave [ἀνδραπόδου]' (*Laws* 966B1–3). We see here the full reach of philosophic demands. The members of the Nocturnal Council must be able to give a full explanatory account and anything that falls short of this seems to be worth little.[93] But the affirmation that believing something without grasping the explanation is fit only for slaves is made by the decidedly non-philosophic Kleinias. He has come a long way from some of his earlier pronouncements and has come close to accepting the Athenian's conception of what is shameful for free human beings. Shame has become directly attached to an awareness of one's own failure to grasp a reasoned explanation.

Shame will thus have a limited role in Magnesia: it cannot serve as the primary motivation for virtuous action in adults, although it can play an important role in the ethical development of younger citizens. This does not, however, exclude shame from the life of virtuous adults. It can provide an additional source of motivation on the side of reason's commands. The reliable presence of such a motivation can be of great practical significance, since circumstances will be such that, from time to time, even in a virtuous person rational deliberation and desire are not fully effective. Even a virtuous person in Magnesia can have too much to drink or be faced with unusually great temptations. And it may be a fact of human psychology that properly trained agents are still subject to an immediate sensitivity to the judgments of others that does not spring from rational deliberation and is not fully informed by it. The Dependency Thesis does not require Plato to hold that the appropriate training of this capacity cannot be good for a virtuous agent. But he has little reason to regard it as an important good in itself. As the education of Kleinias himself shows, a good ethical education will involve a remaking of the citizens' sense of shame. Insofar as shame becomes attached to failing to grasp a rational explanation, it comes to point beyond itself.

4.6 Pleasure

In the *Laws*, Plato repeatedly insists that the topic of pleasure is fundamental to his ethical and political philosophy: '[For] human beings who inquire into laws, almost their entire inquiry concerns pleasures and pains, in cities and in private dispositions. These two springs flow forth by nature, and he who draws from the right one, at the right time, and in the right amount is happy' (*Laws* 636D5–EI).[94] At the end of the first half of the prelude to the whole law code, the Athenian returns to the point.

Now thus far, what has been said describing the practices that are to be followed and the sort of person each should be himself, concerns mainly the divine things; we have not yet discussed the human things, though we must—for we are carrying on a dialogue with human beings, not gods. By nature, the human consists above all in pleasures and pains and desires. From these, of necessity, every mortal animal is, as it were, attached and bound in the most serious fashion. (*Laws* 732D8–E7)

Pleasure is a central topic for lawgivers in at least two ways. First, insofar as they are concerned to bring it about that the citizens have happy lives, they must attend to pleasure, since pleasure is essential to a happy human life (indeed, the happiest life is the most pleasant life). Second, insofar as they are the primary educators of the citizens, they must pay close attention to pleasure, since enjoying the right pleasures is not simply a constituent of the happy life and a concomitant of achieved virtue, but is essential to the development of virtue itself.

The second passage, however, also suggests that pleasure may be too central to human life for our own good. Elsewhere in the *Laws*, Plato holds that if a course of action is painful or not sufficiently pleasant, we may either fail to follow it even if we realize that it is overall better or only do the better thing reluctantly.[95] This immediate and powerful attractiveness of pleasure is especially suspect, since pleasure is not the good and it does not account for the correctness or goodness of things (*Laws* 667B5– 668B7). And as we have also seen, pleasure is a dangerous and seductive force within the soul: it is the main source of akratic action and, perhaps even worse, it tends to distort judgments about what is good both in mature and in immature agents, and even in virtuous people.

Let us begin our discussion by looking back to the *Republic*. Plato's views there have difficulties and obscurities and may not be fully worked out. But they do provide a useful starting point for considering the position of the later dialogues. In a difficult but important passage from Book 9 of the

Republic, Plato seems to understand pleasure as being the replenishment of a lack.[96]

Are not hunger, thirst, and the like some sort of emptyings of the body? They are. And are not ignorance and lack of sense emptiness of the soul? Of course. And would not someone who partakes of nourishment or strengthens his understanding get filled? Certainly. Does the truer filling up fill you with that which is less or that which is more? Clearly, with that which is more. And which kinds partake more of pure being? Kinds of filling up such as filling up with bread or drink or delicacies or food in general? Or the kind of filling up that is with true belief, knowledge, reason, and, in sum, with all of virtue? Judge it this way: That which is related to what is always the same, immortal, and true, is itself of that kind, and comes to be in something of that kind—this is more, is it not, than that which is related to what is never the same and mortal, is itself of that kind, and comes to be in something of that kind? That which is related to what is always the same is far more. And does the being of what is always the same participate more in being than in knowledge? Not at all. Or more than in truth? Not that either. And if less in truth, then less in being also? And is it not generally true that the kinds of filling up that are concerned with the care of the body share less in truth and being than those concerned with the care of the soul? Yes, much less. And do you not think that the same holds of the body in comparison with the soul? Certainly. And is not that which is more, and is filled with things that are more, really more filled than that which is less, and is filled with things that are less? Of course. Therefore, if getting filled with what is appropriate to our nature is pleasure, that which is getting more filled with things that are more enjoys more really and truly a more true pleasure, while that which partakes of things that are less is getting less truly and surely filled and partakes of a less trustworthy and less true pleasure. (*Rep.* 585A8–E4)

On this account, each part of the soul has its own pleasure that consists in the replenishment of its associated natural lack. The Reasoning part's pleasure consists in the replenishment of the soul with knowledge of the Forms, and the Appetitive part's pleasure consists in the replenishment of the body with respect to food, sex, and drink. (Note that in both cases, the pleasure of the part consists in the replenishment of what that part takes as an end or regards as good.) This provides Plato with a criterion for ranking pleasures. Since pleasure consists in the replenishment of a lack, the more real or genuine the replenishment is, the more real or genuine the pleasure is. And if one pleasure is more real or genuine than a second pleasure, then the first is more pleasant then the second. Since knowledge and the soul are more real than food and the body, the replenishment of the Reasoning part is more real than the replenishment of the Appetitive part. Thus the pleasures of the Reasoning part are more real and genuine pleasures than those of the Appetitive part and so are more pleasant.

I shall not examine the details of this argument. But it serves an important purpose in the *Republic* in allowing Plato to argue that the philosophical life, that is, the just life, is the most pleasant life. In the course of doing so, Plato not only argues that the life of the philosopher is far more pleasant than any other sort of life, but also appears to suggest that the pleasures of the lower parts fail to be pleasures at all.[97] Yet even if we allow that some of the Appetitive part's pleasures are real, they fall exceedingly low on the scale of pleasures. Their failure is caused by the defectiveness of what the relevant replenishment consists in, that is, bodily replenishment. In a virtuous person, the Reasoning part of the soul directs both of the lower parts to the best pleasures that they are capable of pursuing and enjoying. But this does not change the basic *sort* of pleasure that they can pursue and enjoy: anything that can be a pleasure for the Appetitive part is such in virtue of being a bodily replenishment.

This view has three significant consequences. First, the pleasures of the lower parts of the soul are primarily of interest only insofar as they soothe the lower parts and render them such as not to interfere with the Reasoning part. Second, Plato makes no explicit room for sensory pleasures of any sort that belong to the Reasoning part. Indeed, it is not clear that his analysis allows for such pleasures.[98] Finally, Plato in the *Republic* shows little concern that philosophers might be seduced by the pleasures of the lower parts of the soul (or that philosophers might be subject to akrasia). This optimism seems reasonable in light of the Book 9 passage, since why would philosophers be enticed by the pleasures, for example, of the Appetitive part? They already have a view about the value and pleasantness of such replenishments and there seems to be no obvious reason why the occurrence of appetitive pleasures should undermine these views (except, perhaps, in cases in which such pleasures or their associated desires so severely disrupt reason that they prevent it from functioning).[99]

In the later dialogues, especially the *Philebus*, Plato's views about pleasure grow more complex. He is increasingly concerned with the diversity of pleasure, the specific natures of its various kinds, and with the dissimilarities among them. Nevertheless, in both the *Philebus* and the *Timaeus*, Plato still seems to treat at least sensory pleasures as intimately related to replenishments or restorations. They do not, however, consist in such replenishments. The pleasure is, instead, a form or kind of perception. This is not to say that pleasure is a feeling that the experiencer perceives; rather, sensory pleasure is itself the perception of a replenishment or restoration.[100]

As we saw in the first half of this chapter, Plato in the late period thinks of perception as a non-conceptualized psychic movement. But Plato also recognizes a broader state that includes conceptualization and belief. He sometimes characterizes as 'appearance' a 'mixture of belief and perception', that is, the acquisition of a belief through or on account of perception.[101] This is the typical state that people are in as a result of their ordinary dealings with the world. For example, a normal perceiver confronted with a red apple in normal viewing circumstances will, *ceteris paribus*, have an appropriate visual perception that is linked with a judgment giving the content of the perception, e.g. 'This is a red apple.' Similarly, in the case of pleasure, the perception involved has content that can be articulated and insofar as pleasure involves both the non-conceptualized movement and the interpretation, the pleasure is representational and has conceptual content. The view that pleasures, broadly construed, have conceptual content is essential to a number of the claims that Plato makes about pleasure in the *Philebus*. For example, it is because pleasures essentially involve concepts or beliefs that Plato can appeal to the content of these concepts or beliefs to classify different kinds of pleasures and to explain why some are contrary to each other. The fact that pleasures have conceptual content also provides the basis for some of the claims that Plato goes on to make in this dialogue about 'false pleasures'.[102]

The idea that pleasure can have conceptual content has important implications for Plato's understanding of pleasure's value and of its place in the good life and in ethical education. Since perception, broadly construed, involves some conceptualized awareness or interpretation, it is open to reason in at least two ways. First, in order to conceptualize the perception in any way at all, the soul must draw upon some of the resources of reason. Minimally, it must draw upon the common property, being, in order to judge that something is F for any F at all. So any contentful awareness requires some contribution from reason. But even more important, the interpretation of the perception is open to further rational influence insofar as it can draw upon additional concepts of reason. Such interpretation will involve the discrimination of various qualities and can vary in the range of qualities discriminated and the precision or clarity with which they are discriminated. In the case of a sensory pleasure that is (partially) constituted by a perception, different qualities of the perception can be conceptualized or made the object of contentful awareness and this can be done in a more or a less fine-grained way. On the *Republic* picture, sensory pleasures were nothing more than restorations of a bodily condition and nothing other than the fact that the bodily condition being restored is relevant to their status as pleasures.[103] On Plato's later view, the pleasure can be (partially) constituted by other features of the perception and its associated conceptualization.

To see in more detail how this might work, let us begin with a passage from the *Philebus*.

> [True pleasures are] those related to colors we call fine and to shapes and to most smells and sounds and in general all those that are based on imperceptible and painless lacks, while their replenishments are perceptible and pleasant . . . By the fineness of a shape, I do not mean what the many might suppose, namely that of a living being or of a picture. What I mean, what the argument demands, is rather something straight or round and what is constructed out of these with a compass, rule, or square, such as plane figures and solids. Those things I take it are not fine in a relative way, as the others are, but are by their very nature forever fine by themselves. They provide their own specific pleasures that are not at all comparable to those of scratching. And colors are fine in an analogous way and import their own kinds of pleasures . . . What I am saying is that those among the smooth and clear sounds that produce a single pure tone are not fine in relation to anything else but in and by themselves and that they are accompanied by their own pleasures which belong to them by nature . . . [T]here is also the less divine class of pleasures connected with smells. But because there is no inevitable pain mixed with them, in whatever way or wherever we may come by them, for this reason I regard them as the counterpart to those others. (*Phil.* 51B3–E4)

It is important to see what this passage by itself asserts. Plato here seems to be thinking of these sensory pleasures, including those pleasures taken in fine colors and shapes (or smells), as kinds of perceptions of restorations. He distinguishes true pleasures here from pleasures that are not true simply in terms of purity. A true pleasure is a pure pleasure, that is, it is a pleasure unmixed with pain. In the case of pleasures taken in fine shapes or colors, it is quite important that the antecedent deprivation is not noticed. For when the antecedent deprivation is noticed, the person is pained and the resulting pleasure is mixed and thus impure. More generally, impure pleasures are those in which the pleasure consists in or is taken in something that essentially involves pain. Most bodily pleasures are impure. For example, the pleasures of quenching one's thirst or of satisfying one's hunger consist in the perception of the restoration of a natural state of balance. These perceptions of restorations do involve a perception of the initial imbalance, so they will, as such, involve pain. There are also impure pleasures which are entirely psychic. For example, malice or envy is, in itself, painful, but it (partially) consists in pleasures taken in the actual or anticipated misfortunes of others.

In the case of seeing a fine color or fine shapes, the pleasure is pure and thus true because the absence of the fine color or shape is not painful. But Plato does not define pure pleasures as those consisting in the appreciation of fineness or good order. Nor does he give a way to distinguish among pure pleasures with respect to their pleasantness. A pure pleasure is more pleasant than any pleasure mixed with pain, but this does not allow us to discriminate with respect to pleasantness among equally pure pleasures.[104] This passage does not allow us to conclude that pure pleasures that consist in a clearer and more precise appreciation of fineness are more pleasant than pure pleasures that involve a less clear and less precise appreciation.

Nevertheless, the central cases of pure pleasure that Plato mentions here consist in the appreciation of the finemaking features of objects. It is worth stressing that the pure pleasures that Plato is concerned with here are sensory pleasures. They are the pleasures taken in plane or solid figures that are constructed with a compass or square, not the pleasures of contemplating the Form of the Circle. These sensory pleasures involve recognizing or appreciating the fineness or good order of a sensory object and this involves not only conceptualizing the perception in terms of non-sensible properties such as straight or spherical, but also in terms of the non-sensible property of fineness. In the *Republic*, sensory pleasures as a class were downgraded as less pleasant than intellectual ones by reference to the criterion of the genuineness of the replenishment involved. In the *Philebus*, sensory pleasures taken in fine objects are no longer downgraded in this way: they, too, count as pure pleasures and Plato gives no further criterion of the degree of pleasantness. The characterization of the pleasures of smell as 'less divine' may suggest that Plato has some further criterion for distinguishing among pure pleasures, but he does not make this explicit here.

Several passages from the *Timaeus* and the *Laws*, however, go further in showing how the classification and ranking of pleasures is related to the extent to which they consist in the appreciation of finemaking properties.

[T]he god invented sight and gave it to us so that we might observe the revolutions of reason [τοῦ νοῦ] in the universe and apply them to the revolvings of our own reasoning [τῆς παρ' ἡμῖν διανοήσεως]. For there is a kinship between them, even though our revolutions are disturbed, whereas the universal orbits are undisturbed. So once we have come to know them and to share in the ability to make correct calculations according to nature, we should stabilize the straying revolutions within ourselves by imitating the completely unstraying revolutions of god. Likewise, the same account goes for sound and hearing—these too are the gods' gifts, given for the same purpose and intended to achieve the same result. Speech was designed for this very purpose and it plays the greatest part in its achievement. And all such composition as lends itself to making audible musical sound is given in order to express harmony, and so serves this purpose as well. And harmony, whose movements are akin to the orbits within our souls, is a gift of the Muses, if our dealings with them are guided by reason [μετὰ νοῦ], not for irrational pleasure [ἡδονὴν ἄλογον], for which people nowadays seem to make use of it, but to serve as an ally in the fight to bring order to any orbit in our souls that has become unharmonized, and make it concordant with itself. Rhythm, too, has likewise been given to us by the Muses for the same purpose, to assist us. For with most of us our condition is such that we have lost all sense of measure, and are lacking in grace. (*Tim.* 47B6–E2)

This passage is difficult and some of its details rest on views of Plato that we can no longer find at all plausible. But the philosophical point that Plato is making does not require that his astrophysics be correct. Plato held that the stars are living beings animated and moved by divine souls. These divine souls are constituted by pure reason and reason possesses an eternal circular psychic motion.[105] The divine souls impart this motion to the stars' bodies which thus travel in circular paths. Our souls too, as we saw in our earlier discussion of the *Timaeus*, are—albeit in a more impure form—composed of the same stuff as the souls of gods and are thus constituted by rotating circles composed of Sameness, Difference, and Being. These circles are distorted by embodiment and sense-perception. In the above passage, Plato claims that sense-perceptions that involve making correct judgments about the revolutions of the stars result in the circles of our own souls becoming better ordered. The perfect circular psychic movement of the souls of the gods which animate the stars produces physical circular motion in the stars. When we perceive this, the appropriate circular motion is re-established in the motions of our own souls. Re-establishing this order is both a causal process in our souls and a cognitive one; coming to true judgments about the stars is, in part, a matter of the circles of our souls regaining their proper form.

Plato goes on to claim that the same is true in the case of harmony. Harmonious or fine sounds embody the same sort of fine or good order that the circles of our souls have in their best or original state (which is an approximation of the fine order of divine souls) and the appreciation of such order re-establishes the proper order in the circles of our souls. It is crucial to note that this is in part a sensory process: it is not simply by thinking of geometric shapes that order is restored. Good order is restored in the motions of the soul that are involved in, and affected by, sense-perception. The process is also surely scalar: the circles of our souls can be more or less distorted and the degree of their restoration depends on our intelligent appreciation of harmonies or of the revolutions of the stars.

In this passage, it might seem that Plato is contrasting such correct sensory appreciation (dealings with the Muses that are guided by reason) with pleasure as such. But, more precisely, what the above passage does is draw an unfavorable contrast between correct sensory appreciation and 'irrational pleasure.' Another passage from the *Timaeus* suggests that not all sensory pleasures need be so irrational. In this second passage, Plato describes how the proper combination of fast and slow or high and low pitched sounds produces harmony.

Sometimes, when the motion they [sounds] produce in us as they move toward us lacks conformity, these sounds are inharmonious; at other times, when the motion does have conformity, the sounds are harmonious. [What happens in the latter case is this.] The slower sounds catch up with the motions of the earlier and quicker sounds as these are already dying away and have come to a point of conformity with the motions produced by the slower sounds that travel later. In catching up with them, the slower sounds do not upset them, even though they introduce another motion. On the contrary, they graft onto the quicker movement, now dying away, the beginning of a slower one that conforms to it, and so they produce a single effect, a mixture of high and low. Hence the pleasure [ἡδονὴν] they bring to fools and the delight [εὐφροσύνην] they afford—by their expression of divine harmony in mortal movement—to the wise.[106] (*Tim.* 80A4–B8)

The terminological distinction that Plato draws here between pleasure for the foolish and delight for the wise should not lead us to think that the latter is not a form of pleasure at all. Consider, for example, a passage from the *Laws*.

[E]very young creature, so to speak, is incapable of remaining calm in body or in voice, but always seeks to move and to cry: young things leap and jump as if they were dancing with pleasure [μεθ' ἡδονῆς] and playing together, and utter all sorts of cries. The other animals, the argument goes, lack perception of the various kinds of order and disorder in motions (the orders which have received the names of 'rhythm' and 'harmony'); to us, in contrast . . . the gods have granted the pleasant perception [αἴσθησιν μεθ' ἡδονῆς] of rhythm and harmony. (*Laws* 653D7–654A3)

In the *Timaeus* passage, Plato distinguishes different pleasures which nevertheless have the same generic object, e.g., sound. In the *Laws* passage, Plato does not attribute pleasure to animals in their perception of movement, but does characterize the human perception of order in movement as a kind of pleasure. In each case, there is a distinction between what intelligent and unintelligent subjects perceive and this distinction is between perceiving the orderliness of certain movements and failing to do so. And in the *Timaeus* passage, this is correlated with a distinction between two kinds of pleasures.[107] This distinction among pleasures thus rests on a distinction between the features noticed in the perception. The preferred pleasures are appreciations, in a sensory mode, of fine or good order.

The order instantiated, for example, in correct harmonies or rhythms can be appreciated to widely varying degrees. But even a quite basic appreciation of harmony or rhythm involves perceiving it as some kind of order and such a perception can constitute a pleasure. Even such a low-level perception of order in harmony involves conceptualizing it in accordance with concepts drawn from reason. More sophisticated pleasures will involve making clearer and more determinate one's grasp of the sort of order involved. But even at the more sophisticated levels, these are still cases of sensory awareness. Sensory pleasures will vary greatly in the extent to which they invite and allow such conceptualization and the elaboration of it. Seeing the revolutions of the stars easily lends itself to conceptualization in mathematical terms, as does perceiving harmony in sound. Yet even the basic and primitive awareness of the rhythmic order of one's own body in movement can draw upon reason's conception of order.

With this as background, let us take up the question of pleasure's role in ethical education. That pleasure has an essential role in such education and that a virtuous person must from childhood on learn to take pleasure in the right things is one of Plato's most prominent assertions about ethical development in the *Laws* and it is perhaps the claim in Plato's ethics about which Aristotle is the most explicitly enthusiastic (e.g. *N.E.* 1104^{b}11–13). Consider one representative passage from the *Laws*.

[I]n children, the first childish perceptions are pleasure and pain, and it is in these first that virtue and vice come into being in the soul . . . Education, I say, is the first virtue that comes into being in children. Pleasure and love, pain and hatred, become correctly arranged in the souls of those who are not yet able to reason, and then, when the souls do become capable of reasoning, these passions can in consonance with reason affirm that they have been correctly habituated in the appropriate habits. This consonance in its entirety is virtue. (*Laws* 653A5–B6)

But even if we accept the claim that a person must take pleasure in the right things in the right way in order to develop a virtuous character, this does not yet tell us why pleasure plays such an essential role in ethical development. And there is more than one way in which we might try to account for this central role. First, there is a straightforward and deflationary account of pleasure's role. On this account, children, given the proper training, are brought to take pleasure in some particular virtuous actions or expressions of virtue. They come to like and find pleasant some particular expressions of virtue and dislike and find unpleasant some particular expressions of vice. These pleasures are either non-conceptualized or, at any rate, are not conceptualized by drawing upon independently given concepts that are (at least partially) constitutive of the concepts of the fine, the good, or of virtue. By seeing new cases as relevantly similar to these early ones with respect to their pleasantness or disagreeableness, children come to form concepts of what is fine or good.[108] They will come to see, e.g., two actions as fine because they are enjoyable or pleasant in the same way. Although the above passage from the *Laws* has sometimes been read in this way, such an interpretation is not consistent with the rest of Plato's ethics. Such an account makes the notion of what is pleasant or pleasant in a certain way explanatorily basic with respect to the concepts of good, fine, or virtue and Plato clearly rejects this view. Pleasantness is not what accounts for the goodness or fineness of things and the concepts of fine, good, and virtue can be specified independently of our finding certain things pleasant or disagreeable in particular ways.

This account does, however, have the attraction of showing why taking pleasure in the right things really is an essential part of becoming virtuous. Even more important, such an account allows experiencing the right pleasures to make a substantive cognitive contribution to becoming virtuous. It does so because the concepts of fineness, goodness, and virtue are given their content by the children's early pleasures, which are themselves independently specifiable. The mere fact that an account makes experiencing the right pleasures essential to becoming virtuous does not entail that the account gives pleasure a substantive cognitive role. After all, experiencing the right sorts of pleasures might be essential to becoming virtuous even if such experiences were not essential for the cognitive aspect of virtue, since a virtuous character also involves the proper disposition of the person's non-rational emotions and desires. We might think, for example, that people could acquire the appropriate concepts of good and fine simply by taking over, on authority, the concepts used by their teachers or that they could acquire them by recollection. Neither of these processes obviously requires that the children experience the right pleasures. Children might acquire the concept *horse* by relying on the instruction of their teachers without experiencing any particular pleasures connected with horses and the recollection of the concept *equal* in the *Phaedo* also seems to require no particular sorts of pleasant experiences. Yet we might hold that in addition to having the right concepts of good and fine, virtuous people must be properly affectively disposed towards virtue. And it seems reasonable to think that if mature virtuous agents are to come to find virtue pleasant, they will need to have, early on, the appropriate pleasures.

This second account gives pleasure an essential role in ethical development only by denying it a cognitive role. So let us consider a third account that allows pleasure a cognitive role, but avoids the problems of our first, deflationary explanation. This new account allows experiencing the right pleasures to make a contribution to the cognitive condition of the virtuous person, but insists that its role is causal rather than substantive. On this view, pleasure fixes the learners' attention on what they are experiencing and encourages them to further exploration of the activity in question. Pleasure encourages us to linger and focus on the activities that we are involved in and to bring to bear on them our capacities for making finer and more accurate discriminations.[109] So taking pleasure in virtuous actions leads us to focus on them and thus to come to see what they have in common and thus what is good or fine about them. The goodness or fineness of the activity is independent of its pleasantness, but the pleasantness fixes our attention on the activity so that we can, by reflecting on the activity, come to appreciate its goodness or fineness. Similarly, finding virtuous actions painful will discourage us from focusing on them and thus learners will fail to develop their abilities to make the right discriminations. On this account, the contribution that pleasure makes to ethical development is causal rather than substantive. Experiences of pleasure might serve to focus our attention on virtuous activities satisfactorily even if we did not take pleasure in these activities for their own sake, or if the pleasures involved had no significant ethical similarities among themselves, or even if they were non-conceptualized. All that matters is that the pleasures play their proper causal role in fixing the learners' attention.

Such an account can explain some of the training that we give to children. We may reward with candy a five-year-old who shares her toys with her younger brother, and Plato himself encourages children to pursue their elementary lessons in arithmetic by setting them problems framed in terms of athletics and letting them practice counting with pretty garlands. And while this account makes experiencing the right pleasures relevant to the cognitive aspect of virtue, it does not give pleasure the wrong priority with respect to the concepts of the fine and the good. Moreover, some versions of it could accommodate the possibility that certain pleasures, for example the *Philebus'* pure pleasures taken in geometrical shapes or pure colors, have conceptual content that may include conceptualization in terms of the fine and the good. After all, what we are trying to explain is the role of pleasure in ethical development; the proponent of this account does not have to claim that the sorts of pleasures that play this causal role in early education are as cognitively sophisticated as any pleasures can be. She should allow that once the concepts of the good and the fine are acquired by the exercise of the person's discriminatory capacities which are brought into play by simple pleasures, these concepts are available for further use. Nothing excludes the possibility that these concepts, once acquired, can be used in conceptualizing more sophisticated pleasures.

Nevertheless, we should not accept this as the basic explanation of the role of pleasure in ethical education. (Although there is no reason to deny that it can explain some ways in which pleasure plays a role in such education.) It has two related defects. First, it does not explain Plato's insistence on a highly specific and determinate regimen of pleasures for the young. As we have seen, their songs, dances, and games are regulated in remarkable detail in order to guide them to the right pleasures. If pleasure's role were only a causal one, there would be no good reason to expect such specificity. (Extrinsic incentives provided, for example, by rewards would also be enough to focus the learner's attention.) Second, although this point is a little hard to state precisely prior to further analysis, the passages from the *Timaeus* and the *Laws*, especially those from the *Timaeus* quoted above, suggest that there is a certain continuity in content between early pleasures and later, more sophisticated ones, and between early pleasures and correct judgments of what is fine and good. Such continuity, if it really obtained, might allow us to give pleasure a substantive role in ethical development without making the mistakes of the first account.

We should begin by noting that the pleasures that Plato presents as fundamental at the start of ethical education are not those of performing the sorts of actions required by virtue. They are not, for example, cases of taking pleasure in paying back debts or resisting temptations. The *Laws'* passages that we have seen stress that the proper education in pleasure must begin very early (*Laws* 653A5–B6, 653D7–654A3). The pleasures of children that Plato focuses on are those taken in the rhythmic movements of their bodies in dance and, more generally, in rhythm and harmony in music. This might seem simply to make our problems more acute. We shall need to explain, it seems, not only how pleasures associated with the early performance of virtuous actions facilitate coming to stand in the right cognitive relation to virtuous actions, but also how pleasures that are not associated with standard examples of virtuous actions enable a person to make a transition into the ethical realm.

This new problem arises from the assumption that there is a discontinuity between the values at stake in these early sensory pleasures and in cases of virtuous actions. But this is an assumption that Plato rejects. At the very earliest stages, the pleasures of young children in rhythm and harmony may well not be sensitive to the properties of order and disorder in movement. Very young humans seem to share the sorts of pleasures that non-human animals are capable of. Nevertheless, fairly early in the child's development, it can respond to the order inherent in harmonies and rhythms. This will, no doubt, be a very dim and indistinct appreciation of the order that accounts for the goodness and fineness of the harmonies and rhythms to which children are exposed. Nor need Plato hold that a child's first dim grasp of fineness and order must in all cases come by this route. (They will also receive an education in mathematics and simple ethical instruction.) But such sensory manifestations of order can be appreciated early on. Furthermore, children's sense of order in harmony and rhythm can undergo increasingly sophisticated development that is not sharply discontinuous. On this account, these sorts of sensory pleasures can make a direct cognitive contribution to ethical development in two ways. First, they might well be the first experiences that trigger a dim awareness of fineness and goodness. But even if they are not, they can provide an important locus for the child's further development of these notions.[110]

There are several important consequences of this account. First, it allows the conceptual content of the pleasure to play a cognitive role in itself. The conceptual content of these sensory pleasures facilitates the learner's acquisition and development of the notions of fineness and goodness. At more advanced stages, enjoying the proper sensory pleasures in the appropriate way can be, in itself, a significant cognitive achievement. Second, as we saw, the *Philebus* seemed to endorse a qualitative distinction among pleasures: pure pleasures are, as such, more pleasant than impure pleasures. The *Philebus*, however, did not explicitly distinguish degrees of pleasure in terms of the extent to which the pleasure's conceptual content involves an adequate appreciation of fineness and goodness. So the pleasures of smelling a rose and those taken in the appreciation of fine shapes or of fine and virtuous actions all count as pure and the *Philebus* gives us no way to distinguish the latter as more pleasant than the former or as being higher pleasures.

The account developed on the basis of the passages we have seen from the *Laws* and the *Timaeus* suggests, however, how Plato might draw such a distinction among pure pleasures. Such a distinction would be especially welcome to Plato, since he holds that the most virtuous life is also the most pleasant life. The purity criterion by itself seems to be much too weak to show that the virtuous life is more pleasant than any unvirtuous life. Even if all the pleasures of virtue are pure pleasures, not all pure pleasures are pleasures of virtue. The purity criterion by itself does not seem to allow us to judge that a less virtuous life composed primarily of, e.g., the pure pleasures of smelling roses, is less pleasant than a more virtuous life containing the pleasures of virtue.[111] It will be easier to defend the claim of the virtuous life to be the most pleasant if we distinguish pleasures qualitatively; at least in part, in terms of the degree to which the object taken pleasure in is itself fine and of the adequacy of one's grasp of its fineness.

There is a final important point to note. As we have seen, a main reason that spirited emotions are a problematic element of ethical education and of a finished ethical character is that a person's early spirited emotions typically involve a false ethical judgment or at least involve a failure to have an appropriate true judgment. This is true even when the person has advanced well beyond the basic stage at which anger is a simple response to the frustration of desire or to apparent harm and instead takes wrongdoing as its object. Even at this more advanced stage, the person will usually think that the wrongdoing that is the object of the anger is voluntary or that whether the wrongdoing is voluntary is not relevant to the appropriateness of anger.

So, as I have argued, anger must be extensively reworked and restricted before it can be an appropriate element of a good ethical character and, even when so reworked, serious questions about its value remain.

The sorts of pleasures that we have been considering do not seem to have these defects: they do not seem typically bound up with false ethical judgments and they seem to be an expression of human excellence rather than of human weakness. In such pleasures the person is directly registering and responding to genuine value properties that things actually have, e.g., to the fineness of a shape or a harmony. (Unlike, for example, the case of the desire for honor which, even when correctly directed toward things that really merit honor, seems to be responsive to something that merely tracks genuine value properties.) One might worry, however, that such properties can most clearly and precisely be known not through experiencing sensory pleasures, but rather by the exercise of non-sensory faculties: they can be, for example, the subject of philosophical investigation and ultimately of adequate definition. So it might be argued that pleasure still shares with anger the significant defect that it involves the partial or incomplete application of reason's resources.

I do not think, however, that such an assimilation of anger to pleasure is convincing. Anger, even when it is appropriately regulated by reason in a virtuous person, does not stem from overall deliberation and, like other spirited emotions, is especially sensitive to self-regarding considerations. Such emotions are useful capacities for human beings to have and this is what we should expect, since the construction of the soul is an example of the Demiurge's providential activity. The fact that anger can proceed without the need for overall deliberation allows for rapid response to circumstances involving a perceived threat to the agent. Moreover, as we have noted, the intense desires that anger typically involves can provide useful motivational support for the commands of reason. In each of these cases, however, anger is useful because of the relatively disadvantageous circumstances that human beings find themselves in. If our reasoning processes were faster or our rational desires were not subject to interference from irrational emotions and desires, these features of anger would simply be defects.

The case of the pleasures we have been considering seems to be importantly different. The worry above was that although sensory pleasures may involve an appreciation of genuine finemaking or goodmaking qualities, the appreciation of such pleasures is not the mode in which these qualities can be most clearly and precisely grasped. In the comparison between rational beliefs and desires and the beliefs and desires that are bound up with spirited emotions, the latter seem to be intrinsically undesirable or dispensable. The desirability of spirited emotions seems to be due to their extrinsic features. They are, for example, less costly in terms of the agent's time and the high motivational strength of their associated desires can have the good consequence of allowing reason's commands to be causally efficacious.

In order to see how similar the case of the pleasures we have been considering is to that of the spirited emotions, we should begin by comparing the grasp of value properties in sensory perception with the clearer and more precise grasp of them in non-sensory apprehension. Is it the case here, too, that the former is intrinsically dispensable or undesirable? If one had the appropriate non-sensory apprehension of these value properties, would it be undesirable or otiose also to have a grasp of these properties in a sensory mode? We might think this, if we held that the capacity for sense-perception itself is undesirable or dispensable for a creature capable of non-sensory apprehension or, at any rate, that the additional capacity for sense-perception is desirable only insofar as it facilitates the creature's getting around in the world.

But there is good reason to doubt that this is Plato's position. According to the *Timaeus*, the orderliness of the perceptible world is the outcome of the Demiurge's providential ordering and the perceptible world is as fine and good as it can be. It is both fine as a whole and it contains many fine things. The perfection of the sensible world is something that can be the object of rational cognition: it is available for recognition by our cognitive capacities. Even the World Soul, which consists simply of a rational element, is capable by its very nature of arriving at the truth about perceptible objects, and doing so is a perfection of its own inherent nature. Although such activity is not cognition at its very best, it is a perfection rather than a defect. So sensory pleasures themselves that consist in a grasp of such truths are an excellence of human nature that is not simply dispensable.[112]

What seems to be more problematic, however, is the desire for pleasure as such. The sorts of pleasures that we have been considering, along with the pleasures of virtue and of contemplation, are, according to the *Philebus*, constituents of the good life. So they could be desired as good on the basis of overall deliberation.[113] But the desire for sensory pleasures as pleasures is distinct from a deliberated desire for the good and such a desire for pleasure is not so obviously an excellence of human nature. It does not seem, for example, to be an exercise of a human capacity that has its own distinctive and appropriate domain. The truth that these are pleasures is open to recognition by the soul's rational capacities and a person could accept this truth while still desiring the pleasure simply for what makes it really deserving of choice, that is, because it is good. This sort of distinction between appropriate pleasures themselves and the desire for these pleasures as pleasures gains support from two further considerations. First, although the *Philebus* counts certain pleasures as themselves constituents of the good life and thus as non-instrumental goods, it does not include as a constituent of the good life the proper disposition of one's desires for pleasures as such.[114] Second, pleasures typically bring with them an undeliberated, immediate inclination or desire to pursue them. But it seems that the genesis of such a desire must be suspect from the point of view of reason. If the awareness that a pleasure may be in the offing simply causally produces a desire for pleasure without being backed up by some sort of judgment that the pleasure is worth pursuing, then this failure seems to be a defect. But there is also something troubling about the possibility that the desire for pleasure involves a judgment that it merits pursuit. The judgment that it merits pursuit is made without overall deliberation and is not made on the criterion of goodness. In this case as well, such mechanisms might be useful for the creature's survival, but are not clearly intrinsically desirable. Although the desire is not formed on the basis of a judgment about overall goodness, the desire still moves the person to act (and can bring about action) and thus competes with rational judgments and desires as a source of action. In moving the agent to act, it plays (or perhaps usurps) the role of a rational desire and a rational judgment of value without clearly deserving to do so.

Second, from reason's point of view, there is something puzzling about the desire for pleasure as such. Consider, for example, the case of certain bodily pleasures such as those associated with hunger and thirst. Since the pleasure is a perception of the restoration involved, it seems that the desire for pleasure as such should be a desire for the perception of the restoration. (However, this desire may not conceptualize its object in these terms.[115]) But the important benefit for the person consists in the restoration of her bodily condition and not the perception of it. In such cases, pleasure may track the beneficial condition, but the desire for it is directed not at this condition itself, but at the agent's awareness of it (cf. *Laws* 667B5–E8). In the case of the higher sorts of sensory pleasures we have considered, it is less clear that the primary benefit consists in the restoration rather than the awareness of it.[116] But even if the perception of the restoration is valuable in its own right and is, perhaps, a greater good than the restoration itself, what such a perception seems to call for is a response to it as good.

I shall close this chapter by considering some of the negative aspects of pleasure. Non-rational motivations are especially dangerous insofar as they present a threat to the workings of rational belief and desire. As we have seen, non-rational motivations can prompt people to act akratically and thus interfere with the exercise of reason, so to speak, from the outside. In such a case, the formation of reasoned judgments and desires is not forestalled nor are they undermined once they have been formed. Rather the rational judgments and desires are simply causally overpowered. And as we have also seen, pleasure's interference with the workings of reason can be more intimate. Pleasure can, for example, focus people's attention on itself and away from other considerations that they would normally take into account. Here people may come to a mistaken judgment about what is overall best in these circumstances, because they ignore considerations that they would normally recognize as relevant and perhaps give excessive weight to pleasure.

But as we saw in our discussion of akrasia, such a mechanism does not seem to explain why people come to be systematically mistaken, rather than just going wrong in particular cases or why they come to have false beliefs about the goodness of various *types* of pleasures. This is especially the case when people already possess knowledge or firm and well-grounded beliefs about what is good. To a greater extent than in the middle period, Plato is concerned in the *Laws* with the corrupting force of pleasure. Even philosophers can give in to the wrong pleasures and once they begin to do so, their judgment of what is good becomes increasingly corrupted. The *Republic* does not suggest that this can happen to philosophers and it is hard to see how it could on the *Republic*'s account. The Reasoning part of the soul in a philosopher has a fixed view about the worth of bodily replenishments and although it will make sure that the appropriate bodily pleasures are pursued, there seems to be no reason for it to revise its own judgments of the good in order to bring them into line with what the lower parts find pleasant.

But the greater complexity of sensory pleasures in the later dialogues opens up more ways for a person to go wrong. In the *Republic*, the picture of sensory pleasures seems to be quite simple: Plato focuses on bodily pleasures such as thirst and hunger in which there is only one salient feature, that is, being filled up again. On the later view, matters are more complex. Even in sensory pleasures, one can attend to different features of the perception. In the case of the pleasures that Plato is more favorable to, one can attend to their formal features, e.g. their possession of a certain structure and order. But even in these cases, the following is true.

(1) The perceptions typically possess order only rather imperfectly.
(2) The very same perceptions possess other features besides order.[117]
(3) There is a limit to how fine-grained one's sensory awareness can be.

Our task is now to provide a plausible route from particular instances of enjoyment or finding pleasant to false general judgments of goodness. Consider a person who enjoys a particular sensory pleasure. She will have a perception of a restoration and will typically have an undeliberated desire for such a pleasure. This immediate desire invites her to pursue this pleasure and since she is a reflective agent, she may ask herself whether doing so is good. She might then apply some independent criterion of goodness to decide whether this pleasure is good. But she may frequently not engage in such an elaborate and explicit process. She might find that this particular pleasure, although not superlatively fine and orderly, is sufficiently fine to be good. Or she might, for example, take the fact that she finds this particular thing pleasant as prima-facie evidence of its goodness. Restorations, after all, are often beneficial to the person and if the pleasure is not obviously an illicit one, its pleasantness might be prima-facie evidence of goodness. Or even if she were not convinced that the pleasure was in fact good, but thought it was neither good nor bad, she might decide it is reasonable to indulge in it in order to avoid the pain of frustration. In both of these latter two cases, the experiencing of the pleasure offers some, although not decisive, reason to think that pursuing it is good. (Repetition may dull the awareness that it is not good in itself, but choiceworthy only to avoid the pain of frustration.) Finally, the experience of the pleasure might by itself tend to cause the person to judge that it is good, perhaps by focusing her attention on the pleasure itself, especially in cases in which the pleasure is not obviously illicit.

But once the particular pleasure is endorsed as good, it may then serve as a standard of judgment for other pleasures. Indeed, it is implausible to think that the person's selection of pleasures as good proceeds in each case by the application—whether or not deductive—of substantive general rules. She will pursue as good other pleasures because she sees them as relevantly similar to the initial ones. There are, at this point, several ways for the person to go wrong (in addition to the case in which her initial judgment that the pleasure was worth choosing is mistaken).

(1) Consider the case in which the pleasure possesses order, but does so imperfectly. The person might be right that this initial pleasure was in fact worth choosing. But she may go wrong in generalizing from it. Since there will be many fairly closely similar, but more defective pleasures available and only relatively few better ones, she may generalize downward (even if she is not aware of doing so). The error will grow worse, if she then proceeds to generalize from the newly selected pleasures as well.

(2) Even if the initial pleasure is good enough to be worth choosing, it has many other features besides those making it worthy of choice and there are limits on how fine-grained our awareness of the features of our perceptions can be. Even philosophers may go wrong in the features that they attend to and make the basis of their judgments of similarity. We should expect these mistakes to be small at first. In attending to a harmony or rhythm, the perception that constitutes the pleasure represents the orderliness of the harmony or rhythm, but it also represents other features. All that may be required to get the process of degeneration started is that the person include in her similarity base some other features than genuine orderliness, say, the intensity of the variations involved in the harmony or rhythm. (This

feature, of course, need not be explicitly conceptualized in terms of intensity.) The person still prizes this feature of the pleasure as part of what constitutes good order in this case.

These errors will not be confined to mistakes about what pleasures are good. Since the person takes herself to be responding to genuine value features, her judgements about what pleasures are good may well lead her to revise her general judgments of goodness and fineness. Once certain features are initially valued in sensory pleasures, they may come to guide one's further choices. Intensity and novelty, for example, may be valued in other sensory pleasures and beyond. A pattern of defective choices may spread quite widely before the person subjects the feature to full-blown rational examination. By the time this occurs, the person's desires may be so strongly and pervasively trained on the mistaken features that they can cloud her judgment while the mistaken conception has become so deeply entrenched that she begins to modify her choices in its direction.

A final point to note is that we can offer some further explanation of why the person initially focuses on pleasures that are defectively fine or orderly and have other features such as intensity that are not finemaking. First, insofar as the perception of a restoration constitutes a pleasure, many experiences will be brought forward as pleasant and immediately desirable. Although well-educated people have learned to select among their pleasures and have reshaped their sense of what is pleasant, they will have a natural tendency to rationalize the attractiveness of these pleasures. But as we also saw in Chapter 3, insofar as memories are involved in certain pleasures they can embody a kind of reasoning that is not fully part of the person's conscious awareness. Early pleasures will not be especially sensitive to genuine value properties of order and fineness. They will, rather, be responsive to, e.g., the size or the intensity of the replenishment and insofar as memories of these are linked to the production of desires, people will be subject to desires for pleasures that have these features. If the detailed workings of the process by which memories produce desires is not fully transparent to the agents' reflection, they may find themselves with desires for pleasures that involve, e.g., intense or novel replenishments, although they do not consciously conceptualize the pleasures as such and instead focus on the fact that they do possess, albeit imperfectly, a certain kind of order. To the extent that this occurs, their ethical judgments will be especially liable to corruption by the processes described above.[118]

5 The Citizens of Magnesia

5.1 Introduction

We have seen so far that Plato's view of non-philosophers in the late period is significantly different from that of the middle period: he is much more optimistic about their capacity to attain genuine virtue. This optimism rests on Plato's view that non-philosophers are capable of appreciating, albeit in an imperfect way, genuine value. As we saw in the last chapter, this view depends on developments in Plato's psychology and epistemology, in particular, on the unification of the soul and on the increased prevalence of the Forms in reasoning. But this development in Plato's ethics also has significant implications for his political theory. We have already considered in some detail one such consequence: because Plato thinks that non-philosophers are capable of genuine virtue, he requires the lawgiver to add preludes to the laws which are to educate the citizens so that they will grasp the reasons for the laws' provisions. In this final chapter, I want to consider more generally the political and social implications of the changes I have discussed so far. Given the way that Plato thinks people are and can be, what sort of political institutions and practices are appropriate for them? In light of what we have seen so far, how should a city and its laws be organized?

5.2 An Overview of Magnesia

Let us begin with a brief overview of the basic social and political institutions of Magnesia. Magnesia is to be a colony founded by the greater part of Crete. It will be located in a part of Crete that has been left empty by an ancient migration and is about ten miles from the sea. The site is basically self-sufficient in resources without having much excess to export. Plato sees this unsuitability for active commerce and distance from the sea as advantages: they discourage the maritime and commercial activities that corrupt cities by fostering a love of money-making in the citizens and by allowing close contact with foreigners who bring innovation and have not received the good ethical education afforded Magnesians.[1]

The city will be relatively populous: its number of households is to remain permanently at 5,040.[2] Immigration and emigration policies are designed to avoid population excess and deficiency. Each household will have an allotment consisting of two plots of land: one nearer the city's center and one nearer its borders. Each household's allotment is intended to be equally productive (*Laws* 737C–E, 745C–D). The households and land are not owned or farmed in common, but 'each shareholder must consider his share to be at the same time the common property of the whole city, and must cherish his land, as part of the fatherland, more than children cherish their mother' (*Laws* 740A3–6). Part of the sense in which the lot is in common is that it is inalienable and cannot be divided or aggregated: the assignment of the lot to a household is intended to support the household throughout the generations. (There are also restrictions on the use of the land.[3])

The only economic inequality that Plato allows is in movable assets. The possible degree of such inequality is, however, sharply limited. Plato establishes four property classes: the members of the top or first class have assets worth between three and four times the value of the lot (and the tools and animals needed to farm it), the second class between two and three times this value, and so on.[4] Anything accumulated over the highest amount will be confiscated by the city (*Laws* 744D–745A). Such assets do not include gold and silver, since these may be possessed only by the city; there will be only a token currency (*Laws* 742A–B). The property classifications are relevant in two ways: (i) some offices are open only to members of higher property classes, and (ii) fines and taxes take property class into account (*Laws* 774B, 955E).

But as we shall see below when we examine the city's offices, these property classes do not play a significant political role. Indeed, P. A. Brunt has plausibly argued that 'the distinctions in wealth that he [Plato] permits turn out to be a sham.'[5] When the Athenian introduces the property classes, he claims that it would be best if all citizens were equal, both with respect to the possession of a lot, and in their movable property, but that it is inevitable that the colonists will arrive with differing amounts of movable goods (*Laws* 744B). Brunt argues that since citizens cannot engage in manufacture or trade (or have their slaves engage in them), the richer citizens have no source of income except the production of their allotment which should tend to be equal to that of the poorer citizens. Thus once wear and tear have taken their toll on the richer citizens' initial stock of movable goods, they will not be able to maintain a significant edge over the less well-off citizens. Moreover, since consumption is regulated and imports of luxuries are banned, differences in property class allow for only small differences in standard of living. Brunt concludes that 'the division into property classes is thus meaningless.'[6] One might resist this judgment by arguing that differences in industry or skill could result in noticeable differences in production and that consumption is not so regulated as to produce uniformity. Nevertheless, Brunt does show that the division into property classes does not allow for great economic inequality in Magnesia.

One important way in which economic inequality is muted in Magnesia is that common meals are introduced for all citizens.[7] At Athens, there were social and political clubs and religious associations that served to foster friendship and social bonds among their members. Although these clubs were by no means restricted to the rich, members of such associations were generally among the better-off. Other cities had common meals for the office-holding class, but these were aristocratic institutions.[8] Crete and Sparta, however, extended these institutions to the entire male citizen body. Aristotle praises this extension and adopts it in the ideal city of the *Politics*. Common meals are beneficial because they (i) provide a locus for edifying conversation and music, and (ii) both express and foster friendship among the citizens.[9] Aristotle criticizes the abolition of private property in the *Republic* as an impractical extreme in seeking to unify the city: 'it is better for possessions to be privately owned, but to make them common property in use' (*Politics* 1263ᵃ38–9). The Cretan and Spartan system of common meals is a better way of making property 'common' (*Politics* 1263ᵇ40–1264ᵃ1).

Although the Athenian approves of Crete and Sparta for instituting common meals, the Magnesian practice differs in a characteristic way from that of Crete and Sparta. These two cities include only men in the common meals, since they adopted the practice for military reasons and their goal continued to be success in war (*Laws* 625A, 633A, 780D). Since the goal of Magnesia's laws is to foster virtue in all, the Athenian requires common meals for all the citizens, both men and women, and intends the meals to foster virtue generally.[10] Plato expects common meals to provide a venue for edifying conversation and music and expects these to foster and help maintain the virtuous condition of the citizens. The simple meals will also help prevent the development of luxurious tastes in food and will help encourage moderation with respect to the other appetites. But perhaps its most important effect is to help to foster a concern for the welfare of others. By helping to support the common meals, citizens are encouraged to see themselves as both responsible for the welfare of their fellows as well as dependent on them.

One indication of this aim is found in Plato's provisions for funding the meals. In Sparta, each citizen had a duty to support the common meals by making a direct contribution to them; in Crete, they were supported by public revenues.[11] In Magnesia, they will be funded by the direct payment of dues by individual citizens.[12] It seems reasonable to expect that the method of individual dues will have a stronger tendency to foster citizens' concern for others: they will have a continuous obligation to contribute directly to the welfare of their fellows. We should note two further points about such a plan. First, Aristotle criticizes the Spartan system because it makes contribution to the common meals a prerequisite for participation in public life and thus tends to exclude the poor from it (*Politics* 1271ª26–37). But the Magnesian system does not have this drawback: the distribution of property lots is intended to insure that no citizen falls into such poverty. Common meals in Magnesia will not exclude any citizens because of poverty nor are they needed to insure the feeding of the citizens: each household's lot will be more than sufficient for that. By requiring common meals, the laws enjoin the citizens to engage in a cooperative venture that publicly expresses their concern for each other. This benefit is not produced at the cost of creating the inherently undesirable situation calling for remedial action in which some citizens do not have the means to support themselves. Second, Plato has good reason to mandate such an institution in Magnesia.

One of the deepest tendencies that Plato thinks human beings have is to satisfy their acquisitive and appetitive desires. Such desires need not take purely egoistic forms, but can consist in giving exclusive or excessive weight to the interest of family and friends. In Magnesia, these dangers are greater than they would be in a city that abolished private families and property. Plato no longer thinks that such abolition is possible.[13] But by allowing the sort of private families and property ownership found in Magnesia, we risk encouraging the growth of selfish tendencies. Relatively severe wealth limitations help limit the citizens' acquisitive desires and common meals take the further step of widening their sphere of concern.

As I shall argue in Section 5.4, citizenship is a fundamental political notion in Plato's later dialogues. Let us begin by seeing how widely Magnesia distributes it. Many inhabitants of Magnesia are not citizens. There is a considerable slave population (including both public and private slaves) and they, of course, are not citizens. Also found within the city are transient foreigners and resident foreigners (metics) who may stay for twenty years.[14] Slaves and foreigners are an economic necessity for the city for they will carry on the trading, manufacturing and menial occupations that are barred to citizens.[15] The lotholders or heads of households are citizens, but citizenship is not restricted to them and owning land is not a necessary condition of citizenship. The sons and heirs of lotholders are called 'citizens' and are liable to military service at age 20, can participate in elections at that age, and can serve in office at 30.[16] They will not inherit the household lot, however, until their father dies. What of women? In Magnesia, the private family is not abolished. Although women lack an independent right to own property, they are liable to military training and service and attend their own common meals (*Laws* 780D). The Athenian holds that they can attain the four cardinal virtues and for this reason requires that they be educated (*Laws* 804D–805A). For Aristotle, women are not citizens of the ideal city, since they are excluded from political office.[17] But in Magnesia, women can participate in elections and hold political office and the Athenian explicitly counts them as citizens (*Laws* 814C2–4). In Section 5.3, I consider in greater detail the *Laws'* complicated views about women. Citizens can, as punishment for certain offenses, lose their citizenship.[18]

Let us turn to the political system or constitution (*politeia*) of Magnesia. This will involve an account of the political offices (*archai*) in Magnesia, of how they are to be filled, and of the laws the officeholders or magistrates (*archontes*) are to administer (*Laws* 751A–B). Magnesia has a rich variety of offices, but the main ones are: the Assembly (*koinos sullogos, ekklēsia*), the Council (*boulē*), the magistrates, especially the guardians of the laws (*nomophulakes*), the courts, and the Nocturnal Council (*nukterinos sullogos*).[19]

The Assembly is the main electoral authority in the city; it is composed of all citizens, or more precisely, all those who have served or are serving in the military (military service begins at age 20, *Laws* 753B and 764A). Although each citizen may participate in every meeting, attendance at most meetings is compulsory only for the top two property classes (*Laws* 764A).[20] The Assembly is responsible for the election of most of the city's officers and magistrates, including members of the Council, the guardians of the laws, various military officials, the examiners or auditors (*euthynoi*), as well as many other more minor magistrates.[21] The other functions explicitly given to it are (i) a role in judging offenses against the public, (ii) making awards of merit, (iii) extending the term of residence for metics, and (iv) passing on proposed changes in the laws, at least those regarding dances and sacrifices.[22] It may also have other responsibilities in connection with foreign affairs.[23]

The Council is composed of 90 members from each property class for a total of 360 members.[24] Men are eligible for office at age 30, women at age 40. The election procedure is quite complicated and combines both ballot and lot; rounds of balloting reduce the candidates for each class to 180, and the final 90 are chosen by lot. The procedure allows—but does not require—members of the upper property classes to have a somewhat greater role in the process. (Participation in the selection of candidates from the upper two property classes is mandatory for all classes; selection of candidates from the lower two property classes is mandatory for the upper two property classes, but optional for the lower two.[25]) Members serve one-year terms. The Council is divided into 12 smaller groups (prytanies), each of which exercises its functions for one month. The Council exercises ordinary administrative powers, such as calling and dissolving the Assembly, receiving foreign ambassadors, supervising elections, and so on. The

Council's functions seem to be more limited than those of the Athenian Council: in Magnesia, the Council does not supervise and audit other magistrates, does not have any power to try cases, and is not explicitly given the power to control the Assembly's agenda.[26]

The guardians of the laws (*nomophulakes*) are composed of 37 citizens, at least 50 years of age who serve from the time of their election until age 70 (*Laws* 755A). Apart from the Nocturnal Council, the guardians of the laws are the most important officials in the city. The first statement of their duties assigns them the responsibilities of (i) 'guarding the laws', (ii) maintaining the property register, and (iii) acting as a court to try those accused of having excess property (*Laws* 754D–E). As Morrow perceptively observes, this passage should not be understood as a full account of their functions, but rather (ii) and (iii) provide an application of (i) with respect to a particular law. We can distinguish four ways in which the *nomophulakes* guard the laws.[27]

(1)   Although they do not seem to have the authority to discipline other magistrates, they are assigned the general task of supervising them and are expected to bring appropriate cases to the attention of the courts or the examiners.

(2)   They exercise wider supervisory powers over citizens in general and, for example, are charged with fining those who spend excessively on feasts, granting permission to travel abroad, and overseeing the care of orphans.

(3)   They possess various judicial functions and are in charge of especially important or difficult cases involving the family, property, and the abuse of laws. These include cases of excess property and the refusal to carry out court judgments; they also hear along with the 'select judges' capital cases and themselves deal with charges against the select judges.

(4)   Perhaps their most important task is the revision and supplementation of the existing laws. The Athenian likens their task to that of the successors of a painter who intends to leave behind him 'the most beautiful possible painting' that 'never gets worse, but always improves over time' (*Laws* 769C1–3). The successors must not only repair decay, but also fill in details only sketched in outline by the original painter and improve upon whatever deficiencies are left by the original painter's shortcomings (*Laws* 769A7–E2). The Athenian

does not specify here how much revision is permitted nor the exact mechanism by which changes or supplementation can be made, and these issues are better addressed after we consider the Athenian's other discussions of changing the law and of the Nocturnal Council. But the Athenian in the passage introducing the *nomophulakes* seems to think that their role is not trivial, since he claims that he and his fellow founders of Magnesia 'should at the same time try our best to make these men lawgivers [νομοθέτας] as well as guardians of the laws [νομοφύλακας]' (*Laws* 770A7–9).

There are some textual difficulties in the passage in Book 6 that establishes the method of selecting the *nomophulakes*, but it seems clear that in the normal course of affairs they are elected by repeated balloting in the Assembly.[28] Two final points concerning the *nomophulakes* raise more general issues. First, the Athenian's willingness to rely on popular election to fill such important offices in the city is evidence of his confidence that the citizens' education—without special supplementation, e.g. by the advanced studies set for the Nocturnal Council—will enable them to make good judgments about candidates and to be motivated to act in accordance with these judgments (*Laws* 751C–D).[29] Second, the *nomophulakes* almost always exercise their powers as a board and not individually.[30] This requirement is in part intended to avoid bias and corruption, but it also reflects a more general insistence by the Athenian that political action be preceded and informed by deliberation.[31] This also suggests something about the abilities developed by the citizens' education and of how Plato thinks of ethical deliberation. The capacity for good ethical deliberation is not simply an ability to apply a general rule inflexibly or a capacity for correct practical judgment that is constituted by an ability to grasp case by case what the right thing to do is without the need for, and the possibility of, giving further reasons or justifications for such decisions.[32] The importance of deliberation suggests rather that the citizens will be able to engage in discussions of reasons for particular decisions and to elaborate their appreciation of the relevant principles by rational discussion.

Let us turn to the court system. Athenians saw their popular courts 'as an organ of the state exactly on a par with the Assembly and the Council . . . sometimes the court is even described as the highest organ of the state'.[33]

As is appropriate for such an organ in a democracy, popular courts in Athens were large: numbers of jurymen ranged from 201 to 2,501.[34] They were arranged by area of competence, not by hierarchy, and there was no higher court to which to appeal: 'Indeed, because the verdict was in a sense the opinion of the *polis* [city], it would have been inconceivable to admit that there could be any higher authority to hear an appeal.'[35]

One of the major innovations in Magnesia is the elaborate structure of appeals in judicial cases. The Athenian distinguishes public and private suits (*Laws* 767B–768C). For both sorts of cases, appeal is possible. In private suits there are three grades of courts. Courts of the first instance are composed of arbitrators chosen from among the friends and neighbors of the litigants. The first stage of appeal is to a 'tribal court'; these are popular courts chosen by lot. The last stage is an appeal to 'select judges' who are elected annually by the full body of all officials. In public suits, the court is the Assembly, although examination and investigation of the case is conducted by three of the higher magistrates. For capital offenses, there is a special court consisting of the guardians of the laws together with the select judges.[36] Finally, magistrates in the normal performance of their duties can act as courts in cases involving disputes below a certain amount.[37]

Here, too, the Athenian's confidence in the capacities of Magnesia's citizens is evident. Citizens, in virtue of their standing in the political community, expect to have a share in the administration of justice.

In regard to crimes against the public, it is necessary, first, that the majority have a share in the decision. For when someone does an injustice to the city everyone suffers the injustice, and they would justly be vexed if they had no share in such trials . . . Even in private suits it is necessary that everyone share [κοινωνεῖν] as much as possible. For anyone who does not share in the right of judging considers himself not at all a sharer in the city itself.   (*Laws* 767E9–768B3)

The Athenian appears to find this a reasonable requirement and designs the system of courts to meet it.[38] The system of appeal and the trial procedures allow for much greater deliberation and more thorough examination than at Athens, but the well-being of Magnesia depends on its citizens being capable of such deliberation and judgment.

In Book 12, the *Laws'* final book, several new political bodies are added or, rather, their position is made more explicit. First, every official in the city is subject to scrutiny (*dokimasia*) of his qualifications for office upon election, and examination and review (*euthuna*) of his conduct in office.[39] In Book 12, the Athenian establishes a body of officials—the examiners—who are to review the conduct of other magistrates in office. They have a position of special responsibility, since wrongdoing by magistrates quickly leads to factional strife that undermines the city (*Laws* 945D). To do their job well, the examiners 'must be in every way amazing men with respect to the whole of virtue' (*Laws* 945E2–3) and 'superior in virtue' to the other magistrates (*Laws* 945C1–2). Nevertheless, no special training is required of them to perform this function and the examiners are chosen by ballot. Three are elected each year by a vote of all the citizens. The minimum age for election is 50 and examiners serve until they are 75.[40]

The second new body has been the source of considerable controversy. The Athenian provides for the establishment of a 'Nocturnal Council' (*nukterinos sullogos*) which is so called because it meets daily from dawn until sunrise 'when everyone would have the most leisure from the rest of their private and common activities' (*Laws* 961B6–8).[41] The Nocturnal Council is first explicitly mentioned in Book 10 where it is assigned an educational function. Those who have violated Magnesia's impiety laws out of ignorance, rather than bad character, are to be imprisoned for five years. During their imprisonment, the members of the Nocturnal Council are to meet with them in order to reform their beliefs by teaching (*Laws* 909A). In Book 12, the Council is assigned the new function of meeting with 'observers' (*theōroi*) upon their return to the city. Observers are citizens over 50 years of age who have been granted permission to travel abroad in order to learn from and about the outside world. The members of the Council are to examine them to see whether their travel has corrupted them and to learn from them any discoveries they have made that are relevant to laws or to education (*Laws* 952B–D).

The Nocturnal Council's membership seems to include: (i) the ten oldest guardians of the laws, (ii) the current supervisor of education and his predecessors, (iii) examiners and other citizens who have won awards of honor, (iv) certain observers who, upon their return, are invited to participate by the Nocturnal Council itself, and (v) each of the above members is to nominate for membership (whose acceptance is subject to the approval of the other members) a younger associate between the ages of 30 and 40.[42]

The rest of the Book 12 passage charges the Nocturnal Council with having knowledge of the goal of the city's laws and with safeguarding the city. The Athenian does not make explicit what the Council's exact power and authority are and I return to this controversial question in Section 5.4.

This examination of the political structure of Magnesia strongly supports Morrow's claim that the property classes do not have an especially significant role.

> In filling of offices these property classes play a very minor part. They are disregarded completely in the selection of the most important officers of the state, viz. the guardians, the euthynoi [the examiners], the educator [supervisor of education], and the members of the court of select judges. They are also disregarded in the selection of generals and other military officers. All citizens are admitted to the assembly and to the popular law courts without consideration of property.[43]

In sum, in Magnesia all citizens have similar political opportunities and responsibilities. (Officials, of course, have special responsibilities, but offices are largely open to all.) All citizens are required to act in a wide variety of social and political functions which call for the display of the virtues. All, for example, are expected to fight for the city and although courage is not limited to the military realm, this is one important facet of courage. (Plato's dismissive remarks about the sort of courage that exists apart from the other virtues should not make us underestimate the importance he attaches to genuine courage displayed by the virtuous person in circumstances of danger.) And this is one area of virtuous activities from which the *Republic's* third class was excluded. All citizens participate in the political life of the city. All are eligible to vote for political offices, to hold most political offices, and to participate in the systems of the courts. And, as we have seen, doing so will require an active exercise of the virtues.

5.3 A Second-Best City: Women, Leisure, the Nocturnal Council, and Changing the Law

An important theme in the *Laws* is how far good political and social institutions can actually be implemented in real-world circumstances, and made compatible with the general constraints imposed by human nature. In this section, I shall consider four of the most significant examples of this tension between what is best and what is possible: (1) the role of women in Magnesia, (2) the degree of leisure had by the citizens, (3) the role of the Nocturnal Council, and (4) the possibility of changing the law.

Women   Scholarly opinion is sharply divided over the political and social place of women in Magnesia. Susan Okin claims that 'despite all his professed intentions in the *Laws* to emancipate women and make full use of the talents he was now convinced they had, Plato's reintroduction of the family has the direct effect of putting them firmly back into their traditional place.'[44] David Cohen, on the other hand, holds that 'it seems reasonable to conclude that in Plato's state [in the *Laws*] women were expected, indeed required, to participate in all aspects of political and civic life.'[45]

Let us begin by considering the *Laws*' programmatic remarks about women. In Book 6, the Athenian urges the lawgiver to pursue 'whatever way a member of the community, whether his nature be male or female, young or old, might ever become a good man [ἀνὴρ ἀγαθός], possessing the virtue of soul that befits a human being [τὴν ἀνθρώπῳ προσήκουσαν ἀρετήν], (*Laws* 770C7–D2). This passage suggests that there is a single virtue, the virtue appropriate to human beings, that makes both men and women virtuous and good.[46] Since the same virtue is to be developed in them, women must share the education given to men.

It shall not be left up to the father's wish to decide who shall attend and whose education shall be neglected, but rather, as the saying goes, 'every man and child insofar as he is able', must of necessity become educated, because they belong more to the city than to those who generated them. Indeed, my law would say all the very same things about females that it says about males, including that females should be trained equally [ἴσα]. I would speak without being at all afraid of the argument that horseback riding and gymnastics are fitting for men, but not fitting for women. For I am persuaded by the ancient stories I have heard, and at this moment, so to speak, I know there are countless myriads of women around the Black Sea—the women called Sarmatians—who are enjoined to handle not only horses, but the bow and the other weapons as well, in equality with men, and who practice them equally . . . [I]f, indeed, it is possible for these things to turn out this way, then the way that they are now arranged in our lands—where it is not the case that all the men with their entire strength, and united in spirit, practice the same things as women—is the most mindless of all. For in this way, almost every city is just about half of what it might be, when with the same expenditures and efforts it could double itself. (*Laws* 804D3–805B1)

The Athenian describes this position as holding that 'our female race must, as much as possible, have a common share in education and the other things along with the race of males' (*Laws* 805C7–D1). Further, the Athenian seems optimistic about the degree of virtue that women can attain: 'a lawgiver must be complete, and not half a lawgiver; to let the female live in luxury, spend money, and follow disorderly pursuits, while supervising the male, is to leave the city with only about half of a completely happy life, instead of double that' (*Laws* 806C3–7). This passage strongly suggests that women are capable of the same degree or extent of happiness that men are and, given the centrality of virtue to happiness, it seems that women can attain the same degree of virtue that men can.

In light of these passages, we should expect that in Magnesia women will share equally in eligibility for holding political offices and in the right to participate in the selection of officeholders. And there are texts that suggest this is the case. In particular, Cohen relies on the following passage from the end of Book 6.

A girl should marry between the ages of sixteen and twenty . . . and a boy between thirty and thirty-five. A woman can enter office at forty, a man at thirty. A man is subject to service in war from the age of twenty until the age of sixty; in whatever military services [χρείαν . . . πρὸς τὰ πολεμικά] it seems women should be employed, each will be ordered to do what is possible and fitting for her, after she has borne children and until she is fifty years old. (*Laws* 785B2–9)

This passage seems to be explicit in allowing women to serve in political offices at age 40. Further, it seems to resolve an earlier ambiguity. As we saw above, the basic electoral qualification in Magnesia is bearing arms for the city and the present passage seems to make it clear that women perform military service. So the only political difference between men and women appears to be that women's eligibility for office starts ten years later.

Further examination, however, suggests that the evidence is more equivocal. First, even the passages noted so far contain ambiguities and qualifications. For example, the passage above stating 40 as the age at which women may hold office does not explicitly state what offices women may hold and this age limit may apply only to the female officials the Athenian mentioned just a little before (*Laws* 784A1–B1), who are solely concerned with the supervision of young married couples. Moreover, it only claims that women will perform some unspecified 'military services', not that their service satisfies the arms-bearing requirement for voting. Second, there are a number of passages in the *Laws* that make, in passing, unfavorable evaluations of women.[47] In recommending common meals for women, for example, the Athenian makes the following comment.

That race of us humans that is by nature more secretive and cunning because of its weakness, the female, was incorrectly left in disorder by the legislator's failure to be firm . . . When one overlooks the disorderliness of women's affairs, what is affected is not only, as one might suppose, a half; in fact, to the degree that our female nature is inferior [χείρων] to that of males as regards virtue [πρὸς ἀρετὴν], by so much would the harm approach being more than double. (*Laws* 781A2–B4)

A passage from the Athenian's discussion of the songs to be used in education is also relevant.

[S]ince what belongs to females is determined by the very way they differ in nature [τῆς φύσεως], one must make use of this difference in order to make clear the difference in the songs. Magnificence [τὸ δὴ μεγαλοπρεπές], then, and whatever inclines to courage [τὴν ἀνδρείαν], ought to be declared to be masculine-looking; whatever leans rather toward the orderly and the moderate [κόσμιον καὶ σῶφρον] should be proclaimed, in legal convention and in speech, as belonging more to the feminine. (*Laws* 802E6–11)

Neither of these first two considerations is, however, decisive. One might well think that the textual ambiguities should be resolved in accordance with Plato's theoretical statements at *Laws* 804D–806C. Nor do the passing negative evaluations of women settle the point. Some may only reflect a negative judgment of the sorts of characters women have developed in Greek society outside of Magnesia. Others, such as the two passages just quoted, seem to go further and make claims about the nature of women.[48] But even these need not undermine the broader interpretation of women's roles in Magnesia. Plato, for example, might think that (a) women are, in general, physically weaker than men and that this weakness makes them more likely than men to develop the skills of deception in order to get their way, (b) women will, even if given the proper education and social encouragement, generally more fully develop cooperative virtues rather than those associated with facing bodily dangers.[49] One could accept (a) and (b) while still holding that with a good education and in the appropriate social environment women can develop honest and courageous characters. Even if one were to hold that men will in general display a higher degree of such virtues or that the highest achievements in these categories will belong to men, one might well think that women's attainments are sufficient to allow them to participate equally with men in selecting candidates for political office and in holding office itself.[50]

A deeper and more troubling worry is raised by Susan Okin. The reintroduction of individual property in Magnesia brings with it a reintroduction of marriage and the family.[51] But these institutions are reintroduced in forms that both fail to recognize and tend to undermine women's status as autonomous citizens. Women lack an independent right to own property, their marriages are arranged by their male relatives, and they are excluded during their childbearing years from certain social and cultural activities, apparently on the assumption that they are to stay at home (e.g. *Laws* 785B2–9). Such restrictions may not be incompatible with allowing women to participate in elections and to hold office at age 40, but they deprive women of personal autonomy to an important degree and would certainly retard their full participation in political and social life. Thus even if Plato does not think that there are significant differences between the nature of men and women or in their capacity for virtue that would justify significantly unequal political roles, his acceptance of private property may commit him to accepting major political inequalities. And such inequalities might obtain either *de jure* or simply *de facto*.

So what should be our overall verdict on the role of women in Magnesia? Perhaps the most suggestive answer is that of Trevor Saunders.

[T]he right question is not, 'Did Plato intend women to hold office in Magnesia?', as if the answer had to be disjunctive, yes or no, but '*Would* he have intended it, once convinced it was feasible?' On his own functional and pragmatic premises, he would surely have regarded any state in which women hold major office successfully as a better state than one in which they do not. In Magnesia, by accident or design, he is not clear whether he envisages it; but he has at any rate left the door open, and would surely be very happy to see the Magnesians walk through it.[52]

Plato's programmatic and theoretical remarks strongly suggest that the natures of men and women and their capacities for virtue are sufficiently equal that there should be substantial political equality. Other than simple backsliding or duplicity on Plato's part, there may be two reasons for the equivocal position of the *Laws*. First, the attitudes that the colonists—both male and female—bring with them are quite unfriendly to such innovations. Second, the return of private property and families tends to bring with it the retention of the traditional sexual division of labor and responsibility that militates against the political and social equality of women. But Plato's political philosophy is not committed to the idea that either of these are inherently desirable or are permanent features of human life. The attitudes of the citizens who have been educated under Magnesian law will presumably be different. Similarly, there are many social and economic arrangements that fall between those sketched for Magnesia and full communism and some of these may, without other bad consequences, encourage a more equal status for women.[53] We can accept the somewhat equivocal nature of the evidence from the *Laws* without undermining Plato's commitment to his programmatic and theoretical remarks.

Leisure   How much leisure do the citizens of Magnesia have? The answer to this is important for our overall understanding of Magnesia, since political activity and other educational and social activities for adults require a substantial amount of leisure time. One of Plato's clearest remarks comes in Book 7.

What then would be the way of life of human beings for whom the necessities were taken care of in due measure, for whom matters pertaining to the arts were handed over to others, and whose farms, assigned to slaves, provided sufficient produce from the things of the land to allow human beings to live in an orderly way? Suppose there were separate common meals arranged for men, and nearby common meals for the members of their families, including female children and their mothers . . . To live lives ordered in this way, is there no necessary and wholly appropriate activity left, but is each of them to live out his life fattened up, like a cow? (*Laws* 806D7–807A6)

As we shall see below, Plato goes on to answer that what is left is the craft of citizenship which will leave the citizen no time for any other. It is clear from elsewhere in the *Laws* that trade, craft, manufacture, and any other sort of wage-earning are forbidden to the citizens, nor are citizens permitted to set their slaves to such work (846D–E and 919D–E).[54] This passage seems to claim explicitly that the citizens will not work the land themselves, but rather that it will be worked by slaves.

Other passages confirm the impression that Plato intends the citizens of Magnesia to have ample leisure and not to be required to spend time working their lots. The Athenian describes this city as one that 'dwells in the greatest leisure [σχολήν . . . μεγίστην]' (*Laws* 832D1–2). The lives of citizens, like those of Olympic athletes, totally lack leisure for any activity except the object of their pursuit (*Laws* 807C4–5). For citizens, this is the full attainment of the virtue of soul and of body and to this goal no other activities should be allowed to pose an obstacle (*Laws* 807D1–2). The pursuit of virtue must take such priority, since for it 'every night and day' is scarcely sufficient time (*Laws* 807D4–5). Indeed, the citizens' great degree of leisure presents a problem for the legislator.

As might be expected, a fear came over me as I reflected on the problem of how someone will manage a city like this, in which young men and women are well reared, and unoccupied with [ἀργοί] the severe and illiberal tasks that do the most to quench wantonness; and where sacrifices, festivals, and choruses are the preoccupation of everyone throughout their whole lives.   (*Laws* 835D6–E2)

Aristotle also supports this reading. According to him, the citizens of Magnesia will live 'in idleness' (ἀργοί, *Politics* 1265ᵃ15–16) and their lives will be free 'from menial tasks' (τῶν ἀναγκαίων, *Politics* 1265ᵃ7–8). Indeed, Aristotle compares their freedom from menial tasks to that of the auxiliaries and guardians of the *Republic* who live off the contributions of the producer class and are not engaged in farming or any other productive activity.[55]

Plato thus seems to intend that all citizens in Magnesia have the leisure necessary to engage in political and a wide variety of social, religious, and educational activities.[56] Certainly how much leisure the citizens would have who lived in an actual city founded in general accordance with the sketch of Magnesia will depend on their geographic and economic circumstances. Depending on these factors and the possibility of finding other institutions that might increase their leisure time, we can imagine a range of cities, basically in accordance with the sketch of Magnesia, that offered varying degrees of leisure time to their citizens. But there are two general conclusions to draw from Plato's discussion.

(1)   Plato intends all citizens to have considerable leisure time to devote to non-economic activities and does not think that such a possibility is excluded by the ordinary social and economic facts of human life.

(2)   Even if external circumstances are unfavorable and reduce the time available for non-economic activities for most citizens, they still have the capacity to benefit from leisure time. The bar to their engaging in and benefiting from non-economic leisure activities would lie in external circumstances, not in their own natures.

The Nocturnal Council   Related difficulties surround the institution that Plato introduces at the end of the *Laws*, the Nocturnal Council. Although the Council is only explicitly introduced at the end of Book 12, it is anticipated earlier.[57] We have considered above its membership and the two functions the Athenian explicitly gives it: the attempt to convert, by conversation, imprisoned atheists and the examination of returning 'observers'. What is especially controversial about the Nocturnal Council is the extent of its other powers. Near the end of the *Laws*, the Athenian comments:

> But in every case, the end each time is not quite the doing of something, nor the acquiring and settling; it is rather when one has discovered a perfect and permanent safeguard for what has been begotten that one ought to believe that whatever needs to be done has been done, and prior to that one must believe that the whole is unfinished.   (*Laws* 960B5–C1)

In the case at hand, such a safeguard requires that something in the city possess knowledge of the goal of legislation (*Laws* 962B5–C2). The requisite knowledge will be that of virtue, specifically, of how virtue is both many and one. This requires knowing the definition of virtue and of the four virtues and thus knowing, for example, why both courage and moderation are rightly called 'virtues' (*Laws* 963C–964A). Similarly, its members should know how the fine and the good are both many and one (*Laws* 966A5–7).

They are also expected to have knowledge about the gods, the soul, and the motions of the stars (*Laws* 966c–968a). As an essential part of this, they will require extensive knowledge of music and mathematics. The Athenian declines to specify further their exact course of studies, but it seems clear that it includes a broad range of philosophical topics as well as studies of more empirical matters concerning law, such as the law codes of other cities. Given the method of selection, not every member of the Nocturnal Council will have a full philosophical education, but many will have attained quite a high level.

The Athenian does not make explicit how the Council is to give institutional effect to its knowledge. The following passage has, however, encouraged some to see the Nocturnal Council as having very great, or even unlimited, powers.

If this divine council should come into being for us, dear friends, the city ought to be handed over to it [παραδοτέον τούτῳ τὴν πόλιν]; of the present-day lawgivers none, so to speak, have any quarrel with this . . . [This will happen if] our men have been accurately selected, fittingly educated, and, once educated, have been lodged in the country's acropolis and made into guardians whose like, with respect to the virtue of safeguarding, we have not seen come into being in our lives previously. (*Laws* 969b2–c3, cf. 960b5–e11 and 961c3–6)

Some scholars have held, on the basis of these passages, that Plato intends the Nocturnal Council to be the main political authority in Magnesia. On this view, either it will have the same powers as did the philosopher kings in the *Republic* to change laws and institutions as it sees fit or the extent of its powers will simply be left to the Nocturnal Council itself to determine.[58] Such an interpretation has, however, quite high costs. As its leading contemporary proponent concedes, 'assigning the [Nocturnal] council this sort of role creates a fundamental break in the argument of the *Laws*. Thus we are forced to postulate some change in Plato's plans as he wrote the work. Presumably, had he lived to complete the work he would have integrated the two parts into a consistent discussion.'[59] But accepting such a flat inconsistency on one of the most fundamental points of the *Laws*' political theory and explaining it by the hypothesis that Plato's death prevented the final revision of the text is an unattractive interpretative strategy and we should seek less radical expedients.

Perhaps the most sustained and impressive effort to do so is that of Glenn Morrow.[60] Morrow offers a persuasive case for thinking that the Nocturnal Council is not an afterthought added in Book 12, but is antici- pated throughout the *Laws*. Moreover, Morrow makes a promising start at explaining the Nocturnal Council's role. This Council is to possess various sorts of knowledge and it must also educate its own members. Even with- out possessing powers beyond those explicitly assigned to it, the Nocturnal Council should exercise a considerable influence on Magnesia's governance. Its members include some of the city's most important offi- cials, including the ten oldest guardians of the laws, the examiners and the current supervisor of education, and the former supervisors (an office that Plato at one point calls 'by far the greatest of the highest offices in the city' (*Laws* 765E1–2, cf. 809A–B)). Plato would certainly expect that these offi- cials' administration of the laws and revision of them—if this is permit- ted—will be informed by their studies. Perhaps even more important, the younger associate members of the Nocturnal Council will come to fill many offices of the state and will exercise an informal, but still significant, influence on other citizens in the deliberations that we have seen play such an important role in Magnesia's system of government, as well as in their other contacts with their fellows. The citizens are to watch the younger associates carefully and honor them if they perform well (*Laws* 952B).

This influence will, in fact, be more significant than is usually realized. Morrow makes the insightful observation—which has largely gone un- noticed—that the younger associates are to retire at age 40, perhaps sooner if their sponsor dies or retires.[61] The fact of retirement means that many more citizens than is usually thought will have undertaken the studies assigned to the Nocturnal Council and will have participated in it. When a younger associate reaches age 40, he will retire and *a new one will take his place*. So the number of people who will have received the philosophically sophisticated education intended for the Nocturnal Council is consider- ably greater than the number of younger associates plus the full members of the Council at any one time. We must include all those who have left the Council at age 40. We can only think of the Nocturnal Council as some- thing like the tiny philosophical elite of the *Republic* separated by a gulf from the rest of the citizens if we ignore this point. Although not every member of the Nocturnal Council will be an accomplished philosopher, the course of education that members go through is quite sophisticated and lasts, on average, five years. A significant number of Magnesians will have had such an education. We should expect that the previous general education will be of a sufficiently high level to allow them to benefit from these advanced studies and we can expect them to diffuse widely throughout the rest of the population what they realize is an extraordinarily valuable possession for any human being.

This informal role of influencing others is, however, the only one that Morrow assigns to the Nocturnal Council. Morrow seems to adopt this solution because Plato does not give it any further formal role in Magnesia's system of government and Morrow is rightly reluctant to see this Council as inconsistent with the elaborate and detailed discussions of political institutions in the earlier books of the *Laws*. We should accept Morrow's unwillingness to attribute major inconsistencies to Plato. This gives us good reason to reject interpretations, such as Klosko's, that give to the Nocturnal Council the same powers as the philosopher kings of the *Republic* or that allow it carte blanche authority to determine the extent of its own powers. Such interpretations are not only inconsistent with myriad earlier provisions concerning Magnesia's political institutions, but are inconsistent with one of the *Laws'* basic political principles. Repeatedly in the *Laws*, Plato emphasizes that allowing any magistrate or political body unchecked authority runs too great a risk of the abuse of power. Such a risk is still too great even if the possessors of power have genuine knowledge: even those with full knowledge are subject to corruption in such circumstances.

But accepting this reasonable point does not entail holding that Plato must be fully explicit about the powers of the Nocturnal Council. We might think Plato would have to be fully explicit, if we held that the *Laws* provided a fully determinate blueprint of the just city. But we should not understand the *Laws* in this way. (I return to this point in the next section.) There is an open texture to the political and social institutions that Plato sketches and we should allow for a range of ways of implementing the basic structure. For example, as we shall shortly see, Plato appears to assign to the 'guardians of the laws' (the *nomophulakes*) some important role in revising

Magnesia's laws. In his Book 12 discussion, Plato describes the members of the Nocturnal Council as 'those who will really be guardians of the laws' (τοὺς ὄντως φύλακας ... τῶν νόμων, *Laws* 966B5). The members of the Nocturnal Council will, if properly educated, be 'made into guardians whose like, with respect to the virtue of safekeeping, we have not seen come into being in our lives previously' (*Laws* 969C2–3). We need not see these claims as a volte-face on Plato's part or as evidence of different chronological strata in the text of the *Laws*. Nor need we see Plato as here canceling his earlier provisions for an elected body of officials known as 'the guardians of the laws'. In any case, there will be a considerable overlap between the members of the Nocturnal Council and the guardians of the laws. The Nocturnal Council includes the ten oldest guardians of the laws. But surely some of the examiners, supervisors of education, and winners of awards of merit who are on the Nocturnal Council will also be guardians of the laws, as should some of those who served as younger associates of the Nocturnal Council. The guardians of the laws are elected, but Plato has stressed that all the citizens will pay attention to those who serve as younger associates and will honor them if they turn out well. We can see members of the Nocturnal Council as both advising and acting together with the guardians of the laws in many different ways in a just and good city. We should thus allow for a range of ways in which the outline of Magnesia sketched above can be realized. They will fall between excluding the Nocturnal Council from any political role at all and seeing its members as philosopher kings in disguise.

Changing the law   There is a similar controversy surrounding the possibility of, and procedures for, changing the law. Some have taken the following passage to show that after a ten-year period of experimentation and revision the entire law code is to be made immutable, except in the case of the unanimous agreement of the citizens.

For it is inevitable that . . . the lawgiver will leave out the small and numerous details; and those who constantly gain experience in them, learning from yearly practice, must make yearly arrangements and corrective changes until what seems to be a satisfactory definition of such customs and practices has been reached. Ten years of sacrificing and dances would be a measured and sufficient period of time to assign for gaining experience in each and every aspect. If the lawgiver is still alive, they can share the common task with him, but if he has died, each of the magistrates should bring to the attention of the guardians of the laws whatever omissions need correcting within their own jurisdictional spheres, and continue to do so until each feature seems perfected in fine fashion; then the customs are to be made unchangeable, and adhered to along with the rest of the laws the lawgiver laid down for them at the beginning. They are never voluntarily to change a single one of them. But if some necessity should ever seem to overtake them, they must consult with all the magistrates and the whole people and all the oracles of the gods. If all these are in harmonious agreement, then the change can be made, but otherwise never in any way. If there is any opposition, the law will be that it always prevails. (*Laws* 772A6–D4)

But this passage has its own ambiguities. Does this requirement of immutability with the closing provision for change apply to all legislation or just to the laws concerning sacrifices and dancing? We should, along with most commentators, prefer the narrower reading.[62] The passage itself in its context points to the narrower construal.[63] Further, as Ritter and England have noted, the provision that the 'oracles of the gods' must agree suggests that this passage refers only to the laws concerning sacrifices and dances.[64] Finally, as Guthrie notes, to toss in a universal rule at the end of a long sentence that is, on any interpretation, explicitly concerned with the regulation of sacrifices and dances would be an 'oddly casual' way for Plato to proceed.

Second, is the requirement that 'all the magistrates and the whole people and all the oracles of the gods' must be in agreement mean that no member of any of these bodies may object or that none of the three bodies may object?[65] If the passage applies only to the restricted subset of laws, answering this may not be essential. But in any case, requiring unanimous agreement of the whole people would surely make change impossible and including 'all the magistrates' along with 'the whole people' would be redundant. Worse, requiring unanimous agreement would be absurd. One might refuse to allow any changes in the original law code; this is a problematic view, but it is a position someone might hold if he thought that the original lawgiver possessed a wisdom far surpassing that of any of his successors. (It would have to be far surpassing, since anything short of infallibility might go wrong and could be corrected even by less talented successors: theoretical and empirical knowledge could make advances and, in any case, circumstances change and cannot be fully anticipated by any lawgiver. Indeed, actually keeping the law the same over time will require interpretation and reinterpretation of it.[66]) But once one allows for some change, requiring universal agreement is simply silly: Plato recognizes that, lamentably, some citizens are stupid, insane, bad, or criminal and it would be absurd to require their agreement if all the other (wiser, better) citizens approve. We have good reason, then, to accept Morrow's view that the requirement is that none of the three bodies may object. But looking at this passage by itself cannot resolve the ambiguities of Plato's views on the possibility of changing the law; we must take into account his other views on related issues. Let us begin by considering Plato's programmatic discussions of change in the laws.

The first passage comes from Book 6. Here the Athenian compares the lawgiver to a painter.

[T]he painter's activity, for example, never seems to finish working on each of the figures, but keeps touching it up or highlighting . . . it never seems to cease its adorning and hence never to reach a point where there can be no further improvement of the painting as regards beauty and clarity . . . [S]uppose someone once took it into his head to paint the most beautiful figure possible, one that would never get worse but would always improve as time went by. Do you not see that since he is mortal, he will have to leave behind a successor, able to make it right if the painting suffers some decay at the hands of time, as well as to make future touch-ups that improve on deficiencies left by his own artistic weaknesses? Otherwise, will not his very great labor last but a brief time? . . . Well then, do you not think that the lawgiver has such a purpose? He first writes his laws with as nearly adequate a precision as he can muster. Then, with the passage of time, as his opinions are tried out in deed, do you suppose there is any lawgiver who is so imprudent as to be ignorant of the fact that he must necessarily have left behind very many such things that require being set right by some follower, if the constitution and order of the city he has founded are always to become in no way worse but instead better?   (*Laws* 769A7–E2)

The expedient the Athenian suggests is to try their best to make the guardians of the laws 'lawgivers as well' (νομοθέτας, *Laws* 770A8). At the beginning of Book 8, the Athenian again refers to the guardians of the laws. In discussing the arrangement of the city's official sacrifices, he remarks 'The interpreters, priests and priestesses, and diviners should get together with the appointed guardians of the laws to arrange whatever the lawgiver is forced to leave incomplete with respect to these matters. These same persons are the ones who must determine just what he has left incomplete' (*Laws* 828B3–7). Earlier in the *Laws* we were told what their task would be: they are to ensure, at all costs, that the constitution fosters complete virtue in the citizens.

> [N]o one of any sort is to be seen giving precedence in honor to any of the other things that are impediments, not even, finally, to the city, if it appears necessary that the alternative to its destruction is either willingly tolerating the slavish yoke of being ruled by worse men or departing the city in exile. All such things must be borne, and suffered, rather than allowing the constitution to be changed into one whose nature it is to make human beings worse. These are the things we agreed to in our previous discussions, and now you must look to both these goals of ours as you pass our laws in review. You should blame those that are not capable of effecting these goals, but those that are capable, you should welcome and, gladly adopting them, live under them. (*Laws* 770D7–771A2)

There are several important points to notice about these passages. To begin, the lawgiver's successors are intended not only to fill in details and remedy decay, but also to correct deficiencies. Their goal is to improve the laws and make them better (and Plato draws no sharp distinction between improving the laws and preventing decay or correcting the bad). Moreover, Plato holds that the need for improvement is not limited to a short period of time, but is a permanent feature of political life. This responsibility requires that the successors be not merely guardians of the laws, but lawgivers as well. (The Athenian's interlocutors are in the process of becoming lawgivers, but have not yet become such, *Laws* 859C2–3, cf. 857E10–858A3.) In order to do this, the successors are to become the pupils of the original lawgivers, but the lawgivers cannot merely order them to carry out and preserve what has been laid down. Since they must also rectify deficiencies, they must come to an intelligent agreement with the lawgivers' principles. This requirement can be quite demanding: in the appropriate circumstances, the successors must be prepared to overturn the constitution or to abandon Magnesia altogether. Finally, the position of the succeeding lawgivers is intended not to be extra-constitutional, but rather they are to have a place within Magnesia's ordinary political structure. And there are a number of passages in the *Laws* that take up these programmatic remarks and assign to the body of elected officials, known as the guardians of the laws, a role in amending and revising the laws.[67]

Plato returns to this topic at the end of the *Laws*. As we have seen, Book 12 elaborates on two institutions that are relevant to the issue of changing the laws. First, there are the officials known as the 'observers'.

[T]here are always among the many certain divine human beings—not many—whose intercourse is altogether worthwhile, and who do not by nature grow any more frequently in cities with good laws than in cities without. These the inhabitant of cities with good laws, if he is incorruptible, must track down . . . in order to place on a firmer footing those legal customs that are finely laid down, and correct [ἐπανορθούμενον] others, if they are lacking [τι παραλείπεται]. For without this observation and search, a city will never remain perfect [τελέως]. (*Laws* 951B4–C4)

The observers upon return are to report to the Nocturnal Council (*Laws* 952B7–9). Although he thinks it will be rare, the Athenian allows for the possibility that such observers will come to Magnesia from other cities. Such an observer will ask 'either to see something fine that is different from the fine things in other cities, or to reveal some such thing to another city' (*Laws* 953C6–D1). Thus the rationale underlying the appointment of the observers explicitly presumes that the laws of Magnesia may need supplementation or revision and allows for them.

Plato proceeds to claim that the constitution of Magnesia needs a 'permanent safeguard' and that this will be the Nocturnal Council (*Laws* 960B5–C1). '[I]f our founding of the country is to have an end, there must be something in it that knows, in the first place . . . our political goal . . . and then in what way it ought to attain this, and who—first among the laws themselves, and then among human beings—gives it advice finely or otherwise' (*Laws* 962B4–9).

The senior members of the Nocturnal Council 'who are an image of reason because they are distinguished by their wise thinking about many matters worthy of discussion, deliberate [βουλεύεσθαι], using the young as assistants in their collective deliberation. Thus both of them in common really save the whole city' (*Laws* 965A1–4). Such guardians 'must be able not only to look to the many, but also to pursue and know the one, and knowing it, to order everything [συντάξασθαι πάντα] with a synoptic view to that' (*Laws* 965B8–10). The Athenian sums up as follows:

Is not this our argument concerning all the serious things, that those who are really to be the guardians of the laws must really know what pertains to the truth about them, and must be capable of interpreting it in speech and following it in deed, judging by the standard of nature what things come into being finely and what things do not? (*Laws* 966B4–8)

Note that as part of their task, the members of the Nocturnal Council are assigned the job of 'interpreting' the truth about the laws; earlier they were described as having to deal 'with the man who needs to know and understand [γνῶναί τε καὶ εἰδέναι]' and thus they must 'be superior to the others in teaching and making entirely clear [διδάσκοντα . . . καὶ πάντως δηλοῦντα] what power vice and virtue have' (*Laws* 964C1–3).[68]

These passages bring together two themes that Plato has stressed. There is a need both to make the city 'perfect' by finding a 'permanent' safeguard for it and there is a need for assuring intelligent examination of the laws. Permanent safeguarding is attained not by rendering the law code itself permanent and immutable, but by insuring that there is an institutional framework in the city that allows for learning new high-level truths and for taking account of circumstances. (This includes both the Nocturnal Council and the observers sent out to learn new truths.) What we still need to do is to see how this is to be given institutional effect in Magnesia.

So let us turn to the considerations that have led some to think that Magnesia's law code is basically unrevisable. First, there are passages in the *Laws* that are more skeptical of change. The most striking comes during Plato's discussion of children's games. Since commentators who think Magnesia's laws are basically immutable typically emphasize this passage, it is worth quoting at length.

[E]veryone is unaware that the character of the games played is decisive for the establishment of the laws, since it determines whether or not the established laws will persist. Where this is arranged, and provides that the same persons always play at the same things, with the same things, and in the same way . . . there the serious customs are also allowed to remain undisturbed. But where the games change, and are always infected with innovation . . . where the young never call the same things dear, where good form and bad form—in the postures of their own bodies or in other things they use—are not always agreed upon, where instead they honor especially the man who continually innovates with something new . . . [there is the greatest ruination for cities]. For, escaping notice, this man transforms the characters of the young, and makes them dishonor the ancient and honor the new . . . Change . . . is much the most dangerous thing in everything except what is bad—in all the seasons, in the winds, in bodily habits, and in the characters of souls . . . Thus, if one were to look at bodies, one would see how they become accustomed to all foods and drinks and exercises, even if at first they are upset by them . . . [and] come to like, be accustomed to, and familiar with, a whole regimen—thriving on it in the best way . . . [I]f someone is ever compelled to change back to one of the reputable diets, he is at first upset with sickness, but then once again with difficulty recovers . . . [T]his very same thing applies to the thoughts of human beings and the natures of their souls. If they are brought up under laws which by some divine good fortune have remained unchanged for a great length of time, if they neither remember nor have heard that things were ever otherwise than they are at present, then the entire soul reverences and fears changing any of the things already laid down. Somehow or other the lawgiver must think up a device by which this situation will prevail in the city. The following is what I at least have discovered . . . everyone thinks that very great and serious harm cannot follow from changes in the games of the young, since these are really just games. So they do not prevent such changes, but give in to and follow them, not taking into account that these boys who practice innovations in their games must necessarily grow up to be men who are different from those the earlier children grew into; being different, they seek a different way of life, and in seeking it they desire different practices and laws; from this it follows that none of them fears the arrival of what was now said to be the greatest evil for cities. There are, indeed, other changes—those affecting outward appearance—that would do less damage; but whatever brings about frequent change in the praise and blame accorded to dispositions is the greatest of all changes, I believe, and would require the most attentive watching. (*Laws* 797A7–D5)

This passage gives us two sorts of reasons for wondering whether Plato in fact intends a radical curtailment or perhaps elimination of change in the laws. First, he makes explicit here, as he does not in the above passages, the costs of change. Second, the remarkable limitations on changes in children's games has led many to think that if even such trivial details are (nearly) permanently fixed, then everything else and, in particular, all of the more important political and social provisions must be too.

But neither reason requires us to see Plato as rejecting—or as having good reason to reject—his theoretical and programmatic remarks about change that we have considered. As to the first consideration, Plato offers several interesting reasons for thinking that change may have considerable unanticipated costs. First, change has intrinsic costs: in the case of physical health, adjusting to a new regimen, even if it is better for the person, is a cost and involves a period of upset. The same should be true in social and political adjustments. Second, it is easy to acquire a taste for novelty that leads to a preference for variety and change, even if it is not clearly for the better. If true, both are good reasons for a conservative bias in revising and changing the law. Even if a proposed new practice would have been better if it had been the one originally chosen, it may nevertheless better, taking the costs of change into account, to stick with the existing policy. What these reasons justify, however, is not a total ban on all change, but a weighing of the gain of change against these somewhat hidden costs. Even if Plato were to draw the conclusion that change should be radically curtailed or banned, these claims do not justify such a conclusion and we can accept them consistently with accepting Plato's earlier theoretical reasons for favoring change in some circumstances.[69] This more moderate and qualified conclusion is the one that Plato does, in fact, draw at the end of the passage: 'whatever brings about frequent change in the praise and blame accorded to dispositions is the greatest of all changes, I believe, and would require the most attentive watching.'

But what of the second point? If Plato is so wary of changes even in children's games, can we not infer that he would simply ban change in all more important matters? Although tempting, this is not a good inference. Change in children's games is especially problematic for two reasons. First, changes in their games, songs, and dances change what they take pleasure in. As we saw in the last chapter, Plato thinks that such changes in pleasure bring with them changes in what the person values as good and fine. Moreover, pleasures have a seductive quality and can bring about changes in what a person values by circumventing or interfering with a person's deliberative capacities. (Note that Plato describes changing children's games as 'using all sorts of pleasures to persuade them', Laws 798E6–7.) These dangers are all the greater in children because their rational capacities are still being developed in quite basic ways. Change in what they take pleasure in damages their chances of attaining the capacity to engage in rational deliberation. Second, even in adults, pleasure is seductive and the wrong pleasures can irrationally bring about changes in basic values or prevent the person from bringing these right judgments appropriately to bear in deliberation. Rational deliberation on these matters is thus especially difficult and we have good reason to be wary of changes, even if they seem to be the outcome of rational deliberation. Plato's views here have an interesting resemblance to, for example, those of some modern theorists concerned with race and gender. They argue that sincere deliberation by well-intentioned, intelligent people is often distorted by (perhaps unconscious) racial and gender stereotypes. Thus some argue that we should impose external constraints on deliberative outcomes. For example, since our judgments about job candidates tend to be irrationally influenced by race and gender in these ways, we should require hiring to approximate the representation of women and minorities in the population.

For Plato, there are special reasons why it will be difficult to assure the rational integrity of deliberation about songs and dances. As we saw in the last chapter, Plato thinks that the goodness of dances and songs is affected not only by the associated content of the accompanying words, but also by the mathematical or quasi-mathematical properties of the music. The value theory that this involves is not well worked out in the dialogues and it seems quite possible that Plato never worked out such a theory in detail (cf. *Laws* 657A4–B8). Rational deliberation in these matters will thus be extraordinarily difficult, even apart from the possibility of its corruption, and would require a highly sophisticated body of specialized knowledge. If Plato had some confidence in the particular judgments he had reached about certain rhythms and harmonies, these considerations would give him good reason for a strong conservative bias in matters concerning dances, songs, and children's games.

A related argument against the permissibility of change is offered by Klosko and Stalley who hold that Plato's praise for Egypt, Crete, and Sparta shows that he is inclined to ban all change. But a more complicated picture emerges from the relevant passages. What Plato especially praises Egypt for is its fixing permanently the fine songs used in education and the fine postures employed in dance and represented in painting and sculpture (*Laws* 656C–657C). These are precisely the areas in which, as we have seen, Plato has special reason to endorse a strong conservative bias.[70] Furthermore, it is quite reasonable for Plato to praise Egypt for putting these matters beyond change, since he thinks that their chances of making reasoned revision in their laws are small: he describes the other aspects of their laws as 'worthless' (φαῦλα, *Laws* 657A5).

Similarly, it is misleading to describe the Athenian's attitude as 'reverence for the long-established codes of Crete and Sparta' and to infer from this that the law code of Magnesia must remain similarly fixed.[71] A fundamental problem for Crete and Sparta is that they lack any adequate understanding of the real goal of law, that is, the fostering of genuine virtue. Sticking to their law codes enforces a certain discipline on the citizens and prevents the even greater evil of emancipating their appetitive desires. But it does not undermine the reasons that the Athenian gives for revising and amending the law code of Magnesia in light of further knowledge.[72]

Third, we might think that changing the laws is envisaged only in minor details or allowed only for a limited period of time. It is true that the Athenian often explicitly notes that certain details will have to be worked out by later lawgivers. But there are also some quite important matters that the Athenian holds must be worked out later, for example, the sort of studies assigned to the Nocturnal Council.[73] Moreover, the Athenian's theoretical principles examined earlier also make it clear that more fundamental change is possible. With respect to the existence of a time limit, we have seen that we should not take the passage at *Laws* 772A6–D4 to establish a ten-year examination period for all laws, but only for those concerning sacrifices and dancing. There are two other passages in which Plato envisages a limited time period for the revision of laws concerning the details of judicial procedure, although he does not establish a precise figure (846B–D, 957B). Other passages that discuss revision do not mention a time limitation and say that amendment and revision should be carried on until the laws seem satisfactory.[74] Since Plato thinks that there are significant hidden costs to changing the laws, change should not be too frequent. Nevertheless, even in the passage at *Laws* 772A–D in which the laws, after the requisite period of revision, are made 'unchangeable' (ἀκίνητα, 772C4) and the Athenian enjoins the citizens 'never voluntarily to change a single one of them' (772c6–7), he immediately goes on to specify a procedure that can be used to change them if need be. So even if we were to interpret Plato as holding what he does not in fact say, that is, that all the laws are to be made unchangeable after a ten-year period of revision, the existence of a procedure for changing the laws allows us to reconcile this with the rest of his theoretical arguments for change in certain circumstances. Indeed, since the future generations raised under Magnesia's laws will be considerably better than the original one, good revisions may be more possible after forty, fifty, or sixty years than in the first ten years of the colony's existence. Plato's views about the importance of education, especially early education, lead to this result, even if we were to think that he himself did not take it fully into account.

Finally, Klosko's view that Magnesia's laws are unchangeable depends on his overall interpretation of the *Laws*. Specifically, he holds that in Magnesia

[e]verything possible is done to prevent the subjects from examining their moral standards . . . The unhappy implication, however, is that the moral status of the state and everyone in it depends on the wisdom of the laws, while no one in the state is able to assess this. Plato undoubtedly wants the Magnesians to take it on faith that their laws meet the requisite standards, but this has to be accepted on faith, in the absence of any means to confirm it.[75]

It is because Klosko thinks that this is the position of the earlier books of the *Laws*, that he sees Book 12 as marking a sharp break in Plato's thought. Because Plato 'cannot break completely with the ideals of his youth' and comes to see late in the composition of the *Laws* the unsatisfactoriness of the early books, he turns the Nocturnal Council into the philosopher rulers of the *Republic*.[76] But we can avoid positing a contradiction in the *Laws* that can be resolved only by finding chronological strata within the text, by rejecting such extreme interpretations of the earlier books and of the Nocturnal Council. I have already argued that Magnesia is designed precisely to avoid the outcome that everyone takes the laws on faith. An understanding of the reasons behind the laws is supposed to be widely diffused in the citizen body and in the Book 6 passage comparing the legislator to a painter (*Laws* 769A–771A), Plato insists on establishing within the city a body that possesses knowledge of the goal of the laws so that it can revise and improve them. Plato's theoretical and programmatic remarks commit him to this and we have not seen good reason to think that he comes to reject these claims.

What, then, are the exact details of Plato's position on changing the laws? Before we try to answer this question, we should heed a salutary warning from Trevor Saunders concerning what he calls 'the documentary fallacy.'

[This fallacy] is to suppose that Magnesia is an exact blueprint, fixed in all its details; and that if something is unclear we have only to inspect the text closely enough to discover a precise Platonic provision lurking between the lines. That is not so: Magnesia is a shifting structure. Plato is to some extent his own worst enemy in this respect. His suspicion of innovation, and his denunciation of change (797a ff.), can all too readily give the impression that Magnesia's institutions are inflexible, to be taken or left as a whole, without any modification at all. But in fact he makes it very clear that they simply stand at one point on a *sliding scale* of political maturity [emphasis in the original]. Magnesia incorporates all sorts of tensions within itself, for example, between election and lot, rich and poor, oligarchical inequality and democratic equality, between discretion and the letter of the law, between private life and public life. Hence the structure he sketches is, like all political structures, capable of improvement; it embodies aspirations . . . [Plato's] laws about sexual conduct envisage that both a higher and a lower standard than the one he sketches are possible (841a–842a). He is apparently prepared to undertake sociological investigation to discover the ingrained moral and social views of prospective and actual Magnesians. Such information will enable him to frame laws embodying the best possible standards of conduct, laws which are not arbitrary, but, if circumstances change, not fixed either. Finally, Magnesia is not a 'closed' society: it has arrangements to enable it to learn from foreign sources how to improve itself.[77]

Moreover, as David Cohen aptly observes, whatever the provisions there are in Magnesia for the amendment of laws, these too can be amended and revised.[78] Both Cohen and Saunders are right that searching for an exact institutional blueprint for the good city in the *Laws* is a mistake. We must be guided by the general principles that Plato enunciates and settle for a rough outline that makes the best sense of all that Plato says.

We have seen that Plato accepts that revision and improvement are possible in any set of laws. Changing circumstances can demand revision and in actual cities the understanding of basic social, political, and ethical principles can always be advanced. We cannot read these claims away. Nevertheless, Magnesia starts with basically good laws and change has its own costs, some of which are not obvious. It is also the case that on some matters, the destabilizing effects of pleasure will make rational deliberation especially difficult. Thus Plato's principles commit him to allowing for revision and improvement of the laws coupled, however, with a conservative bias in favor of existing law (and to making revision more difficult in some areas than others). Thus allowing the laws to be changed, for example, simply by majority vote of the Assembly would seem unacceptable. In the passage at *Laws* 772C–D, Plato sketches a procedure for changing certain religious laws that, reasonably construed, calls for the approval of all the offices in the city, the Assembly, and the oracles. (We may assume that the oracles' approval is not needed in all cases.) There are other passages assigning the task of revising and amending the laws to the elected body of officials known as the guardians of the laws. In Book 12, the Nocturnal Council is seen to have the knowledge necessary for basic revision and improvement.

We cannot reasonably specify all the remaining institutional details. We have seen good theoretical and textual bases for thinking that the laws concerning dances, songs, and children's games will be especially hard to change. There may be other categories of laws that should display a similar conservative bias. Exactly what officials should be involved in each kind of change and how does the procedure work? Where can the proposals for change originate? If the Assembly is involved, does it need to approve by a simple majority of those present and voting or is a super-majority required? If the latter, how high is it? In the offices that must approve, does Plato include, e.g., the select judges? The city-wardens? It is idle to search for an exact answer to all these and related questions in the text.

We might, however, still think it important to press the question concerning the Nocturnal Council. Does it possess sole and complete authority to revise the laws? If not, does it play any but an advisory role? Once again, the open texture of Plato's discussion suggests that he envisaged a range of possibilities. Nevertheless, there is good reason to see Plato as intending something between making the Nocturnal Council the sole authority for all changes in law and excluding it from any official role. The fact that Plato does not explicitly give it a formal role is a weak ground for thinking he intends to deny it any such role. The passage on changing the laws concerning sacrifices gives a place to the agreement of all offices and this should include the Nocturnal Council. Further, the guardians of the laws clearly have a role in the revision of some laws and Plato calls the members of the Nocturnal Council the 'real guardians of the laws' (*Laws* 966B5–6).

On the other hand, giving the Nocturnal Council sole authority is not only never suggested, but it also contradicts earlier explicit provisions about changing some laws. More important, it conflicts with two general principles that Plato advances in the *Laws*. First, as we have noted, Plato is careful to provide a system of checks and balances among the institutions of Magnesia. Granting the Nocturnal Council sole authority runs afoul of this.[79] Second, Plato takes great care to give political deliberation a prominent place in the life of Magnesia and relies on election to fill even the most important offices. (Even if the Nocturnal Council had sole authority, nearly all the senior members are elected officials and this is a considerable difference from the philosopher rulers of the *Republic*.[80]) Giving a role to other bodies of officials and to the Assembly would encourage even wider diffusion of serious political deliberation throughout the city. Given the number of people who will have been younger associates of the Nocturnal Council, many will have some of the capacities needed to engage in serious political deliberation. Their training and the general education of the Magnesians will give them reason to see the knowledge of the Nocturnal Council as entitling it to a special place in such deliberations and Plato emphasizes the educational functions of the Nocturnal Council. Nevertheless, given Plato's views about the possibility of corruption, he has very strong reason not to give the Nocturnal Council sole and absolute authority to change the laws. And, parallel to the case of women, regardless of exactly what role Plato thought officials capable of in Magnesia when it is actually founded, he has every reason to think that a city would be better if it extended widely, with due safeguards, the forums for political deliberation.[81]

5.4 Citizenship and the Boundaries of the City

It is a commonplace that modern political philosophy breaks with classical political philosophy, that is, the political philosophy of Plato and Aristotle, over the issue of what the proper end of the political community or state should be. Classical political philosophy takes as the proper goal of the good city the happiness of all its citizens and, since happiness requires virtue, the proper end of the good city essentially includes fostering virtue in the citizens. A good or just city is a community of the virtuous striving for the attainment of virtue in common. Modern political philosophies reject making the citizens virtuous as a political goal and instead see the end of the state as, for instance, assuring citizens' self-preservation, or more generally, protecting their other natural rights, the attainment of freedom or equality, or the establishment of social justice. Virtue is neither the goal of the political community nor a criterion of membership in it.

This is an unnuanced understanding of modern political philosophy. But we are now in a better position to see that this commonplace account also distorts classical political philosophy. In particular, it overlooks a significant development in Plato's understanding of what a good city is and of what a citizen of a good city should be. The birth of the classical political community occurs, I shall argue, in the *Statesman* and the *Laws* and not in the *Republic* (nor in Aristotle).

Let us understand the position I am attributing to classical political philosophy to be committed to two claims. In the case of a good city,

(1) the end of the laws is that the citizens lead happy and thus virtuous lives, and
(2) a citizen must be capable of sharing in the end of the city's laws and thus of living a virtuous and happy life.

Without some further spelling out of the notion of a political end, there seems to be a gap between (1) and (2). It is not incoherent to think that there is a criterion of membership in the good city that is independent of virtue and happiness, although (1) specifies the goal for the whole city.[82] But a natural way of getting from (1) to (2) is by holding that the end or *telos* of the laws and social institutions itself establishes the appropriate criterion of membership. The content of the *telos* then allows us to specify what is common to the members of the good polis insofar as they are members.[83]

We can see Aristotle make such a move. In the *Nicomachean Ethics*, he gives an account of the end of political science: 'We stated the end of political science to be the best end, and political science spends most of its pains on making the citizens to be of a certain character, that is, good and such as to perform fine actions; (1099^{b}29–32). This understanding of the end of political science underpins Aristotle's conception of citizenship in the *Politics*: 'A citizen is one who shares in ruling and being ruled. He differs under different forms of government, but in the best constitution he is one who is able and chooses to be ruled and to rule with a view to the life of virtue' (*Politics* 1283^{b}42–1284^{a}3). For Aristotle, political association aims at the best end, that is, the proper goal of the good polis is the happiness of all its citizens and, since happiness requires virtue, the proper end of the good city essentially includes fostering virtue in the citizens. Citizens in such a city must be capable of sharing in such a life.

In the *Republic*, Plato holds that the good or just city is made up of three distinct classes—the guardians, the auxiliaries, and the producers—and insists that the members of all three classes are citizens of the city (e.g. 519E4). Nor does 'citizen' (πολίτης) in these passages simply mean 'inhabitant' without carrying any normative implications. As citizens, members of all three classes have a just claim that the laws and the social institutions of the just city aim at doing what can be done for them, that is, take their well-being into account as far as they can. Nevertheless, as I argued in Chapter 1, the members of the lower two classes in the *Republic* are not capable of genuine virtue. This understanding of the capacities of ordinary citizens in the *Republic* has profound implications for the nature and possibility of political association and of the ties that bind the citizens to one another as well as for the nature of good political rule and the dignity and goodness of political activity.[84]

First, as we saw in more detail in Chapter 1, each of the three classes in the *Republic* has its own distinctive end. This does not rule out the possibility that they can nevertheless agree, each from its own perspective, on how the city should be organized, although it does have the result that this agreement will be relatively fragile because the different ends of the three classes always threaten to pull apart. But there is a more important point. The city of the *Republic* would not count for Aristotle as a proper community (*koinōnia*). In a proper political community, the joint work of the citizens is to form an ethical association in which each person can live a life of virtue. This failure of the *Republic*'s just city to constitute a genuine community is reflected in the nature of the ties that bind the citizens together.[85] The philosopher rulers, although they do act on behalf of the other citizens, cannot aim at inculcating genuine virtue in them; non-philosophers will not aim at inculcating genuine virtue in anyone (and their cooperative activities will not be an expression of genuine virtue). The cooperation among the three classes thus lacks a crucial kind of ethical value. Similarly, the ties of friendship that bind the citizens together cannot, except within the first class, be based on virtue. To the extent that political activity is constituted by such cooperation, it too lacks this sort of ethical value. A basic indication of how deep this failure of the *Republic*'s political theory is, from Aristotle's point of view, is that in his own ideal city he assigns the functions performed by the *Republic*'s third class of citizens to non-Hellenic slaves who are merely necessary means to the life of the good city, but are not genuine parts of it.[86]

In the *Republic*, political rule also takes a characteristic form. The same persons always rule and the second and third classes are excluded from deliberative and judicial functions. Such exclusion is quite reasonable, since the members of the lower classes are not fit to participate in ruling: the best aim of political rule is to foster virtue and no one outside of the first class can do this. Nor are the lower two classes even the proper object of good political rule, since desirable qualities fostered in them are not genuine virtues. Since Aristotle thinks that the value of ruling depends on the value of the ruled, the political activities of the ruling class will, insofar as they are directed to the lower two classes, lack an important ethical value (cf. Aristotle *Politics* 1254ª25–8).

In the later dialogues, citizenship and its implications come to be a central concern of Plato's political philosophy. Let us start with the *Statesman*.

The Statesman   The announced task of the *Statesman* is to offer an account of what the ideal statesman (*politikos*) is and, since the ideal statesman is one who possesses the political art (*politikē technē*) or political knowledge (*politikē epistēmē*), the dialogue proceeds by searching for an account of this art or knowledge. Most of the *Statesman* is, however, concerned with the proper philosophical methodology to be used in seeking definitions and in employing the method of collection and division to do so. Nevertheless, in the dialogue's closing pages, Plato provides a sketch of what a city ruled by such a statesman would be like, that is, a sketch of a good or just city.

At 277D1, the Eleatic Stranger, Plato's spokesman in the dialogue, suggests that they will best make progress in their search for an account of the statesman if they make use of a model and proposes weaving as an example. The choice of weaving turns out to be especially apt, since one of the main tasks of the statesman is weaving together the different temperaments or characters found in the city. In particular, Plato claims that there are two basic kinds of people: the courageous and the moderate. These two classes are mutually exclusive and they seem to be jointly exhaustive.[87] Plato provides a brief sketch of these character types.

For those who are especially moderate [διαφερόντως . . . κόσμιοι] are always ready to live the quiet life, carrying on their private business on their own by themselves, associating with everyone in their own city on this basis, and similarly with cities outside their own, being ready in any way to preserve peace of some kind. (*Stsmn.* 307E2–6)

But what about those who incline more to courage [οἱ πρὸς τὴν ἀνδρείαν μᾶλλον ῥέποντες]? Is it not the case that they are always drawing their cities into some war or other because of their desire for a life of this sort which is more intense than it should be . . . ?   (*Stsmn.* 308A4–7)

What is most important to us here is Plato's ethical evaluation of these character types and his account of the role that their possessors should play in a just city. As the above descriptions suggest, these character types are highly flawed.

When [the moderate] do what they want nobody notices that they are being unwarlike and making the young men the same, and that they are perpetually at the mercy of those who attack them, with the result that within a few years they themselves, their children, and the whole city together often become slaves, instead of free men, before they have noticed it.   (*Stsmn.* 307E6–308A2)

On the other hand, the courageous 'make enemies of people who are both numerous and powerful, and so either completely destroy their own fatherlands or else make them into slaves and subject to their enemies' (*Stsmn.* 308A7–9).

Given the deep conflict between these types over what is fine and good, Plato claims that their normal relation to each other will be one of hostility and disagreement over most matters. When they try to live together in a city, their disagreement 'turns out to be a disease that is the most hateful of all for cities' (*Stsmn.* 307D7–8). It is also important to see that Plato does not suggest that either defective character is better than the other: unlike, for example, the timocratic and other defective characters in the *Republic*, the courageous and the moderate are not ranked with regard to virtue and happiness. And if there were a significant difference between the two, we would expect Plato to tell us. If we assimilated the courageous to the *Republic*'s timocratic character, we might expect them to be better (or less bad) than the moderate, but Plato does not say this.[88] Indeed the fact that those with unmodified courage are put to death while those with unmodified moderation are enslaved may suggest that the moderate are less bad than the courageous.

We would not expect a just city to be composed of such people and we find two linked responses by Plato to this problem. He proposes

(i)   to remedy these deficiencies by an ambitious educational program and,

(ii) to use this educational program to redraw radically the boundaries of the city.

Let us begin by considering how the boundaries of the city are redrawn. Political science, like weaving, is a constructive art and Plato states a general principle that applies to all constructive sciences.

[No] constructive science is willing to put together any, even the most worthless, of its products out of bad and good things [ἐκ μοχθηρῶν καὶ χρηστῶν], every kind of science everywhere always casts out [ἀποβάλλει] the bad as far as it can, and takes only the fitting and the good [τὰ δὲ ἐπιτήδεια καὶ χρηστὰ] ... (*Stsmn.* 308C1–5)[89]

Plato then applies this principle to political science: 'In that case, neither will what is by nature truly the political science ever willingly put together a city out of good and bad [ἐκ χρηστῶν καὶ κακῶν] human beings' (*Stsmn.* 308D1–3). Thus it is a necessary condition of membership in a just city that one be a good or virtuous person. The performance of one's social task and the normal duties of citizenship are not sufficient to entitle one to membership. The just city is a city composed of virtuous people. Those who cannot share in *both* courage and moderation, as well as the rest of the virtues, the genuine science of statesmanship excludes or 'casts out' from the city 'by inflicting upon them the punishments of death and exile and the greatest penalties of disenfranchisement' or it at least excludes them from the political community by enslaving them (*Stsmn.* 308E8–309A6). Those who are thus excluded will be people who possess the courageous or the moderate character type insofar as they are unmodified by the education that Plato describes.

What, then, is this education? Those who have been 'correctly educated' (*Stsmn.* 309D3–4) receive into their own souls 'really true and firmly secured opinion about what is fine, just, and good' (τὴν τῶν καλῶν καὶ δικαίων πέρι καὶ ἀγαθῶν ... ὄντως οὖσαν ἀληθῆ δόξαν μετὰ βεβαιώσεως, 309C5–7). True opinions, however, can be 'firmly secured' either because they are supported by reasons and explanations or by non-rational means. Can we tell what Plato has in mind? First, the security that these opinions have seems to be presented as a feature of the opinions themselves and not as something arising from some additional training. If so, their security should result from the fact that they are supported by reasons and explanations. Of course, even reasoned explanations must be properly received and grasped if they are to produce the right state in a person. But why bother inculcating reasoned opinions, if the reasons are not appreciated and do not account for the security of the opinion? Insofar as the courageous and the moderate do grasp the reasons and explanations and integrate them with the rest of their beliefs, they will do more than unthinkingly accept what they are told.[90] Second, Plato describes only those who have the proper nature and have received this education as becoming 'fine' (γενναῖον, *Stsmn.* 309A9–B1). After this education, they no longer possess the one-sided courage and moderation that failed to be virtues. Only then do they share in both 'a courageous character and a moderate character [κοινωνεῖν ἤθους ἀνδρείου καὶ σώφρονος] and the other qualities that tend towards virtue [ὅσα τε ἄλλα ἐστὶ τείνοντα πρὸς ἀρετήν]' (*Stsmn.* 308E9–309A1).

It is because of such an education that they become genuinely courageous and if the moderate acquire these opinions, they become 'truly moderate and wise, so far as wisdom goes in the context of life in a city [ὄντως σῶφρον καὶ φρόνιμον, ὥς γε ἐν πολιτείᾳ]' (*Stsmn.* 309E6–7).[91] In coming to possess genuine courage, moderation, and wisdom, the citizens come to see good reasons for acting in ways other than those toward which their natural disposi-tions would incline them. These citizens have more than the merely formal belief that the scientific ruler should be obeyed; they also have substantive beliefs about what is fine, just, and good. Their natural dispositions are not, however, entirely left behind and even after they have been educated, citizens differ in characteristic ways. Nevertheless, the citizens are sufficiently well educated that they can hold some important political and social offices in the city. These include those of general, orator, public educator, and judge. Plato describes these as 'precious', 'akin to', and 'close to' the science of statesman-ship possessed by the statesman (*Stsmn.* 303D4–304A4).[92]

Given the sameness of the citizens' education and the approximate same-ness of their resulting ethical characters, there is far less political and social differentiation in the good city of the *Statesman* than in the *Republic*. In the *Republic*, the auxiliaries are 'better men' 'by far' than the producers (*Rep.* 405A6–B4, 456D5–E7, and 522A3–B5). In the *Statesman*, all the citizens are good and fine and, with the possible exception of the scientific ruler, there is no such hierarchy of virtue within the citizen class. Or more precisely, although some citizens will be more virtuous than others, the differences of character types do not establish a hierarchy of virtue. There are no classes within the citizen body that are differentiated in terms of the sort of virtue their members can possess. In the *Statesman*, there are no classes of citizens differentiated by the sorts of ultimate ends they pursue or by their social and political functions or by the institutions applying to them. Ordinary mar-riage is envisaged for all citizens, possessions are not held in common, at least all able male citizens perform military service and both the courageous and the moderate serve in political offices on roughly equal terms (*Stsmn.* 311A4–9).⁹³ All citizens are expected to possess a high level of virtue. Given the important place of virtue in happiness, the same conclusion holds, *mutatis mutandis,* for happiness.

Political philosophy occupies a surprisingly small portion of the *Statesman's* text, but this dialogue takes a crucial step. It redraws the boundaries of the city so that the just political association has become a community of the virtuous. Political science takes as its task drawing the citizens of a just or good city together 'by concord and friendship [ὁμονοίᾳ καὶ φιλίᾳ] into a common life [κοινὸν ... τὸν βίον]' (*Stsmn.* 311B9–C1). It is only in this way that political science can bring about a 'happy city' (*Stsmn.* 311C5–6).

The *Laws* decisively carries forward this first step taken by the *Statesman.* To begin, the *Laws* not only excludes those engaged in trade and manufacture from citizenship, but even prohibits citizens from setting their slaves to such tasks under their supervision.

No resident [citizen] shall be numbered among those who engage in technical arts, nor any servant of a resident [citizen]. For a citizen [πολίτης] possesses a sufficient art [τέχνην], and one that needs long practice and many studies [πολλῆς ἀσκήσεως ἅμα καὶ μαθημάτων], in the keeping and conserving of the public system of the city [τὸν κοινὸν τῆς πόλεως κόσμον σῴζων καὶ κτώμενος], a task that demands his full attention. (*Laws* 846D2–7)

This passage from the *Laws* continues to echo and revise the *Republic.*

[T]here hardly exists a human being with sufficient capacity to carry on two pursuits or two arts thoroughly, nor yet to practice one himself and supervise another in practicing a second. So we must lay down this as a fundamental rule in the city: no man who is a smith shall act as a carpenter ... but each several craftsman in the city shall have one single craft, and gain from it his living. This law the city-stewards shall labor to guard, and they shall punish the resident [citizen], if he turn aside to any art other than the pursuit of virtue [τινα τέχνην ... μᾶλλον ἢ τὴν τῆς ἀρετῆς ἐπιμέλειαν]. (*Laws* 846D7–847A6)

The contrast with the *Republic* is unmistakable: there the principle of specialization regulates the entire citizen body. It is precisely by the performance of the art of the smith or joiner that the citizens of the producer class fulfill their political work (*ergon*).[94] In the *Laws*, both joiners and smiths are excluded from citizenship and the citizen is required to practice the art of virtue. The work done by the producer class of the *Republic* is assigned either to aliens or to slaves for the simple reason that their corruption does not directly harm the city (*Laws* 919C2–D2). A producer class of citizens simply no longer exists in the city of the *Laws*. Nor are the auxiliaries present in the *Laws*: all citizens engage in military service and there is no class of citizens whose education is limited to the sort of musical education the auxiliaries received in the *Republic*.

The art of virtue is, however, a very demanding one.

[T]here does remain for men living this life a task that is by no means small or trivial, but rather one that a just law imposes upon them as the weightiest task of all. For as compared with the life that aims at a Pythian or Olympian victory and is wholly lacking in leisure for other tasks, that life we speak of—which most truly deserves the name 'life'—is doubly (rather far more than doubly) lacking in leisure, seeing that it is occupied with the care of the virtue of the body and the soul [ψυχῆς εἰς ἀρετῆς ἐπιμέλειαν]. For there ought to be no other secondary task to hinder the work of supplying the body with its proper exercise and nourishment or the soul with teachings and habits [μαθημάτων τε καὶ ἐθῶν]. Every night and day is not sufficient for the man who is doing this to win from them their fruit in full and ample measure. (*Laws* 807C1–D5)

For the city of the *Laws* to be virtuous, it is not sufficient that each of several functionally defined classes is doing its own job, and thus it is not sufficient that the members of one class perform military service while each of the members of another performs a single art (cf. *Laws* 806C3–7). The entire law code of the city aims at fostering all the virtues in the whole citizen body. Each citizen is required to be virtuous and the boundaries of the political community are constituted by the capacity for and dedication to virtue. Moreover, this very conception of the city and of citizenship is part of the citizens' self-conception: they are educated to see themselves as craftsmen of virtue.[95]

This conception of the good city as a community of the virtuous aiming in common for a life of virtue is not found, I have argued, in the *Republic* nor is it found for the first time in Aristotle's *Politics*. It is constituted in Plato's *Statesman* and *Laws*.[96]

5.5 *The Problems of Citizenship*

This new understanding of what a good city can and should be and of the nature of its genuine members, that is, of the citizens, has deep implications for Plato's political philosophy. In the rest of this chapter, I shall focus on three issues. First, it is an essential part of this conception of the city that it is an association in which the citizens in common aim at leading the good life. To get a first idea of what this requirement comes to, consider Aristotle's complaint in the *Politics* that constitutions that have the wrong political goal and do not aim at making the citizens good and just fail to be genuine cities or communities. In oligarchies, which make the attainment of individual wealth the ultimate end, or in the cities where law is understood as a compact by which men agree not to do injustice to each other, fellow citizens are related to each other in the same way as are members of different cities bound together by commercial treaties: 'They do not concern themselves about what kind of persons the ones in the other city ought to be, nor are they concerned that no one covered by the agreements be unjust or be vicious in any way at all. They are only concerned that they do nothing unjust to one another' (*Politics* 1280ᵇ1–5).⁹⁷ Genuine citizens of a good city have a direct, non-instrumental interest in each others' wellbeing, specifically, they seek in common to develop the virtues in their fellow citizens. As we saw in Chapter 1, Plato seems to think that all the citizens of the good city of the *Republic* were capable of having a noninstrumental interest in others. He appeals, for instance, to generalized family sentiments or a sense of gratitude for benefits received to underpin such a concern. But if the non-philosophical citizens are to aim—as they are in Magnesia—at the genuine well-being of their fellow citizens, that is, aim at making them virtuous, what motivation do they have for doing this? What grounding can we give for the sort and extent of other-regarding concern that Plato demands as a political duty?

Second, Plato and Greek political thought in general held that since a political community must be ordered and structured in an effective way to insure that it functions properly, it must have rulers. But what sort of participation in ruling should citizens expect to have in virtue of being citizens? Early in the *Laws*, Plato characterizes the proper sort of education in Magnesia as follows: 'the education we speak of is the training from childhood for virtue that makes a man eagerly desirous of becoming a perfect citizen, understanding how both to rule and be ruled justly' (*Laws* 643E3–6). Must citizens in the ideal city share equally in rule? Since we have seen that they do not in Magnesia, does this undermine Plato's claim that they are genuine members of the political community?

Third, if not all citizens are expected to participate equally in rule, what sort of political participation do they engage in and how is their reduced form of participation good for them? Can it be an important part of their welfare, if it is reduced to a merely passive level? We might compare citizenship in Magnesia to other reference points. Consider, for example, Pericles' Funeral Oration with its famous praise of the citizens of the Athenian democracy who pursue both public and private matters and work for the common good.

And we ourselves can judge rightly regarding affairs, even if [each of us] does not originate the arguments; we do not consider words to be an impediment to actions, but rather [regard it as] essential to be previously instructed by speech before embarking on necessary actions. We are distinctive also in that we hold that we are simultaneously persons who are daring and who vigorously debate what they will put their hands to. Among other men, ignorance leads to rashness, while reasoned debate just bogs them down.[98]

Aristotle, although he would reject Pericles' claims about democratic Athens, holds that in an ideal city all citizens should share in rule by taking turns in ruling and that they benefit from doing so.[99] Is the role assigned to most citizens in Magnesia so passive that they are not genuine contributors to the political association? Are they active enough to be full citizens? If not, how is their sort of political participation good for them?

5.6 The Question of Motivation

In this section, I shall first consider what sort of other-regarding concern is demanded of citizens in Magnesia and then turn to the three types of considerations Plato appeals to in order to show that citizens will satisfy these demands (with respect to one of them—an appeal to friendship among citizens—I consider in some detail how it is implemented in Magnesia's social and political institutions). As we shall see at the end of this section, once we have identified the most prominent and significant reasons why Plato thinks that citizens have to display the sort of other-regarding concern demanded by Magnesia's laws and institutions, we need to address the yet more basic question of the value to the individual citizens of their political activity and other-regarding concern. In Section 5.7, I consider in greater depth the nature of the political activities of Magnesia's citizens, and in Section 5.8, I turn to the difficult issues surrounding the value of such activity and, more generally, of other-regarding concern.

What is Required In order to see what motivations the citizens of Magnesia can and should have for other-regarding concern, we must first see what is required of them. Specifically, our present concern is with what is required of them insofar as they are citizens and thus with what the laws and social institutions demand. Let us begin by considering some textual evidence: 'We do not call . . . any laws correct that are not established for the sake of what is common [$\tau o\hat{v}\ \kappa o\iota v o\hat{v}$] to the whole city' (*Laws* 715B3–4). So a system of correct laws and social institutions must aim at promoting what is common to the whole city. This is the common good or benefit.[100] Moreover, Plato understands the common good in an explicitly optimizing form. In justifying the restrictions that he imposes on bequests of property, Plato comments: 'I shall legislate with a view to what is best [$\tau\grave{o}\ \beta\acute{\epsilon}\lambda\tau\iota\sigma\tau o v$] for the entire city and family, and with a view to all this, will justly assign a lower rank to what belongs to each individual' (*Laws* 923B4–6). In the theology of Book 10, Plato describes god's goal for the universe by appealing to the paradigm of a craftsman: what a true craftsman should aim at is what is best ($\beta\acute{\epsilon}\lambda\tau\iota\sigma\tau o v$) for the whole with which he is concerned' (*Laws* 903C5–7). Since Plato also conceives of the legislator as a craftsman, the same principle applies to him.

Correct or just laws thus aim at what is common to the whole city, that is, what is best for the whole city. So the good lawgiver tries to optimize and Plato seems to give further content to the notion of optimizing.

The hypothesis that underlies our laws aims at making the [citizens] as happy and as friendly to one another as possible [ὡς εὐδαιμονέστατοι . . . ὅτι μάλιστα]. (*Laws* 743C5–6)[101]

It is not without reason that the laws of Crete are held in especially high esteem by all the Greeks. The reason is that they are correct laws—and they are correct because they make those who use them happy. For they provide all the goods. (*Laws* 631B3–6)[102]

In Book 7, Plato criticizes Crete and Sparta for neglecting the education of women. Such failure to educate the women leaves

the city with only about half of a completely happy life instead of double that. (*Laws* 806C3–7)

Sometimes the law will persuade, and sometimes—when dispositions are recalcitrant—it will persuade by punishing, with violence and justice. Thus, if the gods are willing, the laws will make our city blessed and happy.   (*Laws* 718B2–4)[103]

Thus the lawgiver should strive for what is best in common and that is to make the city or the citizens as happy as possible.[104] More generally, we should take this to be the appropriate aim or goal of Magnesia's laws as well as of all its political and social institutions.[105]

This principle is still indeterminate, however, in several important ways. From at least the time of Bentham through the present day and especially in the past fifty years, the notion of optimizing principles and their justificatory role in morality and in legal systems has received a great deal of analysis.[106] The technical sophistication of present-day discussions of optimizing and maximizing principles far exceeds anything that we might reasonably expect to find in Plato. Moreover, recent debates have made clearer the connection between optimizing or maximizing and other important related issues. Although we can consider the implications of Plato's claims for these issues, we do not find in his texts, e.g., an explicit and thematic discussion of the do/allow distinction or a detailed examination of some of the puzzle cases that may interest us. It does not follow that considering Plato's response to puzzle cases would be unilluminating or that trying to make his claims as complete and precise as possible would be philosophically uninteresting. But I shall not attempt to do this in a thorough way here, and shall instead concentrate on what is most directly relevant to the question of the citizens' motivations.

Let me note very briefly, however, some remaining issues that are especially significant: (1) the place of maximization in justification, (2) the range of the maximization principles, and (3) the form of the maximization principles. First, is the principle of maximizing happiness (however this is to be formulated) the single fundamental justificatory principle of Plato's political philosophy? Are all other goals or aims, sets of laws, and political institutions ultimately justified insofar as they contribute in the appropriate way to the ultimate end of maximizing happiness? Or are there principles of justification that are independent of maximizing happiness?[107] It is clear that not every law (or institutional aim) makes an explicit appeal to happiness and Plato suggests political and legal principles or goals that do not always obviously coincide with maximizing happiness. For example, as we shall see in the next section, a principle of 'political justice' requires that political offices be distributed according to virtue. Some penological principles are explicitly justified only by an appeal to the benefit of the offender and some types of acts seem to be absolutely prohibited. Moreover, some passages, such as *Laws* 743C5–6 quoted above, apparently give equal standing to other goals (in this case, promoting friendship).

To begin, Plato's programmatic remarks about god's action with respect to the universe and about practical rationality as it is displayed in craft production strongly suggest a commitment to optimization as the fundamental justificatory principle. Insofar as lawgivers take these as paradigms, they are committed to trying to bring about the best overall outcomes. This does not yet, however, commit us to any particular criterion for determining what outcomes are best. Given its prominence in Plato's claims about the general goals of laws and institutions, maximizing happiness must be a relevant criterion, but this does not entail that it is the only criterion. There is nothing incoherent in the idea that the principles for determining what is best might be irreducibly plural. Difficulties will arise, however, if the principles give inconsistent results, but this can be avoided in several ways: e.g. (1) the principles might be consistent at least in all the cases that actually must be settled, (2) the areas in which the principles apply might be restricted so as to avoid conflict, or (3) one principle may trump the others, but the trumped principle might still have justificatory force.

For many of the other goals and principles that Plato endorses, it is plausible to think that, although they do not explicitly refer to maximizing happiness, they can be given a 'two-levels' justification. Particular courses of action are evaluated in terms of rules or goals that do not mention happiness, but the system of goals and rules is itself justified in terms of maximizing happiness. Whether or not Plato thinks that some other principles have an independent justificatory force as principles for evaluating laws and institutions, he does give maximizing happiness a certain priority. Other goals, including some important ones, are sometimes overridden by the goal of maximizing happiness, but Plato never suggests that the goal of maximizing happiness should be overridden.[108] So for present purposes, it may be enough that Plato does not allow that laws and institutions should aim at outcomes that do not maximize happiness.

A second important issue is the range of the maximizing happiness principle. If we are to maximize the happiness of the people in the city, *whose* happiness is to be taken into account? Are the laws, for example, only to take into account the happiness of the citizens? Or are they to take into account the happiness of all the individuals in the city? Do women, slaves, and resident aliens count? What of non-residents? Plato does not explicitly and thematically discuss this issue and the evidence is difficult. But his position seems to be that the happiness of citizens is all that the laws are required to aim at: this includes women, but excludes slaves, resident aliens, non-resident aliens, and, more generally, those living in other cities. This requires some qualifications, but is enough for our present purposes.[109] And as we shall see below, such restrictions are also in tension with more universalistic and more fully impersonal principles that Plato himself suggests in the *Laws*.

A third issue concerns the exact form of the maximizing happiness principle. Plato advocates more than merely aiming at bringing people up to a certain minimum level of happiness: he accepts some sort of 'more is better' principle with respect to the happiness of the citizens. Nevertheless, maximizing happiness can be understood in a number of different ways: for instance, as maximizing the aggregate produced by summing the happiness of all citizens or as maximizing the average happiness (total happiness divided by the number of citizens). (These interpretations might come apart only if the number of citizens varies.) More generally, we can conceive of maximizing happiness as 'making as many citizens as possible as happy as possible': a formulation that has two maximands and leaves undetermined how we are to weight numbers of citizens and degrees of happiness.[110] One especially important version of this principle construes the goal as making each citizen as happy as possible and holds that maximizing the happiness of any one citizen is compossible with maximizing the happiness of every other citizen. It is especially difficult to fix upon a single, precise interpretation of maximizing, since, given the rest of Plato's views, it may be the case that some logically distinct principles will, at least in actual or likely cases, be coextensive. Specifically, some straightforward forms of maximizing happiness understood in an aggregating manner will be coextensive with maximizing the happiness of each citizen, if, in fact, maximizing the happiness of any one citizen is compossible with maximizing the happiness of every other citizen.[111]

The most important issue here concerns the possibility of trade-offs among citizens' happiness, so let us turn to focus on the relation between the individual's happiness and that of the rest of the citizens. There are several reasons for thinking that Plato accepts that there is a harmony between the individual's well-being and overall well-being (this is, roughly, the claim that maximizing overall happiness does not require an individual to make sacrifices in his own happiness).[112] The theology of Book 10 seems to hold that there is such a coincidence between what is best for the individual and what is best for the whole at the level of the universe itself. God has arranged the whole universe so that it is in the best possible condition and, in doing so, has brought it about for each soul that 'what is best in your case for the whole turns out to be best for you as well' (Laws 903D2–3). Plato also seems to assert that there is such a coincidence between what is best for the individual and what is best for the whole at the level of the city. It is the fact that any person placed in a position of autocratic power will eventually forget this truth that Plato gives as a reason against any form of autocracy (Laws 875A2–C3). It is implausible that there could be such a coincidence between individual happiness and the happiness of the whole city if Plato held some form of ethical solipsism, but we have seen that he does not. The happiness of others is, in some appropriate way, part of the individual's happiness. Passages that might seem to suggest that there are conflicts between the happiness of individuals and the happiness of the whole city may only claim that there seem to be such conflicts if one has a mistaken conception of individual happiness (especially a conception that is mistaken because it does not give the proper place to the happiness of others).[113]

Moreover, unless such a coincidence between the happiness of the individual and the happiness of the whole city does obtain, Plato faces a very awkward problem. As we have seen, just or correct law requires citizens to act in such a way as to maximize happiness. Plato clearly expects the virtuous citizens of Magnesia to act in accordance with just laws. So virtuous citizens are clearly expected to act in such a way as to maximize happiness. This does not, of course, require that the virtues of individuals are defined in terms of maximizing happiness or acting on behalf of the common good. What it requires is that the demands of an individual's virtue do not conflict with what is required for the common good. Since Plato is a rational eudaimonist, he thinks that a rational person will pursue virtue and the common good only if this is consistent with realizing his or her own (greatest) happiness. If what is best for the individual could come apart from what is best for the whole city, there would be a conflict between what rationality requires for the individual and what rationality requires at the level of the whole. Plato shows no sign of thinking that such a conflict is possible.[114]

What motivates But even if we accept that Plato thinks that there is such a coincidence between the individual's happiness and the happiness of the whole city, we still need to see why such a coincidence obtains. This is especially the case, since we find the requirement that the individual act in such a way as to maximize overall happiness an extremely demanding one.[115] Ordinary common sense (both contemporary and, according to Plato, Greek) finds it obvious that there can be frequent conflicts between my own good and the good of the whole community. Thus for ordinary common sense, requiring the individual to act so as to maximize overall happiness would be extremely demanding: it would require the person, in some cases, to aim at something incompatible with her own greatest happiness. But even if ordinary common sense is wrong—as Plato thinks it is—about the relation between the individual's own happiness and the happiness of the community, the requirement that citizens maximize overall happiness is still quite demanding. Even if there is a coincidence between the two, consistently aiming at maximizing the happiness of the community requires a considerable revision of common-sense beliefs and also requires resistance to, or training of, the less than fully rational desires that do not share this end. Indeed, Plato in the *Laws* seems to think that this goal is too demanding for human nature. Although it would be best, Plato rejects holding women, children, and property in common, since this arrangement makes excessive demands on human nature (*Laws* 739A–E). The citizens living under such a constitution would, however, be happier and would aim at the happiness of their fellows to a greater extent than will the Magnesians.

Nevertheless, the limitations on property, the civic duties, and the highly structured way of life in Magnesia are still quite demanding. What sort of motivation will the citizens have for acting in this way? There are, of course, some quite straightforward reasons for obeying the laws and following the social practices of Magnesia: there are legal and social sanctions for failing to comply. Moreover, the city is a cooperative association and engaging in a pattern of mutually beneficial exchanges can be in individuals' interests, even if they take no interest in the well-being of others for their own sake.

But what we are trying to find is an explanation of how the citizens can be motivated to take an interest in others for their own sake. To begin, consider the rich variety of ways in which the citizens associate intimately with one another. First, there are private households in Magnesia, so there will be ordinary family ties. Since marriage partners are normally restricted to fellow citizens, family ties will extend widely and develop throughout the city. (This is especially so, since marriage partners are to be chosen for the sake of the city, not for one's own pleasure.) Second, there is a vast array of political and social bodies that bring the citizens into close contact with one another: they will eat common meals, come together at frequent religious, social, and athletic gatherings, perform military service together, and work together in the Assembly, the system of courts, and the huge variety of other major and minor offices in Magnesia (e.g. *Laws* 738B–D).

These considerations, although important, do not answer all our questions. First, the formation of close family ties or particular friendships may result in many citizens caring non-instrumentally for the well-being of some others in the city, but it does not guarantee that each citizen cares non-instrumentally for the well-being of all the other citizens. Second, as we saw in Chapter 1, it is not enough even that each citizen care non-instrumentally for the well-being of all others. We may still wonder whether in caring for the well-being of others they really are caring about something of genuine value. What we want to see is whether the ties binding citizens together rest on a response to genuine value.

Let us begin with the first concern. Plato does not think that friendship involving a non-instrumental concern for the friend's well-being must be restricted to intimate relations between two or a few people. In the *Laws*, Plato does not think that holding women, children, and property in common is possible. Nevertheless, if such a community were to come into being, it would be one in which the ties of friendship bound all the members together (*Laws* 739C2–3). Such friendship would involve taking a non-instrumental interest in the well-being of all of one's fellow citizens. But Plato also thinks that a similar, albeit weaker, sort of friendship is possible in actual political communities. In both Athens and Persia when they were well-governed, friendship bound together large parts of the political community—both rulers and ruled—so that they had a non-instrumental concern for each others' well-being. In Persia under Cyrus 'the rulers shared their freedom with the ruled and drew toward equality; as a result the soldiers felt more friendly toward their generals and faced danger with eager spirits . . . Everything prospered for them in those days because of freedom and friendship and a common sharing of reason' (*Laws* 694A6–B6). After Cyrus, the Persians 'destroyed the friendship and community within the city. Once this is corrupted, the policy of the rulers is no longer made for the sake of the ruled and the populace, but instead for the sake of their own rule' (*Laws* 697C8–D3). Although the Persians' interest in others may have been based on a false understanding of what is of value, it still shows that a non-instrumental concern with each others' well-being can bind together—as citizens—the members of an actual political community.

In Magnesia, encouraging friendship among the citizens is one of the main aims of the law. The Athenian holds that

a city should be free and wise and a friend to itself and that the lawgiver should give his laws with a view to these things. (*Laws* 693B3–5)

We said [a back reference to *Laws* 693B3–5] that the lawgiver must in laying down his laws aim at three [goals], namely that the city for which he legislates be free, that it be a friend to itself, and that it possess reason. Those were the goals. (*Laws* 701D7–9)

When he [the legislator] has thus sanctified all these things in an ordered arrangement, he should no longer make any change in what pertains to either dance or song. Thus the same city, with the citizens that are as similar to one another as possible, should experience the same pleasures, and live well and happily. (*Laws* 816C5–D2, cf. 739B8–E3)

Another passage (*Laws* 743C5–6), quoted above, gives the goal of encouraging friendship in the city special prominence by pairing it with the overall goal of maximizing happiness.

But does such non-instrumental concern involve an appropriate response to something that is of genuine value? It is clear that Plato intends this to be true of the sorts of friendship that he is most concerned to foster in the city. He distinguishes several different kinds of friendship and claims that in the best sort, 'friendship is the name we give to the love of those who are like each other in respect of virtue' (*Laws* 837A6–7). This is the sort of friendship that the laws promote in the city and it aims at encouraging the youth to become as virtuous as possible (*Laws* 837D4–6). Thus the parties to such friendships will have a virtue-based aim for their friendship. Not all of these friends' acts will be guided by explicit thoughts of virtue. Their reasons for acting will not always take the form 'Doing X fosters virtue in Y and I am a friend of Y'.[116] But we should expect that both parties have the goal of fostering and maintaining virtue in each other. Thus this form of other-regarding concern is distinct from a generalized benevolence in which one wishes well to others regardless of their virtue. This is a significant difference from the *Republic*, in which the bonds binding citizens together rely on forms of other-regarding concern that do not require a shared conception of virtue and do not aim at developing in all a virtuous character that has a common content.

But is this sort of virtue-based friendship something that binds each citizen to all others or does Plato intend to promote an overlapping series of such friendships throughout the city? The context of the above passage suggests that Plato here has particular friendships between pairs of older and younger people especially in mind. Thus although the law may aim at developing such friendships throughout the city as a whole, we may think that they fail to be genuinely civic or political friendships because they are not intended to bind together each citizen to all other citizens as such.

In the *Republic*, at least within the classes participating in the community of women and children, there is a single kind of tie binding each citizen together with all others: each citizen has a bond of kinship with all others. In Magnesia, private families are retained and some differential concern for the interests of family members is expected. Intimate emotional attachments between two, or at any rate a small number of people, will bind together subgroups of the citizens. Friendships aimed at virtue will be most active and intense among small groups of people, since it is not possible to be equally involved in the development of each person's virtue.

Nevertheless, we should not conclude that the political goal of encouraging friendship in Magnesia is simply to encourage a series of potentially overlapping individual friendships. First, even if Plato accepts that citizens have a differential concern for family and intimate friends, he can allow that friendship still binds together each citizen with all others to some extent. Second, various social institutions in Magnesia aim at widening the sort of concern that one has for family and friends: common meals and the great variety of social groups that exist will serve to extend each person's range of concern. Third, the social and political groups that the citizens participate in have as their explicit goal fostering virtue in the whole citizen body so that each citizen will tend to see his political and social activities as aiming at developing virtue in his fellow citizens as such.

But we might still have two worries. First, does this expansion of the range of friendship stretch the notion of friendship too far? Second, is such friendship still, in some distinctive way, a political sort of friendship? With respect to the first concern, consider, for example, the five marks of friendship that Aristotle gives in the *Nicomachean Ethics*. Friends are known to each other and a friend (i) wishes and does good to his friend for the friend's sake (and is aware that his friend has a similar attitude of well-wishing), (ii) wishes the friend to live for the friend's own sake, (iii) spends time with his friend, (iv) makes the same choices as his friend, and (v) shares his friend's sorrows and joys (cf. *N.E.* 1156ª2–5 and 1166ª2–10). We need not assume that Plato shares exactly this conception of friendship or that it is fully acceptable as it stands, but it is an intuitively plausible account that provides one way of seeing whether Plato's notion of friendship is radically revisionary. We might think that counting as friendship any relation that binds each citizen to his fellow citizens as such must be revisionary, since one cannot 'share one's life and activity with every other citizen just as such'.[117] Furthermore, the lack of a community of families and property in Magnesia imposes a significant restriction on the degree to which citizens share in the same joys and sorrows.

It simply is true that given the size of Magnesia, it is not possible for each citizen to have an intimate personal relationship with all others, and that Plato explicitly accepts that private families and property do restrict the degree to which one citizen can share the joys and sorrows of his fellow citizens. So the sort of 'friendship' that one citizen has for another in virtue of being his fellow citizen cannot satisfy Aristotle's marks of friendship. Nevertheless, the sort of friendship that Plato envisages does better on these criteria than initially seems to be the case. Insofar as each citizen is committed to wishing for the common good for its own sake, he is committed to wishing for the happiness of his fellow citizens for their own sake. A virtuous person may wish well to his fellow citizens even in a badly organized city in which he is the only virtuous person or he might wish well to citizens in distant cities with whom he never has contact. Such benevolence or other-regarding concern lacks the element of shared activity that is an essential feature of friendship as Aristotle describes it. But in Magnesia, the political structure develops and sustains a wide-ranging set of shared activities that aim at fostering virtue in all the citizens. The average citizen will not merely wish well to his fellows, but a considerable part of his life will be bound up in cooperative activities that aim at the common good and thus at fostering and maintaining virtue in all. The cooperative nature of these activities not only allows the individual citizen to realize that his fellow citizens wish him well in return, but also allows for the citizen to 'share his life and activity with every other citizen just as such' in a substantial sense. The wide variety of political and social groups and associations will foster many forms of cooperative and shared activity among the citizens.

In the city of the *Republic*, citizens have fundamental disagreements on what constitutes the good and most citizens are unable to attain the most important goods. This will not be the case in Magnesia. Citizens are, in general, expected to agree on the central importance of virtue and thus can share the ends of their activities to a far higher degree. Their agreement on political and social ends allows them to share in each other's plans and choices. Since they share a conception of the good, they will be able to share in their fellow citizens' actual joys and sorrows in a way that is not possible across classes in the *Republic*. Moreover, Magnesia's citizens will share not only in the activities of those with whom they engage in daily political and social interactions, since they will also see their political and social groups as part of the larger structure of institutions constituting the city. All the citizens share the goal of advancing the common good and will consciously coordinate their activities to do so.

In Magnesia, such shared activities and projects will thus have some of the important features of more intimate friendships. Citizens can share the end of advancing the common good and will act on its behalf in engaging in many forms of activity that occupy a substantial part of their time. With respect to some aspects of their lives, Plato expects that their concern for each others' well-being will fall short of that displayed in more intimate relations. Citizens in Magnesia, it seems, will still be differentially concerned with the material well-being of their households and the well-being, especially the ethical well-being, of their family and close associates. But even here, Plato expects citizens to devote considerable time and energies to advancing the well-being of their fellow citizens as such. The system of common meals and the sharp limitations imposed on wealth show that the citizens will be interested in the material well-being of their fellow citizens. Similarly, citizens devote time and energy to political and social associations aimed at fostering virtue in all.

It is also important to note that Magnesia's political structure does not merely make empirically more likely the shared activities and choices involved in such cooperation. Insofar as any political structure produces, in some way or another, virtuous people, it makes it more likely that there will be people cooperating to advance shared virtuous aims. But in the case of Magnesia, its political organization provides the constitutive structuring of these activities. The political structure of Magnesia makes possible an essentially political form of shared activity, that is, sharing in the business of running the city, supporting its constitution, and furthering its political goals. Nor, as we have seen, should we construe political activity narrowly. The social groups and interactions of the citizens are structured by the laws and have public goals as part of their own self-understanding. As part of sharing in these activities, individual citizens will be responsive to the plans and actions of their fellow citizens, share a commitment to the cooperative activity, and support each other in fulfilling their own parts.[118] This is a pattern of shared activities, plans, and choices that is open only to citizens in their capacities as citizens. Since the particular shared activities have their ends and their constitutive structure established by the city's goals for its citizens, it is reasonable to think of these activities as an expression of friendship that exists between fellow citizens as such.

The rich variety of political and social groups found in Magnesia and their role in the city constitutes another significant difference from the *Republic*. The *Republic* tended to try to foster unity and other-regarding concern by abolishing or ignoring social and political groups that fell below the level of the city as a whole or one of the three social classes as a whole. For example, private families are abolished in the upper two classes, all in the city are invited to see themselves as bound together by family-like sentiments, and small-scale political or social groups are ignored or have no place. But in Magnesia, it is precisely such small groups that provide a main locus for the development and expression of other-regarding concern. To the extent that they involve the sort of cooperation found in the large- and small-scale political deliberation and action that are so prevalent in Magnesia, such shared activities are a kind of friendship concerned with virtue that need not be as hierarchical as the friendships of the old for the young. (I turn to the more general issue of how hierarchical political relations are in Magnesia in the next section.)

Plato also suggests two other related sorts of motivation for other-regarding concern that do not assume an intimate personal context and do not require shared activities. First, the theology of Book 10 invites the citizen to see fostering virtue as sharing in god's plan for the universe as a whole. God has ordered physical bodies as well as souls so that the whole universe attains, as far as possible, virtue and happiness. Each soul is designed to strive 'for what is best in common' and what is best for each soul is also best for the whole (*Laws* 903B4–D3). From these claims, it is only a short step to the conclusion that each soul should adopt the aim of seeking the perfection or virtue of all the other parts of the whole and that this involves fostering virtue in other souls. Plato proceeds to take this step.

But perhaps they [the gods] might be compared to the rulers of armies; it might even be that they are like doctors taking care of a war against diseases in bodies, or farmers fearfully awaiting seasons that are usually difficult for the generation of plants, or those set over flocks. For since we have agreed among ourselves that heaven is full of many good things and also of the opposite, and that there are many more of the latter, we assert that there is an immortal battle of this kind going on, requiring an amazing guard, and that the gods and daimons are our allies, while we in turn are the possessions of the gods and daimons. Injustice and insolence, together with lack of wisdom, destroy us, while what saves us are justice and moderation, together with wisdom—qualities which are among the psychic powers of the gods, but a small portion of which someone would also discern clearly dwelling here in us.[119]   (*Laws* 905E8–906B3)

Plato is not suggesting that our ultimate reason for seeking to advance virtue is that doing so is in accordance with god's plan. Rather, god aims at what is best and it is the fact that this goal is best that should also be our reason for pursuing it.

At least in the case of god, Plato is willing to describe aiming at the good as the expression of love or friendship. In the *Timaeus*, Plato presents god's ordering of the universe for the best as an expression of his love and lack of jealousy.

Why did he who framed this whole universe of becoming frame it? . . . He was good, and one who was good can never become jealous of anything. And so, being free of jealousy, he wanted everything to become as much like himself as was possible . . . The god wanted everything to be good and nothing to be bad so far as that was possible . . . it was not permitted (nor is it now) that one who is supremely good should do anything but what is finest.   (*Tim.* 29D7–30A7)

God's love for the universe consists in his bringing about its best condition.[120]

But also simply within the context of the city, Plato suggests that it is the goodness of virtue—wherever it is located—that gives us a reason to foster it. In the great prelude to the law code as a whole at the beginning of Book 5, the Athenian addresses all the citizens.

The greatest of all evils is one which most men have implanted in their souls, and which each one of them excuses in himself and makes no effort to avoid. It is the evil indicated in the saying that every man is by nature a lover of self [ὡς φίλος αὐτῷ πᾶς ἄνθρωπος φύσει], and that it is right that he should be such. But the truth is that the cause of all errors in every case lies in the person's excessive love of self. For the lover is blind in his view of the object loved, so that he is a bad judge of things just and good and fine [τὰ δίκαια καὶ τὰ ἀγαθὰ καὶ τὰ καλὰ], because he thinks that he should always honor what is his own more than what is true. But the man who is to attain the title 'Great' must love [στέργειν] neither himself nor his own belongings, but things just, whether they happen to be actions of his own or rather those of another man [ἀλλὰ τὰ δίκαια, ἐάντε παρ᾽ αὑτῷ ἐάντε παρ᾽ ἄλλῳ μᾶλλον πραττόμενα τυγχάνῃ].   (Laws 731D6–732A3)

A virtuous person thus must love not only himself, but a virtuous character and virtuous actions wherever they occur. This, too, Plato describes as a kind of friendship.

This same praise [i.e. that of making a man great] should be bestowed on moderation and wisdom, and on any other good possessions that can be given to others as well as possessed by oneself. The one who does the giving should be honored most highly; in the second rank should be put the one who is willing to give, but unable; as for the one who begrudges [φθονοῦντα] certain good things and does not, out of friendship [διὰ φιλίας], voluntarily share them in common with anyone, he should be blamed—though the possession itself should not be dishonored on account of the possessor.   (Laws 730E1–731A2)[121]

The appeal to friendship between citizens as such in a good city, the theological appeal to god's efforts at bringing good order to the universe, and the direct appeal to the value of virtue make it clear that the citizen, motivated in this way to show other-regarding concern, is aiming at something that is of genuine value.

The last issue to take up is why this is in the interest of each citizen. Since this question raises issues about other-regarding concern that go beyond purely political topics, I shall postpone discussion of it to Section 5.8. But here we should note two points of tension in Plato's views. Both the appeal to sharing in god's plan for the universe and the direct appeal to the value of virtue tend to push the requirements of virtue and the requirements of citizenship further in the direction of impartiality than Plato seems to wish to go in the *Laws*. God's concern for virtue in the universe as a whole suggests that the virtuous person should be concerned to foster virtue as such wherever it occurs and not only virtue within his own city. But Plato shows little sign of extending other-regarding concern universally. (Book 10's theology also reminds us that the individual has a life transcending life within the city and that a virtuous life within the city is only a small part of the soul's long progressive growth in virtue. As we shall see at the end of this chapter, this theological fact has significant implications for Plato's political philosophy.)

But even within the city, the direct appeal to promoting virtue wherever it occurs because it is valuable, pushes in the direction of a kind of impartiality. If the value of virtue gives all citizens a reason to foster it in their fellows, there is a prima-facie case for devoting one's time and energy to doing so and not devoting extra time and energy to one's family and intimate friends. There is also pressure to distribute goods so as to foster virtue impartially and this may well militate against income inequalities, private households, and ordinary marriage. One might try to argue that such apparent compromises are, in fact, consistent with an impartial demand. Concentrating on improving those nearest to one is likely to be more efficient than trying to improve strangers and, similarly, individual landownership may be more efficient (allowing a greater surplus to be redistributed). But Plato does not explicitly take this route. Nor, on the other hand, does he attempt to argue that such partiality is justifiable as such. Moreover, it may be the case that such compromises are necessary because of the ways in which even virtuous human motivation, as a matter of psychological fact, falls short of more strongly impartial demands. Private ownership satisfies the desire to have control over one's immediate surroundings, and allowing limited differences in wealth satisfies the desire to have one's rewards closely correlated with effort expended and perhaps even the desire to be comparatively better off. These compromises may still produce very good results, since (i) given the relative unimportance of more wealth once a satisfactory level has been reached, limited differences in wealth may not greatly affect individuals' chances to lead virtuous and happy lives, and (ii) one's bias toward those near and dear to one will, at least in large part, take the form of trying to make them genuinely virtuous people who are thus interested in the well-being of others. Nevertheless, we still need to consider further what sort of impartiality Plato thinks virtue requires.

To the extent that citizens are motivated in the ways that we have considered, Plato has solved two of the problems facing the *Republic*'s theory. First, since citizens aim at each other's virtue and happiness for its own sake, cooperation among them will be more stable. Second, since such cooperation is based on a recognition of the value of virtue, it will be in itself more valuable. Moreover, such cooperation or friendship now has an essentially political aspect: it is manifested (although not exclusively) in the self-conscious support, for the right reasons, of a political structure that aims at virtue in all citizens.

5.7 Political Rule and Citizenship

What implications does this understanding of a just city and its citizens have for the nature of appropriate political rule? We can approach this question by considering Aristotle's understanding of political rule in the just state. The claim that there is a special kind of rule constituting the relations among the citizens of an ideal state is one of the most basic ideas of Aristotle's political philosophy and it is what Aristotle himself sees as perhaps his most fundamental difference from Plato. The *Politics* opens with an argument that the good political community has a special nature and that this requires a distinctive sort of rule. Because Plato has misunderstood the nature of political rule, he has also failed to understand the nature of the good city.

We see that every city is a community of some sort, and that every community is established for the sake of some good . . . Clearly, then, while every community aims at some good, the community that has the most authority of all, and encompasses all the others, aims highest, that is to say, at the most authoritative good of all. This community is the one called a *polis*, the community that is political. Those, then, who think that the positions of statesman, king, household manager, and master of slaves are the same, are not correct. For they hold that each of these differs not in kind, but only in whether the subjects ruled are few or many; that if, for example, someone rules few people, he is a master; if more, a household manager; if still more, he has the position of statesman or king—the assumption being that there is no difference between a large household and a small *polis*. As for the positions of statesman and king, they say that someone who is in charge by himself has the position of king, whereas someone who follows the principles of the appropriate science, ruling, and being ruled in turn, has the position of statesman. But these claims are not true. (*Politics* 1252ᵃ1–16)[122]

For Aristotle, genuine political rule is

(1) exercised over free and equal citizens,
(2) exercised for the common good, and
(3) requires that citizens rule and be ruled in turn because they are free and equal.[123]

Rule exercised by masters over slaves fails to be political, since they are not equal (and the slave is not free). Although such rule may benefit the slave, that is not its goal, and masters rule permanently. But not only the sort of rule exercised by masters over slaves fails to be political. Even sorts of rule that naturally aim at the benefit of the ruled can fail to be political: for example, that in a just kingship or that of a parent over a child or of men over women. In these cases, according to Aristotle, the parties, although free, are not equal and thus permanent rule by the superior is just. In the case in which the parties are equal, as are the citizens of the ideal city, their equality of merit makes permanent rule by one party unjust.

For justice and merit must be by nature the same for those who are by nature similar. Hence, if indeed it is harmful to their bodies for unequal people to have equal food or clothing, the same holds, too, where offices are concerned. The same also holds, therefore, when equal people have what is unequal. Which is precisely why it is just for them to rule no more than they are ruled, and therefore, to do so in turn. (*Politics* 1287ᵃ12–18)[124]

In the ideal city, then, offices will be distributed according to merit and this requires that citizens must rule and be ruled in turn.[125]

That is why reciprocal equality preserves cities, as we said earlier in the *Ethics*, since this must exist even among people who are free and equal. For they cannot all rule at the same time, but each can rule for a year or for some other period. As a result they all rule, just as all would be shoemakers or carpenters if they changed places, and the same people were not always shoemakers and carpenters. (*Politics* 1261ª30–7)

The specific institutional form that this takes in Aristotle's ideal city seems to involve an assembly of all the citizens that has substantial powers and the filling of all offices, both high and low, by lot.[126] The idea that genuine and full citizenship requires ruling and being ruled in turn is also one of the most basic principles of Athenian democratic ideology: whoever does not have a share in ruling, but is permanently ruled over, is not a citizen. Although Aristotelian political theory and Athenian democratic thought differ in quite important ways, both affirm as a fundamental principle this strong connection between sharing in ruling and being a citizen.[127]

Aristotle's claims immediately set two questions for Plato's understanding of political community in the *Laws*. First, Magnesia is ruled for the common good and it is essential to Plato's political vision that all citizens are treated in the ways appropriate to free people. So rule in Magnesia satisfies some of Aristotle's criteria for political rule. But is the political community one of equals? Does the way that political rule is exercised in Magnesia undermine the claim of some citizens to be full members of the political community? Second, Aristotle's view that sharing in rule is just in the ideal city rests on the claim that equality in merit requires equal participation in rule. But it is also an essential part of Aristotle's view that permanent rule by some in the ideal city would unjustly deprive others of something valuable and good for them. Equality in rule is equality in the distribution of a good, not of a burden. Does Magnesia recognize adequately the ways in which political activity is good for the citizens?

Equality of Rule As we have seen, the *Laws* in an early passage enunciates a very strong understanding of the connection between citizenship and ruling: education is supposed to train the person to become a perfect citizen, that is, one who understands both how to rule and be ruled justly (*Laws* 643E3–6). The education for citizenship given to all members of the political community in Magnesia thus seems to conform to the Aristotelian ideal of preparing them for equal shares in ruling. Nevertheless, as we have seen, political rule is not distributed equally in Magnesia. Plato still thinks that there is a very strong connection between knowledge and virtue on the one hand and one's entitlement to rule on the other and that knowledge and virtue are distributed unequally among the citizens of Magnesia.

Plato gives special prominence to the goals of making the city free, a friend to itself and wise. In the case of the first two goals, the primary reference is the entire citizen body. All are to be treated as free insofar as the city's correct constitution aims at the common good and the city provides to the citizens an explanation of the principles supporting the laws governing them.[128] And all are encouraged to share in the sort of friendship we have just considered. It is also true that the city aims at fostering all the virtues in all the citizens and this requires ensuring that they possess wisdom. Nevertheless, in Book 12 Plato makes it clear that this is not all that is required for a city to be wise. In the case of every animal, it is the wisdom in its soul that best assures its salvation. The city's salvation, too, is best assured by the presence of wisdom in it and this requires that there exists within it a body that has knowledge of the city's political goal and of how it is best attained. This is, of course, the Nocturnal Council whose members receive an advanced education. And Plato explicitly links this training with an entitlement to rule. One who does not attain the sorts of knowledge required of members of the Nocturnal Council 'would almost never become an adequate ruler of the city as a whole, but would be an assistant [ὑπηρέτης] for the other rulers' (*Laws* 968A2–4). We have considered earlier in this chapter some of the difficulties surrounding the exact political role of the Nocturnal Council. But the connection between virtue and the entitlement to rule does not rest simply on the interpretation of controversial claims about the Nocturnal Council, but also on general political principles that Plato clearly enunciates.

In Book 6, just after sketching the election procedures for members of the Council, Plato states a basic principle of 'political justice'.

This selection procedure would strike a mean between a monarchic and a democratic constitution, which is the mean the constitution should always aim for. For slaves and masters would never become friends, nor would worthless types and good people, if they were both held equal when it comes to honors [τιμαῖς]. Both these situations fill constitutions with civil strife . . . The ancient pronouncement is true, that 'equality produces friendship' . . . But just what equality can do this? Because this is not very clear, we get into a lot of trouble. For there are two equalities, the same in name, but in many respects almost diametrically opposed in deed. Every city and lawgiver is competent to assign honors [τὰς τιμὰς] according to the one sort—the equality that consists in measure and weight and number—and by the use of the lot applies it in distributions.[129] But it is not so easy for everyone to discern the truest and best equality. For it is the judgment of Zeus, and it assists human beings only to a small degree, on each occasion; still, every bit of assistance it does give to cities or private people brings all the good things.[130] By distributing more to what is greater and smaller amounts to what is lesser, it gives due measure to each according to their nature: this includes greater honors always to those who are greater as regards virtue, and what is fitting—in due proportion—to those who are just the opposite as regards virtue and education. Presumably this is just what constitutes for us political justice [τὸ πολιτικὸν . . . αὐτὸ τὸ δίκαιον]. It is for this that we should now strive, and to this equality that we should now look . . . It is to this that one should look while giving laws, not to the tyranny of the few, or of one, or of some rule by the populace, but always to justice. And this is what has just been described—the natural equality given on each occasion to unequal men. (*Laws* 756E9–757D5)

This passage commits Plato to the following principle for the distribution of political offices.[131]

Distribution according to Virtue: A distribution of political offices to persons is just if and only if it distributes offices to persons in direct proportion to each person's virtue.[132]

This principle presents a very serious threat to the entitlement of most Magnesians to participate in ruling and, especially, to participate equally. According to it, the most important offices in the city should go to the most virtuous and, as Book 12 suggests, this will be especially those with greater knowledge. Plato does not make explicit what the relation is between this principle and the city's ultimate political goal of making the city as happy as possible. But that ultimate goal also presents a threat to the entitlement of most Magnesians to engage equally in ruling. The inevitability of akratic failure, even in philosophers who have absolute power, is an argument against autocracy, but it does not vindicate a conception of citizenship as ruling and being ruled in turn. Moreover, this argument against autocracy is only a prudential one; it does not show that there is something positively good about giving a share in rule to all citizens. Further considerations of political stability may lead us to distribute a share in ruling widely. If most people are excluded from significant participation in ruling, they are less likely to support the constitution. But this, too, is, as it stands, only a prudential argument.

Does the *Laws* have the resources to argue that there is something positively good about giving a share in rule to all citizens? If it does, then the claims of individual citizens to share in rule will not be so easily overridden by, for example, considerations of efficiency. To begin, neither Plato nor Aristotle thinks that being a normal, adult human entitles one to a significant share in ruling. For both of them, a claim to rule must be based on a form of merit that goes beyond this. Distributing a share in ruling widely might be justified if most citizens had something valuable to contribute. We have so far compared Magnesia with Aristotle's ideal city, but this may be a misleading comparison. Aristotle's ideal city gives such an important role in ruling to all citizens because it assumes that all citizens are equal at an extremely high level of virtue. But even if we consider cities that have a citizen body of less uniformly high attainment, Aristotle offers an argument for seeing most citizens as capable of making an important contribution.

But the view that the many rather than the few best people should be in authority would seem to be held, and while it involves a problem, it perhaps also involves some truth. For the many, who are not as individuals excellent men, nevertheless can, when they have come together, be better than the few best people, not individually, but collectively, just as feasts to which many contribute are better than feasts provided at one man's expense. For being many, each of them can have some part of virtue and practical wisdom, and when they come together, the many is just like a single human being, with many feet, hands, and senses, and so too for their character traits and thoughts. That is why the many are better judges of works of music and of the poets. For one of them judges one part, another another, and all of them the whole thing. (*Politics* 1281ᵃ40–1281ᵇ15)

Plato's own views in the *Laws* on the need for expertise in judging works of art suggest that he would not find this argument persuasive.[133] To see whether he is right, let us consider the ways in which collective judgment might bring epistemic benefit.

Most simply, pooled knowledge can increase the factual basis for decisionmaking, and consulting all (or at least many people) may improve the decisionmakers' knowledge of how laws and institutions affect each person and various social groups. Although Plato need not reject such considerations, he does not seem to think they are sufficient by themselves to show the need to involve many people in decisionmaking. In this, he seems to be right. All that they show is that decisionmakers must have the relevant information. Many people might be needed to collect the relevant information and make it available, but this does not show that they must participate in the actual decisionmaking.[134]

We might be able, however, to offer a better argument for collective decisionmaking from either of two other directions. First, if we accepted a moderate form of pluralism about value according to which the goods relevant to human happiness instantiate a reasonable variety of different kinds of goodness, then we might think that different sorts of people would be able to make distinctive contributions to deliberation and decisionmaking. Certain people might better appreciate aesthetic value, others ethical value, and so on. But as we saw in Chapter 2, Plato does not accept this sort of pluralism about value and what he emphasizes in the *Laws* is that truly wise deliberation must be informed by a grasp of what is common to all forms of value. The well-trained member of the Nocturnal Council must 'see what is common to these things [truths about the gods and the soul] and the things that concern the Muse, and should apply this understanding, in a harmonious way, to the practices and customs that pertain to habitual dispositions' (*Laws* 967E2–4).[135]

A second, perhaps more promising, line of argument, does not seek pluralism at the level of value itself, but rather focuses on the side of the potential knower. Even if the best sort of deliberation proceeds from a grasp of what is common to all forms of value, it might be the case that the best available approximation of it results from the pooling of various partial perspectives. In the absence of perfect knowledge, deliberation may best proceed as a collective project among people with differing epistemic strengths and weaknesses. (Such people would have to be reasonably reliable so that strengths rather than weaknesses were combined, they would have to be able and willing to learn from discussion, and there would have to be institutional provisions for such activity.) Moreover, this is a possibility that Plato has good reason to take especially seriously. In the *Statesman*, as we saw, Plato thinks that the differing natural tendencies in people persist despite a uniform education about the good and the fine. Even after people have been educated to a high level, different sorts of considerations will be particularly salient for them and their judgments will still tend, although they have a great degree of overlap, to diverge in characteristic ways. Given only a fairly modest degree of caution about the possibility of moving from high level, quasi-mathematical truths about goodness to more particular judgments, we should expect such variety. Nevertheless, Plato does not explicitly take this line in the *Laws*. And in Book 12's discussion of the Nocturnal Council, he seems confident—more confident, perhaps, than he should be—that the sort of education sketched there can result in a reliable and non-partial grasp of the truth. He does not, however, explicitly reject the above line of argument and it may help ground some of Magnesia's political practices: for example, the important role that Plato gives to collective discussion and deliberation in the exercise of many political offices.

Plato, however, does think that, even in Magnesia, the principle of distributing political offices according to virtue should not be strictly adhered to.

Nonetheless, necessity compels every city to blur the distinction between these two [kinds of equality], if it is to avoid partaking of civil war in some of its parts. For equity and forgiveness [τὸ γὰρ ἐπιεικὲς καὶ σύγγνωμον] whenever they are applied, are always infringements of the perfection and exactness that belong to strict justice.[136] Because of the discontent of the many they are compelled to make use of the equality of the lot, but when they do, they should pray both to the god and to good luck to correct the lot in the direction of what is most just. Thus, of necessity, both equalities ought to be employed, but the type that depends on chance should be employed as rarely as possible. A city that is going to last is compelled, for these reasons, to do things this way.   (*Laws* 757D5–758A4)

It is important to see exactly what concessions this passage does and does not make. What Plato contrasts with the proper sort of equality that distributes offices according to virtue is the use of the lot. A lottery might be a reasonable procedure in Aristotle's ideal city in which all citizens are roughly equal in virtue, but its use in Magnesia is simply a concession to promote political stability. Use of the lot is justified by the danger of the resentment of those not deemed worthy of office; it is not a procedure demanded by justice nor does it tend to promote a better distribution of political offices.[137]

But Plato does not criticize the procedure of filling offices by election as a violation of proportional equality and, as we have seen, employs it as the basic method of filling even the most important offices in Magnesia.[138] What, then, justifies this use of elections? Democratic decisionmaking can be defended in several different ways.[139] First, we might appeal to the intrinsic value of freedom or liberty. Democratic decisionmaking respects or embodies the value of the citizens' freedom because the restraints imposed on citizens are self-imposed. It is thus, we might argue, the best or perhaps the only way to reconcile the need for coercive laws and institutions with the freedom of the people bound by them. But Plato does not make such an argument and would reject one of its basic premises. Freedom, understood as not being subject to rules that one has not consented to or participated in making or as the capability to make and give effect to one's own choices, is not a non-conditional good for Plato. Its value will be dependent on one's possession of virtue.

A second sort of argument appeals to the fundamental value of equality. Political decisions affect, in basic and substantial ways, the lives of all citizens and thus, many have argued, it is reasonable to give them all an equal say in decisionmaking. As we have seen, however, Plato's principle of proportional equality rejects the claim that all citizens are entitled to an equal say. Perhaps then, Plato is only committed to an instrumentalist defense of the use of elections. He may not think that election is preferable because of its intrinsic properties, but rather because it is the procedure, given Magnesia's circumstances, most likely to produce the best outcomes. Plato might reasonably think this if he believed that the citizen body will generally be able to choose fairly well and that non-elective procedures, such as vesting the power to fill all offices in the Nocturnal Council, would both lead to resentment and run the risk of corruption. This line of argument expresses considerable confidence in the ethical capacities and attainments of ordinary citizens: they must be able, with a significant degree of reliability, to recognize differences in virtue and respond appropriately to them.

Such a defense also suggests that Plato takes a crucial step beyond a purely instrumental justification of the use of elections. The principle of distributing offices according to virtue seems to provide a non-instrumental justification for a certain distribution of political offices. But among the positions of political authority and responsibility in Magnesia is the Assembly to which all citizens belong and which plays an important role in the elections to most of the other offices in the city.[140] Thus we can see the ethical capacities of most citizens as not simply providing an instrumental reason to use elections, but rather as a claim of merit. Even if they do not possess knowledge and virtue at the highest levels, citizens are still entitled to an important kind of political participation. This will be all the more significant if distributing offices according to virtue is not only an instrumental means to maximizing the happiness of the city, but is also a principle of justice in itself.

Participation in elections is, however, only one part of political decision-making and it may not require the most fully realized forms of good ethical character. It does not, for example, require the grasp of first principles that might be necessary for some higher forms of substantive deliberation. But it would be a mistake to think that ordinary citizens' political participation in Magnesia is limited to voting. As we have seen, Magnesia has a rich variety of political offices requiring a large number of officeholders and in many such offices, an essential part of their duties will involve deliberation. Most citizens will be expected to engage in deliberation about political and ethical issues, even if such deliberation is not based on a full grasp of first principles.

Nevertheless, we may still find this understanding of citizenship somewhat pallid compared with that of Aristotle's ideal city.

Aristotle's view is that the citizen of a State must have something more than mere passive virtue; he must be able to take a share in guiding its destinies, he must live its full life . . . [The best state is best] because it realizes the highest quality of life— life of the fullest and completest kind. Its citizens must be . . . purposed to live, in the active exercise of all forms of virtue, moral and intellectual; their 'virtuous activity' must be that fully equipped and wholly unimpeded 'virtuous activity' to which alone Aristotle concedes the name of happiness; they must live a life in which the moral virtues work hand in hand with their nobler kin, the intellectual virtues.[141]

Newman's remarks suggest, I think, a deep worry about the political theory of the *Laws*. One of the most attractive features of Aristotle's view is its active conception of citizenship in a good city. Such citizenship requires participation in the governance and life of the community and this activity is an essential part of leading a fully virtuous life. Since such participation is an expression of the person's virtue, it is a major component of, and not just a means to, leading a good life.[142] We have seen that Plato gives citizenship a fundamental place in his later political theory and that Magnesia's citizens are not simply politically passive. The question we must now turn to is whether Plato in the *Laws* understands political activity as a significant component of the ordinary citizen's good and exactly what the goodness of such activity consists in.

The Goodness of Political Activity   That Plato in the *Laws*, like Aristotle, thinks of holding political office as a good, and not a burden, can be seen simply from his statement of the appropriate principle for distributing political office. Plato describes this principle as governing the distribution of 'honors' (*timai*). The same word can refer to a particular kind of honor, that is, political office, and the context makes it clear that this is what Plato has primarily in mind. But the passage need not exclude the broader sense of *timai*. Plato does think that other honors in the city should be distributed according to a person's virtue and it is clear that such honors are good for their recipient and not burdens. This distributive principle does not, however, tell us *why* sharing in political office is good. (We need not think, for example, that the only benefit of political activity is that it is an honor to participate.) This question is particularly pressing in light of the *Republic*. What Plato stresses there is the reluctance of philosophers to engage in ruling. Cities will not be well governed until it is clear that those who are the rulers could have a better life doing something other than ruling and, notoriously, philosophers must be 'compelled' to return to the Cave and rule the city. Upon deeper analysis, we may be able to show that, even in the

Republic, ruling does not involve an overall sacrifice by the philosopher rulers of their happiness and we may be able to find reasons why ruling is, in fact, good for them.[143] Nevertheless, the *Republic's* tone sets the issue for us of how ruling, and political activity more generally, can benefit those who engage in them.

Finding that political activity benefits even ordinary citizens may have further significant political consequences. If such activity were not of benefit to the citizens engaged in it, then minimizing the political activity of some (or perhaps excluding them entirely from political life) would not be a cost that had to be taken into account in the reckoning of overall benefit. Those deprived would not be deprived of a good. But if political activity is good for those engaging in it, then in deciding upon the distribution of political powers and functions we have to take into account the fact that excluding some deprives them of a good. The issue is not only who would rule most efficiently, but how to secure both the goal of effective rule and insure that the good of political activity is well distributed.[144]

In the *Republic,* the political activities of the rulers are based on their knowledge of the Forms and derive at least a large part of their value from being an expression of the philosophers' knowledge (501A–B, 540A–B). But the education afforded to most citizens in the *Laws* does not seem to give them knowledge of the Forms and so their political activity cannot be an expression of such knowledge. Yet even if it is not good because it consists in knowledge of the Forms and action based on such knowledge, their political activity still benefits the citizens. We thus need some other account of how this is so. One way of doing this is to try to establish that the value of good political activity has a certain kind of autonomy from the value realized in contemplation.

There is more than one way in which such autonomy might obtain. To begin, we might return to the *Laws'* medical analogy. There Plato appeals to the status of the patients to justify the doctor's treatment. Because the patients are free people, they should be brought to understand and accept the principles governing their treatment. One way of understanding this is as appealing to the intuition that it is better for the individual to be self-ruled than to be ruled from without. Something like this intuition may account for the immediate attractiveness that the Athenian's interlocutors find in the proposal that the legislator in Magnesia should do what has never been done before and treat the citizens as free people. On such an account, the value of political activity consists in its being an expression of one's capacity to be a self-governing agent.

But as we have also seen, such an account is not sufficient for Plato. Self-governance is valuable for the individual only if it is self-governance in accordance with the right principles. This fact does not yet show that the value of political activity fails to be independent of the value realized in contemplation, since we are not entitled to conclude that self-governance can be in accordance with the right principles only by realizing the sort of value characteristic of contemplation. But self-governance's lack of unconditional value poses in an acute form the issue of the relation of good political activity to the values that guide it.

First, good political activity will be an expression of virtue and an instance of virtuous activity. Even without a high level of theoretical knowledge, most citizens have some grasp of correct ethical principles and co-operate with each other to realize a genuine common good. Indeed, for non-philosophers in Magnesia, the activities that aim at the common good are the primary expressions of their virtue. Since they value virtue for its own sake, they will also value these activities for their own sake. This opens up a range of virtuous political activity not found in the *Republic*: it is still aimed at virtue for its own sake, but is not based on contemplation. Political activity as such, that is, participation in the social institutions of the just city aimed at furthering the common good, is good in itself and forms an important part of each citizen's happiness.

But what is the relation of such activity to the value realized in contemplation? We can immediately see that several ways of sustaining the autonomy of virtuous political activity are not open to Plato. For example, if one thought that the values that guide good ethical activity were not the sorts of things that could be the object of contemplation, then good ethical activity could not instantiate the sort of values realized in contemplation. Similarly, one might think that although value properties could be the object of contemplation, they constitute only a relatively insignificant range of such objects. But Plato rejects both of these views: value properties such as the just and the good are objects of contemplation and value properties are basic in understanding the order and structure of the world.

There are other options that are not so clearly unsatisfactory. One might think, for example, that the essential element of value in contemplation consists in its full grasp of the thing known. Contemplation of value properties will be valuable to the extent that reason fully and precisely grasps their nature. But this full and precise grasp of a thing's nature might not be the way that value properties enter into practical ethical thought. One might hold that ethical activity gains its value, at least in large part, from the quality of the practical deliberation underlying and guiding it. And perhaps the distinctive excellence of practical deliberation is not its full theoretical understanding of the nature of the goal, but rather some feature more intimately linked to action. The distinctive excellence of practical deliberation, on such an account, would consist not in the detail and precision of its understanding of the nature of the end or the value to be realized, but rather in finding the best way to realize an appropriate goal in the given (and perhaps quite complex) circumstances.[145] Alternatively, one might hold that the value of good ethical activity lies not so much in the agents' full understanding of the end nor in their skill in seeing how to realize this end in the circumstances, but rather in the agents' attitude towards the good or in the extent or magnitude of the good aimed at or achieved.[146] On such an account, the primary value of good ethical activity lies in its being an expression of the person's love of the good and commitment to realizing it in action. Or perhaps ethical activity, especially political activity, is particularly valuable insofar as it aims at or achieves a large-scale good (the good of the whole city).

These lines of thought have been sketched only very roughly and they raise issues that receive greater thematic attention in later Greek ethical reflection than in Plato himself. But they once again point to the need for some further consideration of good ethical and political activity and, in particular, of their value.

5.8 The Goodness of Ethical Activity

Let us begin by considering two radical responses to this set of problems. By seeing what is unsatisfactory in them, we can find at least the outlines of a more adequate answer. The first line of thought holds that in order to understand the goodness of ethical activity and the demand that it makes upon the virtuous agent we must ultimately give up the eudaimonist framework. We must justify the goodness of ethical activity by appealing to a notion of goodness that is different from, and can come into conflict with, what is good for the agent. One way of making this idea more concrete is found in Nicholas White.

Plato believes that certain indispensable judgments of value employ a notion of the good . . . that is entirely impartial and non-self-referential. (Indeed, it is seemingly also impersonal, in the sense of not depending on the needs or desires of any human being.) Using this notion, it is possible to make a judgment to the effect that a thing is good non-self-referentially or 'absolutely', not merely good for oneself or conducive to one's happiness. Thus on Plato's view someone can judge that the maintenance of a city-state is good in this way. I think that such judgments are made in *Republic* VII, at the point at which the rulers of Plato's ideal city-state consent to govern it rather than simply engaging in philosophical thinking. Here, as I take it, they give up a happier life in order to serve a sort of good that is more important, civic justice. This is a greater good in a non-self-regarding sense, not something that is good *for them*, or good merely by virtue of sustaining their own happiness.[147]

On this account, ethical activity has an impartial or absolute value that makes a demand upon a virtuous agent, presumably simply in virtue of being rational. It is the absolute goodness of ethical activity that gives us a reason, and sometimes an overriding reason, to act virtuously even when this conflicts with our own good or happiness.

We might also think that the *Laws* itself suggests that Plato is moving in this direction. We could point to the passage that we have already noted several times in which Plato appeals to the value of ethical activity to provide a reason for action for the just person: '[T]he man who is to attain the title "Great" must love neither himself nor his own belongings, but things just, whether they happen to be actions of his own or rather those of another man' (*Laws* 732A2–4). One way in which we might understand this passage is as rejecting eudaimonism's special concern with the agent's own good. Specifically, we might see it as claiming that the just person is equally concerned with goodness wherever it occurs. The special concern that eudaimonism holds that every rational agent has with his or her own good is to be replaced by an impartial concern for goodness wherever it may be instantiated. Such a view could be held in one of two forms depending on how we understand the goodness that the just agent is to promote. On the first interpretation, the just person is supposed to be impartial with respect to people's happiness: he has equal reason to promote the happiness of any person and no special reason to promote his own happiness. On the second interpretation, the just person is supposed to be impartial in promoting non-relational goodness wherever it occurs. Since rational creatures can instantiate such non-relational goodness much more satisfactorily than, e.g., works of art or other non-animate objects, the just person's efforts will be primarily directed towards bringing about happiness. Nevertheless, the object directly aimed at is the promotion of non-relational goodness.

One might object to such an account that it cannot be Plato's view, since Magnesia does not require such impartiality. Even a just person is expected to have greater concern for those close to him and especially for his fellow citizens. This objection, however, is not decisive. We can reconcile such a view of the impartiality required by justice with Magnesia's actual practice in several ways. First, as we have seen, Plato thinks that human nature limits the degree of other-regarding concern that it is possible for a person to have. So although perfect justice might require such impartiality, all that could reasonably be expected even of virtuous people is some approximation to it. Second, we might argue that differential concern with those close to one and with one's fellow citizens can be justified on impartial grounds. There is little or nothing that the citizens of Magnesia can do for the inhabitants of Thrace and given one's greater knowledge of, and ability to affect, those near to one, efforts spent in pursuing their good (or promoting non-relational goodness in them) will be more efficient.

Nevertheless, Plato does not explicitly make such arguments and throughout the *Laws* he seems to take it for granted that a rational person has a special concern for his or her own happiness.[148] And even in the above passage, Plato claims that a just person must love justice wherever it occurs; he does not say that a just person must impartially promote the good. So we should at least attempt to find a solution that is compatible with eudaimonism.

Let us begin by considering a second radical response to our worry. We might think that something like the first picture is inevitable, or at least exceedingly natural, once we start with a certain conception of reason as displayed in ethical activity. Consider, for example, the following line of thought.

When, for instance, on the theoretical level a man looks beyond empirical cases to the [F]orm they exemplify, he is necessarily indifferent as to which of these cases he starts from, or one may say, reads the [F]orm through. And if, as might sometimes happen, different cases can provide readier intellectual access to different aspects of the [F]orm, he launches himself from as many such different cases as possible. Any concentration of interest on one instance above others would suggest that reason, if operating at all, is being limited by some non-rational principle.

If practical and theoretical reason are but two sides of one and the same power, and if in a purely theoretical consideration of, for example, the ideal human soul one would as soon take any particular actual soul as one's starting point as any other, neither giving one's own special priority nor having to have a special reason for *not* giving it special priority: then it would seem that practical reason too cannot in itself differentiate between one's own and other souls as the ground in which the ideal is to be—not this time contemplated, but—realized.[149]

On this view, both practical and theoretical reason are expressions of the same power. Theoretical reason seeks to arrive at a full and complete understanding of truth and, insofar as it does, pays equal attention to all particulars (at least to all particulars of equal epistemic value). Practical reason aims not at contemplating the truth, specifically, the truth about value, but at realizing it. Yet insofar as it is an expression of the same power as theoretical reason, it shares in the universality of reason. Practical reason is thus indifferent as to which particular it takes as its object (except insofar as they differ in their potential to instantiate value). To the extent that practical reason guides a person's life, he has equal reason to promote value wherever it occurs.

On this conception of practical reason and of its relation to theoretical reason, a strongly impartialist conclusion seems to follow. Practical reason is part of a unitary power that is directed as such towards value—it is part of the expression of the unified tendency of reason to grasp the nature of value and to promote it. In both its theoretical and practical expression, reason is impartial. And insofar as it is the excellence of practical reasoning that accounts for most of the value or goodness of good ethical activity, the goodness of ethical activity will lie in its promoting the genuine good wherever it is found. This account, just like White's, seems to reject rational eudaimonism insofar as it denies that rational agents have a special concern with their own good. We thus have similar reasons for seeking a different solution that is compatible with eudaimonism. (The idea, however, that reason inherently involves a sort of impartiality is important and I return to it below.)

The most straightforward response would be to try to avoid the impartialist result by loosening the connection between theoretical and practical reason. Specifically, we could try to give practical reason a greater independence from theoretical reason while still holding that it is the excellence of practical reasoning that gives ethical activity (at least much of) its goodness. Consider as an example of such an account one that holds that practical wisdom's

distinct contribution comes not from an alleged ability to focus understandingly on a goal of transcendent worth, or to formulate a purpose that comprehensively integrates all the values that should matter to us in order of their merited priority— but from its skill in seeing what particular line of action would, from the practical point of view (which includes the moral), be best to adopt in pursuit of some (usually) quite ordinary goal such as anyone might have.[150]

This view leaves it open how other-regarding considerations should enter into practical reasoning, but insofar as it denies that the excellence of reason in its practical aspect consists in its direction toward and pursuit of some hard-to-discern end—such as non-relational value—it suggests a less revisionary account of the aim of practical reason. Its aim will typically be quite 'ordinary' goals. And so by breaking the link between reason in its practical expression and some sort of absolute or transcendental value, we might be able to avoid the resulting impartialist pressure.

But for Plato, at least, we cannot so easily break this link. First, in the *Laws*, Plato stresses that the highest form of political and ethical activity, that is, lawmaking, should be based on something like a contemplative grasp of value. The idea that reason in all its expressions gains its value from its direction toward non-relational value draws further support from our discussion of the *Philebus'* value theory in Chapter 2. Different sorts of knowledge are graded with respect to their goodness for us in terms of their grasp of objective principles of order and value. Second, as we have seen, Plato holds up as a model for good human reasoning god's rational activity. Such activity includes both a full and precise grasp of value and a practical rational impulse to instantiate it in the world. Finally, although the passage at *Laws* 731D–732A in which Plato seems to make a direct appeal to value in explaining the motivation of the just person may not require us to abandon eudaimonism, it does suggest that there is a tight connection between the practical expression of reason and objective value.

We should thus seek an account of the value of ethical activity that accepts an intimate connection between reason and objective and non-relational goodness, while still accepting eudaimonism. I shall first consider one recent subtle and important attempt to explain the place of other-regarding concern in rational activity while accepting eudaimonism and then turn to sketch, at least in outline, an alternative account. In *Plato's Ethics*, Terence Irwin offers an account of why the just person in the *Republic* should be motivated, consistently with rational eudaimonism, to display at least some degree of other-regarding concern, that is, at least as much as is involved in treating the happiness of some other persons as a non-instrumental end of action. In doing so, Irwin appeals to the orientation of reason in its practical aspect toward the fine both in the agent's own life and in the lives of others.

Irwin suggests that in order to understand why the *Republic*'s just person displays the appropriate concern for the interests of others, we must turn to Plato's theory of love in the *Symposium* and the *Phaedrus*.[151] The *Symposium* holds that our basic rational desire, from which our other rational desires derive, is to have the good always, that is, to be immortal in our possession of the good. But the only way for us to be immortal is by propagation and we can distinguish two kinds of propagation: (1) interpersonal, and (2) intrapersonal. Interpersonal propagation, in the first instance, is to be understood as ordinary reproduction bringing a new person into existence. Intrapersonal propagation expresses my future concern for myself. Since, for humans, their characters, personalities, memories, aims, and so on all change over time, we keep ourselves in existence by retaining the appropriate connections between our old 'self' and our new 'self'. This is not to claim that the person really fails to persist over time; rather, a person persists insofar as there are the appropriate causal and qualitative connections between his different temporal stages.

Passage A
What matters, then, in self-concern, as Plato understands it, is the preservation of what I value in myself . . . and the fact that this preservation results from my own action. The presence of these connexions makes it true that the later person is the same person as me, despite the various differences between my present self and my later self. If these connexions were not present, then the future person would not be me. Still, it is not the bare fact that the later person is the same person as me that gives me a reason for self-concern, any more than the bare fact that a person is my 'other half' gives me reason for concern (cf. *Symp.* 205d10–206a2). If it happened—impossibly, in Plato's view—that someone could be my later self without having these connexions with me, we could not understand why I should be concerned about him. When the later person is identical to me, my concern about him is understandable insofar as he preserves (or improves) valuable features of the earlier person.[152] An 'important qualification' of the claim that it is the persistence of such connections that explains personal identity is that insofar as we are rational we want the persistence (or development) in us of what is really fine, not what simply appears fine to us.
. . . I want my future self to have the traits that result from learning more about the fine. The fact that my future self has an outlook that is a rational development of my present values should matter to me.[153]

With this understanding of self-concern in hand, we can now see why a rational person should be concerned about other people.

Passage B
[Plato] has argued that what I value about intrapersonal propagation is the propagation of the valuable aspects of myself in a person who will exist in the future. Now he points out that the person in whom I propagate these aspects of myself need not be me in the future; it may be another person who exists now. I can

therefore achieve what I value about intrapersonal propagation if I propagate these aspects of myself in another person: if I value intrapersonal propagation, I ought to value interpersonal propagation. Indeed, I sometimes ought to prefer interpersonal propagation, since I cannot always ensure my own continued existence, and this limitation may prevent me from fully realizing in myself everything that I might want to realize in myself. In these cases the reasons that lead me to care about intrapersonal propagation should lead me to prefer propagation of these valuable traits in another person.[154]

This is one line of argument for other-regarding concern, but Irwin suggests another. The second appeals to the notion of 'self-expression'. The sort of self-expression that Plato has in mind here, Irwin thinks, can be found in the actions of the *Timaeus'* Demiurge which aim at making the world, including other souls, as good as possible.

Plato seems to assume that the god will want to express his goodness, even when his self-preservation does not require it. The god wants to express his goodness by exercising his capacity to create the sort of goodness that he has, and this desire for self-expression does not depend on any limitation in his capacity to preserve himself.[155]

On the most straightforward reading of this argument, Irwin is suggesting that god has a reason to be concerned about bringing about the good condition of others, although he can assure his own intrapersonal propagation forever. To the extent that we can share something like this motivation, we too would have a reason for some form of other-regarding concern that is independent of the reasons provided by the first argument. And although in mortal human beings—as opposed to god—this aim might compete with other aims that we have, including those involved in self-preservation, it is not obvious that it should have no weight with us and thus Irwin can, I think, reasonably appeal to it.

Are these arguments convincing? I do not intend to argue that they fail completely, that is, that they cannot justify some forms of other-regarding concern. But I do think that we can have reasonable worries about them. Before turning to examine these two lines of argument, let us note what may be a third rationale.

[Plato] agrees that the rational part of the soul must have a holistic outlook, it transcends the limited and one-sided views that are characteristic of the non-rational parts. He now points out that if my rational part has a holistic and comprehensive outlook, it must also be temporally comprehensive and so must look forward to my future interests. He argues that an appropriately comprehensive concern for my present and my future cannot allow my concerns to be confined to myself; for since I cannot always preserve myself, I must seek to propagate the valuable aspects of myself in other people.[156]

On this line of argument, concern for others is justified precisely because I cannot preserve myself forever. By itself, this argument gives us no reason for other-regarding concern, if we could so preserve ourselves. (It does not, of course, deny that there could be such reasons.) But this is too controversial a premiss on which to rest other-regarding concern. In a number of other dialogues besides the *Symposium*, Plato holds that the soul is immortal and identifies the person (the 'I') with the soul. And he accepts that a soul can undergo very great psychological discontinuities while remaining the same soul.[157]

But this strong assumption is not needed for Irwin's two other lines of argument. Consider Passage B above. The argument here is importantly different. Irwin here claims that the reasons that justify my concern with intrapersonal propagation also justify a concern with some sorts of interpersonal propagation. Irwin also claims that since I cannot always insure intrapersonal propagation, I should in these cases prefer interpersonal propagation. But here my failure to survive does not ground the rationality of all my other-regarding concern, rather it gives my other-regarding concern, in the form of interpersonal propagation, a higher priority in certain cases. This is consistent with the idea that the similarities between intrapersonal and interpersonal propagation by themselves justify some degree of concern with interpersonal propagation and thus justify some forms of other-regarding concern. This is a significant advantage over the more controversial argument just considered.

But how, exactly, does this new argument go? The most promising version of Irwin's argument (found in Passages A and B) depends on drawing a distinction between 'what matters' to us in self-concern and identity itself. 'What matters' to me, that is, what it is rational for me to be concerned about, is the improvement or preservation of what I value in a future person along with the fact that the preservation is a result of my action. As Passage

B argues, 'what matters' to me can be secured, even when identity fails, by the right sort of interpersonal propagation. Passage A argues that even when identity does obtain, it could not rationally sustain concern for myself when my future self lacks the appropriate relation to my present self (e.g. when my future self does not improve or preserve what I value).[158] Identity itself is neither necessary nor sufficient for what matters or for self-concern understood in terms of what matters.

But this analysis gives the wrong verdict, and what Plato would think is the wrong verdict, in some very important cases. Since Irwin explicitly allows that improvement in my conception of the fine preserves 'what matters', he avoids an objection that faces some modern theorists who similarly distinguish identity from what matters, e.g., Derek Parfit. Since on Parfit's view what matters is the preservation of psychological connectedness and continuity, it is difficult to see why I should be interested in large psychological changes that constitute an improvement.[159] But on Irwin's view, I have no self-concerned reason to regret ethical degeneration: even if I were identical with the future degenerated self, 'we could not understand why I should be concerned about him.'[160] But this just seems to be the wrong verdict about such cases and seems to be the wrong verdict from Plato's point of view. The philosopher has, for example, good reason to disvalue becoming a worse person and at least one important reason for this is the self-concerned reason that such a decline would be bad *for him*.[161] (And as we shall see, the rationality of such self-interested concern is essential to Plato's later eschatology.) We thus have good reason to reject Irwin's account of what matters as an appropriate analysis of self-concern. But once we reject this account of self-concern, it is natural to explain why I am concerned about or value (or disvalue) the preservation or improvement (or loss or impairment) of fine states of myself by my prudential concern for my own well-being. Yet if we accept this, we no longer have an argument for the rationality of my concern with the establishment or maintenance of fine states in others.

So this leaves us with Irwin's final argument for other-regarding concern that appeals to the claim that god has an interest in self-expression and that, as rational creatures, we should also. The idea that god's motivation in acting toward the world is a paradigm for the actions of the just person plays,

I have argued, an important role in the *Laws*. But here the worry concerns precisely the nature of god's motivation: is it most accurately characterized as a desire for self-expression? Is his basic motivation (1) or (2)?

(1) God wants to make the world as much like himself as possible.

(2) God wants to make the world as good as possible.

We can find both stated in the *Timaeus* (29D7–30C1). In the *Laws*, however, (2) is the form we find. And (2) seems to be the right characterization of god's motivation. It is the fact that god's state is good that explains why he wants to instantiate it elsewhere, not the mere fact that it is *his* nor even the complex fact that it is good and it is his.

We should thus attempt to find another motivation for other-regarding concern that also helps to explain the value of such concern. Since, as we have seen, Plato in the *Laws* does make a direct appeal to the value of virtue in explaining why a just person should be interested in promoting the virtue of another, we should begin by considering whether we can make this a central part of the just person's motivation. There are, however, two important worries that any such attempt must face. First, we have seen that some worry that this abandons eudaimonism. But there is a further and more troubling issue. We might allow that such a direct concern for virtue can be made a part of the agent's happiness and thus made consistent with eudaimonism. But we might think that such a move is only a formal sleight of hand: it is 'a blatant gerrymandering of the notion of happiness to make it include a kind of duty that . . . plainly can be at odds with happiness under any normal construal'.[162] The second, and related, worry concerns just how demanding such a requirement would be. Does it, for example, require the just person to be impartial between promoting his or her own good and the good of any other person?

Let us begin with the first sort of worry. In order to show that such an appeal to the value of virtue does not entail abandoning eudaimonism, we can adopt a fairly common strategy aimed at showing that the eudaimonist need not consider only states of himself to be good for their own sake. Specifically, we can hold that I can choose something other than a state of myself as a part or constituent of my happiness and that in doing so I can also choose it for its own sake.[163] Accordingly, as a first approximation, we can construe the direct appeal to the value of virtue as the claim that promoting the good condition of others (or their well-being itself) is a part of a rational person's happiness, and so non-instrumentally good for that person.

The charge that including other-regarding concern in this way within the person's own happiness makes eudaimonism trivial, or that it begs important questions, is more worrisome. Such a reconciliation would be trivial, if it rested on the idea that anything that a rational person aims at non-instrumentally or anything that matters to her in its own right is part of her happiness or non-instrumentally good for her. Many philosophers have, for example, thought that a rational person must aim at moral action for its own sake or non-instrumentally, but do not see this as showing that aiming at the morally good or right for its own sake is good *for* the rational person or that a rational person should aim at acting morally as part of his or her own happiness. What we need to show is not just that promoting the good of others is rationally or morally required; rather, we need to show that non-instrumentally promoting the good of others forms part of something that it is intuitively reasonable to think of as a person's own good or welfare. The objection that our strategy is question-begging focuses on precisely this question. The critic may claim that although promoting the good of others may make a rationally compelling demand on human beings, such a concern for the well-being of others will inevitably conflict, at least in some cases, with any reasonable understanding of individual welfare or well-being.[164]

For an especially clear instance of why one might think such a conflict inevitable, consider some of Kant's criticisms of eudaimonism. On Kant's view, the standpoint of happiness or of self-interest is the 'natural-social' standpoint which is expressed by my inclinations as they appear under the conditions of social life. Happiness is our well-being as natural creatures and, as such, is the imagined maximal satisfaction of our empirical inclinations.[165] Given this conception of happiness, we may not be able to form a consistent conception of it because of the indeterminate and variable nature of our inclinations. But even if we could, it is surely overwhelmingly likely that happiness, so understood, will often conflict with the demands of morality and especially with other-regarding demands. Matters may even be worse if we take into account our social nature, since Kant tends to think that the conditions of human sociability are such that people's conception of happiness is an expression of their competitive desire to see themselves as superior to others.

But more moderate conceptions of happiness can also give this charge some bite. Julia Annas, for example, provides a bold and ambitious account of how happiness enters quite generally into ancient ethics. According to Annas, ancient ethics begins with the question of how I should live or what my life should be like. This is a question that ordinary people, and not just philosophers, will put to themselves and it is 'the entry point for ethical reflection'.[166] But as the entry point, this standpoint also constrains in important ways the possible answers we can arrive at. Although happiness is not a determinate notion and is given much of its content by reflection on our ethical commitments, we must start from the concerns, commitments, and practical attitudes we have as well-brought up agents. Yet there are two sorts of concerns about the place that a conception such as Annas' allows for other-regarding concern within happiness. First, we might worry about the degree of other-regarding concern, especially other-regarding concern that takes the form of promoting virtue in others, that can be accommodated by such a view. It is reasonable to expect that the ordinary concerns and commitments of well-brought up human beings will include non-solipsistic ends. Moreover, our initial entry point need not be the culmination of our reflection and we should not underestimate the degree to which such reflection might extend our other-regarding concern. Nevertheless, the concern to promote virtue, even if confined to the citizen body, threatens to come into conflict not only with our more narrowly self-interested concerns, but also with our commitments to those especially near to us. More strongly impartial claims will be increasingly difficult to justify.

But there is, I think, a more pressing tension. Perhaps the strongest forms of other-regarding concern that would be embodied in the ordinary commitments of citizens of a Greek city would be those to one's family, household, and close friends. Especially strong ties to others might also grow out of a common commitment with other citizens to risk one's life in defense of the city. But in both of these cases, concern for others may not exclusively take the form of concern with others' virtue. People typically are capable of being deeply concerned with the welfare of their children, family members, or comrades in arms while recognizing that they are not especially virtuous

people and such concern need not always take the form of ethical reformation. Even if, starting from the initial entry point, other-regarding concern
could be extended in scope to include many others, its original sources may
not be fully virtue-based and it is not clear that it will, after we reflectively
systematize and make consistent our ordinary concerns and commitments,
evolve into such a concern. Finally, to the extent that we do find our ordinary
concerns and commitments expressing other-regarding concern in the form
of promoting virtue, we may still legitimately wonder whether this simply
shows that they are not all structured by the ultimate end of our own happiness. Happiness may not be a determinate notion, but we again run the risk
of a merely formal reconciliation, if we expand it to include everything that
upon reflection matters to us.

As we have seen, Kant provides an account of human nature that gives
content to the notion of the good for such a creature. But the content of the
good so developed does not sustain a strong place for other-regarding concern within the individual's happiness. Annas suggests that ancient ethics in
general tries to do without such a tight link between nature and happiness,
in particular, between human nature and an account of the human good.
According to Annas, we give content to our initially indeterminate notion
of happiness by reflecting on and attempting to make consistent our concerns and commitments, not by appealing to theoretical claims about the
nature of human beings. But even if this sort of view could sustain a strong
place for other-regarding concern within a reflective and consistent account
of our commitments, I have argued that we might still reasonably wonder
whether this shows that such other-regarding concern is, in fact, part of our
happiness or good.

So we should consider whether Plato provides an account of human
nature that grounds his conception of the human good or happiness and
explains why our nature is such that other-regarding concern is good for us.
We can begin not directly with an account of the relation between human
nature and the human good, but with an account of the relation between
human nature and other-regarding concern.

Let us return to the theology of *Laws* 10. In it, Plato provides an account
of some of the essential features of souls, especially good souls, and of their
place in the world. To begin, all souls have been designed so that they con-

tribute to the virtue and happiness of the whole universe. This is, however, a fact about the nature of souls that is independent of the individual soul's own aims and intentions. But Plato goes further: it is the nature of a good soul to aim at benefiting, that is, at promoting virtue and happiness (*Laws* 903B4–904B6).

Is there a way of moving from this claim to showing that promoting virtue and happiness is good for the individual soul? Plato here can fairly appeal to a connection between the essential nature of a thing and its well-being or good. It is a truism that what is good for a thing depends on what kind of thing it is. But Plato can also appeal to the stronger claim that the good of a creature consists (at least in large part) in the performance of the sorts of activities that are essential to it. Indeed, the intuitive plausibility of this idea is sufficiently great that it may be able to ground a conception of the human good that calls for revisions, in quite fundamental ways, of our ordinary concerns and commitments. This is a line of thought that we have explored in more detail in Chapter 4. There I argued that Plato holds that the essential nature of the rational aspect of the soul is to seek to stand in the appropriate relation to the truth and, in particular, to the truth about value. I also attempted there to show how we can develop an account of the good condition of non-rational (or, perhaps better, not fully rational) motivations starting from this basis.

We can now develop this idea somewhat further. The central and unifying feature of reason in all its forms for Plato is its orientation toward value. Let us consider three aspects of this. First, there is a cognitive aspect. Reason has an inherent tendency to seek to grasp the truth and, as a basic element of this, to grasp the truth about order and value. This tendency finds its expression both in seeking a full and complete grasp of non-sensible principles of order and value and in seeking the truth about sensibles. Second, there is an affective aspect. Reason is not simply a faculty capable of or tending to grasp the truth, but is moved by its own nature toward the truth. It is not merely the case that certain desires are endorsed from the outside by reason, rather an equally basic expression of reason's own nature is its love of the truth and the good. Finally, there is a practical aspect. It is the faculty of reason that accounts for our practical response to value. Reason seeks to instantiate genuine goodness both in itself and elsewhere.

On this understanding of reason and the nature of the individual soul, we can see why a concern to promote value and, specifically, to promote virtue in others is part of the individual's well-being. Other-regarding concern, insofar as it takes the form of promoting virtue in others, thus is good for the individual in that it is a realization of one of the most basic aspects of his nature. Further, because this is an appropriate response to what is good (i.e. this sort of other-regarding concern embodies both a love of and desire to instantiate what is non-relationally good), it is reasonable to hold that such other-regarding concern is itself non-relationally good.

Such an account is not obviously question-begging, if Plato can support this conception of reason and the identification of ourselves with reason independently of this understanding of human happiness. And although Plato's psychology is not free of normative claims, there is no reason to think that it depends directly on his conception of happiness. This account does not answer all of the questions that we might reasonably raise about the relation between other-regarding concern and happiness, but by considering some of the remaining issues, we can better understand both its strengths and its limitations.

An essential feature of this account is that it attributes a certain sort of unity to reason. Reason is a single faculty or capacity that displays a unified response toward truth and value. Seeking to grasp the nature of the good, loving the good and loving knowledge of it, and seeking to promote the good are equally expressions of the nature or essence of reason. We should thus expect a virtuous agent to seek understanding of the good as well as to promote it. One important way in the later Greek tradition that this account comes under pressure is from views that give greater priority to understanding or contemplating the truth or the good and thus threaten to minimize the place of other-regarding concern.

There are two ways in which this might happen that are worth special attention. First, one might hold that reason is not a single unified capacity or faculty, but rather is composed of at least two more basic capacities. These capacities are distinguished by their different functions and different objects. One accounts for theoretical understanding of first principles and what follows from them. The other is concerned with the cognition of particular individuals and with practical deliberation. We might also hold that theoretical activity is best, because its objects are the best possible objects. If so, then theoretical activity may be seen as the activity of reason *par excellence* and thus given an absolute priority over other expressions of reason.

But even without the separation of reason into distinct faculties, we might think that certain uses of reason are much better or have a much higher priority than others. Such a view is especially plausible if one sees the lower capacities as imperfect or incomplete realizations of the higher capacity. Consider, for example, Plotinus on the relation between good action and contemplation.

All things aim at contemplation and look to this end . . . Men, too, when their power of contemplation weakens, make action a shadow of contemplation and reasoning. Because contemplation is not enough for them, since their souls are weak and they are not able to grasp the vision sufficiently, and therefore are not filled with it, but still long to see it, they are carried into action, so as to see what they cannot see with their intellect. When they make something, then, it is because they want to see their object themselves and also because they want others to be aware of and contemplate it, when their project is realized in practice as well as possible. Everywhere we shall find that making and action are either a weakening or a consequence of contemplation; a weakening if one had nothing in view beyond the thing done, a consequence if he had another prior object of contemplation better than what he made. For who, if he is able to contemplate what is truly real, will deliberately go after its image? The duller children, too, are evidence of this, who are incapable of learning and contemplative studies and turn to crafts and manual work.[167]

Such a view might justify giving contemplation (nearly) absolute priority.

Both of these represent serious challenges to the sort of Platonic position I have sketched. And both are lines of thought that are especially prominent among those who explicitly think of themselves as Platonists or who, at least, are deeply influenced by Plato.[168] But even on the conception I have sketched, problems lurk. Even if reason is unified in the way that I have suggested, for limited creatures such as ourselves, the different expressions of reason threaten to compete with one another. Even if, for example, the capacity to paint is a single, unified capacity, painting portraits competes with painting landscapes. Individuating the capacity more finely does not remove the possibility of conflict: let the capacity be that of painting portraits, still, painting A's portrait competes with painting B's.

So should we still think that the solution sketched represents progress? First, for all other reasonable interpretations of Plato on other-regarding concern, there is a similar problem (and the present interpretation has advantages that the others lack). Consider, for example, Broadie's suggestion that the just person in the *Republic* comes to give equal weight to promoting the good wherever it is found. On this view, we still face a problem concerning how the person can best promote the good. If states of philosophic contemplation have an especially high value, then it may be reasonable, on purely impartial grounds, for a person to devote great amounts of time to developing such states in herself. It may be more difficult to produce such states in others in a reliable way and it would seem that, in any case, one's efforts might well be restricted to quite a small number. If the value of contemplation is sufficiently high, it will tend to crowd out other forms of other-regarding concern.

Similarly, Irwin's proposal faces a problem about the priority of contemplation with respect to other activities. If the value of contemplation is sufficiently high, it may crowd out other-regarding concern, even if we accept Irwin's argument for the claim that other-regarding concern is good in itself. (This danger will be greater, if we do not think that individual mortality makes it necessary for a eudaimonist to seek the good of others.) But even if we accept that a significant degree of other-regarding concern is warranted, we face a similar problem about the possible competition between fostering contemplation in (a few) others and developing different forms of other-regarding concern.

Although the solution I have sketched does not provide a precise account of how to weight the value of contemplation and the value of other expressions of reason, it has important advantages. First, as opposed to some interpretations, it justifies other-regarding concern within a eudaimonist framework. Further, by grounding other-regarding concern in an account of the nature of reason and of the nature of the individual soul, it provides support for thinking that other-regarding concern is not illicitly smuggled into our conception of individual well-being, but has a genuinely important place there in its own right.

Second, even if this account does not establish the precise weight of different goods, the claim that other-regarding concern in the form of promoting the good is a basic expression of reason suggests that such concern should have a significant place in the good life. In particular, it helps to provide a plausible justification for the very sort of other-regarding concern that is required of Magnesia's citizens. As I have argued, the fundamental aim of the laws in Magnesia is to foster the good and virtue of all the citizens. The political association is one in which every citizen is to aim at promoting virtue in all others. Insofar as the political association has this aim, we can see why an individual for whom promoting the good is an important part of his own welfare would give a prominent place in his life to political activity, that is, to supporting and fostering the political association. As I have also argued, it is much less clear why the goal of promoting the good justifies political activity in the *Republic*.

On this account, other-regarding concern is non-relationally good because it is an appropriate response to non-relational value. This, along with certain claims about the nature of reason and human nature, allows us to see the value of other-regarding concern to the person herself. Promoting the good as the basic form of other-regarding concern and ethical activity is not sharply cut-off from the value of contemplation. The value of promoting the good lies not simply in the amount of good produced and thus not simply in the causal powers of the action. Promotion of the good is an activity that, in order to be valuable, must display an intelligent appreciation, although not necessarily a philosophical understanding, of the value promoted. I have argued, especially in Chapter 2, that Plato does expect a virtuous person's promotion of the good in Magnesia to include an intelligent appreciation of the value at stake. I shall not rehearse those arguments here, but they can now be supplemented, in a significant way, by certain aspects of Plato's eschatology. I shall turn to this in the next and final section of this chapter.

But before doing so, we need to return to the topic of impartiality and, specifically, to the question of what sort of impartiality is required by this account of the place and value of other-regarding concern. A commitment to promoting non-relational value or the well-being of others as a non-instrumental end does not entail any particular interpretation of impartiality. To begin, there are several kinds of impartiality that are inconsistent with eudaimonism. First, one might simply abandon the notion of something being good *for* a person.[169] One could simply evaluate courses of action in terms of how well they promote non-relational value and require all agents to pursue the course that best promotes non-relational value. Or one could retain the notion of the good of an individual, but require all agents to give equal weight to their own good and the good of each other person. But if these were the only ways in which a direct concern for value could be made part of a virtuous person's motivation, we might well think that it was a mistake to see Plato as making an appeal to such a direct concern.

These are not, however, the only options. For example, we might evaluate outcomes in terms of how well they promote non-relational value and then identify each person's (greatest) happiness with the outcome that best promotes non-relational value. Similarly, we might start by evaluating outcomes in terms of how well they promote the overall narrow well-being of all individuals, where each individual's narrow well-being excludes the well-being of others. We could then identify each person's greatest happiness with the outcome that best promotes overall narrow well-being. These possibilities show that certain sorts of impartiality or concern with non-relational value or the genuine well-being of others need not be inconsistent with eudaimonism.

Nevertheless, both of these options make far greater demands on the virtuous agent than Plato does and they threaten to trivialize the reconciliation of eudaimonism with other-regarding concern. But it is important to see that Plato is not committed to either of these options by the interpretation that I have sketched. Both of these options rely, for example, on a very strong and controversial assumption about the aggregation of value and the connection it has to the notion of justice or virtue. Roughly, both assume that (a) courses of action can be ranked or evaluated by principles that give equal weight to the good of each person or to each instance of non-relational value, and (b) justice or virtue requires the agent to promote in the appropriate way the best overall course of action.

There are, however, a number of other ways of embodying a notion of impartiality within a conception of justice or virtue. And many such conceptions can allow that a virtuous person has some special concern with his own actions, well-being, or commitments.[170] Nevertheless, we might think that Plato must be committed to a very strong conception of impartiality and, in particular, something more like the simple aggregative principle. First, as we have seen, Plato shows some commitment to what seem to be aggregative principles in specifying the goal of law and in describing god's attitude toward the universe, and individuals are required to obey the law and are invited to share god's perspective. Second, we considered above an argument for a tight connection between reason and the equal promotion of value wherever it occurs, that is, one that holds that for a rational moral agent, because he is identical with reason, there is 'not a fundamental difference between the self and others as possible objects of his action . . . it would be *irrational* to differentiate [between them]'.[171]

Neither line of thought, however, seems decisive. First, Plato's statement of the goal aimed at by law and by god with respect to the universe is not precise enough to commit him to the distinctively strong position held, e.g., by modern consequentialists. Nothing in the relevant passages suggests, for example, that Plato intends to rule out agents' special responsibility for what they do as opposed to what they allow. And a coincidence between individual and overall well-being does not entail that each individual must be impartial between his own good and that of all others. The second point raises deeper issues. Since it is not obvious that prudence is less fundamental a principle of practical rationality than benevolence, the mere fact of our identity with reason would not entail that we are required to give something like equal weight to the promotion of every person's well-being or every instance of non-relational value. We must further fill out the conception of reason that this objection suggests to see why the argument fails.

But to begin we must also note that our identity with reason is not the only metaphysical fact relevant to determining what our good is. Even if each of us is reason, individual souls retain distinct identities and Plato seems to think that this is relevant to understanding their good. Consider, again, the passage from Book 10's theology.

He who supervises everything has put all things together with a view to the salvation and virtue of the whole, and each part suffers and does what befits it, insofar as it can . . . For every doctor and every true craftsman does everything for the sake of the whole, creating a part which strives for what is best in common, for the sake of the whole, and not the whole for the sake of the part. But you complain, ignorant of how what is best in your case for the whole turns out to be best for you as well, by the power of common generation.   (*Laws* 903B4–D3)

In this passage, Plato distinguishes two distinct perspectives from which we can evaluate what happens in the world—that of my own individual good and that of the good of the whole—and claims that there is a coincidence between them. But he does not suggest that the point of view of the individual is somehow illusory or unreal; rather, Plato stresses the soul's retention of its own identity. Moreover, it is not simply the case that souls remain individual particulars, but they are particulars that have a perspective or point of view from which each can evaluate the world.

This fact about the irreducibility of the individual's perspective has often been taken to legitimate the rationality of a special concern for oneself. Consider the famous example of Sidgwick.

It would be contrary to Common Sense to deny that the distinction between any one individual and any other is real and fundamental, and that consequently 'I' am concerned with the quality of my existence as an individual in a sense, fundamentally important, in which I am not concerned with the quality of the existence of other individuals: and this being so, I do not see how it can be proved that this distinction is not to be taken as fundamental in determining the ultimate end of rational action for an individual.[172]

Plato never offers an argument justifying rational eudaimonism, but perhaps the closest he comes to it is in the above passage from Book 10 of the *Laws* which, I think, suggests an intuition similar to Sidgwick's. Even if this is right, it does not yet give any determinate content to the notion of the individual's good. But in light of the actual demands that Plato places on virtuous agents, it is plausible to see Plato taking a second step in accommodating the individual's perspective. Plato can consistently hold that the promotion of the genuine well-being of others is an important constituent of my own good, while allowing that I can give a certain priority to other aspects of my own good.

This should seem intuitively plausible if we consider the following case. Suppose that fairly early on in life, before I made much progress in attaining the sort of rational understanding that is part of virtue, I were reliably informed that by abandoning further education and serving as a chattel slave, I could provide the resources necessary for developing at least two people in far-off Mysia whose virtue would be equal to what I could attain.[173] This is a far greater sacrifice than that which Plato demands of the philosopher rulers in the *Republic*. Both intuitively, and insofar as we draw on passages in the *Laws* that stress that the individual must give the highest priority to the good condition of his own soul, it seems that Plato would hold that I am not required to make such a sacrifice and that insofar as I am rational, I should pursue my own greater perfection.[174] If this is right, then we might also try to explain some of the ways in which the ethical demands upon Magnesians fall short of strong conceptions of impartiality, such as the consequentialist aggregation model, by a similar strategy. Plato may accept that rationality requires a person to have a special concern with his own actions and perfection.[175]

We can now return to Broadie's claims about practical reason in Plato. She argues that as a person's theoretical reason in a 'purely theoretical consideration' of the soul would not take his own soul as an object of inquiry just because it is his own, so a person's practical reason will not seek to promote his own good just because it is his, but will instead promote each individual's good equally.[176] I do not, however, think that this argument is successful. Plato, unlike perhaps Aristotle, does not distinguish a special faculty that is responsible for theoretical reasoning, but is not concerned with particulars and never prompts to action. Reason insofar as it is engaged with first principles is already practical in that it is my seeking to attain and exercise understanding myself. It is an exercise of a capacity of mine that is inherently directed toward my own perfection as a rational creature. In an analogous way, the good exercise of my reason in action involves the promotion of the good based on an appreciation of principles of order and value. As such, it is inherently directed toward my perfection as a rational creature whose responsiveness to the good is an expression of its own powers. Thus in being responsive to the good, I shall love good wherever it occurs, but I cannot see my own efforts to promote it as simply the exercise of a causal power to bring about the good that is made valuable by its product. And insofar as I see my love of the good and promotion of it as the expression of my own essential nature, it is reasonable to give my own perfection a certain priority.

Such an account gives us, very roughly, some outline of the ways in which the promotion of non-relational value or of the well-being of others is restricted in the goals of a virtuous Platonic agent. So how much conflict does this suggest that there can be between my own happiness rationally pursued and the impartial promotion of the well-being of rational agents or non-relational value wherever it occurs? First, this view allows for substantial weight to be given to others' well-being and the promotion of non-relational value within one's own happiness. The example, if persuasive, suggests that huge sacrifices of one's well-being narrowly construed—especially large sacrifices in the good condition of one's own soul—may not be justified by the greater overall benefit. But this does not suggest that a sacrifice in one's well-being narrowly construed can never be outweighed by the components of one's happiness concerned with others. Second, the most important sorts of goods for Plato are not essentially competitive, unlike, for example, the goal of being the richest person in the city. Acting so as to increase my virtue or my rational understanding of the world need not conflict with promoting the virtue of others or their rational understanding of the world. Indeed, it will usually be the case that I can best promote these goals by joining in a cooperative association in which all members aim at fostering the virtue and understanding of all.

Third, Plato need not try to justify as rational or optimal the weight assigned to other-regarding concern by common sense or even by well-educated and reasonably virtuous common sense. In the *Laws*, Plato repeatedly insists that human beings, almost inevitably, are overly partial to their own good and that of those near to them. This is, for example, what makes holding property in common impractical. And holding property in common is much less demanding than giving equal weight to the happiness of every citizen. And, in turn, this is much weaker than the demand to show equal concern for all rational creatures.

Finally, as we have seen, the theology of Book 10 assures us that there is a coincidence between what is best for the individual in the long run and what is best for the whole in the long run. Such a claim is important insofar as it helps to provide assurance about one's ethical direction. As we have seen, Plato thinks that human beings are, almost inevitably, too partial to their own interests and the interests of those near to them. They are too partial in that more other-regarding concern would be more virtuous and thus better for the individual. So expanding the degree or range of one's other-regarding concern would be better for individuals and, for human beings, it will almost always be possible to do more. Plato's theology assures us that there is no inevitable conflict between my best state (which should be considerably different from the way that I am now living) and the best states of other people.

5.9 Transpolitical End

In this final section, I would like to return to two concerns raised earlier. First, our explanation of the Dependency Thesis and of the value of other-regarding concern requires that the virtuous agent have an intelligent, though not necessarily philosophical, appreciation of the values at stake. Although I have argued that Plato aims at fostering such an intelligent appreciation in as many of Magnesia's citizens as possible, there is another perspective from which to evaluate Magnesia's success in doing so.

Second, on the interpretation developed of the value of political activity as an expression of virtue, Magnesia may still seem to come off relatively badly in comparison with Aristotle's ideal city. Plato, we might think, fails to take seriously enough the idea that political activity is good for the person and thus unduly restricts it. The detail and fixity of the law code and the ways in which significant political initiative is shifted to a highly educated elite do not take sufficient account of the possibility that most citizens would benefit from a more active political role. Similarly, Plato overvalues assuring the stability of most citizens' true ethical beliefs and does not give sufficient weight, even on his own principles, to their coming to grasp for themselves the reasons for their beliefs. I have already considered how far these charges are true and some of the reasons for Plato's reluctance to go as far as we might think that he should.

What is most important, however, is that this evaluation of Magnesia omits an essential part of Plato's own understanding of his project. Unless we put the political community itself in the proper context for Plato we shall, I think, inevitably tend to find the political theory of the *Laws* of interest for the way in which it partially anticipates Aristotle, but lament its backsliding into the elitism of the middle period. To better see Plato's own understanding of his project, we must turn to the status of the political community itself. For Aristotle, human beings are political animals in a strong sense. It is natural for them to live together with other humans and engage in complex cooperative activities with each other that include governing the community rightly. It is only in city life that human beings can find the full realization or completion of their nature. The best state affords to as many of its genuine members as possible the locus for the only sort of good life of which human beings are capable. If the best life is at least in part essentially constituted by practical activity in accordance with the virtues of character, the city is required for the full expression of human happiness. And even if the best life is solely contemplative, our lives must begin and end within a city. Humans are born to live and to pass out of existence in a city and it is the only venue in which their nature can be realized: we have no other lives. This simply is not true for Plato. Plato accepts the immortality of the soul and for him the ultimate goal of each human being is transpolitical. Eschatology is an essential part of Plato's vision of human life in the *Phaedo*, the *Republic*, and the *Laws*, and it is an essential part of his understanding of the nature and purpose of political communities.

One of the most striking and significant features of the eschatology of the *Phaedo* and the *Republic* is the destiny of non-philosophic souls. In the *Phaedo*, Plato seems to present two accounts of the soul's afterlife: one that involves reincarnation and one that involves a final judgment. The differences between the two accounts are not, fortunately, relevant to the questions that concern us. Early in the *Phaedo*, Plato draws a stark contrast between the post-mortem fates of philosophers and non-philosophers: '[W]hoever arrives in the underworld unadmitted to the rites and uninitiated, will wallow in the mud, while he who arrives there purified and initiated will dwell with the gods' (*Phd.* 69C5–7). The only people who have been purified and initiated are those 'who have practiced philosophy in the right way' (*Phd.* 69D2–3). Wallowing in the mud, although metaphorical, is clearly a miserable condition, but it is the only fate open to those who have not actually engaged in philosophy correctly.

Later in the *Phaedo*, Plato suggests, instead of the apparent final judgment of this passage, a series of reincarnations. Non-philosophers who lack any sort of virtue will be reincarnated as the appropriate kind of non-human animal. Gluttons will come back as donkeys, the unjust and tyrannic as wolves, hawks, and kites. But Plato also tells us what happens to those who possess non-philosophical virtue.

Are not the happiest even of these [i.e. non-philosophers], and the ones going to the best place, those who have practiced popular and political virtue which they call 'moderation' and 'justice', and which was developed by habit and training, without philosophy or reason? . . . [They are the happiest] because it is likely that they will go back into a political and tame race, either, I imagine, that of bees or wasps or ants, or back again into the very same one, the human race, and that respectable men are born from them . . . But no one may rightly join the company of the gods who has not practiced philosophy and is not completely pure when he departs from life, no one but the lover of learning.   (*Phd.* 82A10–82C1)

As I argued in the first chapter, even on this view in which a final judgment is replaced by a series of reincarnations, there is no possibility of significant improvement for non-philosophers in the afterlife. The best and happiest of non-philosophers live out their lives and then undergo a cycle of transmigrations into the lives of political and tame animals or perhaps, go back again into a 'respectable' human life which Plato treats on an equal footing with the non-human incarnations. But none of these is a life that is worth living for a human being. A genuinely choiceworthy life comes only with philosophy.

In the *Republic*, the eschatological myth is more complex, but the message is much the same. The myth of Er which closes the *Republic* is again committed to reincarnation. After death, souls are judged and then sent through the heavens or under the earth for a period of 1,000 years. All souls that are not incurably bad then make a choice of their next life.

[T]he one who came up first chose the greatest tyranny. In his folly and greed, he chose it without adequate examination and did not notice that, among other evils, he was fated to eat his own children as part of it. When he examined at leisure the life he had chosen, however, he beat his breast and bemoaned his choice. And, ignoring the warning of the Speaker, he blamed chance, daimons, or guardian spirits, and everything else for these evils but himself. He was one of those who came down from heaven, having lived his previous life under an orderly constitution, where he had participated in virtue through habit and without philosophy. Indeed, so to speak, most of those who were caught out in this way were souls who had come down from heaven and were untrained in suffering as a result . . . Because of this and because of the chance of the lottery, there was an interchange of good and evil for most of the souls. If, however, someone pursues philosophy in a sound manner when he comes to live here on earth and if the lottery does not make him one of the last to choose, then . . . it looks as though not only will he be happy here, but his journey from here to there and back again will not be along the rough underground path, but along the smooth heavenly one.   (*Rep.* 619B7–E5)

As I argued in Chapter 1, what this eschatological myth shows is that non-philosophical virtue is not of long-run benefit to its possessor. Habitual virtue does not enable people to make good choices of their next life. Their choice of lives reflects their ethical character and conception of the good and it is because habitual virtue failed to give them any significant appreciation of what is genuinely valuable that they go wrong. Non-philosophical virtue at its best again fails to bring about a good ethical character and, most importantly from the perspective of the myth, does not bring with it ethical progress (or entitlement to such progress) in the afterlife.[177]

In the eschatology of the two great middle-period dialogues, the *Phaedo* and the *Republic*, the fate of non-philosophers reveals the real nature of their lives here and now. Non-philosophers' lives are lived without an apprehension of genuine reality and value. Thus they fail to have good lives and will make significant and enduring progress only by turning to philosophy.

In some of the dialogues following the *Phaedo* and the *Republic*, we find important changes in Plato's eschatology and, especially, in the destiny of non-philosophers. To begin, consider the account of non-philosophers in the *Phaedrus* argued for in Chapter 4. There we saw that Recollection played a significant role in the cognitive development of human beings quite generally. For example, the second-best sort of lovers, who lead a life without philosophy, nevertheless have begun to recollect (in the language of the *Phaedrus*' myth, the wings of their souls have begun to grow). This fact is crucial to their post-mortem fate.

In death they are wingless when they leave the body, but their wings are bursting to sprout, so the prize they have won from the madness of love is considerable, because those who have begun the journey in lower heaven may not by law be sent into darkness for the journey under the earth; their lives are bright and happy as they travel together, and thanks to their love they will grow wings together when the time comes.   (*Phdr.* 256D3–E2)

So according to the *Phaedrus*, the progress that non-philosophers make in this life without turning to philosophy makes their next life better. We may think that Plato exaggerates his optimism in claiming that such progress is inevitable, but we have good reason to see the claim that progress has been made as seriously meant. Some non-philosophers, who have not begun philosophizing, have made genuine and crucial epistemic and thus ethical progress: they have begun to recollect some very important Forms concerned with value, especially the Form of Beauty or the Fine. It is their cognitive progress in this life that entitles them to further progress in the next: their reward is future progress in recollection. This is a decisive break with the *Phaedo* and the *Republic*.

The *Laws* also offers an eschatology. In the course of Book 10's exposition of Magnesia's theology, we find the following passage in the Athenian's defense of the claim that the gods care for human affairs.

He who supervises everything has put all things together with a view to the salvation and virtue of the whole, and each part suffers and does what befits it, insofar as it can . . . Now since soul is always put together with body, sometimes with one, sometimes with another, and undergoes all sorts of transformations . . . no other task is left for [god] except that of transferring the disposition that has become better to a better place, and the worse to a worse place, according to what befits each of them, so that it obtains the appropriate fate . . . Since our king saw that all actions are involved with souls, and that there is much virtue in them, though much vice . . . and since he understood that whatever is good in soul is always beneficial in nature, while the bad is harmful; since he saw all these things, he presumably contrived the situation of each part so that in the whole, virtue would very much triumph, and vice meet defeat, in the easiest and best way. For the sake of the whole he has, in fact, contrived it so that when a certain sort of thing comes into being it must always take a certain place, and then dwell in certain regions. And he has assigned to the wishes of each of us the responsibility for what sort of person comes into being: the way one desires and the character of one's soul just about determines each time, what every one of us, for the most part, becomes . . . So all things that partake of soul are transformed, possessing within themselves the cause of the transformation, and, undergoing transformation, are moved according to the order and law of destiny. For smaller and lesser transformations of dispositions there is lateral movement, when the transformations are greater and more unjust, there is a fall into the depths and the places said to be below, to which people in their fear give the name 'Hades' . . . But when a soul's own wishing and familiarity with others have become strong, and as a result it obtains a large share of vice or virtue—then, when by mingling with a divine virtue it comes to be such in an exceptional degree, it undergoes an especially great transformation in locale and is borne along a hallowed path to some other, better place. And when the opposite things occur, it transfers its own life to the opposite sorts of places . . . He who becomes worse is transported among the worse souls, while he who becomes better is transported among the better, and in life and in every death, suffers and does the things that are appropriate for similars to do to similars.   (*Laws* 903B4–905A1)

The citizen's life lived within the city is thus only a small part of the continuing life of the soul. As in the *Phaedrus*, the process that Plato envisages is one of gradual improvement: better souls move to better lives or places and in doing so their progress in virtue is facilitated.[178] While such progress in virtue need not only be an increase in knowledge, epistemic progress will be part of the improvement: one of the main benefits of associating with good people is the benefit of conversing with and learning from them (*Laws* 728B2–C2).

But what is especially important for us is that this theology allows us to better understand the place of a good political community in human life. Political activity is not simply an instrumental means to further progress in virtue, but neither is a good city the highest venue for virtuous activity. (This may reduce, at least in comparison with Aristotle, the dignity of political activity and the political community.) All virtuous souls are on a path that in the best case will lead them to a life outside the city that involves some form of enriched intellectual understanding (and may also involve expressing this understanding in other-regarding concern: just souls, along with the gods and *daimons* as allies, participate in the effort to bring about the good in the whole universe (*Laws* 906A2–B3)). In light of this goal, the tight restrictions that Plato places on the citizens' lives in Magnesia can be seen to foster ultimate intellectual growth rather than to retard it. The great danger in life is that of sinking down—a failure in virtue results in one's next reincarnation being in a worse place that reduces one's chances of further improvement. In this case, there is a great incentive to keep citizens from going astray. Small progress in this life, for example, some grasp of basic ethical principles, even if quite imperfect, will entitle one to (and enable one to make) further progress. The fear that restrictions on the lives of citizens in Magnesia treats them as merely children, although misplaced, points to an important truth. The education of citizens involves more than teaching them that certain things must be done. They will also receive reasons. But safeguarding them from error and preferring solid progress to risk is justifiable in the hope of their eventually attaining greater rationality. Aristotle, for instance, reconciles citizens' need to rule and be ruled in turn with the permanent rule of adults over non-adults by the fact that non-adults will eventually grow up and take their turn in ruling: being ruled is a necessary stage in coming to be capable of ruling. We can see Plato as having a temporally extended version of this: those with less developed reason in this reincarnation may develop more fully in the coming series of reincarnations. Their tutelage is not a permanent condition and it is not the best that they are capable of. The sort of virtuous life in the city that is open to non-philosophically virtuous citizens in Magnesia is both a genuine expression of rationality and an essential stage in further rational progress.

Insofar as many citizens, both men and women, can come to make such progress, Plato is far more optimistic than Aristotle about the capacity of human beings to attain a good and flourishing state of soul. What Magnesia offers to its citizens is the possibility that non-philosophers—even while remaining non-philosophers—can lead virtuous lives and can make the sort of progress that entitles them to the opportunity of increased happiness.

Notes

Chapter 1 Philosophers and Non-philosophers in the *Phaedo* and the *Republic*

1. The Xenocrates quotation is fragment 3 Heinze and the translation is adapted from Guthrie (1987, vol. 5, p. 482). The reference to compulsion is justified by the parallels from Cicero and Servius. Cf. Isnardi Parente (1982, ad loc.). A similar view is ascribed by Diogenes Laertius to Aristotle (D.L. 5.20). We may think the attribution is unreliable, but that Diogenes found it unsurprising to attribute this to Aristotle tells us something about the currency of such views. The *Protrepticus* quotation is from Ross 13, Düring B46–51 and the translation is adapted from Barnes (1985). The Plotinus quotation is from *Ennead* I. 2. 6–7; I quote, with slight modification, A. H. Armstrong's (1966–88) translation. Controversy surrounds the authenticity of the *Protrepticus* fragments, but the general consensus is in favor of accepting most of the ones in Iamblichus, including those cited. For further discussion, see Düring (1961). For the claim that the philosopher alone is happy, see Ross 4, Düring B8–9; Ross 6, Düring B41, B59–70; Ross 10c, Düring B108–110, and Düring (1961, pp. 15, 32). On Aristotle on non-philosophers in the *Eudemian Ethics*, see Rowe (1971, p. 71 n. 3).

2. Schneewind (1998, p. 4).

3. Schneewind (1998, p. 4).

4. I am simplifying by taking Aquinas to represent the medieval tradition; for a more nuanced treatment, see R. Wood (1997). See Aquinas, *Summa Theologica* 1a.2ae.Q.94 and 2a.2ae.Q.2 and 6. For a start on Aquinas' views, see Davies (1992, pp. 274–96), Fairweather (1954, pp. 21–33), Luscombe (1996), and Potts (1996). I am deeply indebted to Hester Gelber and Rega Wood for their help on this topic.

5. On the relation of civic virtue to happiness and the higher grades of virtue, see Bussanich (1990, especially p. 181) and Dillon (1996a). For the later development of these ideas in Neoplatonism, see Dillon (1990, chs. 14 and 18), (1996b, p. 366), and Wildberg (forthcoming).

6. Translations of the *Phaedo* draw on Gallop (1975), Grube in Cooper (1997), Hackforth (1972a), and Rowe (1993). Translations of the *Laws* draw on Bury (1926) and Pangle (1980); translations of the *Republic* draw on Bloom (1968), Grube revised by Reeve in Cooper (1997), and Shorey (1978).

7. πᾶσαν at *Laws* 739C1 is qualified by ὅτι μάλιστα, but this passage clearly envisages communism, perhaps of differing degrees of stringency, throughout the whole city (e.g. *Laws* 739E–740A suggests that this would include farming in common). Plato's ranking here is: in first place, full communism throughout the entire citizen body; in second place, the constitution of Magnesia that they are now describing (*Laws* 739E, 807B, and 875D); in third place, constitutions approximating the second best one in less favorable circumstances. (See Barker (1960, pp. 370–1 n. 2) against Ritter.) The point that this is not the ideal of the *Republic* was rightly noted long ago by Natorp and recently re-emphasized by André Laks. Barker's (1960, p. 251 n. 1, pp. 370–1 n. 1) only reason for rejecting what he agrees is the clear meaning of the text is that he cannot accept that Plato could have a higher ideal than the *Republic*.

8. Issues of Platonic chronology are once again becoming controversial (e.g., Annas (1999) and Kahn (1996)). For my purposes, I do not need to take a position on the chronological and doctrinal relations between the 'Socratic' or 'early' dialogues and the 'middle-period' dialogues. What I am arguing is that there are significant differences between the *Phaedo* and the *Republic* on the one hand, and the *Laws*, the *Philebus*, the *Statesman*, and the *Timaeus* on the other. I argue that the *Phaedrus* and the *Theaetetus* are more similar to each other than they are to the *Phaedo* and the *Republic* on some important issues in psychology and epistemology and that the epistemological and psychological claims of the *Phaedrus* and, especially the *Theaetetus*, help support the views of the *Laws*, the *Philebus*, the *Statesman*, and the *Timaeus*.

With respect to the *Laws*, we have Aristotle's testimony that the *Laws* is later than the *Republic* (*Pol.* 2.6) and a report in Diogenes Laertius (3.37) that the *Laws* was unfinished at the time of Plato's death. For further discussion of the *Laws'* date, see Guthrie (1987, vol. 5, pp. 321–3), Saunders (1970), Schöpsdau (1994, pp. 135–8), and Stalley (1983, pp. 2–4). As Charles Kahn—who, among contemporary leading Anglo-American scholars, is one of those most sympathetic to a more unitarian view of Plato—has effectively argued, the consensus of many stylometric investigations over the past century confirms (subject to whatever methodological concerns one might have about stylometry itself) that the six dialogues—*Critias, Laws, Philebus, Sophist, Statesman,* and *Timaeus*—form a stylistic group that differs significantly from the other dialogues. A group of four—*Parmenides, Phaedrus, Republic,* and *Theaetetus*—are stylistically similar to each other and are closer to the late group of six than they are to the remaining dialogues. Most scholars taking other considerations into account go further than this with regard to dating. Even Kahn (1996, pp. 47–8) finds it reasonable to date the *Phaedo* and the *Symposium* closely together shortly before the *Republic* and to date the *Phaedrus* and the

Theaetetus in that order between the *Republic* and the late group of six. Leaving aside the question of the relative chronological order of the *Phaedo* and the *Symposium*, the following scholars (in addition to Kahn) accept that these two dialogues precede the *Republic* and that the *Phaedrus* and the *Theaetetus* occur in that order between the *Republic* and the late group of six: Guthrie (1987, vol. 4, pp. 50–1), Kraut in Kraut (1992, pp. 46 n. 57, 47 n. 61), Ross (1953, p. 10), and Vlastos (1991, pp. 46–7). Brandwood (1976, p. xvii) and Ledger (1989, pp. 224–5) accept this order, except for placing the *Theaetetus* just before the *Phaedrus*. For further discussion of the *Phaedrus'* date, see de Vries (1969, pp. 7–11), Nussbaum (1986, pp. 465 n. 7, 470–1 n. 5), and Rowe (1986b, pp. 13–4). For more general recent discussions of stylometry, see also Brandwood (1990), Brandwood in Kraut (1992, pp. 90–120), Fine (1988a), Keyser (1991), (1992), Nails (1992), T. Robinson (1992), and Young (1994).

The main thrust of my argument is that the *Phaedo* and the *Republic* are more similar to each other on the ethical, epistemological, and psychological issues I discuss than they are to the group formed by the *Laws*, *Phaedrus*, *Philebus*, *Statesman*, *Theaetetus*, and *Timaeus*. For the most part, I do not need to take a position on the chronology within these two groups. My claims about the content of particular dialogues are argued for on their own merits and do not depend on a specific chronological order.

9. The argument distinguishing Forms from sensibles is at *Phd.* 74B4–C6. The *Meno* introduces the idea of knowledge gained by Recollection, but, unlike the *Phaedo*, it neither contrasts such knowledge with sense-perception, nor claims that the objects of Recollection are Forms. Indeed, the *Meno* makes no explicit mention of Forms at all. The *Phaedo* asserts that Forms are not grasped by the senses (65D9–10), but by reasoning (65C2–3, 66A1) or thought (65E2–5); cf. 79A1–4. As Kahn (1996, p. 352) rightly notes, this is an advance on the *Symposium* which does not name the faculty of non-sensory apprehension. *Phaedo* 84A9 asserts that Forms are not the objects of opinion (ἀδόξαστον) and implies that sensibles are, cf. 80B3–5. (I shall use 'sensible' to apply to both sensible properties and sensible particulars; I shall distinguish between these only when it seems important to do so.) The *Phaedo* does not make explicit exactly what this contrast comes to and I discuss the issue more fully below in the context of the *Republic's* contrast between knowledge and perception.

10. Sense-perception is necessary for the Recollection of Forms. But Recollection provides a mechanism, distinct from perception, for the acquisition, or active exercise, of certain concepts, beliefs, or knowledge. When people recollect the Form of Equal, they acquire or activate a conception of what equality is. (For more discussion, see Section 4.2.) What is central to Plato's notion of Recollection

is that this conception of equality is neither directly given by a perception (or its content) nor is it built up from the contents of perception (e.g. by abstraction, comparison, or compounding). For excellent modern discussions, see Cowie (1999, pp. 3–32) and Fodor (1981, pp. 257–316). It is plausible that the relation between perception and Recollection is a causal one (the perception 'triggers' the Recollection), but what is most important is that perception neither directly provides the content of concepts recollected nor can one acquire these concepts by various operations (which do not themselves involve concepts acquired by the Recollection of Forms) on the contents of perception.

11. At *Phd.* 68c5–6, Plato, speaking of the ordinary conceptions of these virtues, says that courage 'especially' belongs to philosophers; at 68c8–12 he says that only philosophers have moderation. But as Rowe (1993, p. 147) rightly notes, Plato treats the courage and the moderation of non-philosophers in exactly the same way: both are 'absurd' (*atopos*). Plato here simply appeals to the intuition that one cannot be courageous because of fear or moderate because of immoderation, but these conclusions may rely on the principles later enunciated for adequate explanations (*Phd.* 95E–99D, 100C–103C), see Gallop (1975, pp. 98–102), Gosling and Taylor (1984, pp. 88–91), and Rowe (1993, pp. 147–8). One might think that if honor-lovers sacrifice some pleasures for honor, they should have 'so-called' moderation. But Plato seems either to think that (i) they are acting for the pleasure of honor (*Phd.* 69A1–3), or that (ii) even if they are not acting for the sake of pleasure, the fact that they are acting for the sake of bodily goods makes them immoderate (perhaps because their desire for honor masters or rules them without their engaging in rational deliberation).

12. On the translation, see Rowe (1993 ad loc.).

13. Neither (i) nor (ii), nor anything else in the *Phaedo*, entails that wisdom is the only proper object of pursuit. For further discussion, see Irwin (1977b, pp. 160–4) and Rowe (1993, ad loc.). The passage at *Phd.* 69A–c has sparked a literature, e.g., Gooch (1974), Gosling and Taylor (1984, pp. 87–95), Luce (1944), and Weiss (1987), (1989).

14. I draw on Irwin (1977b, p. 255), although Irwin's original account would, I think unintuitively, count the ultimate end of creating great art for its own sake as solipsistic. I shall ignore distinctions between states and activities and between other people honoring you and your thinking that others honor you.

15. There is a textual difficulty at 82B7. If we read καί (Burnet) rather than ἤ καί (Duke et al.), then we should translate as 'and then back again into the very same one, the human race . . .' . Fortunately, it does not matter much which we read. Even if we think that coming back into the human race is a distinct option that excludes going into the race of bees, wasps, or ants (and is not a further

reincarnation after that as one of these three political creatures), this is just another option that Plato puts on the same level as the other three. There is no hint that there is a special class within those who practiced popular and political virtue who get a vastly better reincarnation, i.e. as respectable men, cf. Rowe (1993, ad loc.). All of the reincarnated souls are 'not at all the souls of the good, but of the worthless [τῶν φαύλων]' (*Phd.* 81D6–7). In either case, the message is the same: these souls either migrate from human to non-human lives and back again without there being much difference between these reincarnations, or it makes little difference which of the four classes the souls go into in their first reincarnation.

16. The 'popular and political virtue' of *Phd.* 82A12–B1 seems to be a type of the slavish virtue (which is merely a façade of virtue) attributed to non-philosophers at 69B7–8. (1) The 'wrong exchange' for virtue mentioned at 69A6 is sufficient for slavish virtue and this is the exchange that all non-philosophers make (68D2–69A4). (2) 82C6–8 seems to describe all those who undergo the transmigrations of 81E–82B as lovers of wealth or honor and this is sufficient for slavish virtue (68C1 ff.). (3) The only people who undergo the transmigrations described at 81E–82B are those who do not have 'good' souls, but rather 'worthless' souls (81D6–7).

17. For a defense of attributing psychological eudaimonism to Plato in these dialogues, see Irwin (1995a, pp. 52–64). I assume in this paragraph that Plato accepts a maximizing form of psychological eudaimonism, since this provides a greater challenge to the possibility of non-instrumental, other-regarding concern. For fine discussions of the general nature of Platonic ethics, see Moravcsik (1980), (1986).

18. The *Phaedo*'s apparent acceptance of possible conflict between the desires of the soul and those of the body (e.g. 68C8–12 and 82C2–6) might allow for akrasia, but Plato does not explicitly recognize it here. Even if the *Phaedo* were to allow for akrasia, there is no reason to think that it holds that all other-regarding concern is akratic.

19. See Ackrill (1980, pp. 18–20), Irwin (1995a, pp. 65–7), and Vlastos (1991, pp. 203–9). For further discussion of the notion of 'parts' of happiness, see Section 5.8.

20. On the connection between *Phd.* 69C–D and 'Orphic' views, see Parker (1983, pp. 281–307). On the relations among *Phd.* 69A–E, the transmigration account at 81A–82D, and the closing myth (107C–115A), see Annas (1982c, pp. 125–9) and Dorter (1982, pp. 78–9 and 166–75).

21. Rowe (1993, p. 288) effectively argues that those referred to at *Phd.* 114B6–7 include only philosophers, although Plato distinguishes two subgroups of philosophers; see also Sedley (1991, p. 378).

22. Cf. *Phd.* 66B3–D1, 68E7, and 79C2–8. In these passages, Plato blames the body and its desires and the senses for non-philosophers' failure to grasp the truth and, in particular, for their failure to grasp the truth about what is really worth pursuing. These are reasonable claims for Plato to make if he holds that perception, and not any grasp of Forms, provides the content of non-philosophers' desires.

23. Such emotions and desires might be incorrectly endorsed by a reasoning capacity not doing its proper job or they might move the person to act without cooperation from reason. For reason opposing bodily desires and emotions, see *Phd.* 94B7–E6; the 'right exchange' passage shows that reason can set a person's ends.

24. Cf. Reath (1989, pp. 52–6); I discuss related ideas more fully in Ch. 3. On the first option, the strength or intensity of desire is a principle of evaluation in its own right; on the second option, strength influences, and even may determine, the principle of evaluation without itself being an evaluative criterion.

25. *Rep.* 441B6 uses the same Homeric passage (*Odyssey* 20.17–18) to describe the conflict between the Reasoning part of the soul and one of the soul's lower parts.

26. For the body as subject, see *Phaedo* 66C7–8, 81B2–5, 83D6–7, and 94B7–E1. This view is accepted by Irwin (1989, p. 235 n. 27) and Price (1995, pp. 36–40) argues effectively for this claim. Bostock (1986, pp. 26–7, 131–3) rejects it, but does not, I think, give us reason to think that it is not the *Phaedo*'s view. Rowe (1993, p. 142) is right that Plato does not claim that the body can perceive or desire apart from the soul, but the fact that the presence of the soul is necessary for the body to be alive and exercise its capacities is consistent with the claim that the body is the subject of perceptions and certain desires. The *Phaedo*'s view is not consistent with that of the *Republic* and has certain costs. But in addition to the strong textual evidence for it, we can see why Plato would have found it attractive. The sorts of desires attributed to the body here are not recognized in the Socratic dialogues (with the possible exception of the *Gorgias*). In the *Republic*, Plato explicitly accepts that recognizing their existence requires attributing them to a subject distinct from the subject of rational desires and so partitions the soul into different subjects. We can see the *Phaedo* as a halfway house: it implicitly recognizes that the same subject cannot have both sorts of desires, but finds another subject, the body, for these desires while retaining the unity of the soul.

27. The faculty of non-sensory apprehension that is responsible for a grasp of Forms is attributed to the soul and not the body in the *Phaedo*, cf. n. 10. The body is not immortal and thus, we can infer, is not capable of Recollection. (As we shall see in Ch. 4, the *Phaedrus* explicitly excludes the lower parts of the soul from Recollection.) So the conceptual content of the body's desires cannot be derived from concepts drawn from an awareness of Forms. Thus whatever role we attribute

to the soul in perception, the only plausible resources left for the body are perception and whatever can be built up from it by psychic operations that do not require an awareness of Forms.

28. The *Phaedo* does not explicitly take a position on whether the body can think that something is good, but it gives us no reason to deny this, cf. Irwin (1977b, p. 322 n. 48.) On whether the lower parts of the soul in the *Republic* can think that something is good, see Section 3.3.

29. I accept Scott's (1987) and (1995, pp. 53–73) arguments for the claim that non-philosophers do not engage in Recollection in the *Phaedo*, see also Section 4.2. By the denial that non-philosophers apprehend the Forms, I mean, as a first approximation, that they do not have concepts of them. Nor do they have concepts of the non-sensible value properties, such as fineness, that things have in virtue of standing in the appropriate relation or tie to Forms. (In the *Phaedo*, Recollection is needed for the acquisition or activation of such concepts, at least while the person is embodied.) This may not rule out the possibility that non-philosophers can have beliefs about Forms or other non-sensible items or refer to them.

30. Fine and Irwin have argued persuasively for this interpretation. To begin, see Fine (1993, pp. 167–8) and Irwin (1977a) and (1995b, pp. 264–5). But also relevant is the general context provided by their discussion of the notion of compresence; see Fine (1993) and Irwin (1995a) under 'compresence' in their indices and Fine (1978) and (1990). Both provide references to other discussions. If we reject this interpretation and hold that non-philosophers do not recognize sensible properties, but only sensible particulars, this will not let them avoid the defect I discuss in the text.

31. This claim is intended to be neutral on the proper analysis of non-sensible property possession, cf. n. 77.

32. Cf. n. 88.

33. The only route that Plato recognizes in the *Phaedo* to attaining the appropriate non-sensible content for one's value concepts is Recollection and non-philosophers do not engage in this. Plato is fairly non-committal on what other concepts can be given by perception or built up from it. Counting honor-lovers as lovers of the body would be especially jarring for Plato's audience, since it is a trope from Homer onwards to contrast the mortality of humans with the imperishability of their fame (*kleos*). See, e.g., Redfield (1975, pp. 34–5).

34. The *Euthydemus* and the *Meno* are both usually dated before the *Phaedo*, although recently the *Euthydemus*' date has become controversial. Scholars dating the *Euthydemus* and the *Meno* before the *Phaedo* include: Brandwood (1976, p. xvii), Irwin (1995a, pp. 12, 362 n. 1), Kahn (1996, pp. 47–8), Kraut in Kraut (1992, p. 46 n. 57), and Vlastos (1991, p. 47). Guthrie (1987, vol. 4, p. 50) prefers the order

Meno–Phaedo–Republic–Euthydemus; Ledger (1989, pp. 224–5) prefers the order *Meno–Phaedo–Euthydemus–Republic*. Also see, Hawtrey (1981). I find it more plausible to date both of these dialogues before the *Republic*, but my interpretation does not require a position on this issue.

35. Irwin (1995a, pp. 141–6) and Scott (1995, pp. 38–52) offer good reasons for considerable caution about the benefits of true belief in the *Meno*.

36. For a fine discussion, see Moravcsik (1992, pp. 14–28).

37. This is not to deny, of course, that a person displaying no form of other-regarding concern might be even worse. We may also differ from Plato on issues connected with autonomy. If other-regarding concern is guided by the other's conception of the good, we may be inclined to see such concern as a significant virtue, even if we think that the conception of the good is flawed. But our intuitions will, I think, less clearly support a favorable evaluation, if we think that the conception of the good is radically mistaken or if we see it as formed in conditions very unfavorable to reasonable reflection. This might be true, for example, of women's and minorities' conceptions of the good that have been formed by the internalization of sexist and racist beliefs or by conceptions of the good growing out of various forms of psychological infirmity. Our evaluation will be least favorable when the person showing the other-regarding concern is aware of the defectiveness of the other's conception of the good. But if the conception of the good is sufficiently defective, we may not think that such other-regarding concern is a significant virtue, even if the person displaying it does not recognize (and is not even culpable for failing to recognize) the defect. For further discussion of autonomy, see Section 2.12.

38. Philosophers love and desire wisdom, e.g. *Phd.* 66D7–E4. Wisdom involves grasping, by reasoning and thought (cf. n. 9), the things that are or the Forms (*Phd.* 65D11–66A8). This especially includes what justice, the fine, and the good are (*Phd.* 65D4–7).

39. Weiss (1987, p. 66 n. 39).

40. *Phd.* 66B6–7, D8, E4–5, 67B8–9, 68B3–4. More generally, see *Phd.* 65C5–9 and D11–E5. *Phd.* 74B2 claims that we—presumably Socrates and some other philosophers—know what the equal is. At *Phd.* 76B10–12, Simmias says that after Socrates' death, no one will be able to give an account of the Forms they have been discussing 'as they deserve' (ἀξίως), cf. 118A17. This does not entail that no one but Socrates (i) can give such an account of some of these Forms, or (ii) can give some sort of account of all these Forms. The *Phaedo* does not offer an explicit theory of what it is to give an account of a Form.

41. Fine and Irwin have plausibly argued that we should understand the Form of F in the *Phaedo* as the property F, rather than as a thing *having* the property F, see

Fine (1980) and (1993, pp. 44–65), Irwin (1977a) and (1977b, pp. 132–76); both Fine and Irwin provide ample references to competing interpretations. My argument, however, does not require me to take a position on this issue. See Moravcsik (1992, pp. 271–90) for penetrating criticisms of many attempts to identify Forms with modern conceptions of properties or universals. Non-semantic accounts of universals, such as that of Fine, seem to respond to these worries.

42. The *Phaedo* does not explicitly exclude the possibility that the philosopher's good consists solely in the contemplation of Forms, but neither does it endorse it, cf. n. 13. To see philosophers' good as consisting solely in the contemplation of Forms gives too little weight to the role of Forms as standards and produces needless conflict with the *Symposium* and the *Republic*.

43. See, e.g., *Gorg.* 513E5–514A3, *Laws* 705D3–706A4, 743C5–6, and *Rep.* 420C1–4.

44. Only the philosopher rulers receive the mathematical and philosophical education described in Books 6–7 (cf. *Rep.* 503B4–5); the auxiliaries receive only a musical and gymnastic education. The citizens who receive a mathematical education, but fail to progress further, do not form a functional class within the city. I keep the now common translations for the lower two classes, although 'money-making' is more accurate for χρηματιστικόν than 'producer' and as A.E. Taylor rightly points out (1928, p. 46), ἐπίκουρος has the clear connotation of a professional police and soldier force rather than the blander 'auxiliary'. Indeed, Plato's most common word for the second class is not ἐπίκουρος, but πολεμικός ('warrior'), and στρατιώτης ('soldier') is also quite common (note the easy interchange of ἐπίκουρος and στρατιώτης at *Rep.* 414B5 and 414D3). Similarly, φύλακες, a general term for the class that defends the city (a few of whose members go on to become philosopher rulers or φύλακες in the most precise sense, *Rep.* 503B5) is too blandly translated as 'guardians'. The choice of φύλακες stresses the police and military functions that these people have in defending the city against enemies both internal and external; Burnyeat's (1999, p. 257 n. 3) 'the Guards' is more apt. For more optimistic views of the auxiliaries, see Gill (1985), (1996, pp. 240–320), and Kamtekar (1998).

45. For present purposes, it does not matter whether we say that the Reasoning part is wise or that people are wise in virtue of their Reasoning part's possession of knowledge. On the necessity of knowledge for the other virtues, see Cooper (1999, pp. 107–14, 139–40) and Irwin (1995a, pp. 223–36). Note also that *tauta* (pointing back) at *Rep.* 442C6 helps show that courage requires knowledge. Allowing someone to possess one of the other virtues without possessing wisdom would violate the Reciprocity of the Virtues (the claim that each virtue requires all the others), see Annas (1999, pp. 120–36) and Cooper (1999, pp. 76–117).

46. We should understand *epistēmē*, in the definition of wisdom at *Rep.* 442C6, in the strict sense in which it contrasts with 'true belief' (*orthē doxa*): (1) Plato has used 'true belief', e.g., at 430B2 where *epistēmē* in the strict sense would be inappropriate; and (2) a major theme of Books 5–7 is the crucial difference between *epistēmē* and true belief. Moreover, the argument whose conclusion is stated at 580A9 ff. (that the just person is happier than the unjust) depends on the fact that the just person is a philosopher and possesses *epistēmē*, as do the arguments that the just person's life is more pleasant at 581A3 ff. At the end of Book 4, Glaucon claims that their inquiry has settled the question of whether the just person is happier. Although Glaucon does not yet recognize that the definition of justice requires *epistēmē* in the strict sense, we should not assume that this claim applies to those with true belief. Two lines of argument might be thought to support the answer at the end of Book 4 that the just person is better off. (I) If justice is psychic health, we might argue that, like physical health, psychic health is so great a good that no other good could compensate for its loss. Without further explanation of what psychic health consists in, this claim is not obviously compelling (see e.g. Irwin (1995a, pp. 254–61)). But also it would be question-begging to assume that the possession of true belief is sufficient for psychic health. Psychic health might reasonably be thought to be a condition in which each part of the soul does its own job well and a Reasoning part that fails to attain *epistēmē* does not do its job well. (II) Suppose that Plato did accept that a just person is one who possesses true belief (rather than *epistēmē*) about the good and whose two lower parts of the soul are appropriately subordinate to this belief. Thus a just person would always know or have true belief about what is best for him and, since the lower parts of his soul are in the proper order, he would always try to act on this knowledge or belief. From this it comes close to following that a just person, in any given circumstances, would be no worse off than an unjust person in the same circumstances (and would usually be better off). Unjust people, after all, either have false beliefs about what is good or are liable to interference from their own emotions and desires. (I leave aside problem cases, e.g., such as whether the person's having true belief or knowledge about the good is compatible with external frustrations of his plans and actions.) Nevertheless, this is a much weaker conclusion than Plato should want, since the argument depends on the just and unjust person being placed in exactly the same circumstances. The above argument would not show that the just person would even usually be better off if the unjust person's circumstances were more favorable. To show this, Plato will appeal to the value of knowledge.

47. We cannot assume that this education results in such people acting virtuously because they value genuine virtue for its own sake. The failure of beasts and slaves might be that they act only out of fear of punishment. Education might

instill 'higher' motives—acting for the sake of honor or out of a desire to obey the law or because one unreflectively accepts society's standards—while still not resulting in an appropriate grasp of virtue.

48. See Adam (1979, ad loc.), Cooper (1999, p. 140), Görgemanns (1960, pp. 114–29), Irwin (1977b, p. 329 n. 26) and Shorey (1978, ad loc.).

49. Also see Irwin (1977b, p. 330 n. 28).

50. This account of the ends of the parts of the soul goes beyond the characterization of the parts in Book 4, but the two accounts are not inconsistent. We should rather see the Book 9 account as supplementing that in Book 4. On victory or honor as the special object of the Spirited part, see Cooper (1999, pp. 276–7). *Rep.* 581D–E suggests that the desires of the Spirited part and of those people ruled by it are not directed at genuine virtue: why else would they count as either not really pleasures or as barely pleasures? Cairns (1993, pp. 391–2) appears to deny, implausibly, that the auxiliaries have happiness as their ultimate end.

51. Here and elsewhere in quotations from the *Republic*, I have omitted the interlocutor's response when it does not seem to affect the point. On τὰ πρῶτα τριττὰ γένη, see Adam (1979, ad loc.). Plato's point is not that these classes fail to be exhaustive, but rather that they can be further subdivided.

52. *Rep.* 580D3–5 reminds us of 435B ff. (discussed in the text below) which shows that the basic capacities of the parts of the soul are the same whether or not the person is in the just city. The classification of the ends of the parts in Book 9 is not restricted to when the soul is in a defective city (so that the Spirited part of the soul might have higher objects in the just city): note that according to Book 9, loving wisdom is the natural object of the Reasoning part.

53. *Rep.* 581B12–C1 suggests that each person is ruled by exactly one part of the soul. But nothing excludes the possibility that the identity of the ruling part might change over time nor does there seem to be any a priori reason why certain parts might not alternate (or even have different spheres of decision-making). This does not affect the point about the nature of the auxiliaries' goal, since, as I argue in the text, their education does not equip their Reasoning part to play its proper role, even in such restricted ways.

54. Cf. *Rep.* 516E8–517E2 and Irwin (1977b, p. 222). See *Rep.* 484C3–D10: those who have not received a mathematical and philosophical education are 'blind' to the fine, the just, and the good, cf. *Stsmn.* 309C5–D4 and *Laws* 890B3–C8.

55. The justification at *Rep.* 520C–521B for the claim that philosophers alone should rule also suggests that the auxiliaries are primarily motivated by honor. If the philosopher rulers are ruled by the Reasoning part and the third class by the Appetitive part, it would be odd to hold that the auxiliaries are not ruled by the Spirited part. And if they were ruled by the Reasoning part, they would find

the lives that they live very frustrating. Finally, Irwin (1977b, pp. 329–30 n. 26) effectively criticizes Kraut's (1973) interpretation of *Rep.* 590C–591E, see also Irwin (1995a, p. 351).

56. See Hourani (1949), Ober (1998, p. 228), and Reeve (1988, pp. 186–91). See also, *Rep.* 456D–E and 405A–B. At *Rep.* 415A7–B3 Plato suggests that future philosophers might be found among the offspring of the two lower classes. This is consistent with my claim that for Plato in the *Republic* no significant improvement (i.e. one that gives them a life well worth living) is possible in people's lives, unless they receive a philosophic education. There might be offspring of, e.g., producers who are capable of benefiting from such an education, but they will actually have good lives only if they receive it.

57. We can allow for some variety in the objects of the Appetitive part, see Cooper (1999, pp. 126–30). If the third class were capable of valuing virtue for its own sake or motivation by honor, we should expect them to be capable of fighting for the city and sharing in the community of property, women, and children.

58. E.g. *Rep.* 586D ff. and 589A ff. The philosopher knows the pleasures of honors and appetitive satisfactions (starting from, but not limited to, childhood), and these pleasures originate in the lower parts.

59. For reasons to reject such a further entity, see Irwin (1995a, pp. 284–8) and Kahn (1987). But even if there were such a further entity, it would seem limited to choosing among the ends of the three parts. For further discussion, see Section 3.2.

60. For a good account of this argument, see Irwin (1995a, pp. 229–30).

61. Also at *Rep.* 583A8, Plato pairs *polemikos* and *philotimos* in describing the timocrat, cf. n. 44.

62. At *Rep.* 421B3–7, Plato says that their aim in establishing the just city is to bring about the greatest happiness for all the citizens. This does not entail, however, that Plato thinks that all the citizens can be made happy. In this passage itself, Plato leaves it as an open question whether the guardians will be happy in a city that is arranged so as to make the whole city as happy as possible (e.g. 421B–D). And Plato in the *Phaedo* clearly does distinguish between better and worse (or unsatisfactory and worse) lives that non-philosophers can live. He even explicitly picks out a group of non-philosophers who are the 'happiest' of non-philosophers—these are the ones reincarnated as ants or bees rather than as wolves or donkeys (*Phd.* 82A11). But, as I have argued, all non-philosophers in the *Phaedo* have very unsatisfactory lives.

63. Translation adapted from that in Barnes (1985).

64. Cf. *Phd.* 69C6. *Borboros* is very rare in Plato and occurs only in this passage from the *Republic*, *Phd.* 69C6 which describes the afterlife of non-philosophers, and *Phd.* 110A6 where it characterizes the place below the surface of the 'true' earth.

And it is only philosophers whose fate in the afterlife is to be on the surface of the true earth or some yet better place, see Rowe (1993, pp. 288–9).

65. We should not see this passage as committing Plato to the claim that anyone who does not actually possess *nous* about the Form of the Good is dreaming and deserves to sleep forever in Hades. Although Plato sometimes seems to suggest that all knowledge requires knowledge of the Form of the Good, there are reasons to see him as holding, rather, that knowledge of the Form of the Good is required for the best sort of knowledge of anything. He even explicitly sometimes allows the state of mind described in the second highest level of the Divided Line to count as a kind of knowledge, e.g. *Rep.* 510A9. (See Fine (1990, pp. 97, 99 n. 27).) The person dreaming at 534C–D has only belief (c6) and thus his state corresponds to one of the two lower sections of the Divided Line; Plato typically associates dreaming with *doxa* (476C2–D6 and 520C6–D1). *Rep.* 533B6–C3 describes mathematicians as dreaming insofar as they rely on hypotheses, but this does not mean that they lay hold only of an image (*eidōlon*) of being or that they have only *doxa*: they do lay hold of being (533B7, cf. 534C5) and Plato reminds us just after 533B–C that their state is not one of *doxa* (533D5–534A1). On sleeping in the *Laws*, see 808B3–C2.

66. *Rep.* 445C4–7, cf. 543C7–544A8. If Plato thought that non-philosophers were capable of virtue or a good second-best, it would be odd that he does not discuss a corresponding constitution. We might find the verdict that any person not satisfying the Book 4 definition has a form of vice to be harsh and incompatible with the idea that some non-philosophers possess a kind of virtue. But the *Phaedo* attributes to non-philosophers a form of virtue (including *politikē* and *dēmotikē* virtue), but what they have, like vice, fails to benefit them. As I have noted, my characterization of non-philosophers in the *Republic* does not require that we see them as really possessing a form of vice, since their failure to possess genuine virtue is sufficient to make it the case that they do not have good lives. But the judgment that they do have a vice may not be as surprising as it initially seems: the claim that their condition is a vice does not entail that they are morally vicious, selfish, or responsible for their condition and is not obviously unreasonable if their most important part, the Reasoning part, is in as bad a condition as the metaphor of the Cave suggests that it is.

67. *Euthydemus* 279A4–B3 presents honor, along with goods of the body, as a Dependent Good. *Philebus* 11D4–6 rules out honor as a plausible conception of happiness, see Hackforth (1972c, p. 12).

68. This is not sufficient for the comparative thesis, since we might think that the just people could have so many evils in their lives that life is of negative value. People who are unjust because they are akratic may not have false beliefs, but will

be tempted to go for the worse option and akrasia, Plato thinks, usually leads to corruption of one's view of the good.

69. On the relation of the argument that the just person has the most pleasant life to the happiness of the just person, see, e.g., Kraut in Kraut (1992, pp. 312–14), Murphy (1951, pp. 207–23), and Gosling and Taylor (1984, pp. 98–101). On the superior truth or reality of the philosopher's pleasures and the status of other pleasures, see Gosling and Taylor (1984, pp. 106–28).

70. Gosling and Taylor (1984, p. 128).

71. Cf. *Rep.* 522A4 with 619C7–8 and *Phd.* 82B2; and 619D8–EI with *Phd.* 69B8. Contra Annas (1982c, p. 135), *Rep.* 619D8–E5 shows that Plato does not expect a philosopher ever to make a bad choice in his next choice of life; 619DI–3 claims only that not all people who passed through heaven make a good choice the next time, not that at least some philosophers make such a bad choice. In certain circumstances, the life chosen by the philosopher may not be happy (*Rep.* 619EI–5), but it will, it seems, be well worth living (619B2–6).

72. What is true is that they avoid the damage of being attached to bad objects, having their worst desires liberated and experiencing the inevitable frustration of such desires.

73. We cannot explain the non-philosopher's bad choice of the tyrant's life simply by invoking his carelessness encouraged by his sojourn in heaven (cf. Annas (1982c, p. 135)): what he regrets overlooking in his haste is that this life includes, e.g., eating his own children. He does not regret his attraction to the specious goods of the tyrant's life. This is not incompatible with the admission of the habitually virtuous to heaven, since the condemnation of the curably unjust to Hades is made on the basis of their acts (*Rep.* 615B and see Adam (1979, ad loc.)). Since the myth promises an account of the prizes and wages given to the just person by the gods, we can assume that the benefits in question will include the sorts of consequences of justice that Plato put aside in Book 2. On the other hand, while suffering in Hades makes them choose more slowly, there is little or no indication that it leads to a concern with virtue for its own sake. (I agree with Saunders (1991, pp. 200–1) that the better choice of those who suffered is not an expression of genuine virtue, but is more narrowly prudential.) This is true even of Odysseus, who chooses the life of a 'private man who minds his own business [ἀπράγμονος]' (620C6–7). The philosopher in the *Republic* is sometimes said to be 'minding his own business', but philosophers are not the only people so described, see, e.g., 565A–B where the members of the largest class in a democracy who cultivate their farms are said to be 'minding their own business' (ἀπράγμονες, 565A2). Indeed, Hirst (1940, pp. 67–8) plausibly suggests that Plato here is drawing on Euripides' lost *Philoctetes* where a world-weary Odysseus ponders an easier and quieter, but

hardly philosophic, life. Of course, nothing excludes the possibility that while leading a quiet life in his next reincarnation, Odysseus might turn to philosophy.

74. There is a large literature on the *Rep.* 5 argument and related issues about Forms and knowledge and belief. See, e.g., Annas (1981, pp. 190–241), Baltzly (1997), N. Cooper (1986), Fine (1978), (1990), (1993, pp. 44–65, 142–96), Gonzalez (1996), Gosling (1960), (1968), Irwin (1977a), Kahn (1981), Moravcsik (1976b), (1979b), Vlastos (1981, pp. 58–75), F. C. White (1984), and N. White (1987b), (1992). Two closely related views are worth noting. First, one might hold that the *Republic* recognizes the existence of 'mathematicals' or 'intermediates' which are non-sensible, but, unlike Forms, are not unique and allow that knowledge can be either of Forms or of mathematicals. (On mathematicals, see, e.g., Annas (1975) and Burnyeat (1987).) Second, one might hold that the Book 5 argument does not establish that no sensible can be known, but rather the more restricted claim that what is known is F and cannot be not-F. For some Fs, the only objects of knowledge would be Forms, e.g. just, so that I cannot know that this action is just. But for other Fs, e.g. man, sensible particulars are such that they are F and cannot be not-F, so that I can know, e.g. that Socrates is a man. For a version of this interpretation, see Annas (1981, pp. 190–215).

75. On the verb 'to be' in Greek, see Brown (1994), (1999), Kahn (1973), and (1981). It is important to note that Kahn's understanding of the veridical use of 'to be' differs significantly from Fine's. On Fine's view, in the veridical use, 'is' applies to the contents of belief and knowledge, that is, to propositions and when so applied, claims that the proposition is true. On Kahn's view, in the veridical use, 'is' applies to objective states of affairs and is to be understood as 'a conjunction of "X exists" and "X is F", for unspecified values of X and F' (Kahn, 1981, p. 130 n. 18). See Kahn (1981, pp. 105–9, 112–15) for how the veridical construction combines with other uses, L. Brown (1994, pp. 214–15) on the place of the so-called 'is' of identity, and Fine (1993, pp. 160–82) and Brown (1994), (1999) on the relation of these distinctions to that between 'complete' and 'incomplete' uses of 'to be'. Both Kahn and especially Brown (1994, pp. 212–28) stress how common overdetermined uses of 'to be' are.

76. If sensible particulars are not impossible entities, we need to qualify the ways in which they are F and not-F. For interpretations that hold that Plato does think that sensible particulars are, in some way, both F and not-F (at least for the range of properties considered in the *Republic* 5 argument which includes the value properties of fine and just), see, e.g., Gonzalez (1996, especially pp. 253–62), Kahn (1981, pp. 113–14), and N. White in Kraut (1992, pp. 277–310, especially pp. 284–5), N. White (1987a), and (1987b). Also see Code (1986), (1988), and M. Frede (1988). Fine and Irwin reject the view that sensible particulars must be both F and not-F

and hold that 'the many Fs' that are both F and not-F are instead sensible or observational property types. See Fine (1993, pp. 142–70), Irwin (1977a), and (1995a, pp. 148–68).

77. All the interpretations considered agree that for Plato value properties are non-sensible. This point is unaffected whether one analyzes property possession as having an immanent character, or having a property trope, or as standing in the appropriate relation, or as having the appropriate non-relational tie, to a transcendent or immanent universal. For further discussion of the metaphysics of property possession, see D. Armstrong (1978), (1989), (1997, pp. 113–19), and Fine (1981), (1983). Note that D. Armstrong (1989, pp. 55, 108–10) no longer accepts the 'fundamental relation regress argument' endorsed in D. Armstrong (1978, vol. 1, ch. 5, sec. 6).

78. For such claims, see Annas (1981, pp. 223–4) who also cites *Rep.* 484B, 521D, 527B, 534A, 585A–586B, and Kahn (1996, pp. 361–2). For Fine's response to such claims, see Fine (1990, pp. 94–106). Especially important is Fine's (1990, pp. 100–1) claim that the Divided Line is a classification of cognitive conditions and not of objects. For an extended argument that the Divided Line offers a division of both cognitive conditions and objects, see Burnyeat (1987, pp. 217–32), who also endorses (p. 225 n. 31) the interpretation of *Rep.* 5 in Kahn (1981). For an argument that the grammar of *Rep.* 509D6–9 shows that Plato's primary division is of kinds of objects (which can be correlated with different states of mind), see Murphy (1951, pp. 156–8).

79. Fine (1990, pp. 85–6) offers reasons independent of her interpretation of the *Rep.* 5 argument for rejecting the traditional interpretation, not all of which are clearly persuasive. One of Fine's reasons for holding that the *Republic* allows for knowledge of sensibles is that at 520C4 Plato claims that the philosopher will, upon his return, know (γνώσεσθε) things in the Cave. But it is not clear how much weight can be placed on this, since Plato in the *Republic* sometimes loosely calls 'knowledge' (*epistēmē*) things that even on Fine's account do not count as knowledge for Plato, see, e.g., N. Cooper (1986, pp. 240–1). Moreover, the verb for 'know' at 520C4 is *gignōskein*, but Plato's typical word for the state he is contrasting with belief is *epistēmē* (*epistasthai*). And it is not clear that the fact that one 'knows' (*gignōskein*) something entails that one has *epistēmē* of it. See Barnes (1975, p. 90) and Lyons (1963, p. 177). This appeal to Plato's phrasing is backed, however, by a more general argument. '[T]his skeptical result [that no one can have knowledge of sensibles] would be quite surprising in the context of the *Republic*, which aims to persuade us that philosophers should rule, since only they have knowledge, and knowledge is necessary for good ruling. If their knowledge is only of Forms—if, like the rest of us, they have only belief about the sensible world—it is unclear why they are specially fitted to rule in this world. They don't know, any more than the

rest of us, which laws to enact' (Fine (1990, p. 86)). Plato might, however, hold that knowledge of Forms will make our judgments of particulars more accurate and reliable, although they do not satisfy the criteria for genuine knowledge (and this is compatible with many different criteria for knowledge).

A second argument is that the denial of the possibility of knowledge of sensibles has highly unintuitive results: 'No one can know, for example, what actions are just or good; no one can know even such mundane facts as that they're now seeing a tomato, or sitting at a table' (Fine (1990, p. 86)). It is unclear, however, that Fine's interpretation has less unintuitive consequences: since, on her view, any know-ledge requires knowledge of Forms (e.g. Fine (1990, p. 86)), only a philosopher could know she's now seeing a tomato, or sitting at a table. (Or if we restrict the argument to relatives, only a philosopher could know that Mount Everest is large.) None of these objections, however, counts against Fine's interpretation of the Book 5 argument itself.

Perhaps the most troubling aspect of the traditional interpretation is that it is intuitively plausible that a person might have the concept F (or even know the def-inition of F) and yet be in a cognitive state with respect to 'F is G' such that either (i) he grasps a truth about F, but does not have *epistēmē* (e.g. he lacks the appropri-ate justification or explanation) or even (ii) he grasps a falsehood. A wide variety of reasonable responses to this worry—some accepting, some rejecting the tradition-al interpretation—are compatible with my position. For some discussion, see Baltzly (1997, pp. 267–8) and Kahn (1996, p. 361 n. 35). Finally, there is one worry about the traditional interpretation that, although common, is misguided. Gonzalez (1996, p. 272), for example, claims that 'sensibles do not exist indepen-dently of the forms, but are only their images or imperfect instantiations. Therefore, forms and sensibles are not completely separate, only extrinsically relat-ed objects: the being of the sensible object is exhausted by its participation in the form, it exists and is what it is only as intrinsically related to the form. On account of this intrinsic relation, in recognizing beautiful bodies as beautiful I can be said to have some awareness of the form of beauty they imitate.' The idea here seems to be that the ontological relation between the Form and the sensible is so intimate that awareness of a sensible brings with it awareness of the Form. But this argument is not obviously persuasive. Consider the Morning Star and the Evening Star. The ontological relation between them is closer than that between Forms and particu-lars on any reasonable interpretation, since the Morning Star is identical to the Evening Star. But it is plausible to think that I can have all sorts of beliefs about the Morning Star, while having no beliefs about the Evening Star. For Aristotle's view on whether some sort of *epistēmē* of particulars is possible, see Burnyeat (1981), Lear (1987), and Leszl (1972).

80. Even the claim that non-philosophers have no knowledge of Forms may conflict with our ordinary modern intuitions. We might, for example, count as instances of knowledge about Forms either (1) or (2): (1) It is not the case that (the Form of F is F and it is not the case that the Form of F is F). (2) Plato wrote about Forms in the *Republic*. (Our view about (2) may, in part, depend on what we think 'Form' refers to in such belief reports.)

81. This is only a rough approximation, since pessimism about non-philosophers might be warranted unless (1) their valuing of things and actions was roughly correct, and (2) their true opinions about value Forms entered into their valuings in an appropriate way.

82. See Irwin (1995a, pp. 154–68, 262–80). The cognitive condition of non-philosophers would not be improved from Plato's point of view if we instead held that they did not recognize any properties at all, either sensible or non-sensible, but only sensible particulars.

83. *Rep.* 522A–525C seems to suggest that a grasp of Forms need not enter into ordinary judgments that, e.g., 'This is a finger' or 'This is large'. Nor does the passage suggest that a recognition and rejection of contradictions as such must involve a grasp of Forms. (For further discussion, see Irwin (1995a, pp. 157–61) and Scott (1995, p. 83).) Nor should we expect that such an ability would require a grasp of Forms: the lower parts of the soul are capable of means–end reasoning and such reasoning seems to require some observance of the Principle of Non-Contradiction. But it is plausible to see the *Republic* as implicitly holding (e.g. 490B) what the *Phaedrus* and the *Timaeus* explicitly assert, that is, that the lower parts of the soul have no contact with the Forms. For further discussion of the *Phaedrus* and the *Timaeus* on this point, see Section 4.2.

84. Most people even in the just city remain in the Cave; this is why the philosopher must re-enter the Cave in order to rule. Fine holds that most people in the *Republic* remain in the cognitive condition represented by the lowest stage of the Divided Line and do not recollect (Fine (1990, p. 102 n. 33); (1993, pp. 138 and 315 n. 62)).

85. Whether the *Republic* is committed to some form of the theory of Recollection is controversial. For a negative answer, see Reeve (1988, pp. 107–10). For an affirmative answer, see, e.g., Irwin (1977b, pp. 140, 218) and (1995b, p. 316); Irwin (1995a, p. 389 n. 18) also holds that *Rep.* 476A along with 493E–494A supports D. Scott's (1995) view of Recollection and Scott holds that non-philosophers do not recollect.

86. See Nussbaum (1980, pp. 87–8) and Vlastos (1991, p. 110) for the view that *Rep.* 537D–539D bans the elenchus for all those below age 30. Irwin (1995a, p. 277) suggests that all that Plato may intend to ban in this passage is people under 30

practicing the elenchus, while allowing it to be practiced upon them. But the bad effects that the passage ascribes to the use of the elenchus involving those under 30 explicitly include the bad effects of having it practiced on them (see 538A–539A and especially, 539B9–C1). Establishing the precise age limit is not important for the issue at hand, however, since the passage does restrict the elenchus to those who have undergone the *Republic*'s extensive mathematical education (537C–D). On this, see Reeve (1988, p. 109), and Irwin (1995b, p. 276) seems to hold that either use of the elenchus is part of 'philosophical training'.

87. I agree with Scott (1995, pp. 53–73) on this point and I discuss Recollection further in Section 4.2. For other discussions of Recollection relevant to the *Phaedo*, see Ackrill (1973), Fine (1992), (1993, pp. 137–8), Moravcsik (1971a), and Rowe (1993).

88. But even consistently with this, we can allow them to have beliefs, and even true beliefs, about value Forms. For example, non-philosophical sight-lovers might accept (T).

(T) Beauty makes every beautiful thing beautiful.

Sight-lovers would, of course, think that Beauty is a cluster of sensible properties. But we might still have reason to hold that 'Beauty' in a non-philosopher's utterance of (T) refers to the non-sensible Form of Beauty and to count his utterance of (T) as expressing a belief about the Form. We might hold that even in his assertion of (T), the sense of 'Beauty' is not, so to speak, determined by what is in his head (but, e.g., by the correct etymology of 'Beauty' or by the views of experts in the community). Since (T) might enter into the actual valuings of non-philosophers, these cases might, strictly speaking, be counterexamples to (v) as formulated in the text. For further discussion, see Section 4.2.

Finally, my interpretation does not hold that ethical and epistemic progress is an all-or-nothing affair in the *Republic*, and the Cave and the Line images show that progress is made in stages. But this is compatible with there being very great differences between certain stages. The basic complaint about non-philosophers is that ordinary ethical habituation or the 'musical' education that the auxiliaries receive fails to turn the person 'toward being' (*Rep.* 521D–523A). It does not give them a grasp of the appropriate non-sensible principles of value and order. So they all remain within the Cave and their mental states fall on the lower half of the Divided Line. Going beyond this point is not the sudden intuitive grasp of all there is to know; one stage, for instance, is the acquisition of a fairly strong mathematical competence. But what *Rep.* 521D–523A shows is that these are higher stages of philosophical education and that normal ethical training and habituation or even the very intensive musical training the auxiliaries receive fall below this.

89. Translations from the *Symposium* draw on Nehamas and Woodruff in Cooper (1997). Cf. n. 8.

90. The exact relation between Plato's claims about bodily and psychic replacement and the view that individual souls remain identical over time need not be specified for our present purposes.

91. Although the *Phaedrus* differs from the *Symposium* in significant respects, it also holds that there is an important link between other-regarding concern and a shared conception of the good. For further discussion, see Ferrari (1987), (1991), Moravcsik (1971b), (1982), O'Brien (1984), Price (1989, pp. 15–102), and Rowe (1986a), (1990). There may, nevertheless, be a possibility of some tension between concern for one's own good and one's efforts to help others secure for themselves the good similarly conceived. On the close affinities between the *Symposium*'s view of the virtue of non-philosophers and that of the *Phaedo* and the *Republic*, see Kahn (1996, p. 272), O'Brien (1984, pp. 188–9), and Price (1989, p. 51).

92. Plato holds that the offspring of members of each class will usually have the nature fitting them to be members of the same class (*Rep.* 415A–C). The education that the children receive may also make it less likely that there will be significant mobility among classes, cf. n. 56. It is clear that a movement downwards is a misfortune for the children and would, *ceteris paribus*, be perceived as such by the parents. Auxiliaries may be content to have their children move up to the guardian class, since the philosopher rulers will receive even greater honors. Given the austerity of the lives of the two upper classes, parents of the producer class would see little reason to desire upward mobility for their children.

93. As we have seen, nothing requires non-philosophers to be ethical solipsists. *Rep.* 580D ff. need not require solipsism. It may simply specify the kind of good each part of the soul values and thus the kind of good valued by the person ruled by that part. This does not exclude the possibility that such a person may display other-regarding concern aiming at securing that type of good for some others.

94. The attempt to see the desire for honor as the desire to do what is honorable must face the problem that Plato describes (*Rep.* 581A9–B3) the Spirited part's motivation as love of honor (*philotimia*) and the desire for good reputation (*eudokimein*) and that he clearly classifies honor and good reputation as things that 'come from' virtue according to the Book 2 classification (*Rep.* 361A–C and 612D–613C). Note that Aristotle in *N.E.* 1095^{a}17–1096^{a}5 distinguishes honor from virtue as two different answers to the question of what happiness is (cf. 1123^{b}20–21), in a passage clearly indebted to the *Republic*.

95. It should be a constraint on a proper interpretation of non-philosophers' motivations in the *Republic* that they think that their own ultimate end consists in their own happiness. Holding that the ultimate end of all of one's actions is one's

own happiness is compatible with holding that virtue and virtuous action are good for their own sake: this is, for example, true of the genuinely just person. It is a greater challenge to show how non-philosophers' conceptions of their ultimate end could be such as to make them think that ordinary virtuous actions and the disposition to perform them are good for their own sake. And optimistic interpretations of non-philosophers' motivations often do not attempt to provide such an account. (Cairns (1993, p. 391) explicitly denies the need for it and sees virtuous non-philosophers, as opposed to Platonically just people, as acting instead on 'conscience'.) But even if we could find some such account, I have argued that no plausible account of non-philosophers' ultimate ends will allow us to see them as holding that genuine virtue is good for its own sake.

96. Either of these goes beyond simply holding that receiving honor is good. On the first option, the auxiliaries wish to be honored for actually living up to the standards as opposed to seeming to; on the second, they desire to be honored for living up to the actual standards of the just city, rather than for living up to the city's standards whatever they might be. (The desire to be honored for living up to the actual standards can be fragile without failing to exist: the actual object of their desire might change when something else is honored in the city.) But insofar as the auxiliaries really are guided primarily by the Spirited part of the soul and so are lovers of honor, Plato does at times suggest that they will not be especially concerned with the source of the honor (*Rep.* 474c–475c, cf. Irwin (1995a, pp. 233–5)).

97. Indeed, to the extent that such motivations focus on others' reactions to the agent and the agent's ranking *vis-à-vis* others, they lead away from reflection on the goodmaking features of things. The fundamental problem with non-philosophers' value concepts is that they do not have the appropriate non-sensible content. As we have seen, Plato's remarks suggest that their content is, in fact, sensible, but this claim is not necessary for his basic complaint. To put the point in terms of the *Phaedo*, even if non-philosophers' operations on sensible content could produce a concept with non-sensible content (e.g. by something like abstraction), they do not recollect the concepts of value properties such as the fine. If we take no position on whether Recollection is the only route to the appropriate content (since, e.g., the *Republic* makes no explicit commitment to Recollection) the problem remains that non-philosophers' value concepts do not have the appropriate content, because of the limitations of their education.

The passage perhaps most favorable to the cognitive accomplishments of non-philosophers concerns the relation between the auxiliaries' musical education and a love of the fine at *Rep.* 401c–402c. But this passage does not say that the auxiliaries love the fine because they grasp that it is genuinely fine. Moreover, the way in which people value the fine is conditioned by their conception of the good. And, as we have seen, the auxiliaries (much less the producers), insofar as their Reasoning parts do not perform their proper job, do not have a correct conception of the good. This does not entail that non-philosophers cannot refer to or have beliefs about the fine nor that they could not value things by means of a concept that is coextensive with the correct concept of the fine. As we have also seen, however, Plato thinks that non-philosophers, as a matter of fact, fail to value the best instances of the fine and the good.

98. On the relation between honor and virtue, see Cooper (1999, pp. 253–80), Korsgaard in Engstrom and Whiting (1998, pp. 203–36), and Whiting (1996, especially her discussion of 'natural virtue' at pp. 178–89).

99. Although it is not often remarked how weak the true belief requirement is in itself: Plato allows true belief about what is to be feared to slaves and animals, *Rep.* 430B2–9, cf. Adam (1979, ad loc.). (The auxiliaries do have something more than just this sort of true belief.)

100. For my present purposes, I can leave indeterminate the exact relation between the happiness of the city and the happiness of the citizens and the precise form of maximizing intended. For further discussion, see Section 5.6.

101. It has seemed to some that Reeve holds such a view and, in particular, holds that each person's happiness consists in that person's own maximal pleasure. See Reeve (1988, pp. 37, 164), Annas (1989), and Kraut (1990, pp. 492–4). But the interpretation of Reeve's views is controversial, see Reeve (1989). The view presented in the text, whether or not that of Reeve, is, however, worth examination.

102. Cf. Reeve (1988, pp. 166–7 and 204–8).

103. Cf. Brink (1990).

104. I agree with Annas (1981, p. 178), Price (1989, p. 179), Reeve (1988, p. 184), Saunders (1985, p. 103), Stalley (1991, p. 186), Vlastos (1994, vol. 2, p. 86), and Waterfield (1994, p. xxxiii) that the producers do not share in the community of women, children, and property. Mayhew (1997, pp. 129–37) agrees that the proposals in *Republic* 5 with respect to women, children, and property do not apply to the producers and that at least some of Plato's arguments for these institutions could only apply to the two higher classes. He argues, however, that the producers' activities with respect to women, property, and especially children, are highly regulated. In his view, 'the strongest evidence' (1997, p. 135) for this claim is the passage at *Rep.* 462A–E which asserts that a community of pleasure and pain holds the city together: but this passage only shows that if the producers could, *ceteris paribus*, share in the community of women, children, and property, the city would be better off. It does not show that Plato in fact thinks this is possible. In any case, Mayhew accepts that the regulation of the producers falls well short of the Book 5 proposals and, to the extent that this is so, the worry noted in the text above still

persists. Finally, the fact that Plato expects auxiliaries to accept the community of women and property does not show that they must be genuinely virtuous: even the concern for honor understood merely as a concern for fame can lead people, as Plato recognizes, to sacrifice material goods and even their lives.

105. On related arguments concerning political obligation, cf. Simmons (1979, pp. 157–90).

106. It is worth noting that the passage at *Rep.* 590C–E which argues that the slavery of other citizens to the best man is for their own benefit and not to their harm does not appeal to the idea that a person in this subordinate condition is just or acts justly. If Plato did accept these claims, they would be the most effective way to show that such rule benefits the one who is ruled by reason from the outside, since Plato has, by this point, argued for the benefit of justice on independent grounds.

107. Since Irwin's account is not intended to apply to non-philosophers (and there may be reasons why it should not directly apply to them), the discussion in the text is not meant as a criticism of it. I discuss Irwin's later view in Irwin (1995b) on related topics in Section 5.8.

108. Irwin (1977b, p. 237).

109. Irwin (1977b, p. 241).

110. Perhaps the most promising way to secure cooperation throughout the city relies on the possibility of habituating the non-philosophic classes not to engage in detailed reflection from their own point of view as to whether such cooperation is in their best interests. (As we have seen, even if cooperation is in their best interests, they may not be able to grasp reliably why this is so.) They will, instead, come to accept that the laws (and the social institutions) are in their best interests and in obeying them, they will act so as to advance the interests of the philosopher rulers. We might still worry that: (1) it may be hard to instill such a disinclination to evaluate political and social institutions and that free-riding or defecting may still be tempting, and (2) the laws and social institutions will not be able to regulate all aspects of these classes' behavior in detail and insofar as their cooperation is not based on an at least somewhat intelligent appreciation of why they are benefited, they (especially the producers) will be liable to go astray where there are gaps in the regulation of their behavior. Nevertheless, such an ingrained idea that following the rulers' advice is better for them than following their own independent calculations may be historically widespread, and societies can endure a relatively high rate of non-compliance or wayward behavior. This may give us some grounds for hope concerning the stability of the just city in the *Republic*, but it does not affect the question of the ethical value of such cooperation. I am indebted to John Cooper for an illuminating discussion of these issues.

111. Cf. Irwin (1990b, p. 80) and Aristotle *N.E.* 1167ᵃ22–ᵇ15.

112. Newman (1985, vol. 1, pp. 427–8). Capitals are in the original; I have transliterated *spoudaioi*. *Spoudaios*, although quite common in the *N.E.*, is difficult to translate. In addition to the sense of 'excellent' or 'worthy of serious attention', there is, according to LSJ, an overtone of earnestness and activity when it is applied to people.

113. Cf. Ober (1998, p. 232), Nightingale (1995, p. 18), and *Rep.* 428C–429A, 431B–C, and 445D.

114. The translation is adapted from Gregor (1996, pp. 53–4), emphasis in the original.

115. This account draws on Korsgaard (1996a, pp. 43–76, especially pp. 56–8), Korsgaard (1998, pp. 206–10), and Reath (1989). For another important interpretation of Kant, see A. Wood (1999).

116. Korsgaard (1998, p. 209) emphasis in the original and (p. 230 n. 10) for Kant's striking optimism about the active reflectiveness of ordinary moral thought.

117. Malcolm (1981, p. 68).

118. Korsgaard (1996a, pp. 259–61), emphasis in the original.

119. This is not to deny the causal role of perception, see n. 10.

120. For the *Republic*, see 588B–590A, 611B–612A.

Chapter 2 Virtue, Goods, and Happiness in the *Laws*

1. Cf. Pangle (1980, pp. 379–80). For Aristotle's criticism of Crete and Sparta, see *E.E.* 8.3 (7.15), *Pol.* 2.9; S. White (1992, pp. 219–46) and Whiting (1996). *Rep.* 544C1–3 classifies Crete and Sparta as timocracies, cf. 545A2–3.

2. *Laws* 714A2 connects 'distribution' (*dianomē*) with *nomos* and *nous*. See England (1921, ad loc.) who plausibly suggests a link with *daimones*; I am indebted to remarks made by André Laks at the 1996 Princeton Colloquium in Ancient Philosophy. For Aristotle on the connection between law and reason, see *N.E.* 1180ᵃ13–24. For the claim that the primary referent of *nous* is not the faculty of reasoning, but rather the good condition of the reasoning faculty, that is, a virtue, see Broadie in Gentzler (1998, p. 294 n. 5) and Menn (1995, pp. 14–18).

3. *Laws* 835E4 speaks of *logos*, rather than *nous*, but cf. 836E4.

4. The *Laws*' cosmology and its relation to that of the *Timaeus* are controversial. For my purposes, I do not need to take positions on whether (1) the creation of the world is intended literally, or (2) soul is the source of all motions or only of all motions within the formed world. For a start on the literature, see Mohr (1985, chs. 2, 7, 8, 9), T. Robinson (1995, pp. xviii–xix, xxiv–xxxii, 59–110, 145–57), and Vlastos (1994, vol. 2, chs. 15, 16).

5. Cf. Menn (1995, pp. 6–13).

6. I remain neutral on whether *nous* can exist apart from souls. See, e.g., Menn (1992), (1995), Mohr (1985, ch. 10), and T. Robinson (1995, pp. xix–xxii, 59–110). Translations of the *Timaeus* draw on Zeyl in Cooper (1997) and Bury (1975).

7. See Menn (1995, pp. 41–2).

8. Laks (1991, pp. 221–3).

9. I accept Ast's emendation at 722C1. See England (1921, ad loc.) for the correct construal of 722B6–7: another course was open to previous lawgivers, besides the exclusive use of force, as far as the uneducated state of the masses would permit. Plato is not suggesting that most of the citizens of Magnesia are a 'mob lacking in education'. *Ochlos* is very pejorative and Plato does not use it to describe the citizens of Magnesia: see 670B8, 700C7, 707E3, 734B6, and 819B2. At 817C5, the *ochlos* hanging around the marketplace might be citizens in other cities, but would be non-citizen metics and slaves in Magnesia.

10. On Kleinias' reply, see Bobonich (1996, pp. 269–73).

11. *Laws* 811C–812A. On education in Magnesia, see Morrow (1960, pp. 297–398).

12. This point is well discussed by Morrow (1960, pp. 343–8). Plato requires only some citizens, the future members of the Nocturnal Council, to pursue these mathematical studies 'with precision' (*akribeias*, 818A1). But in the *Laws*, Plato requires all citizens to pursue mathematics for more than practical reasons, while in the *Republic* the study of mathematics for more than practical purposes marks the decisive distinction between the auxiliaries' musical education and the education of the philosophers. On the pig as a symbol of ignorance, see Burnyeat (1999, p. 231).

13. Cf. *Laws* 819D ff. and the close parallel at *Rep.* 525B ff.: mathematics is the study that especially turns people toward 'truth and being' (525C6).

14. Compare the *Republic*'s straightforward and unsophisticated regulations (337D–392A) against the citizens 'blaspheming' (*Rep.* 381E5, cf. *Laws* 821D2) the gods.

15. The fact that such sophisticated training is part of Magnesia's basic education intended for all gives us further reason to take Plato at his word that Book 10's theological arguments are to be presented to all the citizens. On the astronomical theory suggested here, see G. E. R. Lloyd (1982, pp. 86–94), (1991, pp. 268–9), Mendell (1998), Neugebauer (1969, pp. 153–5), Vlastos (1975, pp. 23–65, especially 49–51, 64–5, 99–102), and Yavetz (1998).

16. Mueller (1980, p. 115). Also see Knorr (1975, pp. 94–6).

17. For discussions of the relation of circular movement to reason that come to different conclusions, see Lee (1976) and Sedley in Fine (1999b, pp. 317–19).

18. For recent discussions of the preludes and related issues, see Bobonich (1991), (1996), Cohen (1993), Cooper (1999, pp. 184–90), Curren (1994), Irwin

(1995a, pp. 349–53), Laks (1990), (1991), (1995), (2001), Morgan (2000, p. 166), Morrow (1953), (1960, pp. 552–60), Nightingale (1993), (1999b), Popper (1971, pp. 139–40), Stalley (1994), Versenyi (1961), and Yunis (1996, pp. 211–36).

19. Laks (1991).

20. See England (1921, ad loc.).

21. Laks (2000, pp. 269–70) offers four cases in which the *Laws* substitutes a humanly possible arrangement for what would be ideally best: (1) the allowance of private property; (2) the rule of law rather than individual rulers to avoid abuses of power; (3) the mixed constitution for the same reason; and (4) 'human' forms of praise, appealing to pleasure, are instituted in contrast to forms of praise appealing to 'honor' and 'reputation'. Cf. Laks (1987). But in all of these cases, Plato makes it as explicit as he can that the ideal is unrealizable and for that reason advocates a 'second-best' alternative for Magnesia. (For (1), see 739E–740A; for (2), see 874E–875D; for (3), see 691C–692A. (4) is the odd man out, since Plato does not suggest doing without appeals to honor, but supplements this with the claim that the just life is the most pleasant life, 732E ff.) Plato does not say anything like this about his programmatic justification for the preludes.

22. Susan Sauvé Meyer made the importance of this point clear to me.

23. The Athenian stresses the novelty of using such preludes in Book 4 (722B–E), which Laks himself accepts as non-hyperbolic and as a model for the actual preludes found in Magnesia.

24. (1) Laks holds that the depiction of the preludes in the medical analogy of Book 4 is consistent with the Hippocratic tradition, but that the medical analogy found in Book 9 goes well beyond this and is thus conscious hyperbole. One consideration that Laks advances in support of this view is that Book 9 goes so far as to picture the doctor 'going back to the general nature of bodies' in his quasi-philosophical discussion with the patient (857D3–4). (a) But 857D3–4 need not be seen as a reference to all physical bodies as opposed to all animate or human bodies, see England (1921, ad loc.). (b) Even if we were to take it as such, there are precedents for thinking that cosmological theory is necessary for understanding illness both in the medical tradition, see, e.g., M. Frede (1987, pp. 225–42), G. E. R. Lloyd (1984, pp. 146–51), and in Plato see, *Tim.* 82A ff. (2) Laks holds that Book 9 is distinctive and hyperbolic in using the language of Platonic dialectic. But we find similar language in Book 4, see 720C3–5. The only word in Book 9 that overlaps with the terminology of Platonic dialectic is *dialegesthai* at 857D1, but this verb is not uncommon in the *Laws* in a non-technical sense, e.g. 648A8. Further, as England (1921, ad loc.) rightly notes, 857D3 echoes 720D3. (3) Laks holds that the Book 9 passage suggests that legislation can be renounced entirely. But Plato does not make so strong a claim. Plato says that the sort of prelude recommended here is a

way of educating the citizens and is not itself legislating or stating laws with their penalties. But nothing in Book 9 suggests that a city can do without laws and in Book 9 itself the Athenian states laws with their penalties (e.g. 864D ff.). From the fact that some in Magnesia need penalties, it does not follow that the Athenian intends to provide rational argument exclusively for an elite group of rulers.

Other criticism has focussed on the Book 10 prelude to the impiety law itself. It is sometimes held that the only intellectually sophisticated discussion that the Athenian offers to the citizens is the prelude in Book 10. But I have argued that this is false, since *Laws* 861C–864C serves the same purpose as a prelude and is addressed to the citizens. But even if the Book 10 prelude were unique—and its length and argumentative detail show why this would not be surprising—we would still have to account for the fact that Plato includes it. A more worrisome criticism is the suggestion that Plato introduces it only as an antidote to widespread false stories about the gods and does not value the rational instruction it provides (a claim that might be thought to find support in 886A–891E, especially 890D–891B; e.g. Annas (1999, pp. 112–14)). But this is not a convincing reading of 886A–891E. (a) The appeal to widespread false beliefs about the gods is a poor justification for providing an intellectually sophisticated argument only in the case of impiety: (1) the only people who would be liable to hear such stories would be the first generation of colonists; if the Athenian valued the arguments only as an antidote and was suspicious about providing rational arguments to most citizens, he should restrict the prelude to the first generation; (2) as we have seen, Plato thinks that many ordinary and fairly respectable ethical views (e.g. Cretan and Spartan) are radically mistaken and thinks that even with the benefit of a Magnesian education, people will tend to be overly partial to their own interests; he thus has similar reasons to provide rational arguments as antidotes on other ethical topics; and (3) as we have also seen in the case of Cretan and Spartan views about the gods' goal for their law codes and in *Republic* 2, Plato thinks that ordinary views about the gods are shot through with serious ethical error, so he should not be willing to rely on ordinary theological views. (b) Despite Plato's occasional praise of primitive innocence (e.g. 679B3–E4), he makes it clear that primitives' lack of the right sort of cognitive sophistication is a serious ethical failure, e.g., 678B1–3 and *Stsmn.* 272B1–D2. Cf. Nightingale (1999a, p. 304). (c) Kleinias does say that giving the Book 10 prelude requires them to go 'outside the realm of legislation [*nomothesia*]' (891D7–8), but (i) he still advocates that they do so, and (ii) we already knew that the sort of education the lawgiver is to provide to the citizens is not in itself legislation (857E4–5). (d) On 634D–635A, see Bobonich (1996, p. 260 n. 22). (e) Members of the Nocturnal Council will study much more intensively a comprehensive group of theological arguments and related topics (*Laws* 967D–968B), but this does not undermine the fact that the Book 10 prelude is intended for all citizens. (f) Although Plato is concerned about the corrupting effects of false beliefs, his pragrammatic remarks about the preludes make it clear that he thinks that the citizens will be better off if they grasp the reasons for their true beliefs. We should thus see him here as ironically downplaying to his interlocutors the importance of education in order to encourage them to assert the need for it themselves, cf. 820C4–D6 and 890DI–891A8.

25. Stalley (1994, p. 171 n. 65).

26. e.g. *Laws* 853B–854A and 880D–E; cf. Yunis (1996, p. 218).

27. Saunders (1991, pp. 210–11). This elaborate and explicit threefold structure should also be borne in mind with respect to *Laws* 854B–C, 873E–874A, and 913CI.

28. I discuss the special studies for members of the Nocturnal Council in Ch. 5.

29. Bobonich (1991), (1996).

30. Both Seneca and, according to Seneca (*Ep.* 94, 38), Posidonius think that the preambles in the *Laws* really do teach. Posidonius, however, disapproves of Plato's proposal and holds that law 'should be a voice, as it were, sent down from the gods'. Posidonius thus holds that the law should be a 'sacred text', but he sees this as a criticism of Plato. Cf. Nightingale (1993).

31. Laks (1991, p. 428), translation mine. Compare Aristotle's views on what results, if we rely on the attitudes of most people. Rhetoric avoids conflict with ordinary beliefs about virtue and happiness, and these beliefs especially concern the value of external goods. So rhetoric will avoid, for example, claiming that virtue is the most important part of happiness or perhaps even that virtue is part of happiness, as opposed to merely a necessary condition of it. See Irwin in Rorty (1996, pp. 142–74).

32. Cf. Aristotle at *N.E.* 1180ª24–ᵇI: Sparta, more or less alone, is concerned with the education of its citizens.

33. For further discussion, see Bobonich (1995b). Other recent studies of the *Statesman* include Gill (1995), Kahn (1995), Lane (1998), and Rowe (1995a), (1995b), (1996).

34. See Rowe (1995b, ad loc.). Translations of the *Statesman* draw on Fowler in Fowler and Lamb (1975) and Rowe in Cooper (1997).

35. For a discussion of the *Statesman* that shares this reading, see Cooper (1999, pp. 165–91).

36. In stating the general principles that justify a particular law, the preludes may help the citizens to know how to apply the law in novel circumstances. Cf. Silverthorne (1975).

37. E.g. *Laws* 631B3–6, 718B2–4, 743C5–6, 806C3–7, and there is further discussion in Section 5.6.

38. Also see *Laws* 660D ff., 696B–697C, and 742D–744A. Note that justice includes wisdom (*phronēsis*), 631C5–8. There will be citizens, to be sure, in whom the law fails to instill the whole of virtue, but Plato never suggests that the laws fail in the case of every non-philosopher. Indeed, he expects that there will be quite a few successes, cf. n. 126.

39. The text is troubled, but I agree with the reading of Burnet, des Places, England, and Saunders. Saunders' note (1972, p. 15) is especially helpful.

40. The virtue of the constitution is secured by making the citizens as virtuous as possible. Note the echo in Aristotle *Pol.* 1253ª27–30.

41. The last two sentences are spoken by Kleinias, but the Athenian immediately endorses them, 963A5.

42. I accept the emendation *paristatai* for the manuscripts' reading *polis ktatai*, see England (1921, ad loc.). But this dispute does not significantly affect the sense; if we keep the manuscripts' reading, we must cash it out along the same lines. See Bobonich (1995a, p. 137).

43. Cf. Bobonich (1995a, p. 137), Brickhouse and Smith (1994, pp. 134–5), Ferejohn (1984, pp. 111–20), and Section 2.12.

44. See Korsgaard (1996a, p. 277).

45. For a helpful discussion, see Korsgaard (1996a, pp. 276–82). Other important discussions include: Darwall (1983, pp. 117–67), Korsgaard (1996b, pp. 132–45), Nagel (1970, pp. 90–8), (1986, pp. 152–63), Parfit (1984, pp. 142–4), and Scheffler (1987), (1988, pp. 1–13, 243–60), (1992, pp. 103–8).

46. Cf. Korsgaard (1996a, pp. 225–74). In these passages, Plato does not seem interested in the question of whether a Dependent Good, even when possessed by a virtuous person, is good in all possible circumstances. Bodily health is not good for a disembodied soul and keen sight would not benefit a virtuous person in a world with no visible objects. Plato seems to be assuming normal human background conditions. I focus for now on the question of necessity. I return to sufficiency in n. 158.

47. Cf. Aristotle *N.E.* 1096ᵇ8–14: instrumental goods do not, as such, participate in the Form of the Good. Cf. N. White (1984).

48. See, e.g., Slote (1983, pp. 61–75).

49. Kleinias shows some verbal inconsistencies over whether the goal of legislation is victory in external warfare alone, victory in both internal and external wars, the courage necessary for such victories, the goods secured by such victories, or the virtue necessary for victory in both. I focus on what seems to be his basic view.

50. This is an 'improved' reinterpretation of Tyrtaeus who is originally presented as only concerned with courage in external wars (*Laws* 629A–630B); literally read, Tyrtaeus 9.13 (Diehl) may suggest that such courage is the whole of virtue.

51. An overall or all-things-considered judgment should take into account both various respects in which a thing is good and temporal considerations. We might also consider the possibility that although most of a person's Dependent Goods are good for that person, their overall balance is negative.

52. The precise sense of *athlios* is not clear, but it at least suggests that such a life is far from worth living. If *athlios* is the polar opposite of 'happy' (*eudaimōn*) and 'happy' describes an optimal state, then this suggests that a Dependent Good is of no benefit at all to an unjust person.

53. Is there is a *tertium quid* between justice and injustice and how would this affect the Dependency Thesis? In Passages A and B Plato seems to treat 'just' and 'unjust' as mutually exclusive and jointly exhaustive: e.g. 660E8–9 and 661C2–4. *Laws* 631B6–C1 appears to claim that if you do not have the virtues, then you will lack the Dependent Goods too. In any case, if Plato thinks that there is a *tertium quid*, and especially if he thinks that this is the category to which most people belong, then we would expect him to discuss it. But he does not mention or suggest the possibility of a *tertium quid* in Passages A and B and this suggests that, even if there are such cases, they are not of great ethical significance.

54. E.g. Annas (1999, pp. 40–51), Brickhouse and Smith (1987), (1994), Ferejohn (1984), Irwin (1986b), (1995b, pp. 52–63), Santas (1994), Striker (1996, pp. 316–24), and Vlastos (1985), (1991, pp. 200–32). Also see *Chrm.* 173A–175A. For a plausible account of one possible important difference between the *Euthydemus* and the *Republic*, see Striker (1996, pp. 320–4).

55. Vlastos (1991, pp. 215, 203 n. 14).

56. Vlastos (1991, p. 225).

57. Vlastos (1991, p. 225).

58. Vlastos (1991, p. 225). The thesis that virtue is the sole component of happiness is open to a stronger objection. Since virtue is identical to knowledge of the good, the thesis that virtue is the only component of happiness is equivalent to the claim that knowledge of the good is the only component of happiness. This idea, although not incoherent, results in an oddly empty account of virtue and happiness. Virtue and happiness would be knowledge of the good, but the only possible good would be this very knowledge of the good. Another way of putting this is that the only thing good by itself would be the knowledge that everything except this very knowledge is at best instrumentally valuable insofar as it contributes to this knowledge.

59. Vlastos (1991, pp. 200, 220).

60. It is no solution to hold that the distinction between wisdom or virtue and other goods is in itself a distinction between moral and non-moral value, since we still must answer the question of whether wisdom consists only in knowledge of

the moral good. Since Vlastos thinks that if virtue were the only component of happiness, we would have reason to act only in cases in which states of affairs are differentiated by their moral values, it seems that he does not include knowledge of non-moral good in the knowledge that comprises virtue.

61. Cf. Moravcsik (1993, pp. 208-9).

62. Vlastos (1991, p. 215).

63. Annas (1999, p. 46 n. 48) rightly notes that the skill and productive analogies are not present in the *Laws*.

64. Cf. Irwin (1995a, p. 56). I take correct use to be necessary for benefiting from a Dependent Good and not merely necessary for happiness. The stronger reading is supported by *Euthd.* 280E4–281A1, 281B4–6, and 281D5–E1.

65. Brickhouse and Smith (1994, pp. 130, 133).

66. The *Euthydemus* holds that, in addition to possession, correct use is necessary to benefit from a Dependent Good (e.g. 280D4–7, cf. *Meno* 88A4–5), but it draws heavily on simple productive examples and does not consider hard cases such as pleasure or the welfare of others. Even if we accept the *Euthydemus* principle, we could hold that, although some use is necessary for any benefit, once some use is made, the Dependent Good has some additional value apart from use. Some of the goods mentioned in *Republic* 2's classification of goods (e.g., harmless pleasures, 357B7–8) seem to have more than use value.

67. One might think that 'use' in the *Euthydemus* and the *Meno* is sufficiently broad that it avoids these problems and that it also includes an appreciation of value. Such a 'use' of, e.g., pleasure might be simply experiencing it. For my present purposes, I do not need to decide whether this is the correct account of these dialogues. My point is that the need for appreciation of value has not been clearly recognized. Once it is, a number of significant philosophical questions, as well as some important connections between the *Laws'* Dependency Thesis and the *Philebus*, come into clearer focus.

68. These should not be confused with *feelings* of satisfaction or contentment, see Kraut (1979, pp. 170, 173).

69. If *a* is F, then there are some features of *a* that make it the case that *a* is F. I shall call these features in virtue of which *a* is F, 'F-making properties' or 'F-makers'. Cf. D. Armstrong (1997, pp. 2–3).

70. Knowledge of the goodmaking properties of things is a much more plausible condition of value than simply knowledge of what is good for me. Why, after all, should knowledge of what is good for me be of significant benefit apart from its correct use in relatively favorable circumstances? Why, for instance, would I be significantly benefited from knowing that pleasure is good if I cannot obtain pleasure? Cf. Kraut in Kraut (1992, pp. 311–37) and Striker (1996, pp. 320–4).

71. See Griffin (1988, pp. 33–4) and Parfit (1984, pp. 493–502). Also on some desire-satisfaction accounts of the good, although agents must desire the relevant object, they do not have to be aware that their desire has been satisfied.

72. I am indebted to John Cooper on this point.

73. Translations of the *Philebus* draw on Fowler in Fowler and Lamb (1975), D. Frede in Cooper (1997), Gosling (1975), and Hackforth (1972c).

74. See ad loc. Bury (1897), D. Frede (1993), and Hackforth (1972c).

75. This judgment is supported by the imaginary reply of the personified pleasures to Socrates' later question of whether they prefer to live alone or with wisdom at *Phil.* 63B7–C3. This passage's apparent implication that the two isolated lives are equally undesirable is not necessarily Plato's own position, since it is the pleasures themselves who are speaking and their stress on the idea that the best form of knowledge especially knows about pleasure suggests that they are not entirely reliable spokesmen for Plato. Similarly, the initial rejection of both unmixed lives at *Phil.* 20B–C need not commit Plato to the claim that the two unmixed lives are equally undesirable. All that Plato needs for the argument at that point is that neither unmixed life is the good life; he does not need to establish that they are equally lacking in value. And Plato does accept a significant asymmetry between them: the life of unmixed pleasure is that of a mollusk, while the unmixed life of reason is a god's life. The latter life might not be possible for us to live and it might not satisfy some of the desires and needs we actually have; thus a mixed life is better for us than an unmixed life of reason. But this does not entail that such an unmixed life of reason, if we could live it, would be deeply undesirable or that knowledge without pleasure has no value for us. The different values of knowledge and pleasure, however, cannot be established by this direct appeal to intuitions (either Protarchus' or our own) and requires the philosophical theory developed in the rest of the *Philebus.*

76. (a) is mentioned first and separately (*Phil.* 21B6–9); Protarchus seems to hold that calculating the way to obtain future pleasure is only instrumentally valuable to *having* the pleasure (21B2). Plato's back reference, at *Phil.* 60D8–E1, to the counterexample does not mention calculation about the future.

77. *Phil.* 11B4, cf. 60A7–B1. On Protarchus' relation to Eudoxus, see Gosling (1975, pp. 139–42), Gosling and Taylor (1984, pp. 157–64). On Eudoxus, see Aristotle *N.E.* 1172^{b}9–25, Diogenes Laertius 8.86–91.

78. I adopt Gosling's (1975) translation, we may also translate 'everything that knows it hunts for it . . .'

79. *Phil.* 60D4–E1 claims that one would not wish to have anything at all, including, but not limited to, pleasure, without knowledge. Plato thus explicitly holds that all goods, not just pleasure, are subject to a knowledge requirement. The

weakest interpretation of such knowledge would require knowing that one has the possession, but self-conscious possession is hardly sufficient to make something even *prima facie* desirable. Interpreting this as the knowledge that the possession is pleasant would render pointless Plato's proceeding to ask whether we wish to have the life of reason without any pleasure (*Phil.* 60EI–3). It is thus plausible to construe this knowledge as the awareness that what one has is good.

80. Eudoxus appeals to the alleged fact that all animals, and not just humans, pursue pleasure to support the claim that pleasure is the good, cf. n. 77.

81. Very roughly, we might distinguish three steps in the development of the notion of an ultimate end. Let us start with a set of desires. Their objects are already intentionally characterized, so we have exercised our ability to discriminate and identify objects. We then recognize that our desires have, more or less, a certain pattern: the satisfaction of some has no further end in view; others are 'for the sake of' something else. A second step is a normative step: we conclude that some objects of our desires should be treated as ends of action and we try to make our ends of action into a consistent whole. This step need not involve sophisticated reasoning; we might simply have a brute preference for certain ends, or we might adopt certain ends because our desires for these objects are especially frequent or intense. Finally, we can try to develop objective standards to determine what ends really are worth desiring.

82. Irwin (1995a, p. 334) makes the interesting suggestion that hedonists might agree that some form of rational consciousness is needed in the good life, but hold that what is good in such a life consists solely in the pleasures taken in rational consciousness and not at all in rational consciousness itself. Plato, however, might not think that this is a genuine possibility. Presumably agents would have to be aware of the pleasure taken in rational consciousness for this pleasure to be desirable. If they are not aware of this pleasure, then it too should be subject to the counterexample. But if agents must be aware of the pleasure taken in rational consciousness, then the hedonist seems committed to separating the single intentional act of being aware of a pleasure into two components, the awareness and the pleasure one is aware of, and attributing value solely to the latter. While it would not be obviously unreasonable to attribute value to some state of affairs apart from one's awareness of it, the counterexample shows that the hedonist does not do this with regard to pleasure. It is less clear that it is acceptable to attribute no value to pleasure unless one is aware of it, but to hold that within the act of being aware of pleasure only the pleasure has value. But it does seem that, in response to the counterexample, all that hedonists need do is attribute value to their knowledge of pleasure, they need not, and will not, attribute value to any other kind of knowledge. Thus we can at least conclude that they do not value knowledge as such, that

is, they do not value knowledge for the characteristics that make it knowledge. Thus the counterexample does not show that knowledge as such has any value.

83. There is a considerable literature on the issues surrounding *peras* and *apeiron*; important contributions include Cooper (1999, pp. 150–64), Gosling (1975), Meinwald (1998), Moravcsik (1979a), (1992, pp. 213–49), and Striker (1970). I accept Cooper's (1999, pp. 150–5) account of good things as mixtures.

84. Cf. ad loc. D. Frede (1993) and Poste (1860).

85. *Phil.* 64C5–7 emphasizes that these are the cause of the goodness of the good life. The inclusion of truth at *Phil.* 64D9–65A3 is prepared for by the assertion at 64B2–3 that truth is a necessary condition of a mixture being a mixture at all. On the relation between measure and fineness, see Gosling (1975, pp. 134–6) and Hackforth (1972c, p. 133); on the distinction between fineness and proportion at *Phil.* 66A4–C2 and the apparent absence of truth from this passage, see ad loc. Bury (1897), Gosling (1975), and Hackforth (1972c). Also see Aristotle, *Meta.* 1078ᵃ31–ᵇ36 and Cooper (1999, pp. 273–6).

86. Cf. Murphy (1938, pp. 117–18).

87. Irwin (1995a, p. 334).

88. Irwin (1995a, p. 338).

89. *Pace* Hackforth (1972c, p. 36), καὶ μᾶλλον ἔτι at *Phil.* 22D5 is not a rejection of the claim at 22D3–4 that νοῦς is the αἴτιον of the mixed life; rather, it picks up οὐκ ἀμφισβητῶ πω at 22C7–8. τούτου at 22D4 does not point forwards to the claim that reason is more akin to what makes the mixed life good, but rather, as is typical, backwards to the claim that reason is the cause of the mixed life (and thus deserves second place). (If Hackforth were right, we should expect *toutou de* instead of the more inferential *toutou dē*.) I am indebted to Liz Asmis and Christian Wildberg for discussion of this issue.

90. At *Phil.* 23B6–9, Socrates claims that in order to establish that reason deserves second place, he needs his fourfold classification of 'all the things that now exist in the universe' (*Phil.* 23C4–5) and he returns to this point at *Phil.* 27C3 ff. after distinguishing and enumerating the four genera: the determinant, the indeterminate, the mixture, and the cause of the mixture. In particular, Socrates claims that by answering the question of which genera reason and pleasure belong to, he will answer the question of which deserves second place. Protarchus sees where this line of argument is leading (*Phil.* 28B1–C5): once reason is established as the cause of the mixed life, this will be sufficient to establish that it deserves second place. Socrates' reiteration of the idea that simply by establishing the genera to which pleasure and reason belong, we establish which deserves second place, shows that he has not given up (1). *Phil.* 30D10 ζητήσει picks up ἐζητοῦμεν at 27C5; 30D10 ἀπόκρισιν points to 28A4–7, but 28A4–7 is part of the section beginning at 27C3.

91. *Phil.* 22D4–E3 συγγενέστερον καὶ ὁμοιότερον, 64C5–9 προσφυέστερον καὶ οἰκειότερον; reason is also said to be οἰκειότερον καὶ προσφυέστερον (67A10–12, cf. 11D11–12A4) to the good or mixed life than pleasure is. Also see *Phil.* 65A7–66C2.

92. I have changed a question into a statement where assent is clearly expected and is given.

93. A pure white is 'whiter' (*leukoteron*) than a mixed white (53B5) and pure pleasure is 'more pleasant' (*hēdiōn*) than a mixed pleasure (53C1). In both cases, a pure F is more F than an impure one; a pure F is a genuine F or an F without qualification. Similarly, pure knowledge is 'more fully' (*mallon echomenon*) knowledge than a less pure kind (55D6). Cf. *Phil.* 56B4–6: more accurate (*akribēs*) knowledge is 'more of an art' (*technikōteran*) than less accurate knowledge. On the link between accuracy and purity, see 56A7, B5, C5–6, 57B6, C1–3, C7, D1. For a helpful discussion of the connections among Plato's criteria, see Cooper (1999, pp. 156–8).

94. Impurity does not seem to require a mixture of F with the opposite of F. Pure pleasures are free of pain, but pure white is free of admixture with any other color, not just with black. This allows for the possibility that impure forms of knowledge are mixed, if either ignorance or false belief is present. Purity also seems to involve some notion of a continuum or a comparison class: the purity of a pure white is undermined if it is mixed with some other color, not just by having some non-color property.

95. This is what we should expect, since being a correct mixture of the determinant and the indeterminate makes something a good thing and impure forms of knowledge and pleasure are less good than pure forms. On the connection between impurity and indeterminacy, see Cooper (1999, pp. 151–7, 162–3) and Fine (1993, pp. 100–1). Fine rightly connects such indeterminacy with compresence. But we need a notion of compresence that is narrower than Fine's notion of 'broad compresence', since pure pleasures as well as impure pleasures are both pleasant and not-pleasant in the broad sense, because everything but the property of F is F and not-F in the broad sense. A narrower notion of compresence (that still is not Fine's 'narrow compresence') seems, intuitively, to be what is needed to capture the example that Fine uses to show the need for a notion broader than narrow compresence. Fire in the *Timaeus* (49C–51D) is both fire and not-fire, but no sensible sample of fire is both fire and not-fire in the narrow sense. The problem with fire is that each sample has bits of earth and other elements mixed in with it. Sensible samples of fire will be broadly compresent with respect to being fire, but this is too broad a notion to capture this point about fire. Even if a sensible sample were entirely unmixed with anything else, it would still be broadly compresent with respect to being fire, since any sensible sample of F is in broad compresence with respect to

being F (like Socrates with respect to being a man, a sensible sample of fire is in broad compresence in virtue of having coincidents).

96. Cf. *Rep.* 525D–526A and Burnyeat (1987, pp. 225–7).

97. *Phil.* 58A1–5, 59A8–D6, 61D10–E4. Cf. Fine (1993, pp. 97–101); the claim that the Form of F is purely and determinately F does not entail that the Form cannot be described as indeterminate in some respects.

98. See Cooper (1999, pp. 156–7) on the ways that the subject matters of empirical sciences are less determinate. This is not inconsistent with the possibility that sensibles might be described determinately with respect to some properties and that knowledge of them is possible (at least in some respects) on the basis of knowledge of Forms.

99. Cf. *Phil.* 59C5–6 with *Laws* 896B10–D8. *Phil.* 59C2–D8 goes beyond, in the expected direction (53A9–B1, C1–2), 58B9–D8. The final ranking at 66A4 ff. makes it clear that this is a value ranking.

100. *Phil.* 52C2 ff. and see Fine (1993, pp. 100–1).

101. Cf. *Phil.* 59A11–B5. The inferiority of the objects of the inferior kinds of knowledge with respect to accuracy, truth, and fixity can be explained by the notion of indeterminacy and a kind of compresence rather than strictly by temporal change, cf. n. 95.

102. The sentence does not assert the existence of such a faculty, but the context shows that Plato accepts it. We might also translate 'loves the truth and goes to all lengths for its sake'.

103. Note that this picks up the characterization of the limit (*peras*) at *Phil.* 25A6–B2 and thus helps to show that this is non-relational goodness.

104. The epistemic value of a pure or true F holds on more than one reasonable interpretation of the notion of purity: see, e.g., Code (1994); Cooper (1999, pp. 156–60); Fine (1993, pp. 46–61 and 100–1), and Kahn (1981).

105. *Phil.* 66B8–C2. Since knowledge is a non-instrumental part of the good life, the knowledge in the good life instantiates the goodmakers.

106. Nothing is more measured than knowledge and reason, *Phil.* 65D9–10 and, as we have seen, knowledge involves a grasp of measure. Reason and wisdom are the finest things, *Phil.* 59C8–9. In the middle period, Plato claims that the soul or its reasoning part is capable of knowing the Forms because it is like the object known: *Phd.* 79D1–7, *Rep.* 490A8–B7, cf. *Symp.* 211D8–212A2. In the *Timaeus* (35A ff.), we find the difficult but related idea that the reasoning aspect of the soul is composed, at least in part, of Forms.

107. We should note two points about Plato's views on causation. First, Plato is not concerned here to show that reason is a sufficient condition for the goodness of all Dependent Goods. Cf. nn. 46, 158. Second, one might appeal to the *Phaedo's*

notion of a 'clever cause' to suggest that reason in virtue of being a cause need not be a necessary condition, since clever causes are not necessary conditions. Indeed, it seems that clever causes are such that it can be true that not only a particular clever cause is the cause of a certain effect, but the opposite of this clever cause can cause the same effect (fever is a clever cause of disease, but so is hypothermia). But the notion of a clever cause is too weak to capture what Plato intends to assert about the role of reason in the good life. From the opening mollusk counterexample to the closing discussion (*Phil.* 60C6–E5), Plato is explicit that he is trying to show the necessity of reason. This attempt fits well with the causal principle that like causes like which we have independent reason to ascribe to Plato. We might also think that even instances of causal explanation by clever causes are made true by the holding of the appropriate instance of like causing like, although this will often require considerable care in specifying the cause and effect. For example, 'fever causes disease' is made true in virtue of the fact that excess heat in certain parts of the body causes certain internal structures of the body to become excessively hot and this is a form of disease. On Plato on causation, see Annas (1982a), Fine (1987), Gallop (1975), A. C. Lloyd (1976), Makin (1990–1), Morris (1985), Sedley (1998b), and C. Taylor (1969).

108. I follow Cooper (1999, pp. 161–3).

109. Such pleasures, insofar as they benefit the person, are subject to a twofold regulation by reason. As we shall see in more detail in Ch. 4, the perception of order itself involves an exercise of reason and reason is also involved in the appreciation of this order as such.

110. For a fine analysis of the pleasures of health, see Cooper (1999, pp. 160–3).

111. Moderation, when isolated from the other parts of virtue, deserves no honor, but only 'speechless silence' (*Laws* 696D11–E1), and does not benefit its possessor (710A5–B2).

112. Most, if not all, of the value of health consists in (1) its enabling various other beneficial activities, and (2) the healthful and good pleasures that such a state involves. Knowing that health advances all of one's activities is not enough for the sort of knowledge required for benefit, since this is open to unjust people. They think that health is good because it allows unjust activities and involves, for example, certain intense unmixed pleasures. But neither of these benefits the person. We can thus see why the intuitively plausible idea that sickness is worse for the unjust than the just, because the unjust pursue projects that are more easily affected by sickness, is mistaken. The projects the unjust would otherwise engage in are not beneficial to them. Similarly, we might think that the exercise of sight, insofar as it is a utilization of a basic human capacity, would benefit both the just and unjust. But the unjust do not use sight in order to appreciate genuine value, and since

reason is inherently directed towards value, they are not exercising a distinctively human capacity. I am indebted to Sally Haslanger and Martha Nussbaum for discussion of these issues.

113. *Laws* 688A–689C and for related modern discussions, see Chisholm (1986), Lemos (1994, pp. 73–7), and Nozick (1981, pp. 505–51).

114. We might, for example, need to know something about the medium of instantiation (and we can remain neutral on whether knowledge of the general account of goodness when conjoined with the relevant knowledge about the medium of instantiation is always sufficient to specify deductively an account of goodness in the particular case).

115. In the *Laws*, Plato gives exactly this sort of explanation of the value of a Dependent Bad in the only example discussed in detail: immortality is bad for an unjust person and a shorter life is preferable because it is 'a lesser bad' (661C1–5).

116. In the *Euthydemus*, Plato claims that it is preferable for people without knowledge to lack the Dependent Goods, since they will make fewer mistakes and thus will be less harmed (*Euthd.* 280E5–281A1, 281B8–D2, especially C2). We should not cash out harm in terms of losing Dependent Goods, since losing them would not harm the unjust person. The idea that a Dependent Bad could benefit unjust people would conflict with the *Euthydemus*' claims (280E5–6) that knowledge is necessary for correct use and that if people use a thing incorrectly they are harmed.

117. It might be good for a person to grasp correctly why the bad is bad, but (i) having this piece of knowledge does not require having the Dependent Bad, and (ii) unjust people fail to grasp why the bad is bad. The reasons in the text provide a general explanation of why Dependent Bads are preferable for the unjust and this seems to be what Plato intends—he does not suggest that their preferability depends on very special circumstances. Cases in which the Dependent Bad, in the form of punishment, leads to ethical reform do not seem to be the main cases Plato has in mind. Some Dependent Bads are not plausible punishments (e.g., ugliness and bad sight would seem to require punishments that maim and these would be inappropriate for free citizens) and others that sometimes might be punishments (e.g. poverty) often afflict people without being penalties, and such penalties do not always lead to reform.

118. The *Euthydemus* and the *Meno*, like the *Laws*, hold that health is only good for the virtuous person. Cf. Vlastos (1985, p. 17 n. 55) where he distinguishes the Socratic conception of happiness in which health is only good for the virtuous person from the 'Platonic [i.e. Plato from the middle period on, including the *Republic*] and Aristotelian conceptions of happiness (where, e.g., health is good, so far as it goes, for all persons, regardless of their moral character)'. Vlastos (1991, pp. 200–32) omits this claim.

119. This does not entail that there is any stretch of time during which people would be better off overall if they had not been just; Plato holds that people are always worse off being unjust no matter how long they continue to live, cf. Kraut in Kraut (1992, p. 337 n. 31). It is consistent with this claim that there can be short-run losses of other goods that are only made up in the long run. That Plato is concerned here with the long-run, overall balance of benefits is shown by the 'either during his lifetime or after he had died' qualification at *Rep.* 613A6–7. Plato's point is not simply about the virtuous person's good use of apparent evils; what use could a virtuous person make of human illnesses when dead?

120. We might argue that although Plato holds the Dependency Thesis in the *Republic*, he does not choose to rely on it in his arguments for justice. Plato might want to show that, even if an unvirtuous person could benefit from goods other than virtue, a just person would always be better off. He might choose to argue in this way because he wants to show someone, whose view is that only goods other than virtue are of any real value, that (i) virtue is a good, and (ii) virtue is vastly more important for any human being than all other goods. This allows Plato to engage effectively someone who might resist (or might even not be able to understand) the stronger claim contained in the Dependency Thesis. (I am indebted to John Cooper for making this possibility clear.) Even if Plato were following such a strategy, it is puzzling that he does not make his support for the Dependency Thesis clearer. Yet I do not think that the evidence allows us to establish clearly what the *Republic*'s position is with respect to the Dependency Thesis. Other relevant passages include the following. (1) *Rep.* 491A–492A and 495A–B assert that many goods can, when a person does not receive a proper education, corrupt the soul by leading it away from philosophy. These goods are thus on the whole bad for the person, but the passages do not clearly claim that they are of no benefit at all to the person or that their only benefit is the degree to which they lead the person to philosophy. (2) *Rep.* 505A distinguishes two cases in which people do not benefit: (a) if they know other things without knowing the good, (b) if they possess all things without possessing the good. Even if (a) claims that the value of all forms of knowledge is dependent on knowing the good, this does not exhaust the range of Dependent Goods; (b) seems to be the weak claim that what you have must be good if you are to benefit. (3) Perhaps the most promising passage is *Rep.* 505D11–506A2, especially if we construe 505E3–4 as 'miss [the benefit from other things] even if there is some benefit from other things' rather than as 'miss [the good] even if there is some benefit from other things'. Yet even on the former translation, it is not obvious exactly what positive requirement Plato here asserts for benefit. He claims that one misses the benefit from other things if one is 'at a loss' as to what the good is and has no 'settled opinion' about it. But it is not clear how

much or what kind of knowledge is necessary to avoid these two faults. We may, however, think it best not to press this passage too far. We might see it as a slight overstatement, especially if the above claim that all other knowledge without knowledge of the good fails to benefit is also a slight overstatement, cf. Ch. 1, n. 65. (4) *Rep.* 589D–590A and *Rep.* 591C–592A do not clearly assert dependency and are consistent with the idea that the value of virtue is so much greater than that of the Dependent Goods that virtue is always the decisive consideration.

121. We might accept that each part of the soul has its own built-in objective or end, but still doubt whether the notion of 'good for a part of the soul' really has application. For my present purposes, I remain neutral on this question as I remain neutral on what the *Republic*'s position on the Dependency Thesis ultimately is. But Plato does explicitly characterize wisdom (whether or not he is to be taken literally) as knowledge of what is good for each of the three parts and for the community formed by all three (*Rep.* 442C5–8). For some who do think that 'good for a part of the soul' has application in the *Republic*, see Irwin (1995a, pp. 245–7) and Reeve (1988, pp. 142–3, 153–9).

122. *Rep.* 586D claims that when the lower parts pursue the pleasures recommended by the Reasoning part, they will attain their most beneficial pleasures, but this does not show that the lower parts cannot attain any beneficial pleasures without the Reasoning part's guidance and even when the lower parts attain their best pleasures, they will not enjoy those pleasures proper to the Reasoning part. Each part might also need the awareness that its desires were satisfied, but this is far less than the Dependency Thesis requires. Nor is the *Republic*'s ordinal ranking of lives at 580A–C obviously consistent with the *Euthydemus*' apparent claim (281B–C) that one is less harmed if, when lacking knowledge, one also lacks moderation and courage.

123. See, especially, the claim at *Rep.* 581D10–E4 that the pleasures of the lower parts are 'very far from pleasure' retaining *tēs hēdonēs* at E2. This point explicitly concerns pleasure and not goodness and the relation of this argument to the evaluation of the happiness of lives is controversial; but the passage offers some reason for thinking that a similar claim is true about the goodness of the satisfactions of the lower parts. The text here is troubled; I agree with Shorey (1892, p. 366), against Adam, that we should put a question mark after μανθάνοντα at 581E2 and retain τῆς ἡδονῆς and construe it with οὐ πάνυ πόρρω.

124. Plato pursues two distinct strategies that he does not distinguish sharply. First, he allows true belief, as well as knowledge, to be a satisfactory leader of the other virtues: *Laws* 688B1–4, cf. 689B2–3, 653A7–B1, and 644D1–3 (also see *Ep.* 7 342C5). Second, he sometimes allows that some form of true belief can qualify as wisdom: 689C6–E2, cf. 710A5–B2. See the helpful discussion in Irwin (1995a,

pp. 347–53). The important question is whether the *Laws* accepts that true belief of the right sort can embody an appropriate grasp of non-sensible value properties and I defend this claim in Chs. 3 and 4. Stalley (1983, p. 48) suggests that Plato's use of *phronēsis* for the virtue of wisdom is significant and that he is here anticipating Aristotle's usage. But we should not accept this suggestion. In the *Laws*, as elsewhere in his corpus, Plato frequently interchanges *phronēsis* and *sophia* and their cognates: 689D2, D4, D5, D7, 696C8, and 710A6. Guthrie (1987, vol. 5, pp. 478–9) attributes such a distinction to Xenocrates, not Plato; also see Saunders (1962, p. 46) and A. E. Taylor (1929, pp. 246–51).

125. Compare Plato's narrower and broader uses of *epistēmē* and *nous* in the *Philebus* (e.g. 21B–22A and 58A–59E, especially 59C–D) and cf. Broadie in Gentzler (1998, p. 294).

126. For the aim of the laws as instilling complete virtue and Plato's expectation that it will succeed in many cases, see, e.g., *Laws* 630C, 631C–D, 641B–C, 647C–D, 705E–706A, 707D, 731E–732B, 734E–735A, 742C–743C, 770C–771A, 790B, 807C–E, 817B–C, 818C–D, 822E–823A, 853B–C, 876C–D, 878A–B, 913B–C, 921D–922A, 945B–E, 946E–947B, and 963A. Also see Vlastos (1981, pp. 14, 426). For happiness, see, e.g., 790B and 947B.

127. Cf. Irwin (1995a, pp. 349–53).

128. Korsgaard (1996a, p. 259). On types of realism in ethics, see Korsgaard (1996b, pp. 28–48, 205–8, 245–6).

129. On the ideal of assimilation to god (*homoiōsis theōi*), see especially Sedley in Fine (1999b, pp. 309–28).

130. Berlin (1977, p. 131) and cf. Ober (1998, pp. 6–7).

131. See, e.g., Korsgaard (1996a, pp. 335–62). For further discussion, see Christman (1989).

132. Cf. Bobonich (1996, pp. 262–81).

133. More precisely, Plato does not think that it is unconditionally good for people's choices and actions to be determined by their own beliefs and desires, not even their beliefs about and desires for the overall good. As we shall see in Ch. 4, however, Plato does acknowledge one way in which self-determination can be unconditionally good. In the *Timaeus*, Plato suggests that *nous* at its best is a form of self-determining activity and that failures in rationality can be understood as the effects of external forces that impinge upon and distort *nous* and to that extent leave us passive.

134. It is plausible to see *Rep.* 518B–E as evidence that the *Republic* accepts the theory of Recollection, cf. Ch. 1, n. 85. If so, 518D10–E2 tells us something quite important about the conceptual content of the lower two parts of the soul. What it suggests is that the condition of the lower two parts of the soul, even in a

courageous and moderate person, does not involve any concepts based on Recollection.

135. Sedley in Fine (1999b, p. 323).

136. Courage and moderation properly understood should include a good state of the Reasoning part of the soul, see Ch. 1, Section 1.11. Plato's fundamental worry about the emotions, insofar as they consist in certain conditions of the lower parts of the soul or in non-rational motivations, is not that they are not within the agent's control, but that their objects lack serious value.

137. For further discussion, see Section 5.8. Good choice of particulars will require a grasp of the appropriate universal, if we think of practical deliberation as moving deductively from the universal to the particular. But good choice of particulars may require grasp of the appropriate universal, even if one rejects a deductivist (or a rule/case) conception of practical deliberation. Even on a specificationist account, a grasp of the universal might be necessary in order to set the range within which further specification occurs.

138. Burnyeat (1987, pp. 238–9).

139. Or perhaps, quasi-mathematical: e.g., all ethical properties are specifiable in terms of some continuum plus determinants that are mathematical ratios or proportions.

140. See Bobonich (1995b, pp. 315–19).

141. See, e.g., *Laws* 662D–E and Irwin (1995a, pp. 343–5). For further discussion, see Section 5.8. I speak of 'greatest happiness' here without meaning to prejudge the completeness issue.

142. For other instances of the necessity claim, see *Laws* 716A2–B5. This passage may seem to offer a distressingly instrumentalist reason to be just and a restricted view of what justice is. But the passage illustrates a recurrent rhetorical strategy in the *Laws*. This is the first address to the colonists who have been educated in ordinary Greek cities and have thus received a very defective ethical education. The first address is at a simpleminded level, but points beyond itself. Plato offers this as part of an account of assimilation to god, but as we have seen, citizens will later come to recognize that this involves grasping the rational order of the world and joining with god to bring about justice in the world, 742E4–743C4, 874D2–5. By the 'nurture and education of the soul', Plato means the nurture and education which produces virtue, cf. 854E5–6. It is thus virtue whose presence makes life livable and without virtue, life is not worth living (899D8–E4 (cf. 905B–C), and 906A2–B2).

143. The necessity of virtue for happiness is much less controversial if happiness is understood in a maximalist fashion. Appealing to differences in weight between the value of virtue and that of other goods is more problematic if we recognize

degrees of virtue and hold that the more virtuous one is, the better off one is, no matter how other goods and bads are distributed. We would then have to claim that the smallest difference in virtue outweighs the largest possible difference in other goods.

144. It is difficult to find a passage that clearly commits Plato to the claim that A is happier than B and both A and B are happy. Relevant passages include *Gorg.* 478D–E, *Rep.* 465D ff., and *Symp.* 195A6. I am indebted to David Johnson for these references and discussion of them.

145. I discuss the notion of a part or component of happiness further in Section 5.8.

146. The sufficiency thesis would not, however, follow trivially: e.g., if a minimum length of time is necessary for happiness, a person might attain virtue, but fail to be happy. The claim that happiness consists in virtue is weaker than the claim that virtue is the only non-instrumental good, since if there are a plurality of non-instrumental goods, happiness might consist in some proper subset of them.

147. Annas (1999, pp. 31–51). Although I argue against some of Annas' claims, I have learned a great deal from her work.

148. Cf. Irwin (1995a, p. 346).

149. Annas (1999, p. 44).

150. Annas (1999, p. 38) seems to accept this point about the *Philebus*, cf. Irwin (1995a, pp. 335–7). The *Euthydemus'* apparent claim (280A) that wisdom is sufficient for success in art is explicitly rejected in the *Laws* (708E–709E). On the *Menexenus* (cf. Annas (1999, pp. 40–1)), 247A seems to suggest that parents are better off, i.e. happier, if their children are good. I have argued above in the text that in the *Republic*, (1) the external goods that come from justice affect one's happiness (612A ff.), and (2) the person's happiness is affected by the satisfaction of the desires of the lower parts of the soul.

151. Annas (1999, p. 42) seems to suggest that virtuous activity (in addition to the condition of soul that constitutes virtue) is necessary for happiness (this is why external goods are pursued and non-vice evils rejected) and to understand virtuous activity in a fairly normal sense, that is, it does not occur wholly within the agent's body. But this view faces problems in accounting for, e.g., the happiness of the just person on the rack. Annas thus sometimes seems to go further and attribute to Plato the full-blown Stoic view of indifferents, e.g. Annas (1999, pp. 44, 48–9). And on Annas' interpretation of the Stoics, they handle rack cases by appealing to their metaphysics of action and identifying the virtuous activity necessary for happiness with something that goes on entirely within a person's body, Annas (1992b, pp. 98–102), (1993, pp. 398–405). But a theory of indifferents and such a theory of action are very strong theses to attribute to Plato without explicit textual evidence.

152. Other relevant passages include the following: (1) *Laws* 662c ff. seems to suggest that the most virtuous life available to a person is the happiest life available to him. This may not be enough to show that virtue is sufficient for happiness: (a) even if the most virtuous life available to a person is the happiest life available to him, this does not entail that such a life is happy, and (b) waiving (a), the passage entails that the most virtuous life is happy, but not that the virtuous life is happy. (2) 829A1–5 suggests that one cannot prevent oneself from suffering injustice unless one becomes 'completely good'. Although Plato goes on to discuss war, he cannot be implying that the virtuous are immune from suffering injustice because they are invincible fighters (cf. *Laws* 638A). Rather we might interpret the passage along the lines that Vlastos suggests for a similar passage from the *Apology*. Vlastos (1985, pp. 9–10) interprets the claim at *Ap.* 30c5–d5 that a good person cannot be harmed as meaning that the good person can suffer no significant harm. The idea here is that although there are goods other than virtue, virtue is sufficient for happiness, so that harm done to virtuous people, as long as it did not impair their virtue, would still leave them happy. This is a possible reading of the *Laws* passage, but the Greek, in any case, does not say that becoming completely virtuous guarantees suffering no injustice, but only that it is a necessary condition, see England (1921, ad loc.). (3) At 906A2–B2, Plato claims that injustice destroys us, while justice 'saves or preserves [*sōizei*] us'. This seems compatible, however, with the idea that virtue guarantees that we are not miserable, although it is not sufficient for happiness. (4) *Laws* 742E4–743C4, if one takes *schedon* at 742E4 literally, it suggests that virtue is not sufficient for happiness.

153. *Laws* 660E2–3 loses its point unless we construe the participle as causal (note the parallel at 660E6) and is so translated by R. Bury, Saunders, and A. E. Taylor.

154. Cf. Annas (1999, pp. 44–5).

155. Their primary evidence consists of several passages from the early dialogues that seem to suggest that a sufficient degree of ill health could render the life of even the virtuous person not happy and, indeed, not worth living. (See Brickhouse and Smith (1987), (1989, pp. 163–7), Irwin (1977b, p. 100), (1986b), Kraut (1984, pp. 37–9), and Vlastos (1991, pp. 200–32).) Important passages include *Crito* 47E and *Gorgias* 512A–B (cf. 505A). My primary concern here is with the *Laws* and I take no position on the interpretation of the early dialogues, but let me note the following two points: (1) we can explain, consistently with the claim that virtue is sufficient for happiness, the idea that a sufficient degree of ill health may prevent one's life from being happy. As Vlastos (1985, p. 8 n. 62) suggested, Plato's point may be that extreme ill health affects the soul and destroys or disrupts its virtuous condition. (2) Allowing that a virtuous person might have a life that is not worth living

has some troubling consequences. Consider a person *P* who is virtuous and a person *S* who is more virtuous than *P*. (I assume here that virtue comes in degrees, cf., e.g., *Laws* 757C, 854D–E.) It seems clear that Plato would say that *S* is better off, i.e. happier, than *P*. (This is suggested by Plato's argument that one should never do an injustice because any act of injustice makes one's soul worse, e.g., *Ap.* 28B–D, *Crito* 47A–49B.) Now suppose that *S* has a degree of ill health that makes *S*'s life not worth living. Given the assumption that the more virtuous people are, the better off they are, it still follows that *S* is better off than *P*. Since *S*'s life is both better than *P*'s life and not worth living, it follows that *P*'s life is not worth living no matter what other goods *P* has. A similar argument can be made for any person *P* except someone who is such that there can be no one more virtuous, i.e. someone who is maximally virtuous. It thus follows that no life, except the most virtuous possible life, is worth living.

156. Indeed, *Laws* 874D2–5 seems to claim that virtue is sufficient to make one's life worth living, but it is not clear how far we should press this passage.

157. See Kraut in Kraut (1992, pp. 311–37) and, e.g., *Laws* 726A–728C.

158. Let us take up the issue of sufficiency. In the *Laws*, the two most elaborate and detailed statements of the Dependency Thesis (631B–D, 660E–661E) do not stress that virtue is sufficient to benefit from Dependent Goods. One sign of this is that Plato asserts that Dependent Goods benefit the just person without asserting that virtue guarantees correct use or that the Dependent Goods *always* benefit the just person. And, in the *Laws*, unlike the *Euthydemus*, Plato does not hold that wisdom makes good luck unnecessary, cf. n. 150; also see n. 46. *Laws* 660E–661E claims that the just person can be happy with relatively few Dependent Goods, but we do not have to hold that the *Laws* intends to assert the sufficiency of virtue for benefit that made the *Euthydemus'* position so open to counterexamples. The explanation of the Dependency Thesis that I have offered shows why, although virtue may not be strictly sufficient for benefit, it typically suffices.

159. In several passages in the *Laws*, Plato employs a rough trichotomy of goods: (1) goods of the soul, (2) goods of the body, and (3) goods concerned with property and wealth. See *Laws* 870A6–C1 and cf. 697B2–6, 717C2–6, 726A–728D, 743D–E. Cf. Aristotle *E.E.* 1218^{b}32–4, *N.E.* 1098^{b}12–20, *Pol.* 1323^{a}25–1324^{a}4, especially 1323^{b}7–29, *Protrep.* Ross 11, Düring B21; also see Cooper (1999, pp. 292–311), and Kraut (1997, pp. 53–9). This trichotomy in Plato is not fully elaborated; we are not told, for example, whether it is exhaustive or where, if anywhere, virtuous action or the welfare of others is classified. *Laws* 870B5–6 does not claim either that (a) virtue of the soul is the only psychic good and virtue of the body is the only bodily good, or (b) that the only psychic good which bodily goods are 'for the sake of' is virtue. *Laws* 870B4–5 states Plato's point in general terms: wealth is for the sake

of the goods of the body and we are to supply (on the strength of 870B3–4) the corresponding point that bodily goods are for the sake of psychic goods. The claim that wealth is third after the virtue of the body and the soul logically follows, since bodily virtue is a bodily good and the virtue of the soul is a psychic good. Plato singles out these goods—the virtue of the body and the virtue of the soul—because of their special importance within their particular classes, but his claim does not entail and should not be read as suggesting either (a) or (b). On a strict interpretation of this passage, wealth is instrumental only to bodily goods, but this is surely too restrictive; wealth might also be instrumental to psychic goods.

Goods in the second and third categories are Dependent Goods. 'Goods of the soul' include virtue which is an Independent Good, but could include other goods of the soul, e.g. pleasure. The most important new point that this passage seems to add is that the lower two kinds of goods 'are for the sake of' the goods of the soul. Plato thus seems to be claiming that the lower two sorts of goods are of value only insofar as they are used in good psychic activity or instrumentally contribute to psychic goods. This goes beyond Plato's previous claims that such goods are Dependent Goods. But this is also apparently the position of the *Philebus*, since the only components of happiness it recognizes are psychic states.

Chapter 3 Parts of the Soul and the Psychology of Virtue

1. The *Republic* does not offer an analysis of the nature of a psychic subject, psychic affections and activities, or of the relation obtaining between them. And as we shall see, the Principle of Contraries relies upon our intuitive understanding of the relation between a subject and its affections and activities. We should thus understand the claim that the parts of the soul are agent-like as the claim that psychic affections and activities stand to the parts of the soul in the same relation that we pre-reflectively think they stand in to the person who has them.

2. For desires and pleasures, see, e.g., 580D3–587E4; for *boulesthai* and *ethelein*, e.g., 437B1–C10 and 439A1–D2. For beliefs, e.g., 442B5–D1 and 574D1–575A7; for persuasion and agreement, e.g., 442B5–D1, 554C11–E5, and 589A6–B6. Also see Annas (1981, pp. 109–52), Burnyeat (1976, pp. 203–22), Joseph (1935, pp. 41–82 and 156–78), and Moline (1981, pp. 52–78). All three parts are capable of at least some form of means–end reasoning, including that involving practical goals: 580E2–581A7, cf. Annas (1981, pp. 129–30, 139, 218–20), Lesses (1987), and Moline (1981, pp. 59–61). On the *Republic*'s view, also see Gill (1996, pp. 240–75) and Penner (1990); for the analogy with bodily health, see Moravcsik (1976a), (2000), and (2001). On possible hints of psychic complexity in the *Gorgias*, see Irwin (1995a, pp. 114–17).

3. On the 'divided self' in Greek poetry, see Gill (1996, pp. 175–239).

4. Nor does Plato suggest that (i) all that the literal attribution of, e.g., belief comes to is the presence of certain patterns in behavior, or (ii) that attributing beliefs to the parts is justified because the parts are part of a larger system which is the proper subject of beliefs and the parts bear some appropriate relation to whatever it is that really does the believing, e.g., they have a prominent causal role in belief production.

5. Dennett (1981, pp. 123–4), cf. Dennett in Guttenplan (1994, p. 240).

6. The interpretation of Dennett is controversial, but for one plausible view, see McLaughlin and O'Leary-Hawthorne (1994). For richer contemporary accounts of intentional systems, see, e.g., Mark Johnston in MacDonald and MacDonald (1995, pp. 459–60 n. 25) who holds that a system capable of having intentions 'should have some capacity for practical reasoning and have a means of representing its own desires and beliefs, a means of representing possible outcomes of action and the extent to which they serve its desires, and a capacity to act upon what it has judged to be the best alternative'; and Fred Dretske (1992), (1995) who argues that literally true attributions of beliefs and desires to a system requires that the system have internal representations.

7. For ἐθέλειν in the sense of ability or capacity, see *Phdr.* 230D and *Rep.* 370B. Thus we do not need the actual existence of contraries to show lack of unity; the possibility of them is sufficient. The Principle of Contraries does not by itself allow us to establish that any two given beliefs and desires belong to the same part, since two desires might fail to be contraries in the sense specified by the Principle, yet still belong to different parts (e.g. the rational desire to refrain from drinking and the appetitive desire to go to sleep). In order for the parts of the soul to play the role that they do in the *Republic*, Plato needs to account for (a) the grouping of different desires together into one part, (b) the attribution to each part of some particular end or set of ends (580D–581A), and (c) the attribution to each part of some awareness of what goes on in the other parts and outside the agent.

8. Price (1995, pp. 41, 53–5) and Woods (1987, pp. 33–4). Price (1995, pp. 56–7), however, also seems to suggest that Plato's views in the *Republic* are inconsistent and that his 'explicit' view treats the parts of the soul as 'subjects'.

9. If properly applied, this principle need not introduce a vicious regress or inconsistencies. I accept Irwin's (1995a, pp. 229–30) account, but see also Williams (1973) and Wilson (1976).

10. Note that affections (*pathē*) are ascribed here to the parts of the soul.

11. At *Rep.* 435C9–D5, Socrates remarks that they will not accurately apprehend 'this' using their present methods, but that a 'longer and fuller path' is necessary. In the context, 'this' must refer to the question of whether the soul has three forms in it, but when Plato refers back to this passage at 504B1 ff., the question that needs a

longer path concerns the definition of the virtues. For discussion, see Adam (1979) on 435D. But 435C9–D5 does not justify reading away as merely metaphorical the attribution of beliefs and desires to the parts of the soul.

1.   In the *Republic*, Plato sometimes says that an account he provides is metaphorical or given through an image (e.g. 506E, 514A, 588B). He never uses such language to describe the conclusions of the Book 4 argument.

2.   435C9–D5 does not say that a deeper inquiry would lead to a different result, it rather claims that the Book 4 argument will not settle the question 'accurately' (*akribōs*, 435D1). This is compatible with the idea that the Book 4 argument establishes the correct result, but does not do so in the epistemically best way. This is a point that we cannot appreciate until we reach the metaphysics and epistemology of Books 5–7. There we learn that all knowledge requires knowledge of the Form of the Good (507D11–E2, 508E3) or at least that the best sort of knowledge does (505A, 508A5). Plato there holds that knowledge requires knowing a Form and requires an ability to give an account (531E, 534B); he also sketches the way in which dialectic must give its accounts (509D–511E, note especially 511E2–4). The Book 4 argument falls well short of these requirements and thus is not the most accurate way of settling the question. A more accurate way might, for example, explicitly employ the correct definition of 'soul'.

3.   I have argued that Plato does not suggest at 435C9–D5 that the conclusion of the Book 4 argument is false. And so he gives us no suggestion of what the 'true' account is. But if he rejects the Book 4 argument, it does not follow that he thinks the parts of the soul are not agent-like; he might, instead, hold that there are four agent-like parts. So even if we were to dismiss the conclusions of the Book 4 argument, we could not infer that Plato rejects agent-like parts of the soul. Although Book 10 may suggest that the only part of the soul that exists discarnate is the Reasoning part, Book 10 does not suggest that talk of agent-like parts while the person is embodied is metaphorical. The Book 4 argument is one of the two most detailed and careful arguments in the *Republic* (along with that at 475E–480A); we should not discard its conclusions without strong reason.

12.   People are at least the more basic subjects and, within ordinary assumptions, are the basic subjects. They may even be strictly the proper subjects of spiritedness, if being spirited is a quality possessed by a person in virtue of the condition of more than one part of the soul.

13.   Note that ὧδε at *Rep.* 436B5 is picked up by πῶς at B7 and that πῶς is answered by the statement of the Principle of Contraries (436B8–C1).

14.   See Burnyeat (1976, pp. 29–39) for a convincing argument that for Plato the claim that a person F's with X entails that X is what does the F-ing or is the subject

of F-ing. On the other side, see Price (1995, p. 54). Price's view that 'a person F's with X' entails that X is 'an aspect of [a person] in respect of which [she] do[es] it', fits very awkwardly the option that Plato considers (eventually to reject) at 436B1 that we learn, grow angry, and desire the pleasures of nutrition 'with the whole soul'. Price's view would seem to make the whole soul into an 'aspect' of the person, but this seems hard to reconcile with, e.g., the claim that the discarnate soul continues to possess knowledge (and that it is because of some special features of the soul that it can possess knowledge).

15. A point rightly emphasized by Stalley (1975).

16. I accept Adam's understanding of *Rep.* 436D7–E1. I keep the by now common translation of *peripheres* at 436E2–4 as 'circumference', although it is not at all clear that this is correct. Cf. *Parm.* 137E5–6, 137E–138A1, and *Phil.* 51C3–4; of lines and surfaces, *peripheres* just means 'round' or 'curved' and this seems to be its meaning at *Rep.* 436E. Once understood this way, there is no temptation at all to think of *to peripheres* as the subject of motion (as it must be on Price's and Woods' interpretation). I am indebted to Reviel Netz for discussion and help on this point.

17. Price (1995, pp. 41, 54) holds that Plato accepts the legitimacy of such reversals, cf. Woods (1987, pp. 34–6).

18. More precisely, *Rep.* 436D1 does not explicitly use 'part', but uses the locution τὸ μέν τι/τὸ δέ.

19. Another strategy is to say that X moves *kata* Y *just means* that Y is a part of X and that Y moves. Greek allows such a distributive use of *kata*, *LSJ* s.v. B II. But we have several reasons for not construing Plato this way here. (1) Consider how the *kata* locution is introduced in this passage. Plato introduces this as a case in which 'tops stand still as a whole at the same time that they are in motion when with the peg fixed in one point they revolve' (436D5–7). The next clause generalizes this to 'any other case of something moving around in a circle in the same place [*allo ti kuklō(i) periion en tē(i) autē(i) hedra(i)*]' (436D7). The 'in the same place' qualification is necessary to distinguish the case of rotation on an axis from the case of something revolving in a circle. Now consider *Rep.* 436E3–4. Here the top is moving in a circle (*kuklō(i) kineisthai*) and doing this *kata to peripheres*. This would be ambiguous if it merely stated that the circumference was moving in a circle, since the circumference might be revolving in a circle around a fixed point in a plane. In doing so, it would sweep out an annulus. It is not ambiguous, if *kata to peripheres* specifies the direction of motion, that is, that the top is moving in a circle with respect to its own circumference, that is, rotating, not revolving. (2) In the head/rest of the body counterexample, Plato rejects the description that *ho autos* moves and stays at rest. He does not replace this description with the *kata* terminology (or suggest that it can be so replaced), but with

two different subjects (*to men/to de*) having contraries. But if *kata* were construed in a distributive sense, Plato's preferred description would be equivalent to saying the same man (*ho autos*) moves *kata* his hands and rests *kata* his body. If this were right, Plato at 436B10–C1 should not so sharply distinguish between the option of one thing suffering incomplete contraries from the option of more than one thing suffering contraries. Two distinct things (X and Y) suffering complete contraries could fall under the case of one thing having X and Y as parts and suffering one contrary *kata* X and the other contrary *kata* Y. (3) The distinction between being *pros* something and *kata* something is essential in the case of motion in order to distinguish between motion toward something and motion with respect to something. If *kata* specifies the part moving, then moving *pros* X will have to cover both kinds of movement. The *pros* clause in the Principle will have to rule out both moving and not moving with respect to something and moving and not moving toward something. But then the same thing can move and not move *pros* the same thing: the circumference of a rotating sphere moves *pros* the axis (because the circumference rotates around it) and does not move *pros* the axis (because the sphere neither contracts nor expands). (4) In any case, if *kata* is used distributively so as to specify the different subjects of rest and motion, it is simply equivalent to the part option. But then the question at 436C5–6 should be answered yes, instead of no, because of cases such as that of the spinning top. (Given that we allow that, e.g., the circumference moves when the top rotates and stands still with respect to the axis.) *Pros* would then have to do the work seen in the top example, but there is no sign that it does this.

20. More precisely, as long as the center point of the top does not move with respect to any of the three axes (e.g. the top does not move up/down on its axis and does not undergo translation in the plane perpendicular to the axis), the top occupies the same space.

21. On the other construal of the head and hands example, the conflict would be the very complicated case of willing or intending or desiring that one part of the body move and that another part stay still. At *Rep.* 436C5, C9, C11, and D1, ἵστημι is in the perfect and thus is intransitive. Since the head and hands example is just a special case of 436C5–6, we should understand it to involve being at rest and in motion. κινέω at 436C5 and C11 and D1 may be either passive or middle, but the passive is standard for being in motion, cf. *Soph.* 250B2. The accusatives at 436C10 are accusatives of respect and this is made clearer by 436D1.

22. The position of γε in 439B5 stresses τὸ αὐτό and emphasizes that Plato's conclusion is that the *same thing* is not acting. γε rarely intrudes in unified phrases such as τὸ αὐτό and its position here makes it clear that the important words are τὸ αὐτό and not τῷ αὐτῷ. See Denniston (1981, pp. 146–7).

23. Note how this too picks up the language of the head/hands case and the statement of the Principle of Contraries: τὰ αὐτά and ἕτερά at *Rep.* 436B5–6 and B8–10; also cf. 439B8–11 with 436C11–D1.

24. Note that there is no *kata* or *pros* qualification here.

25. The archer is perhaps an unfortunate example because it can be tempting to think of this not as a spatial case, but as a case of action or the initiation of action which has a psychic component and there is no need to partition the soul to handle these cases (but then Plato does not think that one has to partition the soul to handle them). Plato picks a simple case of physical motion that involves the vocabulary of pushing and pulling, perhaps because these notions recur in his characterization of desire (cf. 439B9–11 with 437C3–9).

26. We need not worry here about the deep metaphysics of sensible objects: e.g. whether sensible things are just bundles of properties or tropes (at, perhaps, some position in the Receptacle) or whether they include some further element of particularity.

27. Despite occasional loose language suggesting that the person is something over and above the three parts of the soul (e.g. *Rep.* 443C9–444A2, 550A4–B7, and 553B7–D7), the Book 4 account does not allow for such an entity and we can explain the claims that Plato makes without invoking it, see Irwin (1995a, pp. 285–8) and Kahn (1987, pp. 79–81). A distinct person over and above the three parts would be hard to distinguish from the Reasoning part to the extent that a person is a rational actor and has the capacities of the Reasoning part. It would also undermine the role of the parts of the soul in explaining a person's choices and threatens to lead to a pointless regress.

28. On language linking this to earlier passages, cf. n. 23. Also note that the contrast marked by μὲν/δέ at *Rep.* 439C5–7 is picked up at 439D4–8 and combined with the dative construction, cf. 436A8–B2.

29. ὡρίσθω at *Rep.* 439E2 picks up 436B2 and B5.

30. For further criticisms of Price, see Bermudez (1996) and Cooper (1995). Price (1995, pp. 40–57) also suggests that the part does not *have* desires and beliefs, but *is* a 'home' or a 'field' of desires and beliefs. On this account, the unitary soul is the subject of all beliefs and desires and thus, e.g., desires drink and rejects it at the same time. These predicates are, however, relativized so that they are 'with respect to' (*kata*) different parts (*eidē*) of the soul and thus can be had by the same subject. I have argued that this interpretation misrepresents Plato's argument in Book 4, but we have other reasons to reject this account. First, Plato in *Republic* 4 and elsewhere speaks of the parts as doing contraries or having affections (*pathē*), cf. n. 10 and *Tim.* 69C6–D4. Second, Price's interpretation imposes a further, quite substantive, restriction on the possession of contraries over and above the Principle of

Contraries. Once relativized to different parts, the Principle should allow, e.g., incompatible beliefs. Because Price finds this unsatisfactory, he demotes apparently incompatible beliefs to half-beliefs. But we do not have textual evidence for this sort of supplement to the Principle of Contraries.

31. I do so for convenience and do not mean to suggest that Plato would describe every conative affection as an *epithumia*, cf. Irwin (1995a, p. 205).

32. The only explicit comment on this point in the literature is Adam (1979, ad loc.): 'One part of the soul asks, and the other answers.' But this is not right; the soul, or—as the argument will soon show—more precisely, the part of the soul, nods assent to itself (437c5). The opposites described here are done by different parts of the soul. The assent and dissent are activities of different parts and the assent and dissent each go on entirely within one part. Although communication among the parts is possible, assent and dissent are inherently part of the representation of a desire. If all cases of desire are describable as a kind of assent or dissent, then the notion of assent involved cannot be too complex. Plato here does not explicitly argue that assent and dissent are genuine contraries and he does not analyze the nature of their opposition. Nevertheless, he treats the question as one concerning the compatibility of two psychological or propositional attitudes (accepting a proposition or asserting a positive imperative and rejecting a proposition or asserting a negative imperative) and he does not assimilate the impossibility of the same thing doing both of these to the impossibility of the same proposition being true and false.

33. On whether the strength of a desire can be defined, non-vacuously, in causal terms see n. 39. We might try to refine the above account by specifying a non-dispositional property grounding this capacity.

34. For some contemporary discussions of agent-causation, see Clarke (1993), Kane (1996), O'Connor (1993), and W. Rowe (1987). I discuss related issues further in Section 4.2.

35. The example is indebted to Fred Dretske; for an important discussion of a related issue in a contemporary, naturalistic context, see Dretske (1992).

36. Insofar as a command is linguistic it can invite deliberation and rational evaluation, even if it does not stem from them. Hare (1963, pp. 67–79) sees intentions as self-commands, but Plato's commands here are just desires and do not have the role of intentions (i.e. they do not settle the person on something); rather Plato's commands give content to the desire and provide a link, but not a decisive link, to action, cf. Mele (1995, pp. 20–1, 71–6). On the point that intentions are more tightly and more normatively linked to action than desires, see Bratman (1987) and (1999).

37. Cf. Mele (1992, pp. 46–85). I shall usually omit from now on the 'try to do' qualification. The most interesting and problematic cases of akratic action, in con-

temporary accounts, are those in which the person acts voluntarily or intentionally. (See Mele (1987, pp. 3–49) and, for an influential skeptical challenge to the possibility of such cases, Watson (1977).) Plato does not try to develop a technical notion of voluntary or intentional action that is intended to capture, as an important desideratum, action that is not psychologically compelled. (In the sense of the 'Socratic paradox', any action that is contrary to what is, in fact, best for the person is involuntary (*akōn*), so all akratic action is involuntary. Since this includes *any* action proceeding from a false judgment about what is best, this notion of involuntary action is quite distinct from what we think of as psychological compulsion.) But the *Republic* recognizes cases of knowledgeable action against an overall best judgment and does not suggest that all of these are due to psychological compulsion.

38. Thinking of desires as tugs does not require or even suggest that the desire lacks intentional content. One might think that the assent or dissent specifies the content of a desire while the description of it as a pull merely attributes strength to the desire. (Even this would not suggest that Plato thought that desires had no intentional content, since he describes them as both forms of assent or dissent and as pulls.) But this does not seem to be Plato's idea here: even when described as a tug or a pull, the desire is directed toward some object and this may specify its intentional content (e.g. 439A9–B1). This also leaves open the possibility that a desire's content affects its strength. Cf. Velleman (1989, pp. 190–6) on the distinction between the strength a desire has independently of its significance being grasped and the strength it has because its significance is grasped.

39. On the notion of the strength of a desire, see Gosling (1990, pp. 174–85), Mele (1987), (1990), and (1992), Penner (1978), Santas (1966), Thalberg (1985), and Watson (1977, pp. 329–30).

40. Plato never explicitly makes this claim. Cf. Davidson's (1980, p. 23) well-known principle P1: 'If an agent wants to do X more than he wants to do Y and he believes himself free to do either X or Y, then he will intentionally do X if he does either X or Y intentionally.'

41. Mele (1995, p. 16) usefully distinguishes four ways of preventing best judgment from coming apart from motivational strength once we have recognized both: (1) a best judgment causes highest motivational strength, (2) highest motivational strength causes a best judgment, (3) a common cause causes both highest motivational strength and best judgment, and (4) there is a conceptual connection between best judgment and highest motivational strength.

42. I assume that there is a desire for what is overall best going along with the belief about what is overall best.

43. *Rep.* 442B5–D1 and 589A6–B6 (cf. 554E3–5) show that this is persuading the Appetitive part. Since the agreement includes the Spirited part, the Spirited part

too should be able to make overall judgments about what is best for itself. λόγος here must mean more than 'speech' and should mean something like 'reasoning' or 'argument', since suppression by compulsion and fear could involve speech. For the construction with ἄμεινον, see 463D and *LSJ*. Also see n. 2.

44. With respect to Aristotle, John Cooper (1999, pp. 244–6) makes the important point that it is conceptual overlap or the sameness of conceptual content between reason and the non-rational desires that allows reason to persuade non-rational desires, for example, by drawing anger's attention to the broader features of the action or to long-run considerations. This does not require that there be full overlap between the concepts of reason and those found in non-rational motivations (some concepts of reason may not be shared by the non-rational motivations). Indeed, we can loosen somewhat the requirement for conceptual overlap. We might allow, for example, that two speakers can successfully communicate even if they have different conceptions of the concept used in communication. Suppose you think of water as H_2O, and I think of it as the odorless, tasteless liquid that freezes at winter temperatures. You and I will, even without awareness of the difference in our conceptions, be able to have successful linguistic interactions about water in a wide range of circumstances. Similarly, a token of 'justice' in a rational judgment or desire may have an interpretation associated with it different from that associated with a token of 'justice' in a non-rational motivation.

45. If, when it is not persuaded by the Reasoning part, the Appetitive part has an overall judgment that it is best to act in accordance with its own strongest desire and this judgment conflicts with the overall judgment of the Reasoning part, we could explain the agent's akratic action as the result of a conflict between two parts of the soul each of which acts in accordance with its own overall judgment. As I argue below, however, the possibility of conflict within, e.g., the Appetitive part is a problem for this strategy. Cf. A. Walker (1989, p. 663).

46. Irwin (1995a, p. 215), Lesses (1987), and Price (1995, pp. 50–1).

47. Cf. *Rep.* 442A5–7 which describes the Appetitive part as 'by nature [*phusei*] most insatiable for money'; also see 551A, 553C–D, 555A, 558D, 561A, 572C, and 573D. On an initial reading, 580E–581A seems quite straightforward. Plato here attributes a love of money to the Appetitive part of the soul and explains that it loves money because money is a means of satisfying its other desires. This seems to show that Plato attributes to the Appetitive part at least the ability to make means–end judgments about the usefulness of money in satisfying some desires. But another reading of this passage is possible. Let us call this the 'Capture Interpretation'. (I am indebted to Charlotte Stough for discussion of this idea.) The Capture Interpretation is based on a passage that occurs in Plato's description of the origin

of an oligarchic man. Such a man is born of a timocratic father and in his youth sees his father suffer various political and financial misfortunes. Chastened by the experience of his father, the son 'thrusts love of honor and the spirited part head-long out of the throne of his soul . . . such a man now puts the appetitive and money-loving part on the throne, and makes it the great king within himself . . . he also makes the reasoning and spirited parts sit by it on the ground on either side and be slaves, letting the one [i.e. the Reasoning part] neither calculate about nor consider anything but where more money will come from less' (*Rep.* 553B8–D4, cf. 442A7–B3). The key idea of this interpretation is that the Appetitive part itself never engages in means–end reasoning and never holds any means–end beliefs: all such reasoning is done by the Reasoning part. In the case of money, the Appetitive part forces the Reasoning part to carry out means–end calculations (hence, 'Capture' Interpretation) but never itself holds any means–end beliefs.

There are, however, decisive reasons for rejecting this interpretation: (1) Plato never says that it is the Reasoning part that realizes that money is an instrument for the satisfaction of the Appetitive part's desires. Note again *Rep.* 553B8–D4, which is the most detailed discussion in the *Republic* of the capture of the Reasoning part. The task set here for the Reasoning part is not that of determining how to satisfy the Appetitive part's desires for food, drink, and sex, but rather, the task of deter-mining how to make the most money. (The Reasoning part is to consider, for example, whether to buy internet or biotechnology stocks.) Thus the only passage that might be thought to support the Capture Interpretation suggests instead that the Appetitive part on its own realizes that money is instrumental to the satisfac-tion of its desires and then sets the Reasoning part to calculate the best ways of making money, cf. *Rep.* 442A5–7: the Appetitive part's love of money is natural to it. (2) Once we try to fill out the details of the Capture Interpretation, it is very dif-ficult to avoid attributing some kind of means–end reasoning to the Appetitive part. (a) To begin, Plato does not depict the capture or co-opting of the Reasoning part as merely the effect or outcome of the activity of the Appetitive part; rather, the Appetitive part *tries* (*Rep.* 442B2) to enslave the Reasoning part. How could we explain such an attempt without attributing to the Appetitive part something like the belief that capturing the Reasoning part is a means to attaining its own goals? (b) More generally, there seems to be no plausible way to explain the genesis of the Appetitive part's desire for money without ascribing at least some means–end beliefs to it. Consider the following argument.

Fact 1: The Appetitive part desires drink.

Fact 2: The Reasoning part believes that money is the way to satisfy this desire. (I leave aside whether we must attribute to the Reasoning part the belief that money is the *best* way to satisfy the desire for drink.)

On the Capture Interpretation, from Fact 1 and Fact 2, Fact 3 is supposed to follow:
Fact 3: The Appetitive part desires money.

But how does this happen? If we say that the Reasoning part explains to the Appetitive part the relation between money and drink and that the Appetitive part acts because it grasps this explanation, we cannot avoid attributing means–end beliefs to the Appetitive part. So let us suppose that the Reasoning part simply issues the following imperative to the Appetitive part: 'Desire money!'. The problem now is to explain why the Appetitive part accepts this imperative: after all, the Appetitive part, at least on some occasions in some people, does not accept the imperatives of the Reasoning part. The only plausible explanation for the Appetitive part's acceptance of this imperative is that the Appetitive part comes to see the relation between the Reasoning part's imperative and what the Appetitive part already wants. Finally, there is one further problem with this last suggestion that the Appetitive part accepts the Reasoning part's imperative 'Desire money!'. The problem is that even in some people whose Reasoning part has not been captured by their Appetitive part, their Appetitive part is still unruly and, in particular, may still desire money (*Rep.* 571B–572B). But if the Reasoning part has not been captured, it will not issue the imperative 'Desire money!' and we shall need another way to explain the Appetitive part's desire for money. The Appetitive part must either do the means–end reasoning itself or come to grasp the Reasoning part's belief—not obey its imperative—that money is instrumental to the satisfaction of its desires. And this requires that the Appetitive part have at least some means–end beliefs.

48. The lower parts do not have the appropriate concepts to appreciate the good condition of the Reasoning part and will not attribute value to the goods valued by the other parts, *Rep.* 581C–E.

49. This passage expands the account given of the parts of the soul in Book 4, but is not inconsistent with it. The need for expansion is clearer once we see how weak the Book 4 account is and that the Principle of Contraries is not enough to establish the unity of a part of the soul, cf. n. 7.

50. *Rep.* 558D–559D and Reeve (1988, pp. 135–6).

51. Even if some prompting by the Reasoning part is necessary for the lower parts to be reliably successful, the lower parts must have the appropriate concepts allowing them to respond to the Reasoning part's communications. Persuasion of the lower parts includes the sort of education that results in long-term effects, but this, too, will involve acquiring and retaining the appropriate beliefs and persuasion on a particular occasion is also possible. Cf. Gill (1997).

52. On Davidson's (1982) and (1986) theory, for example, the location of two psychic items in different subsystems does not explain their failure to interact

rationally, since subsystems are functionally defined in terms of rational interaction, see Mele (1987, pp. 76–8) and Pears (1984, pp. 84–7).

53. For a contemporary defense of this claim, see Haksar (1991, pp. 1–58); for an influential denial, see Parfit (1984).

54. Plato does not try to work out in detail what the epistemic differences might be between the Appetitive and the Spirited parts. But the most important fact about them is explained by their shared epistemic limitation.

55. Cf. Ch. 1, n. 88.

56. Irwin (1995a, p. 216). But cf. 'Only the rational part has desires that rest on a conviction about what is best, not on the strength of other desires' (p. 216) and, especially, pp. 293 and 295.

57. Irwin (1995a, p. 215, emphasis added).

58. E.g. Irwin (1995a, pp. 220–1).

59. Irwin (1995a, pp. 215, 234).

60. Irwin (1995a, p. 290).

61. It also seems that the Spirited part could suffer conflicts that satisfy the intuitive description of contrariety 'as such'. Irwin characterizes this contrariety between the Spirited and the Appetitive parts (which suffices to license the Principle of Contraries) as follows: the impulses of the Spirited part 'are opposed not just to an appetite but to acting on appetite, as such, on this occasion. The spirited impulse is not merely an aversion to the particular appetite; it opposes the agent's tendency to be guided by appetite to this degree' (Irwin 1995b, p. 212). Consider the following case that draws on Irwin's description of the parts. The Spirited part has an immediate desire for justice, but it is not committed to virtue if the cost is dishonor (p. 234); that is, when the cost of virtue is dishonor, the Spirited part prefers honor or thinks that it is, on the whole, better (cf. p. 215). In this case, it seems reasonable to say that the Spirited part opposes not just a particular desire it has, but also acting on immediate desires, as such, on this occasion; or that it opposes the agent's tendency to be guided by immediate good-dependent desires to this degree. Angry impulses also seem to provide cases of such conflict. In some cases in which it is more virtuous and more honorable (and thus better) to refrain from acting on an angry impulse, the Spirited part will have a desire that opposes acting on the angry impulse, as such, on this occasion and it will oppose the agent's tendency to be guided by angry impulses to this degree. It is thus not clear that Irwin's intuitive characterization of 'contrariety as such' succeeds in avoiding splitting within the Spirited part. Other interpretations could be considered, e.g., contrariety 'as such' occurs in cases in which the opposing desire rejects the object of the opposed desire as not the sort of thing that should be taken into account at all (and thus also rejects the opposed desire itself). This allows us to

sustain a distinction between the Spirited and Appetitive parts and, arguably, to avoid a division within the Spirited part or the Appetitive part (honor, etc. are always *relevant*). But since Irwin thinks that the Reasoning part in its judgments of the good does take into account, within proper limits, the objects of the lower parts, this will not distinguish the Reasoning part from the lower parts. Further, if, e.g., the Spirited part ever acts on a desire for its short-run good against its desire for its long-run good, i.e. what is overall good, there is what seems to be akrasia within the lower parts without the explicit application of the Principle of Contraries.

62. Plato characterizes thirst in Book 4 both as a desire for drink (437D11, an object) and for drinking (439B1, an action). Insofar as thirst is characterized as a desire to drink, it has affinities with a desire for pleasure understood as a restoration which is Plato's standard conception of pleasure in the *Republic*, see Gosling and Taylor (1984, pp. 105–28) and *Rep.* 439D8. For further discussion in connection with the *Philebus*, cf. Section 4.6.

63. Cf. Mele (1987, pp. 75–84), Pears (1984, pp. 87–106), and Walker (1989, p. 664).

64. Cf. Irwin (1995a, pp. 214–16).

65. On this issue, see Gardner (1993, pp. 40–84), M. Johnston in MacDonald and MacDonald (1995, pp. 433–5), and Pears (1984), (1991).

66. Cf. Gardner (1993, p. 80).

67. Cf. Peacocke in Peacocke (1994, pp. xix–xx).

68. On similar issues with respect to self-deception, see Pears (1991).

69. As Gardner (1993, pp. 73–6) argues, one serious problem for partitioning theories is explaining the origin of the subsystem. The idea that the lower parts are 'added on' gives Plato an explanation of their origin, but, I have argued, at a high cost. A natural way of trying to avoid this is to see the Reasoning part developing a kind of internal complexity that does not involve the emergence of different subjects. This is the sort of account, I argue in Ch. 4, that we find in the later dialogues.

70. The further claim that the lower parts are not part of me does not follow from the claim about my identity with the Reasoning part after death: the lower parts might be essential to me for a phase of my existence, or even if they were always inessential, they might still be parts of *me*. But seeing the lower parts as more alien or external to me than this is fostered by understanding them as genuine subjects. Also see Plato's description of the soul as a creature composed of a human (the Reasoning part) grown together with two non-human animals (a lion and a hydra-headed beast) that has an external cover in the shape of a human (*Rep.* 588B–591A). Cf. Annas (1999, pp. 134–6) and Gill (1997).

71. This is particularly troubling, if the cooperation of *thumos* is usually necessary for reason winning, cf. Sedley (1992).

72. The important point concerns access to epistemic resources: the lower parts do not have access to the Forms or concepts derived from an awareness of them (cf. Alcinous 25.5); the Reasoning part can draw on both the resources of perception and those of an awareness of Forms. Plato in the *Republic* does not try to anatomize in full detail the functions of the parts in the process of perception. Cf. Burnyeat (1976, pp. 33–6), Price (1995, pp. 70–1), and Reeve (1988, pp. 303–4).

73. See Fodor (1996) and (1998b, pp. 127–42).

74. The beliefs, desires, and emotions associated with each part interact rationally to a significant degree and insofar as these groups of psychic items do so and are goal-structured, they provide a more or less coherent viewpoint. If we do not entirely reject the idea of a subject of mental states, then it is not unreasonable to explain the structure of these beliefs and desires and their associated epistemic capacities by attributing them to distinct subjects, cf. n. 53. The particular form in which Plato accepts innate concepts may also be relevant. If the Reasoning part is to recollect, it must pre-exist; the claim that the lower parts do not pre-exist would provide a good explanation of why they do not recollect. Once we try to work out the details of such a theory, significant costs and difficulties may arise, but the initial move is not unnatural and is plausibly thought to have considerable explanatory power.

75. The first quotation is Fortenbaugh (1975, p. 23); the second, Saunders (1962, p. 37). Also see Belfiore (1986), Rees (1957), and Roberts (1987). On the later history of psychic division, see Vander Waerdt (1985a) and (1985b).

76. The application of the Principle of Contraries requires neither akratic action nor actual akratic conflict, since the mere possibility of akratic conflict is sufficient for its application. Thus a perfectly harmonious soul still has these parts. Indeed, even the possibility of akratic conflict may not be necessary for the Principle of Contraries, since inconsistent explicitly held non-action-guiding beliefs would seem to license its application.

77. The passage's details show that calculation (*logismos*) is included among the affections that are or exert a pulling force. At 644E1, $\tau\alpha\hat{\upsilon}\tau\alpha$ in $\tau\alpha\hat{\upsilon}\tau\alpha$ $\tau\grave{\alpha}$ $\pi\acute{\alpha}\theta\eta$ points backwards to 644C6–D3 and *logismos* is explicitly mentioned at 644D2. The pull of calculation is included among the 'pulling forces' ($\tau\hat{\omega}\nu$ $\H{\epsilon}\lambda\xi\epsilon\omega\nu$) at 644E5. Are these $\H{\epsilon}\lambda\xi\epsilon\iota\varsigma$ the *pathē* at E1? That the $\H{\epsilon}\lambda\xi\epsilon\iota\varsigma$ of E5 refer to the *pathē* at E1 (or to their exertion of force) is shown by Plato's basic characterization of the *pathē* at E2–3: they 'draw' us and 'pull against' ($\mathring{\alpha}\nu\theta\acute{\epsilon}\lambda\kappa o\upsilon\sigma\iota\nu$) each other. The word choice of $\H{\epsilon}\lambda\xi\epsilon\iota\varsigma$ simply draws out the notion of pulling ($\H{\epsilon}\lambda\kappa\omega$) in $\mathring{\alpha}\nu\theta\acute{\epsilon}\lambda\kappa o\upsilon\sigma\iota\nu$. Although the demonstrative does not occur at E5, the article in Greek can have a demonstrative force (e.g. Kühner and Gerth, (1955, sec. 461.8)); $\tau\hat{\omega}\nu$ $\H{\epsilon}\lambda\xi\epsilon\omega\nu$ is

translated, I think appropriately, as 'these' affections by Bury (1926), Saunders in Cooper (1997), and A. E. Taylor (1960). We should not be troubled by the idea that calculation is classified as a *pathos*, rather than, e.g., some sort of activity; *pathos* is quite a general term (that includes having a false belief, *Tht.* 187D3, cf. *Phil.* 49A4–5, and also see *Tht.* 196B9). In any case, we should distinguish between the activity of forming a belief or a calculation and the state of having a belief or calculation. The latter is passive in a way that the former is not. Plato draws a similar distinction at *Tht.* 191D4–192A4 and characterizes having a *doxa* (which is itself the outcome of a process of silent speech) as a *pathos*, *Soph.* 264A4–B4. I would like to thank Terry Irwin and André Laks for discussion of these issues.

78. *Laws* 644E1 taken with 645D6–7 shows that Plato here classifies *thumos* as a *pathos* of the soul and Plato goes out of his way to distinguish clearly between an affection (*pathos*) of the soul and a part (*meros*) of the soul (863B3). Note also the use of the plural at *Laws* 645D6–7 and 934A5. Cf. Saunders (1962, pp. 38–41). At 644C6–7, pleasure and pain are described as 'two foolish counselors (*sumboulō aphrone*)'. (Cf. *Tim.* 69D2–3 where boldness (*tharros*) and fear (*phobos*) are described as *sumboulō aphrone*.) But this description is immediately rejected as unclear at 644D4–6 and Plato replaces it with the puppet image. In any case, Plato never in the *Laws* or elsewhere treats pleasure and pain as agent-like parts, i.e. as the subjects of mental states and activities.

79. Such conflict can produce akratic action and tends to lead to mistaken views of the good, see *Laws* 902A6–B2, *Phdr.* 237D5–238C4, and *Rep.* 430E5–431B7. I am indebted to Eric Hutton for discussion of these issues.

80. *Soph.* 227A–230E. On the *Philebus*, see Rees (1957, p. 112).

81. Whether *Laws* 10 understands the soul as a self-moving thing or as a kind of motion, it does not suggest a partitioning of the soul into agent-like parts.

82. Those who may still be inclined to think that the *Laws* passage is, at least by itself, compatible with agent-like parts of the soul, although it is not evidence for them, may find my interpretation of Plato's later position the best overall explanation of his later views in light of the argument in Section 4.2 that the *Theaetetus* excludes the possibility that the parts of the soul could, as they did in the *Republic*, have conceptual powers.

83. We should probably understand 'perception' (*aisthēsis*) at 645E1 as a conceptualized state, that is, more precisely as a mixture of *aisthēsis* and belief (*doxa*), cf. Ch. 4, n. 43. There is no suggestion that drunkenness takes away all belief and leaves the person with a contentless drive. Should we include (some tokens of) all things weakened by drink among the golden cords? If so, it is interesting to find at least certain perceptual beliefs associated with calculation, although Plato does not make much of this here.

84. In the *Laws*, 'akrasia' (ἀκράτεια), 'akratic' (ἀκρατής), and 'self-controlled' (ἐγκρατής) are most commonly used with regard to pleasure and pain: 636C6, 710A8, 840C5, 886A9, and 908C2–3. But these are not the only things with regard to which one can have or lack self-restraint: other items (see 869A2–3 and 934A3–6) include fears (φόβοις), desires (ἐπιθυμίαις), envious emotions (φθόνοις), and spirited emotions (θυμοῖς).

85. What is the relation between these affections and the agent's actions? Can, for example, calculation, fear, or spirited emotion 'lead' or draw a person to perform a certain action without being combined somehow with a desire? Plato does not address this issue, but some of the affections he mentions simply are desires: e.g. ἐπιθυμίαι and ἔρως. For other affections which are not desires, it is plausible that each instance of the affection is associated with an appropriate desire. For example, the affection of envy might be associated with a desire to improve one's own position vis-à-vis others (or diminish that of others). And with regard to calculation, we can associate the agent's overall judgment with the desire for what he believes best for himself overall.

86. On the necessity of the eventual corruption of autocrats, even those with the sort of knowledge had by philosophers, see Vlastos (1981, pp. 204–17) and (1994, vol. 2, pp. 102–3). One might reject this interpretation and argue that *Laws* 875C3–D5 shows that a person who really has genuine *epistēmē* will not be akratic; note that *epistēmē* does not occur in 875A1–C3. Plato might still think that such genuine *epistēmē* is so rare (875D2–3) that he abandons the autocratic rule of philosopher-kings. It may be difficult to settle this point with certainty, but I incline to accepting Vlastos' view for three reasons. (1) 691C5–D4 and, especially, 713C4–D3 seem to claim that anyone who rules as an autocrat—implicitly including those with genuine *epistēmē*—would be corrupted and it is reasonable that such corruption would begin with akrasia. (2) 689B2–4 explicitly includes *epistēmē*; the fact that this is described as 'ignorance' does not, I think, suggest that a person in this state suffers any cognitive deficiencies. Plato's point is, rather, that (a) such a state is not sufficient for the virtue of wisdom (*phronēsis*, *Laws* 645E1–2), and (b) such *epistēmē* will soon be lost. (3) In Section 3.9, I suggest some theoretical reasons that would allow for akrasia, even in one possessing *epistēmē*.

87. Cf. Mele (1987, pp. 7–8) and Rorty (1980b).

88. England (1921, ad loc.).

89. Cf. Charles (1984, p. 168), Matthews (1966), and Rorty (1980b).

90. Cf. Broadie (1991, pp. 79–80), Cooper (1975, pp. 5–10), Charles (1984, pp. 138–43), Irwin (1986a, pp. 78–9), and Mele (1981).

91. Instead of 'overturning many things' we might translate 'often brings about ruin' which would help avoid the implication that anger always works

through akrasia. The point of 'irrational' (*alogistos*) seems to be that no calculation goes on.

92. We should accept Saunders' (1991, pp. 261–3) arguments that this is still a case in which the person at the time of action is trying to kill, not a case in which he is just trying to wound but goes too far. Although regret is neither necessary nor sufficient to show the absence of prior deliberation, it is reasonable to think that regret, when it occurs, will often be in the absence of prior deliberation.

93. See Saunders (1973b), (1991, pp. 225–42), and Woozley (1972).

94. Anger is a state that involves a mixture of pleasure and pain (*Phil.* 47E–48A) and this helps to explain its strong motivational effects. Although the desire for retaliation involved in anger need not be a desire for pleasure or to avoid pain, pleasure and pain will typically provide further motivation.

95. Cf. *Tim.* 86B1–C3 where pleasure and pain are said to make a person unable to see or hear correctly (*orthōs*).

96. Cf. *Tim.* 86B1–88B5 and Saunders (1991, pp. 168–72).

97. Pears (1984, pp. 8–9).

98. *Laws* 649C8–D2 and 863B6–9 suggest that pleasure can cause a change in, not just a destruction of, the agent's overall judgment; see Section 4.6.

99. It is not essential that the mistake result in or involve a false judgment, but these are easy illustrations. See Pears (1984) and contrast the important and influential argument in Nisbett and Ross (1980, pp. 228–48), that many sorts of erroneous and damaging beliefs for which theorists have offered motivational explanations are better explained by non-motivational factors.

100. Cf. Chappell (1995, pp. 201–7) and Rist in Reverdin (1975, pp. 103–17). For contemporary discussions of self-control or willpower that see it as an ethically neutral power, see Mele (1987, pp. 54–5) and R. Roberts (1984).

101. For a related regress worry concerning volition, see Ryle (1949, pp. 66–7) and for one way to avoid it, Brand (1970, pp. 10–11).

102. Hobbes (1994, Part 1, ch. 6, paras. 50–3, p. 33), capitalization and emphasis in the original, but I have slightly modified the punctuation; Schopenhauer (1999, pp. 31–2), emphasis in the original. Both of these are cited in Dent (1984, p. 96).

103. Some prominent options that involve nothing more than beliefs and desires include: (1) the appropriate belief all by itself, without the addition of any desire, can produce action, (2) the appropriate belief requires the addition of a desire which is an independent existence to produce action, and (3) the appropriate belief requires the addition of a desire to produce action, but the desire is caused by the belief; the desire's ability to motivate is explained by and does not explain the belief's ability to motivate. For contemporary discussions of these options in the case of moral beliefs, see Dancy (1993, pp. 1–17) and Smith (1996, pp. 1–15).

104. Sedley (1992, pp. 146–8).

105. *Laws* 647E10 ff. The *Republic* refers to an ability or capacity (*dunamis*) in discussing courage (429B8–C3, 430B2–5), but cashes this out in terms of the states of the Spirited part of the soul; in particular, in terms of the firmness of the beliefs in the Spirited part (430A3–5 and 430B8 if we accept Stobaeus' μόνιμον). Cf. *Defs.* 412B3, 412C1–2, 412A3, and Sedley (1992). Plato in the *Republic* does not recognize something like an intention or a decisive acceptance that is the ultimate proximal generator of action. Accepting intentions as non-reducible psychological items in addition to beliefs and desires does not obviously eliminate the possibility of weakness of will, since, for example, some philosophers think that it is possible intentionally to act akratically. Nevertheless, one might think that weakness of will would be much more common if there were no intentions, since intentions provide a mechanism that (typically) brings strength of desire into line with evaluation. See, e.g., Mele (1992, pp. 172–96).

106. For a forceful contemporary argument against 'hydraulic' accounts of action and, specifically, against accounts of akrasia that rely simply on the possibility of a misalignment between evaluative ranking and motivational force, see Wallace (1999). Wallace argues that such accounts leave the agent too passive in that it is not up to the agent to determine whether such alignment obtains; Wallace suggests that we also need to acknowledge volitions, which unlike the given desires of the hydraulic account, are directly under the control of the agent. For a related worry about analyzes of action that leave the person passive insofar as action is traced to the operation of forces within us, see Velleman (1992) which offers a more reductive account of self-determination than Wallace.

107. The basic idea is that there is a gap between the agent's final belief about and desire for the overall best and the particular action performed. But there are several ways of filling this out depending on exactly what we think is missing. Theorists have stressed the need for: (a) something to initiate, sustain, and monitor the action, (b) something plan-like for carrying out the action so as to coordinate with other actions, and (c) something that terminates deliberation or practical reasoning and commits the agent to a particular action. We would also need to show that such gaps cannot be filled by further beliefs and desires, but require something not reducible to them. For arguments that more than beliefs and desires are required, see Bratman (1987), (1999), and Mele (1992). We can now note an important refinement to our discussion of the role of, e.g., shame in supporting rational motivations. In a case of akratic conflict, the agent might find that her feelings of shame are either not engaged or are too weak to tilt her motivational balance in favor of her rational desire. She might then actively undertake to increase the force of her motivations associated with shame by, for example, focusing her

attention on the imagined reaction of others to her acting badly. Insofar as the person focuses her attention on certain considerations that will interact with her disposition to feel shame or brings such considerations to mind (cf. *Tim.* 71A–D), she is active with respect to her beliefs, desires, and emotions. Thus even enlisting shame on the side of rational motivations may involve a form of the unreduced agency that I go on to discuss below. I am grateful to Stephen Darwall for helping me to see this point.

108. We might think that such language should be taken no more seriously than Plato's earlier habit of occasionally speaking of the person as an entity over and above the soul and the body or over and above the three parts of the soul. For examples, see Price (1995, pp. 35, 38). I agree that such earlier language should not be understood literally (n. 27), but it is wrong to assimilate this case to it. In the case of the *Republic*, positing the person as an entity over and above the parts of the soul that chooses among them is an unexplanatory addition. The parts of the soul were intended to provide an explanation of the choices we make and a fourth subject, in addition to the three parts of the soul, has no distinctive explanatory function. But in the present case, a subject over and above psychic states and activities may reasonably be thought to have real functions. First, it provides a subject and a principle of unity for psychic states and activities. Second, it is a source of agency with respect to psychic states and activities. We may ultimately decide (e.g. for Humean or naturalistic reasons) that a psychic subject is not needed to play these roles. But it is not clear that this objection is correct and the postulation of a psychic subject (unlike the earlier cases) is not obviously unexplanatory.

109. Richard Taylor, for example, distinguishes between trying to recall a name and being reminded of the name in Brand (1970, p. 51). Also see Frankfurt in Rorty (1976, pp. 239–51, especially 240–1). Thalberg (1978) suggests ways of canceling our apparent commitment to such activity.

110. For discussion of this idea, see Strawson (1994, pp. 111–14).

111. *Phdr.* 245C5–246A2 and *Laws* 10, especially 893B1–899D2. On Plato, see Bett in Fine (1999b, pp. 425–49), Hankinson (1990), Mohr (1985, ch. 8), Price (1990), T. Robinson (1995, pp. xviii–xix, 111–18, 145–55), Skemp (1967, pp. 74–115), and Waterlow (1988, especially pp. 209, 213, 232, 236–7). Waterlow (1988, p. 209) argues that Plato is at least committed to the claim that 'every causal series of changes must have a causally first member, and that this first member is a change in which the being that changes is itself the source of its change.' For discussion of self-motion in Aristotle and the later tradition, see Gill and Lennox (1994).

112. See A. E. Taylor's (1928) helpful note ad loc. It would be wrong to think that the point of 77C3–5 is that the plant's body does not move and so the plant lacks self-motion for the simple reason that plants' bodies *do* move. It is thus plausible to

connect the lack of self-motion with the claim at 77B7–C3 that its genesis has not given to it a motion (κίνησις) of revolving in itself around itself. If this is right and self-motion requires self-rotation, then the point does not concern *bodies* at all. Plato does not think that only whirling dervishes are genuine self-movers. The point concerns the (part of the) soul. Since the part between the midriff and navel, the Appetitive part, is passive, it lacks genuine self-motion. Cf. 46D5–E2 and the striking 89E3–90A2, especially E6–8. For a discussion of related issues in some Neoplatonists, see Lautner (1994).

113. For a fascinating discussion of the notion of 'active powers' of the mind in 18th-cent. philosophy, see Schneewind (forthcoming).

114. The lack of causally sufficient prior conditions may not distinguish the case of self-motion from that of the physical world, since Plato may not accept that there is a necessitated causal order of physical events, cf. Sorabji (1980, pp. 59–69).

115. E.g. in Calcidius *De Fato* 156 we find an especially intimate connection between the self-motion of reason on the one hand and choice and approval on the other, see Boeft (1970, p. 38).

116. Cf. nn. 84, 98.

117. This is not to say that they always disappear entirely. For example, in some cases of perceptual illusion, I may reason to a belief that *p*, but when not focusing on this conclusion I may judge not-*p* suggesting that I have retained at least an inclination to believe not-*p*. Related considerations have led some, e.g., Stampe (1987), to see desire as analogous to perception in involving a non-doxastic notion of appearance. While having reasoned to, and still focusing on, the conclusion that the stick is straight, I can consistently hold that it 'looks bent' or 'seems bent'. Similarly, it is suggested that desire is a form of awareness that involves the same notion of seeming. Specifically, my desiring that *p* involves it seeming to me as if it would be a good thing if *p* obtained. And this is, in the same way, consistent with my *believing* that it is not the case that it would be a good thing if *p* obtained.

118. This echoes closely *Rep.* 439B3–5 in which the Appetitive part is described as directing the person toward drink. Insofar as this is a desire for replenishment, it seems to be a desire for pleasure on the *Philebus'* understanding of such bodily pleasures; a similar point is made independently by Todd Ganson in an unpublished paper. I am indebted to Peter Railton for discussion of related issues.

119. Megillus accepts the broadening of courage to include resistance to desires and pleasures at *Laws* 633D4, but Kleinias allows that a person could be courageous but immoderate at 662A4.

120. *Laws* 633C8–D3. Although cast in the form of a question here, the claim is endorsed at 634A1–4 and 635C3–D6. Plato sometimes only mentions resistance to fear when speaking of courage (e.g. 791B10–C2 and 963E3–8), but explicitly rejects

such a restriction here. For courage in the face of pleasures, cf. *Rep.* 429C7–430B5 and 442B11–C3.

121. Since Plato thinks of the virtues as relatively stable conditions of soul, it seems best to construe courage in the *Laws* as the state of soul that grounds the agent's disposition to struggle or resist fears, pleasures, and so on. On the possibility of differences between men and women with respect to courage and moderation, see Section 5.3.

122. Plato's language sometimes suggests that courage is a scalar phenomenon and that the greater one's capacity to resist akratic impulses, then, *ceteris paribus*, the more (completely) courageous one is (e.g. *Laws* 647C7–D7). The *ceteris paribus* clause is necessary because we do not want to hold that people are more courageous if they actually have and resist frequent strong akratic impulses. It is sufficient that, for example, they could resist great fears if they had them. But if this is right, should we allow that the virtuous person might have misdirected or inappropriately strong desires and fears? As we have already seen, Plato in the *Laws* stresses that human psychology is such that it is (nearly) impossible for anyone to be fully guided by reason: a community of property would be a better arrangement, but it is not possible and perhaps even well-trained philosophers would be corrupted by pleasure if they had autocratic power. As we shall see in more detail in Section 4.6 Plato thinks that pleasures in particular provide ineradicable sources of akratic impulses that may also tend to undermine the person's judgments about the good and the fine.

123. On the Reciprocity of the Virtues, or as it is sometimes called, 'the unity of the virtues', see Annas (1993, pp. 73–82), Badhwar (1996), Cooper (1999, pp. 76–117), Foot (1978) and (1983), Irwin (1988), (1995b), Kraut (1988), Lemos (1994), McDowell (1979), Nagel (1980, pp. 128–41), Penner (1973), Telfer (1989–90), Walker (1993), and Watson (1984).

124. E.g. courage: *Laws* 630A1–D1, 696B1–C1, 963C5–E9; moderation: *Laws* 696D4–E3, 709E6–710B6. For the *Statesman*, see Bobonich (1995b) and Cooper (1999, pp. 165–91).

125. This ability or capacity is improved by practice and training and in Books 1 and 2 Plato proposes drinking parties (*symposia*) to foster it. Wine will be used to increase the force of akratic impulses well beyond their usual intensity (*Laws* 646A–650B, 671A–E). Plato's language here is drawn heavily from physical training (e.g. 647D2). Part of this improvement will be in the psychic analogue of increased physical strength: with practice, the person will be able to resist stronger desires. But just as physical strength is not the only skill developed in bodily gymnastics, psychic strength is not the only product of such training. The person will develop some skills in resisting akratic impulses (cf. 635D1–4 and England's note ad loc.

with 647C10–D7), e.g. knowing how to employ other desires and emotions in the aid of resistance.

126. Although this is not a full discussion of the possibility of possessing wisdom and lacking either courage or moderation (the lack of either of these would also entail a lack of justice), let me note a few points. Obviously, one could define any of the virtues, e.g. wisdom, so that its possession requires the presence of the others, but this seems to make the Reciprocity of the Virtues trivial. It would be more interesting if, for example, we could show that the intrinsic properties the Reasoning part has in a fully virtuous person could not be had by the Reasoning part, if either of the lower parts were not in their virtuous condition. (I put the point in terms of the *Republic*'s psychology, since this worry faces both the *Republic* and the *Laws*. A similar argument could be made explicitly in terms of the *Laws*' psychology.) It might well be the case that the condition of the lower parts could not be (very) defective during the person's ethical education, but once wisdom is acquired, might not the good condition of the lower parts be undermined in some way? Perhaps one's moderation might be undermined by exposure to novel or very great pleasures. This might undermine harmony without (at least immediately) producing change in the knowledgeable state of the Reasoning part. Nevertheless, we might have several reasons for thinking that this is not a counterexample to the Reciprocity of the Virtues. Let me mention one line of argument that I think is not clearly successful and one that is more promising. First, we might argue that the state of the Reasoning part in the person lacking either moderation or courage would have to be different from the state of the Reasoning part in a fully virtuous person, because the former would have to count the frustration of the person's strong bad desires as a cost, and this would make its views of good and bad different from the views of the Reasoning part in a fully virtuous person. But (i) it is not clear that the person need count this frustration as more than instrumentally bad, and (ii) if it is non-instrumentally bad, then the Reasoning part in both persons should take account of it—just as it should take account of, e.g., the cost of undergoing some sort of bodily pain in order to do some virtuous action. The cognitive state of the person does not seem to be relevantly different in these cases. A better reason, I think, for not seeing this as a counterexample is that Plato thinks of virtues as fairly stable states and, as we shall see in more detail in Section 4.6, he thinks that a defective condition of the lower parts will tend to undermine judgments about the good.

127. For moderation perhaps in the service of defective ends, see *Laws* 839E5–840B1, cf. 696D4–E3, and 709E6–710B6; compare the account of courage at 963C5–E9. If moderation is restricted to self-control in the face of pleasures, it seems to be a proper part of courage as it is characterized at 633C8–634A4; if it is construed more broadly as also including resistance to fears, desires, and so on, it

seems to be identical with such courage. Plato sometimes requires wisdom for moderation, e.g., 710A5–B2 and 734A8–B6. But moderation so conceived is still hard to distinguish from courage, if we hold that genuine courage must be guided by wisdom. We might try to distinguish courage and moderation by claiming that the ability to resist that we find in both is dependent on different psychological states: e.g. courage and moderation might have different causal origins or the ability to resist might be grounded in two different psychological states. Perhaps the most plausible form of this view would be close to the conception of moderation as consonance that I go on to discuss in the text.

128. *Laws* 689A5–E2 calls such consonance 'wisdom'; Plato later claims that such a state is moderation (710A5–8), cf. 653A5–C4. This conception of moderation as consonance is similar to moderation at *Republic* 442C10–D1. The *Republic* also seems to suggest a different conception of moderation (e.g. 430E6–9) which is similar to the other conception of moderation found in the *Laws* according to which it is an ability to resist fears and pleasures.

129. See Section 2.6.

130. It is reasonable to think that the intrinsic properties the lower parts have in a fully virtuous person could not be had by the lower parts if the Reasoning part lacked wisdom (I assume here that some forms of true belief are sufficient for wisdom). In particular, it is reasonable to think that the content of the lower parts' beliefs and desires must be different in these cases. The person lacking wisdom will (or would in certain circumstances) make different choices and this will show up in the content of the beliefs and the desires of the lower parts. One might object that someone could perform all the same actions that a virtuous person would, but for different reasons. So long as the beliefs and the desires of the lower parts do not reflect the reasons for action (e.g. are of the form 'This action is best' or 'This action is to be done'), they might be identical with those of the virtuous person. But it is at least true that different counterfactuals are true of the lower parts in the wise person and in the non-wise and it is reasonable to think that the different counterfactuals are made true by different facts about the lower parts. The lower parts should include some beliefs about why things are good or desires directed at certain features of objects: e.g. contrast the desire for drink as a necessary pleasure with the desire for the pleasures of intense replenishments.

Chapter 4 Parts of the Soul and Non-rational Motivations

1. Again, Section 1.12 provides a more precise formulation of this claim. What is essential to my argument is that in the middle period non-philosophers' ends are not correctly set by reason; I do not need to claim that they must take honor or pleasure as their ultimate ends, or that they are ruled by lower parts of the soul.

2. On dating, see Ch. 1, n. 8.

3. See A. E. Taylor (1928, ad loc.). It does not affect the point, if we think that the seed or marrow is the ensouled creature.

4. κωφός ('deaf') can simply mean 'senseless', 'stupid', or 'mute (e.g. *Tht.* 206D9),' and see Thompson (1868, ad loc.). In tragedy, a *kōphon prosōpeion* (*prosōpon*) is a mute figure, *LSJ* s.v. 2a. It is thus a conflict, at the level of the myth's imagery, that the black horse is described as conversing with the charioteer and the good horse. I am indebted to Julia Annas on this point.

5. Alcinous 30.3, H184; cf. 25.5, H178 where Alcinous claims that the irrational parts of the soul do 'not make use of reason [*logismōi*] or judgment [*krisei*] . . . nor yet of general concepts . . . [nor do they have] any conception at all of intelligible reality [*tēs noētēs phuseōs*]'. In this passage, Alcinous attributes to the irrational parts only *phantasia* which, on his conception of it, is common to all animals; see the helpful notes by Dillon (1995) and Whittaker (1990) ad loc.; the latter notes the connection with the *Timaeus* and that this view is widespread among the Middle Platonists. The translation is from Dillon (1995).

6. I agree with Scott (1995, p. 16) and others against Fine (1993, p. 138) that the theory of recollection is a theory of innateness, specifically, a theory of innate concepts or beliefs. Plato in discussing recollection does assert that certain psychic items, that is, certain mental particulars, are innately in the soul (e.g. *Phd.* 73A9, 75B5, *Phdr.* 249C6–7). We might hold that this is simply a convenient manner of speaking, rather than a literal truth claim, if we thought that it was clearly wrong to hold that conceptual abilities are grounded in concepts that are mental particulars. But I think that Plato is not clearly wrong—and, in fact, was right—to hold that conceptual abilities are grounded in concepts as mental particulars. In this, I agree with Fodor against, e.g., Peacocke who is perhaps the leading contemporary proponent of the idea that concepts are epistemic capacities. See Fodor (1998a), (1998b, pp. 27–34), Margolis and Laurence (1999, pp. 3–8), and Peacocke (1992).

7. Scott (1995, p. 19).

8. Scott (1995, p. 77). For Scott, the non-lover is the non-philosopher.

9. *Phdr.* 249B5–6 and 249E4–250A1 show that every human soul has seen some Forms in one of its transits; 248E5–249A1 implies that all souls eventually regain their wings, cf. 250C1–6. *Phdr.* 248C3–6 says that every soul that becomes embodied has failed to see any of the Forms in the immediately prior transit; this applies to the philosopher and shows that a failure to see any Forms in the transit prior to embodiment does not prevent recollection while embodied. In thinking about the *Phaedrus*, I have benefited from an unpublished paper by Myles Burnyeat. The *Timaeus* (41E1–2) and the *Phaedrus* thus agree that all human souls have seen the Forms.

10. But cf. Hermias' scholia (Couvreur (1901)) on *Phdr.* 248D and 248E.

11. This link will be causal rather than inferential. Recollecting will not be noticing that one's experience is already conceptualized in accordance with buried knowledge, but making one's buried knowledge available. Once available, it can be applied to other items. In the *Phaedrus*, at least, recollection is seen as involving the actualization of the concept the person is initially unaware of, not merely a disposition to form certain ideas under appropriate conditions.

12. I agree with de Vries (1969) and Hackforth (1972b) ad loc. that neither *Phdr.* 248C6 nor any other passage in the *Phaedrus* provides an explanation of the soul's fall from original perfection.

13. Verdenius (1955, ad loc.) comparing 248B4, rightly takes κακίας at 248C7 as weakness. All that we need is that a failure of knowledge is at least partially responsible. For further argument, see Price (1989, p. 74), cf. Hackforth (1946).

14. *Phdr.* 250A1–5. Indeed, we could even allow that bad desires were the primary determinant of the person's degree of knowledge as long as the person's degree of Form awareness still played, at least in some respects, an independent role in the choice of life.

15. See de Vries (1969, ad loc.). For wings beginning to grow: 256D3–5, cf. 249A7–B1, 249D4–7, 251A1–D7, especially 251B6–D2, and 255D1–2.

16. The urge to see this as a kind of philosophic life is nearly overpowering, see Hackforth (1972b, p. 109) rightly rejecting such a claim by Wilamowitz.

17. Cf. Scott (1995, p. 77).

18. If you accept this principle, then it may also be tempting to think that in recollecting the Form of F, the only Form that, so to speak, enters one's thoughts, is the Form of F. This may again, at least to some extent, be suggested by the case of the Form of the Equal in the *Phaedo*. It would be easy to believe that in coming to think that sensible equals are not identical to the Form of the Equal, the only Form that one thinks of is the Form of the Equal (and, perhaps, the Form of the Unequal, if there is one). But this is an implausible general thesis. First, the Form of F may itself be internally complex in such a way that thinking of it requires thinking of more than one Form. The Form of Triangle, for example, presumably bears some intimate relation to, say, the Forms of Line and Three (if there are such Forms). (It is controversial how far Plato recognized that Forms have such complexity in the middle period. And even if he did hold that Forms were complex in this way, it is a separate question how far recollection as described in, e.g., the *Phaedo* makes room for such complexity.) Recollecting, even indistinctly, the former might plausibly be thought to involve recollecting the latter. Second, Forms seem to have significant necessary connections with other Forms, even in cases which are not obviously instances of internal complexity. For example, the truths that justice is fine or that

justice is good are presumably made true by the relations—whatever the appropriate analysis of these may be—that hold among the Forms of Justice, Fine, and Good. There is no reason to think that the definition of a Form specifies all such necessary connections. Third, Plato's later metaphysics emphasizes that Forms stand in complicated relations of superordination and subordination: e.g. the Form of Justice and the Form of Virtue. Knowing one Form may require knowing its location within a very complicated structure, but some awareness of some of these relations may be involved even in dim recollection: recollecting justice may involve seeing it as a virtue. Fourth, it might also be the case that recollecting the Form of F requires various kinds of reasoning, e.g. distinguishing F from various other items. And if, for example, Sameness, Difference, and Being are Forms, they might be thought to be involved in many or all of these judgments, even if one is not explicitly thinking of them as Forms. As we shall see below, Plato in the *Theaetetus*, the *Timaeus*, and the *Sophist* thinks that some highly abstract Forms are involved in all (or almost all) thought. The *Phaedrus'* myth does not provide an account of these issues and its explicit focus is exclusively on the Form of Beauty. But the *Phaedrus* does emphasize that all souls see a number of Forms with varying degrees of distinctness and that the recollection of beauty brings with it widespread effects in a person's thinking. Further, the *Phaedrus* rejects the simple principle of recollection in the text above and allows that people can recollect a Form without having awareness of the Form as such. Thus the *Phaedrus* leaves open the issue of how far other Forms (and which other Forms) might be involved in recollecting Beauty or engaging in other kinds of thought. Indeed as we have seen, the 'descent of lives' passage suggests that recollection, to one degree or another, of a fairly indeterminate range of Forms is involved in much human thought and choice.

19. Cf. the lovers of sights and sounds in *Republic* 5 and *Phaedo* 81B1–C2, 83D4–E3.

20. Cf. Ch. 1, n. 29.

21. E.g. Scott (1995, p. 63).

22. Cowie (1999, pp. 27–31).

23. I leave aside tightening of the statement of this; e.g. we should require that *G* is the only possible candidate for *greater than* and is not composed out of the concepts *greater than* and *physical length* and so on.

24. The idea that a concept is a mental representation having structure that specifies the necessary and sufficient definitional features for its correct application has been, until the past few decades, the predominant theory of concepts for rationalists and empiricists alike. Moreover, such a theory has many attractive features, one of the most important of which is a natural account of compositionality. 'Prototype' theories of concepts, one of the most popular rivals to the classical

view, have serious difficulties with respect to compositionality. See Margolis and Laurence (1999, pp. 3–81). The above account requires that the concept F specify the definition of F and that this involves specifying necessary and sufficient conditions; this is not to claim that any correct specification of necessary and sufficient conditions for being F counts as an adequate definition of F.

25. This epistemic defect of non-philosophers is consistent with the claims that (i) everyone has all of the innate concepts there are, and (ii) some experience they can undergo while embodied, e.g. the elenchus, might bring these concepts to light, that is, make them available to the person. (The *Phaedrus'* account of the differences in the number and clarity of Forms seen might suggest, however, that for some people only a restricted range of innate concepts or beliefs can be made available in a given embodiment.)

26. Such a view will seem disastrously misguided if one holds both: (1) philosophers and non-philosophers can share the same belief about Forms, and (2) the content of a belief is determined by the speaker's conceptions or mental representations. Consider two believers, A and B. Suppose A is astronomically sophisticated and can recognize Hesperus whenever she sees it, realizes that it is identical with Phosphorus and the planet Venus, and so on. Suppose B thinks that Hesperus is a different star from Phosphorus and thinks that Hesperus is a star that is sometimes, including sometimes at night, visible from somewhere on earth. A and B have two different ways of thinking about Hesperus or conceptions of it or two different mental representations of it. We can analyze this state of affairs in more than one way. Consider the following claim: (p) Hesperus is sometimes visible in the night sky. We might deny that A and B both believe that p because their conceptions of Hesperus are quite different. This may motivate a denial of (1). But we do not have to do this. We can allow that both believe that p, because, e.g., B's conception of Hesperus has the appropriate causal links to Hesperus or because she intends to defer to experts. We can now accept (1), but deny (2). If we accept (1) and deny (2), there is no obvious general problem for the possibility of successful communication understood as the transmission of information. It is worth noting, however, that there may be a problem for the transmission of knowledge in certain cases. If knowledge about Hesperus, for example, requires thinking about Hesperus in the right way, that is, by the appropriate conception, then even if B were to accept some true claim about Hesperus made by A, even on the basis of quite good evidence about A's reliability in astronomical matters, she might fail to know this claim. This may provide support for some of Plato's claims about the difficulty of knowledge transmission. I am indebted to K. Taylor (1997) for the example. Nor does even the denial of (1) preclude the pragmatic success of many instances of communication. Suppose Plato denies that the philosophically or scientifically

unsophisticated have beliefs about fire, because they are totally unaware of the Form of fire or are totally unaware that fire has a microstructure (much less have any idea of what that microstructure is). Nevertheless, a cold philosopher can, with great confidence, expect the right result when she requests of a naïve person 'Please make a fire'. This is also true if their roles are reversed.

27. Cf. Fine (1977, pp. 296–9). Important discussions of the *Cratylus* include Annas (1982b), Barney (1997), (1998), Irwin (1982), Kahn (1982), Kretzmann (1971), Mackenzie (1986), Reeve (1998), Schofield (1982), Sedley (1998a), Silverman (1992), and Williams (1982). For general discussions of Platonic chronology, including the *Cratylus*, see Ch. 1, n. 8.

28. The *Phaedrus* does not require articulate knowledge of what the fine is in order to have some grasp of the real essence of the fine. In this case, it may be difficult to tell whether a person does have such a grasp. In the case of mad lovers, what seems to be required is at least a recognition that the fineness of the thing in question has a kind of value that is not dependent on our desires and interests. But although there may be cases that are hard for us to classify, Plato can hold that there is always a determinate answer to the question of whether the person has a grasp of the fine. Non-mad lovers fail because their beliefs about, and responses to, the fine are not the outcome of recollection of the Form of the Fine. To have the concept of the fine, one's concept must have the right sort of causal ancestry: it must be the outcome of recollection. Seeing the Forms produces memories of them in the soul of the person which remain unconscious or inactive until triggered. What makes M a memory of the Form F is that it was produced by seeing the Form F and Plato leaves the notion of seeing a Form unanalyzed. Actively having the concept F requires having a triggered memory of F. Having such a triggered memory will ground one's ability (1) to discriminate F things, and (2) to have certain beliefs about F. But Plato might not hold that it is a necessary condition of having the concept that one be able to distinguish it from all related concepts. He can thus allow people to go wrong about the concepts that they possess.

29. Fine (1977, p. 297).

30. Sedley (1998a).

31. Again, Plato could retreat to allowing that some operation (such as abstraction) on sensory contents can result in the formation of a concept with non-sensible content, but hold that only by accessing innate concepts do you get the non-sensible concept with the correct content, i.e. the content appropriately corresponding to the objective, non-sensible property.

32. In objection, Gassendi suggested that we might get some other concepts from experience, e.g. *straight line*, and by abstraction or composition form the concept *chiliagon*. Descartes claims that sense-experience could not provide *straight*

line either, since the world contains only approximations to straight lines, see Cowie (1999, pp. 35–6).

33. This sentence has often been emended, but we can keep the consensus of the manuscripts, see Verdenius (1955) and de Vries (1969) ad loc. Scott (1995, pp. 77–8 n. 26) accepts Verdenius' (1955) understanding of 249B6–C1 so that we do not need to emend the text. But Scott suggests that Verdenius accepts that *legomenon* = *logos* = the man. This equivalence is extremely important for Scott's interpretation, since he appeals to the parallel with *Rep.* 476B10–11 to show that Plato in *Phdr.* 249B7 is discussing a philosopher 'going' to what he recognizes as a Form. But this is not Verdenius' view, since he identifies a *legomenon* with a *logos*; but does not identify either with a man: 'the subject of *ion* is not *eidos* but a *legomenon*, which is much the same as a *logos*, and it is this *logos* which proceeds from a number of perceptions to a concept' (Verdenius (1955, p. 280), I have transliterated the Greek). Verdenius translates *legomenon* as 'something that is expressed'. Verdenius' view is also accepted by de Vries (1969) on 249B7–C1.

34. E.g. of hippocentaurs at *Phdr.* 229D6 and of songs at 237A7. *Idea* too is metaphysically unloaded up to and throughout the myth, see especially 251A3. On *eidē* and *genē* in the *Phaedrus*, see Hackforth, (1972b, p. 147 n. 1).

35. We can remain agnostic about the exact nature of these Forms: e.g. whether they are paradigmatic, separate, or everlasting. We can also remain neutral about the exact relation between natural joints and Forms: we do not need to assume that there is a one-to-one correspondence between natural joints and Platonic Forms. See the helpful discussions in Fine (1993, pp. 44–65 and 120–41).

36. The reference to 'perceptions' in the second half of the sentence also suggests that what we are dealing with at least includes relatively low-level cognitive states. The movement is from many acts of perception to a single *eidos* arrived at by reasoning. Plato's phrasing stresses the fact that the starting point is many particular acts of perception. (See de Vries (1969) on 249B7–C1.) This would be a quite inaccurate and misleading way of characterizing how the philosopher comes to have knowledge of the Form for Plato, especially after the *Republic*. (Nor is the *Phaedo* a closer parallel, since it is important there that a single perception is involved, cf. Rowe (1993, pp. 172–3), Scott (1995, pp. 62–3).)

What sort of grasp or understanding does Plato have in mind in Passage 1? This single sentence underdetermines an interpretation and the *Phaedrus* does not provide a detailed epistemology. But since the sentence immediately following Passage 1 characterizes this process as recollection, it should include the other cases of recollection that the myth recognizes. (Restricting 249C1–4 to full-blown philosophical knowledge (*epistēmē*) of the Form would threaten to deny recollection even to philosophers far advanced on the path to understanding.) Thus it should include the many humans (including many non-philosophers) who are mad lovers and so recollect the Fine, even if they have no beliefs about the Form of the Fine as such. This suggests that Plato is not thinking of a highly sophisticated cognitive state. If we understand Plato's point here parallel to the recollection of the Fine, the claim is that being human involves the ability to begin to make at least some correct discriminations among the basic kinds in the world. How many discriminations a human must make and how accurately, he does not tell us. Doing so requires more than we can get from perception, it also requires recollection of the Forms. Exactly what perception fails to give us and how much it can give us is left indeterminate by the text. But Plato does make recollection necessary for a grasp of basic kinds in the world that does not yet involve explicit recognition of the Forms.

So how pervasive is recollection in the *Phaedrus*? The dialogue provides no definitive answer, but we have seen that it is certainly not confined to philosophers or philosophical reflection. On the most plausible reading of the descent of lives passage, recollection in some form is part of all human lives; it is certainly part of the lives of all mad lovers. (*Phdr.* 266B3–5 also suggests a weak reading, cf. *Soph.* 259E5–6. For discussion, see Fine (1993, pp. 135–6) and Moravcsik (1992, pp. 200–12).) We will also see it as more pervasive, once we see that recollecting the Form of F need not involve an explicit recognition of a Platonic Form, and that it may require recollecting other Forms as well. Some recollection is involved in any sort of human cognition that grasps the basic kinds of things in the world in a way that goes beyond what other animals can do.

37. Cf. Fine (1993, pp. 120–41) on 'the object of thought' argument. Nothing in the present interpretation of the *Phaedrus* entails (or even, I think, suggests), e.g., that a person can only think of what exists. The *Phaedrus* does not tell us whether Plato thinks that (1) whenever a person has a general thought, she thinks of something that exists, or (2) whenever a person has a thought, she thinks of something that exists. If Plato holds that all thoughts have a propositional structure that involves the notion of being, then he might (and would, for example, on Burnyeat's interpretation of the *Theaetetus*) accept (1) and (2), since any thought would involve the 'common' (*koinon*) of being.

38. See Price (1995, p. 80) and Thompson (1868, pp. 72–4).

39. Cf. *Phdr.* 249B7–C1. Note that the non-actual possibility considered here is that it has some *aisthēsis* of *logos*. On the text, see A. E. Taylor (1928, ad loc.).

40. *Rep.* 442B5–D1 and 589A6–B6 (cf. 554E3–5) show that this is persuading the Appetitive part.

41. All the cognitive work involved in conceiving of the ends of the Appetitive part as good and in choosing such a life as a goal would have to be done by the Reasoning part. If so, the Reasoning part must have some inclinations within it to

such a life or there must be a purely causal link between the Appetitive part's desires and the Reasoning part's judgments.

42. Cf. Ch. 3, n. 47.

43. The image's 'bilious colors' (χολώδη χρώματα, *Tim.* 71B7–8) that suffuse the liver are drawn from the liver's own bitterness (71B2) and the bitter is associated with the contraction of the soft and moist (65C1–E4). (1) In light of Plato's mention of *phantasmata*, we might think that he intends to attribute *phantasia* to the Appetitive part and that this is a capacity for having contentful states that is independent of belief or *doxa*. But given the *Sophist's* (264B2) conception of *phantasia* as a combination of *doxa* and *aisthēsis*, *phantasia* cannot provide an epistemic resource that is independent of *doxa*. Since *Tim.* 70E5–71B5 and, especially, 77B3–C5 deny *doxa* to the Appetitive part, it cannot possess *phantasia* either. (2) If images are to be the bearers of content *for* the Appetitive part, then the Appetitive part will need the capacity to grasp and process them. But this requires the implausible attribution to the Appetitive part of a quasi-perceptual system that perceives these images. Moreover, on the *Timaeus'* account, perceiving something as such and such is due to the Reasoning part (cf. n. 56). The images or signs (*sēmeia*) on the liver signify something both when the creature is alive and when it is dead (although when it is dead, the signs are too obscure to signify clearly, *Tim.* 72B6–C1). But in either case, the images signify something to a *logos*-possessing interpreter. (3) Even for Appetitive desires, this pictorial theory of content seems much too impoverished. How would the Appetitive part represent a pleasant or even a sweet drink, a desire for water rather than for other colorless, odorless liquids, or the complicated structure of desire involved in means–end reasoning? The idea that the Appetitive part thinks pictorially, although lacking belief, seems to be another instance of rhetorical exaggeration in Timaeus' speech (as is, perhaps, the idea that the soul is literally composed of parts of Forms, cf. n. 52). This leaves Plato with a problem that he—like many other philosophers, both ancient and modern—does not fully face, that is, explaining the capacities and behavior of non-human animals while denying them belief. For a superb exploration of these issues in antiquity, see Sorabji (1993). At *Tim.* 70B6, the claim that 'every sentient part of the body' responds to the information passed on by reason that an injustice has been done is needlessly problematic if it is interpreted as meaning that the body itself grasps the significance of what comes from reason. It does make good sense, however, if Plato's point is that reason's thoughts can bring about certain bodily changes, e.g. motions in the blood. Similarly, at *Tim.* 70D8–71B5, the claim that the Appetitive part responds to 'the power of thoughts which proceed from reason' does not mean that the Appetitive part is a cognitive subject that grasps the significance of reason's thoughts. What it means, rather, is that reason's thoughts can, in

these cases, produce the non-conceptualized psychic motions that, when conceptualized, are fully fledged tokens of, e.g., fear and desire.

44. On the text, see A. E. Taylor (1928, ad loc.).

45. *Tht.* 189E3–190A8, cf. *Soph.* 263E3–264A3, and *Phil.* 38B12–39B2. We should not be worried that *doxa* is treated here as the outcome of a process and thus that denial only of *doxa* might allow for some preceding silent *logos*. There is no reason to see Timaeus as distinguishing sharply between *doxa* and *logos*, cf. Passage A. Timaeus' contrast is between anything linguistic and something non-linguistic.

46. Plato has no desire to naturalize belief, see *Tim.* 46C7–E6.

47. We can distinguish the claim that sensory experience has a non-conceptualized aspect or component from the further claim that sensory experience has a non-conceptualized aspect or component that involves awareness. See Dretske (1995). But in neither case do we need to posit a separate subject of such states.

48. The Demiurge sets 'each as it were in a chariot [ὄχημα]' (*Tim.* 41E1–2); the otherwise pointless reference to a chariot seems designed to recall the *Phaedrus'* account of Recollection. Skemp (1947, p. 56) holds that *doxa* is limited to the immortal part of the soul.

49. See, e.g., *Rep.* 523A5–525A5. For discussion, see Burnyeat (1976), Fine (1988b), and M. Frede (1987, pp. 3–8).

50. See Ch. 3, n. 72 and *Rep.* 490B2–7.

51. On this issue, see Burnyeat (1976), (1990), Cooper (1970), Fine (1988b, pp. 25–6), D. Frede (1989), (1996), M. Frede (1987, pp. 3–8), Kahn (1981), and Kanayama (1987).

52. It is composed of a mixture of the Forms of Being, Sameness, and Difference (i.e. indivisible (ἀμέριστος) and unchangeable Being, Sameness, and Difference), and the bodily counterparts of these: being, sameness, and difference which are divisible or distributed in bodies (μεριστός, 35A1 ff.). See, e.g., Cornford (1937) and A. E. Taylor (1928) on 35A1 ff., and D. Frede (1996, pp. 34–41).

53. Silverman (1990a, p. 150).

54. Cf. *Tht.* 156B2–7. Pleasure and pain insofar as they are just perceptions (*aisthēseis*) would be unconceptualized; with regard to fear, cf. *Tim.* 71B5.

55. Cf. *Tim.* 45C7–D3 and 67A7–B5. For the etymology of *aisthēsis*, see A. E. Taylor (1928) on 43C5–7.

56. *Tim.* 64B may not be totally decisive, but see 69C6–D6, 45C7–46A2 and cf. *Phil.* 33D2–34A8 and *Tht.* 186B11–C2. See L. Brisson (1999), Ostenfeld (1982, p. 330 n. 188), and Silverman (1990a).

57. Given the *Sophist's* conception of *phantasia* as 'a mixture of perception and belief' (σύμμειξις αἰσθήσεως καὶ δόξης, 264B2), it cannot provide an epistemic resource that is independent of belief.

58. *Alogos* also carries the sense of lacking the proper mathematical ratio, see A. E. Taylor (1928, ad loc.).

59. Cf. *Tim.* 89E3–90D7. On *atelēs* at 44C3, see A. E. Taylor (1928, ad loc.) and cf. *Phd.* 69A6–D4 and *Phdr.* 248B4–5. The *Timaeus* also suggests other reasons, connected with the passage at 77B6–C5, as to why the lower parts, insofar as they are purely passively receptive in the act of perception, cannot attain belief or *logos*. This passage may help to explain that passivity: insofar as the soul undergoes motion coming from the outside, it is passive.

60. When the revolutions attain the correct shape, the soul is 'intelligent' (*emphrona*, 44B7); a state that should include correct ethical beliefs that are then reinforced by education. The 'greatest illness' (45C1–2), which they avoid, is an ethical failure, cf. 86B2–87B8 and 90D1–7.

61. One might still press the worry of why Plato retains in the *Timaeus*, at least on the surface, the partitioning of the soul and characterizes the unconceptualized affections in the Appetitive part as desires. (1) The language of partitioning offers a useful way of classifying and referring to psychic phenomena. At some points in the *Timaeus*, what is important for Plato's purposes is, for example, the different natures of the objects pursued by spirited emotions and appetitive desires (90A–C). When Plato claims, e.g., that footed animals spring from people who have ignored philosophy and 'followed the lead of the parts of the soul that are in the chest' (91E5–6), the language of partitioning is convenient and we need not see any commitment at all to the existence of parts of the soul as agent-like subjects. (And Timaeus' speech often makes use of metaphors that are not literally intended, e.g. the personification of the genitals.) (2) When the *Timaeus* does focus on the nature of the soul, we find two things. First, at 77B–C it makes it entirely explicit that Plato rejects the parts of the soul as found in the *Republic*. The Appetitive part in the *Timaeus* is no longer anything that can have beliefs. Second, the *Timaeus* also makes it quite clear that the parts of the soul could no longer have the sort of resources that they did in the *Republic*. Perception in the *Timaeus*, strictly speaking, is an unconceptualized psychic movement and the conceptualization of it is done by a single entity or faculty, reason. So Plato is clear in the *Timaeus* that there is no room for parts of the soul as subjects of beliefs or as conceptualizers of perception. (3) So what of Plato's characterization of the unconceptualized affections in the Appetitive part as desires? Plato is seriously committed to the important point that desires have an unconceptualized aspect, just as perception does. But as in the case of perception, this is not the end of the story. Plato characterizes 'perception' (*aisthēsis*) strictly as a unconceptualized psychic movement, but his psychology gives a crucial role to contentful perceptual awareness. Although Plato does not develop in the *Timaeus* a technical terminology to mark this distinction,

he provides an account of how contentful awareness is arrived at through the conceptualization of reason. It is reasonable to see, e.g., desire, fear, and pleasure as quite similar. (Indeed, it must be the case with respect to pleasure insofar as Plato thinks of pleasure as a kind of perception.) Plato's psychology gives a role to a contentful impulse toward a thing (or a contentful aversion in the case of fear). I have argued that we should see reason as playing a similar role here and should not be surprised that Plato does not develop a technical terminology here either. (4) Perhaps the greatest remaining impetus to accepting some role for parts of the soul as subjects insofar as they have unconceptualized psychic movements is Timaeus' localization of them in parts of the body. It is difficult to determine how seriously committed Plato is to such localization. (Cf. Plato's greater diffidence at *Laws* 898D9–899A6 concerning the location of the soul with respect to the body.) But we could accept (1) the localization of certain psychic faculties or affections in particular bodily regions, or (2) give some parts of the body an especially important causal role in the transmission of bodily movement to the soul without thinking that the soul is composed of different subjects, some of which are havers of unconceptualized psychic movements. Finally, even if one were to think that the *Timaeus* accepts, or at least does not reject, soul parts understood as the ultimate subjects of unconceptualized psychic movements (despite what I argued is the philosophical unattractiveness of this idea), this would not greatly affect my interpretation. Such vestigial soul parts would no longer be relevant to action in the way that they are in the *Republic*, as I argue below in connection with the *Theaetetus*.

62. Even if the correct chronological order is *Phaedrus–Theaetetus–Timaeus*, the *Theaetetus* may be more explicit on this issue than the *Timaeus*.

63. Such further judgments might even include thinking that 'X is really red', if this involves, for example, thinking about the conditions of perception. A thinner interpretation would allow perception some form of simple conceptual labeling that is subpropositional, e.g. 'red' rather than 'This is red'.

64. The commons may be Forms, even if they do not have all the features that middle-period Forms do. Plato might also think that the commons have features beyond what the argument at *Tht*. 184B–186E establishes.

65. Cooper (1970, pp. 124–9) rightly stresses against Cornford that Plato is not concerned here with how we come to have explicit knowledge of the Forms.

66. Burnyeat (1990, p. 58).

67. *Tim*. 77B3–C5 suggests that activity in the form of self-motion is necessary for (a) having some sort of self-awareness, and (b) forming and having beliefs. Plato here does not provide an argument for these claims. But, first, even if nonconceptualized perceptual affections are a purely passive impingement, any operation on them (including bringing concepts to bear upon them and thus making

them the object of contentful awareness) would seem to be an act of the soul's circles of same and different and Plato has independent reasons for thinking that the soul is a self-mover. But there is also some intuitive pull to the idea that taking a state as an object of awareness or thought is inherently 'active' rather than 'passive'. It will, for example, include the sorts of activities involving the *koina* discussed above. What seems to be needed is the presence of a cognizer and manipulator of input whose operations are not cashed out entirely in terms of the causal interaction of beliefs, desires, or other *pathē*. And in the late dialogues, Plato stresses the activity of the soul and presents the soul as an unreduced cognizer and manipulator of input. On the activity of the soul in conceptualizing perception, see Burnyeat (1976), Cooper (1970), and M. Frede (1987, pp. 3–8). On the role of the soul as an initiator of inquiry and operator on psychic contents, see the discussion of the *Theaetetus'* metaphors of the Aviary and the Wax Block in Burnyeat (1990, pp. 99–100) and McCabe (1994, pp. 291–7). On related issues in later Platonism, see Lautner (1994).

68. The point does not concern, so to speak, the range of the vocabulary open to the Spirited or Appetitive parts, but rather their conceptual resources. The lower parts do not have the conceptual resources necessary to respond to something because they grasp that it is, e.g., genuinely just or good.

69. Cf. Section 2.12.

70. In the *Republic*, the tripartitioning of the soul was a central element in Plato's argument that having a just soul is a great good for the person. This claim about the goodness of justice is not, however, undermined by the later unified view of the soul. First, in the *Republic*, the harmonization of the parts of the soul under the guidance of the Reasoning part is good for the person because it prevents akratic conflict and action and allows the person to avoid the perhaps painful frustration of the desires that the lower parts would have if they were not under the guidance of the Reasoning part. On the later view, both of these points still apply to the harmonization of the non-rational motivations under the guidance of reason. Second, on the *Republic* view, justice is a great good for a person because it is a condition of psychic health. Since it is still the case on the later view that justice requires wisdom, reason in a just person will be in a healthy state because the person's rational capacities stand in the appropriate relation to truth. With respect to the non-rational motivations, Plato has even better reasons to see their good condition as a great good for the person on his later view. As I have argued, given the cognitive limitations of the lower parts in the *Republic*, there are important concerns about how valuable the good condition of these parts is in itself. Since, on the later view, non-rational motivations, under the guidance of reason, can be informed by reason at least to a significant degree, their good condition is more valuable.

71. *Logos* at 42D1 has overtones of 'measure' and 'proportion', cf. A. E. Taylor (1928, ad loc.).

72. See Sedley in Fine (1999b, p. 323) for an interesting argument that *peri tēn genesin* at 90D1–2 should be translated 'concerned with becoming', rather than 'at our birth'.

73. Cf., e.g., Irwin (1995a , pp. 252–4).

74. For a related contemporary point about the motivational force of ethical judgments, see Korsgaard (1996a, pp. 311–34).

75. I have benefited from the important series of articles in Cooper (1999, pp. 118–37, 138–49, 237–52, 253–80, and 406–23).

76. One might object that Plato's claim here is not that one should not feel anger against curable criminals, rather the claim is that one's anger should be restrained (*aneirgonta*, 731D1). The person will continue to feel anger against curable criminals, but will not act on it and will also feel pity. This is the point, one might suggest, of the closing remark that the good person should 'be always at once [*hekastote*] passionate [spirited] and gentle' (731D4–5, the translation is Bury's (1926)). But we should not accept this objection. (1) As England (1921, ad loc.) rightly points out, *hekastote* does not suggest that the person is spirited and gentle on the same occasions; it is, rather, used distributively—'as occasion demands'— and is so translated by Saunders (1976) and A. E. Taylor (1960). (2) Another passage from the *Laws* also helps to make it clear that good people are supposed to extinguish their anger, not just override it or keep from acting upon it. In Book 10, the Athenian grows angry in his imaginary conversation with a young atheist, but checks himself and says that he and his fellow founders must speak with the young atheist 'without spiritedness [*athumos*] . . . let us speak gently, quenching our anger [*sbesantes ton thumon*]' (888A5–6). (3) We should not expect Plato to allow that a good person can, except in certain very difficult circumstances, be angry when anger is inappropriate: such a state of character would seem to be, at best, a form of continence, rather than virtue. (4) On the idea that this sort of persuasion of non-rational motivations, as opposed to retaining them while blocking their expression in action, requires that the non-rational motivation comes to share part of reason's evaluative outlook, see Cooper (1999, pp. 254–5, 260–1). (5) Thus we might well prefer Saunders' (1976) translation of the claim at 731D1 that the virtuous person should 'restrain' (*aneirgonta*) his *thumos* as 'restrain and abate' (cf. Saunders (1991, pp. 151–2 and 180)) or A. E. Taylor's (1960) 'curb and tame'. Or, perhaps, Plato's claim at 731D1 is that we must restrain not the particular angry impulse, but that we must restrain our thumotic capacity so that it does not issue in anger or the anger is extinguished on this occasion. This thumotic capacity for anger is still a part of a virtuous person's character, since there are appropriate occasions for anger. But this

capacity must be educated so that it finds expression against the right objects. For another instance of such education in which it is clear that certain types of anger are extinguished in a virtuous character, see *Soph.* 227D4–230E4, especially 230B4–D4. I am indebted to Rachel Barney for discussion of these issues.

77. Cf. Nussbaum (1994, pp. 412–17, 424).

78. Cf. Cooper (1999, pp. 130–2, 420–3).

79. It is anger's limitation to a narrow range of considerations that is crucial, not that it prompts immediately to action. In Book 9 of the *Laws*, Plato considers two men, one of whom acts immediately, while the other does not act on the spur of the moment but still acts on anger. One is like the involuntary agent, the other like the voluntary; but neither is fully voluntary and the failure results from not acting out of fuller deliberation (866D5–867C2).

80. Cf. Ch. 3, n. 90.

81. One might think that the penal code itself suggests that Plato is rather pessimistic about how many offenders are incurable and too willing to take behavior as an accurate gauge of the condition of the soul.

82. Cf. Mackenzie (1981, pp. 209–10) and Saunders (1991, pp. 181–4).

83. Cf. Chisholm (1986) and Nozick (1981, pp. 399–473, 505–51).

84. I do not wish to deny that anger can be, in a way, a perfection of our rational nature. Anger is a permanent feature of our embodied existence. It is, at least usually, an externally driven process: the person perceives some slight and anger is an immediate response to it that involves some non-conceptualized aspect (e.g. the intensity of the associated desire). To the extent that reason succeeds in providing the right conceptualization of this immediate registration of the slight, this shaping by reason is a perfection of our rational nature. What seems still to be a weakness is whatever purely passive element persists, e.g. the intensity of the remaining desire. For an argument that Aristotle gives a much more positive account of *thumos*, see Cooper (1999, pp. 253–80).

85. See Cairns (1993, pp. 382–92); his criticism of Fortenbaugh's (1975, pp. 32, 27–8) claim that the *Republic* associates shame with the Reasoning part is convincing. On shame in the *Laws* and its superiority to other expressions of spirit, see Walsh (1963, pp. 49–52).

86. Again, the criminal law shows that Plato does not expect all to be virtuous and the first colonists' education will be defective. Shame, in particular, is intended to provide stop-gap motivations when rational considerations are not fully available or not fully effective; see e.g. *Laws* 646E10–650B10.

87. In the case of honor, the attempt to refashion the motivation is fairly straightforward. The problem with the desire for honor in the *Republic* was that it was directed not at the value of the activity in question, but rather at people's reac-

tion to it or, at least, that the desire for honor did not include an appreciation of what makes the thing in question truly deserving of honor. But honors are not dispensed with in Magnesia. In the general exhortation to the citizens in the *Laws*, however, Plato tries to refashion the motivation of honor to shift the person's focus from receiving honor to the activity of honoring one's own soul (*Laws* 726A2–727A2, 728C6–D2). Plato here attempts to remold the desire so that it no longer aims merely at excelling in competitive exertion to a state that involves a direct awareness of value. Honoring one's soul involves a recognition of what is fine or valuable; it becomes a desire to develop in one's own soul the qualities and characteristics that are genuinely valuable and deserving of honor. Although Plato does not try to do away with the incentive of being honored, he seems to think that the initial desire for being honored can also be retrained so as to take directly as its object what is honorable.

88. See *Laws* 646E10–650B10 and 698B4–700C4. Here I can only touch on some aspects of the role of shame in the *Laws*. For recent discussions of shame both inside and outside a Greek context, see Nussbaum in Rorty (1980a, pp. 395–435), Redfield (1975, pp. 115–19), G. Taylor (1985, pp. 85–107), and Williams (1993, pp. 75–102).

89. See e.g. *Laws* 700A3–701C4. Plato stresses the connection of this sort of shame to deference to a superior and the ethical significance of this deference more than other Greek writers who link shame (*aidōs, aischunē*) and fear (*deos, phobos*); cf. Edmunds (1975, pp. 59–70, 217–25) and Williams (1993, p. 196 n. 24).

90. I agree with Irwin (1977b, pp. 329–30) and Reeve (1988, pp. 48–9, 100) that this applies to both lower classes; for a different interpretation, see Kraut (1973).

91. There are three related reasons for shame here: (1) that you previously had a false belief, (2) that you previously thought that you knew although you did not, in fact, know, and (3) that you still lack an adequate grasp of the truth.

92. Cf. *Tht.* 167D5–168B2 and *Soph.* 230B4–E4. The elenchus is not restricted to philosophers in the early dialogues and seems not to be restricted to them in the *Sophist*.

93. Cf. 964B3–968B2 which draws the contrast between the philosopher and the non-philosopher more unfavorably than any other passage in the *Laws*. What should we make of the reference to *dēmosias aretais* ('the public virtues or excellences') at 968A2? This does not suggest that all but the philosophic rulers of the Nocturnal Council have only a qualified form of virtue of the sort had by non-philosophers in the *Phaedo* and the *Republic*. First, note that in the 368 Stephanus pages of the *Laws*, this is the only reference to *dēmosia aretē*. If Plato had really wanted to claim that all but the philosophic members of the Nocturnal Council have only this qualified form of virtue, it would be quite surprising to find him

introducing such a major claim and one that is in conflict with the rest of the *Laws* in so offhand a manner. Some, however, have suggested that the *dēmosia aretē* of this passage is the same thing as the 'popular virtue' (*dēmōdēs aretē*) of 710A5–B2. But this cannot be right. First, *dēmōdēs aretē* is characterized by Plato as that found in beasts and children: it is a self-restraint, with regard to pleasures, that might not be directed to the right ends. Plato in the *Laws* never claims that the ordinary citizens of Magnesia have only *dēmōdēs aretē* and he expects that the virtue of ordinary citizens will be directed to the right ends and that they will have some sort of rational support for their beliefs. Second, *dēmōdēs aretē* is contrasted by Plato himself with having one's moderation directed by true belief, so this could not be the sort of moderation that ordinary citizens have (689A1–E2).

What, then, is the meaning of the phrase *dēmosia aretē*? *dēmosia*'s basic meaning is 'belonging to the state or people', 'public'. *To dēmosion*, for example, often means 'the public treasury', e.g. *Rep.* 465D6–7 and *Laws* 774D5. Also see, *Laws* 884A8, 909D9, 910C1, C5, 921D8, 952E5, and 957A4. Although *dēmosios* is found fairly frequently in Plato, he never, except here, uses it to qualify *aretē*. Perhaps the closest occurrence is at *Prot.* 325B5 and 326E2–3 in Protagoras' speech; here the distinction is not between two grades of virtue, rather, the common phrase, *idiai kai dēmosiai*, describes virtue as it is expressed in, or relates to, private and public life, cf. *Rep.* 599D6. (For a use of *dēmosios* that is quite similar to the one that I suggest here, see *Rep.* 577B2 where Plato refers to *dēmosiois kindunois* which are, as Shorey (1978) aptly renders it, 'the hazards of public life'.) We can make further progress by considering Plato's use here of *aretē*. *Aretē* is, of course, the word that Plato uses to refer to the cardinal virtues of individuals—courage, justice, moderation, and wisdom—but it also has in Plato, as well as other Greek writers, the general meaning of 'excellence'. It can be used to refer to any good quality of a person or a thing. (1) And in this very passage describing the Nocturnal Council, Plato does use *aretē* in this sense. At 961D5, where Plato refers to the *aretē* of the head and of the soul and claims that this *aretē* is what secures safekeeping (*sōtēria*) for every animal, *aretē* clearly means 'excellence', not 'cardinal virtue'. (Saunders (1976) translates it as 'functioning satisfactorily' and A. E. Taylor (1960) as 'perfection'.) At 962D1–3, the Athenian says that the present argument suggests that the Nocturnal Council must have 'every virtue' (or 'the whole of virtue', *pasan aretēn*). It is not clear what it would mean for the Council to have every cardinal virtue, although it might mean that each of its members should possess each of the cardinal virtues. But it is better to see this as a back reference to 961D5, since this is the place where the present argument might suggest this claim. The idea then would be that the Council must possess every excellence that is necessary for securing the safekeeping of the city. In particular, it must possess the excellence of the 'head' and of the 'soul' which includes the good condition of sight and hearing (961D1–E6); cf. the analogy at 964D3–965A7 where Plato compares the younger members of the Nocturnal Council to the head and senses and the older members to the soul or the mind. At 969C2–3, Plato says that if the guardians of the Nocturnal Council are properly educated they will be 'guardians whose like with regard to the virtue of safekeeping [*pros aretēn sōtērias*]' have never been seen before. Here again *aretē* must mean 'excellence', not 'cardinal virtue': the safekeeping of the state will require the cardinal virtues, but is not itself one of the cardinal virtues. (England (1921) and A. E. Taylor (1960) rightly translate *aretē* here as 'perfection'. Because they think that *aretē* must mean 'cardinal virtue', Ast, Stallbaum, and Winckelmann (see England (1921) ad loc.) all suggest various elaborate and implausible ways of emending or construing the text in order to avoid the claim that there can be an *aretē* of safekeeping.) (2) We should also note that *aretē* at 968A2 is in the plural. David Blank (forthcoming) makes the very surprising but brilliant observation that the plural usage of *aretē* is quite rare in Plato. As Blank observes: out of 644 uses of the lexeme *aretē*, Plato uses the plural only in fifteen cases. Seven of these are in the passage from the *Meno* in which Meno claims (against Socrates) that there are different *aretai* of different kinds of people: children, women, and 'very many other *aretai*' (*Meno* 72A1). Of the eight other uses, two (*Rep.* 618B1, *Crit.* 109C1) clearly refer not to moral virtues, but to fine deeds and qualities in general; 6 (*Tim.* 87D1, *Soph.* 251A10, *Laws* 968A2, *Prot.* 323A8, *Phil.* 49A1, and *Rep.* 518D9) are very general statements referring not only or especially to the moral virtues. Blank's analysis supports the present interpretation of *dēmosias aretais*. (3) If we construe *aretē* simply as 'excellence', we can give good sense to the phrase and avoid the conflict noted above with the rest of the *Laws*: *dēmosiai aretai* are the 'public excellences', i. e. those good traits that allow one to function well in public or political life. Plato's claim then is that rulers, in addition to whatever other more obvious public or political excellences they need in order to rule well, must possess the sort of advanced theoretical knowledge he has just sketched. This fits the context of Plato's discussion of the Nocturnal Council: the question he is asking is what sort of knowledge is necessary for exercising the highest sort of political functions, not what sort of knowledge is necessary for virtue. Moreover, if *dēmosiai aretai* were low-grade forms of virtue, such as the 'popular virtue' (*dēmōdēs aretē*) of 710A5–B2, Plato would not claim, as he does, that the quasi-philosophic members of the Nocturnal Council need to have the sort of advanced theoretical knowledge he has just sketched '*in addition*' (968A2–3) to such virtues. This is, however, a perfectly appropriate claim, if *dēmosiai aretai* are public or political excellences. Thus, properly construed, Plato's use of *dēmosia aretē* does not imply that ordinary citizens have only a low-grade form of virtue.

94. 'Distress' may be a better translation for *lupē* than 'pain', but it does not easily pluralize.

95. *Laws* 662D1–664C2 and 732D8–734E2. Even if the requirement is that a person would not choose something other than the most pleasant life, this does not entail that pleasure is the only (or the most important) feature that makes such a life good or that the person is motivated only (or predominantly) by considerations of pleasure, cf. Irwin (1995a, pp. 342–5).

96. For the *Republic's* position on pleasure, see Gosling and Taylor (1984, pp. 103–28).

97. Cf. Ch. 2, n. 123.

98. Such sensory pleasures are at least not among the pleasures of the Reasoning part that the Book 9 argument (585A–E) appeals to in order to vindicate the superior pleasantness of the philosopher's life. We may find the claim that the *Republic* makes no room for sensory pleasures belonging to the Reasoning part especially plausible, if we think that unmixed bodily pleasures (584B5–8) are nevertheless not really true pleasures. See Gosling and Taylor (1984, pp. 111–15). And even if the *Republic* allows for sensory pleasures belonging to the Reasoning part, they do not, as I shall argue below, play the important role in ethical learning that they do in the later dialogues.

99. The danger is greatest for non-philosophers, see *Rep.* 429E7–430B5.

100. See Gosling and Taylor (1984, pp. 134–42, 178–83). We need not hold that all pleasures are perceptions of a replenishment.

101. For discussions, see Barney (1992, pp. 286–93), Cooper (1970, p. 133 n. 13), M. Frede (1987, pp. 3–8), Lycos (1964), and Silverman (1990b).

102. E.g. D. Frede (1985), (1993, pp. xlv–liii), and Irwin (1995a, pp. 319–21, 328–30). The debate on false pleasure in the *Philebus* has generated a considerable literature: see, especially, Gosling and Taylor (1984, pp. 429–53) with references to the earlier literature, including some important papers by Gosling, Penner (1970), and Williams (1959).

103. Perhaps along with sensory features of the restoration, such as its speed, size, and intensity (which are plausibly seen as sensory on the *Republic's* view). I leave aside further potential defects in sensory pleasures such as insatiability and the tendency to lead to false beliefs, cf. Gosling and Taylor (1984, pp. 111–22).

104. Gosling and Taylor (1984, pp. 135, 141). On Plato's restrictiveness about pure pleasures here, see D. Frede (1993, pp. liii–lv) and Gosling (1975, pp. 121–2). Worries about how well the purity criterion tracks valuable pleasures are not restricted to the pleasures of smell. Consider someone experiencing pleasure after unsuspectingly eating a brownie laced with LSD. In this case, there are no antecedent pains associated with a desire or a craving for such pleasures.

105. See Sedley in Fine (1999b, pp. 316–20).

106. Cf. A. E. Taylor (1928, ad loc.) and *Prot.* 337C1–4. On Plato's more favorable view of Prodicus' distinctions outside of the early dialogues, see Irwin (1995a, p. 373 n. 29).

107. Cf. Aristotle, *E.E.* 1230^{b}38–1231^{a}4. Despite some terminological variation in Plato, Gosling and Taylor (1984, pp. 178–92) argue convincingly that his view in the *Philebus* and the *Timaeus* is that pleasure *is* a form of perception.

108. My discussion of some of these possibilities is indebted to David Charles' fine article in Heinaman (1995, pp. 135–72).

109. Cf. Charles (1984, pp. 182–3) and Charles in Heinaman (1995, pp. 152–3). It is true that pain can also concentrate the mind, but although it may, in some sense, focus our attention on what we are doing, it focuses it on the wrong features of the activity. Pain also discourages us, in general, from engaging in the activity again and thus prevents us from getting to know it better. I am indebted to John Cooper on this point.

110. We could allow that philosophers in the *Republic* have good sensory pleasures, but these pleasures do not play this sort of role in their ethical learning.

111. See Gosling and Taylor (1984, pp. 140–3).

112. Plato's view is that sensible objects possess fineness and goodness to a sufficient degree that the sensory apprehension of them is valuable, even if it is less valuable than the apprehension of intelligibles. (That the sensible objects possess these features to a significant degree is an important qualification. It is not enough that there are truths to be known about sensible objects, since merely knowing truths may lack any (serious) value. Any true proposition, for example, entails non-denumerably many other true propositions, but there seems to be little, if any, value in knowing the entailments formed by the reiterated addition of disjuncts.) This is importantly different from certain later views of sensory pleasure, such as, for example, Baumgarten's. Baumgarten holds that the aesthetic is the perfection of sensitive cognition and that the perfection of sensory cognition is clear, but confused or indistinct representation. But for Baumgarten, the indistinctness of the sensible is good in itself, because it has a richness that is lacking in the more distinct ideas of reason: see Gregor (1983).

113. Insofar as pleasure taken in virtuous activity includes more than, e.g., thinking of the Form of the Fine, it will seem to include the pleasure of apprehending a fine particular.

114. In the case of the desire for something as good, when the thing is in fact good, the desire for it is backed by a true judgment that the object is worthy of pursuit. In the case of a desire for pleasure as pleasant, there may be a corresponding true judgment that the object of pursuit is in fact pleasant. But insofar as the desire

for the object as pleasant carries with it an implicit judgment that the object is worthy of pursuit because it is pleasant, the case is more problematic. We might accept that pleasure is, at least in certain cases, a sign of goodness so that the desire for a particular pleasure might involve a true judgment that the thing is, *ceteris paribus*, worth pursuing. What is less clear is that reason can approve of an implicit judgment that the object is worth pursuing simply because it is pleasant (and not because it is good).

115. Gosling and Taylor (1984, pp. 178–83).

116. Especially if, for example, the restoration involved in the perception of fine sounds is the massed return of bodily parts in the ear, cf. Gosling and Taylor (1984, pp. 180–2).

117. With respect to (1), the claim that physical objects typically possess order and proportion only imperfectly and approximately is a humdrum truth about production and does not entail the controversial metaphysical thesis that every sensible F is only imperfectly F. With respect to (2), this claim will be true even of pure sensory pleasures and will be all the more true of good appetitive pleasures, if there are such (as is plausibly argued by Cooper (1999, pp. 160–3)).

118. And it is reasonable to think that fully virtuous people (or those nearly so) would be most likely to succumb first to novel, subtle pleasures.

Chapter 5 The Citizens of Magnesia

1. Disapproval of maritime activity is not a Platonic eccentricity: Aristotle agrees with Plato's statement of the disadvantages of the sea, but allows a port, suggesting that its disadvantages can be overcome by strictly regulating contact with foreigners (*Politics* 1327ᵃ11 ff.).

2. *Laws* 737E ff. and see Brunt (1993, p. 247). The number 5,040 is evenly divisible by every number from 1–10 inclusive and—conveniently for calculation—has 59 divisors and is evenly divisible by 12, which is a common unit in Magnesia. Golding and Golding (1975, p. 353) estimate Magnesia's population at about 50,000 plus resident aliens.

3. On the proper characterization of landownership in Magnesia, see Morrow (1960, pp. 105–7). For limitations on the lotholder's testamentary powers, see *Laws* 877C–E and 923A ff. Brunt (1993, p. 279) notes that these are one of Plato's 'most radical deviations from normal usage [which would] surely [be] unacceptable to most Greeks'. The fact that the lot is reassigned, if heirs fail, is one important reason why it is the property of the city, and not in the possession of individuals. On the concept of private property see, Honoré (1961) and Waldron (1990, pp. 26–61).

4. Some have interpreted Plato to mean that the highest class has only between two and three times the value of the lot, i.e. their total property taking the notion-

al value of the lot into account would be worth up to four times the value of the lot. The interpretation that they may have *movable assets* up to four times the value of the lot is held by Aristotle (*Politics* 1265^{b}22 and 1266^{b}7) and is convincingly argued for by Morrow (1960, p. 131 n. 112). This is important, since the other interpretation reduces the lowest class to the level of subsistence farmers and thus significantly reduces their chances for political participation or leisurely activity.

5. Brunt (1993, p. 265).

6. Brunt (1993, p. 265, 265 n. 61) lists passages in the *Laws* limiting consumption.

7. On the differences between the Cretan and the Spartan methods of supporting common meals, see Morrow (1960, pp. 389–98) and Jones (1990, pp. 489–91).

8. Figueira (1984, pp. 97–8).

9. Kraut (1997, pp. 109–10); see Morrow (1960, p. 322) on Plutarch, Xenophon, and others on common meals.

10. Aristotle (*Politics* 1274^{b}11) claims that common meals for women are peculiar to Plato.

11. Aristotle, *Politics* 1271^{a}27–37.

12. *Laws* 955E3–4 and 847E2–848B6, but see 842B1–8. For discussion, see Morrow (1960, pp. 395–6).

13. *Laws* 739B8–740A2, cf. 736C5–737B9 and see Laks (2000, pp. 269–73). It is not clear, I think, whether Plato holds that a community of property is simply impossible, given human nature, or that it is so demanding that it is extremely unlikely—although not absolutely impossible—that a city having a community of property could persist. (Aristotle in *Politics* Book 2, ch.5 may more clearly take the first option.) Even in the latter case, one might reasonably think that we should not even attempt to found such a city. *Laws* 739B8–E1 suggests that Plato also thinks that if such a city could exist, it would be better than Magnesia (and that its citizens would be happier, as they would be if all were to attain philosophical understanding). The *Republic* and the *Laws* both accept the formal principles that the best city is the one that is most unified and is the happiest, but differ in the ways in which they specify these goals.

14. Barker (1960, p. 376) and Morrow (1941, p. 39).

15. Plato would probably not bestow citizenship on metics even when, owing to population loss, outsiders must be granted Magnesian citizenship; see Morrow (1941, p. 39).

16. See Morrow (1960, pp. 112–13).

17. On women in Aristotle's political theory, see F. Miller (1995, pp. 240–5).

18. See Saunders (1991, pp. 275, 277–8).

19. On Plato's terminology for the Assembly, see Morrow (1960, p. 157 n. 4).

20. On the purpose of this provision, see Morrow (1960, pp. 158–9).

21. For details, see Morrow (1960, pp. 156–64).

22. On (i), see Morrow (1960, pp. 264–70); (iv) is discussed further below.

23. On the Assembly in general, see Morrow (1960, pp. 156–65, 174–6, and 229) and Piérart (1973, pp. 89–121).

24. All members of the household are counted as being from the same property class. For further discussion, see Morrow (1960, pp. 165–78).

25. It is not clear that this results in the overrepresentation of the higher property classes, see Stalley (1983, p. 118).

26. See Morrow (1960, pp. 165–78) and Piérart (1973, pp. 89–121), especially (pp. 108 ff.) for an argument that Plato, more consistently than Aristotle, assigns only deliberative functions to the Assembly and Council.

27. Morrow (1960, pp. 195–215) and Piérart (1973, pp. 152–208).

28. Morrow (1960, pp. 204–6 and 238–40) following Wilamowitz sees an inconsistency in Plato's proposals, but Saunders (1970) offers a plausible way of avoiding this.

29. Saunders (1970, p. 235) rightly notes this.

30. Even when a guardian acts alone, the determination of a penalty requires a board, Morrow (1960, p. 203).

31. E.g. *Laws* 855D–856A and see Morrow (1960, pp. 244–5, 280–2).

32. The latter is one plausible way of understanding John McDowell's position on practical reason, see Wallace (1991).

33. Hansen (1991, pp. 178–80).

34. Hansen (1991, p. 187).

35. Todd (1995, p. 89).

36. On the difficulties surrounding some of the details, see Morrow (1960, p. 269). Plato (*Laws* 957A) notes that these provisions are open to revision.

37. Plato differs from Athens in giving more power to magistrates, see Stalley (1983, pp. 113–16).

38. Contra Morrow (1960, pp. 254), Plato endorses this claim, see 768A3.

39. Morrow (1960, pp. 215–19).

40. On the number of examiners, see Barker (1960, pp. 400–1) and Morrow (1960, pp. 223–5).

41. 'Dawn Council' would be a more accurate translation (*Laws* 951D6–7); Luc Brisson (2001) happily suggests 'Le Collège de Veille' (Vigilance Committee or Board) which both avoids the sinister connotations of 'Nocturnal Council' and distinguishes it from the Council.

42. Its composition is described in two passages, *Laws* 951D4–E5 and 961A1–B6. Morrow (1960, pp. 503–4) seems right to attribute little significance to the small differences in the two accounts.

43. Morrow (1960, p. 133), and see Stalley (1983, pp. 118–20). On the notion of the 'mixed constitution', see Morrow (1960, pp. 521–43) and Stalley (1983, pp. 116–20).

44. Okin (1979, p. 50).

45. Cohen (1987, p. 37). Both Cohen and Okin are quoted in Saunders (1995, p. 591). For related discussions, see Annas (1976), Morrow (1960, pp. 113, 121, 157, 168, 329–31, 393–4), Smith (1983), Stalley (1983, pp. 104–6), and Vlastos (1994, vol. 2, pp. 133–43).

46. The point is emphasized by the irony of ἀνὴρ at 770D1; similarly, note the playful order of men and women at *Laws* 805A7.

47. Saunders (1995, p. 604 n. 8): 637C, 694D–E, 731D, 790A–B, 817C, 909E, 917A, 934E, 944D–945A.

48. On the notion of nature, see Annas (1993, pp. 135–41), Kamtekar (forthcoming), Okin (1979, pp. 63–70), and Smith (1983).

49. I do not mean to claim that Plato clearly holds (b). Indeed, the above passages and *Laws* 794D5–795D5 may suggest that he holds a more egalitarian position about women's nature.

50. For a more pessimistic reading of these passages, see Levin (2000). Levin's account does not, I think, give sufficient weight to the *Laws*' theoretical and programmatic remarks about women, and goes wrong in thinking that the *Laws*' view of human nature is unrelievedly more pessimistic than the *Republic*'s.

51. Okin (1979, p. 44).

52. Saunders (1995, p. 604).

53. Newman (1985, vol. 1, pp. 179–80, 195) argues that in the *Laws* the household has only a shadowy existence and sees *Laws* 794A–C as promising, even in Magnesia as originally constituted, something like daycare for children over 3.

54. See Brunt (1993, pp. 263–4). Such activities would take too much of the citizens' time and tend to foster their acquisitive desires.

55. Morrow's (1960, pp. 152, 531) arguments for the claim that most citizens do work their land are well answered by Brunt (1993, pp. 273–4) and Guthrie (1987, vol. 5, p. 345); also see Barker (1960, pp. 374–5). Property classes affect some political duties and the less well-off might have to devote more time to the supervision of their plots, even if they do not engage in labor themselves. But, as Morrow himself agrees, property qualifications do not play a large political role in Magnesia. On Greek views on the compatibility of estate management with leisure time, see Brunt (1993, p. 264), Johnstone (1994), and Ober (1998, p. 341 n. 88).

56. Plato, unlike Aristotle (see Kraut (1997, p. 203–9)), thinks that the education of adults is possible and necessary. In order to do so, Plato proposes to

use music (*Laws* 659B–C), the preludes, mathematics, including the study of incommensurable magnitudes, and astronomy.

57. *Laws* at 632C4–6 and 818A1–3. *Laws* 818A does not say that mathematics and astronomy are reserved for a few, but that they should be labored over with precision (*akribeia*) by few. Morrow (1960, pp. 343–50) is right that Plato requires mathematical studies for all citizens, including study of incommensurable magnitudes and mathematical astronomy. And see Carone (1996, pp. 347–8).

58. Barker (1960, pp. 406–10) seems to hold the former. Klosko (1988, p. 84) argues for the weaker view that the Nocturnal Council is intended to hold 'some unspecified high political office'. This is compatible with an extremely wide range of possibilities.

59. Klosko (1988, p. 85). Klosko (1988, p. 86) claims that the presence of other inconsistencies in the *Laws* should make us more willing to accept this inconsistency. But some of the problems Klosko offers as evidence are hardly serious (whether men can marry at 25 or 30) and others, such as the procedure for selecting guardians of the laws, may not, in fact, be inconsistencies, see Saunders (1970). I accept Cherniss' construal of 968C5; Cherniss (1953, pp. 373–4) and Morrow (1960, p. 513 n. 22) offer convincing arguments for construing *tōn toioutōn* at *Laws* 968C3–4 as referring to the knowledge or education necessary for the Nocturnal Council and not their general political authority. Also note the context: at 968B1, the Athenian refers to the 'entire education' he has been suggesting for the Nocturnal Council and claims that he has long experience and made long investigation *peri ta toiaut'*, 968B7–8. *Ta toiauta* here clearly refers to these studies proposed for the Nocturnal Council; Kleinias urges that they 'proceed along the path' along which god is conducting them (968B10–11): the reference here is to the Athenian's point that study of the stars, which are moved by divine souls, leads men to pursue and grasp the studies he recommends (966D6–968B1). Kleinias then says that they must discover and state the way (*tropos*) that this would correctly come about (968C1–2), that is, the correct way to proceed on the path along which god is conducting them. *Tōn toioutōn* then follows immediately at 968C3–4 and refers to what precedes, that is, to these studies and their arrangement. Following directly after this, *ta toiauta* at C6 must refer (1) to the same things as *tōn toioutōn* at C3–4, and (2) to the education of the Nocturnal Council, since what its proper arrangement requires is 'schooling with full discussion' (C6).

60. Other interpretations which agree with Morrow that the description of the Nocturnal Council in Book 12 is not inconsistent with the rest of the *Laws* and does not attribute to it the function and power of the philosopher rulers of the *Republic*, include Guthrie (1987, vol. 5, pp. 368–75), Kahn (1961) and (1995), Laks (2000, pp. 283–4), Piérart (1973, pp. 229–34), and Stalley (1983, pp. 112, 133–6).

61. Morrow (1960, p. 504). The younger associates could not play their role as the 'senses' of the older members if they remained permanently on the Council.

62. Those accepting a narrower reading of this passage include England (1921, ad loc.), Guthrie (1987, vol. 5, p. 368), Morrow (1960, p. 571 n. 54), Piérart (1973, p. 206), and Stalley (1983, p. 82). Piérart (1973, pp. 206, 405–7) rightly points out that Plato is especially concerned to avoid change in religious matters. Klosko (1988, p. 82) holds that the narrower interpretation of this passage is 'preferable', although he believes there are other reasons to think that Plato intends to ban change quite generally.

63. *Laws* 772A7, B4, B6. If we were to adopt the broader construal, then we should with Ast reject θυσιῶν τε καὶ χορειῶν at 772B6, but there is no textual support for this.

64. In both the *Republic* and the *Laws*, oracles are assigned only rather minor functions concerned with the details of ritual and religious laws, see Morrow (1960, pp. 402–7).

65. For a defense of this interpretation see Morrow (1960, p. 571). Even if one were to think that *panta ton dēmon* at *Laws* 772D1 literally means 'every member of the people', it would be better, for the reasons noted above, to see this as a rhetorical exaggeration.

66. The magistrates might well be highly averse to changing how the law is to be applied in certain tried and tested circumstances, but, nevertheless, need to meet a new case where it is not immediately obvious how the law ought to be applied and it is in such cases that they will need to interpret the law. The new case may make them need to re-examine old cases and possibly revise how the law is to be applied in cases similar to the old ones. So, even with an extremely strong bias against changing the application of the law, once it has been well tested, it is nevertheless possible that something will crop up that will be problematic for the old application and will force them to reconsider and make the appropriate changes. I am indebted to Laura Maguire for this suggestion.

67. Passages assigning the *nomophulakes* the task of revising and completing the laws include, *Laws* 769A7–771A4, 779C5–D2, 816C1–D2, 828B3–7, 835A2–B4, 840E2–7, 846B6–C8, 847D1–7, 849E1–6, 855D1–4, 871C3–D2, 917E2–918A5, 920B3–C7, 957A1–C1. As Klosko (1988, pp. 83–4) rightly notes, 957A–C shows that the younger lawgivers of 846B–C, 855C–D are the *nomophulakes*. As Piérart (1973, pp. 204–7) notes, if the provision at 772A–D applies to all laws, these tasks must take place before the final establishment of the city (or, with Klosko, we might see this as evidence of a fundamental inconsistency in the *Laws*). But if we adopt Morrow's more moderate interpretation of 772A–D, we need not think that all

revision and completion must take place before the final establishment of the city and, as I have argued, Plato's programmatic remarks about preserving and revising the laws along with the consideration that future generations of Magnesians should be greatly ethically superior to the first generation (especially the very first generation), support Morrow.

68. This echoes Glaucon's and Adeimantus' demand in the *Republic* (358B3–6 and 366E5–9) that Socrates make clear what power justice has.

69. *Laws* 797A–D explicitly allows that change in what is bad is not just permitted, but not dangerous (797E1–2). The more concerned Plato is with the possibility that change can be motivated by beliefs and desires whose defectiveness or irrationality is not obvious and that change has unforeseen consequences, the more inclined he will be to view it as dangerous, even if permissible, and to heighten his rhetoric against it. Compare Broadie (1991, pp. 388–98) on Aristotle's strategy in recommending contemplation and Tessitore (1996, pp. 4–6).

70. Even in this passage, the conclusion that Plato states is more moderate: fine laws will not allow poets to teach whatever forms of rhythm or tune they like best regardless of their consequences for the citizens' virtue (656C1–7) and the laws will require the poets to portray virtuous people (660A3–8).

71. Stalley (1983, p. 82), cf. Klosko (1988, p. 82) on Egypt.

72. Cf. Bobonich (1996, p. 260 n. 22).

73. For instances concerned with details, see *Laws* 772A–C, 828B, 835A, 843E, 918A with 920B–C, 957A–B. But Stalley (1983, p. 82) is not right to limit envisaged instances of changing the law to just details, see *Laws* 818E5–7 and 968C3–7. They will legislate later on mathematical studies and concerning the Nocturnal Council, but these are not just details.

74. *Laws* 846C2–8 and 957A2–B5: we cannot determine how long such a period might be. The Athenian does not say that a similar provision applies to all other laws and, e.g., 820E, 828B–D, 835A, 843E, 855D, and 968C–E do not state any time limit on revision (not even the 'until satisfactory' provision).

75. Klosko (1986, pp. 233–4).

76. Klosko (1988, pp. 85–8). Klosko's position may undergo some change: (1986, p. 323) holds that they are 'not easily to be altered'; (1988, p. 87) holds that they are 'all but impossible to change'.

77. Saunders (1995, p. 603), and see Saunders (1986, pp. 207–8) on the interplay between the laws and the characters of citizens in Magnesia and how this could lead to adjustment of the laws.

78. D. Cohen (1993, p. 314).

79. On the rule of law, see D. Cohen (1995, pp. 32–57), Morrow (1960, pp. 544–72), and Ober (1998).

80. Morrow (1960, pp. 503–4): observers and perhaps some citizens who have received awards of merit might not be elected.

81. There are a vast range of possible ways for Magnesia to meet these desiderata: the Nocturnal Council could be given sole power of origination for changes, it could be given veto power, and so on.

82. See Newman (1985, vol. 3, pp. 372–3).

83. If the difference between happy and non-happy lives is small, then such a restriction seems less reasonable. The deep disparities in treatment that result from such a restriction appear more justifiable if the difference is great. Aristotle seems to hold that the excluded are merely means to the good life of the polis (*Politics* 1328ᵃ21 ff.) and this suggests that he thinks the difference between the two groups is great.

84. Cf. Wolin (1960, pp. 56–8).

85. Cf. *Laws* 739A3–740A2, which claims that in a unified city the citizens delight in the laws responsible for this unity, with *Rep.* 464A1–9, where the common delights are in the same women and children and their welfare. On Aristotle, see, e.g., Keyt (1991, pp. 124–6), Miller (1995, pp. 54–6), and Schofield (1996), (1999, pp. 82–159).

86. See Newman (1985, vol. 4, p. 425).

87. Bobonich (1995b, pp. 313–16).

88. The *Statesman's* distinction of character types is neither identical nor coextensive with the *Republic's* division of three basic character types and classes: see Bobonich (1995b).

89. The addition of 'no' is justified by the context.

90. Plato stresses that such opinion is 'divine' (*Stsmn.* 309C7), and for each citizen, it is an internal bond that 'binds the eternal part of their souls with a divine bond, to which that part is akin' (309C1–2). Although we should not read into the *Statesman* the *Republic's* theory of parts of the soul, according to the *Timaeus* (69C5–D6) and Book 10 of the *Republic* (611A ff.), the immortal part of the soul is the rational part. And if the divine bond of true opinion is akin to the rational part, these true opinions should be supported by reasons and not just trained emotions and habits. Note also that the bond of true opinion binds or works on the rational part of the soul alone and not on the mortal part (*Stsmn.* 309C1–3).

91. Cf. Rowe (1995b, ad loc.).

92. See Cooper (1999, pp. 172–82).

93. Cf. Bobonich (1995b, pp. 322–9), Cooper (1999, pp. 184–5), and Skemp (1952, pp. 42–6).

94. Cf. *Rep.* 406A–407B, but I have argued in Ch. 1 that Plato in the *Republic* does not think that genuine virtue can be developed in all the citizens. On the

notion of one's political *ergon* in the *Republic*, see Broadie (1991, p. 118) and Vlastos (1994, pp. 69–103).

95. The practices of having citizenship descend by inheritance and be maintained throughout life are in tension with the continuation of a community of the virtuous. Although Plato provides for stripping citizenship as a punishment for some criminal offenses, constant screening would be entirely impractical: it would impose far too high demands on the accuracy and honesty of the testing procedure and great strains on the social fabric by mid-life exclusion. Since the family is preserved, it would also impose high demands on the willingness of people to do the virtuous thing even at a severe cost to their own kin. For these reasons, maintenance of a community of the virtuous requires political mechanisms for dealing with non-ideal conditions. One way of meeting some of these worries would be to require that no class in the good city with a specifiable social role should be incapable of virtue, while excluding individuals only in cases of serious failures in virtue. Also see Saunders (1962).

96. In the *Politics*, Aristotle famously enunciates a view of the good city as one that exists 'for the sake of the good life' and for the sake of enabling its citizens to lead good lives (*Politics* 1252^{b}29–30). This understanding of what a city is determines how its boundaries must be drawn. '[N]ot all the things that are necessary for cities to possess are to be counted as parts of a city . . . but whenever there is one thing that is for another's sake and another for whose sake it is, there is nothing in common except that one produces what the other receives. . . . The city is a community of similar people, and its object is the best possible life. And since the greatest good is happiness, and this is some perfect activity or employment of virtue, and since it has come about that some men can share in it, but others can have little or none of it, it is clear that this is why there arise different kinds and varieties of cities and constitutions. For as each set of people pursues happiness in a different manner and by different means, they make for themselves different modes of life and different constitutions' (*Politics* 1328^{a}24–^{b}1). Aristotle also makes clear the consequences of this for the best constitution: '[T]he citizens must not live a mechanic or mercantile life (for such a life is ignoble and contrary to virtue), nor yet must those who are to be citizens in the best city be farmers (for leisure is needed both for the development of virtue and for political activity)' (*Politics* 1328^{b}33–1329^{a}2); '[T]he mechanic class has no share in the city, nor has any other class that is not a "craftsman of virtue" [τῆς ἀρετῆς δημιουργόν]' (*Politics* 1329^{a}19–21).

97. For a fine discussion of this passage, see Cooper (1999, pp. 365–70).

98. Thucydides 2. 40. 2–3. The translation is by Ober (1998, p. 88).

99. Aristotle, *Politics* 1259^{b}5–6, 1261^{a}30–1261^{b}16, 1278^{a}40–^{b}5, 1279^{a}8–13, 1287^{a}10–18, 1288^{a}1–2, 1325^{b}3–10, and 1332^{b}12–29; see Irwin (1990b) and Kraut (1997, pp. 70–3, 133–8).

100. Even in this passage, it seems that Plato is claiming that correct laws are established for the sake of the common good, which is to be construed as the greatest happiness of the citizens to whom the law applies. At *Laws* 713A9 ff., Plato refers to the old story that human beings were once ruled by Zeus' father, Kronos. Kronos' rule was 'very happy' (713B2–3); he provided good laws and justice (713E1–2) and thus made men happy (713E3). (This last clause suggests that what made Kronos' rule 'happy' was that people under it were happy.) Plato also makes it clear that the same principles apply to law nowadays: the best laws now in existence imitate Kronos' rule (713A9–B4 and 713E3–714A2). Note that Plato freely shifts here between 'correct' (*orthoi*, 715B3) laws and 'good' laws (*eunomia*, 713E2). On laws and institutions aiming at the good or the best, see 628A–C, 646C–D, 664A, 697B–D, 875A–B (and the common good), 903C, and 923B. On 'faction-states' which do not aim at the common good, but only at the good of some part of the city, see 712E–713A and 832B–D. On aiming at happiness, see 858D.

101. *Laws* 743C7 shows that Plato is thinking of citizens here.

102. I take γάρ at 631B5 as confirmatory and causal and the participle, ἀποτελοῦντες, as stating the reason that the laws are correct.

103. I do not think that Plato intends to draw any important distinction between 'blessed' (*makarios*) and 'happy' (*eudaimōn*) here; cf. Nussbaum (1986, especially pp. 329–33) and Newman (1985, vol. 3, p. 310).

104. Also see *Laws* 664A2–3, 665C2–5, 683B3–4, 697A10–C2, 701E1–702B1, 709C5–9, 768A1–4, 829E7–830A1, 831A1–3, 839C6–D1, 858C10–D9, 945E3–6, and 958A2–3. For further discussion, see Morrison (2001), Neu (1971), and Vlastos (1994, vol. 2, pp. 63–103).

105. They will, however, have to be extended: we cannot simply collapse the evaluation of institutions and practices into the evaluation of laws. For example, we might think that we could always evaluate the correctness of any social practice, P, by evaluating a law requiring P. But this would be a mistake. The state of affairs in which P operates without the law's sanction and that in which it operates with the law's sanction are two distinct outcomes and may differ in terms of happiness. For example, citizens, although they may be willing to act in accordance with P, may resent its being made compulsory and their resentment and possible efforts to frustrate the law would affect the total amount of happiness. Plato is quite clear about this point, e.g., *Laws* 788A–790B.

106. See e.g. Scheffler (1988), (1992), and Slote (1989).

107. 'Appropriate' need not be instrumental. Two other aims of law that Plato stresses in the *Laws* are: (1) inculcating all the virtues in the citizens, and (2) making the city free, wise, and friendly to itself (693B3–E3, 694A3–B6, and 701D7–E8), cf. Vlastos (1994, vol. 2, p. 99 n. 117). In both cases, it is plausible to think that these

goals are justified by their contribution to making the city as happy as possible. Also see, 738E1–2, 739B8–E2, and 816C7–D2.

108. This, for example, seems to be the most plausible interpretation of the exceptions that Plato makes to the proportional equality principle of political justice, cf. n. 132. Also see *Laws* 715B2–4 where the criterion for correct law—including laws regulating the structure and filling of the city's offices—is that they aim at the common good or what is best overall for the citizens.

109. Slaves, resident aliens, transient aliens, and those living in other cities are treated quite differently, although in no case is their happiness seen as part of the goal of the city's laws (e.g. *Laws* 631B3–6, 743C5–6). Slaves are clearly the least protected group, although even in their case, there are restrictions on how they can be treated (776B5–778A5, especially 777C7–E6, and 936B3–8). On this important and underexplored topic, see Morrow (1941), (1948), (1960), (1976), and Vlastos (1981, pp. 147–63). Also, as for example the provisions for making the lot inalienable show, the city is concerned for the happiness of future generations of citizens.

110. Cf. Scheffler (1987, pp. 59–60 and 77–9). Plato's theory may have the resources necessary to develop a theory of degrees of happiness. We could try to give content to the idea of degrees of happiness in at least two ways: (1) we might hold that virtue itself is a scalar quality and that if a person possesses the proper degree of virtue, she is happy, but that it is still possible for the same person to be more virtuous and thus happier, or (2) leaving aside the question of whether virtue is a scalar quality, we could hold that a person who is virtuous is therefore happy, but that the more non-instrumentally valuable Dependent Goods she possesses, the happier, *ceteris paribus*, she would be. Cf. section 2.13.

111. On Aristotle, see Nussbaum (1988) and Charles (1988).

112. Cf., e.g., Brink (1990).

113. E.g. *Laws* 736C5–E4 and 923A2–C5. More difficult is 735A–736B where Plato envisages scarcity requiring forced emigration. Plato does not try to clarify this notion of a coincidence between the individual's happiness and the city's. He might think that in any given circumstances in a just city, there are some accessible outcomes in which each citizen is optimally happy. (Note that this allows for the possibility that there are two outcomes A and B such that although neither A nor B is optimal, B is a highly ranked outcome in which the city is happier than in A, although some people will have to make a sacrifice of happiness in B in comparison to A.) But even if such an outcome is possible if all act justly, worries remain. If some act unjustly, is it the case that if all the remaining citizens act justly they can be optimally happy in these circumstances? Or might third-party injustice ever produce cases in which even if all the remaining citizens act justly, some can only optimize their happiness at the expense of others not optimizing? For related ideas

in connection with Aristotle, see Cooper (1999, pp. 356–77) and Irwin (1990a, pp. 389–406).

114. *Rep.* 420B3–C4, 421B3–C5, and *Laws* 923B4–6 at least seem to suggest the counterfactual that if maximizing the happiness of the city required making some citizens less happy than they could be, a good lawgiver would choose to maximize the happiness of the city.

115. See, e.g., Scheffler (1988) and (1992).

116. Insofar as people can be benefited without being made more virtuous, virtuous friends' justification for some of their actions need not be promoting virtue in the other. A virtuous friend should, however, be willing to give up the attempt to benefit when doing so would impair the friend's virtue. But even here, the desire to benefit is a motivation independent of increasing the friend's virtue.

117. Annas in Patzig (1990, p. 241). On political friendship, see Annas in Patzig (1990, pp. 243–9), Cooper (1999, pp. 356–77), and Irwin (1990b).

118. On the notion of cooperative activity or shared agency, see Bratman (1999, pp. 93–161).

119. 'Ally' at 906A6 is *summachos*, literally, one who fights together or alongside of.

120. On the argument, see Irwin (1995a, pp. 308–10). Also see *Phdr.* 247A7, *Laws* 635B1 (where 'jealousy' (*phthonos*) is opposed to 'good will' (*eunoia*)), and Mills (1985).

121. It is this sort of friendship that Plato in the very opening pages of the *Laws* claims that the best lawgiver will foster in the city (*Laws* 627D11–628D1). This is a friendship among virtuous people, not a generalized benevolence for all regardless of virtue.

122. Aristotle's complaint seems to have *Stsmn.* 258E8–259D5 especially in mind, cf. Xenophon *Memorabilia* III. iv. 12, III. vi. 14.

123. I am indebted here to Kraut (1997, pp. 63, 72, 106, 133, 135–7). On (1), see *Politics* 1255^{b}20, 1259^{b}5–6, 1277^{b}7–9; on (2), see *Politics* 1279^{a}28–9; on (3), see *Politics* 1259^{b}4–5, 1261^{a}30–^{b}6, 1279^{a}8–10, 1279^{b}4–5, 1287^{a}11–14, 1288^{a}1–2.

124. Cf. *Politics* 1259^{b}5–6, 1261^{a}30–1261^{b}4, 1279^{a}8–10, 1287^{b}41–1288^{a}2, 1332^{b}16–27.

125. Cf. *Politics* 1326^{b}14–16 and 1332^{b}26–7.

126. For the assembly, see Kraut (1997, p. 134) and for the lot, *Politics* 1332^{b}26–7. I am indebted to Richard Kraut for discussion on this point.

127. On Aristotle on citizens, see Kraut (1997) and Miller (1995). Also see Ober (1998, pp. 300–1) and Schofield (1996).

128. On freedom in Plato, see the fine discussion in Moravcsik (1983).

129. *Timē* often means 'political office' and, as the context shows, this is primarily what Plato has in mind here.

130. This sentence, 757B7–C1, suggests a justification of the principle of proportional equality in terms of the benefit of its application; the claim that 'it brings all the good things' is strikingly similar to Plato's earlier justification of Crete's laws (631B3–6).

131. See Harvey (1965) and Ober (1998, pp. 279–80).

132. For forward-looking justifications of the distribution of honor and offices, see *Laws* 648B–C, 691B–C, 694B, 697B–C, 711B–D, 715B–C, 728C–D, 730D–E. For a further exception to the above principle, see 759B4–7. Saunders (1972, pp. 31–2) offers what may, on the whole, be the most plausible interpretation of the difficult passage at 744A8–D1, but cf. Stalley (1983, pp. 118–19).

133. See *Laws* 700A7–701C4, although Magnesia's citizens will be better than those of Athens.

134. The epistemic gain from pooled information and collective discussion will be especially great, if people's judgments are likely to be initially biased by self-interest, but they are able and willing to correct their judgments through rational discussion. For further discussion, see J. Cohen (1986), and Waldron (1995). Arguments that appeal to the idea that group discussion improves the average participant's judgments differ from arguments appealing to Condorcet jury theorems. The latter show that if the average individual's competence of getting the correct answer is above 50 percent, then the probability of a simple majority getting a correct answer increases rapidly as the size of the group increases. These arguments do not rely on the idea that deliberation preceding voting increases individual competence or issues in better-informed group judgments.

135. 'The Muse' is philosophy, see Cherniss (1953, p. 377 n. 1). Even if generic similarity is compatible with a considerable variety of species, Plato stresses finding what is common.

136. On 'equity', see Saunders (2001).

137. The most straightforward justification for using the lot would be that it maximizes happiness even if it infringes the principle of distribution according to virtue; one could also argue that, since resentment will tend to lead to large-scale bad changes in the distribution of offices, the use of the lot maximizes, in the long run, the match between virtue and political office.

138. Elections are intended as a way of choosing the best people, see *Laws* 751C4–D5, 945B3–946C3, and Stalley (1983, pp. 118–22).

139. I use 'democratic' in the modern sense in which voting counts as a democratic method of decisionmaking. On the understanding of democracy in Greek political thought, see Ober (1998); see also Christiano (1996).

140. On reconciling proportional equality in Aristotle with the requirement that citizens rule and be ruled, see Ober (1991, especially pp. 130–1). In the passage

at hand, Plato is discussing the Council and not the Assembly, but the principle should also apply to the Assembly, even if Plato does call membership in the Assembly an office (*archē*).

141. Newman (1985, vol. 1, p. 427).

142. I intend this to be neutral on whether Aristotle holds a contemplative or an inclusivist conception of happiness.

143. For a start on the extensive literature, see E. Brown (2000), Kraut (1993), and N. White (1986).

144. A point made in connection with Aristotle by Irwin (1990b).

145. Such reasoning need not be deductive or limited to means–end calculation. This suggestion is influenced by Broadie (1987) and (1991, pp. 179–265). But as we shall see below, it does not represent Broadie's views about Plato and I do not claim that it accurately reflects all of Broadie's views about Aristotle.

146. Cf. Striker in Patzig (1990, pp. 99–100).

147. N. White (1999, pp. 511–12) emphasis in original.

148. See Section 2.13.

149. Waterlow (1972, pp. 31 and 33). Emphasis in original.

150. Broadie in Gentzler (1998, pp. 301–2).

151. Irwin (1995a, pp. 307–17).

152. Irwin (1995a, p. 308).

153. I am not sure how strong a claim Irwin (1995a, p. 308) intends by the requirement that what matters to me in self-concern includes (i) that my future self have an outlook that is a rational development of my present outlook, and (ii) that this results from my own action. One might think that it is empirically highly unlikely that an ethical change that did not satisfy (i) and (ii) could result in, e.g., a better appreciation of genuine value; or one might think that, even if an ethical change that did not satisfy (i) and (ii) had such a positive result, the person would be better off if (i) or (ii) were satisfied. But if I could make such a positive change without satisfying (i) or (ii), why should I not attach some value to it?

154. Irwin (1995a, p. 309).

155. Irwin (1995a, p. 309).

156. Irwin (1995a, p. 310).

157. *Laws* 721B6–c6 does not claim that interpersonal propagation is the only way for a person to be immortal, see 713E8 and 959B3–4. The identity of the person with the soul is necessary for the coherence of Plato's accounts of the afterlife, see 959A4–B7 and T. Robinson (1995, pp. 125–7).

158. This is quite important to the argument, since suppose that 'what matters' to me is my future welfare, in particular, what matters to me is that I am as well-off as possible. On this supposition, I should still care about developing and retaining

a virtuous character, since virtue is the most important component of what is good for me. But then the inference to the rationality of other-regarding concern is no longer clear. Why does concern for *my* future well-being rationalize concern with others' well-being? It is this gap which, I take it, Irwin is trying to fill.

159. Cf. Brink in Dancy (1997, pp. 119–21).

160. Irwin (1995a, p. 308).

161. On degeneration in the *Laws*, see 875A1–C3, 904E4–905C4.

162. N. White (1999, pp. 510–11).

163. The idea that happiness has parts such as virtue or the interests of others has recently come under sophisticated and probing criticism by Richard Kraut in connection with Aristotle. (Kraut (1989), and also see Annas (1992a), (1993, pp. 223–325), (1995), Irwin (1991), (1995b), and N. White (1995), (1999).) Since Plato might use such a notion even if Aristotle does not, I shall leave aside the aspects of Kraut's criticisms that depend on the interpretation of the *Nicomachean Ethics* and focus on those that seem to carry over to Plato. (1) What we can call the 'Composite View' holds that Plato thinks that (a) virtue is good for its own sake, and (b) virtue is good for the sake of happiness. One way for both (a) and (b) to be true is if virtue is good both for its own sake and for the sake of its consequences (so that virtue is good for the sake of happiness in that it is causally productive of good(s) that (at least partially) constitute happiness). But the Composite View holds that there is another way in which (a) and (b) can be true. X can be 'for the sake' of Y when Y is a whole of which X is a part. In particular, we can choose something for its own sake when we choose it as a part of happiness and not as being causally productive of happiness. In this case 'the very features of it that make it choiceworthy for its own sake also make it a part of happiness; in choosing it for the features that make it part of happiness we are also choosing it for its own sake' (Irwin (1995b, p. 291)). Note that this does not entail that everything chosen for its own sake is chosen as part of happiness. (2) Kraut has two objections to this view that concern us here. (A) Kraut holds that to do or choose X 'for its own sake' is to take X as something that '*by itself* provides a reason for action' (Kraut (1989, p. 137, emphasis in original)). To hold that I can do X 'for its own sake' because X itself is part of my happiness is to conflate self-interested and non-self-interested reasons for action and is 'unintelligible' (1989, p. 137). What Kraut seems to be requiring here is that we understand 'X is good for its own sake' as X is non-relationally good or morally right or something similar, but ruling out that it can be understood as the claim that, e.g., X is a final (i.e. non-instrumental) good for me. But Plato is willing to talk about desiring X 'for its own sake' (*hautou heneka*) when it is clear that what he means is that the person desiring X 'for its own sake' thinks of X as a final (i.e. non-instrumental) good for himself that contributes to his happiness. We

find this, for example, in the division of goods at the beginning of *Republic* 2 (357B4–358A6). Plato's distinction between Independent and Dependent Goods in the *Laws* makes it even clearer that Independent Goods are kinds of goods for the agent and are desired as such. Note that the Composite View need not endorse the counterfactual that if, e.g., virtue were not part of a person's happiness, he should not rationally pursue it. We might think that since virtue is an essential part of happiness, we cannot really make sense of this counterfactual. (B) Kraut makes the good point that we should not see happiness as a 'mere aggregate' of goods without some structure and argues that a conception of happiness as a composite of all non-instrumentally valuable goods is flawed. But not all forms of the Composite View are committed to these claims. Happiness is to be understood as an optimal state and thus as the optimal composite. And Plato does provide some guidance about the nature of the composite: according to the Dependency Thesis, other goods are not choiceworthy unless they are accompanied by virtue, and the passage at *Laws* 870A–B suggests that non-psychic goods are valuable only insofar as they contribute to psychic goods. This is not to claim that Plato provides a fully determinate account of the relations among various goods and in the case of the good of others, I indicate some of the indeterminacy that remains. But this does not undermine our reasons for attributing a Composite View to Plato. (3) On Kraut's interpretation, in addition to (a) goods that contribute to happiness and (b) reasons for action that are entirely unconnected with my happiness, there are things that are non-instrumental goods for me that do not contribute to my happiness. (Kraut (1989, pp. 162–70), cf. Irwin (1991).) But this category of goods is quite mysterious: if they are non-instrumentally good for me why do they not contribute to my happiness or improve my overall well-being? On the account sketched, Plato's theory of Dependent Goods has a more natural way of accommodating goods other than virtue: when possessed by a virtuous person, they are non-instrumentally good for her and thus make her happier. For other criticisms of Kraut's views, see Irwin (1991). (4) By adopting a composite view, we can accommodate Plato's insistence that the just person must seek to advance the interests of others compatibly with eudaimonism. We can allow the strong implication of, e.g., *Laws* 662D–E, that a person rationally should seek to advance her greatest happiness and hold that advancing the interests of others directly contributes to her happiness as a part of it. (5) Finally, there is a 'swamping' problem. If we allow that the good of others is a significant component of the person's happiness, do we not run the risk of having to count as happy an unjust person living in a good city because of the happiness of the rest of the citizens? The Dependency Thesis provides a way to avoid this problem. Even if the good of others is good for a person it is a Dependent Good and thus only good for a just person. We may still, however, worry about possible trade-offs between my own virtuous condition and the contribution to my happiness of the good of others. Above, in considering the case of the use of chattel slavery to further the virtue of others, I suggest some rough indications of how Plato might think about such cases.

164. Such critics usually do insist on the actual existence of such conflict. But although such conflict makes the problem more acute, it is not necessary to undermine the inclusion of the welfare of others within the agent's own happiness. Even if the two do not conflict, we still need to justify such inclusion.

165. This account is indebted to A. Wood (2001), although the view in the text should not be assumed to be Wood's.

166. Annas (1993, p. 27). My discussion has benefited from Cooper (1999, pp. 427–48).

167. Plotinus *Enneads* III. 8. 1 and III. 8. 4. I quote, with some modification, Armstrong's (1966–88) translation. The point made in the passage is independent of whether Plotinus recognizes different faculties within reason.

168. These views can be prominent in a thinker even if he does not endorse them, so the first line of thought is important for Aristotle even if he is an inclusivist.

169. E.g. G. E. Moore (1989, pp. 97–105).

170. See, e.g., Baier (1958, pp. 187–213), Gert (1998, pp. 130–54), and Scheffler (1992, pp. 98–114).

171. Waterlow (1972, pp. 34 and 34). Emphasis in original. Strictly, in the first part of the sentence quoted, Waterlow is considering whether or not there is such a fundamental difference, but the context, I believe, shows that she intends to endorse the claim that for Plato there is not.

172. Sidgwick (1981, p. 498), capitals in the original. It is controversial whether Sidgwick also recognizes a second equally fundamental principle of rationality, that of morality or benevolence, or whether this second principle is a fundamental principle of morality rather than rationality. For discussions, see Brink (1990), (1992), and Frankena (1992).

173. It is not satisfactory to argue that even if my goal is simply to maximize the overall good, I should foster virtue in myself because I cannot directly bring about a virtuous condition of soul in others (I can only provide them with the opportunities to become virtuous). Leaving aside the point that fostering virtue in myself does not guarantee that I shall achieve it, if my aim is to maximize overall good, then it seems reasonable to take into account both the size of possible outcomes and the probability of the outcome obtaining.

174. For passages that seem to suggest that I should give highest priority to the good condition of my own soul, see 726A1–728C8 and 730E1–731B3.

175. This does not seem to provide an intrinsic justification for special concern with those with whom one stands in a close relationship, such as parents, friends, or fellow citizens. *Rep.* 421B–C claims that the happiness of no one class in the city should receive special concern or weight. The *Republic*'s community of women and children seems to suggest that Plato there holds that people would be ethically better off if they did not recognize special responsibilities to (biological) family members. Related passages in the *Laws*, such as 731D6–732A3, may also suggest that Plato would not want to offer an intrinsic justification for such sorts of special concern. If this is right, Plato would be committed to a fairly strong form of impartiality. Although we are not required to be impartial between our own well-being and that of others, within that component of our happiness that is composed of the well-being of others it is best for us to give equal weight to the promotion of each other person's well-being.

176. Waterlow (1972, pp. 31 and 33).

177. In neither the *Phaedo* nor the *Republic* is it the case that if a person is a non-philosopher, then all his following lives will not be good. (After all, every philosopher starts as a non-philosopher.) In the *Phaedo*, if we accept reincarnation, it is not impossible that a non-philosopher reincarnated as a 'respectable man' can convert to philosophy; just as in the *Republic* it is possible for a non-philosopher to choose a life in which he will convert to philosophy. But in neither case do non-philosophers make the epistemic or ethical progress that entitles them to, or makes it more likely, that they will make progress in the next life.

178. See England on *Laws* 903D1, E3, 904D5, D6, and Saunders (1973a) and (1991, pp. 202–7).

References

ACKRILL, J. 1973. 'Anamnesis in the *Phaedo*: Remarks on 73c–75c.' In Lee, Mourelatos, and Rorty (1973), pp. 177–95.

——1980. 'Aristotle on Eudaimonia.' In A. Rorty (1980a), pp. 15–33.

ADAM, J. 1979. *The Republic of Plato*. Cambridge: Cambridge University Press.

ANNAS, J. 1975. 'On Intermediates.' *Archiv für Geschichte der Philosophie* 57, pp. 146–66.

——1976. 'Plato's *Republic* and Feminism.' *Philosophy* 51, pp. 307–21.

——1981. *An Introduction to Plato's Republic*. Oxford: Clarendon Press.

——1982a. 'Aristotle on Inefficient Causes.' *Philosophical Quarterly* 32, pp. 311–26.

——1982b. 'Knowledge and Language: The *Theaetetus* and the *Cratylus*.' In Schofield and Nussbaum (1982), pp. 95–114.

——1982c. 'Plato's Myths of Judgment.' *Phronesis* 27, pp. 119–43.

——1989. Review of Reeve (1988). *Times Literary Supplement*. June 2–8, 1989, p. 600.

——1992a. 'The Good Life and the Good Life of Others.' In E. F. Paul, F. D. Miller, and J. Paul (eds.) *The Good Life and the Human Good*. Cambridge: Cambridge University Press, pp. 133–48.

——1992b. *Hellenistic Philosophy of Mind*. Berkeley: University of California Press.

——1993. *The Morality of Happiness*. Oxford: Oxford University Press.

——1995. 'Prudence and Morality in Ancient and Modern Ethics.' *Ethics* 105, pp. 241–57.

——1999. *Platonic Ethics, Old and New*. Ithaca: Cornell University Press.

ARMSTRONG, A. H. 1966–88. *Plotinus*. 7 vols. Cambridge, Mass.: Harvard University Press.

ARMSTRONG, D. 1978. *Universals and Scientific Realism*. 2 vols. Cambridge: Cambridge University Press.

——1989. *Universals: An Opinionated Introduction*. Boulder, Colo.: Westview Press.

——1997. *A World of States of Affairs*. Cambridge: Cambridge University Press.

BADHWAR, N. 1996. 'The Limited Unity of Virtue.' *Noûs* 30, pp. 306–29.

BAIER, K. 1958. *The Moral Point of View*. Ithaca: Cornell University Press.

BALTZLY, D. 1997. 'Knowledge and Belief in *Republic* V.' *Archiv für Geschichte der Philosophie* 79, pp. 239–72.

BARKER, E. 1960. *Greek Political Theory: Plato and his Predecessors*. London: Methuen.

BARNES, J. 1975. *Aristotle's Posterior Analytics*. Oxford: Clarendon Press.

——(ed.) 1985. *The Complete Works of Aristotle*. 2 vols. Princeton: Princeton University Press.

BARNEY, R. 1992. 'Appearances and Impressions.' *Phronesis* 37, pp. 283–313.

——1997. 'Plato on Conventionalism.' *Phronesis* 42, pp. 143–62.

——1998. 'Samson Agonistes: The Case of the *Cratylus* Etymologies.' *Oxford Studies in Ancient Philosophy* 16, pp. 63–98.

BELFIORE, E. 1986. 'Wine and *Catharsis* of Emotions in Plato's *Laws*.' *Classical Quarterly*, ns 36, pp. 421–37.

BERLIN, I. 1977. *Four Essays on Liberty*. Oxford: Oxford University Press.

BERMUDEZ, J. 1996. Review of Price (1995). *Mind* 105, pp. 357–62.

BLANK, D. forthcoming. 'Good as Gold: The Unity of Virtue in the *Protagoras*.'

BLOOM, A. 1968. *The Republic of Plato*. New York: Basic Books.

BOBONICH, C. 1991. 'Persuasion, Compulsion and Freedom in Plato's *Laws*.' *Classical Quarterly*, ns 41, pp. 365–88.

——1994. 'Akrasia and Agency in Plato's *Laws* and *Republic*.' *Archiv für Geschichte der Philosophie* 76, pp. 3–36.

——1995a. 'Plato's Theory of Goods in the *Laws* and the *Philebus*.' *Proceedings of the Boston Area Colloquium in Ancient Philosophy* 11, pp. 101–39.

——1995b. 'The Virtues of Ordinary People in Plato's *Politicus*.' In Rowe (1995c), pp. 313–29.

BOBONICH, C. 1996. 'Reading the *Laws*.' In Gill and McCabe (1996), pp. 249–82.

—— 2001. 'Plato and the Birth of Classical Political Philosophy.' In Lisi (2001), pp. 95–106.

BOEFT, J. D. 1970. *Calcidius on Fate: His Doctrines and Sources*. Leiden: Brill.

BOSTOCK, D. 1986. *Plato's Phaedo*. Oxford: Clarendon Press.

—— 1988. *Plato's Theaetetus*. Oxford: Oxford University Press.

BRAND, M. 1970. *The Nature of Human Action*. Glenview, Ill.:Scott, Foresman and Company.

BRANDWOOD, L. 1976. *A Word Index to Plato*. Leeds: W. S. Maney & Son.

—— 1990. *The Chronology of Plato's Dialogues*. Cambridge: Cambridge University Press.

BRATMAN, M. 1987. *Intention, Plans, and Practical Reason*. Cambridge, Mass.: Harvard University Press.

—— 1999 . *Faces of Intention*. Cambridge: Cambridge University Press.

BRICKHOUSE, T. C. and SMITH, N. D. 1987. 'Socrates on Goods, Virtue, and Happiness.' *Oxford Studies in Ancient Philosophy* 5, pp. 1–27.

—— 1989. *Socrates on Trial*. Princeton: Princeton University Press.

—— 1994. *Plato's Socrates*. Oxford: Oxford University Press.

BRINK, D. 1990. 'Rational Egoism, Self, and Others.' In Flanagan and Rorty (1990), pp. 339–78.

—— 1992. 'Sidgwick and the Rationale for Rational Egoism.' In Schultz (1992), pp. 199–240.

BRISSON, L. 1999. 'Plato's Theory of Sense Perception in the *Timaeus*: How it Works and What it Means.' *Proceedings of the Boston Area Colloquium in Ancient Philosophy* 13, pp. 147–76.

—— 2001. 'Le Collège de veille (*nukterinos sullogos*).' In Lisi (2001), pp. 161–77.

BROADIE, S. 1987. 'The Problem of Practical Intellect in Aristotle's *Ethics*.' *Proceedings of the Boston Area Colloquium in Ancient Philosophy* 3, pp. 229–52.

—— 1991. *Ethics with Aristotle*. Oxford: Oxford University Press.

BROWN, E. 2000. 'Justice and Compulsion for Plato's Philosopher-Rulers.' *Ancient Philosophy* 20, pp. 1–18.

BROWN, L. 1994. 'The verb "to be" in Greek Philosophy: Some Remarks.' In Everson (1994), pp. 212–36.

—— 1999. 'Being in the *Sophist*: A Syntactical Enquiry.' In Fine (1999a), pp. 455–78.

BRUNT, P. A. 1993. *Studies in Greek History and Thought*. Oxford: Clarendon Press.

BURNET, J. 1901–7. *Platonis Opera*. 5 vols. Oxford: Oxford University Press.

—— 1980. *Plato's Phaedo*. Oxford: Oxford University Press.

BURNYEAT, M. 1976. 'Plato on the Grammar of Perceiving.' *Classical Quarterly*, ns 26, pp. 29–51.

—— 1981. 'Aristotle on Understanding Knowledge.' In E. Berti (ed.) *Aristotle on Science*. Padua: Antenore, pp. 97–139.

—— 1987. 'Platonism and Mathematics: A Prelude to Discussion.' In Graeser (1987), pp. 213–40.

—— (ed.) 1990. *The Theaetetus of Plato*. Indianapolis: Hackett.

—— 1999 . 'Culture and Society in Plato's *Republic*.' In *The Tanner Lectures on Human Values*, 20. Salt Lake City: University of Utah Press, pp. 215–324.

BURY, R. 1897. *The Philebus of Plato*. Cambridge, Mass.: Harvard University Press.

—— 1926. *Laws*. 2 vols. New York: G. P. Putnam's Sons.

—— 1975. *Plato: Timaeus, Critias, Clitophon, Menexenus, Epistles*. Cambridge, Mass.: Harvard University Press.

BUSSANICH, J. 1990. 'The Invulnerability of Goodness: The Ethical and Psychological Theory of Plotinus.' *Proceedings of the Boston Area Colloquium in Ancient Philosophy* 6, pp. 151–94.

CAIRNS, D. 1993. *Aidôs*. Oxford: Clarendon Press.

CALVO, T. and BRISSON, L. (eds.) 1996. *Interpreting the Timaeus and the Critias*. Sankt Augustin: Academia Verlag.

CARONE, G. 1996. 'The Ethical Function of Astronomy in Plato's *Timaeus*.' In Calvo and Brisson (1996), pp. 341–9.

CHAPPELL, T. D. J. 1995. *Aristotle and Augustine on Freedom*. St. Martin's Press.

CHARLES, D. 1984. *Aristotle's Philosophy of Action*. Ithaca: Cornell University Press.

CHARLES, D. 1988. 'Perfectionism in Aristotle's Political Theory: Reply to Martha Nussbaum.' *Oxford Studies in Ancient Philosophy*, suppl. vol., pp. 185–206.

CHERNISS, H. 1953. Review of G. Müller, *Studien zu den platonischen Nomoi. Gnomon* 25, pp. 367–79.

CHISHOLM, R. 1986. *Brentano and Intrinsic Value*. Cambridge: Cambridge University Press.

CHRISTIANO, T. 1996. *The Rule of Many*. Boulder, Co.: Westview Press.

CHRISTMAN, J. 1989. *The Inner Citadel*. Oxford: Oxford University Press.

CLARKE, R. 1993. 'Towards a Credible Agent-Causal Account of Free Will.' *Noûs* 27, pp. 191–203.

CODE, A. 1986. 'Aristotle: Essence and Accident.' In R. Grandy and R. Warner (eds.) *Philosophical Grounds of Rationality*. Oxford: Oxford University Press, pp. 411–39.

—— 1988. 'Reply to Michael Frede's "Being and Becoming in Plato".' *Oxford Studies in Ancient Philosophy*, suppl. vol., pp. 53–60.

—— 1994. 'Vlastos on a Metaphysical Paradox.' *Apeiron* 27, pp. 85–98.

COHEN, D. 1987. 'The Legal Status and Political Role of Women in Plato's *Laws*.' *Revue internationale des droits de l'antiquité* 34, pp. 27–40.

—— 1993. 'Law, Autonomy, and Political Community in Plato's *Laws*.' *Classical Philology* 88, pp. 301–18.

—— 1995. *Law, Violence and Community in Classical Athens*. Cambridge: Cambridge University Press.

COHEN, J. 1986. 'An Epistemic Conception of Democracy.' *Ethics* 97, pp. 26–38.

COOPER, J. 1970. 'Plato on Sense-Perception and Knowledge (*Theaetetus* 184–186).' *Phronesis* 15, pp. 123–46.

—— 1975. *Reason and the Human Good in Aristotle*. Cambridge, Mass.: Harvard University Press.

—— 1995. Review of Price (1995). *Times Literary Supplement*. October 20, 1995, p. 32.

—— (ed.) 1997. *Plato: Complete Works*. Indianapolis: Hackett.

—— 1999 . *Reason and Emotion*. Princeton: Princeton University Press.

COOPER, N. 1986. 'Between Knowledge and Ignorance.' *Phronesis* 31, pp. 229–42.

CORNFORD, F. 1937. *Plato's Cosmology*. London: Routledge & Kegan Paul.

COUVREUR, P. 1901. *Hermiae Alexandrini in Platonis Phaedrum Scholia*. Paris: É. Bouillon.

COWIE, F. 1999. *What's Within?* Oxford: Oxford University Press.

CURREN, R. 1994. 'Justice, Instruction and the Good: The Case for Public Education in Aristotle and Plato's *Laws*.' *Studies in Philosophy and Education* 13, pp. 1–31.

DANCY, J. 1993. *Moral Reasons*. Oxford: Blackwell.

—— (ed.) 1997. *Reading Parfit*. Oxford: Blackwell.

DARWALL, S. 1983. *Impartial Reason*. Ithaca: Cornell University Press.

DAVIDSON, D. 1980. *Essays on Actions and Events*. Oxford: Oxford University Press.

—— 1982. 'Paradoxes of Irrationality.' In R. Wollheim and J. Hopkins (eds.) *Philosophical Essays on Freud*. Cambridge: Cambridge University Press, pp. 289–305.

—— 1986. 'Deception and Division.' In J. Elster (ed.) *The Multiple Self*. Cambridge: Cambridge University Press, pp. 79–92.

DAVIES, B. 1992. *The Thought of Thomas Aquinas*. Oxford: Clarendon Press.

DE VRIES, G. J. 1969. *A Commentary on the Phaedrus of Plato*. Amsterdam: Hakkert.

DENNETT, D. 1981. *Brainstorms*. Cambridge, Mass.: MIT Press.

DENNISTON, J. D. 1981. *The Greek Particles*. Oxford: Clarendon Press.

DENT, N. J. H. 1984. *The Moral Psychology of the Virtues*. Cambridge: Cambridge University Press.

DES PLACES, É. and DIÈS, A. 1951–1956. *Platon, Oeuvres Complètes*, vols. XI–XII. Paris: Les Belles Lettres, Budé edn.

DILLON, J. 1990. *The Golden Chain*. Aldershot: Variorum Press.

—— (ed.) 1995. *Alcinous: The Handbook of Platonism*. Oxford: Clarendon Press.

—— 1996a. 'An Ethic for the Late Antique Sage.' In L. Gerson (ed.) *The Cambridge Companion to Plotinus*. Cambridge: Cambridge University Press, pp. 315–55.

—— 1996b. *The Middle Platonists: 80 B.C. to A.D. 220*. Ithaca: Cornell University Press.

DORTER, K. 1982. *Plato's Phaedo: An Interpretation*. Toronto: University of Toronto Press.

DRETSKE, F. 1992. *Explaining Behavior*. Cambridge, Mass.: MIT Press.

—— 1995. *Naturalizing the Mind*. Cambridge, Mass.: MIT Press.

DUKE, E. A., HICKEN, W. F., NICOLL, W. S. M., ROBINSON, D. B., and STRACHAN, J. C. G. 1995. *Platonis Opera*. Vol. 1. Oxford: Clarendon Press.

DÜRING, I. 1961. *Aristotle's Protrepticus*. Göteborg: Elanders Boktryckeri Aktiebolag.

EDMUNDS, L. 1975. *Chance and Intelligence in Thucydides*. Cambridge, Mass.: Harvard University Press.

ENGLAND, E. B. 1921. *The Laws of Plato*. 2 vols. Manchester: Manchester University Press.

EVERSON, S. (ed.) 1994. *Companions to Ancient Thought: 3 Language*. Cambridge: Cambridge University Press.

FAIRWEATHER, A. M. 1954. *Nature and Grace: Selections from the Summa Theologica of Thomas Aquinas*. Philadelphia: Westminster Press.

FEREJOHN, M. 1984. 'Socratic Thought-Experiments and the Unity of Virtue Paradox.' *Phronesis* 29, pp. 105–22.

FERRARI, G. 1987. *Listening to the Cicadas*. Cambridge: Cambridge University Press.

—— 1991. 'Moral Fecundity.' *Oxford Studies in Ancient Philosophy* 9, pp. 169–84.

FIGUEIRA, T. 1984. 'Mess Contributions and Subsistence at Sparta.' *Transactions of the American Philological Association* 114, pp. 87–109.

FINE, G. 1977. 'Plato on Naming.' *Philosophical Quarterly* 27, pp. 289–301.

—— 1978. 'Knowledge and Belief in *Republic* V.' *Archiv für Geschichte der Philosophie* 60, pp. 121–39.

—— 1980. 'The One over Many.' *Philosophical Review* 89, pp. 197–240.

—— 1981. 'Armstrong on Relational and Non-Relational Realism.' *Pacific Philosophical Quarterly* 62, pp. 262–71.

—— 1983. 'Relational Entities.' *Archiv für Geschichte der Philosophie* 65, pp. 225–49.

—— 1987. 'Forms as Causes: Plato and Aristotle.' In Graeser (1987), pp. 69–112.

—— 1988a. 'Owen's Progress: A Critical Notice of *Logic, Science and Dialectic*.' *Philosophical Review* 97, pp. 373–99.

—— 1988b. 'Plato on Perception.' *Oxford Studies in Ancient Philosophy*, suppl. vol., pp. 15–28.

—— 1990. 'Knowledge and Belief in Republic V–VII.' In S. Everson, (ed.) *Companions to Ancient Thought: 1 Epistemology*. Cambridge: Cambridge University Press, pp. 85–115.

—— 1992. 'Inquiry in the *Meno*.' In Kraut (1992), pp. 200–26.

—— 1993. *On Ideas: Aristotle's Criticisms of Plato's Theory of Forms*. Oxford: Oxford University Press.

—— (ed.) 1999a. *Plato 1: Metaphysics and Epistemology*. Oxford: Oxford University Press.

—— (ed.) 1999b. *Plato 2: Ethics, Politics, Religion and the Soul*. Oxford: Oxford University Press.

FLANAGAN, O. and Rorty, A. (eds.) 1990. *Identity, Character, and Morality*. Cambridge, Mass.: MIT Press.

FODOR, J. 1981. *Representations*. Cambridge, Mass.: MIT Press.

—— 1996. *The Modularity of Mind*. Cambridge, Mass.: MIT Press.

—— 1998a. *Concepts*. Oxford: Clarendon Press.

—— 1998b. *In Critical Condition*. Cambridge, Mass.: MIT Press.

FOOT, P. R. 1978. *Virtues and Vices*. Oxford: Blackwell.

—— 1983. 'Moral Realism and Moral Dilemma.' *Journal of Philosophy* 80, pp. 379–98.

FORTENBAUGH, W. 1975. *Aristotle on Emotion*. London: Duckworth.

FOWLER, H. N. and LAMB, W. R. M. 1975. *The Statesman, the Philebus and the Ion*. Cambridge, Mass.: Harvard University Press.

FRANKENA, W. 1992. 'Sidgwick and the History of Ethical Dualism.' In Schultz (1992), pp. 175–98.

FREDE, D. 1985. 'Rumpelstiltskin's Pleasures: True and False Pleasures in Plato's *Philebus*.' *Phronesis* 30, pp. 151–80.

—— 1989. 'The Soul's Silent Dialogue: A Non-Aporetic Reading of the *Theaetetus*.' *Proceedings of the Cambridge Philological Society* 215, pp. 20–49.

—— 1993. *Plato: Philebus*. Indianapolis: Hackett.

—— 1996. 'The Philosophical Economy of Plato's Psychology: Rationality and Common Concepts in the *Timaeus*.' In Frede and Striker (1996), pp. 29–58.

FREDE, M. 1987. *Essays in Ancient Philosophy*. Minneapolis: University of Minnesota Press.

—— 1988. 'Being and Becoming in Plato.' *Oxford Studies in Ancient Philosophy*, suppl. vol., pp. 37–52.

FREDE, M. and STRIKER, G. 1996. (eds.) *Rationality in Greek Thought*. Oxford: Clarendon Press.

GALLOP, D. 1975. *Plato's Phaedo*. Oxford: Clarendon Press.

GARDNER, S. 1993. *Irrationality and the Philosophy of Psychoanalysis*. Cambridge: Cambridge University Press.

GENTZLER, J. (ed.) 1998. *Method in Ancient Philosophy*. Oxford: Clarendon Press.

GERT, B. 1998. *Morality: its Nature and Justification*. Oxford: Oxford University Press.

GILL, C. 1985. 'Plato and the Education of Desire.' *Archiv für Geschichte der Philosophie* 67, pp. 1–26.

—— 1995. 'Rethinking Constitutionalism in *Statesman* 291–303.' In Rowe (1995c), pp. 292–312.

—— 1996. *Personality in Greek Epic, Tragedy, and Philosophy*. Oxford: Clarendon Press.

—— 1997. 'Did Galen Understand Platonic and Stoic Thinking on Emotions?' In J. Sihvola and T. Engberg-Pedersen (eds.) *The Emotions in Hellenistic Philosophy*. Dordrecht: Kluwer, pp. 113–48.

GILL, C. and McCABE, M. (eds.) 1996. *Form and Argument in Late Plato*. Oxford: Oxford University Press.

GILL, M. L. and LENNOX, J. G. (eds.) 1994. *Self-Motion*. Princeton: Princeton University Press.

GOLDING, M. P. and GOLDING, N. H. 1975. 'Population Policy in Plato and Aristotle: Some Value Issues.' *Arethusa* 8, pp. 345–58.

GONZALEZ, F. 1996. 'Propositions or Objects? A Critique of Gail Fine on Knowledge and Belief in Republic V.' *Phronesis* 41, pp. 245–75.

GOOCH, P. 1974. 'The Relation between Wisdom and Virtue in *Phaedo* 69a6–c3.' *Journal of the History of Philosophy* 12, pp. 153–9.

GÖRGEMANNS, H. 1960. *Beiträge zur Interpretation von Platons Nomoi.* Zetemata 25. Munich: Beck.

GOSLING, J. C. B. 1960. '*Republic* V: Ta Polla Kala.' *Phronesis* 5, pp. 121–39.

—— 1968. 'Doxa and *Dunamis* in *Republic* V.' *Phronesis* 13, pp. 119–30.

—— 1975. *Plato: Philebus.* Oxford: Clarendon Press.

—— 1990. *Weakness of the Will.* London: Routledge & Kegan Paul.

GOSLING, J. C. B. and TAYLOR, C. C. W. 1984. *The Greeks on Pleasure.* Oxford: Clarendon Press.

GRAESER, A. (ed.) 1987. *Mathematics and Metaphysics in Aristotle.* Bern: Haupt.

GREGOR, M. J. 1983. 'Baumgarten's *Aesthetica.*' *Review of Metaphysics* 37, pp. 357–85.

—— 1996. *Practical Philosophy: Immanuel Kant.* Cambridge: Cambridge University Press.

GRIFFIN, J. 1988. *Well-Being.* Oxford: Clarendon Press.

GUTHRIE, W. K. C. 1987. *A History of Greek Philosophy.* Vols. 4 and 5. Cambridge: Cambridge University Press.

GUTTENPLAN, S. (ed.) 1994. *A Companion to the Philosophy of Mind.* Oxford: Blackwell.

HACKFORTH, R. 1946. 'Moral Evil and Ignorance in Plato's Ethics.' *Classical Quarterly* 40, pp. 118–20.

—— 1972a. *Plato's Phaedo.* Cambridge: Cambridge University Press.

—— 1972b. *Plato's Phaedrus.* Cambridge: Cambridge University Press.

—— 1972c. *Plato's Philebus.* Cambridge: Cambridge University Press.

HAKSAR, V. 1991. *Indivisible Selves and Moral Practice.* Edinburgh: Edinburgh University Press.

HANKINSON, R. J. 1990. 'Implications of Immortality.' *Proceedings of the Boston Area Colloquium in Ancient Philosophy* 6, pp. 1–27.

HANSEN, M. 1991. *The Athenian Democracy in the Age of Demosthenes.* Oxford: Blackwell.

HARE, R. M. 1963. *Freedom and Reason.* Oxford: Oxford University Press.

HARVEY, F. D. 1965. 'Two Kinds of Equality.' *Classica et Mediaevalia* 26, pp. 101–46.

HAWTREY, R. 1981. *Commentary on Plato's Euthydemus.* Philadelphia: American Philosophical Society.

HEINAMAN, R. (ed.) 1995. *Aristotle and Moral Realism.* London: UCL Press.

HEINZE, R. 1965. *Xenokrates.* Hildesheim: Georg Olms.

HENRY, P. and SCHWYZER, H. R. 1964–1983. *Plotini Opera.* 3 vols. Oxford: Clarendon Press.

HIRST, M. 1940. 'The Choice of Odysseus (Plato *Republic* 620C–D).' *Classical Philology* 35, pp. 67–8.

HOBBES, T. (ed. E. Curley) 1994. *Leviathan.* Indianapolis: Hackett.

HONORÉ, A. M. 1961. 'Ownership.' In A. G. Guest (ed.) *Oxford Essays in Jurisprudence.* Oxford: Oxford University Press, pp. 107–47.

HOURANI, G. F. 1949. 'The Education of the Third Class in Plato's *Republic.*' *Classical Quarterly* 43, pp. 58–60.

IRWIN, T. 1977a. 'Plato's Heracliteanism.' *Philosophical Quarterly* 27, pp. 1–13.

——1977b. *Plato's Moral Theory.* Oxford: Oxford University Press.

——1982. 'Aristotle's Concept of Signification.' In Schofield and Nussbaum (1982), pp. 241–66.

——1986a. 'Aristotelian Actions.' *Phronesis* 22, pp. 68–89.

——1986b. 'Socrates the Epicurean?' *Illinois Classical Studies* 11, pp. 85–112.

——1988. 'Disunity in the Aristotelian Virtues.' *Oxford Studies in Ancient Philosophy,* suppl. vol., pp. 61–78.

——1989. *Classical Thought.* Oxford: Oxford University Press.

——1990a. *Aristotle's First Principles.* Oxford: Oxford University Press.

——1990b. 'The Good of Political Activity.' In Patzig (1990), pp. 73–98.

——1991. 'The Structure of Aristotelian Happiness.' *Ethics* 101, pp. 382–91.

——1995a. *Plato's Ethics.* Oxford: Oxford University Press.

——1995b. 'Prudence and Morality in Greek Ethics.' *Ethics* 105, pp. 284–95.

ISNARDI PARENTE, M. 1982. *Senocrate-Ermodoro Frammenti.* Naples: Bibliopolis.

JOHNSTONE, S. 1994. 'Virtuous Toil, Vicious Work: Xenophon on Aristocratic Style.' *Classical Philology* 89, pp. 219–40.

JONES, N. 1990. 'The Organization of the Kretan City in Plato's *Laws.*' *The Classical World* 83, pp. 473–92.

JOSEPH, H. 1935. *Essays in Ancient and Modern Philosophy*. Oxford: Clarendon Press.

KAHN, C. 1961. 'Plato's Cretan City.' *Journal of the History of Ideas* 22, pp. 418–24.

—— 1973. *The Verb 'Be' in Ancient Greek*. Dordrecht: Reidel.

—— 1981. 'Some Philosophical Uses of "to be" in Plato.' *Phronesis* 26, pp. 105–34.

—— 1982. 'Language and Ontology in the *Cratylus*.' In Schofield and Nussbaum (1982), pp. 152–76.

—— 1987. 'Plato's Theory of Desire.' *Review of Metaphysics* 41, pp. 77–103.

—— 1995. 'The Place of the *Statesman* in Plato's Later Work.' In Rowe (1995c), pp. 49–60.

—— 1996. *Plato and the Socratic Dialogue*. Cambridge: Cambridge University Press.

KAMTEKAR, R. 1998. 'Imperfect Virtue.' *Ancient Philosophy* 18, pp. 315–39.

—— forthcoming. 'Distinction without a Difference? Plato on "Genos" vs. "Race".' In J. Ward (ed.) *Traditional Philosophers on Race*. Oxford: Blackwell.

KANAYAMA, Y. 1987. 'Perceiving, Considering, and Attaining Being (*Theaetetus* 184–186).' *Oxford Studies in Ancient Philosophy* 5, pp. 29–81.

KANE, R. 1996. *The Significance of Free Will*. Oxford: Oxford University Press.

KEYSER, P. 1991. Review of Ledger (1989). *Bryn Mawr Classical Review* 2.7.3.

—— 1992. Review of Brandwood (1990). *Bryn Mawr Classical Review* 3.1.12.

KEYT, D. 1991. 'Three Basic Theorems in Aristotle's *Politics*.' In Keyt and Miller (1991), pp. 118–41.

KEYT, D. and MILLER, F. (eds.) 1991. *A Companion to Aristotle's Politics*. Oxford: Blackwell.

KLOSKO, G. 1986. *The Development of Plato's Political Theory*. London: Methuen.

—— 1988. 'The Nocturnal Council in Plato's *Laws*.' *Political Studies* 36, pp. 74–88.

KNORR, W. 1975. *The Evolution of the Euclidean Elements*. Dordrecht: Reidel.

KORSGAARD, C. 1996a. *Creating the Kingdom of Ends.* Cambridge: Cambridge University Press.

—— 1996b. *The Sources of Normativity.* Cambridge: Cambridge University Press.

KRAUT, R. 1973. 'Reason and Justice in Plato's *Republic.*' In Lee, Mourelatos, and Rorty (1973), pp. 207–24.

—— 1979. 'Two Conceptions of Happiness.' *The Philosophical Review* 88, pp. 167–97.

—— 1984. *Socrates and the State.* Princeton: Princeton University Press.

—— 1988. 'Comments on "Disunity in the Aristotelian Virtues", by T. H. Irwin.' *Oxford Studies in Ancient Philosophy,* suppl. vol., pp. 79–86.

—— 1989. *Aristotle on the Human Good.* Princeton: Princeton University Press.

—— 1990. Review of Reeve (1988). *Political Theory* 18, pp. 492–6.

—— (ed.) 1992. *The Cambridge Companion to Plato.* Cambridge: Cambridge University Press.

—— 1993. 'Return to the Cave: *Republic* 519–521.' *Proceedings of the Boston Area Colloquium in Ancient Philosophy* 7, pp. 43–62.

—— 1997. *Aristotle Politics Books VII and VIII.* Oxford: Clarendon Press.

KRETZMANN, N. 1971. 'Plato on the Correctness of Names.' *American Philosophical Quarterly* 8, pp. 126–38.

KÜHNER, R. and GERTH, B. 1955. *Ausführliche Grammatik der griechischen Sprache.* 2 vols. Hanover and Leipzig: Hahnsche Buchhandlung.

LAKS, A. 1987. 'Raison et plaisir: pour une caractérisation des *Lois* de Platon.' *La Naissance de la raison en Grèce. Actes du Congrès de Nice,* pp. 291–303.

—— 1990. 'Legislation and Demiurgy: On the Relationship between Plato's *Republic* and *Laws.*' *Classical Antiquity* 9, pp. 209–29.

—— 1991. 'L'Utopie législative de Platon.' *Revue philosophique,* pp. 416–28.

—— 1995. 'Prodige et médiation: esquisse d'une lecture des *Lois.*' *Le Temps philosophique,* pp. 11–28.

—— 2000. 'The *Laws.*' In Rowe and Schofield (2000), pp. 258–92.

—— 2001. 'In What Sense is the City of the *Laws* a Second Best One?' In Lisi (2001), pp. 107–14.

LANE, M. 1998. *Method and Politics in Plato's Statesman.* Cambridge: Cambridge University Press.

LAUTNER, P. 1994. 'Rival Theories of Self-Awareness in Late Platonism.' *Bulletin of the Institute of Classical Studies* 39, pp. 107–16.

LEAR, J. 1987. 'Active Episteme.' In Graeser (1987), pp. 149–74.

LEDGER, G. 1989. *Re-Counting Plato*. Oxford: Clarendon Press.

LEE, E. N. 1976. 'Reason and Rotation: Circular Movement as the Model of Mind (*nous*) in Later Plato.' In Werkmeister (1976), pp. 70–107.

LEE, E. N., MOURELATOS, A. P. D., and RORTY, R. (eds.) 1973. *Exegesis and Argument*. New York: Humanities Press.

LEMOS, J. 1994. 'The Unity of the Virtues and its Defenses.' *The Southern Journal of Philosophy* 32, pp. 85–106.

LEMOS, N. 1994. *Intrinsic Value*. Cambridge: Cambridge University Press.

LEPORE, E. and McLAUGHLIN, B. (eds.) 1985. *Actions and Events*. Oxford: Blackwell.

LESSES, G. 1987. 'The Divided Soul in Plato's *Republic*.' *History of Philosophy Quarterly* 4, pp. 147–61.

LESZL, W. 1972. 'Knowledge of the Universal and Particular in Aristotle.' *Review of Metaphysics* 26, pp. 278–313.

LEVIN, S. 2000. 'Plato on Women's Nature: Reflections on the *Laws*.' *Ancient Philosophy* 20, pp. 81–97.

LISI, F. (ed.) 2001. *Plato's Laws and its Historical Significance*. Sankt Augustin: Academia Verlag.

LLOYD, A. C. 1976. 'The Principle that the Cause is Greater than its Effect.' *Phronesis* 21, pp. 146–56.

LLOYD, G. E. R. 1982. *Early Greek Science: Thales to Aristotle*. Cambridge: Cambridge University Press.

——1984. *Magic, Reason and Experience*. Cambridge: Cambridge University Press.

——1991. *Methods and Problems in Greek Science*. Cambridge: Cambridge University Press.

LUCE, J. 1944. 'A Discussion of *Phaedo* 69a6–c2.' *Classical Quarterly* 38, pp. 60–4.

LUSCOMBE, D. E. 1996. 'Natural Morality and Natural Law.' In N. Kretzmann and A. K. J. Pinborg (eds.) *The Cambridge History of Later Medieval Philosophy*. Cambridge: Cambridge University Press, pp. 705–19.

LYCOS, K. 1964. 'Aristotle and Plato on "Appearing".' *Mind,* ns 73, pp. 496–514.

LYONS, D. 1963. *Structural Semantics.* Oxford: Publications of the Oxford Philological Society.

McCABE, M. 1994. *Plato's Individuals.* Princeton: Princeton University Press.

MacDONALD, C. and MacDONALD, G. (eds.) 1995. *Philosophy of Psychology.* Oxford: Blackwell.

McDOWELL, J. 1979. 'Virtue and Reason.' *The Monist* 62, pp. 330–50.

MACKENZIE, M. M. [McCABE] 1981. *Plato on Punishment.* Berkeley: University of California Press.

—— 1986. 'Putting the *Cratylus* in its Place.' *Classical Quarterly,* ns 36, pp. 124–50.

McLAUGHLIN, B. and O'LEARY-HAWTHORNE, J. 1994. 'Dennett's Logical Behaviorism.' *Philosophical Topics* 22, pp. 189–258.

MAKIN, S. 1990–1. 'An Ancient Principle about Causation.' *Proceedings of the Aristotelian Society* 91, pp. 135–52.

MALCOLM, J. 1981. 'The Cave Revisited.' *Classical Quarterly,* ns 31, pp. 60–8.

MARGOLIS, E. and LAURENCE, C. (eds.) 1999. *Concepts: Core Readings.* Cambridge, Mass.: MIT Press.

MATTHEWS, G. 1966. 'Weakness of Will.' *Mind,* ns 75, pp. 405–19.

MAYHEW, R. 1997. *Aristotle's Criticism of Plato's Republic.* Lanham: Rowman & Littlefield.

MEINWALD, C. 1998. 'Prometheus's Bounds: *Peras* and *Apeiron* in Plato's *Philebus.*' In Gentzler (1998), pp. 165–80.

MELE, A. 1981. 'The Practical Syllogism and Deliberation in Aristotle's Causal Theory of Action.' *The New Scholasticism* 55, pp. 281–316.

—— 1987. *Irrationality.* Oxford: Oxford University Press.

—— 1990. 'Errant Self-Control and the Self-Controlled Person.' *Pacific Philosophical Quarterly* 26, pp. 19–30.

—— 1992. *Springs of Action.* Oxford: Oxford University Press.

—— 1995. *Autonomous Agents.* Oxford: Oxford University Press.

MENDELL, H. 1998. 'Reflections on Eudoxus, Callippus and their Curves: Hippopedes and Callippopedes.' *Centaurus* 40, pp. 177–275.

MENN, S. 1992. 'Aristotle and Plato on God as Nous and as the Good.' *Review of Metaphysics* 45, pp. 543–73.

—— 1995. *Plato on God as Nous.* Carbondale: Southern Illinois University Press.

MILLER, F. 1995. *Nature, Justice, and Rights in Aristotle's Politics.* Oxford: Clarendon Press.

MILLS, M. 1985. '*Phthonos* and its related *Pathê* in Plato and Aristotle.' *Phronesis* 30, pp. 1–12.

MOHR, R. 1985. *The Platonic Cosmology.* Leiden: Brill.

MOLINE, J. 1981. *Plato's Theory of Understanding.* Madison: University of Wisconsin Press.

MOORE, G. E. 1989. *Principia Ethica.* Cambridge: Cambridge University Press.

MORAVCSIK, J. 1971a. 'Learning as Recollection.' In G. Vlastos (ed.) *Plato 1: Metaphysics and Epistemology.* Garden City, NY: Doubleday, Anchor, pp. 53–69.

—— 1971b. 'Reason and Eros in the "Ascent"-passage of the *Symposium.*' In J. P. Anton and G. L. Kustas (eds.) *Essays in Ancient Greek Philosophy.* Albany: State University of New York Press, pp. 275–302.

—— 1976a. 'Ancient and Modern Conceptions of Health and Medicine.' *Journal of Medicine and Philosophy* 1, pp. 337–48.

—— 1976b. 'Recollecting the Theory of Forms.' In Werkmeister (1976), pp. 1–20.

—— 1979a. 'Forms, Nature and the Good in the *Philebus.*' *Phronesis* 24, pp. 81–101.

—— 1979b. 'Understanding and Knowledge in Plato's Philosophy.' *Neue Hefte für Philosophie* 15/16, pp. 53–69.

—— 1980. 'On What We Aim at and How We Live.' In D. Depew (ed.) *The Greeks and the Good Life.* Indianapolis: Hackett, pp. 198–235.

—— 1982. 'Noetic Aspiration and Artistic Inspiration.' In J. Moravcsik and P. Temko (eds.) *Plato on Beauty, Wisdom and the Arts.* Totowa, NJ: Rowman and Littlefield, pp. 29–46.

—— 1983. 'Plato and Pericles on Freedom and Politics.' *Canadian Journal of Philosophy*, suppl. vol. 9, pp. 1–7.

MORAVCSIK, J. 1986. 'Plato's Ethics as Ideal Building.' *Proceedings of the Boston Area Colloquium in Ancient Philosophy* 2, pp. 1–21.

—— 1992. *Plato and Platonism.* Oxford: Blackwell.

—— 1993. Review of Vlastos (1991). *Mind* 102, pp. 206–10.

—— 2000. 'Health, Healing, and Plato's Ethics.' *The Journal of Value Inquiry* 34, pp. 7–26.

—— 2001. 'Inner Harmony and the Human Ideal in *Republic* IV and IX.' *The Journal of Ethics* 5, pp. 39–56.

MORGAN, K. 2000. *Myth and Philosophy from the Presocratics to Plato.* Cambridge: Cambridge University Press.

MORRIS, M. 1985. 'Socrates' Last Argument.' *Phronesis* 30, pp. 223–48.

MORRISON, D. 2001. 'The Happiness of the City and the Happiness of the Individual in Plato's *Republic.*' *Ancient Philosophy* 21, pp. 1–24.

MORROW, G. 1941. 'Status of Aliens in Plato's *Laws.*' *Scientia* 70, pp. 38–43.

—— 1948. 'Plato and the Law of Nature.' In M. R. Konvitz and A. E. Murphy (eds.) *Essays in Political Theory presented to G. H. Sabine.* Ithaca: Cornell University Press, pp. 17–44.

—— 1953. 'Plato's Conception of Persuasion'. *Philosophical Review* 62, pp. 234–50.

—— 1960. *Plato's Cretan City.* Princeton: Princeton University Press.

—— 1976. *Plato's Law of Slavery in its Relation to Greek Law.* New York: Arno Press.

MUELLER, I. 1980. 'Ascending to Problems: Astronomy and Harmonics in *Republic* VII.' In J. Anton (ed.) *Science and the Sciences in Plato.* Delmas, NY: Caravan Books, pp. 103–22.

MURPHY, N. R. 1938. 'The "Comparison of Lives" in Plato's *Philebus.*' *Classical Quarterly* 32, pp. 116–24.

—— 1951. *The Interpretation of Plato's Republic.* Oxford: Clarendon Press.

NAGEL, T. 1970. *The Possibility of Altruism.* Princeton: Princeton University Press.

—— 1980. *Mortal Questions.* Cambridge: Cambridge University Press.

—— 1986. *The View from Nowhere.* Oxford: Oxford University Press.

NAILS, P. 1992. 'Platonic Chronology Reconsidered.' *Bryn Mawr Classical Review* 3.4.17.

NEU, J. 1971. 'Plato's Analogy of State and Individual.' *Philosophy* 46, pp. 238–54.

NEUGEBAUER, O. 1969. *The Exact Sciences in Antiquity*. 2nd edn. Dover.

NEWMAN, W. L. 1985. *The Politics of Aristotle*. 4 vols. Salem, New Hampshire: Ayer Reprint.

NIGHTINGALE, A. 1993. 'Writing/Reading a Sacred Text: A Literary Interpretation of Plato's *Laws*.' *Classical Philology* 88, pp. 279–300.

——1995. *Genres in Dialogue: Plato and the Construct of Philosophy*. Cambridge: Cambridge University Press.

——1999a. 'Historiography and Cosmology in Plato's *Laws*.' *Ancient Philosophy* 19, pp. 299–326.

——1999b. 'Plato's Lawcode in Context: Rule by Written Law in Athens and Magnesia.' *Classical Quarterly*, ns 49, pp. 100–22.

NISBETT, R. and ROSS, L. 1980. *Human Inference: Strategies and Short-comings of Social Judgment*. Englewood Cliffs: Prentice-Hall.

NOZICK, R. 1981. *Philosophical Explanations*. Cambridge, Mass.: Harvard University Press.

NUSSBAUM, M. 1980. 'Aristophanes and Socrates on Learning Practical Wisdom.' *Yale Classical Studies* 26, pp. 43–97.

——1986. *The Fragility of Goodness*. Cambridge: Cambridge University Press.

——1988. 'Nature, Function, and Capability: Aristotle on Political Distribution.' *Oxford Studies in Ancient Philosophy*, suppl. vol., pp. 148–84, 207–14.

——1994. *The Therapy of Desire*. Princeton: Princeton University Press.

OBER, J. 1991. 'Aristotle's Political Sociology: Class, Status, and Order in the *Politics*.' In C. Lord and D. O'Connor (eds.) *Essays on the Foundations of Aristotelian Political Science*. Berkeley: University of California Press, pp. 112–35.

——1998. *Political Dissent in Democratic Athens*. Princeton: Princeton University Press.

O'BRIEN, M. 1984. '"Becoming Immortal" in Plato's *Symposium*.' In D. Gerber (ed.) *Greek Poetry and Philosophy: Studies in Honor of Leonard Woodbury*. Chico, Calif.: Scholars Press, pp. 185–205.

O'CONNOR, T. 1993. 'Indeterminism and Free Agency: Three Recent Views.' *Philosophy and Phenomenological Research* 53, pp. 499–526.

Okin, S. 1979. *Women in Western Political Thought*. Princeton: Princeton University Press.

Ostenfeld, E. 1982. *Forms, Matter, and Mind*. Dordrecht: Kluwer.

Pangle, T. 1980. *The Laws of Plato*. New York: Basic Books.

Parfit, D. 1984. *Reasons and Persons*. Oxford: Clarendon Press.

Parker, R. 1983. *Miasma*. Oxford: Clarendon Press.

Patzig, G. (ed.) 1990. *Aristoteles' 'Politik'*. Göttingen: Vandenhoeck and Ruprecht.

Peacocke, C. 1992. *A Study of Concepts*. Cambridge, Mass.: MIT Press.

—— (ed.) 1994. *Objectivity, Simulation and the Unity of Consciousness*. *Proceedings of the British Academy* 83.

Pears, D. 1984. *Motivated Irrationality*. Oxford: Oxford University Press.

—— 1991. 'Self-Deceptive Belief Formation.' *Synthèse* 89, pp. 393–405.

Penner, T. 1970. 'False Anticipatory Pleasures: *Philebus* 36a3–41a6.' *Phronesis* 15, pp. 166–78.

—— 1973. 'The Unity of Virtue.' *Philosophical Review* 82, pp. 35–68.

—— 1978. 'Thought and Desire in Plato.' In G. Vlastos (ed.), *Plato 2: A Collection of Critical Essays*. Notre Dame, Ind.: University of Notre Dame Press, pp. 96–118.

—— 1990. 'Plato and Davidson: Parts of the Soul and Weakness of Will.' In D. Copp (ed.) *Canadian Philosophers: Celebrating Twenty Years of the CJP*, *Canadian Journal of Philosophy*, suppl. vol. 16. Calgary: University of Calgary Press, pp. 35–74.

Piérart, M. 1973. *Platon et la cité grecque*. Brussels: Académie Royale de Belgique.

Popper, K. 1971. *The Open Society and its Enemies*. Vol. 1. Princeton: Princeton University Press.

Poste, E. 1860. *The Philebus of Plato*. Oxford: Oxford University Press.

Potts, T. C. 1996. 'Conscience.' In N. Kretzmann and A. K. J. Pinborg, (eds.) *The Cambridge History of Later Medieval Philosophy*. Cambridge: Cambridge University Press, pp. 687–704.

Price, A. 1989. *Love and Friendship in Plato and Aristotle*. Oxford: Clarendon Press.

—— 1990. 'Comments on Hankinson.' *Proceedings of the Boston Area Colloquium in Ancient Philosophy* 6, pp. 28–33.

—— 1995. *Mental Conflict*. London: Routledge & Kegan Paul.

REATH, A. 1989. 'Hedonism, Heteronomy and Kant's Principle of Happiness.' *Pacific Philosophical Quarterly* 70, pp. 42–72.

REDFIELD, J. 1975. *Nature and Culture in the Iliad*. Chicago: University of Chicago Press.

REES, D. 1957. 'Bipartition of the Soul in the Early Academy.' *Journal of Hellenic Studies* 77, pp. 112–18.

REEVE, C. D. C. 1988. *Philosopher-Kings*. Princeton: Princeton University Press.

—— 1989. Letter. *Times Literary Supplement* August 11–17, 1989, p. 873.

—— 1998. *Plato Cratylus*. Indianapolis: Hackett.

REVERDIN, O. (ed.) 1975. *De Jamblique a Proclus*. Tome XXI. Fondation Hardt. Vandoeuvres.

ROBERTS, J. 1987. 'Plato on the Causes of Wrongdoing in the *Laws*.' *Ancient Philosophy* 7, pp. 23–37.

ROBERTS, R. 1984. 'Will Power and the Virtues.' *Philosophical Review* 93, pp. 227–47.

ROBINSON, T. 1992. 'Plato and the Computer.' *Ancient Philosophy* 12, pp. 375–82.

—— 1995. *Plato's Psychology*. 2nd edn. Toronto: University of Toronto Press.

RORTY, A. (ed.) 1976. *The Identities of Persons*. Berkeley: University of California Press.

—— (ed.) 1980a. *Essays on Aristotle's Ethics*. Berkeley: University of California Press.

—— 1980b. 'Where Does the Akratic Break Take Place?' *Australasian Journal of Philosophy* 58, pp. 333–46.

—— (ed.) 1996. *Essays on Aristotle's Rhetoric*. Berkeley: University of California Press.

ROSS, W. D. 1953. *Plato's Theory of Ideas*. 2nd edn. Oxford: Clarendon Press.

—— 1955. *Aristotelis Fragmenta Selecta*. Oxford: Oxford University Press.

ROWE, C. J. 1971. *The Eudemian and Nicomachean Ethics: A Study in the Development of Aristotle's Thought*. Cambridge: Cambridge Philological Society.

—— 1986a. 'The Argument and Structure of Plato's *Phaedrus*.' *Proceedings of the Cambridge Philological Society*, ns 32, pp. 106–25.

ROWE, C. J. 1986b. *Plato: Phaedrus.* Warminster: Aries & Phillips.

—— 1990. 'Philosophy, Love, and Madness.' In C. Gill (ed.) *The Person and the Human Mind: Issues in Ancient and Modern Philosophy.* Oxford: Oxford University Press, pp. 227–46.

—— 1993. *Plato: Phaedo.* Cambridge: Cambridge University Press.

—— 1995a. 'Introduction.' In Rowe (1995c), pp. 11–28.

—— 1995b. *Plato: Statesman.* Warminster: Aries & Phillips.

—— (ed.) 1995c. *Reading the Statesman: The Proceedings of the Third International Symposium Platonicum.* Sankt Augustin: Academia Verlag.

—— 1996. 'The *Politicus*: Structure and Form.' In Gill and McCabe (1996), pp. 153–78.

ROWE, C. J. and SCHOFIELD, M. (eds.) 2000. *The Cambridge History of Greek and Roman Political Thought.* Cambridge: Cambridge University Press.

ROWE, W. 1987. 'Two Concepts of Freedom.' *Proceedings of the American Philosophical Association* 62, pp. 43–64.

RYLE, G. 1949. *The Concept of Mind.* New York: Barnes and Noble.

SANTAS, G. 1966. 'Plato's *Protagoras* and Explanations of Weakness.' *Philosophical Review* 75, pp. 3–33.

—— 1994. 'Socratic Goods and Socratic Happiness.' *Apeiron* 27, pp. 37–52.

SAUNDERS, T. J. 1962. 'The Structure of the Soul and the State in Plato's *Laws.*' *Eranos* 60, pp. 37–55.

—— 1970. 'The Alleged Double Version in the Sixth Book of the *Laws.*' *Classical Quarterly*, ns 20, pp. 230–6.

—— 1972. *Notes on the Laws of Plato. Bulletin of the Institute of Classical Studies*, suppl. no. 28, University of London.

—— 1973a. 'Penology and Eschatology in Plato's *Timaeus* and *Laws.*' *Classical Quarterly*, ns 23, pp. 232–44.

—— 1973b. 'Plato on Killing in Anger: A Reply to Professor Woozley.' *Philosophical Quarterly* 23, pp. 350–6.

—— 1976. *Plato: the Laws.* Harmondsworth: Penguin.

—— 1985. *Aristotle: The Politics.* Harmondsworth: Penguin.

—— 1986. ' "The RAND Corporation of Antiquity"? Plato's Academy and Greek Politics.' In J. H. Betts *et al.* (eds.) *Studies in Honour of T. B. L. Webster I.* Bristol: Bristol Classical Press, pp. 200–10.

—— 1991. *Plato's Penal Code.* Oxford: Oxford University Press.

—— 1995. 'Plato on Women in the *Laws*.' In A. Powell (ed.) *The Greek World*. London: Routledge & Kegan Paul, pp. 591–609.

—— 2001. '*Epieikeia*: Plato and the Controversial Virtue of the Greeks.' In Lisi (2001), pp. 65–94.

SCHEFFLER, S. 1987. *The Rejection of Consequentialism*. Clarendon Press.

—— (ed.) 1988. *Consequentialism and its Critics*. Oxford: Oxford University Press.

—— 1992. *Human Morality*. Oxford: Oxford University Press.

SCHNEEWIND, J. B. 1998. *The Invention of Autonomy*. Cambridge: Cambridge University Press.

—— forthcoming. 'The Active Powers.' In Knud Haakonssen (ed.) *The Cambridge History of 18th-Century Philosophy*. Cambridge: Cambridge University Press.

SCHOFIELD, M. 1982. 'The Dénouement of the *Cratylus*.' In Schofield and Nussbaum (1982), pp. 61–81.

—— 1996. 'Sharing in the Constitution.' *Review of Metaphysics* 49, pp. 831–58.

—— 1999. *Saving the City: Philosopher-Kings and Other Classical Paradigms*. London: Routledge & Kegan Paul.

SCHOFIELD, M. and NUSSBAUM, M. (eds.) 1982. *Language and Logos*. Cambridge: Cambridge University Press.

SCHOPENHAUER, A. (ed. G. Zöller, tr. E. Payne) 1999. *Prize Essay on the Freedom of the Will*. Cambridge: Cambridge University Press.

SCHÖPSDAU, K. 1984. 'Zum Strafrechtsexkurs in Platons *Nomoi*.' *Rheinisches Museum für Philologie* 127, pp. 97–132.

—— 1994. *Platon Nomoi (Gesetze) Buch I–III*. Göttingen: Vandenhoeck & Ruprecht.

SCHULTZ, B. (ed.) 1992. *Essays on Henry Sidgwick*. Cambridge: Cambridge University Press.

Scott, D. 1987. 'Platonic Anamnesis Revisited.' *Classical Quarterly*, ns 37, pp. 346–66.

—— 1995. *Recollection and Experience*. Cambridge: Cambridge University Press.

SEDLEY, D. 1991. 'Teleology and Myth in the *Phaedo*.' *Proceedings of the Boston Area Colloquium in Ancient Philosophy* 5, pp. 359–83.

SEDLEY, D. 1992. 'Commentary on Mansfeld.' *Proceedings of the Boston Area Colloquium in Ancient Philosophy* 6, pp. 146–57.

——1998a. 'The Etymologies in Plato's *Cratylus.*' *Journal of Hellenic Studies* 118, pp. 140–54.

——1998b. 'Platonic Causes.' *Phronesis* 43, pp. 114–32.

SHOREY, P. 1892. Review of Jowett, *The Dialogues of Plato. American Journal of Philology* 13, pp. 349–72.

——1978. *The Republic.* 2 vols. Cambridge, Mass.: Harvard University Press.

SIDGWICK, H. 1981. *The Methods of Ethics.* 7th edn. Indianapolis: Hackett.

SILVERMAN, A. 1990a. 'Plato on Perception and the "Commons".' *Classical Quarterly*, ns 40, pp. 148–75.

——1990b. 'Plato on Phantasia.' *Classical Antiquity* 10, pp. 123–47.

——1992. 'Plato's *Cratylus*: The Naming of Nature and the Nature of Naming.' *Oxford Studies in Ancient Philosophy* 10, pp. 61–81.

SILVERTHORNE, M. J. 1975. 'Laws, Preambles and the Legislator in Plato.' *The Humanities Association Review* 26, pp. 10–20.

SIMMONS, A. J. 1979. *Moral Principles and Political Obligations.* Princeton: Princeton University Press.

SKEMP, J. B. 1947. 'Plants in Plato's *Timaeus.*' *Classical Quarterly* 41, pp. 53–60.

——1952. *Plato, The Statesman.* London: Routledge & Kegan Paul.

——1967. *The Theory of Motion in Plato's Later Dialogues.* 2nd edn. Amsterdam: Adolf M. Hakkert.

SLOTE, M. 1983. *Goods and Virtues.* Oxford: Oxford University Press.

——1989. *Beyond Optimizing: A Study of Rational Choice.* Cambridge, Mass.: Harvard University Press.

SMITH, M. 1996. *The Moral Problem.* Oxford: Blackwell.

SMITH, N. 1983. 'Plato and Aristotle on the Nature of Women.' *Journal of the History of Philosophy* 21, pp. 467–78.

SORABJI, R. 1980. *Necessity, Cause, and Blame.* London: Duckworth.

——1993. *Animal Minds and Human Morals.* Ithaca: Cornell University Press.

STALLEY, R. 1975. 'Plato's Argument for the Division of the Reasoning and Appetitive Elements in the Soul.' *Phronesis* 20, pp. 110–28.

—— 1983. *An Introduction to Plato's Laws*. Indianapolis: Hackett.

—— 1991. 'Aristotle's Criticism of Plato's *Republic*.' In Keyt and Miller (1991), pp. 182–99.

—— 1994. 'Persuasion in Plato's *Laws*.' *History of Political Thought* 15, pp. 157–77.

STAMPE, D. 1987. 'The Authority of Desire.' *Philosophical Review* 96, pp. 335–81.

STRAWSON, G. 1994. *Mental Reality*. Cambridge, Mass.: MIT Press.

STRIKER, G. 1970. *Peras und Apeiron*. Göttingen: Vandenhoeck & Ruprecht.

—— 1996. *Essays on Hellenistic Epistemology and Ethics*. Cambridge: Cambridge University Press.

TAYLOR, A. E. 1928. *A Commentary on Plato's Timaeus*. Oxford: Oxford University Press.

—— 1929. 'Plato and the Authorship of the "Epinomis".' *Proceedings of the British Academy* 15, pp. 235–317.

—— 1960. *Plato: the Laws*. London: J. M. Dent and Sons.

TAYLOR, C. 1969. 'Forms as Causes in the *Phaedo*.' *Mind* 78, pp. 45–59.

TAYLOR, G. 1985. *Pride, Shame and Guilt*. Oxford: Clarendon Press.

TAYLOR, K. 1997. 'Same Believers.' *Philosophical Issues* 8, pp. 357–69.

TELFER, E. 1989–90. 'The Unity of the Moral Virtues in Aristotle's *Nicomachean Ethics*.' *Proceedings of the Aristotelian Society* 90, pp. 35–48.

TESSITORE, A. 1996. *Reading Aristotle's Ethics: Virtue, Rhetoric, and Political Philosophy*. Albany: State University of New York Press.

THALBERG, I. 1978. 'Mental Activity and Passivity.' *Mind* 87, pp. 376–95.

—— 1985. 'Questions about Motivational Strength.' In Lepore and McLaughlin (1985), pp. 88–103.

THOMPSON, W. H. 1868. *The Phaedrus of Plato*. London: Whittaker.

TODD, S. C. 1995. *The Shape of Athenian Law*. Oxford: Clarendon Press.

VANDER WAERDT, P. 1985a. 'The Peripatetic Interpretation of Plato's Tripartite Psychology.' *Greek, Roman and Byzantine Studies* 26, pp. 283–302.

—— 1985b. 'Peripatetic Soul-Division, Posidonius, and Middle Platonic Moral Psychology.' *Greek, Roman and Byzantine Studies* 26, pp. 373–94.

VELLEMAN, J. D. 1989. *Practical Reflection*. Princeton: Princeton University Press.

VELLEMAN, J. D. 1992. 'What Happens When Someone Acts?' *Mind* 101, pp. 461–81.

VERDENIUS, W. 1955. 'Notes on Plato's *Phaedrus*.' *Mnemosyne* 8, pp. 265–89.

VERSENYI, L. 1961. 'The Cretan Plato.' *Review of Metaphysics* 15, pp. 67–80.

VLASTOS, G. 1975. *Plato's Universe*. Seattle: University of Washington Press.

—— 1981. *Platonic Studies*. 2nd edn. Princeton: Princeton University Press.

—— 1985. 'Happiness and Virtue in Socrates' Moral Theory.' *Topoi* 4, pp. 3–22.

—— 1991. *Socrates, Ironist and Moral Philosopher*. Ithaca: Cornell University Press.

—— 1994. *Studies in Greek Philosophy*. 2 vols. Princeton: Princeton University Press.

WALDRON, J. 1990. *The Right to Private Property*. Oxford: Clarendon Press.

—— 1995. 'The Wisdom of the Masses.' *Political Theory* 23, pp. 563–84.

WALKER, A. 1989. 'The Problem of Weakness of Will.' *Noûs* 23, pp. 653–76.

WALKER, A. D. M. 1993. 'The Incompatibility of the Virtues.' *Ratio* 6, pp. 44–62.

WALLACE, R. J. 1991. 'Virtue, Reason, and Principle.' *Canadian Journal of Philosophy* 21, pp. 469–95.

—— 1999. 'Addiction as Defect of the Will: Some Philosophical Reflections.' *Law and Philosophy* 18, pp. 621–54.

WALSH, J. 1963. *Aristotle's Conception of Moral Weakness*. New York: Columbia University Press.

WALZER, R. (ed.) 1934. *Aristotelis dialogorum Fragmenta*. Florence: G. C. Sansoni.

WATERFIELD, R. 1994. *Plato: Republic*. Oxford: Oxford University Press.

WATERLOW, S. [Broadie] 1972. 'The Good of Others in Plato's *Republic*.' *Proceedings of the Aristotelian Society* 73, pp. 19–36.

—— 1988. *Nature, Change, and Agency in Aristotle's Physics*. Oxford: Clarendon Press.

WATSON, G. 1977. 'Skepticism about Weakness of the Will.' *Philosophical Review* 86, pp. 316–39.

—— 1984. 'The Virtues in Excess.' *Philosophical Studies* 46, pp. 57–74.

WEISS, R. 1987. 'The Right Exchange: *Phaedo* 69a6–c3.' *Ancient Philosophy* 7, pp. 57–66.

—— 1989. 'The Hedonic Calculus in the *Protagoras* and the *Phaedo.*' *Journal of the History of Philosophy* 25, pp. 511–29.

WERKMEISTER, W. H. (ed.) 1976. *Facets of Plato's Philosophy.* Assen: Van Gorcum.

WHITE, F. C. 1984. 'The Scope of Knowledge in *Republic* V.' *Australasian Journal of Philosophy* 62, pp. 339–54.

WHITE, N. 1984. 'The Classification of Goods in Plato's *Republic.*' *Journal of the History of Philosophy* 22, pp. 393–421.

—— 1986. 'The Ruler's Choice.' *Archiv für Geschichte der Philosophie* 68, pp. 22–46.

—— 1987a. 'Forms and Sensibles: *Phaedo* 74B–C.' *Philosophical Topics* 15, pp. 197–214.

—— 1987b. 'Perceptual and Objective Properties in Plato.' *Apeiron* 22, pp. 45–65.

—— 1992. 'Plato's Metaphysical Epistemology.' In Kraut (1992), pp. 277–310.

—— 1995. 'Conflicting Parts of Happiness in Aristotle's Ethics.' *Ethics* 105, pp. 258–83.

—— 1999 . 'Harmonizing Plato.' *Philosophy and Phenomenological Research* 49, pp. 497–512.

WHITE, S. 1992. *Sovereign Virtue.* Stanford: Stanford University Press.

WHITING, J. 1996. 'Self-Love and Authoritative Virtue: Prolegomenon to a Kantian Reading of *Eudemian Ethics* VIII 3.' In J. Whiting and S. Engstrom (eds.) *Aristotle, Kant and the Stoics: Rethinking Happiness and Duty.* Cambridge: Cambridge University Press, pp. 162–99.

WHITTAKER, J. (ed.) 1990. *Alcinoos, Enseignement des doctrines de Platon.* Paris: Les Belles Lettres.

WILDBERG, C. forthcoming. 'Porphyry, *Sententiae* 32 and the Grades of Virtue.'

WILLIAMS, B. 1959. 'Pleasure and Belief.' *Proceedings of the Aristotelian Society Supplement* 33, pp. 57–72.

—— 1973. 'The Analogy of the City and Soul in Plato's *Republic.*' In Lee, Mourelatos, and Rorty (1973), pp. 196–206.

—— 1982. 'Cratylus' Theory of Names and its Refutation.' In Schofield and Nussbaum (1982), pp. 83–93.

WILLIAMS, B. 1993. *Shame and Necessity.* Berkeley: University of California Press.

WILSON, J. 1976. 'The Argument of *Republic* IV.' *Philosophical Quarterly* 26, pp. 111–24.

WOLIN, S. 1960. *Politics and Vision.* Boston: Little, Brown.

WOOD, A. 1999. *Kant's Ethical Thought.* Cambridge: Cambridge University Press.

—— 2001. 'Kant versus Eudaimonism.' In P. Cicovacki (ed.) *Kant's Legacy: Essays in Honor of Lewis Beck White.* Rochester, NY: University of Rochester Press, pp. 261–82.

WOOD, R. 1997. *Ockham on the Virtues.* West Lafayette, Ind.: Purdue University Press.

WOODS, M. 1987. 'Plato's Division of the Soul.' *Proceedings of the British Academy* 73, pp. 23–48.

WOOZLEY, A. D. 1972. 'Plato on Killing in Anger.' *Philosophical Quarterly* 22, pp. 303–17.

YAVETZ, I. 1998. 'On the Homocentric Spheres of Eudoxus.' *Archive for History of Exact Sciences* 52, pp. 221–78.

YOUNG, C. 1994. 'Plato and Computer Dating.' *Oxford Studies in Ancient Philosophy* 12, pp. 227–50.

YUNIS, H. 1996. *Taming Democracy.* Ithaca: Cornell University Press.

Index of Passages

General Index